Cryptography and

CRYPTOGRAPHY
AND
NETWORK SECURITY

PRAKASH C. GUPTA
Former Head
Department of Information Technology
Maharashtra Institute of Technology
Pune

PHI Learning Private Limited

Delhi-110092
2015

₹ 450.00

CRYPTOGRAPHY AND NETWORK SECURITY
Prakash C. Gupta

ISBN-978-81-203-5045-8

Published by Asoke K. Ghosh, PHI Learning Private Limited, Rimjhim House, 111, Patparganj Industrial Estate, Delhi-110092 and Printed by Mohan Makhijani at Rekha Printers Private Limited, New Delhi-110020.

Contents

Preface

During last decade, there has been increasing dependence of both organizations and individuals on computing systems and the public Internet for business applications and social networking. While this dependence has enhanced the operational efficiency and ease of communications, the security associated with the exchange of information has become crucial. The security concerns relate to

- privacy and authenticity of information as it is transported across the network, and
- vulnerability of the computing resources and network to the adversarial attacks.

Network Security as a subject addresses all these concerns. It encompasses security protocols and tools to protect the information, computing systems and the network. It is a complex subject because it draws on a variety of disciplines, discrete mathematics, cryptography, network architecture and security algorithms. The purpose of this book is to introduce this subject as a comprehensive text which is self contained and covers all the aspects of network security.

Audience

The book is written for both academic and professional audience. Professionals who did not had formal introduction to the subject as a student but at present their job profiles demand knowledge of the subject will find this book a useful reference.

As a textbook, it is intended as a one semester course for undergraduate course for computer science, information technology, electronics and communication disciplines. The subject is also included in the curricula of several postgraduate programs. This book fits into their requirements also as an introductory textbook.

Book Structure

The content of text is spread over twenty-three chapters and is structured so as to provide a systematic development of the subject. Primarily, it is organized as follows:

- Symmetric-key cryptography (Chapters 2 to 7).
- Asymmetric-key cryptography (Chapters 8 to 10).
- Message authentication and digital signatures (Chapters 11 to 13).

- Cryptographic-key distribution mechanisms (Chapters 14 and 15).
- Security protocols (Chapters 16 to 20).
- Network security threats and tools, malware (Chapters 21 to 23).

Cryptography has its foundations in discrete mathematics. Required mathematical background is introduced as needed. It is spread over three chapters and covers principles of modular arithmetic, algebraic structures, prime numbers and discrete logarithms. This background is essential for the purpose of this textbook and does not require additional resources/books.

Each chapter is divided into sections and subsections to facilitate design of the curriculum as per the academic needs. The text contains numerous examples and illustrations that enhance conceptual clarity. Each chapter has set of problems at the end of chapter that inspire the reader to test his understanding of the subject. Answers to most of the problems are given at the end of the textbook.

In addition, the book includes three appendices that provide supplementary information, glossary of terms and frequently used acronyms. Recommended supplementary reading material is referenced at the end of each chapter. This book contains the most recent Protocol standards as currently applicable.

Acknowledgements

I am thankful to the following institutions which extended full access to their library resources without which this project would not have been possible:

1. San Jose State University Library, San Jose, USA
2. Symbiosis Centre of Information Technology, Pune
3. Balaji Institute of Telecom Management, Pune

I would like to thank the editorial and production teams of PHI Learning, Delhi for the excellent job and timely publication of book.

Prakash C. Gupta
prakashcgupta0911@gmail.com

Abbreviations

AES	Advanced Encryption Standard	DSS	Digital Signature Standard
AH	Authentication Header	EAP	Extensible Authentication
AKM	Authentication and Key		Protocol
	Management	EAPOL	EAP Over LAN
AP	Access Point	EAPOL-KCK	EAPOL Key Confirmation Key
API	Application Programming	EAPOL-KEK	EAPOL Key Encryption Key
	Interface	ECB	Electronic Code Book (mode)
ARP	Address Resolution Protocol	ECC	Elliptic Curve Cryptography
AS	Authentication Server	ECDSA	Elliptic Curve Digital Signature
BSS	Basic Service Set		Algorithm
CCSP	ChangeCipherSpec Protocol	ESP	Encapsulating Security Payload
CA	Certification Authority	ESS	Extended Service Set
CBC	Cipher Block Chaining (mode)	FIPS	Federal Information Processing
CCMP	CTR with CBC-MAC Protocol		Standard
CFB	Cipher Feedback (mode)	FTP	File Transfer Protocol
CHAP	Challenge Handshake Authen-	GCD	Greatest Common Divider
	tication Protocol	GF	Galois Field
CR	Carriage Return	GIF	Graphics Interchange Format
CRC	Cyclic Redundancy Check	HTML	Hypertext Markup Language
CRL	Certificate Revocation List	HTTP	Hypertext Transfer Protocol
CRT	Chinese Remainder Theorem	IBSS	Independent BSS
CTR	Counter (mode)	ICMP	Internet Control Message
DDoS	Distributed DoS		Protocol
DES	Data Encryption Standard	ICV	Integrity Check Value
DH	Diffie–Hellman	IDEA	International Data Encryption
DNS	Domain Name System		Algorithm
DoS	Denial of Service	IDS	Intrusion Detection System
DS	Distribution System	IKE	Internet Key Exchange
DSA	Digital Signature Algorithm	IP	Internet Protocol

ISAKMP	Internet Security Association and Key Management Protocol	PRF	Pseudo Random Function
		PSK	Pre-shared Key
IV	Initialization Vector	PTK	Pairwise Transient Key
KDC	Key Distribution Centre	PWC	Proactive Worm Containment
LF	Line Feed	QOS	Quality of Service
LLC	Logical Link Control	RA	Registration Authority
LPDU	LLC Protocol Data Unit	RADIUS	Remote Authentication Dial-in User Service
MAC	Media Access Control		
MAC	Message Authentication Code	RFC	Request for Comments
MBR	Master Boot Record	RSN	Robust Security Network
MD	Message Digest	SA	Security Association
MIC	Message Integrity Code	SAD	Security Association Database
MIME	Multipurpose Internet Mail Extensions	SHA	Secure Hash Algorithm
		S/MIME	Secure MIME
MPEG	Moving Picture Experts Group	SMTP	Simple Mail Transfer Protocol
MPDU	MAC Protocol Data Unit	SPD	Security Policy Database
MSDU	MAC Service Data Unit	SSL	Secure Socket Layer
MSK	Master Session Key	STA	Station (wireless)
MTA	Message Transfer Agent	TCP	Transmission Control Protocol
MUA	Message User Agent	TGS	Ticket Granting Server
NAT	Network Address Translation	TK	Temporal Key
NLFSR	Non-Linear Feedback Shift Register	TKIP	Temporal Key Integrity Protocol
OFB	Output Feedback (mode)	TLS	Transport Layer Security
OTP	One Time Pad	TOS	Type of Service
PAP	Password Authentication Protocol	TSC	TKIP Sequence Counter
		TTL	Time to Live
PGP	Pretty Good Privacy	UDP	User Datagram Protocol
PKCS	Public Key Cryptography Standard	URL	Uniform Resource Locator
		VPN	Virtual Private Network
PKI	Public Key Infrastructure	WEP	Wired Equivalent Privacy
PMK	Pairwise Master Key	WLAN	Wireless LAN
PPP	Point-to-Point Protocol	WPA	Wi-Fi Protected Access

1

Introduction to Network Security

The purpose of this chapter is to introduce some network security concerns, basic security services and terminology. We begin this chapter with the introduction of the lead cast, Alice, Bob and the unnamed adversary who is a constant threat to secure communication between Alice and Bob. We examine the threats posed by the adversary and outline the required security services. Thereafter, we introduce the basic mechanisms used for providing the security services. Finally, before we close the chapter, we have a look at the organization of the rest of the book.

1.1 SECURITY GOALS

During the last two decades, the public Internet and computers have revolutionized our life styles, business styles, modes of our social interactions, education and entertainment. This change also saw emergence of new set adversaries who are now constant threat to secure communications and information infrastructure essential for the changed life styles.

Our primary security requirements are three—privacy, integrity and availability.

- Privacy is the most basic requirement. Be it the information being transmitted or stored information, we want to protect its confidentiality.
- We want to assure that the adversary does not modify the information. We would like to have an integrity-check of information so that any modification is immediately revealed.
- Information is useful only if it is available to us. The adversary can impact availability of information by attacking the information resource or the access to information resource.

To understand the adversarial threats to security of our information, let us first define our cast consisting of the communicating entities, the adversaries and trusted entities.

1.1.1 The Cast

The basic communication scenario is depicted in Figure 1.1(a). It has the following entities:

Communicating entities: We will call them Alice and Bob. They want to communicate with each other.

An adversary: The adversary is the villain having malicious intent and is a constant threat to secure communication between Alice and Bob. The adversary is known by several names such as attacker, opponent, eavesdropper or intruder in different contexts.

The adversary can be a passive adversary or an active adversary. A *passive* adversary is the one which is capable only of reading and copying information. An *active* adversary, on the other hand, may also transmit, alter, or delete information.

Trusted entity: The trusted entity enjoys the trust of all the legitimate communicating entities. He plays several different roles that support communication between Alice and Bob.

Alice, Bob, the adversary and the trusted entity are seemingly persons, but we use these names to refer to software entities that communicate with each other. Alice could be the client, Bob could be a server and the adversary could be a malicious program.

These entities interact over the public Internet or over a private network (Figure 1.1). In Figure 1.1(b), Bob is on a private network. Alice as a remote authorized user on the Internet accesses Bob for service. The adversary is typically on the Internet but he can be an internal user on the private network as well.

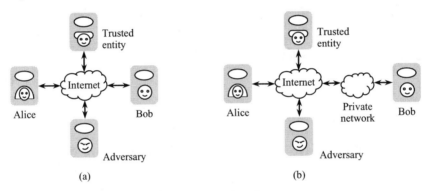

Figure 1.1 The Cast.

1.1.2 Adversarial Attacks

Our security goals, privacy, integrity and availability are constantly under threat from the following forms of adversarial attacks.

Snooping and Traffic Analysis

Snooping (or eavesdropping) refers to unauthorized access to information. For example, an adversary may monitor the data being exchanged between Alice and Bob [Figure 1.2(a)]. The adversary does not modify the content or interfere with the exchange of data. He merely copies the data for his own benefit.

Even if the contents of a message are masked using encryption, mere act of exchange of messages may be useful information for the adversary. Consider that an army unit sends an encrypted message 'Calm at the border' daily at 0800 hours. An adversary may not understand the message, but if there is any change in content, timing or size of message, the change would readily come to his notice. This act of adversary is referred to as traffic analysis.

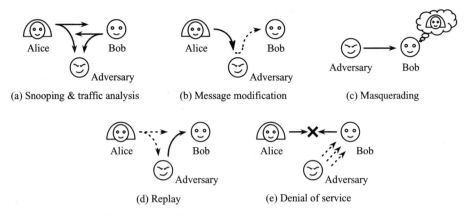

Figure 1.2   Threats to secure communication.

Message Modification

An adversary may intercept a message, modify the contents and release the message to its original destination [Figure 1.2(b)]. The modification may be in the form of alteration, deletion or reordering the contents of a message to the benefit of the adversary. Encryption of a message does not protect it against modification.

- The adversary may achieve his goal by reordering the encrypted message blocks. For example, the adversary may copy the encrypted block containing salary amount of his boss against his own name.
- The adversary may alter some of the bits of the encrypted message without any specific goal. The decrypted message will be some unintelligible stream of bytes.

Masquerading

Masquerading is impersonating someone. The adversary impersonates an authorized entity (e.g. Alice) to access a resource (e.g. Bob) [Figure 1.2(c)]. A masquerading attack would include some other forms of attack as well. For example, the adversary may copy the initial messages of Alice (e.g. her user ID and password) to Bob. He later impersonates Alice and replays the copied authentication messages to access Bob.

Replay

The adversary obtains a copy of a message sent by Alice to Bob and later replays the message [Figure 1.2(d)]. Replay can be used for inserting fraudulent messages in the ongoing session between Alice and Bob, or for authentication as mentioned under masquerading.

Denial of Service

Denial of service (DoS) is an interruption of a service either because the system is incapacitated or because it becomes inaccessible temporarily [Figure 1.2(e)]. DoS attack may

- incapacitate a system by using up all its available memory so that the system does not respond to the service requests, or
- clog the access network so that the system may not be able to communicate.

To amplify the impact of the attack, the adversary may engage several 'zombies' which launch the attack on targeted entity simultaneously when triggered by the adversary. Such attack is called distributed DoS attack (DDoS).

1.2 SECURITY SERVICES

Knowing our security goals, and possible line of attack of the adversary, we are in a position to define our security services requirements[1] (Figure 1.3):

- Data confidentiality
- Data integrity
- Authentication
- Access control
- Non-repudiation

The last security service requirement is not due to the adversary as we shall shortly see.

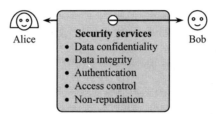

Figure 1.3   Security services.

Data Confidentiality

The most basic security requirement is privacy of communications. This service protects the data from disclosure to unauthorized entities. Confidentiality as service covers even its broader aspect, traffic confidentiality. Traffic confidentiality refers to confidentiality of communicating entities and confidentiality of volume of data.

Data Integrity

Data integrity service is designed to protect data from modification, insertion, deletion, or reordering. Data integrity service provides means for integrity verification. It is to be noted that data confidentiality does not ensure its integrity.

Authentication

Authentication service has two aspects: peer-entity authentication and data-origin authentication.

- Peer-entity authentication refers to proving identity of a communicating entity (e.g. Alice) to the other entity (e.g. Bob).
- Data-origin authentication service provides means to verify the source of data.

---

1. This categorization is based on ITU-T X.800 specification for the Open System Interconnection (OSI) Reference Model. The specification also defines the security services provided by the protocol layers of the model.

Note the subtle difference in peer-entity authentication and data origin authentication. Peer-entity authentication may be done once at the beginning of a communication session. Each message exchanged thereafter during the session requires to be verified for its origin.

Access Control

Access control service protects against unauthorized access to a resource. Access is further qualified in terms of read, write and execute rights. Access control service works in tandem with authentication service since granting entitled access right to an entity requires prior authentication of the entity.

Non-repudiation

We tend to assume that security issues arise due to the adversary only. It is possible that the receiver may alter a delivered message to his advantage, or the sender may later deny having sent the message. Thus there can be dispute between its sender and the receiver. Non-repudiation service protects interests of the sender and the receiver. This service ensures that the sender cannot deny transmission of a message or repudiate contents of the transmitted message and the receiver cannot deny receipt of a message.

1.3   SECURITY MECHANISMS

Security services described earlier are provided by implementing security mechanisms as listed below:

- Encryption mechanism
- Digital signature mechanism
- Data-integrity verification mechanism
- Data-origin verification mechanism
- Entity authentication mechanism
- Notarization mechanism
- Access control mechanism

Encryption Mechanism

Encryption mechanisms provide data confidentiality by transforming the data so that its content becomes incomprehensible. Encryption mechanisms are keyed algorithms, i.e., a key is required to execute the algorithm (Figure 1.4). These algorithms are divided into two categories: symmetric-key and asymmetric-key algorithms. Symmetric-key algorithms require same key for encryption and decryption. Asymmetric-key algorithms have two different keys: one for encryption and the other for decryption.

Encryption mechanisms also complement a number of other security mechanisms. For example, asymmetric-key encryption algorithm can be used for generating digital signature.

Figure 1.4 Encryption mechanism.

Digital Signature Mechanism

Digital signature is electronic equivalent of conventional signature. Digital signature on a message gives it ownership of the signer. Signature algorithm uses asymmetric keys for generating and verification of the digital signature. The signer puts his signature on the message using his private key, a secret known only to the signer (Figure 1.5). The signature is verified using the other key, which is called public key and is not a secret.

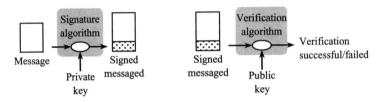

Figure 1.5 Digital signature.

Digital signature is used for verification of message integrity and its source. The sender cannot repudiate the ownership and content of the signed message. Digital signature mechanism also finds application as entity authentication mechanism.

Data Integrity Mechanism

Data integrity mechanism consists of generating a checksum of the message using a hash algorithm [Figure 1.6(a)]. The checksum is called digest and is sent along with the message. The receiving entity verifies integrity of the message using the appended digest [Figure 1.6(b)]. It computes the digest of the received message and compares it with the appended digest. If they match, the verification is successful.

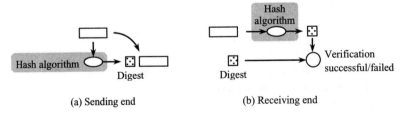

Figure 1.6 Message integrity.

Data-origin Authentication Mechanism

Data-origin authentication mechanism is usually linked with data integrity mechanism. For data-origin authentication, a keyed hash algorithm is used for computing the digest [Figure 1.7(a)]. The digest is called message authentication code (MAC). The key is shared between the sender and the receiver. The receiver verifies the MAC using the same secret key [Figure 1.7(b)]. Successful verification implies that

- the message integrity is intact and
- the message has come from a source that knows the secret key.

Note the difference between MAC and digital signature. MAC does not provide non-repudiation service.

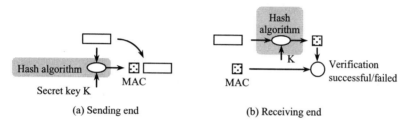

(a) Sending end   (b) Receiving end

Figure 1.7   Integrity and data-origin authentication.

Entity Authentication Mechanism

Entity authentication mechanism provides proof of identification of an entity to the peer entity. The proving entity submits the proof in the form of something known to it, something owned by it, or something inherent in it. For example,

- Alice submits her ID and password as proof of something known to her [Figure 1.8(a)].
- Alice transforms the challenge sent by Bob using the private key owned by her [Figure 1.8(b)]. Bob verifies the transformed challenge using her public key.
- Alice submits her fingerprint as inherent proof of her identification.

(a) Password   (b) Challenge-response

Figure 1.8   Entity authentication.

Notarization Mechanism

Notarization mechanism involves a third entity that is trusted by all the communicating entities (Figure 1.9). The trusted entity plays several roles in different protocols. For example, it may distribute certificates that bind an identity (e.g. Alice) to the public-key. Alice can attach her notarized public-key certificate to her signed message for Bob. Bob verifies her signature on the message using Alice's public key given in the certificate (Figure 1.5).

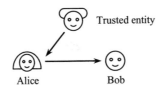

Figure 1.9   Notarization.

Other roles of the trusted entity may include:

- authentication of Alice to Bob,
- issuing secret encryption key to Alice and Bob for their communication session,
- issuing a 'ticket' to Alice for availing the service provided by Bob. Alice produces the ticket when she avails the service.

Access Control Mechanism

Access control mechanism is closely linked to entity authentication. After Alice proves her identity to Bob, Bob determines her entitled access rights and provides her access to the requested resource as per her entitlement, e.g. Alice entitlement may be 'read only'. Access control mechanisms also report unauthorized access attempts as part of a security audit trail.

These mechanisms are implemented as part of different security protocols. We study these security mechanisms and the protocols in this book.

1.4   ORGANIZATION OF THE BOOK

As a subject, network security spans over several specialized fields—cryptography, information technology and computer networks. Understanding of cryptography concepts requires some mathematical background consisting of modular arithmetic, algebraic structures, prime numbers and discrete logarithms. The subject matter of this book is, therefore, organized such that the reader gradually and systematically builds up his knowledge base without feeling handicapped at any stage of learning.

Part One: The first part of the book consists of Chapters 2 to 7. These chapters describe symmetric-key ciphers. Chapter 2 and Chapter 5 lay mathematical foundations required for the subsequent chapters.

Chapter 2   Mathematical Foundations I (Modular Arithmetic)
Chapter 3   Classical Encryption Techniques
Chapter 4   Symmetric-key Ciphers I (DES)
Chapter 5   Mathematical Foundations II (Finite Fields)
Chapter 6   Symmetric-key Ciphers II (AES)
Chapter 7   Symmetric-key Ciphers III (Stream Ciphers and Modes of Operation)

Part Two: The second part of the book has Chapters 8 to 10. We focus on asymmetric-key cryptography in these chapters. Chapter 8 provides the mathematical background required for understanding asymmetric-key cryptography. We study prime numbers, Fermet's and Euler's theorems, Chinese Remainder Theorem, quadratic congruence and discrete logarithms in this chapter. Chapter 9 presents RSA, Rabin and ElGamal cryptosystems. Elliptic curve cryptography (ECC) has become important in recent years. We devote a full chapter, Chapter 10, to ECC.

Chapter 8   Mathematical Foundations III (Prime Numbers)
Chapter 9   Asymmetric-key Cryptosystems
Chapter 10 Elliptic Curve Cryptography

Part Three: Moving ahead, we describe authentication and digital signature mechanisms in part three of the book, which consists of Chapters 11 to 13. We examine structure of hash algorithms in Chapter 11. We study several digital signature schemes, including one based on ECC, in Chapter 12. Chapter 13 is devoted to entity authentication. We also introduce concept of zero-knowledge proof and describe Fiat-Shamir protocol in this chapter.

Chapter 11   Message Authentication
Chapter 12   Digital Signature
Chapter 13   Entity Authentication

Part Four: The fourth part is devoted to key distribution methods. It has the following two chapters.

Chapter 14   Symmetric-key Distribution
Chapter 15   Public-key Distribution

Symmetric key distribution protocols, namely, DH key exchange, Needham–Schroeder key distribution protocol, Otway-Rees key distribution protocol and Kerberos are described in Chapter 14. Public key infrastructure (PKI) required for distribution of public keys is discussed in Chapter 15.

Part Five: This part of the book consists of the following five chapters where we study specific implementation of security protocols.

Chapter 16   Email Security
Chapter 17   Transport Layer Security (TLS)
Chapter 18   IP Security
Chapter 19   Internet Key Exchange (IKE)
Chapter 20   Wireless LAN Security

Security implementation at the application level is tailored to the requirements of the application. Since email is the most widely used Internet application, we study its security implementation in Chapter 16. Chapter 17 describes TLS protocol that implements security at the Transport layer. Security implementation at the IP layer is described in Chapters 18 and 19. Chapter 20 describes security protocols of wireless LANs.

Part Six: This part consisting of Chapters 21, 22 and 23 forms the last part of the book. We describe various threats to network and information security and network tools to counter these threats in these chapters.

Chapter 21   Network Vulnerabilities
Chapter 22   Firewalls and Intrusion Detection Systems
Chapter 23   Malware

Finally we have several appendices that provide supporting material referenced in the some of the chapters of the book.

1.5   SUMMING UP

In this introductory chapter of the book, we identified a framework of security requirements.

- Adversarial attacks on information and communications infrastructure are constant threat to privacy, integrity and availability of information. The attacks can take many forms and include snooping, masquerading, replay, message modification or denial of service.
- To counter the attacks, the security services required are data confidentiality, data integrity, entity authentication, and access control. In addition, non-repudiation service is required to resolve the disputes between the communicating entities.
- The security services are provided by implementing security mechanisms.
  - Encryption mechanism
  - Digital signature mechanism
  - Data-integrity and data-origin verification mechanism
  - Entity authentication mechanism
  - Notarization mechanism
  - Access control mechanism
- Security infrastructure may also require a centralized trusted entity that authenticates communicating entities, and distributes
  - notarized digital certificates,
  - secret encryption keys and
  - tickets for accessing the resources.

We begin the study of cryptography with an introduction to modular arithmetic in the next chapter.

Key Terms		
Access control	Denial of service	Non-repudiation
Authentication	Digital signature	Replay
Data confidentiality	Encryption	Snooping
Data integrity	Entity authentication	Traffic analysis
Data-origin authentication	Masquerading	

RECOMMENDED READING

Douligeris, C. (Ed), Serpanos, D. N., *Network Security, Current Status and Future Directions*, IEEE Press, John Wiley & Sons, Hoboken, NJ, USA, 2007.

Forouzan, Behrouz A., *Cryptography and Network Security*, Tata McGraw-Hill, New Delhi, 2007.

Security Architecture for Open Systems Interconnections for CCIT Applications, ITU-T X.800, International Telecommunication Union, Geneva, 1991.

Kaufman, C., Perlman, R. and Spenciner, M. *Network Security, Private Communication in a Public World*, Prentice-Hall of India, New Delhi, 2007.

Singh, S., *The Code Book: The Science of Secrecy from Ancient Egypt to Quantum Cryptography*, Anchor Books, NY, USA, 1999.

Stallings, W., *Cryptography and Network Security*, Prentice-Hall of India, New Delhi, 2008.

PROBLEMS

1. Suppose that Chess-king organizes online chess tournaments. He announces the first round of live match between grandmasters Alice and Bob (Figure 1.10). The first round is free for all viewers, but the viewers must register for watching the game on their computers. The grandmasters make chess-moves on their computers connected to the Internet. Identify the security services required for the communication between
   (a) a grandmaster and the game server.
   (b) a viewer and the game server.

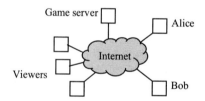

Figure 1.10 Problem 1.

2. The second round of the match between Alice and Bob of Problem 1 is a paid service for viewers. Payment is made at the time of registration using credit card. Identify any additional security service, if required, between a viewer and the game server.

3. The final round of the match between Alice and Bob of Problem 2 allows the viewers to opt for betting on the outcome of the match. Betting option can be chosen at the time of registration and bet can be raised during the game. Identify any additional security service, if required, between a viewer and the game server.

2

Mathematical Foundations I
(Modular Arithmetic)

Cryptography has its foundations deeply embedded in mathematics. The mathematical background required for the purpose of this book consists of three parts: modular arithmetic, finite fields and prime numbers. This chapter covers the first part—modular arithmetic. We begin this chapter with the basic concepts of modular arithmetic and then illustrate these concepts using simple examples of encryption and decryption. We also introduce Euclid's algorithm for determination of greatest common divisor and Bezout's identity for determination of multiplicative inverses in this chapter.

2.1 MODULAR ARITHMETIC

We are familiar with arithmetic that deals with infinite set of integers denoted by the set Z = {..., −2, −1, 0, 1, 2, ...}, and the arithmetic operations addition, subtraction, multiplication and division. Modulo-n arithmetic is based on

- finite set of non-negative integers from 0 to $n-1$ and
- binary[1] arithmetic operations—multiplication, addition and subtraction. Note that we have not included division as part of modulo arithmetic since it is not a binary operation.

It is ensured that the result of any of these operations is always mapped to the set of integers from 0 to $n-1$. Modular arithmetic defines modulo operator, for this purpose.

2.1.1 Modulo Operator

Given any positive or negative integer a from set Z = {..., −2, −1, 0, 1, 2, ...} and a positive integer n, we define a mod n (read a modulo n) to be the remainder r of division of a by n.

a mod $n = r$

For example, if $a = 11$ and $n = 7$, we have

11 mod 7 = 4

---

1. A binary operation has two inputs and one output. Division is not a binary operation because it results in two outputs—remainder and quotient.

We are not interested in the quotient and therefore we ignore it. Here n is called *modulus*. The remainder r is called *residue* and must always be a positive integer. We may need to use a negative quotient when dividing a by n to get a positive remainder.

Example 1   Determine result of the following modulo operations:

(a) 26 mod 17
(b) −35 mod 13
(c) −14 mod 19

Solution

(a) Dividing 26 by 17, we get remainder 9. Thus, 26 mod 17 = 9.
(b) Dividing −35 by 13, using quotient −3, we get remainder 4. Thus, −35 mod 13 = 4.
(c) Dividing −14 by 19, using quotient −1, we get remainder 5. Thus, −14 mod 19 = 5.

2.1.2   Set of Residues

Since the residue r can have integer values from 0 to $n-1$, the mod-n operator maps a positive or negative integer from set of integers Z to an element in the set $Z_n = \{0, 1, 2, ..., n-1\}$. Z_n is called the *set of residues*. Figure 2.1 shows such mapping for modulus equal to 7.

Figure 2.1   Set of residues.

2.1.3   Congruence

Two integers a and b from set $Z = \{..., -2, -1, 0, 1, 2, ...\}$ are said to be congruent modulo n if

a mod $n = b$ mod n

In other words, a and b map to the same element of the set $Z_n = \{0, 1, 2, ..., n-1\}$. Such congruence is expressed using the congruence symbol ≡.

$a \equiv b \quad (\text{mod } n)$

The phrase (mod n) is added to indicate that the congruence relationship is valid under mod n operation. Thus,

$-3 \equiv 4 \equiv 11 \equiv 18 \equiv 25 \quad (\text{mod } 7)$

Example 2   Select the numbers that are congruent modulo 13 in the set $\{17, 28, -9, 51, 56\}$.

Solution   Computing the residues modulo 13, we get

17 mod 13 = 4   28 mod 13 = 2   −9 mod 13 = 4
51 mod 13 = 12   56 mod 13 = 4
Thus, $17 \equiv -9 \equiv 56 \quad (\text{mod } 13)$

2.1.4 Modular Arithmetic Operations

In modulo n arithmetic, addition, subtraction and multiplication are carried out in usual manner, and the result of these operations is mapped to $Z_n = \{0, 1, 2, ..., n-1\}$. Instead of writing $a + b$, we write $(a + b)$ mod n to emphasize that the result must be mapped to Z_n.

The following examples illustrate the application of arithmetic operations modulo 17:

$(14 + 11)$ mod $17 = 25$ mod $17 \quad = 8$ (mod 17)
$(13 - 8)$ mod $17 \ = 5$ mod $17 \quad = 5$ (mod 17)
$(3 - 7)$ mod $17 \ \ = (-4)$ mod $17 = 13$ (mod 17)
(14×2) mod $17 = 28$ mod $17 \ \ = 11$ (mod 17)

2.1.5 Properties of Modular Arithmetic for Integers in Z_n

If a, b and c are elements of Z_n, the following properties of the arithmetic operations in Z_n are observed.

Commutative law $\quad (a + b)$ mod $n = (b + a)$ mod n
$\qquad\qquad\qquad\quad (a \times b)$ mod $n = (b \times a)$ mod n

Associative law $\qquad [(a + b) + c]$ mod $n = [a + (b + c)]$ mod n
$\qquad\qquad\qquad\quad [(a \times b) \times c]$ mod $n = [a \times (b \times c)]$ mod n

Distributive law $\qquad [(a \times (b + c)]$ mod $n = [(a \times b) + (a \times c)]$ mod n

2.1.6 Properties of Modular Arithmetic for Integers in Z

In all the above examples, the binary operation was carried out on integers from set Z_n. If the integers are from set $Z = \{..., -2, -1, 0, 1, 2, ...\}$, we can either first map them to Z_n and then apply the binary operation, or first carry out the operation and then map the result to Z_n. In other words, if a and b are from Z, then

$[(a$ mod $n) + (b$ mod $n)]$ mod $n = (a + b)$ mod n
$[(a$ mod $n) - (b$ mod $n)]$ mod $n = (a - b)$ mod n
$[(a$ mod $n) \times (b$ mod $n)]$ mod $n = (a \times b)$ mod n

To prove any of the above equalities, let $a = pn + r$ and $b = qn + s$. Thus,

$(a + b)$ mod $n = (pn + r + qn + s)$ mod n
$\qquad\qquad\qquad = (r + s)$ mod n
$\qquad\qquad\qquad = a$ mod $n + b$ mod n

Other equalities can be proven in the similar manner. We deal with very large numbers in cryptography. These properties of modular arithmetic enable us to handle large numbers with ease.

Example 3   If $a = 58$, $b = 73$, find $(a \times b)$ mod 7.

Solution (58×73) mod $7 = \{(58$ mod $7) \times (73$ mod $7)\}$ mod 7
$\qquad\qquad\qquad\qquad = (2 \times 3)$ mod $7 = 6$

Example 4   Compute 12^{10} mod 7.

Solution 12^{10} mod 7 $= 5^{10}$ mod 7 $= 25^5$ mod 7 $= 4^5$ mod 7 $= 16 \times 16 \times 4$ mod 7
$$= 2 \times 2 \times 4 \text{ mod } 7 = 2$$

2.2   ADDITIVE INVERSE

In conventional arithmetic, two numbers a and b are additive inverse of each other, if $a + b = 0$. For example, -7 is additive inverse of 7. In modular arithmetic, two numbers a and b in Z_n are additive inverse of each other, if

$$(a + b) \text{ mod } n = 0$$

For example, 3 and 4 of Z_7 are additive inverse of each other since $(3 + 4)$ mod 7 = 0. Additive inverse b of a is given by

$$b = (n - a) \text{ mod } n$$

Each integer of Z_n has its additive inverse in Z_n. For example, the additive inverse pairs of $Z_9 = \{0, 1, 2, 3, 4, 5, 6, 7, 8\}$ are $(0, 0)$, $(1, 8)$, $(2, 7)$, $(3, 6)$, $(4, 5)$.

2.2.1   Encryption and Decryption Using Additive Inverse

To demonstrate a simple application of additive inverse for encryption and decryption, let us represent each letter of English alphabet by an integer that corresponds to its position in the alphabet. Thus 7 corresponds to H if we start with A = 0. All the letters are represented by set Z_{26}. Encryption is carried out by modulo 26 addition of numerical representation of a letter and a fixed number called key. If the key is 20, H is encrypted as:

$(7 + 20)$ mod 26 = 1, which corresponds to letter B.

For decryption, we use the encryption algorithm with the additive inverse of the key. The additive inverse of 20 is 6 in Z_{26}. Therefore, letter B is decrypted as under.

$(1 + 6)$ mod 26 = 7, which is letter H.

Example 5

(a) Encrypt NET if the key is 11.
(b) Decrypt YPE if the key is 11.

Solution

(a) N = 13 $\Rightarrow$ (13 + 11) mod 26 = 24 $\Rightarrow$ Y
    E = 4 $\Rightarrow$ (4 + 11) mod 26 = 15 $\rightarrow$ P
    T = 19 $\Rightarrow$ (19 + 11) mod 26 = 4 $\Rightarrow$ E

(b) Additive inverse of 11 modulo 26 is 15.

    Y = 24 $\Rightarrow$ (24 + 15) mod 26 = 13 $\Rightarrow$ N
    P = 15 $\Rightarrow$ (15 + 15) mod 26 = 4 $\Rightarrow$ E
    E = 4 $\Rightarrow$ (4 + 15) mod 26 = 19 $\Rightarrow$ T

2.3 MULTIPLICATIVE INVERSE

Like additive inverse, we can also define multiplicative inverse in modular arithmetic. Two numbers a and b of $Z_n = \{0, 1, 2, ..., n-1\}$ are multiplicative inverse of one another, if

$$(a \times b) \bmod n = 1$$

For example, multiplicative inverse of 4 in Z_9 is 7 because

$$(4 \times 7) \bmod 9 = 28 \bmod 9 = 1$$

Not all elements of Z_n have the multiplicative inverse. It turns out that a number a will have multiplicative inverse in Z_n, if a and n do not have any common factor other than 1. In other words, their greatest common factor (gcd) is 1. Such numbers are called *relatively prime* or *coprime*. In the above example, 4 and 9 are coprime numbers. Therefore, 4 has a multiplicative inverse in Z_9. Only 1, 2, 4, 5, 7 and 8 in Z_9 are coprime to 9 and have multiplicative inverse. Subset of such numbers in Z_n is denoted as Z_n^*. Thus $Z_9^* = \{1, 2, 4, 5, 7, 8\}$.

Example 6 Find multiplicative inverse pairs of Z_{10}.

Solution $Z_{10} = \{0, 1, 2, 3, 4, 5, 6, 7, 8, 9\}$
   The coprimes of 10 in Z_{10} are 1, 3, 7 and 9. We can find multiplicative inverse pairs by trial.

$$(1 \times 1) \bmod 10 = 1$$
$$(3 \times 7) \bmod 10 = 1$$
$$(9 \times 9) \bmod 10 = 1$$

Thus multiplicative inverse pairs are (1, 1), (3, 7) and (9, 9).
   It is interesting to note that some of the elements are multiplicative inverse of themselves. If the number of elements in Z_n^* is large, searching multiplicative inverse pairs manually can be laborious task. Multiplicative inverse pairs are determined using Extended Euclidean algorithm, described later in this chapter. An important point to note is that, if modulus n is a prime number, then all elements of Z_n except 0 are coprimes to n, and therefore they have multiplicative inverse.

2.3.1 Encryption and Decryption Using Multiplicative Inverse

Just like additive inverse pairs, multiplicative inverse pairs can be used as keys in cryptography for encryption and decryption. As before, we represent all the letters of English alphabet as elements of set Z_{26}. We will use the multiplicative inverse pair (3, 9) of Z_{26} as the key. Letter H is encrypted using key 3 as:

$$(7 \times 3) \bmod 26 = 21, \text{ which corresponds to the letter V}$$

Decryption is carried out using the multiplicative inverse of the encryption key.

$$(21 \times 9) \bmod 26 = 189 \bmod 26 = 7, \text{ which corresponds to H.}$$

2.4 MATRICES

A matrix is an array of $l \times m$ elements arranged in l rows and m columns [Figure 2.2(a)]. A *square matrix* has equal number of rows and columns [Figure 2.2(b)]. An *identity matrix* is a square matrix with 1s on the main diagonal and 0s elsewhere [Figure 2.2(c)].

$$\begin{bmatrix} a_{11} & \cdots & a_{1m} \\ \vdots & \ddots & \vdots \\ a_{l1} & \cdots & a_{lm} \end{bmatrix} \qquad \begin{bmatrix} 5 & 1 & 8 \\ 2 & 0 & 6 \\ 3 & 4 & 1 \end{bmatrix} \qquad \begin{bmatrix} 1 & 0 & 0 \\ 0 & 1 & 0 \\ 0 & 0 & 1 \end{bmatrix}$$

(a) $l \times m$ matrix (b) 3×3 square matrix (c) 3×3 identity matrix

Figure 2.2 Various matrix types.

We are interested in matrices having only integers as their elements. We define the following arithmetic operations for matrices:

Equality Two matrices A and B of the same size can be equal, if their corresponding elements are equal, i.e., if $a_{ij} = b_{ij}$ for all i and j.

Addition and subtraction When two matrices A and B of the same size are added, the matrix C = A + B has its elements $c_{ij} = a_{ij} + b_{ij}$ for all i and j. Subtraction is defined in similar way. Matrix C = A – B has its elements $c_{ij} = a_{ij} - b_{ij}$ for all i and j. If we add a matrix A to itself, we get C = A + A = 2A. Thus, $nA = A + A + \ldots$ n times.

$$A = \begin{bmatrix} 2 & 0 & 1 \\ -3 & 7 & 4 \end{bmatrix} \qquad B = \begin{bmatrix} 3 & 5 & 1 \\ 9 & 2 & -5 \end{bmatrix} \qquad A + B = \begin{bmatrix} 5 & 5 & 2 \\ 6 & 9 & -1 \end{bmatrix}$$

Multiplication Two matrices A and B can be multiplied as C = A × B only if the number of columns in A is same as the number of rows in B. If size of A is $l \times m$ and size of B is $m \times p$, matrix C has size $l \times p$. The element c_{ij} of C is given by

$$c_{ij} = a_{i1} \times b_{1j} + a_{i2} \times b_{2j} + \ldots a_{im} \times b_{mj}$$

$$A = \begin{bmatrix} 2 & 0 & 1 \\ -3 & 7 & 4 \end{bmatrix} \qquad B = \begin{bmatrix} 3 & 2 \\ 1 & 0 \\ 1 & 2 \end{bmatrix} \qquad A \times B = \begin{bmatrix} 7 & 6 \\ 2 & 2 \end{bmatrix}$$

Inverse of a matrix If A and B are square matrices, and A × B = I (Identity matrix), B is called inverse of A and is written as A^{-1}.

2.4.1 Modular Arithmetic of Matrices

In cryptography, we want all elements of a matrix to belong to set $Z_n = \{0, 1, 2, \ldots, n - 1\}$. Therefore, we carry out all the arithmetic operations on matrices modulo n. We also define additive and multiplicative inverses. Recall that we need additive and multiplicative inverses for decryption. Additive inverse B of matrix A is such that A + B = 0 (mod n). Similarly, multiplicative inverse B of a square matrix A is such that A × B = I (mod n). It is interesting to note that if we use modulo n arithmetic, multiplicative inverse of a matrix A exists in Z_n, if determinant |A| and modulus n are coprime.

Example 7

(a) Determine if matrix B is additive inverse of matrix A modulo 7.

$$A = \begin{bmatrix} 3 & 2 & 1 \\ 0 & 5 & 6 \\ 1 & 4 & 0 \end{bmatrix} \quad B = \begin{bmatrix} 4 & 5 & 6 \\ 0 & 2 & 1 \\ 6 & 3 & 0 \end{bmatrix}$$

(b) Determine if matrix B is multiplicative inverse of matrix A modulo 7.

$$A = \begin{bmatrix} 5 & 1 \\ 2 & 4 \end{bmatrix} \quad B = \begin{bmatrix} 1 & 5 \\ 3 & 3 \end{bmatrix}$$

Solution

(a)
$$A + B = \begin{bmatrix} 3 & 2 & 1 \\ 0 & 5 & 6 \\ 1 & 4 & 0 \end{bmatrix} + \begin{bmatrix} 4 & 5 & 6 \\ 0 & 2 & 1 \\ 6 & 3 & 0 \end{bmatrix} = \begin{bmatrix} 0 & 0 & 0 \\ 0 & 0 & 0 \\ 0 & 0 & 0 \end{bmatrix} \text{(mod 7)}$$

B is additive inverse of A.

(b)
$$A \times B = \begin{bmatrix} 5 & 1 \\ 2 & 4 \end{bmatrix} \times \begin{bmatrix} 1 & 5 \\ 3 & 3 \end{bmatrix} = \begin{bmatrix} 1 & 0 \\ 0 & 1 \end{bmatrix} \text{(mod 7)}$$

B is multiplicative inverse of A.

2.5   GREATEST COMMON DIVISOR (GCD)

We say a non-zero integer a is a divisor of another integer b provided there is no residue after the division. When a is divisor of b, we express this fact by $a \mid b$. We are interested in finding the greatest common divisor of two numbers. Greatest common divisor has some interesting cryptographic applications, which we examine later as we proceed. It is defined as follows:

A *positive* integer c is said to be the greatest common divisor (written as gcd) of a and b, if

1. c is divisor of a and b.
2. any divisor of a and b is also a divisor of c.

From the definition, it follows that

- gcd (a, b) = gcd $(-a, b)$ = gcd $(a, -b)$ = gcd $(-a, -b)$, since the greatest common factor is a positive integer. For example, gcd (48, 60) = gcd (48, –60) = gcd (–48, –60) = 12.
- gcd $(a, b) = a$ if $a \mid b$, i.e., if a is divisor of b.
- gcd $(a, 0) = a$, since a always divides 0.

2.5.1 Euclid's Algorithm

Euclid's algorithm for finding the greatest common divisor is based on the theorem that gcd (a, b) = gcd $(b, a \bmod b)$. We assume that a is larger than b without loss of generality. The proof of this theorem is based on the following observations:

1. If $a \bmod b = r$, we can write $a = qb + r$. Every common divisor of a and b must also divide the residue $r = a - qb$. Thus all the common divisors for a and b are also the divisors of b and r.
2. If b and r have any common divisor other than those at (1) above, it should divide $qb + r$ as q is an integer. Therefore, it must divide a also.
3. Thus set of common dividers of a and b is also the set of common dividers of b and r. In other words, gcd (a, b) = gcd $(b, a \bmod b)$

This theorem can be used recursively to determine gcd of two integers.

Example 8 Find gcd of 70 and 38.

Solution   gcd $(70, 38)$ = gcd $(38, 70 \bmod 38)$ = gcd $(38, 32)$
= gcd $(32, 38 \bmod 32)$ = gcd $(32, 6)$
= gcd $(6, 32 \bmod 6)$ = gcd $(6, 2)$
= gcd $(2, 6 \bmod 2)$ = gcd $(2, 0)$

Thus, gcd $(70, 38)$ = 2

2.5.2 Bezout's Identity

Euclid's algorithm determines gcd of two given integers a and b. Bezout's identity extends Euclid's algorithm for determining the multiplicative inverses. It states that when a and b are any pair of positive integers, the following must always hold for some integers l and m:

$$\gcd (a, b) = a \times l + b \times m$$

For example, if $a = 16$ and $b = 6$, we have gcd $(16, 6) = 2$ and we can write $2 = 16 \times (-1) + 6 \times 3$. If a and b are coprime, gcd of a and b is 1, and therefore, we can write

$$a \times l + b \times m = 1$$

Let us consider this equation modulo b.

$$(a \times l) \bmod b + (b \times m) \bmod b = 1 \bmod b \Rightarrow (a \times l) \bmod b = 1$$

Thus l must be multiplicative inverse of a in Z_b.
Similarly, if we consider the equation $a \times l + b \times m = 1$ modulo a, we get

$$(a \times l) \bmod a + (b \times m) \bmod a = 1 \bmod a \Rightarrow (b \times m) \bmod a = 1$$

Thus, m must be multiplicative inverse of b in Z_a. In other words, given two coprimes a and b, if we can express them in the form $a \times l + b \times m = 1$, then the coefficients l and m of a and b are their multiplicative inverses in Z_b and Z_a respectively. Extended Euclid's algorithm described next enables us to express coprimes a and b in this form.

2.5.3   Extended Euclid's Algorithm

We use the same Euclid algorithm as before to find the gcd (a, b), but now we write the residue at each step in the following form:

Residue $= a \times l + b \times m$

Eventually when the residue becomes 1 (which will happen when a and b are coprime), we can get the multiplicative inverses as coefficients of a and b. We illustrate the algorithm with the following example.

Let the two coprimes be 32 and 17. The steps of Euclid's algorithm for determining the gcd of these numbers are given below:

$$
\begin{aligned}
\gcd(32, 17) = \gcd(17, 15) \quad & \text{Residue } 15 = 1 \times 32 + (-1) \times 17 \\
= \gcd(15, 2) \quad & \text{Residue } 2 = 1 \times 17 - 1 \times 15 \\
& = 1 \times 17 - 1 \times (32 - 17) \\
& = (-1) \times 32 + 2 \times 17 \\
= \gcd(2, 1) \quad & \text{Residue } 1 = 1 \times 15 - 7 \times 2 \\
& = 1 \times (1 \times 32 - 1 \times 17) - 7 \times \{(-1) \times 32 + 2 \times 17\} \\
& = 8 \times 32 + (-15) \times 17
\end{aligned}
$$

Thus multiplicative inverse of 32 in Z_{17} is 8. The multiplicative inverse of 17 in Z_{32} is $(-15) \bmod 32$ which is 17.

2.6   SUMMING UP

This chapter covered the first part of the mathematical background required cryptography—modular arithmetic.

- We define $a \bmod n$ (read a modulo n) to be the remainder r of division of a by n, i.e., $a \bmod n = r$. The mod n operator maps a positive or negative integer from set of integers Z to an element in the set $Z_n = \{0, 1, 2, \ldots, n-1\}$, called set of residues.
- Integers a and b are said to be congruent modulo n if $a \bmod n = b \bmod n$.
- If a, b and c are elements of Z_n, the following properties of the arithmetic operations in Z_n are observed.

  Commutative law $(a + b) \bmod n = (b + a) \bmod n$, $(a \times b) \bmod n = (b \times a) \bmod n$
  Associative law $[(a + b) + c] \bmod n = [a + (b + c)] \bmod n$, $[(a \times b) \times c] \bmod n = [a \times (b \times c)] \bmod n$
  Distributive law $[(a \times (b + c)] \bmod n = [(a \times b) + (a \times c)] \bmod n$

- a and b in Z_n are additive inverse of each other if $(a + b) \bmod n = 0$
- a and b of Z_n are multiplicative inverse of one another if $(a \times b) \bmod n = 1$
- Bezout's identity states that when a and b are any pair of positive integers, then for some integers l and m, $\gcd(a, b) = a \times l + b \times m$.
- Extended Euclid's algorithm is used to determine multiplicative inverse in Z_n.

We will see simple applications of modular arithmetic in Chapter 3. We will build on the concepts learnt in this chapter in Chapter 5, where we study algebraic structures.

Key Terms		
Additive inverse	Congruence	Modulus
Associative law	Distributive law	Multiplicative inverse
Bezout's identity	Euclid's algorithm	Set of residues
Commutative law	Greatest common divisor	

RECOMMENDED READING

Dummit, D. and Foote, R., *Abstract Algebra*. John Wiley & Sons, Hoboken, NJ, 2004.

Durbin, J., *Modern Algebra*, John Wiley & Sons, Singapore, 2005.

Forouzan, Behrouz A., *Cryptography and Network Security*, Tata McGraw-Hill, New Delhi, 2007.

Stallings, W., *Cryptography and Network Security*, Prentice-Hall of India, New Delhi, 2008.

Trappe, W., Washington, L., *Introduction to Cryptography and Coding Theory*, Pearson Prentice-Hall, NJ, 2006.

──────(PROBLEMS)──────

1. Find: (a) 25 mod 7, (b) −35 mod 11, (c) −6 mod 8, (d) 23 mod 23.
2. Select the numbers that are congruent modulo 7 in the set {17, 13, −4, 27, 50}.
3. If $a = 43$, $b = 37$, find $(a \times b)$ mod 7.
4. Find: (a) 14^4 mod 12, (b) 81^{15} mod 11.
5. Determine additive inverse pairs of Z_{17}.
6. Encrypt 'WORK' using additive modular arithmetic when the encryption key is 11.
7. Decrypt PUKPH which has been encrypted using additive modular arithmetic. The encryption key is 7.
8. Find multiplicative inverse pairs of Z_{12}.
9. Encrypt the letter 'P' using multiplicative modular arithmetic when the encryption key is 7.
10. Decrypt the letter 'S' which has been encrypted using multiplicative modular arithmetic and encryption key equal to 7.

11. Determine the additive inverse of matrix A modulo 9.

$$A = \begin{bmatrix} 3 & 2 & 1 \\ 0 & 5 & 6 \\ 1 & 4 & 0 \end{bmatrix}$$

12. Determine if matrix B is multiplicative inverse of matrix A modulo 7.

$$A = \begin{bmatrix} 3 & 1 \\ 2 & 4 \end{bmatrix} \qquad B = \begin{bmatrix} 6 & 2 \\ 2 & 4 \end{bmatrix}$$

13. Find the gcd using Euclid's algorithm.
    (a) 105, 66
    (b) 42, 60
    (c) 12, 84

14. Find the multiplicative inverse using Extended Euclid's algorithm.
    (a) 26 modulo 31
    (b) 28 mod 45

15. Determine the multiplicative inverse of 5 in Z_{11}, Z_{12}, and Z_{13}. It is to be noted that the inverse of an integer depends completely on the modulus, i.e., if the modulus changes, the inverse changes. This fact is crucial for the RSA cryptosystem, which is introduced in Chapter 9.

3

Classical Encryption Techniques

This chapter introduces symmetric-key ciphers that have been used in past, before advent of computing technology. These ciphers are not used today, but they are good starting point for understanding the principles of encryption. We begin this chapter with elemental terms and definitions from cryptography. The classical ciphers are categorized as substitution ciphers and transposition ciphers. We examine the various encryption schemes in these two categories. The emphasis is on laying conceptual foundations of encryption principles that would be used later in building modern ciphers.

3.1 TERMINOLOGY OF CRYPTOGRAPHY

The word *cryptography* comes from two Greek words meaning 'secret writing'. It is the science of converting a message into a coded form that hides the information contained in the message. We encrypt a message before its transmission so that an eavesdropper may not get the information contained in the message. The original unencrypted message is called *plaintext*. The encrypted message is called *ciphertext*.

There are many ways of carrying out encryption. These are called *cryptography systems* or *ciphers*. A cryptography system consists of two components (Figure 3.1):

1. A set of complementary algorithms, encryption algorithm (E) and decryption (D) algorithm
2. Cipher key (K)

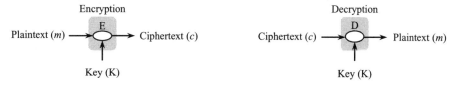

Figure 3.1 Symmetric-key encryption.

It is possible to have an algorithm that works without a key, but then each user will require different and secret encryption algorithm. Use of the cipher key overcomes this problem. Each user has a secret cipher key. A message is encrypted using well-known encryption algorithm and the cipher key. The same key is used for decryption. Therefore, the user shares his key with the other user to whom he sends his encrypted message.

If the message is *m*, encryption algorithm is E and the cipher key is K, the encrypted output *c* is usually written as:

$$c = E(K, m)$$

Similarly, for decryption algorithm D, we write

$$m = D(K, c)$$

Since the encryption and decryption algorithms are well known, strength of a cryptography system is determined by the number of possible keys. If someone tries to decrypt a ciphertext by guessing the key, he is required to make large number of trials. *Key-space* is the total number of all possible keys that can be used in a cryptography system. For example, DES (Data Encryption Standard) algorithm is based on 56-bit key. Its key space is of size 2^{56} ($\approx 7.2 \times 10^{16}$), which is a very large number.

3.1.1   Symmetric-key and Asymmetric-key Encryption

If the key for decryption is same as that used for encryption, we refer such encryption as *symmetric-key encryption*. Figure 3.1 depicts a symmetric encryption system. The sender and the receiver must have a common secret key between them.

We can also have *asymmetric-key encryption* system. It uses a pair of keys. A message encrypted with one of these keys can be decrypted using only the other key. These keys are not deducible from each other. Each user is assigned one pair of such keys. He makes one of these keys known publicly. This key is called *public key* (K_P). All the senders use this public key to encrypt the messages for him. The owner of the public key decrypts the received ciphertext using his other key, which is known only to him and is called *private key* (K_R). As shown in Figure 3.2, Alice uses Bob's public key (K_{BP}) for encrypting a message for him. Bob uses his private key (K_{BR}) for decrypting the message received from Alice.

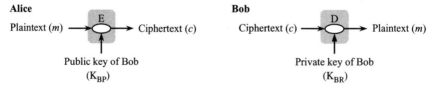

Figure 3.2   Asymmetric-key encryption.

Asymmetric-key encryption has one basic advantage over symmetric-key encryption. Key distribution is very simple since only public key (K_P) is to be shared and public key is not a secret. For example, Bob can publish his public key on his visiting card or web page. There are other important applications of asymmetric key in cryptography. We will learn these later.

3.1.2 Cryptanalysis

Every cryptography system has its weak points. *Cryptanalysis* is the art of deciphering an encrypted message without complete knowledge of the key required for decryption. An attempted cryptanalysis is called a *cryptanalytic attack*. The goals of a *cryptanalyst* can be:

- recovery of partial or full reconstruction of the message from ciphertext. For example, if a firm always prefixes its name in all its messages, the cryptanalyst will be able to partially decrypt the message using encrypted name of the firm as the first hint.
- inferring some contextual information from the ciphertext without breaking the encryption. For example, Alice sends a fixed encrypted message 'Love you' to Bob daily at a fixed time. If the ciphertext is different on a particular day, the cryptanalyst gets some contextual information.
- inferring the key for decryption of future messages.
- finding weakness of a cryptography system for its exploitation.

A cryptanalyst can attack a cryptography system in several ways to achieve his goals. We discuss these later in the chapter.

3.2 CLASSICAL ENCRYPTION METHODS

There are two basic ways of encrypting a message:

- Substitution
- Transposition

Substitution: Substitution means replacing a symbol of the plaintext with another symbol. For example, COMPUTER may be encrypted as DPNQVUFS. Here each letter has been substituted by its next letter in the alphabet.

Transposition: Transposition means rearranging the order of appearance of the symbols of the message. For example, COMPUTER may be encrypted as CMUEOPTR, in which letters at odd positions have been written first. Transposition is also referred to as *permutation*.

The encryption key defines the values of parameters used by encryption and decryption algorithms. An encryption system may have multiple stages of substitution and transposition. We describe in the following sections some classical encryption schemes that demonstrate the application of substitution and transposition techniques.

3.3 SUBSTITUTION CIPHERS

Substitution has been the most common method of encryption. Some of the popular substitution ciphers are listed as follows:

1. Shift cipher
2. Monoalphabetic cipher
3. Playfair cipher

4. Hill cipher
5. Polyalphabetic ciphers
   (a) Vigenere cipher
   (b) One time pad

Substitution is not restricted to substituting one character at a time. Substitution rule can also be done for a group of consecutive characters of the plaintext. Playfair and Hill ciphers are examples of such ciphers.

3.3.1 Shift Cipher

The earliest documented substitution cipher was used by Julius Caesar. His cipher involves substituting each letter of the message with a letter which is three places later. Thus D is replaced with G. The alphabet is wrapped around at Z so that Y becomes B. Thus the word MAYOR is encrypted as PDBRU.

We can express this algorithm mathematically by representing each letter of the alphabet by an integer that corresponds to its position in the alphabet. The entire English alphabet can be represented by integers from 0 to 25. Thus 4 represents letter E, if we start with A = 0. If m and c are the variables representing message and ciphertext respectively, we can now express the encryption and decryption functions as under.

$$c = E(3, m) = (m + 3) \bmod 26$$
$$m = D(3, c) = (c - 3) \bmod 26$$

We use modulo 26 addition because the ciphertext is to be wrapped around letter Z. Note that the key is 3 here. A more general version of this cipher that allows for any amount of shift is called shift cipher. The amount of shift is determined by the key K.

$$c = E(K, m) = (m + K) \bmod 26$$
$$m = D(K, c) = (c - K) \bmod 26$$

For example, if the key K = 5, the word NEW is encoded as given below.

$$N \Rightarrow m = 13 \quad c = (13 + 5) \bmod 26 = 18 \Rightarrow S$$
$$E \Rightarrow m = 4 \quad c = (4 + 5) \bmod 26 = 9 \Rightarrow J$$
$$W \Rightarrow m = 22 \quad c = (22 + 5) \bmod 26 = 1 \Rightarrow B$$

3.3.2 Monoalphabetic Substitution Cipher

Shift cipher described earlier is much too simple. Its key space contains only 25 values for the key. A cryptanalyst can readily try all possible values of the key to decrypt the ciphertext. We can make the task of cryptanalyst more difficult by allowing arbitrary substitution of letters. Table 3.1 shows one example of arbitrary substitution. 'NETWORK' is encrypted as 'FTZVGKA' using the substitution alphabet.

TABLE 3.1 Monoalphabetic Substitution Ciphers

Regular alphabet	A	B	C	D	E	F	G	H	I	J	K	L	M	N	O	P	Q	R	S	T	U	V	W	X	Y	Z
Substitution alphabet	Q	W	E	R	J	Y	U	I	K	P	A	S	D	F	G	R	T	O	L	Z	X	C	V	B	N	M

There can be (26! − 1) such substitution alphabets. The sender and the receiver agree on one substitution alphabet for encryption and decryption.

Example 1 Substitution alphabet of a monoalphabetic cipher is derived from the phrase THE QUICK BROWN FOX JUMPS OVER A LAZY DOG ignoring the second occurrences of the letters. Decrypt the ciphertext QBSEXAFV.

Solution The substitution alphabet is derived from the given phrase as shown below (Table 3.2).

TABLE 3.2 Substitution Table of Example 1

Regular alphabet	A	B	C	D	E	F	G	H	I	J	K	L	M	N	O	P	Q	R	S	T	U	V	W	X	Y	Z
Substitution alphabet	T	H	E	Q	U	I	C	K	B	R	O	W	N	F	X	J	M	P	S	V	A	L	Z	Y	D	G

Substituting the letters from regular alphabet for ciphertext QBSEXAFV, we get the plaintext DISCOUNT.

Cryptanalysis of monoalphabetic substitution cipher entails trying each of the (26! − 1) substitution alphabets. 26! is a very large number (> 4×10^{26}). Cryptanalysts, therefore, take a more intelligent approach, which is based on statistical analysis, and is referred to as statistical attack.

3.3.3 Statistical Attack

Substitution methods described earlier retain some statistical characteristics of the plaintext in the ciphertext. For example, the relative frequency of occurrence of a letter or a combination of letters in English text remains same after substitution. Table 3.3 shows typical frequency distribution of letters in English text. Cryptanalyst exploits these characteristics to decrypt

TABLE 3.3 Frequency Distribution of Letters in English Text

Single letter											
E	12.702	S	6.327	U	2.758	P	1.929	Q	0.095
T	9.056	H	6.094	M	2.406	B	1.492	Z	0.074
A	8.167	R	5.987	W	2.360	V	0.978		
O	7.507	D	4.235	F	2.228	K	0.772		
I	6.996	L	4.025	G	2.015	J	0.153		
N	6.749	C	2.782	Y	1.974	X	0.150		
Double letter										
TH	3.15	ES	1.45	EN	1.20	IS	1.06	HA	0.84
HE	2.51	ON	1.45	ND	1.18	AR	1.01	SE	0.84
AN	1.72	EA	1.31	OR	1.13	OU	0.96	ET	0.80
IN	1.69	TI	1.28	TO	1.11	TE	0.94	AL	0.77
ER	1.54	AT	1.24	NT	1.10	OF	0.94	RI	0.77
RE	1.48	ST	1.21	ED	1.07	IT	0.88	NG	0.75

the ciphertext. He computes the frequency distribution of the letters in the ciphertext and establishes their original identities. A more comprehensive analysis can be done by comparing frequency distribution of diagrams (combinations of two letters) and trigram (combinations of three letters) as well. It is, of course, necessary that the ciphertext should be sufficiently long to reveal its statistical characteristics.

Shift cipher and monoalphabetic cipher are based on single-letter substitution. These ciphers are easy to break using statistical methods. Instead of single letter substitution, we can do multiple-letter substitution. For example, combination two or more letters of plaintext can be mapped to a combination of ciphertext letters. It is seen that multiple letter substitution reduces retention of statistical features of plaintext in the ciphertext. We examine two such substitution ciphers next.

3.3.4 Playfair Cipher

The Playfair cipher is a substitution cipher in which two letters are encrypted at a time. Substitution is made using a 5 × 5 matrix of letters and a key phrase known to the sender and intended receiver. The matrix is formed as under:

- The key phrase is first entered in the matrix left to right starting with the first cell at the top-left corner. Letters that appear second time and spaces in the key phrase are omitted.
- The rest of the matrix is filled with the remaining letters in alphabetic order.
- The letters I and J are assigned the same cell to accommodate all the 26 letters of alphabet in the matrix.

For example, if the key phrase is 'NETWORK SECURITY', the resulting matrix is as shown below.

N	E	T	W	O
R	K	S	C	U
I/J	Y	A	B	D
F	G	H	L	M
P	Q	V	X	Z

Substitution is done in pairs as per the following rules:

- The message is divided into pairs of letters. Repeating letters that fall in the same pair are separated with a filler letter, say X. For example,

LEAVE AT TEN ⇒ LE AV EA TX TE NX

- Note that we have padded the message with the filler X in order to make its length even, and have suppressed the spaces.
- If the two letters of a pair fall in the same row of the matrix, they are replaced by letters to the right in the row. The first element of the row circularly follows the last element of the row. The same rule holds for the letters falling in the same column. Thus

AV ⇒ HT

TE ⇒ WT

- If the two letters of a pair fall in different rows and different columns, each letter of the pair is replaced with the letter that is in the same row but in the column of the other letter. For example,

$$LE \Rightarrow GW$$

$$NX \Rightarrow WP$$

Thus 'LEAVE AT TEN' is encrypted as GWHTTYWVWTWP. Decryption is carried out in a similar manner. While decrypting, one must resolve I/J ambiguity, figure out the padding characters and add spaces to get a meaningful message.

Playfair cipher was thought to be unbreakable for many decades, but it was easily broken. The cryptanalysis of the Playfair cipher is aided by the fact that a diagram and its reverse will encrypt in a similar fashion. That is, if AB encrypts to XY, then BA will encrypt to YX.

3.3.5 Hill Cipher

The Hill cipher takes a mathematical approach to multiletter substitution. A numerical value is assigned to each letter of alphabet. For example, the integers 0 through 25 can be assigned to the letters A through Z of the plaintext. Let us assume three letters of the plaintext are to be substituted at a time. The encryption key K in this case consists of a 3×3 matrix of integers.

$$K = \begin{bmatrix} k_{11} & k_{12} & k_{13} \\ k_{21} & k_{22} & k_{23} \\ k_{31} & k_{32} & k_{33} \end{bmatrix}$$

The ciphertext vector $c = \begin{bmatrix} c_1 \\ c_2 \\ c_3 \end{bmatrix}$ corresponding to the vector $m = \begin{bmatrix} m_1 \\ m_2 \\ m_3 \end{bmatrix}$ is obtained by

$$c = Km \bmod 26$$

Decryption is carried out using multiplicative inverse of K modulo 26.

$$m = K^{-1}c \bmod 26$$

Recall from Chapter 2 that multiplicative inverse modulo 26 will exist if determinant |K| and 26 are coprime. Hill cipher has very large key space since the matrix elements can be chosen from a large set of integers. But it becomes totally insecure, if the plaintext and ciphertext pairs are known. The key matrix can be calculated easily from known m and c pairs.

Example 2 Encrypt the word DESIGN using Hill cipher key $\begin{bmatrix} 9 & 4 \\ 5 & 7 \end{bmatrix}$.

Solution Since the key is 2×2 matrix, we encrypt the letters in pairs. The pairs DE, SI and GN are represented numerically as vectors $\begin{bmatrix} 3 \\ 4 \end{bmatrix}$, $\begin{bmatrix} 18 \\ 11 \end{bmatrix}$ and $\begin{bmatrix} 6 \\ 13 \end{bmatrix}$ respectively. Multiplying these vectors to the key, we get

$$\begin{bmatrix} 9 & 4 \\ 5 & 7 \end{bmatrix} \times \begin{bmatrix} 3 \\ 4 \end{bmatrix} \bmod 26 = \begin{bmatrix} 17 \\ 17 \end{bmatrix}$$

$$\begin{bmatrix} 9 & 4 \\ 5 & 7 \end{bmatrix} \times \begin{bmatrix} 18 \\ 11 \end{bmatrix} \bmod 26 = \begin{bmatrix} 24 \\ 11 \end{bmatrix}$$

$$\begin{bmatrix} 9 & 4 \\ 5 & 7 \end{bmatrix} \times \begin{bmatrix} 6 \\ 13 \end{bmatrix} \bmod 26 = \begin{bmatrix} 2 \\ 17 \end{bmatrix}$$

Converting the numerical values of the multiplication to the respective letters, we get the encryption as RRYLCR.

3.4 POLYALPHABETIC SUBSTITUTION CIPHERS

Monoalphabetic cipher uses one substitution alphabet for encrypting the entire message. This cipher is susceptible to statistical attack. We can improve it by using multiple substitution alphabets to encrypt a message. Such ciphers are called *polyalphabetic* ciphers. The key determines which substitution alphabet is to be used to encrypt a letter of the message. Same letter may be encrypted differently at different locations in the message. Vigenere cipher and One-time pad cipher described next are examples of polyalphabetic substitution cipher.

3.4.1 Vigenere Cipher

In Vigenere cipher, each letter of the encryption key denotes the ciphertext letter corresponding to letter A. The rest of the alphabet is given shift by the same number of places. In the example given below, the key is 'DECADE'. The key is repeated till it covers the entire message. Each plaintext letter is encrypted based on the shift as determined from the corresponding key letter above.

TABLE 3.4 Example of Vigenere Cipher

Reference	A	A	A	A	A	A	A	A	A	A	A	A	A	A
Key	D	E	C	A	D	E	D	E	C	A	D	E	D	E
Shift	3	4	2	0	3	4	3	4	2	0	3	4	3	4
Plaintext	A	T	T	A	C	K	B	L	U	E	A	R	M	Y
Ciphertext	D	X	V	A	F	O	E	P	W	E	D	V	P	C

Since a letter is encrypted differently at its each occurrence in the message, one would expect that the relative frequency distribution would be effectively destroyed in the Vigenere cipher. But a great deal of the input statistical distribution still shows up in the output. The reasons are as follows:

- The key consists of words from English text. Therefore, the letters of the key will have the frequency distribution of English text.

- The encryption rule is repeated at intervals equal to the key length. In above example, every sixth letter is encrypted using the same shift value. Thus the ciphertext consists of six interspersed encrypted messages, each encrypted using a monoalphabetic cipher.

To break the Vigenere cipher, one first tries to determine the length of the encryption key using the above insights. Once it is done, the rest of cryptanalysis involves identifying the original letters based on the frequency distribution.

3.4.2   One-time Pad

Vigenere cipher can be improved by

- using key as long as the message to avoid repeating the key word,
- using random sequence of letters as the key, and
- using a new key for every message so that the key is not repeated ever.

Such a scheme would be unbreakable because ciphertext bears no relationship to the plaintext. It appears simple conceptually, but it requires the sender and receiver to have same sequence of key letters. This is achieved by using a key pad, called *one-time pad*. It contains a random sequence of letters. The sender and receiver both have a copy of the pad. If the message is 300 characters long, first 300 characters from the pad are taken as the key. The sender encrypts each letter of the message as in the Vigenere cipher using the 300-letter key. The receiver decrypts the ciphertext using the first 300 letters from his copy of the pad. Both, the sender and the receiver, cross the used letters of the pad. For the next message, next set of letters is used from the pad.

One-time pad is considered the perfect cipher as it is unbreakable without the key. But it has some major limitations that make it not so useful in practice:

- There is continuous consumption of key pad as the messages are sent. Publication and distribution of the key pads are tricky problems from the security angle.
- The key pads of the sender and the receiver must be identical all the time. Consider a situation when an encrypted message is lost during transit. These key pads would no longer remain identical for future messages.

3.5   TRANSPOSITION CIPHERS

In transposition ciphers, the letters of plaintext remain same, but their original sequence is changed in a systematic way. One simple way could be to write the message along the rows of a matrix and read it column by column. Spaces in plaintext are omitted and last row is completed using a filler character, say X. The key determines the sequence in which columns are read. The following example illustrates the process.

Message: Guard leaves at fifteen hours.   Key: 5263174

5	2	6	3	1	7	4
G	U	A	R	D	L	E
A	V	E	S	A	T	F
I	F	T	E	E	N	H
O	U	R	S	X	X	X

Ciphertext: DAEXUVFURSESEFHXGAIOAETRLTNX

Cryptanalysis of transposition ciphertext is fairly simple. It involves determining whether transposition cipher has been used. The basic characteristics of a transposition cipher are as follows:

- It does not alter single-letter frequency distribution.
- The letters are not substituted.
- It does not preserve the frequency distribution of diagrams and trigrams.

Thus if the single-letter frequency distribution of ciphertext matches to that of English language, and frequency distribution of diagrams does not, it is assumed that transposition cipher has been used. Cryptanalysis thereafter involves arranging in the ciphertext in form of a matrix and playing around with column positions to determine the plaintext. Since number of columns may not be known, all possible values are tried. A transposition cipher can be made more secure by performing multiple rounds of transposition and using different key for each round.

3.6   CRYPTANALYTIC ATTACKS

A cryptanalyst can attack a cryptosystem in several ways. His approach depends on the resources available to him and his goals. We assume that he knows the encryption and decryption algorithms, but he does not know the key. He may have access to the source or the receiver of the ciphertext. Access implies that the source or the receiver may respond to him, if he sends a message to them. Remember that the entities, source and receiver, mentioned below may not be persons. These would be computing systems in today's scenario. We can define the following types of attacks.

3.6.1   Ciphertext-only Attack

The biggest challenge for a cryptanalyst is when he has only ciphertext with him. He has two alternatives: brute-force attack and statistical attack.

Brute-force attack: Brute-force attack consists of trying the entire key-space on the available ciphertext until a meaningful message is obtained. On average, the cryptanalyst will have to try half the keys to get success. Brute-force attack is blunted by keeping the key-space large so that it may not be practically possible to try all the keys. For example, if the key size is 128 bits, there are $2^{128} = 3.4 \times 10^{38}$ possible keys. If it takes 1 μs to try one key, it would take 5.4×10^{24} years to break a ciphertext.

Statistical attack: Apart from the brute-force attack, the other alternative is to use statistical means. The cryptanalyst correlates the statistical characteristics of the available ciphertext to those of its plaintext. To use this approach, he must have some idea of the type of plaintext and enough ciphertext to derive its statistical characteristics.

3.6.2 Known-plaintext Attack

In this case, the cryptanalyst has one or more plaintext (m) and ciphertext (c) pairs <m, c>. Such pairs become available in number of ways:

- Ciphertext may contain encrypted but well-known names, banners or other pieces of information.
- An event that bears some relation to the ciphertext occurs. Suppose intercepted ciphertext is about attack on a city, and attack occurs. Thus part of the plaintext becomes known.

The cryptanalyst tries to deduce the key from plaintext–ciphertext pairs for decrypting future messages.

3.6.3 Chosen-plaintext Attack

The cryptanalyst somehow manages the source to encrypt a plaintext chosen by him. The plaintext is so chosen that, its ciphertext would reveal the structure of the key. Or he may ask the source to encrypt several guesses of plaintext of the available ciphertext. Then he matches the ciphertexts to identify the true plaintext. He may impersonate a genuine receiver to make the sender encrypt his plaintext.

3.6.4 Chosen-ciphertext Attack

In this case, the cryptanalyst somehow manages to get a chosen-ciphertext decrypted by the source or the receiver. To achieve this objective he may impersonate a genuine source or receiver. Having received the plaintext–ciphertext pair, he tries to deduce the key for future use.

A cryptography system should be able to withstand all the above types of attacks. An *unconditionally secure* system can withstand the attacks irrespective of the amount of time and ciphertext available to the cryptanalyst. Usually, cryptography systems are *computationally secure* in the sense that the time required for the computations exceeds the useful lifetime of the information.

3.7 SUMMING UP

In this chapter, we introduced some classical methods of encryption to get familiar with the terminology and principles of cryptography.

- The unencrypted message is called plaintext. The encrypted message is called ciphertext.
- If the key for decryption is same as that used for encryption, we refer such encryption as symmetric-key encryption.

- Asymmetric-key encryption uses two different keys, the public key is for encryption and the private key is used for decryption.
- In a substitution cipher, a character is substituted by another character as decided by the encryption key.
- In transposition cipher, the plaintext letters are rearranged based on some rule parameterized by the cipher key.
- Cryptanalysis is the art of deciphering an encrypted message without complete knowledge of the key required for decryption.
  - When the cryptanalyst has access to ciphertext only, he uses statistical attack, or brute-force attack.
  - In the known-plaintext attack, cryptanalyst uses one or more plaintext–ciphertext pairs for analysis.
  - In chosen-ciphertext attack, the cryptanalyst somehow manages to get a ciphertext decrypted by the source or the receiver by impersonation.
  - In chosen-plaintext attack, the cryptanalyst somehow manages the source to encrypt a plaintext chosen by him. The plaintext is so chosen that, its ciphertext would reveal the structure of the key.

In the next chapter, we use these concepts to build modern symmetric-key block ciphers.

Key Terms		
Asymmetric-key encryption	Cryptanalysis	Public key
Brute-force attack	Known-plaintext attack	Shift cipher
Chosen-ciphertext attack	Monoalphabetic cipher	Statistical attack
Chosen-plaintext attack	One-time pad	Substitution cipher
Cipher key	Plaintext	Symmetric-key encryption
Ciphertext	Polyalphabetic ciphers	Transposition cipher
Ciphertext-only attack	Private key	

RECOMMENDED READING

Forouzan, Behrouz A., *Cryptography and Network Security*, Tata McGraw-Hill, New Delhi, 2007.

Kahn, D., *The Codebreakers, The Story of Secret Writing*, Scribner, New York, 1996.

Kaufman, C., Perlman, R. and Spenciner, M., *Network Security, Private Communication in a Public World*, Prentice-Hall of India, New Delhi, 2007.

Kumar, I., *Cryptology*, AP Press, Laguna Hills, CA, 1997.

Paar, C. and Pelzl, J., *Understanding Cryptography, A Textbook for Students and Practitioners*. Springer (India) Pvt. Ltd., New Delhi, 2009.

Stallings, W., *Cryptography and Network Security*, Prentice-Hall of India, New Delhi, 2008.

Trappe, W., Washington, L., *Introduction to Cryptography and Coding Theory*, Prentice-Hall, NJ, 2006.

-------- (PROBLEMS) --------

1. A shift cipher has key K = 5.
   (a) Encrypt the word ROUTE.
   (b) Decrypt ciphertext FWRD.

2. The most frequent letter in a ciphertext is H. The encryption function is $c = (m + K)$ mod 26. Determine the key K.

3. A generalization of shift cipher known as affine cipher is $c = (am + b)$ mod 26.
   (a) Encrypt the word ARMY for $a = 3$ and $b = 5$.
   (b) Decrypt ciphertext LVOR for $a = 3$ and $b = 5$.
   (c) What are all the allowed values of a in the encryption function $(am + b)$ mod 26?
   (d) If GO maps to TH in an affine cipher $c = (am + b)$ mod 26, determine the valid key (a, b).

4. Affine cipher $c = (am + K)$ mod 26 maps I to P and F to Q. What will be the ciphertext of letter L?

5. The key of Vigenere cipher is VECTOR. Encrypt HOW IT WORKS.

6. Alice and Bob generate substitution alphabet by writing keyword followed by rest of the unused letters of the regular alphabet in sequence. They agree on the keyword GLORY. Alice wants to send the message MEET ME AT EIGHT. How does she encrypt it?

7. A cryptanalyst finds that letter Q is the most frequent letter in the ciphertext. The second most frequent letter is J. If the encryption function is $E(K, m) = (am + K)$ mod 26, determine a and K.

8. Determine the frequency distribution of letters and decrypt the following ciphertext:

   ZIJ UGCJOFDJFZ IQL IKAJR RXZN GF KDHGOZ GY QSS ZNHJL GY QXZGDGWKSJ HQOZL ZIKL QDJFRDJFZ VKSS IQCJ KDHQEZ GF GXO DQOUKFL VJ FJJR ZG OJCKLJ ZIJ JBHQFLKGF HSQFFJR ZIKL NJQO EIKJY IQL QUOJJR ZG OJCKLJ ZIJ ZQOUJZL

9. Construct a Playfair cipher using the keyword GENERAL.
   (a) Encrypt the message GOOD MORNING.
   (b) Decrypt the message DNVTUMEAGUIKKN.

10. Encrypt the word STRONG using each of the three Playfair cipher matrices shown as follows. Examine the matrices closely and generalize your observations.

N	E	T	W	O
R	K	S	C	U
I/J	Y	A	B	D
F	G	H	L	M
P	Q	V	X	Z

(a)

O	N	E	T	W
U	R	K	S	C
D	I/J	Y	A	B
M	F	G	H	L
Z	P	Q	V	X

(b)

Z	P	Q	V	X
O	N	E	T	W
U	R	K	S	C
D	I/J	Y	A	B
M	F	G	H	L

(c)

11. Encrypt ARMY using Hill cipher, if key $K = \begin{bmatrix} 5 & 1 \\ 2 & 7 \end{bmatrix}$.

12. A Hill cipher machine uses a 2×2 matrix K. It gives ciphertext HC for input BA and GT for input ZZ. What is the matrix K?

13. Determine the multiplicative inverse of the key K of Problem 11. Decrypt the ciphertext RPGK using the multiplicative inverse.

14. Encrypt BAD using Hill cipher, if $K = \begin{bmatrix} 8 & 5 & 1 \\ 2 & 4 & 9 \\ 4 & 1 & 8 \end{bmatrix}$.

15. The adversary carries out a chosen-plaintext attack on a mod 26 affine cipher using plaintext HAHA. The ciphertext is NONO. Determine the encryption function.

16. Encrypt the message 'SECRET MASTER KEYS' using double transposition and 4×4 matrix. First transpose the columns according to $(1, 2, 3, 4) \rightarrow (2, 4, 1, 3)$. Then transpose the rows according to $(1, 2, 3, 4) \rightarrow (4, 1, 2, 3)$. The ciphertext is read row by row.

17. Alice and Bob use a shorter alphabet of the following eight symbols. 3-bit binary representation of a symbol is in brackets.

    A(000)   I(001)   L(010)   M(011)   N(100)   P(101)   S(110)   T(111)

    They have one-time key pad IMPLSTSANLI and use XOR of bits of a symbol with respective bits of the key for encrypting the symbol. Encrypt the message 'MAIL STAMP'.

18. If Alice encrypts the message SLAM as PAIN, what is the one-time key pad? Assume the alphabet of Problem 17 is used.

19. Alice uses Vigenere cipher for encryption of her messages to Bob. When her message is very confidential she uses Vigenere cipher two times using two different keys. The first key word is DUAL and the second key word is CIPHER. Her confidential message is 'Meet me at Park Street'.
    (a) What is the encrypted message sent by Alice to Bob?
    (b) Derive a Vigenere key that directly maps her plaintext message to her encrypted message sent by Alice to Bob. How is the key related to the keys used by Alice in respect of its value and size of the key word?
    (c) Does the Alice's double encryption approach really effective?

20. A ciphertext encrypted with Vigenere cipher contains three occurrences of the letter sequence DHESUIGI starting at positions 37, 1283 and 2291. Which is the probable length of the key? (*Hint:* Distance between repeat occurrences is multiple of key size.)

21. The following text is encrypted using shift cipher. Determine the shift key and decrypt the ciphertext.
    Y M J N S H W J F X J I Z X J T K H T R U Z Y J W F S I H T R R Z S N H F Y N T S
    X D X Y J R X G D N S I Z X Y W D M F X N S H W J F X J I Y M J W N X P T K U W T U
    W N J Y F W D N S K T W R F Y N T S

22. We assume that the attacker manages Alice somehow to provide ciphertext of a few pieces of plaintext using affine cipher $c = (am + b) \bmod n$. Show how the attacker computes the key (a, b) of the cipher using two plaintext–ciphertext pairs, (m_1, c_1) and (m_2, c_2). What does the attacker ensures while choosing m_1 and m_2?

4

Symmetric-key Ciphers I
(Data Encryption Standard)

We introduced notion of symmetric-key cipher in Chapter 3. There are two categories of symmetric-key ciphers—block ciphers and stream ciphers. In this chapter, we focus on principles and structural design of symmetric-key block ciphers. We begin the chapter with cryptographic considerations in choosing appropriate block size and key size of block ciphers. We look at block cipher design based on multiple rounds of encryption. We study Feistal block cipher structure and Data Encryption Standard (DES) which is based on this cipher structure. We end the chapter with triple DES which replaced DES to meet the challenge of the current state of computing technology.

4.1 BLOCK CIPHERS

A symmetric-key block cipher encrypts n-bit block of plaintext into n-bit block of ciphertext using a key K (Figure 4.1). A message having more than n bits is divided into n-bit blocks and the last block having fewer than n bits is padded suitably to make n-bit block. Encryption and decryption are carried out taking one block at a time.

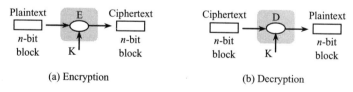

        (a) Encryption   (b) Decryption

Figure 4.1   Block cipher.

There are two ways of transforming a block of plaintext into a block ciphertext—substitution and transposition.

Substitution

Recall the substitution ciphers we studied in Chapter 3. Each letter of the English alphabet is mapped to another letter. In the same manner, a block substitution cipher maps an n-bit block

37

to another n-bit block. For example, we can do substitution transformation simply by adding n-bit key to n-bit plaintext blocks using XOR binary operation (Figure 4.2).

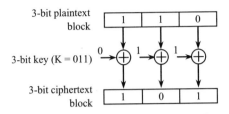

Figure 4.2   Block substitution based on XOR operation.

We can adopt more sophisticated approach for block substitution—random mapping an n-bit block to another n-bit block. Recall that similar approach was adopted in classical monoalphabetic cipher where the alphabet was mapped to a random sequence of letters. There are 2^n possible different plaintext n-bit blocks, and there can be altogether $2^n!$ different mappings (Figure 4.3). These $2^n!$ mappings would require a $\lceil \log_2 2^n! \rceil$ bits long key.

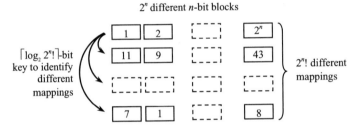

Figure 4.3   Substitution transformation using random mapping.

Let us consider the following example:

For block size of 3 bits, there are $2^3 = 8$ different blocks which can be mapped in $2^3!$ $= 40320$ ways. 40320 mappings will require key size of $\lceil \log_2 2^3! \rceil = 16$ bits to give unique identity to each mapping.

Transposition

Basic transposition transformation of an n-bit block involves shuffling its n bits without changing the number of 1s and 0s in the block [Figure 4.4(a)]. An n-bit block can be shuffled in $n!$ ways [Figure 4.4(b)]. The required key size is $\lceil \log_2 n! \rceil$ bits. For example, if the block size is 3 bits, there can be $3! = 6$ possible transformations. These six possible transformations can be identified using a key having 3 bits.

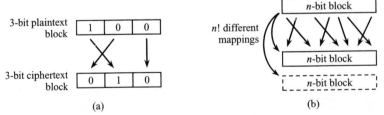

Figure 4.4   Transposition transformation.

Some important observations to note are as follows:

(a) For block size of n bits, the possible substitution mappings are $2^n!$ in number and the full-key size is $\lceil \log_2 2^n! \rceil$. A smaller key size would imply that we use a subset of $2^n!$ possible mappings. The same holds true for transposition transformation as well. The full key size is $\lceil \log_2 n! \rceil$ in this case.

(b) The transposition transformations are subset of $2^n!$ substitution mappings.

(c) In case of full-size key encryption transformation, multiple rounds of encryption using different keys do not result in a stronger cipher. In Figure 4.5, plaintext block m is encrypted to ciphertext block c using keys K_1 and K_2 in two rounds. As shown in Figure 4.5(b), it is always possible to find key K_3 that directly encrypts m to c since we are using full-size key. Thus for the adversary, m is encrypted as c using key K_3. The effort required for brute-force attack on c is equivalent to that for single round of encryption.

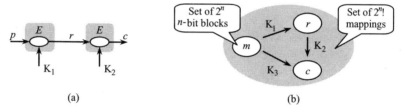

(a) (b)

Figure 4.5 Multiple rounds of encryption.

Consider a shift cipher $c = (m + K) \bmod 26$, where c and m are elements of English alphabet represented as integers from 0 to 25, and K is a full-size key, i.e., it can have values 0 to 25. Let us assume that $m = 12$ is encrypted in two rounds with $K_1 = 6$ and $K_2 = 10$. Thus we have

$r = (m + K_1) \bmod 26 = (12 + 6) \bmod 26 = 18$
$c = (r + K_2) \bmod 26 = (18 + 10) \bmod 26 = 2$

But if m is directly encrypted in one round using $K_3 = 16$, we get

$c = (m + K_3) \bmod 26 = (12 + 16) \bmod 26 = 2$

Therefore, the two rounds of encryption have not resulted in a stronger cipher. But if we restrict the key space to say 0 to 10, then the above encryption carried out in two rounds requires the adversary to find the two round keys.

4.2 BLOCK CIPHERS USING MULTIPLE ROUNDS

Simple random substitution has two issues:

- If the block size (n) is kept too small, compilation of statistics of 2^n different blocks becomes feasible. For example, there are only 256 different blocks, if $n = 8$. Therefore, simple substitution block cipher becomes vulnerable to the statistical attack, similar to the one on monoalphabetic cipher.

- It is possible to thwart the statistical attack by keeping the block size sufficiently large, at least 64 bits. When $n = 64$, the number of different blocks is 18446744073709551616. In such a large block space, the statistical characteristics of the plaintext get diffused and statistical attack becomes infeasible.
- The substitution cipher for block size of 64 bits requires key length of $\lceil \log_2 2^{64}! \rceil \approx 2^{70}$ bits. Such large key-size is impractical. Shorter key would mean that we use a subset of $2^n!$ possible mappings and reduce the effort required to break the code using the brute-force attack.

We address these issues by

- using block size of 64 bits or more,
- using key size of 256 bits or less, and
- doing multiple rounds of encryption.

For example, a common block cipher DES has block of 64 bits, the key size of 56 bits and 16 rounds of encryption. Note that multiple rounds of encryption are effective, since we are using a small fraction of total key space, $2^{56} \approx 7.2 \times 10^{16}$ keys out of total $2^{2^{70}}$ keys[1], required for random mappings. Figure 4.6 depicts the basic structure of such a block cipher scheme.

- In each round, the encryption function R (called round function) uses a different round key K_i (also called subkey) generated from the cipher key K.
- The round function R consists of a *product cipher*. Product cipher is a combination of two or more simple ciphers (e.g. substitution and transposition) executed in sequence in such a way that the product is cryptographically stronger than the individual component ciphers.
- Decryption is also carried out in the same number of rounds, but using the inverse function R^{-1} in each round and reversing the order of usage of the round keys.

Some of the important parameters and design features that determine the structure of a block cipher with multiple rounds are as follows:

Block size: Small block size makes the cipher prone to statistical attack. Large block size results in reduced speed of encryption/decryption. Block size of 128 bits is considered adequate for the current status of computing technology.

Cipher key (K):   Larger cipher key size implies greater security because effort for brute-force attack is increased. Key size of 64 bits or less is considered inadequate in the current status of computing technology. Key size of 128 bits is considered secure.

Round function R and number of rounds: The round function R is so chosen, each additional round of encryption gives more security. The round function R and number of rounds together determine the speed of execution of the block cipher. A slow encryption algorithm may impact on performance of an application. DES and AES that we describe in this book, have 16 and 10 rounds respectively.

---

1. Required key size is $\lceil \log_2 2^n! \rceil \approx 270$ for $n = 64$.

Round keys: Algorithm for generating the round key should have complex relationship between the cipher key (K) and the round key (K_i).

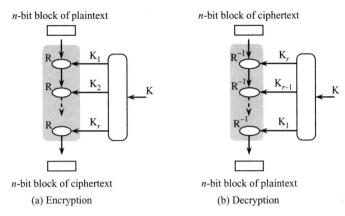

n-bit block of plaintext   *n*-bit block of ciphertext

n-bit block of ciphertext   *n*-bit block of plaintext

      (a) Encryption   (b) Decryption

Figure 4.6 Block cipher based on multiple rounds.

4.2.1 Diffusion and Confusion

Attempts of a cryptanalyst are directed towards finding a correlation between plaintext and ciphertext, and between the key and ciphertext. It was proposed by Claude Shannon in 1945 that any cryptographically secure system requires two fundamental attributes—diffusion and confusion.

Diffusion: Diffusion refers to dispersing the statistical structure of plaintext so that it is not reflected in the statistical structure of the ciphertext. In the context of block ciphers, it implies that changing one bit of an *n*-bit plaintext block should cause wide spread changes in its *n*-bit ciphertext block.

Confusion: In order to foil cryptanalytic attacks on the cipher key, there should be very complex (or confusing) relationship between the statistical characteristics of the ciphertext and the cipher key. A cryptographically secure system requires that changing even one bit of the cipher key should cause wide spread changes in the ciphertext.

These two fundamental attributes are built into every round of a block cipher.

4.2.2 Structure of Round Function R

Figure 4.7 shows some basic structures of round function R and its inverse R^{-1}. For the sake of explanation, we refer the input as plaintext *m*, the output as ciphertext *c* and the key as K. We are aware from Figure 4.6(a) that function R actually takes the output of previous round and the round key as inputs to produce the output for the next round.

    (a) In Figure 4.7(a), the ciphertext is given by $c = m \oplus K$ and the plaintext is given by $m = c \oplus K$. This is the simplest model but has no confusion and diffusion. Changing any one bit of the plaintext or of the key reflects as change in corresponding bit of the ciphertext.

(b) In Figure 4.7(b), function f is applied to the plaintext m and then the key K is added as the secret parameter so that $c = f(m) \oplus K$. Function f is so chosen that each bit of the plaintext m gets diffused to most of the bits of the ciphertext c. Decryption is carried out as $m = f^{-1}(c \oplus K)$, where function f^{-1} is inverse of function f. Thus function f must be invertible. This scheme introduces diffusion, but there is no confusion. Changing any one bit of the key reflects as change in corresponding bit of the ciphertext.

(c) In Figure 4.7(c), the ciphertext is given by $c = m \oplus g(K)$. Function g scrambles the key K before it is added as the secret parameter. It is so chosen that changing even a single bit of the key changes the ciphertext almost entirely. This scheme introduces confusion, but there is no diffusion. Changing any one bit of the plaintext reflects as change in corresponding bit of the ciphertext. Note that decryption does not require scrambling function g to be invertible as $m = c \oplus g(K)$.

(d) Confusion and diffusion can be introduced by combining the last two structures as shown in Figure 4.7(d). Ciphertext and plaintexts are given by $c = f(m) \oplus g(K)$ and $m = f^{-1}[c \oplus g(K)]$ respectively. Note that function f must be invertible and function g need not be invertible.

Thus diffusion and confusion can be introduced by suitable structural design of the round function R and proper choice of functions f and g. Horst Feistel did pioneering work in structural design of block ciphers. He demonstrated that both diffusion and confusion could be achieved using one non-invertible function g. We look at Feistal cipher structure in the next section.

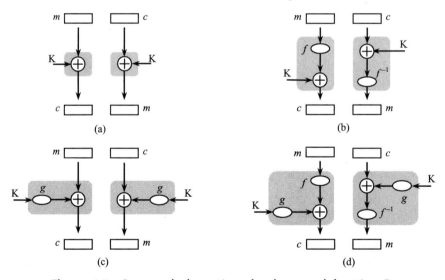

Figure 4.7   Structural alternatives for the round function R.

4.2.3   Feistel Cipher Structure

Feistal's approach to structural design of the round function is shown in Figure 4.8. A block is encrypted in at least two rounds and using only a non-invertible scrambling function g. Encryption consists of the following steps:

(a) The plaintext block m is divided into two halves, m_1 and m_2.

(b) m_1 is encrypted as $c_1 = m_1 \oplus g(K_1, m_2)$ in the first round. Function g is a non-invertible function that scrambles the key K_1 and m_2.

(c) m_2 is encrypted as $c_2 = p_2 \oplus g(K_2, c_1)$ in the second round.

(d) Concatenation $c_1 \| c_2$ is the ciphertext of block m.

Step (b) diffuses bits of the second half m_2 and key K_1 into c_1. Step (c) diffuses bits of c_1 (thus of m_1) and key K_2 into c_2. For decryption, the above steps are carried out in reverse order [Figure 4.8(b)]. c_2 is decrypted first to get $m_2 = c_2 \oplus g(K_2, c_1)$. Then we decrypt c_1 to get $m_1 = c_1 \oplus g(K_1, m_2)$. Concatenation $m_1 \| m_2$ is the decrypted plaintext block. Note that decryption does not require function g to be invertible.

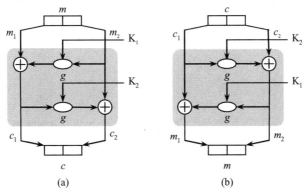

Figure 4.8 Feistel encryption scheme.

Interesting feature of this scheme is that encryption and decryption algorithms are same except for a small difference. Encryption follows the sequence m_1 and then m_2. Decryption, on the other hand, follows the reverse sequence, c_2 and then c_1. If c_1 and c_2 are swapped by the encryption algorithm, the decryption algorithm will be exactly same as the encryption algorithm (Figure 4.9). The keys K_1 and K_2, however, still need to be used in reverse order for decryption.

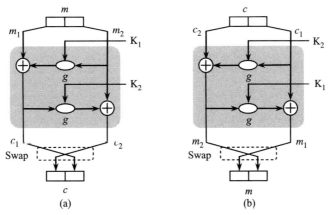

Figure 4.9 Feistel encryption scheme with swapping.

Figure 4.10(a) depicts the Feistel cipher structure consisting of 16 rounds and swapping at the tail end. The decryption algorithm shown in Figure 4.10(b) is same except that round keys are used in reverse order.

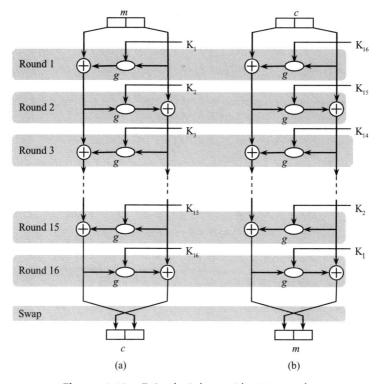

Figure 4.10   Feistel cipher with 16 rounds.

Data Encryption Standard (DES) is a block cipher based on Feistal structure with 16 rounds. We discuss this cipher in the next section. In Chapter 6, we shall study another important block cipher Advanced Encryption Standard (AES). AES uses the structure shown in Figure 4.7(d) for its round function. DES and AES block ciphers are widely used in the industry.

4.3   DATA ENCRYPTION STANDARD (DES)

Data Encryption Standard (DES) was published in 1975 and adopted as standard in 1977 by NIST. DES was broken in 1999, which resulted in NIST issuing a new directive that required organizations to use Triple DES. Triple DES is three consecutive applications of DES. Triple DES continues to enjoy wide usage in commercial applications. To understand triple DES, we must first understand the basic DES.

- DES is a block cipher with block size of 64 bits and key size of 56 bits.
- It is based on Feistel cipher structure with 16 rounds of encryption (Figure 4.10).
- Each round key is 48 bits long and is derived from the 56-bit DES key.

Figure 4.11 shows the overall structure of DES algorithm for encryption. It consists of the following stages:

(a) Initial permutation
(b) Sixteen rounds of encryption
(c) Swapping
(d) Final permutation

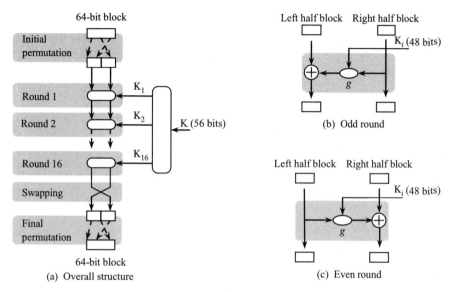

Figure 4.11 Basic structure of DES.

Initial permutation: The 64-bit input block is subjected to an initial permutation as shown in the form of a matrix below. Permutation spreads each input octet over the eight output octets. For example, the input bits 1 to 8 (first octet) occupy the last bit position in each of the output octets.

First output octet →

$$\begin{bmatrix} 58 & 50 & 42 & 34 & 26 & 18 & 10 & 2 \\ 60 & 52 & 44 & 36 & 28 & 20 & 12 & 4 \\ 62 & 54 & 46 & 38 & 30 & 22 & 14 & 6 \\ 64 & 56 & 48 & 40 & 32 & 24 & 16 & 8 \\ 57 & 49 & 41 & 33 & 25 & 17 & 9 & 1 \\ 59 & 51 & 43 & 35 & 27 & 19 & 11 & 3 \\ 61 & 53 & 45 & 37 & 29 & 21 & 13 & 5 \\ 63 & 55 & 47 & 39 & 31 & 23 & 15 & 7 \end{bmatrix}$$

First input octet

Encryption round Each round is based on Feistel cipher structure and encrypts one of the two halves received as output of the previous round. Figures 4.11(b) and 4.11(c) depict an odd and an even round of encryption respectively. An odd round encrypts left-side half block and an even round encrypts right-side half block. Encryption is carried out by XORing the 32-bit output of function *g* that scrambles the other half-block with the round key. The scrambling function *g* is described later.

Swapping: The two halves of the block at the end of round 16 are swapped. As mentioned earlier, swapping enables the encryption and decryption algorithms to be the same except for the order of usage of the round keys.

Final permutation: The 64-bit output after swapping is subjected to final permutation which is inverse of initial permutation. Note that at the time of decryption, the initial permutation restores the bits of the encrypted block to their original places.

The decryption algorithm is same as the encryption algorithm except that the round keys are used in reverse order.

4.3.1 Scrambling Function *g*

Scrambling function *g* is a non-invertible function having three stages—expansion (E), substitution (S) and permutation (P) (Figure 4.12). It takes two inputs: 48-bit round key K_i, and 32-bit half block as inputs to generate 32-bit scrambled output. This output is XORed with the other 32-bit half block to encrypt the half block.

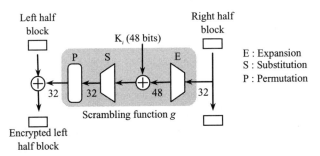

Figure 4.12 Scrambling function of DES.

Expansion (E): The first stage of function *g* expands 32 bits of the right half block to 48 bits. This is achieved by dividing the right half block into eight 4-bit words and then expanding each of these words to 6 bits as shown in Figure 4.13. The expanded 48-bit is then XORed with the 48-bit round key K_i.

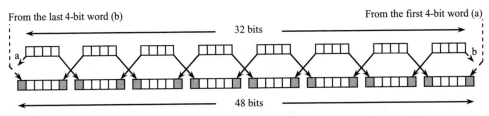

Figure 4.13 Expansion function (E) of DES.

Substitution (S): The 48-bit output produced by the previous step is broken into eight 6-bit words. Each 6-bit word is substituted with a 4-bit using eight different S-boxes, one for each word (Figure 4.14). The eight S-boxes together produce a 32-bit output.

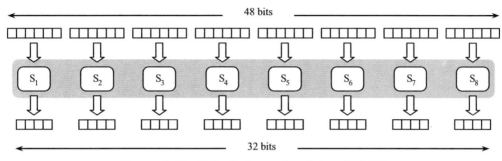

Figure 4.14 Substitution using S box in DES.

The eight S-boxes are basically eight different 4×16 lookup tables containing 4-bit substitution words. The first and the last bit of the 6-bit input word determine one of the four rows and the middle 4 bits determine one of 16 columns of the lookup table. The lookup table of S_1 box is given below (Table 4.1). For example, if the input to S_1 box is 010101, it produces output 12 (1100), corresponding to first (01) row and tenth (1010) column.

TABLE 4.1 Lookup Table of Substitution Box S_1

	0	1	2	3	4	5	6	7	8	9	10	11	12	13	14	15
0	14	4	13	1	2	15	11	8	3	10	6	12	5	9	0	7
1	0	15	7	4	14	2	13	1	10	6	12	11	9	5	3	8
2	4	1	14	8	13	6	2	11	15	12	9	7	3	10	5	0
3	15	12	8	2	4	9	1	7	5	11	3	14	10	0	6	13

Two important points to be noted are:

- The outer two bits that determine the row of a lookup table are function of the adjacent 6-bit words. Thus substitution facilitates diffusion and confusion.
- There are sixty-four different 6-bit input words and these are mapped to sixteen 4-bit output words. Thus four different input words map to the same output word. In other words, substitution is non-invertible.

Permutation (P): Finally, the 32-bit output of the S-boxes is passed through a fixed permutation P that scrambles the output bits. The permutation table is shown below (Table 4.2). It gives the location of input bit in the output bits. For example, seventeenth bit of the input is placed in the second bit position of the output.

TABLE 4.2 Permutation Table

16	7	20	21	29	12	28	17	1	15	23	26	5	18	31	10
2	8	24	14	32	27	3	9	19	13	30	6	22	11	4	25

4.3.2 Round Key Generation

DES specifies key length of 64 bits. These 64 bits consist of 56-key bits and 8-odd parity check bits. Every eighth bit in 64-bit key is a parity bit. The 56-key bits are used for generating sixteen 48-bit round keys as described below (Figure 4.15).

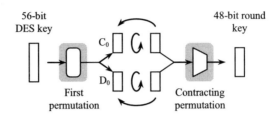

Figure 4.15 Round key generation.

(a) 56-key bits are subjected to first permutation as given below (Table 4.3). For example, 49th bit of the key takes the second bit position after first permutation. Note that bit numbers 8, 16, 24, 32, 40, 48, 56 and 64 are missing because there are parity bits. The original numbers of the rest of the bits are mapped to new locations as indicated in Table 4.3.

TABLE 4.3 First Permutation for Round Key Generation

C_0	57	49	41	33	25	17	9	1	58	50	42	34	26	18
	10	2	59	51	43	35	27	19	11	3	60	52	44	36
D_0	63	55	47	39	31	23	15	7	62	54	46	38	30	22
	14	6	61	53	45	37	29	21	13	5	28	20	12	4

(b) The 56-bit output after permutation is split into two halves of 28 bits each, C_0 and D_0 (Table 4.3).

(c) Each half is rotated left by one or two bits depending on the round number. In round numbers 1, 2, 9 and 16, the rotation is by one bit. The other rounds have two-bit rotation. Thus for round one, C_0 and D_0 are individually rotated by one bit.

(d) The two halves are concatenated and subjected to contracting permutation to get 48-bit round key K_1 (Table 4.4). Note that bits of the two halves are numbered 1 to 56 and bit numbers 9, 18, 22, 25, 35, 38, 43 and 54 are discarded.

TABLE 4.4 Contracting Permutation for Round Key Generation

14	17	11	24	1	5	3	28	15	6	21	10	23	19	12	4
26	8	16	7	27	20	13	2	41	52	31	37	47	55	30	40
51	45	33	48	44	49	39	56	34	53	46	42	50	36	29	32

(e) Next round key is obtained by further rotating the two halves of step (c) by one or two bits depending on the round number and then applying contracting permutation.

4.3.3 Weak and Semi-weak Keys

The only difference in DES encryption and decryption algorithms is that the round keys K_1 to K_{16} are used in reversed order. If the round key K_1 is equal to K_{16}, K_2 is equal to K_{15} and so on, running encryption algorithm second time with the same key will decrypt the ciphertext. DES key that generates the round keys with this property is a weak key. There are four weak keys in the DES key space of 2^{56}. Table 4.5 lists the four weak keys of DES. Keys have been written in hexadecimal notation with their parity bits.

TABLE 4.5 Weak Keys of DES

(Hexadecimal)

0101	0101	0101	0101
1F1F	1F1F	0E0E	0E0E
E0E0	E0E0	F1F1	F1F1
FEFE	FEFE	FEFE	FEFE

If two different DES keys K and K' generate round keys such that K_1 is equal to K'_{16}, K_2 is equal to K'_{15} and so on, then $E[K', E(K, p)] = p$. In other words, a ciphertext block generated using K can be decrypted by repeat encryption using K'. Such keys are semi-weak keys. There are six pairs of semi-weak keys (Table 4.6).

TABLE 4.6 Semi-weak Key Pairs

(Hexadecimal)

First key of the pair				Second key of the pair			
01FE	01FE	01FE	01FE	FE01	FE01	FE01	FE01
1FE0	1FE0	0EF1	0EF1	E01F	E01F	F10E	F10E
01E0	01E1	01F1	01F1	E001	E001	F001	F001
1FFE	1FFE	0EFE	0EFE	FE1F	FE1F	FE0E	FE0E
011F	011F	010E	010E	1F01	1F01	0E01	0E01
E0FE	E0FE	F1FE	F1FE	FEE0	FEE0	FEF1	FEF1

4.3.4 Strength of DES

DES with its 16 rounds of encryption has robust design, but it has its strong and weak points as listed below:

- The substitution step is very effective as far as diffusion is concerned. It has been shown that if just one bit is changed in the 64-bit input data block, 34 bits of the output ciphertext block get altered on average.
- The manner in which the round keys are generated from the DES key is also very effective as far as confusion is concerned. It has been shown that changing one bit of the DES key alters on average 35 bits of the output ciphertext block.
- The 56-bit DES key means a key space of $2^{56} \approx 7.2 \times 10^{16}$ keys. Assuming that, on the average half the keys need to be tried for a brute force attack, a machine trying one

key per microsecond would take 1142 years to break the code. However, a parallel-processing machine trying 1 million keys simultaneously would need only about 10 hours for the brute force attack.

4.3.5 Double DES

56-bit key of DES is considered inadequate against brute force attack. One alternative is to apply multiple DES encryptions on a block of plaintext using different 56-bit keys [Figure 4.16(a)]. For example, if we use two keys K_1 and K_2, double encryption implies that

$$c = E[K_2, E(K_1, m)], \; m = D[K_1, D(K_2, c)]$$

Apparently there is increase in key size from 56 bits to 112 bits, and therefore, brute force attack would require 2^{112} tries. This inference would be correct, if it is not possible to find another key K_3 such that

$$c = E[K_2, E(K_1, m)] = E(K_3, m)$$

If this were the case, double encryption using keys K_1 and K_2 is equivalent to single encryption using key K_3. On the face of it, possibility of existence of K_3 cannot be ruled out.

Recall that DES with its 56-bit key makes use of a small subset of these mappings, about 7.2×10^{16} mappings. It has been shown that a set of 7.2×10^{16} mappings obtained by 2^{56} DES keys is not closed under functional composition $E[K_2, E(K_1, p)]^2$. In simple words, it implies that double encryption using keys K_1 and K_2 will generate a mapping that cannot be obtained by single encryption using key K_3 [Figure 4.16(b)].

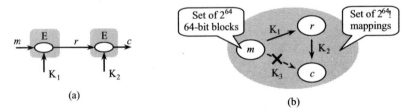

Figure 4.16 Double DES.

Meet-in-the-Middle Attack: For double DES encryption, a cryptanalyst takes a different approach. He does not make 2^{112} tries. He deploys 'meet-in-the-middle attack' as described below:

(a) He manages to get plaintext–ciphertext pair (m, c), where $c = E[K_2, E(K_1, m)]$. He knows that there exists a value r such that

$$r = E(K_1, m)$$
$$c = E(K_2, r)$$

(b) He encrypts the plaintext block m using all the possible values for key K_1. Since DES uses 56-bit key, he tries 2^{56} key values. One of the encrypted values is r.

---

2. Refer to Chapter 4 for closure property.

(c) Simultaneously, he decrypts the ciphertext block c using all the possible values for key K_2. In this case also, one of the decrypted values will be r.

(d) He picks up the key pairs (K_1, K_2) that generate same value on encryption of m using K_1 and on decryption of c using K_2. He may get several such key pairs. He keeps these key pairs for the next step.

(e) He manages to get another plaintext–ciphertext pair (m', c'), where $c' = E[K_2, E(K_1, m')]$. He encrypts m' and decrypts c' using only the key pairs obtained in the previous step (d) and matches the outputs. It can be shown that he will succeed in getting the right pair of keys (K_1, K_2) in this attempt with probability $1 - 2^{-16}$.

Therefore, the effort required for cryptanalysis of double DES using 'meet-in-the-middle' attack is of the order of 2^{57}, which is merely an order more than that for single DES.

4.3.6 Triple DES

Since double DES does not provide the level of security expected from a cipher with 112-bit key, another stage of DES encryption can be added. Triple DES, as it is called, can be configured in two ways:

(a) Triple DES with three different keys (3DES3)
(b) Triple DES with two different keys (3DES2)

Triple DES with Three Different Keys (3DES3)

Figure 4.17(a) depicts the first alternative which consists of three stages—an encryption stage using key K_1, a decryption stage using key K_2, and finally another encryption stage using key K_3. This is also referred to as EDE encryption, where EDE stands for encryption-decryption-encryption.

The decryption stage between two encryption stages does not weaken the resulting cryptographic system in any way. Recall that DES encryption and decryption algorithms are same. Encrypting a plaintext block with one key and then decrypting the output using another key amount to double encryption. Therefore, EDE encryption with three different keys is a three-stage encryption.

There is an important reason for inserting a stage of decryption between two stages of encryption. It makes 3DES3 backward compatible with single DES by setting key $K_1 = K_2$.

3DES3 is also susceptible to meet-in-the-middle attack, but it is still considerably more secure than single DES. The three keys can be found in about 2^{112} computations of DES. But its $56 \times 3 = 168$-bit secret key for encryption make it unwieldy for many applications. Some examples of internet applications that have adopted 3DES3 are PGP and S/MIME.

Triple DES with Two Different Keys (3DES2)

Triple DES with two keys is a popular alternative to the single DES. It uses EDE encryption with keys K_1 and K_2 as shown in Figure 4.17(b). It becomes backward compatible with single DES when $K_1 = K_2$. As regards its security, some theoretically possible cryptanalytic attacks have been suggested, but 3DES2 is still considered as secure as 3DES3.

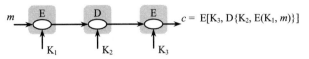

(a) Triple DES with 3 keys (3DES3)

$$c = E[K_3, D\{K_2, E(K_1, m)\}]$$

(b) Triple DES with 2 keys (3DES2)

$$c = E[K_1, D\{K_2, E(K_1, m)\}]$$

Figure 4.17 Triple DES.

The principal drawback of triple DES is that it is slow because of its three stages of encryption. Secondly, triple DES uses block size of 64 bits. From the point of view of efficiency and security, larger block size is desirable.

4.4 SUMMING UP

We started this chapter with introduction to block ciphers and covered one of the most used symmetric-key block cipher, Data Encryption Standard (DES).

- Block ciphers become vulnerable to statistical attack when block size is less than 64 bits. Random block substitution and transposition ciphers require very long key for block of 64 bits. Multiple rounds of encryption are used to address these issues.
- Diffusion and confusion are two important characteristics of block ciphers.
  - Diffusion implies dispersing the statistical structure of plaintext so that it is not reflected in the statistical structure of the ciphertext.
  - Confusion implies there is little correlation between the bits of cipher key and the bits of ciphertext.
- Feistel cipher structure is based on non-invertible round function. DES uses Feistel cipher structure. DES has 56-bit cipher key, 64-bit block size, and 16 rounds of encryption. There are four weak keys and six pairs of semi-weak keys in the key space of 2^{56} keys.
- DES remained a successful and proven cipher till 1998. However, its 56-bit key size proved inadequate with the development of parallel processing technology.
- Set of mappings obtained by 2^{56} DES keys is not closed under functional composition. Therefore, double DES and triple DES are possible. But double encryption is vulnerable to meet-me-in-the-middle attack. Therefore, DES has been replaced with triple DES.
- Triple DES is used in EDE mode (encryption, decryption, encryption) using two or three keys. The decryption stage in the middle enables backward compatibility of triple DES to DES when its encryption key of the first stage is same as the decryption key of the middle stage.

We study another block cipher, AES (Advanced Encryption Standard) in Chapter 6. But before that we need to learn some mathematics first. We introduce algebraic structures in Chapter 5.

<table>
<tr><td colspan="3" align="center">**Key Terms**</td></tr>
<tr><td>Block cipher</td><td>Expansion permutation</td><td>S-box</td></tr>
<tr><td>Confusion</td><td>Feistel cipher structure</td><td>Triple DES</td></tr>
<tr><td>Diffusion</td><td>Meet-in-the-middle attack</td><td>Weak and semi-weak keys</td></tr>
<tr><td>Double DES</td><td>Round keys</td><td></td></tr>
</table>

RECOMMENDED READING

Coppersmith, D., The Data Encryption Standard (DES) and Its Strength against Attacks, *IBM Journal of Research and Development*, Vol. 38, pp. 243–250, 1994.

Data Encryption Standard, Federal Information Processing Standard publication #46, U.S. Department of Commerce, NIST, 1977.

Data Encryption Standard (DES), Federal Information Processing Standard publication #46–3. U.S. Department of Commerce, NIST, 1999.

Forouzan, Behrouz A., *Cryptography and Network Security*, Tata McGraw-Hill, New Delhi, 2007.

Kaufman, C., Perlman, R. and Spenciner, M., *Network Security, Private Communication in a Public World*, Prentice-Hall of India, New Delhi, 2007.

Menezes, A., Oorschot, P. and Vanstone, S., *Handbook of Applied Cryptography*, CRC Press, FL, USA, 1997.

RFC 4772, *Security Implications of Using the Data Encryption Standard (DES)*, IETF, 2006.

Rhee, M., *Internet Security*, John Wiley & Sons, West Sussex, UK, 2003.

Schneier, B., *Applied Cryptography*, John Wiley & Sons, New York, 1996.

Stallings, W., *Cryptography and Network Security*, Prentice-Hall of India, New Delhi, 2008.

Stinson, D., *Cryptography: Theory and Practice*, CRC Press, FL, YSA, 2006.

Trappe, W., Washington, L., *Introduction to Cryptography and Coding Theory*, Prentice-Hall, NJ, 2006.

Vaudenay, S., *A Classical Introduction to Cryptography*, Springer, NY, USA, 2006.

(PROBLEMS)

1. Substitution table for encryption of a 4-bit block cipher is shown below. Ciphertext for a given plaintext is located at the intersection of
   - row determined by the outer two bits of plaintext and
   - column determined by the middle two bits of the plaintext.

(a) What is the ciphertext corresponding to plaintext block 0111?

(b) Construct decryption table on the same lines.

	00	01	10	11
00	1011	1101	0011	0101
01	0110	0000	1110	1001
10	1000	0111	0100	0001
11	0010	1010	1100	1111

2. A 16-bit transposition cipher maps the 4×4 plaintext matrix to 4×4 ciphertext matrix using the following rule:

"Shift circularly the bits of a row towards left by an amount equal to the row number (0, 1, 2, 3). For example, third row is rotated by two positions."

16-bit plaintext and ciphertext words are written as 4×4 matrix columnwise, i.e., first four bits go into first column and so on.

(a) Encrypt the plaintext word 1100 1010 1001 1110.

(b) Decrypt the ciphertext word 1000 1110 0100 1100.

3. A 16-bit block cipher has two stages—substitution stage followed by transposition stage. The cipher divides a 16-bit plaintext into four 4-bit words and uses encryption table of Problem 1 for substitution. The transposition rule is same as in Problem 2. Encrypt the word 1000 0011 1100 0001.

4. Sixteen rounds keys of a Feistal cipher exhibit the following relationships:

$$K_1 = K_{16}, K_2 = K_{15}, K_3 = K_{14}, ..., K_8 = K_9$$

A 64-bit block consisting of the word NETWORKS is encrypted twice using the above cipher to increase the level of security. What is the encrypted output after double encryption?

5. Consider a DES-like encryption in which all the round keys are K of n bits. The input plaintext block of $2n$ bits is divided into two equal sized blocks M_0, M_1. A round of encryption with input blocks M_i, M_{i+1} gives an output M_{i+1}, M_{i+2} where

$$M_{i+2} = M_i \oplus f(K, M_{i+1}),$$

$$f(K, M_{i+1}) = K \oplus M_{i+1}$$

(a) If there are only two rounds, can you determine the key K and the plaintext block, if an encrypted block is available?

(b) Suppose there are three rounds. Do the three rounds make the system more secure?

6. (a) Let $\bar{x}$ denote the complement of string x. Show that if the DES key K encrypts m to c, then $\bar{K}$ encrypts $\bar{m}$ to $\bar{c}$. (*Hint:* Show that input to S-box, and therefore, its output does not change by taking these complements. Then just work through the encryption algorithm.)

(b) The above complementation property of DES can be extended to 3DES with two keys K_1 and K_2. Show that if $E[K_1, E[K_2, E[K_1, m]]] = c$, then

$$E[\overline{K}_1, E[\overline{K}_2, E[\overline{K}_1, m]]] = \overline{c}$$

7. (a) If the DES key $K = 111 \ldots 111$, show that if $E(K, m) = c$, then $E(K, c) = m$. (*Hint:* Determine the round keys.)

   (b) Find another key with the same property.

8. Consider a triple DES scheme with two keys K_1, K_2 as shown in Figure 4.18.

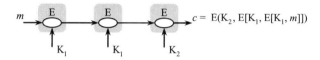

Figure 4.18   Problem 8.

Describe the steps of meet-in-the-middle attack on this scheme. (*Hint:* Choose K_1, K_2 pairs such that $E[K_1, E[K_1, m]] = D[K_2, c]$.)

9. We can consider affine cipher $c \equiv am + b \pmod{26}$ as a double encryption, where the first encryption is multiplying the plaintext m using key a and the second encryption is a shift cipher using key b. Show that the meet-in-the-middle attack on the affine cipher as double encryption takes at most 38 encryption/decryption steps.

10. Given a plaintext–ciphertext pair, the brute force attack takes on average 2^{55} DES encryption computations to determine the key. Show that the average number of computations can be reduced to half using the complementation property of DES, if we have two plaintext cipher text pairs (m, c) and $(\overline{m}, \overline{c})$.

11. Consider a Feistel cipher with four rounds, each pair of rounds having the structure as shown in Figure 4.8(a). The plaintext block is denoted as $m = (L_0, R_0)$. Determine the ciphertext block c in terms of L_0, R_0, and the round key K_i of the following round functions.

   (a) $g(x, K_i) = 0$
   (b) $g(x, K_i) = x$
   (c) $g(x, K_i) = K_i$

12. Alice and Bob have access to two secure block ciphers, cipher X and cipher Y. Cipher X uses a 64-bit key, and cipher Y uses 128-bit key. Alice prefers cipher X, but Bob wants the security of a 128-bit key, and prefers cipher Y. As a compromise, they encrypt each message twice, using two independent 64-bit keys. Is the solution as secure as the security provided by cipher Y?

13. An important property which makes DES secure is that the S-boxes are nonlinear, i.e., $S_1(x_1) \oplus S_1(x_2) \neq S_1(x_1 \oplus x_2)$. Verify this property when $x_1 = 101010$, $x_2 = 010101$.

5

Mathematical Foundations II
(Finite Fields)

We introduced modular arithmetic for set of integers in Z_n in Chapter 2. In this chapter, we extend these concepts into another branch of mathematics known as abstract algebra. Abstract algebra deals with sets and abstract mathematical operations on the elements of the sets. We start with basic algebraic structure group, and develop it further to ring and finally to field. Finite field, in particular, is of interest to us for cryptography because it is associated with additive and multiplicative binary operations. We discuss Galois field $GF(p^n)$ and its application for encryption of binary data using algebraic polynomials.

5.1 BINARY OPERATION

We are familiar with basic binary operations of arithmetic—addition and multiplication. Subtraction is a special case of addition in which addendum is a negative number. We want to extend the concept of binary operation to elements of a set. Since elements of a set may not be numbers, we do not want to restrict the concept of binary operation to arithmetic addition and multiplication. We will use the symbol '•' to represent a generalized binary operation. Thus, $c = a \bullet b$ expresses that output c is obtained when binary operation • is applied on elements a and b.

Let us consider the following example:

Let $a = [3\ 2\ 1]$, $b = [2\ 3\ 1]$ and the binary operation • on pair (a, b) be permutation of b as per a. Then

$a \bullet b = [1\ 3\ 2]$
$b \bullet a = [2\ 1\ 3]$

Note that $a \bullet b \neq b \bullet a$

Since $a \bullet b$ may not be equal to $b \bullet a$, we need to introduce another concept, ordered pair. *Ordered pair* is pair of elements of a set in the given order. Thus pair (a, b) is different from pair (b, a).

5.1.1 Properties of Binary Operation

A binary operation has the following properties:

Commutative law: A binary operation • is said to satisfy commutative law, if

$$a • b = b • a$$

Associative law: A binary operation • is said to satisfy associative law, if

$$(a • b) • c = a • (b • c)$$

For Example:

1. Consider set of integers $Z = \{..., -2, -1, 0, 1, 2, ...\}$. Addition and multiplication operations are commutative and associative in Z. For example,

   Commutative law $3 + 5 = 5 + 3 = 8$ $3 \times 5 = 5 \times 3 = 15$

   Associative law $(3 + 5) + 7 = 3 + (5 + 7) = 15$ $(3 \times 5) \times 7 = 3 \times (5 \times 7) = 105$

2. Multiplication of two matrices is not commutative.

$$\begin{bmatrix} 1 & 2 \\ 3 & 4 \end{bmatrix} \times \begin{bmatrix} 5 & 6 \\ 0 & -2 \end{bmatrix} = \begin{bmatrix} 5 & 2 \\ 15 & 10 \end{bmatrix} \qquad \begin{bmatrix} 5 & 6 \\ 0 & -2 \end{bmatrix} \times \begin{bmatrix} 1 & 2 \\ 3 & 4 \end{bmatrix} = \begin{bmatrix} 23 & 34 \\ -6 & -8 \end{bmatrix}$$

5.2 GROUP

A set G is called a group, if a binary operation • on each ordered pair (a, b) of elements of G follows the following four axioms:

Closure $c = a • b$ belongs to G for any a, b in G.

Associative law $a • (b • c) = (a • b) • c$ for any a, b, c in G,

Identity element   There exists an identity element e in G such that $a • e = e • a = a$ for every a in G.

Inverse element   There is an inverse element a' in G such that $a • a' = a' • a = e$ for each element of G.

A group is denoted as $\{G, •\}$ to indicate the associated binary operation. Some definitions associated with the concept of group are given below:

Order of a group: The *order* of a group, denoted as $|G|$, is the number of elements in the group.

Finite and infinite groups: If a group has finite number of elements, it is called a *finite group*. A group having infinite number of elements is called *infinite group*.

Subgroup: A subset H of a group G is a *subgroup* of G, if H is also a group in itself with the same binary operation (•) as that of G.

5.2.1 Cyclic Group

Repeated application of the binary operation is termed as exponentiation so we can write $a^3 = a \bullet a \bullet a$. Further, we define $a^0 = e$, the identity element. A group G is *cyclic*, if every element of G can be expressed as exponentiation[1] (g^n) of an element g in G. The element g that generates the group G is called the *generator* of the group. For example, let the group be $\{Z_6, +\}$ where $Z_6 = \{0, 1\ 2, 3, 4, 5\}$ and the group operation $\bullet$ is arithmetic addition. This is a cyclic group with the generator element as 1 because as all the elements of the group can be expressed as exponentiation of 1.

$$1^0 = 0$$
$$1^1 = 1$$
$$1^2 = 1 + 1 = 2$$
$$1^3 = 1 + 1 + 1 = 3$$
$$1^4 = 1 + 1 + 1 + 1 = 4$$
$$1^5 = 1 + 1 + 1 + 1 + 1 = 5$$

5.2.2 Abelian Group

A group is called *abelian* group, if it satisfies commutative law also, i.e., $a \bullet b = b \bullet a$ for any a, b in G. An abelian group is also called as *commutative group*.

Example 1   Is the set of residues $Z_7 = \{0, 1, 2, 3, 4, 5, 6\}$ an abelian group for the addition (+) operation?

Solution   We pick up randomly three elements $a = 4$, $b = 5$, $c = 6$ of Z_7 for illustration.

Closure	$a + b = (4 + 5) \bmod 7 = 2$ which is in Z_7. The closure property holds.
Associative law	$a + (b + c) = \{4 + (5 + 6)\} \bmod 7 = 1$
	$(a + b) + c = \{(4 + 5) + 6\} \bmod 7 = 1$
	Since $a + (b + c) = (a + b) + c$, the associative law holds.
Identity element	Element 0 in Z_7 is the identity element, since $a + 0 = 0 + a = a$.
Inverse element	Every element of Z_7 has its inverse in Z_7. For example, 5 is inverse of 2 since $(2 + 5) \bmod 7 = 0$, which is the identity element of Z_7.
Commutative law	Commutative law is satisfied, since $(4 + 5) = (5 + 4)$.

Thus Z_7 with addition operation is an abelian group.

Example 2   Given set S = {[1 2 3], [1 3 2], [2 1 3], [2 3 1], [3 1 2], [3 2 1]} and binary operation $\bullet$ that carries out permutation of an element in S according to another element in S. Determine whether S is abelian group.

---

1. The word 'exponentiation' does not necessarily imply that the binary operation is multiplication. It simply means that the binary operation is applied multiple times.

Solution We will check whether the axioms of an abelian group are satisfied. We will make this check on randomly picked elements of set S, a = [3 2 1], b = [2 3 1], c = [2 1 3].

Closure	$a \bullet b$ = [3 2 1] $\bullet$ [2 3 1] = [1 3 2]
	Since [1 3 2] is in S, the closure property holds.
Associative law	$a \bullet (b \bullet c)$ = [3 2 1] $\bullet$ ([2 3 1] $\bullet$ [2 1 3])
	= [3 2 1] $\bullet$ [1 3 2] = [2 3 1]
	$(a \bullet b) \bullet c$ = ([3 2 1] $\bullet$ [2 3 1]) $\bullet$ [2 1 3]
	= [1 3 2] $\bullet$ [2 1 3] = [2 3 1]
	Since $a \bullet (b \bullet c) = (a \bullet b) \bullet c$, the associative law holds.
Identity element	[1 2 3] is the identity element e in S, since
	[3 2 1] $\bullet$ [1 2 3] = [1 2 3] $\bullet$ [3 2 1] = [3 2 1]
Inverse element	Every element in S has its inverse in S. For example, a' = [2 3 1] in
	S is inverse of a = [3 1 2], since
	$a \bullet a'$ = [3 1 2] $\bullet$ [2 3 1] = [1 2 3] = e.
	Thus S with binary permutation operation $\bullet$ is a group.
Commutative law	$a \bullet b$ = [3 2 1] $\bullet$ [2 3 1) = [1 3 2]
	$b \bullet a$ = [2 3 1] $\bullet$ [3 2 1] = [2 1 3]
	Since $a \bullet b \neq b \bullet a$, S is not an abelian group.

We have been using the symbol $\bullet$ for group operation to emphasize the fact that it can be any binary operation. We saw one abstract example of binary operation in Example 2. In the next section, we introduce second binary operation. Representing these operations by abstract symbols without assigned names is very inconvenient. Therefore, from now onwards, we will use symbol + in place of $\bullet$ and denote a group as {G, +}. The identity element of the group is written as 0 in place of 'e'. It is reiterated that + and 0 are merely notations and do not imply arithmetic addition or numerical 0.

5.3 RING

If we can define one more operation on an abelian group, we have a *ring*, provided the elements of the set satisfy some properties with respect to this new operation also. A ring is typically denoted as {R, +, ×} where

- R denotes the set of elements,
- '+' is the operation with respect to which R is an abelian group, and
- '×' is the additional operation needed for R to form a ring.

It is re-emphasized that '+' and '×' are merely notational symbols of the two binary operations. They are referred to as addition operation and multiplication operation respectively. But they may not refer to arithmetic addition and multiplication.

R is abelian group with respect to the addition operation (+), and therefore, its elements satisfy properties relating to closure, associative law, addition identity element, additive inverse element and commutative law. For {R, +, ×} to be a ring, the following properties are satisfied with respect to the multiplication operation (×):

Closure	If a and b belong to R, then $c = a \times b$ is also in R.
Associative law	$a \times (b \times c) = (a \times b) \times c$ for all a, b, c in R.
Distributive law	$a \times (b + c) = a \times b + a \times c$ for all a, b, c in R.
	$(a + b) \times c = a \times c + b \times c$ for all a, b, c in R.

5.3.1 Commutative Ring

A ring {R, +, ×} is called *commutative ring*, if it satisfies the *commutative law* in respect of the second binary operation (×), i.e., $a \times b = b \times a$ for all a, b in R.

We showed in Section 5.2.2 that the set of residues $Z_7 = \{0, 1, 2, ..., 6\}$, is an abelian group with addition operation. Let us check if it is a commutative ring with arithmetic addition and multiplication operations. We pick up randomly three elements: $a = 2$, $b = 5$ and $c = 6$ of Z_7 for illustration and check its properties with respect to multiplication operation.

Closure	$a \times b = (2 \times 5) \bmod 7 = 3$
	Since 3 is in Z_7, the closure property holds.
Associative law	$a \times (b \times c) = \{2 \times (5 \times 6)\} \bmod 7 = 4$
	$(a \times b) \times c = \{(2 \times 5) \times 6\} \bmod 7 = 4$
	Since $a \times (b \times c) = (a \times b) \times c$, the associative law holds.
Distributive law	$a \times (b + c) = 2 \times (5 + 6) \bmod 7 = 1$
	$a \times b + a \times c = (2 \times 5 + 2 \times 6) \bmod 7 = 1$
	Since $a \times (b + c) = a \times b + a \times c$, the distributive law is satisfied.
Commutative law	Commutative law is satisfied, since $(2 \times 5) = (5 \times 2)$.

Thus Z_7 with arithmetic addition and multiplication operations is commutative ring.

5.4 FIELD

A commutative ring becomes a field (denoted as F) when the following additional properties are defined with respect to the multiplication operation (×):

Identity element	There exists a multiplication identity element symbolically represented as 1 in F such that $a \times 1 = 1 \times a = a$ for every a in F.
Inverse element	There is a multiplicative inverse element b in F such that $a \times b = b \times a = 1$ for each element of F, except for the addition identity element 0 of F. Multiplicative inverse of a is written as a^{-1}.

We have now three algebraic structures namely groups, rings and fields. Table 5.1 summarizes their properties. Fields, in particular, are of interest to us.

- A field supports two binary operations: addition and multiplication.
- Each element has additive inverse.
- Each element (except 0, the addition identity element) has multiplicative inverse.

These properties allow us to do subtraction and division. Subtraction amounts to addition of additive inverse and division amounts to multiplication by the multiplicative inverse.

TABLE 5.1 Properties of Groups, Rings and Fields

Property	Group	Ring		Field	
	+	+	×	+	×
Closure	√	√	√	√	√
Associative law	√	√	√	√	√
Commutative law	√(*)	√	√(*)	√	√
Identity element	√	√	–	√	√
Inverse	√	√	–	√	√

*Commutative group and a commutative ring satisfy commutative law for the respective binary operation

Example 3   (a) Show that the set of residues $Z_7 = \{0, 1, 2, ..., 6\}$ is a field with arithmetic addition and multiplication operations.

(b) Evaluate $(4 + 6)$, $(5 - 3)$, (4×6), $(4 \div 5)$.

Solution

(a) As shown in Section 5.3.1, set of residues $Z_7 = \{0, 1, 2, ..., 6\}$ is commutative ring with arithmetic addition and multiplication operations. For it to be a field,

- it should have multiplicative identity element 1. It has 1 as one of the elements.
- all its non zero elements should have multiplicative inverse in Z_7. Since all the non zero elements are coprime to 7, and they have multiplicative inverse in Z_7.

Therefore, the set of residues $Z_7 = \{0, 1, 2, ..., 6\}$ is a field with arithmetic addition and multiplication operations.

(b) $(4 + 6) = 10 \bmod 7 = 3$
$(5 - 3) = [5 + (-3)] \bmod 7 = [5 + 4] \bmod 7 = 2$
$(4 \times 6) = 24 \bmod 7 = 3$
$(4 \div 5) = (4 \times 5^{-1}) \bmod 7 = (4 \times 3) \bmod 7 = 5$

5.4.1 Galois Finite Fields

If the number of elements in a field is finite, it is called *finite field*. Finite fields find application in cryptography and are of interest to us. Galois was the first mathematician who did indepth study of finite fields. Therefore, finite fields are called Galois Fields (GF).

Galois proved a very important characteristic of finite fields. He showed that the order (i.e. number of elements) of a finite field is always p^n where p is a prime number and n is a positive integer. A finite field of order p^n is written as GF(p^n). When $n = 1$, we have a finite field GF(p) having prime number of elements. When $p = 2$, we have a finite field GF(2^n) having 2^n number of elements. These two types of finite fields find application in cryptography as applied to digital systems.

5.4.2 Finite Fields of Type GF(*p*)

We showed in Example 3 that the set of residues Z_7 is a field with addition and multiplication operations. Set of residues $Z_p = \{0, 1, 2, ..., p - 1\}$, when p is a prime number, is always a finite field under arithmetic addition and multiplication operations. This is so because all the elements of Z_p (except 0) are coprime to p, and therefore, have multiplicative inverse in Z_p. The number of elements in Z_p is p, which is a prime number. Thus Z_p with addition and multiplication operations constitutes a finite field of the type GF(*p*). For example, $Z_2 = \{0, 1\}$ with modulo 2 addition and multiplication operations is a finite field of the type GF(2).

Addition operation	$1 + 0 = 1$, $1 + 1 = 0$, $0 + 0 = 0$
Multiplication operation	$1 \times 0 = 0$, $1 \times 1 = 1$, $0 \times 0 = 0$
Additive inverse pairs	(0, 0), (1, 1)
Addition identity element	0
Multiplicative inverse pair	(1, 1)
Multiplication identity element	1

5.4.3 Finite Fields of Type GF(2^n)

As we saw in Chapter 3, encryption and decryption involve two basic operations—addition and multiplication. We also need additive and multiplicative inverses for decryption. We would like to have an algebraic structure in form of a finite field for encryption and decryption because it permits us to

- define two binary operations (addition and multiplication) and
- have additive and multiplicative inverses to carry out decryption.

Suppose we like to have an encryption system for 8-bit bytes. To construct a finite field of the 8-bit bytes, there are two alternatives for us. We can construct the field of the type GF(*p*) or GF(2^n).

GF(p): We can represent the bytes as decimal numbers, just like we represented alphabet as integers from 0 to 25 in Chapter 3. The 256 bytes can be represented as integers from 0 to 255. If we attempt to define the finite field of the type GF(*p*), we need to discard some of the bytes to have prime number of elements in the field. For example, we can have 251 elements as 251 is the highest prime number less than 255. It implies that we need to declare 5 bytes invalid. We do not want to do that.

GF(2^n): The second alternative for us is to constitute a finite field of the type GF(2^n). In this case, we retain 8-bit byte as an element of the set, so that total number of elements is 2^8.

We also need to define addition and multiplication binary operations appropriately to satisfy the required properties of a finite field. For binary operations, we represent a string of 8-bits of a byte as a polynomial and then define binary operations on the polynomial. The next section deals with these concepts. The finite field so constructed will be of the type GF(2^n) with $n = 8$.

5.5 ALGEBRAIC POLYNOMIAL

An algebraic polynomial is an expression of the form $a_n x^n + a_{n-1} x^{n-1} + \ldots + a_1 x + a_0$, where $a_0, a_1, \ldots, a_n$ are the coefficients and x is the variable. When $a_n \neq 0$, we have a polynomial of degree n. We have no interest in evaluating the value of the polynomial for any specific value of x. We are interested only in polynomial arithmetic which deals with the addition and multiplication of polynomials. For example, if $f(x) = 2x^2 + 3x + 3$ and $g(x) = x + 4$,

$$f(x) + g(x) = 2x^2 + 4x + 7$$
$$f(x) \times g(x) = 2x^3 + 11x^2 + 15x + 12$$

5.5.1 Polynomials over a Field

We can define polynomials whose coefficients belong to a finite field. It is common to use the phrase 'polynomial over a field' to convey the same meaning. When we add or multiply polynomials, we ensure that the coefficients of the resulting polynomials also belong to the same field.

Let us consider the set of all polynomials over the finite field Z_7 with addition and multiplication operations. We use modulo 7 arithmetic when we add and multiply the coefficients of these polynomials. If $f(x) = 5x^2 + 4x + 6$ and $g(x) = 5x + 6$,

$$f(x) + g(x) = 5x^2 + 2x + 5 \quad (\text{mod } 7)$$
$$f(x) \times g(x) = 4x^3 + x^2 + 1 \quad (\text{mod } 7)$$

5.5.2 Representation of Binary Data by Polynomials

Algebraic polynomials can be used to represent blocks of binary data. An n-bit block is represented by a polynomial of degree $n - 1$ having coefficients equal to the bit values. For example, 11010101 is represented as below.

$$f(x) = 1x^7 + 1x^6 + 0x^5 + 1x^4 + 0x^3 + 1x^2 + 0x + 1$$

or $\qquad f(x) = x^7 + x^6 + x^4 + x^2 + 1$

Note that
- the most significant bit is the coefficient of the highest power of x.
- the power of x merely defines the position of the bit.
- the coefficients of polynomials are always 0 or 1.
- we need to use modulo 2 arithmetic when we add or multiply the coefficients.

$$
\begin{array}{llc}
1 + 0 = 1 & 1 \times 0 = 0 & (\text{mod } 2) \\
0 + 1 = 1 & 0 \times 1 = 0 & (\text{mod } 2) \\
1 + 1 = 0 & 1 \times 1 = 1 & (\text{mod } 2) \\
0 + 0 = 0 & 0 \times 0 = 0 & (\text{mod } 2)
\end{array}
$$

In other words, we have defined the coefficients of the polynomials over GF(2).

Consider the following example:

If $f(x) = x^2 + x + 1$ and $g(x) = x + 1$ are defined over GF(2), then

$$f(x) + g(x) = x^2 + x + 1 + x + 1 = x^2$$

$$f(x) \times g(x) = (x^2 + x + 1) x + x^2 + x + 1 = x^3 + 1$$

5.5.3 Set of Polynomials

Now, we can represent set of n-bit words as set of polynomials. For example, if $n = 3$, the set of binary words and corresponding set of polynomials are as under:

$$S = \{000, 001, 010, 011, 100, 101, 110, 111\}$$

$$\equiv \{0, 1, x, x + 1, x^2, x^2 + 1, x^2 + x, x^2 + x + 1\}$$

Having defined set of polynomials that represents n-bit words, we need to define addition and multiplication operations for this set. These basic operations are essential for encryption and decryption.

5.5.4 Modular Arithmetic for Set of Polynomials

In cryptography, we want that that an n-bit word is encrypted as another n-bit word. Since an n-bit word is represented by a polynomial of degree $n - 1$, addition or multiplication of two polynomials must also be of degree $n - 1$. While addition of two polynomials satisfies this requirement, their multiplication results in a polynomial of higher degree. For example, if we multiply two elements (100) and (101), which are represented as x^2 and $x^2 + 1$, we get

$$(100) \times (101) \equiv x^2 \times (x^2 + 1) = x^4 + x^2 \equiv (10100)$$

The two elements (100) and (101) belong to set S of 3-bit words, but the product (10100) does not. Therefore, we must use modular polynomial arithmetic. It is no different from what we learnt in Chapter 2, except that we deal with polynomials instead of integers.

Example 4 Determine $x^2 \times (x^2 + 1) \bmod (x^3 + x^2 + 1)$

Solution $x^2 \times (x^2 + 1) = x^4 + x^2$

To determine the product modulo $(x^3 + x^2 + 1)$, we divide the product by $x^3 + x^2 + 1$.

$$
\begin{array}{r}
x + 1 \\
x^3 + x^2 + 1 \overline{)\, x^4 + x^2} \\
\underline{x^4 + x^3 + x} \\
x^3 + x^2 + x \\
\underline{x^3 + x^2 + 1} \\
x + 1
\end{array}
$$

$$x^2 \times (x^2 + 1) \bmod (x^3 + x^2 + 1) = x + 1$$

Alternatively, the modulo operation can be performed by grouping the dividend as multiple of the modulus. This is done by adding and subtracting (subtracting is same as addition) powers of x as given below:

$$x^2 \times (x^2 + 1) \bmod (x^3 + x^2 + 1) = (x^4 + x^2) \bmod (x^3 + x^2 + 1)$$

We can simplify it by adding $x^3 + x + x^3 + x$, which is in fact zero.

$$(x^4 + x^3 + x + x^3 + x + x^2) \bmod (x^3 + x^2 + 1) = [x(x^3 + x^2 + 1) + x^3 + x + x^2] \bmod (x^3 + x^2 + 1)$$
$$= (x^3 + x + x^2) \bmod (x^3 + x^2 + 1)$$
$$= (x^3 + x^2 + 1 + 1 + x) \bmod (x^3 + x^2 + 1) = x + 1$$

If we replace back binary words in this example, we get

$$(100) \times (101) \bmod (1101) = (011)$$

Thus modulo (1101) multiplication of (100) and (110) from set S of 3-bit words gives the product (011), which is also in set S.

5.5.5 Irreducible Polynomial

A polynomial $f(x)$ over field F (i.e. whose coefficients are from field F) is called *irreducible*, if and only if it cannot be expressed as a product of two polynomials, both over field F and of degree lower than that of $f(x)$. In simple words, a polynomial is irreducible, if it does not have a divisor of degree lower than itself. Taking analogy of prime numbers, an irreducible polynomial can be called *prime polynomial*. We want the modulus polynomial to be an irreducible polynomial, so that all the elements of the polynomial set, except the 0 element, have their multiplicative inverse in the set. Table 5.2 lists the irreducible polynomials of degrees 1 to 4.

For Example,

1. $f(x) = x^3 + 1$ over GF(2) is reducible polynomial because it can be written as product of two polynomials, both over GF(2).

$$(x + 1) \times (x^2 + x + 1) = x^3 + x^2 + x + x^2 + x + 1 = x^3 + 1 = f(x)$$

2. $f(x) = x^3 + x + 1$ is an irreducible polynomial because of the following reasons:

   - Being polynomial of degree three, if $f(x)$ can be factored, one of its factors must be of degree one.
   - The only polynomials of degree one over GF(2) are x, $x + 1$. It is evident that x is not a factor of $f(x)$. By dividing $f(x)$ by $x + 1$, we can show that it is also not a factor of $f(x)$.
   - Thus $f(x)$ does not have any factor of degree one, and therefore, it is irreducible.

TABLE 5.2 Irreducible Polynomials

Degree	Irreducible Polynomial
1	$x + 1$, x
2	$x^2 + x + 1$
3	$x^3 + x^2 + 1$, $x^3 + x + 1$
4	$x^4 + x^3 + x^2 + x + 1$, $x^4 + x^3 + 1$, $x^4 + x + 1$

5.5.6   Finite Field GF(2^n)

Let us return to finite field of the type GF(2^n). We have defined addition and multiplication operations required for GF(2^n) using polynomials. Let us examine if GF(2^n) is, in fact, a finite field. We will assume $n = 3$ for the sake of illustration and then generalize the conclusions for any value of n. For modulus $(x^3 + x + 1)$, which is a irreducible polynomial, we have the following set of possible residues:

$$S = \{0, 1, x, x + 1, x^2, x^2 + 1, x^2 + x, x^2 + x + 1\}$$

This set constitutes a finite field of type GF(2^3) with modulo $(x^3 + x + 1)$ addition and multiplication operations. We can verify that all the properties listed in Table 5.1 for constituting a finite field are satisfied.

- Closure, associative law and commutative law in respect of addition and multiplication operations are satisfied.
- The addition identity element is 0 and multiplication identity element is 1.
- Each element of set S is additive inverse of itself. For example,

$$(x^2 + x + 1) + (x^2 + x + 1) = 0$$

- All elements of sets S except 0 have the multiplicative inverse modulo $(x^3 + x + 1)$ in set S. For example, multiplicative inverse of $x^2 + x$ is $x + 1$ which is in set S.

$$(x^2 + x) \times (x + 1) \bmod (x^3 + x + 1) = (x^3 + x^2 + x^2 + x) \bmod (x^3 + x + 1)$$
$$= (x^3 + x) \bmod (x^3 + x + 1) = 1$$

We can determine multiplicative inverses using extended Euclid's algorithm. The process is exactly the same as for the integers. Example 5 illustrates the algorithm.

Example 5   Determine multiplicative inverse of x^2 in GF(2^3) defined with modulus $x^3 + x + 1$ using extended Euclid's algorithm.

Solution

$$\gcd (x^3 + x + 1, x^2) = \gcd (x^2, x + 1) \quad \text{Residue } x + 1 = 1 \times (x^3 + x + 1) + x \times x^2$$
$$= \gcd (x + 1, x) \qquad \text{Residue } x = x^2 + x \times (x + 1)$$
$$= x^2 + x \times [(x^3 + x + 1) + x \times x^2]$$
$$= x \times (x^3 + x + 1) + (x^2 + 1) \times x^2$$
$$= \gcd (x, 1) \qquad \text{Residue } 1 = (x + 1) + x$$
$$= [(x^3 + x + 1) + x \times x^2]$$
$$+ [x \times (x^3 + x + 1) + (x^2 + 1) \times x^2]$$
$$= (1 + x) \times (x^3 + x + 1)$$
$$+ (x^2 + x + 1) \times x^2$$

Thus, we get multiplicative inverse of x^2 in GF(2^3) as $x^2 + x + 1$ for modulus $x^3 + x + 1$.

We can now revert from polynomial representation to binary words. In the above example, we have computed multiplicative inverse of 100 modulo 1011 as 111. Table 5.3 lists all the 3-bit words, their respective additive and multiplicative inverses modulo 1011 and 1101.

TABLE 5.3 Additive and Multiplicative Inverses of 3-bit Words

3-bit word	Additive inverse	Multiplicative inverse	
		Modulus 1011	Modulus 1101
000	000	—	—
001	001	001	001
010	010	101	110
011	011	110	100
100	100	111	011
101	101	010	111
110	110	011	010
111	111	100	101

The set of 3-bit words along with modular addition and multiplication operations constitutes a field. It implies we can add or multiply any two elements of the set, and the result of the operation always remains within the set. Subtraction and division can be performed using additive and multiplicative inverses. Example 6 illustrates the application of these concepts for encryption and decryption based on affine cipher.

Example 6 (a) Encrypt $m = (101)$ using affine cipher $c = Mm + N$, $M = (110)$, $N = (011)$. All the binary operations are modulo (1101) over $GF(2^3)$.

(b) Decrypt c obtained in (a) above.

Solution (a) We use modular polynomial arithmetic to compute c.

$$c = (110) \times (101) + (011) \quad \mod (1101)$$
$$= (x^2 + x) \times (x^2 + 1) + x + 1 \quad \mod (x^3 + x^2 + 1)$$
$$= x^4 + x^3 + x^2 + x + x + 1 \quad \mod (x^3 + x^2 + 1)$$
$$= x(x^3 + x^2 + 1) + x^2 + x + 1 \quad \mod (x^3 + x^2 + 1)$$
$$= x^2 + x + 1 = (111)$$

(b) To decrypt c, we need additive inverse of N and multiplicative inverse of M. These are obtained from Table 5.3.

$$-N = (011), \quad M^{-1} = (010)$$

m can now be computed using $m = [c + (-N)] \times M^{-1}$.

$$m = [(111) + (011)] \times (010) \quad \mod (1101)$$
$$= (x^2 + x + 1 + x + 1) \times x \quad \mod (x^3 + x^2 + 1)$$
$$= x^3 \quad \mod (x^3 + x^2 + 1)$$
$$= x^2 + 1 = (101)$$

We can define $GF(2^n)$ in similar fashion for n-bit words. We need an irreducible polynomial of degree n as modulus for multiplication operation. AES (Advanced Encryption Standard), which we study in Chapter 6, is based on GF(2^8) and uses irreducible polynomial $x^8 + x^4 + x^3 + x + 1$ as the modulus.

5.5.7   Generator for GF(2^n)

It must have been noticed that modular polynomial arithmetic is not very convenient for processing elements of GF(2^n). It can be shown that the non-zero elements of GF(2^n) form a cyclic group under multiplication. Recall from section 5.2.1, that in a cyclic group, all the elements of the group can be expressed as powers of the generator element g. This representation facilitates computations involving multiplication and multiplicative inverses. For example, $g^2 \times g^3$ is simply g^5. To develop the concept, let us consider set S of 3-bit words represented as a set of polynomials.

$$S = \{000, 001, 010, 011, 100, 101, 110, 111\}$$
$$\equiv \{0, 1, x, x + 1, x^2, x^2 + 1, x^2 + x, x^2 + x + 1\}$$

We claim that each non-zero element of the above polynomial can be expressed as g^n, where g is the generator. If we take the element 'x' of the set as the generator (i.e. $g = x$) and determine other elements, we get Table 5.4. It lists all the elements of set S as powers of the generator and corresponding polynomial and binary forms. Example 7 illustrates the computation of the element g^5.

TABLE 5.4   Various Representations of GF(2^3)

g^n	Modulus $x^3 + x + 1$ (1011)		Modulus $x^3 + x^2 + 1$ (1101)	
	Polynomial	Binary	Polynomial	Binary
0	0	(000)	0	(000)
g^0	1	(001)	1	(001)
g^1	x	(010)	x	(010)
g^2	x^2	(100)	x^2	(100)
g^3	$x + 1$	(011)	$x^2 + 1$	(101)
g^4	$x^2 + x$	(110)	$x^2 + x + 1$	(111)
g^5	$x^2 + x + 1$	(111)	$x + 1$	(011)
g^6	$x^2 + 1$	(101)	$x^2 + x$	(110)

Example 7   If the generator $g = x$, compute the element g^5 of GF(2^3) under multiplication modulo $x^3 + x + 1$.

Solution $g^5 = x^5 \bmod (x^3 + x + 1) = x^2 x^3 \bmod (x^3 + x + 1)$
$$= x^2(x^3 + x + 1 + x + 1) \bmod (x^3 + x + 1)$$
$$= x^2(x + 1) \bmod (x^3 + x + 1)$$
$$= (x^3 + x^2) \bmod (x^3 + x + 1)$$
$$= (x^3 + x + 1 + x + 1 + x^2) \bmod (x^3 + x + 1)$$
$$= x^2 + x + 1 \quad (111)$$

Example 8 If the generator $g = x$, compute g^7 under multiplication modulo $x^3 + x + 1$.

Solution We use Table 5.4 for various powers of the generator.

$$g^7 = g^6 g = (x^2 + 1)\, x \bmod (x^3 + x + 1) = (x^3 + x) \bmod (x^3 + x + 1) = 1$$

When we multiply two elements, we may get powers of g higher than 6. For example, $g^4 \times g^5 = g^9$. Example 8 shows that $g^7 = 1$, and therefore, $g^9 = g^2 = g^{9 \bmod 7}$. Thus $g^i = g^{i \bmod 7}$ in GF(2^3) for any integer i. We can further generalize this result to GF(2^n) as $g^i = g^{i \bmod p}$, where $p = 2^n - 1$.

Example 9 If the generator $g = x$, compute g^{19} under multiplication modulo $x^3 + x + 1$.

Solution We use Table 5.4 for various powers of the generator.

$$g^{19} = g^{19 \bmod 7} = g^5 = x^2 + x + 1 = (111)$$

Example 10 (a) Encrypt $m = (101)$ using affine cipher $c = Mm + N$, M = (110), N= (011). All the binary operations are modulo (1101) over GF(2^3).
    (b) Decrypt c obtained in (a) above.

Solution (a) We express m, M and N in g^n using Table 5.4.

$p = g^3$, M $= g^6$, N $= g^5$

$c = g^6 g^3 + g^5 = g^9 + g^5 = g^2 + g^5 = x^2(1 + x^3) = x^2 x^2 = g^4 = (111)$

(b) $m = [c + (-N)] \times M^{-1}$, where $c = g^4$, $-N = N = g^5$ and M $- 1 = g^{-6}$

$m = [g^4 + g^5] \times g^{-6} = g^{-2} + g^{-1} = g^5 + g^6 = g^3(g^2 + g^3) = x^3(x^2 + x^3) = x^3 = g^3 = (101)$

5.6 SUMMING UP

In this chapter, we introduced algebraic structures, group, ring and field. Algebraic structures enable abstract binary operations on a finite set of integers.

- A set {G, •} is called a group, if the binary operation • on each ordered pair (a, b) of elements of G is closed, follows associative and distributive laws, and the group has an identity element and inverse element for each element of the group.
  - The *order* of a group, denoted as |G|, is the number of elements in the group.
  - A group G is *cyclic*, if every element of G can be expressed as exponentiation (g^n) of an element g in G. The element g that generates the group G is called the *generator* of the group.
  - A group is called *abelian* group, if it satisfies commutative law also.
- An abelian group becomes ring {R, +, ×} when it has another binary operation that has properties of closure, associative and distributive laws. A ring {R, +, ×} is called *commutative ring*, if it satisfies the *commutative law* in respect of the second binary operation (×).

- A commutative ring becomes a field when there are identity element and inverse element for every element of the field with respect to the second operation ($\times$).
- Finite fields are called Galois Fields (GF). The order of a finite field is always p^n where p is a prime number and n is a positive integer. A finite field of order p^n is written as GF(p^n). GF(p) and GF(2^n) find application in digital systems.
- An n-bit block is represented by a polynomial of degree $n - 1$ having coefficients equal to the bit values. A polynomial is irreducible, if it does not have a divisor polynomial of degree lower than itself.
- We can define GF(2^n) for n-bit words, using an irreducible polynomial of degree n as modulus. It can be shown that the non-zero elements of GF(2^n) form a cyclic group under multiplication and each element of GF(2^n) can be expressed as g^n, where g is the generator.

We will find extensive use of these concepts in the following chapters:

Chapter 6   Advanced Encryption Standard (AES)
Chapter 8   Mathematical Foundations III
Chapter 10   Elliptic Curve Cryptography (ECC)

Key Terms		
Abelian group	Cyclic group	Identity element
Additive inverse	Distributive law	Irreducible polynomial
Algebraic polynomial	Field	Multiplicative inverse
Associative law	Finite group	Order of a group
Binary operation	Galois field, GF(p), GF(2^n)	Ordered pair
Commutative group	Generator	Ring
Commutative law	Group	Subgroup

RECOMMENDED READING

Dummit, D. and Foote, R., *Abstract Algebra*. John Wiley & Sons, Hoboken, NJ, 2004.

Durbin, J., *Modern Algebra*, John Wiley & Sons, Singapore, 2005.

Forouzan, Behrouz A., *Cryptography and Network Security*, Tata McGraw-Hill, New Delhi, 2007.

Stallings, W., *Cryptography and Network Security*, Prentice-Hall of India, New Delhi, 2008.

──────── (**PROBLEMS**) ────────

1. Can the set of residues $Z_6 = \{0, 1, 2, 3, 4, 5\}$ form a group for the multiplication ($\times$) operation?

2. Is the group $G = \{1, 2, 3, 4, 5, 6\}$ under multiplication modulo 7 cyclic with generator 3?

3. If $f(x) = x^3 + x + 1$ and $g(x) = x^2 + x + 1$ are defined over GF(2), compute

   (a) $f(x) + g(x)$

   (b) $f(x) \times g(x)$

   (c) $f(x) + g(x) \mod (x^2 + x + 1)$

   (d) $f(x) \times g(x) \mod (x^3 + x^2 + 1)$

4. Simplify the following expressions with coefficients in Z_7:

   (a) $(5x^2 + 2x + 1) \times (3x + 1)$

   (b) $(5x^2 + 5x + 2) + (2x^2 + 3x + 4)$

   (c) $(x^2 + 5x + 2) - (2x^2 + 3x + 4)$

5. Show that the following polynomials over GF(2) are reducible:

   (a) $x^2 + 1$

   (b) $x^3 + 1$

6. Determine gcd of the following polynomials:

   (a) $x^4 + x^2 + x + 1$, $x^3 + 1$ over GF(2)

   (b) $x^5 + x^4 + 1$, $x^3 + 1$ over GF(2)

7. Determine using extended Euclid's algorithm multiplicative inverse of (101) with

   (a) modulus 1011.

   (b) modulus 1101.

8. Determine using extended Euclid's algorithm multiplicative inverse of $x^3 + x + 1$ in GF(2^4) with modulus ($x^4 + x + 1$).

9. Encrypt $m = (110)$ using affine cipher $c = Mm + N$, where M = (011), N = (101). All the binary operations are modulo (1011) over GF(2^3).

10. Decrypt c obtained in Problem 9 above.

11. If the number of non-zero elements in GF(2^n) is a prime number, any non-zero element can be the generator. GF(2^3) has 7 non-zero elements under modulo $x^3 + x + 1$.

    (a) If the generator $g = x + 1$, compute the elements of GF(2^3) under multiplication modulo $x^3 + x + 1$.

    (b) Determine the binary element generated by g^{23}.

6

Symmetric-key Ciphers II
(Advanced Encryption Standard)

Algebraic structures introduced in Chapter 5 are the mathematical foundation of the block cipher Advanced Encryption Standard (AES) that we describe in this chapter. AES cipher was introduced in 2001 when technological advancements in computing technology made DES cipher vulnerable to attacks. We begin the chapter with basic features and overall structure of AES. Each round of encryption/decryption and key expansion schedule of AES are described in detail with examples. We conclude the chapter with comments on security and implementation aspects of AES.

6.1 ADVANCED ENCRYPTION STANDARD (AES)

The Advanced Encryption Standard (AES) was published by NIST in 2001 and was intended to replace DES and Triple DES. Its basic features are as follows:

- AES is a block cipher with a block length of 128 bits.
- AES provides three levels of security using three cipher key sizes—128, 192, or 256 bits.
- Number of encryption rounds is related to the size of the cipher key.

      128-bit key   10 rounds
      192-bit key   12 rounds
      256-bit key   14 rounds

  The round key is always 128 bits long irrespective of the cipher key size.
- AES is a non-Feistel cipher. To achieve required degree of diffusion and confusion, each round of encryption and decryption is based on the structure shown in Figure 6.1. Recall that this structure was introduced in Chapter 4. Encryption function f introduces diffusion and is invertible. Function g introduces confusion and is not required to be invertible.

As noted above, AES provides three levels of security using cipher key sizes of 128, 192 and 256 bits. We restrict description of AES to 128-bit cipher key in this chapter. The structure of AES algorithm for the other key sizes remains same except for the number of rounds.

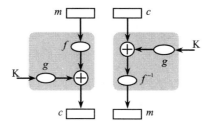

Figure 6.1 Structure of an encryption/decryption round of AES.

6.1.1 State Array and Word

AES uses notion of state array and word. A 128-bit data block of 128 bits is depicted as a 4×4 square matrix of 16 bytes. The bytes of the block are arranged sequentially column-wise, i.e., the first four bytes occupy the first column. The 4×4 matrix of input plaintext undergoes several rounds of encryption to get finally 4×4 matrix of output ciphertext. After each round of encryption, the 4×4 matrix is called *state array* or simply *state* [Figure 6.2(a)].

Similarly the 128-bit cipher key is depicted as 4×4 square matrix of 16 bytes. This key is expanded into a 44 column matrix [Figure 6.2(b)]. Each column of matrix is referred to as a *word*. Schedule of 44 columns provides 11 round keys, each consisting of four words, i.e., 16 bytes or 128 bits.

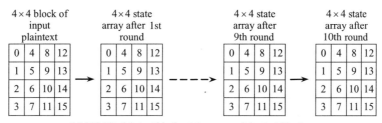

Figure 6.2 State array and key words.

6.1.2 Overall Structure of AES

Figure 6.3 shows the structure of AES cipher for 128-bit cipher key. Only the encryption rounds have been shown in the figure. We will look at the decryption rounds later.

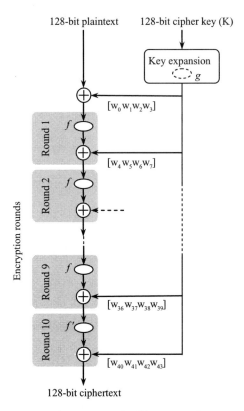

Figure 6.3   Structure of AES encryption rounds.

(a) There are ten rounds of encryption for 128-bit cipher key. The structure remains same for other key sizes, except that additional encryption rounds get added.

(b) Key expansion schedule generates eleven 128-bit round keys from the cipher key K. Each round key consists of four words. For example, the first round key is $[w_0$ w_1 w_2 $w_3]$.

(c) Key expansion schedule embeds the scrambling function g which diffuses each bit of the cipher key K into some bits of several round keys. When round keys are added to the state arrays, each bit of the cipher key gets diffused into several bits of the cipertext block.

(d) Each encryption round consists of transformation of input state using function f followed by round key addition. Function f is so designed that each bit of the input state is diffused into several bits at the output. Note that transformation by function f does not require the round key and as such provides no security till round key is added after this transformation. Therefore, each round has a stage of round key addition.

(e) The encryption function f consists of several stages of substitution and permutation transformations. Each of these transformations is reversible. The decryption rounds (not shown in the figure) have inverse transformation stages in reverse order as we shall see shortly.

(f) The first round is preceded by an additional stage of round key addition. Without this stage, the transformation carried out by function f in the first round will lose its purpose. This is so because this transformation is keyless and can be easily reversed without knowledge of the key.

Note that the tenth round incorporates round key addition as the last stage. The decryption algorithm, which follows reverse order of encryption transformations, will automatically have a preceding key addition stage.

(g) The round function of the last round is slightly different as we shall see later. This is a consequence of AES structure and is required to make cipher reversible.

6.2 ENCRYPTION ROUND

Each round of encryption has the following four stages of transformation (Figure 6.4). The last round is an exception. It does not have MixColumns transformation stage.

(a) Substitute bytes (SubBytes)
(b) Shift rows (ShiftRows)
(c) Mix columns (MixColumns)
(d) Add round key (AddRoundKey)

All these transformations are invertible. The first three stages carry out substitution and permutation at byte and bit levels. The round key as secret parameter is added in the last stage of a round.

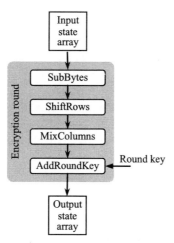

Figure 6.4 Composition of an encryption round.

6.2.1 Substitute Bytes (SubBytes) Transformation

Each byte b of the input state is transformed into byte b' by a substitution process defined by the following equation:

$$b' = Mb^{-1} + N$$

where

- M and N are constant matrices given below.

$$
M = \begin{bmatrix}
1 & 0 & 0 & 0 & 1 & 1 & 1 & 1 \\
1 & 1 & 0 & 0 & 0 & 1 & 1 & 1 \\
1 & 1 & 1 & 0 & 0 & 0 & 1 & 1 \\
1 & 1 & 1 & 1 & 0 & 0 & 0 & 1 \\
1 & 1 & 1 & 1 & 1 & 0 & 0 & 0 \\
0 & 1 & 1 & 1 & 1 & 1 & 0 & 0 \\
0 & 0 & 1 & 1 & 1 & 1 & 1 & 0 \\
0 & 0 & 0 & 1 & 1 & 1 & 1 & 1
\end{bmatrix}, \; N = \begin{bmatrix} 1 \\ 1 \\ 0 \\ 0 \\ 0 \\ 1 \\ 1 \\ 0 \end{bmatrix}
$$

- Multiplicative inverse b^{-1} is determined modulo (100011011) using irreducible polynomial $x^8 + x^4 + x^3 + x + 1$. The multiplicative inverse of byte (00000000) is taken as (00000000).
- All additions are modulo 2, i.e., XOR operation.

The following example illustrates computation of the substitution byte using the above equation. Take note of the order of bits of b and b' in the example. The LSB is written first in the above computation.

To determine the substitution byte for (00001100), we first determine multiplicative inverse of (00001100) modulo (100011011) using irreducible polynomial $x^8 + x^4 + x^3 + x + 1$. The multiplicative inverse is determined using Extended Euclid's algorithm (Chapter 5). Multiplicative inverse of (00001100) is (10110000). We leave the inverse computation as an exercise.

Next we compute the substitution byte b' as follows:

$$
b' = \begin{bmatrix}
1 & 0 & 0 & 0 & 1 & 1 & 1 & 1 \\
1 & 1 & 0 & 0 & 0 & 1 & 1 & 1 \\
1 & 1 & 1 & 0 & 0 & 0 & 1 & 1 \\
1 & 1 & 1 & 1 & 0 & 0 & 0 & 1 \\
1 & 1 & 1 & 1 & 1 & 0 & 0 & 0 \\
0 & 1 & 1 & 1 & 1 & 1 & 0 & 0 \\
0 & 0 & 1 & 1 & 1 & 1 & 1 & 0 \\
0 & 0 & 0 & 1 & 1 & 1 & 1 & 1
\end{bmatrix} \times \begin{bmatrix} 0 \\ 0 \\ 0 \\ 0 \\ 1 \\ 1 \\ 0 \\ 1 \end{bmatrix} + \begin{bmatrix} 1 \\ 1 \\ 0 \\ 0 \\ 0 \\ 1 \\ 1 \\ 0 \end{bmatrix} = \begin{bmatrix} 1 \\ 0 \\ 1 \\ 1 \\ 1 \\ 0 \\ 0 \\ 1 \end{bmatrix} + \begin{bmatrix} 1 \\ 1 \\ 0 \\ 0 \\ 0 \\ 1 \\ 1 \\ 0 \end{bmatrix} = \begin{bmatrix} 0 \\ 1 \\ 1 \\ 1 \\ 1 \\ 1 \\ 1 \\ 1 \end{bmatrix}
$$

$b' = (11111110)$

The SubBytes transformation is inherently resistant to cryptanalytic attacks because of its following design features:

- SubBytes is nonlinear transformation because multiplicative inverse of b is used.
- Matrix M is so designed that each bit of the substituting byte b' is determined by five bits of the substituted byte b.
- Vector N is so chosen that a byte b does not map to itself or its complement $\bar{b}$.

AES defines a fixed 16×16 lookup table called S-box for SubBytes transformation (Table 6.1). A byte represented as {xy} in hexadecimal is substituted with the byte at the intersection of row x and column y.

TABLE 6.1   SubBytes Transformation Table (S-box)

		0	1	2	3	4	5	6	7	8	9	A	B	C	D	E	F
								y									
x	**0**	63	7C	77	7B	F2	6B	6F	C5	30	01	67	2B	FE	D7	AB	76
	1	CA	82	C9	7D	FA	59	47	F0	AD	D4	A2	AF	9C	A4	72	C0
	2	B7	FD	93	26	36	3F	F7	CC	34	A5	E5	F1	71	D8	31	15
	3	04	C7	23	C3	18	96	05	9A	07	12	80	E2	EB	27	B2	75
	4	09	83	2C	1A	1B	6E	5A	A0	52	3B	D6	B3	29	E3	2F	84
	5	53	D1	00	ED	20	FC	B1	5B	6A	CB	BE	39	4A	4C	58	CF
	6	D0	EF	AA	FB	43	4D	33	85	45	F9	02	7F	50	3C	9F	A8
	7	51	A3	40	8F	92	9D	38	F5	BC	B6	DA	21	10	FF	F3	D2
	8	CD	0C	13	EC	5F	97	44	17	C4	A7	7E	3D	64	5D	19	73
	9	60	81	4F	DC	22	2A	90	88	46	EE	B8	14	DE	5E	0B	DB
	A	E0	32	3A	0A	49	06	24	5C	C2	D3	AC	62	91	95	E4	79
	B	E7	CB	37	6D	8D	D5	4E	A9	6C	56	F4	EA	65	7A	AE	08
	C	BA	78	25	2E	1C	A6	B4	C6	E8	DD	74	1F	4B	BD	8B	8A
	D	70	3E	B5	66	48	03	F6	0E	61	35	57	B9	86	C1	1D	9E
	E	E1	F8	98	11	69	D9	8E	94	9B	1E	87	E9	CE	55	28	DF
	F	8C	A1	89	0D	BF	E6	42	68	41	99	2D	0F	B0	54	BB	16

6.2.2   Shift Rows Transformation (ShiftRows)

SubBytes transformation does not alter location of a byte in a 4×4 state array. It merely substitutes an alternative byte in the same location. Shift rows transformation alters the location of bytes of a state array. ShiftRows introduces row-wise circular left shift in the state array obtained as output of SubBytes transformation. The row number (0, 1, 2, 3) determines the extent of byte rotation (Figure 6.5). Thus the first row of the state is not altered and the last row is rotated by three bytes.

Recall that bytes of 128-bit plaintext block are mapped column-wise to 4×4 matrix, i.e., first four bytes go in the first column of the state. ShiftRows transformation spreads out the four bytes of one column to four different columns thereby carries out permutation at byte level.

Before				After				
01	42	8C	12	01	42	8C	12	No shift
19	5A	09	13	5A	09	13	19	1-byte left circular shift
27	6D	10	14	10	14	27	6D	2-byte left circular shift
3E	A7	11	15	15	3E	A7	11	3-byte left circular shift

Figure 6.5   Shift rows transformation.

6.2.3 Mix Columns Transformation (MixColumns)

After SubBytes and ShiftRows transformations, a byte retains its identity as a substituted byte in a different location in the state array. Mix columns transformation scrambles the bits of a column of the state array. This transformation involves multiplication of a column u by a constant 4×4 matrix C. The multiplication is modulo (100011011), i.e., using irreducible polynomial $x^8 + x^4 + x^3 + x + 1$.

$$v = C \times u \bmod (100011011)$$

where matrix C is given as follows. The elements of C are represented in hexadecimal.

$$C = \begin{bmatrix} 02 & 03 & 01 & 01 \\ 01 & 02 & 03 & 01 \\ 01 & 01 & 02 & 03 \\ 03 & 01 & 01 & 02 \end{bmatrix}$$

Let us consider the following example.

If the first column of the state array after ShiftRows transformation has the elements {63}, {F2}, {7D}, {D4} in hexadecimal, the first byte of the state array on MixColumns transformation is computed as given below:

$$[\{02\} \times \{63\} + \{03\} \times \{F2\} + \{01\} \times \{7D\} + \{01\} \times \{D4\}] \bmod (100011011)$$

Now,

$\{02\} \times \{63\}\bmod (100011011) = 00000010 \times 01100011 \bmod (100011011) = 11000110$
$\{03\} \times \{F2\}\bmod (100011011) = 00000011 \times 11110010 \bmod (100011011) = 00001101$
$\{01\} \times \{7D\}\bmod (100011011) = 00000001 \times 01111101 \bmod (100011011) = 01111101$
$\{01\} \times \{D4\}\bmod (100011011) = 00000001 \times 11010100 \bmod (100011011) = 11010100$

Thus,

$$[\{02\} \times \{63\} + \{03\} \times \{F2\} + \{01\} \times \{7D\} + \{01\} \times \{D4\}] \bmod (100011011)$$

$$= 01100010 = \{63\}$$

6.2.4 Add Round Key (AddRoundKey)

All the three previous transformations were carried out without using the round key. The last transformation of a round is AddRoundKey transformation in which 128 bits of the state array are XORed with 128 bits of the round key. The resulting output state array is the encrypted form of the state array at the input of the round.

Figure 6.6 shows structure of encryption rounds of AES with various transformations in every round. Note that the tenth round has only three stages of transformation. MixColumn transformation is missing from this round. Figure 6.6 also depicts the structure of decryption rounds which we describe in the next section.

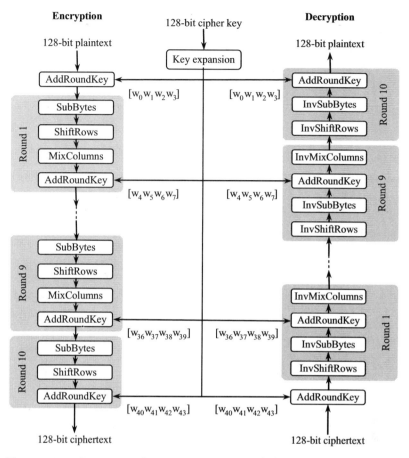

Figure 6.6 Structure of AES encryption and decryption rounds.

6.3 DECRYPTION ROUND

Each decryption round consists of the following inverse transformations (Figure 6.6):

(a) Inverse shift rows transformation (InvShiftRows)
(b) Inverse substitute bytes transformation (InvSubBytes)
(c) Add round key transformation (AddRoundKey)
(d) Inverse Mix columns transformation (InvMixColumns)

Some important observations are as follows:

• The overall structure of AES decryption follows the reverse order of transformations of AES encryption from start to the tenth round.
• AddRoundKey precedes the first round of decryption for the reason given earlier. Due to this the order of transformations within a decryption round appears to have been altered.

- Round keys for decryption are same as those for encryption. But the order in which they are applied is reversed.
- Inverse of AddRoundKey transformation is identical to AddRoundKey transformation because XOR operation is its own reverse (A ⊕ A ⊕ B = B). Therefore, decryption algorithm has AddRoundKey transformation in place of InvAddRoundKey transformation.

Let us look at the various transformations within a decryption round.

6.3.1 Inverse Shift Rows Transformation (InvShiftRows)

In inverse shift rows transformation, each byte in a row of the state array is shifted circularly to right by 0, 1, 2 or 3 bytes, depending on its row number (Figure 6.7). Recall that ShiftRows transformation had circularly shifted the bytes of row to left.

Before					After				
01	42	8C	12		01	42	8C	12	No shift
5A	09	13	19		19	5A	09	13	1-byte right circular shift
10	14	27	6D		27	6D	10	14	2-byte right circular shift
15	3E	A7	11		3E	A7	11	15	3-byte right circular shift

Figure 6.7 Inverse shift rows transformation (InvShiftRows).

6.3.2 Inverse Substitute Bytes Transformation (InvSubBytes)

InvSubBytes retraces the steps of SubBytes transformation in reverse order—subtract N and multiply by M^{-1} to get b^{-1} and take multiplicative inverse of b^{-1}.

$$M^{-1}(b' - N) = M^{-1}(Mb^{-1} + N - N) = M^{-1}(Mb^{-1}) = b^{-1}$$

Remember that subtraction modulo 2 amounts to addition and is XOR operation. The matrix M^{-1} is given below.

$$M^{-1} = \begin{bmatrix} 0 & 0 & 1 & 0 & 0 & 1 & 0 & 1 \\ 1 & 0 & 0 & 1 & 0 & 0 & 1 & 0 \\ 0 & 1 & 0 & 0 & 1 & 0 & 0 & 1 \\ 1 & 0 & 1 & 0 & 0 & 1 & 0 & 0 \\ 0 & 1 & 0 & 1 & 0 & 0 & 1 & 0 \\ 0 & 0 & 1 & 0 & 1 & 0 & 0 & 1 \\ 1 & 0 & 0 & 1 & 0 & 1 & 0 & 0 \\ 0 & 1 & 0 & 0 & 1 & 0 & 1 & 0 \end{bmatrix}$$

Multiplicative inverse of b^{-1} is computed modulo (100011011). Extended Euclid's algorithm can be used for this purpose. Here again AES defines a fixed 16 × 16 lookup table called Inverse S-box (Table 6.2) for determining b from a given b'. As before, hexadecimal representation {xy} of b' determines the location of byte b at the intersection row x and column y of this table.

TABLE 6.2 InvSubBytes Transformation Table (Inverse S-box)

		0	1	2	3	4	5	6	7	8	9	A	B	C	D	E	F
									y								
	0	52	09	6A	D5	30	36	A5	38	BF	40	A3	9E	81	F3	D7	FB
	1	7C	E3	39	82	9B	2F	FF	87	34	8E	43	44	C4	DE	E9	CB
	2	54	7B	94	32	A6	C2	23	3D	EE	4C	95	0B	42	FA	C3	4E
	3	08	2E	A1	66	28	D9	24	B2	76	5B	A2	49	6D	8B	D1	25
	4	72	F8	F6	64	86	68	98	16	D4	A4	5C	CC	5D	65	B6	92
	5	6C	70	48	50	FD	ED	B9	DA	5E	15	46	57	A7	8D	9D	84
	6	90	D8	AB	00	8C	BC	D3	0A	F7	E4	58	05	B8	B3	45	06
x	**7**	D0	2C	1E	8F	CA	3F	0F	02	C1	AF	BD	03	01	13	8A	6B
	8	3A	91	11	41	4F	67	DC	EA	97	F2	CF	CE	F0	B4	E6	73
	9	96	AC	74	22	E7	AD	35	85	E2	F9	37	E8	1C	75	DF	6E
	A	47	F1	1A	71	1D	29	C5	89	F6	B7	62	0E	AA	18	BE	1B
	B	FC	56	3E	4B	C6	D2	79	20	9A	DB	C0	FE	78	CD	5A	F4
	C	1F	DD	A8	33	88	07	C7	31	B1	12	10	59	27	80	EC	5F
	D	60	51	7F	A9	19	B5	4A	0D	2D	E5	7A	9F	93	C9	9C	EF
	E	A0	E0	3B	4D	AE	2A	F5	B0	C8	EB	BB	3C	83	53	99	61
	F	17	2B	04	7E	BA	77	D6	26	E1	69	14	63	55	21	0C	7D

To carry out InvSubBytes transformation of $b' = (11111110)$, we proceed as follows:

$$
b^{-1} =
\begin{bmatrix}
0 & 0 & 1 & 0 & 0 & 1 & 0 & 1 \\
1 & 0 & 0 & 1 & 0 & 0 & 1 & 0 \\
0 & 1 & 0 & 0 & 1 & 0 & 0 & 1 \\
1 & 0 & 1 & 0 & 0 & 1 & 0 & 0 \\
0 & 1 & 0 & 1 & 0 & 0 & 1 & 0 \\
0 & 0 & 1 & 0 & 1 & 0 & 0 & 1 \\
1 & 0 & 0 & 1 & 0 & 1 & 0 & 0 \\
0 & 1 & 0 & 0 & 1 & 0 & 1 & 0
\end{bmatrix}
\times
\left\{
\begin{bmatrix}
0 \\ 1 \\ 1 \\ 1 \\ 1 \\ 1 \\ 1 \\ 1
\end{bmatrix}
+
\begin{bmatrix}
1 \\ 1 \\ 0 \\ 0 \\ 0 \\ 1 \\ 1 \\ 0
\end{bmatrix}
\right\}
=
\begin{bmatrix}
0 & 0 & 1 & 0 & 0 & 1 & 0 & 1 \\
1 & 0 & 0 & 1 & 0 & 0 & 1 & 0 \\
0 & 1 & 0 & 0 & 1 & 0 & 0 & 1 \\
1 & 0 & 1 & 0 & 0 & 1 & 0 & 0 \\
0 & 1 & 0 & 1 & 0 & 0 & 1 & 0 \\
0 & 0 & 1 & 0 & 1 & 0 & 0 & 1 \\
1 & 0 & 0 & 1 & 0 & 1 & 0 & 0 \\
0 & 1 & 0 & 0 & 1 & 0 & 1 & 0
\end{bmatrix}
\times
\begin{bmatrix}
1 \\ 0 \\ 1 \\ 1 \\ 1 \\ 0 \\ 0 \\ 1
\end{bmatrix}
=
\begin{bmatrix}
0 \\ 0 \\ 0 \\ 0 \\ 1 \\ 1 \\ 0 \\ 1
\end{bmatrix}
$$

Multiplicative inverse of b^{-1} modulo (100011011) gives $b = (00001100)$.

6.3.3 Inverse Mix Columns (InvMixColumns)

Inverse mix columns transformation (InvMixColumns) unscrambles the bits a column of the state array. A scrambled column v of the state array is multiplied by a constant C^{-1} to get unscrambled column u. Recall that constant C was used earlier in encryption algorithm.

$$C^{-1} \times v = C^{-1} \times C \times u \bmod (100011011) = u$$

Multiplication is modulo (100011011), i.e., using irreducible polynomial $x^8 + x^4 + x^3 + x + 1$. C^{-1} is given as:

$$C^{-1} = \begin{bmatrix} 0E & 0B & 0D & 09 \\ 09 & 0E & 0B & 0D \\ 0D & 09 & 0E & 0B \\ 0B & 0D & 09 & 0E \end{bmatrix}$$

6.4 KEY EXPANSION IN AES

As shown in Figure 6.6, the state array of 4 × 4 bytes is XORed with the round keys at the start of the encryption algorithm and in each of the ten rounds. The eleven XOR stages require eleven round keys each of (4 × 4) bytes. In other words, AES algorithm requires a key schedule of 44 words, w_0 to w_{43}, as shown in Figure 6.8. AES key expansion algorithm constructs this schedule from the 128-bit AES cipher key. The key expansion algorithm also contains a scrambling function g which diffuses each bit of the cipher key into several bits of the round keys. The steps involved in construction of the key schedule are described below:

(a) The 128-bit AES cipher key is copied into the first four words of the key schedule. The first four bytes of the key (k_0 to k_3) occupy the first column of the key schedule; next four bytes occupy the second column and so on.

128-bit AES cipher key

k_0	k_4	k_8	k_{12}
k_1	k_5	k_9	k_{13}
k_2	k_6	k_{10}	k_{14}
k_3	k_7	k_{11}	k_{15}

Expanded key (44 words for 11 round keys)

w_0	w_1	w_2	w_3	...	w_{43}
k_0	k_4	k_8	k_{12}		
k_1	k_5	k_9	k_{13}		
k_2	k_6	k_{10}	k_{14}		
k_3	k_7	k_{11}	k_{15}		

Figure 6.8 AES key expansion.

(b) The next four words (w_4 to w_7) for the first encryption round are computed from (w_0 to w_3) as given below.

$$w_4 = w_0 + g(w_3) \qquad w_5 = w_1 + w_4 \qquad w_6 = w_2 + w_5 \qquad w_7 = w_3 + w_6$$

where addition is modulo 2, i.e., XOR operation. The process is iterated for the rest of round key words as shown in Figure 6.9(a).

Scrambling function g consists of the following transformations [Figure 6.9(b)]:

RotWord It performs one-byte circular rotation on four-byte word, so that the first byte becomes the last byte.

SubWord It substitutes each byte of the word with the byte from the S-box used in encryption algorithm (Table 6.1).

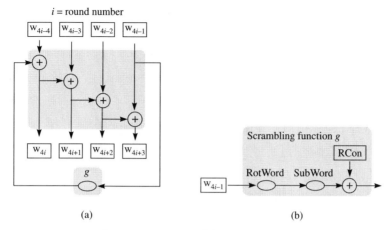

Figure 6.9 Round key generation.

XOR The bytes obtained in step (b) are XORed with a round constant (RCon). The value of RCon depends on the round number as shown in Table 6.3.

TABLE 6.3 Round Constants for Key Expansion

Round	RCon (Hexadecimal)				Round	RCon (Hexadecimal)			
1	01	00	00	00	6	20	00	00	00
2	02	00	00	00	7	40	00	00	00
3	04	00	00	00	8	80	00	00	00
4	08	00	00	00	9	1B	00	00	00
5	10	00	00	00	10	36	00	00	00

Note that the three rightmost bytes of RCon are always zero. RCon for ith round is written as $[RC_i\ 0\ 0\ 0]$, where

$$RC_i = 1 \qquad \text{for } i = 1$$
$$RC_i = 02 \times RC_{i-1} \quad \text{for } i > 1$$

The multiplication is performed modulo (100011011).

Example 1 Given the key of round 7 as {62 83 3E B6 04 9F B3 95 C5 9C B9 AD F7 81 3B 74}, compute the first four bytes of the key of round 8.

Solution

w_{28} = {62 83 3E B6}
w_{29} = {04 9F B3 95}
w_{30} = {C5 9C B9 AD}
w_{31} = {F7 81 3B 74}
$g(w_{31})$ = $RCon_8 \oplus [SubWord[RotWord[w_{31}]]]$
    = $RCon_8 \oplus [SubWord[RotWord\{F7\ 81\ 3B\ 74\}]]]$

$$= RCon_8 \oplus [SubWord\{81\ 3B\ 74\ F7\}]$$
$$= \{80\ 00\ 00\ 00\} \oplus \{0C\ E2\ 92\ 68\}$$
$$= \{8C\ E2\ 92\ 68\}$$
$$w_{32} \quad = \{62\ 83\ 3E\ B6\} \oplus \{8C\ E2\ 92\ 68\}$$
$$= \{EE\ 61\ AC\ DE\}$$

6.4.1 Characteristic Features of the Key Expansion Algorithm

Key expansion algorithm has been designed taking into account known cryptanalytic attacks.

- With the inclusion of nonlinear SubWord transformation, it is not possible to find the cipher key or round key, if part of cipher key or round key is known. Nonlinearity also prohibits determination of round key differences from cipher key differences.
- No matter how similar to each other, two different cipher keys produce several different round keys.
- Each bit of the cipher key is diffused into several round keys.
- Usage of round constant, RCons, eliminates any symmetry in key expansion.
- There are no weak or semi weak keys in AES.
- Key expansion routine can be easily implemented on wide range of processors.

6.5 SECURITY AND IMPLEMENTATION ASPECTS OF AES

AES was developed after DES. Designers of AES took into account the known attacks on DES and its security limitations while designing AES.

- The known attacks on DES when tested on AES could not break security of AES. Unlike DES, there are no weak keys in AES.
- 128-bit cipher key of AES renders any brute force attack impractical with the current technology. AES with 256-bit key will be able to sustain threat of brute force attack even with the projected technological growth of near future.
- AES with 128-bit block size provides strong resistance to statistical attacks.
- AES can be implemented in software, hardware and firmware. Its simple design makes processing very fast. It can even be implemented using 8-bit processor.

6.6 SUMMING UP

In this chapter, we covered AES, a symmetric-key block cipher which is considered secure in the current state of computing technology.

- AES has block length of 128 bits. A 128-bit data block is depicted as a 4×4 square matrix of 16 bytes, called state array in AES.
- AES provides three levels of security using three cipher key sizes—128, 192, or 256 bits. Number of encryption rounds is 10, 12 or 14 rounds for key sizes of 128, 192, 256 bits respectively.

- Each round of encryption has four stages of transformation: SubBytes, ShiftRows, MixColumns and AddRoundKey. The last round does not have MixColumns transformation. All these transformations are invertible. The first round is preceded by an additional stage of AddRoundKey.
- The overall structure of AES decryption follows the reverse order of transformations of AES encryption.
- 128-bit cipher key of AES renders any brute force attack impractical with current technology. 128-bit block size provides strong resistance to the statistical attack.

We have covered two widely deployed block ciphers DES and AES. In the next chapter, we will study various ways of using these block ciphers.

Key Terms		
AddRoundKey transformation	RotWord transformation	State array
Key expansion	Round constant (RCon)	SubBytes transformation
MixColumns transformation	ShiftRows transformation	SubWord transformation

RECOMMENDED READING

Advanced Encryption Standard (AES), Federal Information Processing Standards Publication #197.U.S. Department of Commerce, NIST, 2001.

Forouzan, Behrouz A., *Cryptography and Network Security*, Tata McGraw-Hill, New Delhi, 2007.

Kaufman, C., Perlman, R. and Spenciner, M., *Network Security, Private Communication in a Public World*, Prentice-Hall of India, New Delhi, 2007.

Paar, C. and Pelzl, J., *Understanding Cryptography, A Textbook for Students and Practitioners*. Springer (India) Pvt. Ltd., New Delhi, 2009.

Stallings, W., *Cryptography and Network Security*, Prentice-Hall of India, New Delhi, 2008.

Trappe, W., Washington, L., *Introduction to Cryptography and Coding Theory*, Prentice Hall, NJ, USA, 2006.

Vaudenay, S., *A Classical Introduction to Cryptography*, Springer, NY, USA, 2006.

(PROBLEMS)

1. Show that $\{73\} \times \{a5\} = \{e3\}$ mod (100011011).

2. Compute the substitution byte for $\{01\}$ and verify the entry in the S-box.

3. (a) Rewrite the plaintext $p = \{00\ 01\ 02\ 03\ 04\ 05\ 06\ 07\ 08\ 09\ 0A\ 0B\ 0C\ 0D\ 0E\ 0F\}$ as initial 4×4 state matrix.
   (b) Show the contents of the state matrix initial AddRoundKey stage, if K = $\{01\ 01\ 01\ 01\ 01\ 01\ 01\ 01\ 01\ 01\ 01\ 01\ 01\ 01\ 01\ 01\}$.

4. The 128-bit key in AES consists of all 0s.
   (a) Determine the first round key $[w_4 \ w_5 \ w_6 \ w_7]$.
   (b) Show that $w_8 = w_{10}$.
   (c) Show that $w_9 = w_{11}$.

5. The 128-bit key in AES consists of all 1s.
   (a) Determine the first round key $[w_4 \ w_5 \ w_6 \ w_7]$.
   (b) Show that $w_8 =$ Complement w_{10}.
   (c) Show that $w_9 =$ Complement w_{11}.

6. Compute the substitution byte for {CB} using SubBytes transformation of AES. The multiplicative inverse of {CB} is {04} for modulus (100011011).

7. If $a = \{57\}$ and $b = \{A2\}$, show that SubByte $(a \oplus b) \neq$ SubByte $(a) \oplus$ SubByte (b). Use Table 6.1.

8. If the round key of eighth round is {EA D2 73 21 B5 8D BA D2 31 2B F5 60 7F 8D 29 2F}, calculate the first four bytes of the round key of ninth round.

9. What is the output of the first round of AES if the plaintext consists of 128 ones, and the first round key also consists of 128 ones? Use Table 6.1 for SubBytes transformation.

7

Symmetric-key Ciphers III
(Stream Ciphers, Modes of Operation)

This chapter forms the last part of our discourse on symmetric-key ciphers. We begin the chapter with introduction to symmetric stream ciphers which differ from block ciphers in many ways. There are two categories of stream ciphers: synchronous and self synchronizing stream ciphers. We study their structure and operation in general. RC4, a synchronous stream cipher is then described in detail. We move over to modes of operations of the block ciphers. We had deferred discussion on this topic, since some of these modes of operation can facilitate use of block ciphers as stream ciphers.

7.1 STREAM CIPHERS

Unlike block ciphers which use same secret key to encrypt different blocks, stream ciphers use a stream of keys to encrypt data. One-time pad (OTP) described in Chapter 3 is a classical equivalent of modern day stream ciphers. Recall that

- OTP uses a random sequence of alphabetic characters as stream of keys to encrypt a message.
- Each key is used once to encrypt a character and discarded. Therefore, as many keys are required as the message size.
- Decryption requires the same stream of keys.

A modern stream cipher attempts to capture the spirit of the one-time pad. It uses a cryptographically secure pseudo random key stream for encryption and decryption as shown in Figure 7.1.

A plaintext word m_i is encrypted using the current key word k_i. Decryption of the ciphertext word c_i requires the same key word k_i.

$$c_i = E(k_i, m_i), \qquad m_i = D(k_i, c_i)$$

where

- m_i, c_i and k_i are r-bit words. Word length r can be 1 bit or more. Typically it is 8 bits (one byte).

- encryption (E) and decryption (D) functions are bit-wise XOR operation, i.e., $c_i = k_i \oplus m_i$ and $m_i = k_i \oplus c_i$.
- the key stream $(k_1, k_2, \ldots)$ is a cryptographically secure pseudo random sequence of r-bit words.

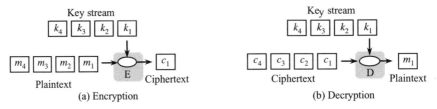

Figure 7.1   Stream cipher.

Note that the security of the stream cipher depends entirely on the security of the key stream $(k_1, k_2, \ldots)$. The key stream is generated using a secret seed key and a cryptographically strong pseudo random sequence generator.

The following characteristics of stream ciphers make them suitable for several applications.

- A stream cipher with a properly designed key stream generator can be as secure as a block cipher.
- Stream ciphers are almost always faster than block ciphers. Their algorithms require far shorter code. Hardware implementation of a stream cipher is much simpler.

Stream ciphers are used in applications that require secure channel for transmission of a stream of data. Block ciphers are more suitable for the applications that deal with blocks of data such as file transfers, data base, email, etc.

Stream ciphers can be divided into two broad categories depending on the way the key stream is generated.

(a) Synchronous stream ciphers
(b) Self synchronizing stream ciphers

We examine these two categories of stream ciphers in brief before going into specific examples of stream ciphers.

7.2   SYNCHRONOUS STREAM CIPHERS

The key stream $(k_1, k_2, \ldots)$ in a synchronous stream cipher is generated using a seed key K and is independent of the plaintext and ciphertext (Figure 7.2). The encrypting end and the decrypting end use the same seed key and ensure that their key streams are always in synchronism. Synchronization is essential so that a plaintext word is encrypted and subsequently decrypted using the same key word.

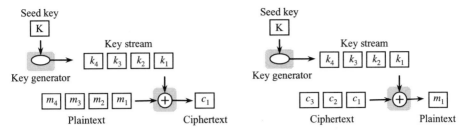

Figure 7.2 Synchronous stream cipher.

The key stream generator is a clocked finite state machine whose internal state S_i is updated at each clocking instant (Figure 7.3).

- Function f determines the next state S_{i+1} from the current state S_i and seed key K.
- Function g generates key k_i from the current state S_i and the seed key K.

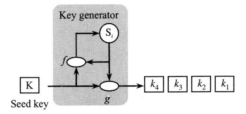

Figure 7.3 Synchronous key stream generator.

Example 1 Figure 7.4 shows four cell linear feedback shift register (LFSR) that generates pseudo random 1-bit key stream k_i. Each cell is capable of storing one bit which is transferred to the next cell on right when it is clocked. The four cells store the seed key 0110 initially. Write the sequence of first 20 bits of key stream k_i when the LFSR is clocked.

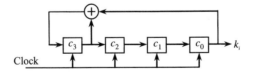

Figure 7.4 Four stage linear feedback shift register.

Solution State transitions when the four cells are clocked are shown in Table 7.1. Input state of each cell is transferred into the cell when it is clocked. The resulting key stream at the output of cell c_0 is 01100100011110101100......

The key stream generated in Example 1 appears to be a random sequence. But note that LFSR comes back to initial state after fifteen state transitions. Thereafter the key sequence is repeated. Thus the key stream is periodic with period of 15 bits.

TABLE 7.1 State Transition of the Four Cell LFSR

State	c_3	c_2	c_1	c_0	State	c_3	c_2	c_1	c_0
Initial	0	1	1	0	10	0	1	1	1
1	0	0	1	1	11	1	0	1	1
2	1	0	0	1	12	0	1	0	1
3	0	1	0	0	13	1	0	1	0
4	0	0	1	0	14	1	1	0	1
5	0	0	0	1	15	0	1	1	0
6	1	0	0	0	16	0	0	1	1
7	1	1	0	0	17	1	0	0	1
8	1	1	1	0	18	0	1	0	0
9	1	1	1	1	19	0	0	1	0

The feedback shift register is called linear feedback register because the feedback bit to the input of cell c_3 is function of *fixed subset* of the outputs of all the cells. The linear feedback register as stream key generator is simple to implement in hardware and software, but its key stream is vulnerable to attacks.

It is possible to have non-linear feedback shift register (NLFSR) where feedback function *f* is *not fixed subset* of the outputs of all the cells (Figure 7.5). By introducing nonlinearity, complexity is enhanced. However, the security of NLFSRs is yet to be fully analyzed mathematically.

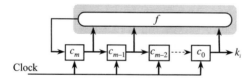

Figure 7.5 Synchronous key stream generator.

7.2.1 Characteristic Features of Synchronous Stream Cipher

Generic characteristics of the synchronous stream ciphers are given below. We will take up a specific example of synchronous stream cipher, RC4, later in the chapter and examine its performance against these characteristics.

Periodicity of key stream: The finite state machine model of the key generator has a very important attribute—the key stream is periodic, i.e., the sequence of key words is repeated after a certain length of the key stream. If the period of repetition of the key stream is too short, then different parts of a plaintext message will be encrypted by the same stream of keys. This constitutes a severe security weakness of a synchronous stream cipher as explained below:

- Knowledge of part of plaintext message allows recovery of the corresponding portion of the key stream. The cryptanalyst, knowing that the recovered key stream is reused later, can successfully decrypt the rest of the ciphertext message.

- Two ciphertext parts can be XORed to give a stream of data that is XOR of two plaintext messages and is independent of the key. This information supplemented with the statistical properties of the plaintext can be used by cryptanalytic to derive the plaintexts and the key stream.

Periodicity of a key stream is usually specified in bits, or as time period along with the bit rate. It should be long enough to ensure that repetition of key stream is overwhelmingly unlikely during encryption of a message or a stream of messages.

Synchronization requirements: If a ciphertext word is lost or an extra word is added during transmission, the synchronization of key stream at the decrypting end is lost and decryption fails. Therefore, synchronous stream ciphers implement resynchronization mechanisms. These mechanisms are based on re-initialization or placing special markers at regular intervals in the ciphertext. Synchronization is re-established when a marker that identifies the particular state at that instant is received.

Error propagation: Synchronous stream cipher encrypts each plaintext word independent of the previous ciphertext word. If an error occurs during transmission of an encrypted data unit, the error does not propagate to the successor word on decryption. In self synchronizing stream ciphers, as we shall see later, a transmission error propagates to the successor word on decryption.

Dispersal of plaintext statistics: While the above characteristic restricts propagation of errors, it makes synchronous stream cipher vulnerable to statistical attacks because there is no dispersal of statistical characteristics of the plaintext.

Active attacks: As a consequence of above characteristics, an active adversary can attack a synchronous stream cipher in number of ways.

- He can cause loss of synchronization by deleting or inserting extra ciphertext words.
- An attacker is able to make controlled changes in parts of the ciphertext by bit-flipping. For example, if he comes to know ciphertext byte 10110110 represents plaintext byte 1, he can change plaintext from 1 to 3 by inverting the second right most bit of the ciphertext to 0. This change would not affect other bytes of the data stream and is likely to go undetected.

7.3 SELF SYNCHRONIZING STREAM CIPHER

Unlike synchronous stream cipher, a self synchronizing stream cipher has the capacity to resume correct decryption, if the key streams at the encrypting and decrypting ends fall out of synchronization. It uses key stream $(k_1, k_2, \ldots)$ which is function of the ciphertext. The key stream is generated using a seed key K and a fixed number of previous ciphertext words [Figure 7.6a)].

$$k_i = g(c_{i-t}, c_{i-t+1}, \ldots, c_{i-1}; K)$$

Key stream at the decrypting end is generated in the same manner using the same seed key K.

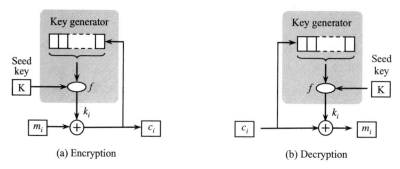

(a) Encryption   (b) Decryption

Figure 7.6   Self synchronizing stream cipher.

Since the key stream is function of a fixed number of preceding ciphertext words, synchronization of key stream is disturbed when a ciphertext word gets deleted, or corrupted by transmission errors. Key stream remains disturbed till the corrupted ciphertext word is in the key generator. If the stream key is function of t ciphertext words, t number of wrong key words will be generated. Thus decryption of these many ciphertext words fails. Thereafter correct decryption resumes.

7.3.1   Characteristic Features of Self Synchronizing Stream Cipher

Following are the generic characteristics of self synchronizing stream ciphers:

Self synchronization: As explained earlier, the key generator self synchronizes in the event of transmission errors. Till re-establishment of synchronization, some of the plaintext words are received corrupted.

Limited error propagation: If the state of a self synchronizing stream cipher depends on t previous ciphertext words, transmission error in a ciphertext word is propagated up to t subsequent ciphertext words on decryption, after which correct decryption resumes.

Active attacks: Recall that an attacker could make controlled changes in a ciphertext word with little likelihood of detection in synchronous stream cipher. But in self synchronizing stream cipher, modification of a ciphertext word, insertion of extra word or deletion of a ciphertext word by an active adversary results in incorrect decryption of several successor ciphertext words. Thus any such attack is more likely to be detected.

Dispersal of plaintext statistics: Self synchronizing stream cipher disperses the statistical properties of plaintext. This is so because each ciphertext word influences the encryption key of the following plaintext. Hence, self synchronizing stream ciphers are more resistant to statistical attacks than synchronous stream ciphers.

The most common self synchronizing stream ciphers are implemented using block ciphers in cipher-feedback (CFB) mode of operation. We will describe this implementation of self synchronizing stream cipher later in the chapter.

7.4 RC4

RC4 was designed by Ron Rivest for RSA Security in 1987. It is a byte-oriented synchronous stream cipher. The size of its cipher key can be from 1 byte to 256 bytes (8 to 2048 bits). RC4 algorithm consists of two parts—initialization and key stream generation.

Initialization: During initialization, the cipher key K is used as seed key to generate a state vector S of 256 bytes. Initialization requires the following steps:

(a) The 256-byte state vector S is set to values 0 to 255 with its elements S(0) = 0, S(1) = 1, ..., S(255) = 255 (Figure 7.7).

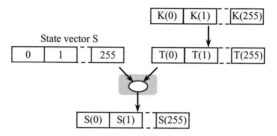

Figure 7.7 Initialization of state vector S.

(b) A temporary vector T of 256 bytes is created using the cipher key K such that its element $T(i) = K(i)$. If the cipher key K is less than 256 bytes, the key bytes are repeated until they fill the T vector.

(c) The T vector is used for initial permutation of the state vector S using the following algorithm:

```
/*Initial Permutation of S*/
j = 0;
for i = 0 to 255 do
  j = [j + S(i) + T(i)] mod 256;
  swap [S(i), S(j)];
```

Let us understand the above algorithm with an example. Consider RC4 stream cipher for 3-bit bytes with state vector S of 8 bytes and 5-byte cipher key K = [1 2 3 4 5]. To start with, we put S = [0 1 2 3 4 5 6 7] and T = [1 2 3 4 5 1 2 3].

(a) First iteration with $i = 0$, $j = 0$
$j = [j + S(i) + T(i)]$ mod 8 = [0 + 0 + 1] mod 8 = 1
Swapping S(0) and S(1), we get S = [1 0 2 3 4 5 6 7]

(b) Second iteration with $i = 1$, $j = 1$
$j = [j + S(i) + T(i)]$ mod 8 = [1 + 0 + 2] mod 8 = 3
Swapping S(1) and S(3), we get S = [1 3 2 0 4 5 6 7]

Rest of the iterations up to $i = 7$ are carried out in similar manner. Table 7.2 gives the results of these iterations for $i = 0$ to 7. The state vector S is initialized to [6 0 1 4 3 7 5 2] after these iterations.

TABLE 7.2   Initialization of State Vector S

	j	0	1	3	0	4	1	7	7	
i	T	S	S	S´	S	S	S	S	S	S
0	1	0	1	1	2	2	2	2	2	6
1	2	1	0	3	3	3	0	0	0	0
2	3	2	2	2	1	1	1	1	1	1
3	4	3	3	0	0	4	4	4	4	4
4	5	4	4	4	4	0	3	3	3	3
5	1	5	5	5	5	5	5	7	7	7
6	2	6	6	6	6	6	6	6	5	5
7	3	7	7	7	7	7	7	5	6	2
$j = j + S(i) +$ $T(i)$ mod 8	1	3	0	4	1	7	7	0		

Key Stream Generation: The state vector S after initial permutation is used for generating the random key stream k as given below.

```
/* Key Stream Generation */
i, j = 0;
while (true)
i = (i + 1) mod 256;
j = [j + S(i)] mod 256;
swap [S(i), S(j)];
t = [S(i) + S(j)] mod 256;
k = S(t);
```

For the state vector S = [6 0 1 4 3 7 5 2] obtained on initialization in the previous example, let us generate key stream for encrypting plaintext bytes 3, 6, 0, 2.

(a) First iteration with $i = 0$, $j = 0$, S = [6 0 1 4 3 7 5 2]

  $i = (0 + 1)$ mod 8 = 1

  $j = [0 + S(1)]$ mod 8 = 0

  Swapping [S(1), S(0)], we get S = [0 6 1 4 3 7 5 2]

  $t = [S(1) + S(0)]$ mod 8 = [6 + 0] mod 8 = 6

  $k = S(6) = 5$

(b) Second iteration with $i = 1$, $j = 0$, S = [0 6 1 4 3 7 5 2]

  $i = (1 + 1)$ mod 8 = 2

  $j = [0 + S(2)]$ mod 8 = [0 + 1] mod 8 = 1

  Swapping [S(2), S(1)], we get S = [0 1 6 4 3 7 5 2]

  $t = [S(2) + S(1)]$ mod 8 = [6 + 1] mod 8 = 7

  $k = S(7) = 2$

Continuing in the same manner, we get $k = 4$ for $i = 2$ and $k = 7$ for $i = 3$. Table 7.3 depicts the results of these iterations. The first four bytes of the key stream are 5, 2, 4, 7. Ciphertext bytes 6, 4, 4, 5 are obtained by XOR of the plaintext with the key stream bytes (Figure 7.8).

TABLE 7.3 Key Stream

j	0	0	1	5
S(0)	6	0	0	0
S(1)	0	6	1	1
S(2)	1	1	6	6
S(3)	4	4	4	7
S(4)	3	3	3	3
S(5)	7	7	7	4
S(6)	5	5	5	5
S(7)	2	2	2	2
$i = i + 1 \bmod 8$	1	2	3	4
$j = j + S(i) \bmod 8$	0	1	5	0
$t = S(i) + S(j) \bmod 8$	6	7	3	3
$k = S(t) \bmod 8$	5	2	4	7

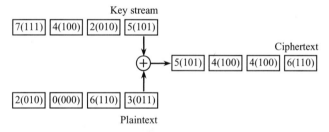

Figure 7.8 Encryption of plaintext.

7.4.1 Analysis of RC4

RC4 has both strong and weak points.

- Analysis has shown that periodicity of stream key of RC4 is overwhelmingly likely to be greater than 10^{100} bits. With cipher key size of 128 or more, RC4 is believed to be secure against the reported attacks on it.
- RC4 has large number of weak keys which can be detected and exploited with high probability.
- It has been reported that first few bytes of RC4 are strongly correlated to the cipher key and can be exploited to determine the cipher key.

- Being a synchronous cipher, RC4 is prone to bit-flipping attack for making predictable changes in the plaintext. Therefore, RC4 should be used along with message integrity checking measures.
- When implemented in software, RC4 is pretty fast algorithm. It is used in
  - SSL/TLS transport layer security protocol to protect internet traffic.
  - WEP (Wired Equivalent Privacy) and WPA (WiFi Protected Access) protocols. These protocols are part of IEEE 802.11 Wireless LAN standard to provide security to wireless networks.

7.5   MODES OF OPERATION OF BLOCK CIPHERS

DES and AES as block ciphers encrypt and decrypt a block of data at a time. Block size is 64 bits in DES and 128 bits in AES. A message is likely to be longer than one block. Therefore, message encryption, in general, involves encryption of a sequence of multiple blocks. Encrypting individual blocks of a message as independent entity may not meet security requirements. For example, if the message contains repetitive data and the data blocks are independently encrypted using a block cipher, the encrypted blocks will also be repetitive. In other words, structure of the plaintext message is reflected in the encrypted message. Secondly, the attacker can easily rearrange the sequence of ciphertext blocks to achieve his objective without even breaking the cipher.

For encrypting a sequence of data blocks of a message, the following five modes of operation have been devised:

1. Electronic codebook mode (ECB)
2. Cipher block chaining mode (CBC)
3. Cipher feedback mode (CFB)
4. Output feedback mode (OFB)
5. Counter mode (CTR)

Each mode of operation is a different scheme for application of underlying block cipher to a sequence of data blocks. The underlying block cipher can be DES, Triple DES or AES. As we shall shortly see, each mode has different characteristics features in terms of security, throughput and sensitivity to errors. An application can adopt one of these modes of operation based on its requirements.

7.5.1   Electronic Codebook Mode (ECB)

Electronic codebook (ECB) is the most basic mode of operation. The message is divided into blocks of required size. If needed, the last fragment of the message is padded to get full block. Each block is encrypted independently using the cipher key K (Figure 7.9). Decryption is carried out using the same key and each ciphertext block is decrypted independently.

This mode is referred to as the electronic codebook mode because, for a given cipher key, there is a fixed mapping between the input blocks of plaintext and the output blocks of ciphertext.

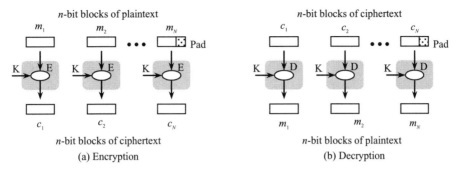

Figure 7.9 Electronic codebook (ECB) mode of operation.

Characteristic Features of ECB

Generic characteristics of ECB mode of operation are given below.

- Identical plaintext blocks result in identical ciphertext blocks.
- Blocks are encrypted independent of other blocks. Therefore, reordering ciphertext blocks is possible. It results in re-ordered plaintext blocks on decryption.
- One or more bit errors in a ciphertext block affect decryption of that block only. Neither the error is propagated to the next block nor decryption of the next block affected.

Security Issues of ECB

Following are the security issues of ECB mode of operation:

- Since identical blocks of plaintext produce identical blocks of ciphertext, ECB not very secure for plaintext containing repetitive information. An attacker can easily make out the structure of a message. For example, the following salary list when encrypted using ECB mode will contain repeating ciphertext block for IT DEPT, which will enable the attacker to identify the structure of the message.

PC GUPTA	IT DEPT	80000.00
B SINGH	IT DEPT	50000.00
TS RAO	IT DEPT	10000.00

- Since encryption of a block is independent of other blocks, an attacker can manipulate a message by rearranging or replacing ciphertext blocks. In the above example, the attacker can easily manipulate his salary because he is aware of the structure of the encrypted message. He can rearrange or substitute encrypted salary data blocks.
- Any change in repetitive pattern of ciphertext block gives out a hint to the attacker that there is some change in prevailing status.

Applications of ECB

ECB is used primarily for secure transmission of short pieces of information, such as an encryption key. Another area of its application is data storage in encrypted form and its retrieval. Since each data block is encrypted independently, an encrypted record can be retrieved from the middle, decrypted, and re-encrypted after its modification without affecting other records.

7.5.2 Cipher Block Chaining Mode (CBC)

ECB mode is insecure when there is repeating pattern of data in the plaintext because the pattern is reflected in the ciphertext. Cipher Block Chaining (CBC) mode of operation overcomes this deficiency of ECB mode. It does not generate identical ciphertext blocks for identical plaintext blocks. Figure 7.10 shows the CBC mode of operation.

- The current block of plaintext is XORed with the previous ciphertext block. The output of XOR operation is encrypted using the block cipher.

$$c_i = E(K, c_{i-1} \oplus m_i)$$

- Decryption is a two-step process as shown in Figure 7.10(b).
    - The ciphertext block is decrypted using the key K.
    - The decrypted output is XORed with the previous ciphertext block to get the plaintext message.

$$c_{i-1} \oplus D(K, c_i) = c_{i-1} \oplus D[K, E(K, c_{i-1} \oplus m_i)] = c_{i-1} \oplus c_{i-1} \oplus m_i = m_i$$

For decrypting the first ciphertext block, the initialization vector is used in place of c_{i-1}.

The chaining scheme shown in the figure needs an initialization vector (IV) for the first invocation of the encryption algorithm. The size of initialization vector is same as the block size. Since the initialization vector is required for decryption also, the encrypting and decrypting entities need to establish a common initialization vector in addition to the cipher key between them.

- Alice can choose a random number as initialization vector and communicate it to Bob along with the secret key.
- Alice and Bob can independently generate initialization vector as part of cipher key establishment process[1].

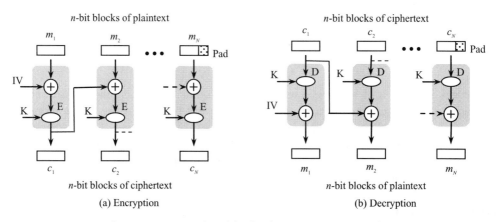

Figure 7.10   Cipher block chaining (CBC) mode.

---

1 Refer to generation of key material in TLS, Chapter 17.

Characteristic Features of CBC Mode

Generic characteristics of CBC mode of operation are as follows:

- In CBC mode, the ciphertext block for any given plaintext block becomes a function of all the previous ciphertext blocks. Therefore,
  - repeating patterns of data are not exposed after encryption.
  - rearranging the order of ciphertext blocks is not possible. The ciphertext blocks can be decrypted in the same sequence as they were generated.
- An error in ciphertext block c_i affects decryption of blocks c_i and the following c_{i+1}. But the error is not propagated beyond c_{i+1}.
- If a ciphertext block c_i is lost, the following ciphertext block c_{i+1} will be not decrypted properly, but the loss will not affect decryption of the ciphertext blocks beyond c_{i+1}. Therefore, CBC mode is self synchronizing.

Security issues of CBC Mode

Following are the security issues of CBC mode of operation:

- CBC mode is prone to bit-flipping manipulation. Since $m_i = c_{i-1} \oplus D(K, c_i)$, if some of the bits of c_{i-1} are inverted, the corresponding bits of decrypted p_i in the same positions will get inverted. Thus an attacker can make predictable changes in the plaintext of a block by inverting the bits of the previous ciphertext block. For example, consider the third record of the salary list.

  TS RAO   IT DEPT   10000.00

  To convert 1 (00000001) to 3 (00000011), the attacker inverts the corresponding bit of the previous encrypted block. The block containing the salary data will be decrypted as 30000.00. The doctored ciphertext block will give some garbled characters on decryption, but these are likely to be ignored.
- There is need to protect the initialization vector from attack. If the attacker can fool the decrypting entity into using a different initialization vector, he can make predictable changes in the first block of plaintext because $m_1 = IV \oplus D(K, c_1)$. By inverting the required set of bits in the IV, he can invert the respective bits of the decrypted plaintext block.
- If same initialization vector is used for transmitting a repeating message, the ciphertext blocks will also be repetitive. The attacker would readily come to know whenever the repeating message is changed. Therefore, initialization vector needs to be regenerated for every new session so that repeating message is encrypted differently at different instances of its transmission.

Applications of CBC Mode

CBC mode is a general purpose mode of operation of block ciphers for the messages having size greater than the block size. Another important application of CBC mode is message authentication. Since the last encrypted block of a message is function of all the earlier blocks of the plaintext message, this block is taken as keyed hash of the message, called message authentication code (MAC). MAC is transmitted along with the plaintext message for validating integrity of the message and the source (Figure 7.11). We will study this application in detail later in Chapter 11.

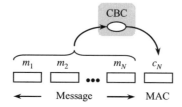

Figure 7.11 CBC mode for message authentication.

ECB and CBC modes of operation can be used for encrypting a message divided into blocks having the size as determined by the underlying block cipher, 64 bits for DES and 128 bits for AES. The next two modes, namely, cipher feedback mode (CFB) and output feedback mode (OFB) enable these block ciphers to be used for encrypting smaller blocks of data.

7.5.3 Cipher Feedback Mode (CFB)

Figure 7.12 depicts the CFB mode of operation. We assume that the block size for encryption is n bits and the plaintext to be encrypted is available in units of s bits, $s < n$. CFB mode is a chained mode of operation like CBC mode and requires n-bit initialization vector. Basic steps of CFB mode of operation are as follows:

(a) The n-bit initialization vector (IV) is stored in the n-bit shift register.
(b) The contents of the shift register are encrypted using the block cipher and cipher key K.
(c) The s most significant bits from the encrypted output are retained and the rest are discarded.
(d) s bits of the plaintext are XORed with the retained s-bit encrypted output of the previous step to get the first s-bit ciphertext block.
(e) The contents of the shift register are moved by s bits to the left (discarding the leftmost s bits) and s-bit ciphertext block produced in the previous step is inserted as the rightmost bits.
(f) Step (b) onwards are repeated for encryption of next s bits of the plaintext.

Note that:
- ciphertext produced at any stage depends on ciphertext produced in all previous stages just as in CBC mode.
- if $s = 8$, a block cipher (e.g. AES) can be used for encrypting 8-bit bytes.

Decryption involves XORing the received ciphertext with the same bits that were used for encryption. Therefore, decryption process also goes through the same steps (a) to (f) listed above. Figure 7.12(b) shows the chaining scheme for decryption. Note that decryption also uses the encryption function (E) of the underlying block cipher.

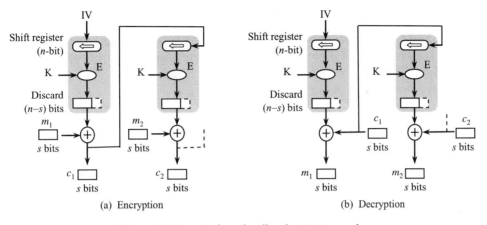

Figure 7.12 Cipher feedback (CFB) mode.

Characteristic Features CFB Mode

Generic characteristics of CFB mode of operation are as follows:

- CFB mode of operation enables encryption of s-bit data blocks ($s < n$) using n-bit underlying block cipher.
- As in CBC mode, the chaining mechanism makes ciphertext block c_i to depend on preceding blocks. Consequently,
  - rearranging order of the ciphertext blocks affects decryption of a message.
  - repeating plaintext blocks are encrypted differently.
  - ciphertext does not expose the plaintext data pattern.
- One or more bit errors in an s-bit ciphertext block affect the decryption of that block and the next n/s ciphertext blocks because that ciphertext block will persist in the shift register for next n/s ciphertext blocks.
- As in CBC mode, CFB mode is self synchronizing after an error occurs. But it requires n/s ciphertext blocks to recover.
- Each execution of encryption algorithm yields only s bits of ciphertext output. Thus throughput is reduced by a factor of n/s as compared to CBC.

Security Issues of CFB Mode

Following are the security issues of CFB mode of operation:

- Just like CBC mode, CFB mode is also prone to bit manipulation. The attacker can cause predictable bit changes in decrypted plaintext block by altering corresponding bits of its ciphertext block. But several following blocks also get garbled on decryption. This increases the likelihood of detection of bit manipulation attack.
- CFB mode is vulnerable to known—plaintext attack, if the IV and the key are fixed. Therefore, the initialization IV needs to be a randomly generated number for each new session.

Application of CFB as Self Synchronizing Stream Cipher

Unlike CBC mode, CFB mode allows encryption of block sizes smaller than the underlying cipher block size. If $s = 8$, CFB mode can encrypt plaintext bytes. Further, note the similarity in structures of CFB mode and self synchronizing stream cipher (Figure 7.6). The s-bit output after encryption using block cipher is function of

- cipher key K, and
- previous n/s ciphertext blocks.

This s-bit output is equivalent to key stream $(k_1, k_2, \dots)$ of the self synchronizing stream cipher. As mentioned above, CFB mode is also self synchronizing. Therefore, CFB mode of operation makes a block cipher to be used as self synchronizing stream cipher.

7.5.4 Output Feedback Mode (OFB)

The structure of output feedback mode (OFB) is shown in Figure 7.12. It is similar to the structure of CFB mode except that s bits from the output of block cipher algorithm are fed back to the shift register. This results in making the s-bit block which is XORed with the plaintext block independent of ciphertext. OFB mode, like CFB mode, uses encryption algorithm (E) of the underlying block cipher for decryption.

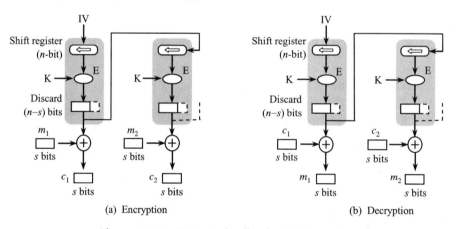

(a) Encryption (b) Decryption

Figure 7.13 Output feedback (OFB) mode.

Characteristic Features of OFB Mode

Generic characteristics of OFB mode of operation are as follows:

- Like CFB mode, OFB mode of operation enables encryption of s-bit data blocks ($s < n$) using n-bit underlying block cipher.
- OFB mode also has a chaining mechanism like CBC and CFB modes. Consequently,
  - repeating plaintext blocks are encrypted differently.
  - ciphertext does not expose the plaintext data pattern.

- As the chaining mechanism of OFB mode is independent of ciphertext blocks,
  - rearranging order of the ciphertext blocks affects decryption of the rearranged blocks only.
  - one or more bit errors in any ciphertext block are not propagated to the following block.
- Unlike CFB mode, OFB mode is synchronous mode of operation. If a block is lost or additional block is inserted, further decryption is not possible.
- Like CFB mode, OFB also has reduced throughput per execution of the encryption algorithm.
- Since the output of encryption function E is independent of plaintext or ciphertext blocks, the encrypted values can be pre-computed. As the plaintext blocks arrive, they are XORed with pre-encrypted values. The same applies to decryption also.

Security issues of OFB Mode

Following are the security issues of OFB mode of operation.

- OFB mode is vulnerable to bit manipulation attack just like CFB mode. Since OFB mode does not use the manipulated ciphertext block in decryption of the following block, the following block of data is unaffected. Therefore, the attack has less likelihood of detection.
- OFB mode is vulnerable to known plaintext attack, if the IV and the key are fixed. Therefore, the initialization vector IV needs to be a randomly generated number for each new session.

Applications of OFB Mode

Like CFB mode, OFB mode is stream oriented mode of operation. Note the similarity in structures of OFB mode and synchronous stream cipher shown in Figure 7.2. The s-bit output of the encryption function (after discarding $n - s$ bits) is XORed with the s bits of plaintext in Figure 7.13. Thus this s-bit output is equivalent to key stream $(k_1, k_2, ...)$ of the synchronous stream cipher shown in Figure 7.2. Also note that each stream key k_i is function of seed key and previous state in Figure 7.3. Similar is the case in Figure 7.13. Thus, if $s = 8$ bits, byte-by-byte encryption and decryption like synchronous stream cipher is possible.

Unlike, CFB mode, OFB mode does not propagate errors to the following block after decryption. Therefore, it finds application in those areas where error occurrence is more likely.

7.5.5   Counter Mode (CTR)

In the counter (CTR) mode of operation, an n-bit counter is used, if the block size is n bits. Figure 7.14(a) shows the encryption process which consists of the following steps:

(a) The counter is initialized to an initial value r which is encrypted using cipher key K.
(b) The encrypted count value r' is XORed with a block of the plaintext m_1 to produce the block of ciphertext $c_1 = r' \oplus m_1$ of the same size.

(c) The counter value r is incremented by a predefined value (typically 1) for each plaintext block, so that every block is XORed with a different r'.

For decryption, the same stream of encrypted counter values is generated using the predefined initial value, incremental value and cipher key K [Figure 7.14(b)]. The encrypted counter values are XORed with the ciphertext blocks to get the decrypted plaintext blocks. Note that only the encryption algorithm of the underlying block cipher is used both for encryption and decryption.

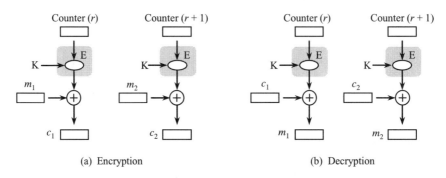

(a) Encryption   (b) Decryption

Figure 7.14   Counter (CTR) mode.

Characteristic Features and Applications of CTR Mode

Generic characteristics, security aspects and applications of CTR mode of operation are given below:

- In the chaining mechanisms, CBC and CFB, a block can be encrypted (or decrypted) only after the complete encryption (or decryption) of previous block. On the other hand, the several counter values can be encrypted in parallel in CTR mode, thereby increasing the throughput of block cipher algorithm.
- Just like in OFB mode, encrypted counter values can be computed in advance. As the plaintext becomes available, it can be XORed with the pre-encrypted counter values. The same applies to decryption also.
- As in OFB mode, an error in ciphertext block is reflected in the decrypted plaintext block but it is not propagated to subsequent plaintext blocks in CTR mode. But a missing ciphertext block results in loss of synchronization of counter values.
- It has been theoretically established that CTR mode is at least as secure as the other modes.
- If it is required to decrypt just one block of data from the stored encrypted data, the chaining modes would require that all the previous blocks be also decrypted. CTR mode is useful in such situations. It allows decryption of individual block of data independently. Thus CTR mode finds application in data storage in encrypted form.

7.6   SUMMING UP

In this chapter, we covered symmetric-key stream ciphers and modes of operation of block ciphers.

- Stream ciphers encrypt individual bytes of a message using a cryptographically secure pseudo random stream of keys.
- In synchronous stream cipher, the key stream $(k_1, k_2, ...)$ is generated using a seed key K. The key stream is independent of the plaintext and ciphertext.
- The key stream of synchronous stream cipher is periodic. Its periodicity is kept long enough to avoid repetition of key stream during encryption of a message.
- RC4 is a byte-oriented synchronous stream cipher. Its cipher key can be from 1 byte to 256 bytes. It has periodicity greater than 10^{100} bits.
- In self synchronizing stream cipher, the key stream is generated using a seed key K and a fixed number of previous ciphertext words. The self synchronizing stream cipher can be implemented using CFB mode of operation of block ciphers.
- Message consisting of multiple blocks is encrypted using one of the following five modes of operation of the block ciphers:
  - Electronic codebook mode (ECB)
  - Cipher block chaining mode (CBC)
  - Cipher feedback mode (CFB)
  - Output feedback mode (OFB)
  - Counter mode (CTR)
- These modes of operation differ in respect of their vulnerability to adversarial attacks and sensitivity to transmission errors.
- ECB mode is suitable for short messages. CFB and OFB modes can be used as stream ciphers. CTR mode finds application in storage of encrypted bulk data. CBC mode is a general purpose mode of operation of block ciphers for the messages having multiple blocks.

With this chapter we have covered structure and modes of operation of major symmetric-key block and stream ciphers. We are yet to cover symmetric-key distribution. We will take up this topic in Chapter 14, since it requires knowledge of some new concepts of cryptography.

Key Terms		
Cipher block chaining mode	Linear feedback shift register	RC4 stream cipher
Cipher feedback mode	Modes of operation	Self synchronizing stream cipher
Counter mode	Output feedback mode	Stream cipher
Electronic codebook mode	Periodicity of key stream	Synchronous stream cipher

RECOMMENDED READING

Forouzan, Behrouz A., *Cryptography and Network Security*, Tata McGraw-Hill, New Delhi, 2007.

Kaufman, C., Perlman, R. and Spenciner, M., *Network Security, Private Communication in a Public World*, Prentice-Hall of India, New Delhi, 2007.

Menezes, A., Oorschot, P. and Vanstone, S., *Handbook of Applied Cryptography*, CRC Press, FL, USA, 1997.

Schneier, B., *Applied Cryptography*, Wiley India, New Delhi, 1996.

Stallings, W., *Cryptography and Network Security*, Prentice-Hall of India, New Delhi, 2008.

Trappe, W., Washington, L., *Introduction to Cryptography and Coding Theory*, Prentice-Hall, NJ, USA, 2006.

Vaudenay, S., *A Classical Introduction to Cryptography*, Springer, NY, USA, 2006.

---(**PROBLEMS**)---

1. Write the first 20 bits of key sequence generated by four-cell LFSR shown in Figure 7.15, if the seed key is 0001.

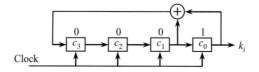

Figure 7.15 Problem 1.

2. The 256-byte cipher key of RC4 is chosen as [0, 0, 255, 254, ..., 2]. What will be the state vector S after initialization using the cipher key?

3. Consider RC4 stream cipher for 2-bit bytes with state vector S of 4 bytes.
   (a) Determine the initialized value of the state vector S, if the cipher key K = [2 0 1 3].
   (b) Determine the first four bytes of the key stream.

4. Suppose that the block size is 64 bits and plaintext consists of 32 bytes of data, B_1 to B_{32}. Encryption is carried out using ECB mode.
   (a) If an error occurs in the first encrypted unit during transmission, which of the decrypted bytes can be in error?
   (b) If the first encrypted unit lost during transmission, will rest of the decrypted be correct?
   (c) If the first encrypted unit gets interchanged with the second unit, which of the decrypted bytes can be in error?

5. Do Problem 4, if the mode of operation is CBC.

6. Do Problem 4, if CFB in byte oriented mode is used.

7. Do Problem 4, if OFB in byte oriented mode is used.

8. Do Problem 4, if CTR mode is used.

9. The padding bytes are added in the last block of message to create full sized block. An indication needs to be given to the receiver so that he could identify and remove the pad bytes from the last part of decrypted message. This can be done in several ways. One possible scheme is to make each padding byte equal to the number of padding bytes added. For example, if 5 pad bytes are added, these five pad bytes can be 00000101. To develop this scheme further, answer the following questions.

   (a) If the last block of decrypted message consists of the following eight bytes, identify and strip off the pad bytes

$$9 \quad 11 \quad 6 \quad 13 \quad 3 \quad 3 \quad 3 \quad 3$$

   (b) If the length of original message is multiple of block length, should the message still be padded? If so what should be value of padding byte(s)?

10. In CBC mode, it is observed that two encrypted blocks $c_i = c_j$. Compute $c_{i-1} \oplus c_{j-1}$ in terms of plaintext blocks m_i and m_j. What does the result convey?

11. Alice sends encrypted messages by using the OFB mode of operation with a secret key K and fixed IV value. The adversary somehow manages to get a plaintext–ciphertext pair sent by Alice.

   (a) How does the adversary carry out the known plaintext attack to decrypt the other transmitted messages?

   (b) If Alice changes over to CFB or CBC mode of operation, does she defeat the adversarial known plaintext attack?

12. Recall that CBC mode encrypts a plaintext block m_i as $c_i = E(K, c_{i-1} \oplus m_i)$, where K is the key, c_{i-1} is the previous encrypted block. Suppose the encryption function is modified as $c_i = c_{i-1} \oplus E(K, m_i)$.

   (a) What is the decryption rule?

   (b) Give security limitations of this mode as compared to CBC mode.

13. Lazy Alice uses always use the same IV instead of choosing IVs at random.

   (a) Describe a security problem this creates if CBC mode is used.

   (b) Describe a security problem this creates if CTR mode is used.

   (c) If the same IV is always used, which is more secure, CBC or CTR mode?

14. In 3DES(EDE), the DES encryption(E)/decryption(D) algorithm is applied three times using three different keys K_1, K_2 and K_3. CBC mode using 3DES(EDE) as block cipher can be configured in two ways (Figure 7.16). In Figure 7.10(a), the output of cascaded 3DES algorithm chained to the encryption of the next block. In Figure 7.10(b), the CBC mode is cascaded 3 times. The output of each stage of DES encryption is chained to the encryption of next block. Note that in the second case each cascaded stage of mode of operation requires a different IV. Which of the two options is better from the point of view of (a) security, and (b) performance?

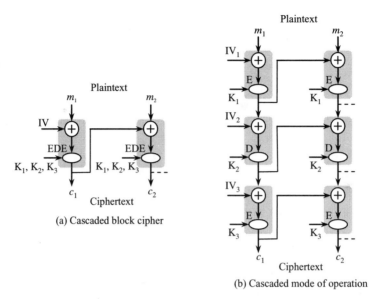

Figure 7.16   Problem 14.

15. When the message size is not multiple of block size, the left over segment of the message is suitably padded to get full-size block. As a result the size of ciphertext increases by an amount equal to the number of padding bytes. In some application, this size increase is not desirable. For example, if the ciphertext is to be allocated same memory buffer as the plaintext. Ciphertext stealing (CTS) mechanism is used to retain the size of the message. Figure 7.17 illustrates CTS mechanism used in ECB mode.

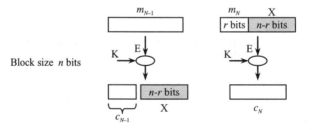

Figure 7.17   Problem 15.

Let us assume that the leftover segment of the message m_N has r bits ($r < n$). As shown in the figure, the right $n - r$ bits (X) of the previous encrypted output are stripped and attached to m_N to get full-sized block which is encrypted like any other block. The size of ciphertext remains same as the c_{N-1} block has r bits.

(a) Describe how these two ciphertext blocks c_{N-1} and c_N are processed to recover m_{N-1} and m_N.

(b) Design CTS scheme for CBC mode of operation.

8

Mathematical Foundations III
(Prime Numbers)

In this chapter, we extend the concepts of modular arithmetic and algebraic structures to primality testing of numbers and solving quadratic congruence. Cryptography and asymmetric key cryptography, in particular, is based on prime numbers. Large part of this chapter deals with prime numbers and associated theorems that find application in cryptography. We discuss Chinese Remainder Theorem and its applications for solving linear and quadratic congruence. Discrete logarithm is introduced in the last.

8.1 PRIME, COPRIME AND COMPOSITE NUMBERS

A positive integer $p > 1$ is a prime number if and only if it has only two *distinct* divisors, 1 and itself. A *composite* number, on the other hand, has more than two divisors including 1 and itself. Thus 2, 3, 5, 7, 11, 13 are examples of prime numbers and 4, 6, 8, 9, 10 are examples of composite number. Note that integer 1 is not a prime number because it does not have two distinct divisors. Thus the smallest prime number is 2. Integer 1 is not composite number also because it has only one divisor, itself.

Two positive integers m and n are called *coprime* numbers if and only if the gcd (m, n) = 1. Thus, 4 and 9 are coprimes but 6 and 9 are not coprimes. Integer 1 is coprime to every positive integer. Coprimes are also called *relatively prime*.

8.1.1 Number of Primes

We are interested in knowing

- if there is a limit after which prime numbers cease to exist and
- what is the number of primes $\pi(n)$ less than a given integer n.

To answer the first question, let us assume that the largest prime is p. Let P = $2 \times 3 \times \dots \times p$ be the product of all primes. P is obviously greater than p and is not a prime number. Note that

- P + 1 is either a prime, in which case P + 1 a prime greater than p or

– P + 1 is not a prime. Let us assume that it has a prime factor q. If $q \le p$, then q must be one of the factors of P also. If q is a common factor of P + 1 and P, it must also divide [(P + 1) – P]. Since [(P + 1) – P] = 1, q cannot be any integer other than 1. Thus P + 1 and P cannot have any common prime factor $q \le p$. In other words, P + 1 must have a prime factor greater than p.

In either case, there always exists a prime number greater than the prime number p. So the set of prime numbers is infinite.

We do not have answer to the second question, but it has been shown that the number of primes $\pi(n)$ less than a given large integer n has the following limits:

$$\frac{n}{\ln n} < \pi(n) < \frac{n}{\ln n - 1.08366}$$

8.2 FERMAT'S AND EULER'S THEOREMS

Two very important theorems of number theory are Fermet's theorem and Euler's theorem. These theorems play very important role in cryptography.

8.2.1 Fermat's Little Theorem

Fermat's little theorem states that if p is a prime number and a is any positive integer, then

$$a^p \equiv a \ (\text{mod } p)$$

In other words, $a^p - a$ will always be divisible by p. Another simplified form of Fermat's little theorem states that if p is a prime number and a is any positive integer, coprime to p, then

$$a^{p-1} \equiv 1 \ (\text{mod } p)$$

Note that we have imposed an additional condition on a in this form of the Fermat's little theorem—a must be coprime to p. Let us verify Fermat's theorems for $a = 5$ and $p = 3$.

(i) $5^3 \equiv 125 \equiv 2 \ (\text{mod } 3)$
     $5 \equiv 2 \ (\text{mod } 3)$
     Thus $a^p \equiv a \ (\text{mod } p)$
(ii) $5^{3-1} \equiv 25 \ \text{mod } 3 \equiv 1 \ (\text{mod } 3)$
     Thus $a^{p-1} \equiv 1 \ (\text{mod } p)$

The following example illustrates the application of Fermat's little theorem.

Example 1   Find 4^{15} mod 13.

Solution 4^{15} mod 13 = $4^2 \times 4^{13}$ mod 13 = $4^2 \times 4$ mod 13 = 12

8.2.2 Euler's Totient Function

Euler's totient function is denoted as $\phi(n)$. For a given positive integer n, $\phi(n)$ is the number of positive integers less than n that are coprime to n. For example, $\phi(6) = 2$ since 1 and 5 are the only two integers less than 6 that are coprime to 6. Two important properties of $\phi(n)$ for cryptography are given below:

1. If n is prime, $\phi(n) = n - 1$ since all the positive integers less than n are coprime to n. For example, $\phi(7) = 6$.
2. If p and q are prime numbers with $p \neq q$ and $n = pq$, then

$$\phi(n) = \phi(pq) = \phi(p)\phi(q) = (p - 1)(q - 1)$$

To prove the second property, we need to look for coprimes of n in set $S = \{1, 2, ..., n - 1\}$. There are $(n - 1)$ elements in this set. Elements $p, 2p, ..., (q - 1)p$ of this set are obviously not coprimes of n because p is a common factor between n and each of these $(q - 1)$ elements. Similarly, the elements $q, 2q, ..., (p - 1)q$ are not coprimes of n. Since p and q are prime numbers, all the rest of the elements of set S are coprimes of n. Thus

$$\phi(n) = (n - 1) - (p - 1) - (q - 1) = pq - p - q + 1 = (p - 1)(q - 1) = \phi(p)\phi(q)$$

Example 2   What is the number of coprimes of 35 in the set Z_{35}?

Solution Z_{35} consists of positive integers from 0 to 34. The number of positive coprimes to 35 and less than 35 can be calculated using Euler's totient theorem.

$$\phi(35) = \phi(5) \times \phi(7) = 4 \times 6 = 24$$

8.2.3 Euler's Theorem

Euler's theorem states that for every positive integer n and every a that is coprime to n, the following must be true:

$$a^{\phi(n)} \equiv 1 \ (\text{mod } n)$$

where $\phi(n)$ is totient of n. Note that when n is a prime, $\phi(n) = n - 1$. In this case, Euler's theorem reduces the Fermat's little theorem. Let us consider the following example:

The four positive coprimes of 8 and < 8 are 1, 3, 5 and 7. Therefore $\phi(8) = 4$. Let us verify Euler's theorem for $a = 3$ which is coprime to 8.

$$a^{\phi(8)} = 3^4 \text{ mod } 8 = 81 \text{ mod } 8 = 1$$

8.3   TESTING FOR PRIMALITY

We do not have any infallible formula or algorithm that can generate prime numbers. When we need a large prime number, we select a random number, and test it for primality. There are several tests, some of which are deterministic but less efficient. The rest are probabilistic which indicate with a good measure of probability that a number is prime or composite. In other words,

- if the number to be tested is actually a prime number, probabilistic methods indicate that the number is prime.
- if the number to be tested is actually a composite number, probabilistic methods may declare that the number is prime. The probability of such happening is very low, but not zero.

Of the primality tests described below, divisibility test and AKS algorithm are deterministic tests for primality. The rest are probabilistic tests for primality.

8.3.1   Divisibility Test

This is a deterministic approach, but it can be used only for small integers. Theoretically, to check whether a number n is a prime or not, we need to divide it by all primes starting with 2. If it is divisible by any prime number $< \sqrt{n}$, then it is not prime. It is not necessary to test beyond $\sqrt{n}$ because a prime factor $> \sqrt{n}$ would mean the other factor would be $< \sqrt{n}$.

8.3.2   Fermat's Primality Test

Fermat's little theorem states that if a is coprime to a prime n, then

$$a^{n-1} \equiv 1 \ (\text{mod } n)$$

This theorem always holds good for all prime numbers, but it does not say that if the above congruence is true, then the number n must be prime. It is possible that some combinations of the base a and a composite number n may satisfy the above relation. For example, 561 is a composite number, but the above congruence is satisfied for base $a = 2$. To improve the reliability of the test, we need to test a number with several different bases.

8.3.3   Square Root Primality Test

The square roots of 1 (mod n) are always 1 and $n - 1$ since

$$1^2 \bmod n = 1$$

$$(n - 1)^2 \bmod n = (n^2 - 2n + 1) \bmod n = 1$$

Square root primality test says that if n is a prime number, then these are the only two square roots of 1 (mod n) in $Z_n = (0, 1, 2, \ldots, n - 1)$. If n is not prime, there may be other square roots of 1 in Z_n.

In other words, if n is prime, the following equation is satisfied by only two elements of Z_n, 1 and $n - 1$:

$$x^2 \equiv 1 \ (\text{mod } n)$$

Note that reverse is not true, i.e., if 1 and $n - 1$ satisfy the equation, it does not imply n is prime. To test primality of a number n, we test the above equality for all the elements of Z_n.

- If any element of Z_n other than 1 and $n - 1$ satisfies the above equation, n is declared as composite.
- If only 1 and $n - 1$ satisfy the above equation, n is can be considered prime, but it may be composite.

Example 3   Conduct square root primality test, if n is equal to

(a) 7

(b) 8

(c) 6

Solution   (a) $Z_7 = (0, 1, 2, 3, 4, 5, 6)$

$0^2 \bmod 7 = 0$ $1^2 \bmod 7 = 1$ $2^2 \bmod 7 = 4$ $3^2 \bmod 7 = 2$ $4^2 \bmod 7 = 2$
$5^2 \bmod 7 = 4$ $6^2 \bmod 7 = 1$

Elements 1 and 6 only satisfy the equation $x^2 = 1 \bmod 7$. Thus 7 can be considered as prime.

(b) $Z_8 = (0, 1, 2, 3, 4, 5, 6, 7)$
$0^2 \bmod 8 = 0$ $1^2 \bmod 8 = 1$ $2^2 \bmod 8 = 4$ $3^2 \bmod 8 = 1$ $4^2 \bmod 8 = 0$
$5^2 \bmod 8 = 1$ $6^2 \bmod 8 = 4$ $7^2 \bmod 8 = 1$

Elements 1, 3, 5 and 7 satisfy the equation $x^2 = 1 \bmod 8$. Therefore, 8 is surely composite.

(c) $Z_6 = (0, 1, 2, 3, 4, 5)$
$0^2 \bmod 6 = 0$ $1^2 \bmod 6 = 1$ $2^2 \bmod 6 = 4$ $3^2 \bmod 6 = 3$ $4^2 \bmod 6 = 4$
$5^2 \bmod 6 = 1$

Note that elements only 1 and 5 satisfy the equation $x^2 = 1 \bmod 6$. But we know that 6 is not prime.

As seen in the above example, square root test is not a deterministic primality test. If we get square root of 1 other than 1 and $n - 1$, only then we can say with surety that n is composite.

8.3.4   Miller–Rabin Algorithm for Primality Testing

Miller–Rabin algorithm for primality testing is based on Fermat's and square-root tests to determine, if the given number is a prime number. It is also not a deterministic test, but gives the result with high probability. Miller–Rabin algorithm is based on the following considerations:

- The number n to be tested for primality is always odd because even numbers cannot be prime. Therefore, $n - 1$ is always even and can be written as product of an odd number m and power of 2.

$$n - 1 = 2^k m$$

- If we choose positive number a such that $1 < a < n - 1$, we rewrite Fermat's test for primality of an integer n using a as the base as under.

$$a^{n-1} \equiv 2^k m \equiv 1 (\bmod n)$$

Note that we have excluded $a = 1$ or $n - 1$ because a^2 mod $n = 1$ for these values of a irrespective of n being prime or composite.

Let us consider the following sequence of numbers. Note that each number is square root of the following number. The last number is square root of a^{n-1} mod n.

$$a^m \text{ mod } n, \ a^{2m} \text{ mod } n, \ a^{2^2 m} \text{ mod } n, \ a^{2^3 m} \text{ mod } n, \ ..., \ a^{2^{k-1} m} \text{ mod } n$$

Fermat's primality test for n to be a prime number requires that

- either it must be the case that the first number satisfies a^m mod $n = 1$, in which case every number in the sequence is 1;
- or it must be the case that one of the numbers in the sequence is $n - 1$, which would then make all the subsequent numbers equal to 1 because $(n - 1)^2$ mod $n = 1$.

If neither condition is true, then n is definitely not a prime. However, if either conditions is true for a given $a < n$, then n is likely to be prime with a very high probability. It has been shown that probability of n not being prime is 1/4. To increase the probability of n being a prime, one can repeat test with different randomly selected a.

The algorithm consists of the following steps:

(a) Determine k and m from $n - 1 = 2^k m$.
(b) Choose base a, $1 < a < n - 1$.
(c) Compute $x = a^m$ mod n. If x is 1 or $(n - 1)$, declare n as prime with high probability. Else move to the next step.
(d) Compute x^{2^i} mod n for $i = 1$ to $(k - 1)$. If x^{2^i} is $(n - 1)$ at any stage, declare n as prime with high probability. Else, n is declared as composite at the end.

Example 4   Test 121 for primality using Miller–Rabin algorithm and base $a = 10$.

Solution   We have $n = 121$, $n - 1 = 120$, $120 = 15 \times 2^3$, $m = 15$, $k = 3$.
Now,

$$10^{15} \text{ mod } 121 = 43 \qquad 10^{15 \times 2} \text{ mod } 121 = 34 \qquad 10^{15 \times 4} \text{ mod } 121 = 67$$

Thus, 121 is composite.

Example 5   Test 97 for primality using Miller–Rabin algorithm and base $a = 10$.

Solution   We have $n = 97$, $n - 1 = 96$, $96 = 3 \times 2^5$, $m = 3$, $k = 5$.
Now,
$$10^3 \text{ mod } 97 = 30; \qquad 10^{3 \times 2} \text{ mod } 97 = 27$$
$$10^{3 \times 4} \text{ mod } 97 = 50; \qquad 10^{3 \times 8} \text{ mod } 97 = 75$$
$$10^{3 \times 16} \text{ mod } 97 = 96 = n - 1$$

Therefore, 97 is a prime number with high probability.

8.3.5 AKS (Agrawal, Kayal, Saxena) Algorithm

The Agrawal–Kayal–Saxena (AKS) algorithm was announced in 2002. It is based on the following generalization of Fermat's little theorem. This generalization states that if a number a is coprime to another number p, $p > 1$, then p is prime if and only if the polynomial $(x + a)^p$ obeys the following equation:

$$(x + a)^p \equiv x^p + a \pmod{p} \tag{8.1}$$

We can expand the binomial $(x + a)^p$ as follows using binomial expansion:

$$(x + a)^p = x^p + \binom{p}{1} x^{p-1} a + \binom{p}{2} x^{p-2} a^2 + \cdots + a^p \tag{8.2}$$

where binomial coefficients are given by

$$\binom{p}{i} = \frac{p!}{i!(p - i)!} \tag{8.3}$$

Since all the binomial coefficients are multiple of p,

$$\binom{p}{i} \bmod p = \frac{p!}{i!(p - i)!} \bmod p = 0$$

Since p is prime number, we use Fermat's theorem to say

$$a^p \equiv a \pmod{p}$$

Therefore, Eq. (8.2) reduces to Eq. (8.1). We can also show that if p is not prime, Eq. (8.1) does not hold. Therefore, AKS is a deterministic primality test.

For primality testing of the number p, we need to compute binomial coefficients given by (8.3) and show that these all are equal to 0, which is a computationally complex task. However, computational complexity of AKS algorithm has been considerably reduced since its announcement in 2002.

8.4 CHINESE REMAINDER THEOREM (CRT)

The Chinese remainder theorem says that if there is a set of linear congruent equations of a variable x with moduli m_1, m_2, m_3, ..., m_k which are pairwise relatively prime, then there is a unique solution to the equations. For example, the following two equations with moduli 3, 5 which are pairwise relatively prime have unique solution for the variable x.

$x \equiv 2 \pmod{3}$

$x \equiv 3 \pmod{5}$

The solution is $x = 8$. It can be verified—8 mod 3 = 2 and 8 mod 5 = 3. In general, for a set of k congruent equations $x \equiv a_i \pmod{m_i}$, $i = 1$ to k, the CRT solution involves the following steps:

(a) Determine $M = m_1 \times m_2 \times m_3 \times \ldots \times m_k$.
(b) Determine $M_1 = M/m_1$, $M_2 = M/m_2$, ..., $M_k = M/m_k$.

(c) Determine multiplicative inverses M_i^{-1} modulo m_i.

(d) Calculate x using

$$x = (a_1 \times M_1 \times M_1^{-1} + a_2 \times M_2 \times M_2^{-1} + \cdots + a_1 \times M_k \times M_k^{-1}) \bmod M$$

Example 6   Solve the following congruent simultaneous equations:

$x \equiv 2 \pmod 3$

$x \equiv 3 \pmod 5$

$x \equiv 2 \pmod 7$

Solution $M = 3 \times 5 \times 7 = 105$, $M_1 = 105/3 = 35$, $M_2 = 105/5 = 21$, $M_3 = 105/7 = 15$

$M_1^{-1} \bmod 3 = 35^{-1} \bmod 3 = 2$

$M_2^{-1} \bmod 5 = 21^{-1} \bmod 5 = 1$

$M_3^{-1} \bmod 7 = 15^{-1} \bmod 7 = 1$

$x = (2 \times 35 \times 2 + 3 \times 21 \times 1 + 2 \times 15 \times 1) \bmod 105 = 23$

This example of CRT can be viewed from another angle. Given congruent equation $x \equiv 23 \pmod{105}$, where modulus 105 can be expressed as product of three pairwise relatively prime numbers, $3 \times 5 \times 7$, we can split this congruence into three congruent equations with moduli 3, 5 and 7 as given below.

$x \equiv 23 \pmod 3 \equiv 2 \pmod 3$

$x \equiv 23 \pmod 5 \equiv 3 \pmod 5$

$x \equiv 23 \pmod 7 \equiv 2 \pmod 7$

8.4.1   Applications of CRT in Cryptography

The two main applications of CRT that we describe in this text are as follows:

(a) CRT is very useful for manipulating very large integers. We are talking about integers with over 150 decimal digits, that is, numbers potentially larger than 10^{150}.

(b) CRT is used for solving quadratic congruent equation of the form $a_2x^2 + a_1x + a_0 \equiv 0 \pmod n$. We describe quadratic congruence in the next section.

Let us illustrate the first application using the following example:

Suppose we need to find $z = x + y$, where $x = 1000$, $y = 983$ using a system that accepts numbers less than 20. We can express x and y using pairwise relatively prime moduli 11, 13 and 17.

$x \equiv 10 \pmod{11}$ $y \equiv 4 \pmod{11}$

$x \equiv 12 \pmod{13}$ $y \equiv 8 \pmod{13}$

$x \equiv 14 \pmod{17}$ $y \equiv 14 \pmod{17}$

We can now write

$z = x + y \equiv 3 \pmod{11}$

$z = x + y \equiv 7 \pmod{13}$

$z = x + y \equiv 11 \pmod{17}$

Next we solve the above equations for z using CRT. We have

$M = 2431$, $M_1 = 221$, $M_2 = 187$, $M_3 = 143$, $M_1^{-1} = 1$, $M_2^{-1} = 8$, $M_3^{-1} = 5$

$z = (3 \times 221 \times 1 + 7 \times 187 \times 8 + 11 \times 143 \times 5) \bmod 2431 = 1983$

8.4.2 Quadratic Congruence

Quadratic congruence implies congruent equation of the type $a_2x^2 + a_1x + a_0 = 0 \pmod n$. Simplified form of this congruence as given below is of our interest.

$$x^2 \equiv a \pmod n$$

We are interested in finding solution of the above equation. In general, modulus n is a composite number. We restrict n to be product of different prime numbers, i.e., $n = p_1p_2p_3 \ldots p_k$. From the comment given at the end of Example 6, we can split the quadratic congruence $x^2 \equiv a \pmod n$ into a set of k quadratic congruences as given below:

$x^2 \equiv a \pmod{p_1}$
$x^2 \equiv a \pmod{p_2}$
...
$x^2 \equiv a \pmod{p_k}$

In other words, the problem of quadratic congruence with composite number as modulus is reduced to finding solution to k quadratic congruent equations, each with a different prime number. Therefore, let us first focus on solving a quadratic congruent equation with a prime number as modulus.

8.4.3 Quadratic Congruence Modulo a Prime p

A quadratic congruent equation $x^2 \equiv a \pmod p$, when p is prime, may or may not have a solution. Euler criterion given below resolves this issue.

(a) If $a^{(p-1)/2} \bmod p \equiv 1$, the equation has a solution.
(b) If $a^{(p-1)/2} \bmod p \equiv -1$, the equation has no solution.

We make another assumption to restrict the complexity of mathematics to the level required for this text. Odd prime numbers (i.e., 2 is excluded) can be expressed as $p = 4i + 1$ or $p = 4i + 3$, where i is an integer. We assume that modulus p is a prime number of the type $p = 4i + 3$. If this be so, then the quadratic congruence $x^2 \equiv a \pmod p$, when p is prime number, has the following solutions:

$$x \equiv \pm a^{(p+1)/4} \pmod p$$

Example 7   Solve the following quadratic congruent equations:

(a) $x^2 \equiv 2 \pmod{11}$
(b) $x^2 \equiv 4 \pmod 7$

Solution   (a) Let us first check, if the quadratic congruence has a solution using Euler's criterion.

$$a^{(p-1)/2} \bmod p = 2^{(11-1)/2} \bmod 11 = 32 \bmod 11 \equiv 10 \equiv -1 \ (\bmod\ 11).$$

Therefore, the solution does not exist.

(b) Using Euler's criterion to verify existence of solution, we get

$$a^{(p-1)/2} \bmod p = 4^{(7-1)/2} \bmod 7 = 64 \bmod 7 \equiv 1 \ (\bmod\ 11).$$

Therefore, the solution does exist. Solving the quadratic congruence, we get

$$x \equiv \pm a^{(p+1)/4} \ (\bmod\ p) = \pm 4^{(7+1)/4} \bmod 7 = \pm 16 \bmod 7 \equiv \pm 2 \ (\bmod\ 7)$$

$$x \equiv 2 \ (\bmod\ 7) \ \text{and} \ x \equiv 5 \ (\bmod\ 7)$$

8.4.4   Quadratic Congruence Modulo a Composite

To find solution to quadratic congruence modulo a composite number of the type $n = p_1 p_2 p_3$ ... p_k, let us go back to Section 8.4.2 and proceed in the following manner:

(a) Split the quadratic congruence $x^2 \equiv a$ (mod n) into k quadratic congruences $x^2 \equiv a$ (mod p_i), i = 1 to k.

(b) Find the pair of solutions of each quadratic congruence $x^2 \equiv a$ (mod p_i) as described in Section 8.5.3.

(c) From the k pairs of solutions, make 2^k sets of linear congruences of the type $x \equiv r$ (mod p_i).

(d) Solve each set of k linear congruences using CRT to determine x. We get 2^k solutions of x.

In cryptography, we use a large composite number n which is the product of only two prime numbers p and q. Therefore, solution to quadratic congruence has four answers as illustrated by Example 8.

Example 8   Find solution to the quadratic congruence $x^2 \equiv 25$ (mod 77), where modulus $77 = 7 \times 11$.

Solution   The quadratic congruence $x^2 \equiv 25$ (mod 77) can be split as given below:

$$x^2 \equiv 25 \ (\bmod\ 7) \equiv 4 \ (\bmod\ 7)$$

$$x^2 \equiv 25 \ (\bmod\ 11) \equiv 3 \ (\bmod\ 11)$$

It can be verified using Euler's criterion that the solutions exist for both the above congruences.

Solving $x^2 \equiv 4$ (mod 7), we get

$$x \equiv \pm 4^{(7+1)/4} \bmod 7 \equiv \pm 16 \ (\bmod\ 7) \equiv \pm 2 \ (\bmod\ 7)$$

$$x \equiv \pm 3^{(11+1)/4} \bmod 11 \equiv \pm 27 \ (\bmod\ 11) \equiv \pm 5 \ (\bmod\ 11)$$

Thus we have four sets of linear congruences as shown in Table 8.1.

TABLE 8.1 Four Sets of Linear Congruences to be Solved (Example 8)

First set	Second set	Third set	Fourth set
$x \equiv 2 \pmod 7$	$x \equiv 2 \pmod 7$	$x \equiv -2 \pmod 7$	$x \equiv -2 \pmod 7$
$x \equiv 5 \pmod{11}$	$x \equiv -5 \pmod{11}$	$x \equiv 5 \pmod{11}$	$x \equiv -5 \pmod{11}$

We solve these four sets of congruences using CRT. The results are given below:

First set $x = (2 \times 11 \times 2 + 5 \times 7 \times 8) \bmod 77 = 16$

Second set $x = (2 \times 11 \times 2 - 5 \times 7 \times 8) \bmod 77 = 72$

Third set $x = (-2 \times 11 \times 2 + 5 \times 7 \times 8) \bmod 77 = 5$

Fourth set $x = (-2 \times 11 \times 2 - 5 \times 7 \times 8) \bmod 77 = 61$

8.5 DISCRETE LOGARITHM

We are familiar with logarithm in arithmetic. If $y = a^x$, then exponent $x = \log_a y$, where a is called the base of logarithm. Discrete logarithm is an analogous function in modular arithmetic. It is defined for a multiplicative group $G = \{Z_n^*, \times\}$, where Z_n^* is set of coprimes of n. If a and b are two elements of Z_n^* such that $b \equiv a^i \pmod n$, we define discrete logarithm of b to the base a as $i = \log_{a,n} b$. Note that we have inserted n in this notation to emphasize the fact that multiplicative group is defined modulo n.

Before we digress any further, let us review the relevant properties of a multiplicative group of Z_n^*.

8.5.1 Multiplicative Group

Multiplicative group $G = \{Z_n^*, \times\}$, is defined over Z_n^* which consists of elements that are coprime to n. The multiplicative identity element e of the group is 1. If n is prime number p, elements of Z_p^* are integers from 1 to $p - 1$. Let us look at some definitions and properties associated with the multiplicative group.

(a) *Order of the group:* Order of a group, $|G|$, is the number of elements in Z_n^*. Since the number of coprimes is $\phi(n)$, $|G| = \phi(n)$. For example, if $n = 8$, set of coprimes of 8 is $Z_8^* = \{1, 3, 5, 7\}$. Therefore, order of the group $G = \{Z_8^*, \times\}$ is 4. If n is prime number p, $|G| = p - 1$.

(b) *Order of an element:* Order of an element a of the group is the smallest i such that $a^i = e = 1$. Take note of the word 'smallest' because there would be other higher values of i satisfying this condition.

Example 9   Find order of elements of $Z_{10}^* = \{1, 3, 7, 9\}$.

Solution   Order of element 1 is 1 since $1^1 \bmod 10 = 1$

     Order of element 3 is 4 since $3^4 \bmod 10 = 1$

     Order of element 7 is 4 since $7^4 \bmod 10 = 1$

     Order of element 9 is 2 since $9^2 \bmod 10 = 1$

Note that 9^4 mod $10 = (9^2$ mod 10×9^2 mod $10)$ mod 10 is also equal to 1. But we take the smallest value of the exponent satisfying this condition for the order of an element.

(c) *Primitive roots:* The element of Z_n^*, which has the order equal to $\phi(n)$, is called primitive root of the group. In Example 9, the primitive roots of the group $G = \{Z_{10}^*, \times\}$ are elements 3 and 7 since their order $= \phi(10) = 4$.

A multiplicative group $G = \{Z_n^*, \times\}$ may not have any primitive root. It can be shown that multiplicative group $G = \{Z_n^*, \times\}$ has at least one primitive root if n is 2, 4, p^i, $2p^i$ where p is an odd prime and i is an integer.

We are interested in primitive roots because only a primitive root can be the base of discrete logarithm.

(d) *Number of primitive roots:* Number of primitive roots is given by $\phi(\phi(n))$. Since $G = \{Z_{10}^*, \times\}$ has $\phi(10) = 4$, the number of its primitive roots is $\phi(4)$ which is 2. We saw in the last example that the two primitive roots of $G = \{Z_{10}^*, \times\}$ are 3 and 7.

(e) *Cyclic group:* A cyclic group has a generator g which can generate all the elements of Z_n^* repeated application of multiplicative operator, i.e., $Z_n^* = \{g^1, g^2, ..., g^{\phi(n)}\}$. Each primitive root is a generator.

There is an interesting observation to take note of. Since Z_n^* is set of coprimes of n, g is coprime of n. Thus using Euler's theorem, we can say $g^{\phi(n)} \equiv 1 \equiv g^0 \pmod{n}$ and $Z_n^* = \{g^0, g^1, g^2, ..., g^{\phi(n-1)}\}$. Following example verifies this observation.

$Z_{10}^* = \{1, 3, 7, 9\}$ with multiplicative operator is a cyclic group with two generators, 3 and 7.

3^1 mod $10 = 3$	3^2 mod $10 = 9$	3^3 mod $10 = 7$	3^4 mod $10 = 1$
7^1 mod $10 = 7$	7^2 mod $10 = 9$	7^3 mod $10 = 3$	7^4 mod $10 = 1$

8.5.2   Multiplicative Group $G = \{Z_p^*, \times\}$

We saw above that if we have a multiplicative group $G = \{Z_n^*, \times\}$ with $n = 2, 4, p^i$, or $2p^i$,

- there will always be at least one generator g, and
- any element x of Z_n^* can be expressed as $x = g^i$ where $0 \le i \le \phi(n-1)$.

If we choose the generator g as the base of discrete logarithm, we can write discrete logarithm of any x in Z_n^* as:

$$i = \log_{g,n} x$$

But discrete logarithm is defined only for the elements of Z_n^* which consists of coprimes of n. This limitation is overcome, if n is chosen to be a prime number p. Let us consider the multiplicative group $G = \{Z_p^*, \times\}$.

- There is always at least one primitive root in Z_p^*. Refer to Section 8.5.1(c).
- Z_p^* is cyclic with the primitive root is the generator g. All the elements of Z_p^* can be expressed as exponentiation g^i.
- Z_p^* consists of all the integers from 1 to $p - 1$.
  $Z_p^* = \{1, 2, ..., p - 1\} = \{g^0, g^1, g^2, ..., g^{p-2}\}$.

Let us take an example. If $p = 7$, we can show there are two generators, 3 and 5. If we select 5 as generator,

$$Z_7^* = \{1, 2, 3, 4, 5, 6\}$$
$$= \{5^0, 5^4, 5^5, 5^2, 5^1, 5^3\}$$

We can write the discrete logarithms to base 5 of the elements of Z_7^* as given below.

$\log_{5,7} 1 = 0$; $\log_{5,7} 2 = 4$; $\log_{5,7} 3 = 5$; $\log_{5,7} 4 = 2$; $\log_{5,7} 5 = 1$; $\log_{5,7} 6 = 3$.

8.5.3 Discrete Logarithm over $G = \{Z_p^*, \times\}$

It is clear from previous section, multiplicative group $G = \{Z_p^*, \times\}$ makes it possible define discrete logarithm for any x, $1 \le x \le p - 1$. Table 8.2 is the logarithm table for $p = 11$. Z_{11}^* has four primitive roots, 2, 6, 7 and 8, any of which can be used as the base.

TABLE 8.2 Logarithmic Table Modulo 11

x	$\log_{2,11} x$	$\log_{6,11} x$	$\log_{7,11} x$	$\log_{8,11} x$
1	10	10	10	10
2	1	9	3	7
3	8	2	4	6
4	2	8	6	4
5	4	6	2	8
6	9	1	7	3
7	7	3	1	9
8	3	7	9	1
9	6	4	8	2
10	5	5	5	5

We would like x to have any integer value, not limited to the range $1 \le x \le p - 1$. We know that modulus p maps an integer x (excluding 0 and multiples of p)[1] to Z_p^*. Therefore, we can say

$$\log_{g,p} x \equiv \log_{g,p} (x \bmod p)$$

Example 10 Compute $\log_{2,11} 16$ using Table 8.2.

Solution $\log_{2,11} 16 \equiv \log_{2,11} (16 \bmod 11) \equiv \log_{2,11} 5 = 4$

---

1. We have excluded 0 and multiple of p because these integers modulo p are equal to 0, and we do not determine logarithm of 0.

8.5.4   Properties and Applications of Discrete Logarithm

Discrete logarithm to the base g, the generator of Z_p^* is similar to arithmetic logarithm. We have listed below some of the properties of discrete logarithm. These can be readily verified using modular arithmetic.

$\log_{g,p} 1 = 0 \bmod (p - 1)$

$\log_{g,p} g = 1 \bmod (p - 1)$

$\log_{g,p} xy = \log_{g,p} x + \log_{g,p} y \bmod (p - 1)$

$\log_{g,p} x^y = y \log_{g,p} x \bmod (p - 1)$

Discrete logarithm is fundamental to many cryptographic algorithms based on modular exponentiation. For example, Diffie–Hellman algorithm in cryptography uses exponentiation to hide a secret number x as number y using

$$y = g^x \bmod p$$

Discrete logarithm of y can give the secret number x. But given y, g and p, it is very difficult to compute $x = \log_{g,p} y$, when p is a vary large prime number. The difficulty is of the same order of magnitude as that of factorizing a large number.

8.6   SUMMING UP

Our objective in this chapter was to learn some topics from number theory. These are essentially required for asymmetric-key cryptography.

- A positive integer $p > 1$ is a prime number, if it has only two *distinct* divisors, 1 and itself. Two positive integers m and n are called *coprime* or *relatively prime numbers*, if their gcd $(m, n) = 1$.
- Fermat's little theorem states that if p is a prime number and a is any positive integer, then $a^p \equiv a \pmod{p}$.
- Euler's totient function $\phi(n)$ gives the number of positive integers less than n that are coprime to n. Euler's theorem states that for every positive integer n and every a that is coprime to n, the following must be true:

$$a^{\phi(n)} \equiv 1 \pmod{p}$$

- Methods for testing primality are (a) divisibility test, (b) Fermat's test, (c) square root test, (d) Miller–Rabin algorithm and (e) AKS algorithm.
- The Chinese remainder theorem (CRT) says that if there is a set of linear congruent equations of a variable x with moduli m_1, m_2, m_3, ..., m_k which are pairwise relatively prime, then there is a unique solution to the equations. CRT is used for solving quadratic congruence $x^2 \equiv a \pmod{n}$.
- Discrete logarithm is defined for a multiplicative group G = $\{Z_n^*, \times\}$. If a and b are two elements of Z_n^* such that $b \equiv a^i \pmod{n}$, we define discrete logarithm of b to the base a as $i = \log_{a,n} b$.

- The element of Z_n^*, which has the order equal to $\phi(n)$, is called primitive root of the group. Number of primitive roots is given by $\phi(\phi(n))$. Only a primitive root can be the base of discrete logarithm.

Key Terms		
Chinese remainder theorem	Euler's theorem	Primitive roots
Composite	Fermat's theorem	Quadratic congruence
Coprime	Miller–Rabin algorithm	Relatively prime
Discrete logarithm	Prime number	Totient function

RECOMMENDED READING

Dummit, D. and Foote, R., *Abstract Algebra*, John Wiley & Sons, NJ, USA, 2004.

Durbin, J., *Modern Algebra*, John Wiley & Sons, NJ, USA, 2005.

Forouzan, Behrouz A., *Cryptography and Network Security*, Tata McGraw-Hill, New Delhi, 2007.

Stallings, W., *Cryptography and Network Security*, Prentice-Hall of India, New Delhi, 2008.

Trappe, W., Washington, L., *Introduction to Cryptography and Coding Theory*, Prentice-Hall, NJ, USA, 2006.

Yan, Song Y., *Primality Testing and Integer Factorization in Public-Key Cryptography*, Springer, NY, USA, 2009.

──────(**PROBLEMS**)──────

1. Show that an odd prime is in the form $4k + 1$ or $4k + 3$, where k is a positive integer. (*Hint:* Express a positive integer as $4k + i$.)

2. Determine the number of coprimes of n in the set Z_n, if n is equal to
   (a) 17
   (b) 77
   (c) 30

3. Show that Euler's totient $\phi(p^n) = p^n - p^{n-1}$ if p is a prime number. (*Hint:* Number of coprimes = p^n − number multiples of $p \leq p^n$.)

4. Using the result of Problem 3, calculate number of the coprimes of the following numbers:
   (a) 81
   (b) 240

5. Use Fermat's theorem to compute the following:
   (a) $7^{14} \bmod 13$
   (b) $5^{-1} \bmod 23$

6. User Fermat's theorem to determine x when $x^{85} \equiv 6 \pmod{29}$.

7. 165 is coprime to 14. Compute $165^{\phi(14)} \bmod 14$ to verify Euler's theorem.

8. Conduct square root primality test on number 11.

9. Conduct Miller–Rabin primality test on the following numbers. Use 2 as the base.
   (a) 73   (b) 49   (c) 61

10. An integer gives remainders 3, 3 and 0 on division by 7, 13 and 12 respectively. Find the integer using CRT.

11. Solve the following linear congruences for x using CRT:
    (a) $x \equiv 4 \pmod 5$; $x \equiv 10 \pmod{11}$
    (b) $x \equiv 2 \pmod 7$; $x \equiv 3 \pmod 9$

12. Solve the following quadratic congruences, if the solution exists:
    (a) $x^2 \equiv 3 \pmod{11}$
    (b) $x^2 \equiv 7 \pmod{19}$
    (c) $x^2 \equiv 12 \pmod{17}$

13. Solve the following quadratic congruences:
    (a) $x^2 \equiv 36 \pmod{77}$
    (b) $x^2 \equiv 23 \pmod{77}$

14. For the multiplicative group $G = \{Z_{13}^*, \times\}$,
    (a) find order of the group.
    (b) find order of each element in the group.
    (c) find the primitive roots of the group.
    (d) make table of discrete logarithms for each primitive root as the base.

15. For the multiplicative group $G = \{Z_{12}^*, \times\}$,
    (a) find order of the group.
    (b) find order of each element in the group.
    (c) find the primitive roots of the group.

16. Miller–Rabin algorithm evaluates the numbers $a^{2^i m} \bmod n$ for $i = 1$ to $(k-1)$ sequentially to test primality of n. If any of these numbers is $n-1$, then all the rest of numbers will be 1 being modulo n square of previous number. But it would be so even if any of these numbers is 1. Justify why we have chosen $n-1$ and not 1.

17. Solve the following linear congruence for x (*Hint:* Multiply both sides by multiplicative inverse making the coefficients of x equal to 1.):
    $2x \equiv 1 \pmod 3$
    $3x \equiv 1 \pmod 5$
    $5x \equiv 1 \pmod 7$

18. Compute the following logarithm values by computing powers of the base 2 modulo 13:
    (a) $\log_{2,13} 3$
    (b) $\log_{2,13} 11$

19. Mr. Mathematical Grandpa forgets his age, but he knows that his age was multiple of three a year ago, it will be multiple of 5 in two years, and it will be multiple of 7 in four years. What is his age?

9

Asymmetric-key Cryptosystems

The concept of asymmetric-key was introduced by Diffie and Hellman in their pioneering paper[1] published in 1976. Since then, several asymmetric-key cryptography schemes have been proposed. Of these, three important asymmetric-key cryptosystems that find wide application in computing environment today are described in this chapter. We begin the chapter with a brief introduction to asymmetric-key cryptography and its usefulness vis-à-vis symmetric-key cryptography. Then we describe RSA, Rabin and ElGamma cryptosystems in detail. Algorithm, security aspects, implementation issues and applications of each cryptosystem are discussed with examples.

9.1 ASYMMETRIC-KEY CRYPTOGRAPHY

Unlike symmetric-key cryptography, where same key is used for encryption and decryption, asymmetric-key cryptography[2] is based on a pair of keys. A message is encrypted with one of these two keys. The encrypted message can be decrypted using only the other key. Each user owns one such pair of keys and he advertises one of the two keys publicly. This key is called *public key*. The owner keeps the other key with himself. This key is called *private key*. Public and private keys are used for confidentiality and for authentication.

Confidentiality: Figure 9.1(a) illustrates the use of public and private keys for confidentiality. Alice wants to send a message to Bob, encrypts it with his (Bob's) public key. Bob can decrypt the received message with his private key. Bob encrypts the reply to Alice using her (Alice's) public key and Alice decrypts the received message with her private key. The adversary does not have the private keys, and therefore, he cannot decrypt these messages.

Authentication: Figure 9.1(b) illustrates the use of public and private keys for authentication. When Alice wants to send a message to Bob, she encrypts the message with her private key.

---

1. Diffie, W. and Hellman, M., New Directions in Cryptography, IEEE Transactions on Information Theory, November 1976.
2. Asymmetric-key cryptography is also known as public-key cryptography.

Bob decrypts the received message using Alice's public key. If he recovers the message[3], he concludes that Alice was indeed the source of the message. No one else could have encrypted the message with Alice's private key. Note that confidentiality is not the aim here. The adversary too can easily decrypt the message using Alice's public key, which is well known.

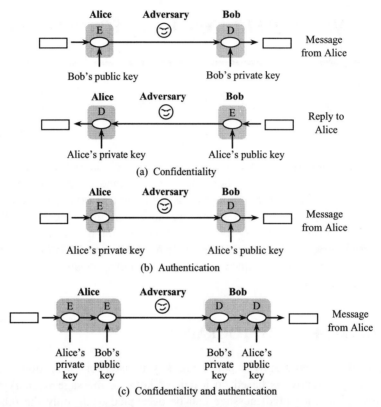

Figure 9.1 Asymmetric-key cryptography.

Figure 9.1(c) shows the basic scheme when both confidentiality and authentication are required. Alice encrypts the message twice, first using her private key and then using Bob's public key. Bob decrypts the message twice, first using his private key and then using Alices's public key. Note that encryption/decryption algorithm is used four times to achieve confidentiality and authentication.

9.1.1 Requirements for Asymmetric-key Cryptography

The intended applications of an asymmetric-key cryptosystem as described earlier lay out the following requirements that the cryptosystem must fulfill:

---

3. Recovery of the message is implied, if the decrypted content passes certain criteria. We will study these in Chapter 11.

- It should be computationally easy to generate a pair of public and private keys.
- It should be computationally easy to encrypt a message using public key and to decrypt it using private key.
- It should be computationally infeasible for the adversary to decrypt a ciphertext with the knowledge of public key.
- It should be computationally infeasible for the adversary to deduce private key with the knowledge of public key.

Security of asymmetric-key cryptosystem lies in the security of private key which is not deducible from public key, though these keys are mathematically generated from a common set of parameters.

9.1.2 Asymmetric-key Cryptography vs. Symmetric-key Cryptography

We can examine asymmetric-key versus symmetric-key issue from several aspects as described below.

Number of keys: Symmetric key cryptography requires large number of secret keys. If there are n users of symmetric key system, each user must maintain $(n-1)$ secret keys with the rest $(n-1)$ users. In all $n(n-1)/2$ secret keys are required among n users. Asymmetric-key cryptography requires lesser number of keys, n pairs of keys for n users.

Key distribution centre[4]: In symmetric-key cryptography, each pair of users must establish a secret key between them. They can either exchange the key using some secure means or they can generate a common secret key independently using a secure key generating algorithm. If there is large number of users, a key distribution centre (KDC) is required to be established.

In asymmetric-key cryptography, public-key part of key-pair can be easily distributed because it is not secret. Private-key part is never shared with any user, and therefore, is not to be distributed. But when the number of users is large, a centralized agency, called certification authority (CA)[5], is needed for public key certification and verification. Public key verification is required because an imposter can easily advertise his public key as the public key of some other user.

Computational overhead: Symmetric-key algorithms are based on substitution and transposition of bits/bytes. These algorithms are fast and can encrypt/decrypt large volume of data efficiently. Asymmetric-key algorithms are based on complex mathematical functions and are slower than the symmetric-key algorithms. Therefore, application of asymmetric-key cryptography is limited to encryption of short messages.

Security: With the current state of computational technology, security of a cryptosystem depends largely on the size of its key, be it symmetric-key or asymmetric-key system. With the growth of technology, both asymmetric-key and symmetric-key systems would require larger key size.

---

4. We will study key exchange methods and key distribution centre in Chapter 14.
5. We will study CAs in Chapter 15.

In short, asymmetric-key cryptography does not make the symmetric-key cryptography obsolete. Both have their merits and are indispensable for security of information systems.

- Encryption of bulk messages requires symmetric-key cryptography.
- Asymmetric-key cryptography is used for secure exchange of secret key of symmetric-key cryptosystem. After successful exchange of secret key, the users change over to symmetric-key cryptosystem for secure exchange of their bulk messages.
- Asymmetric-key cryptography is also used for message authentication as mentioned in the last section.

9.2 RSA CRYPTOSYSTEM

RSA cryptosystem is named after its inventors Rivest, Shamir and Adleman. It was first published 1978 and has since been the most widely accepted and implemented asymmetric-key cryptosystem. RSA is a block cipher in which the plaintext and ciphertext are represented as integers less than 2^{1024} (309 decimal digits). The encryption scheme of RSA is based on modulo n exponentiation of the message m using encryption exponent e.

$$c = m^e \bmod n$$

The sender (Bob), who encrypts the message m, has the values $\{e, n\}$, called public key of its owner (Alice). Note that public key has two parts e and n. Public key is same for all the senders who want to send message to its owner (Alice). Decryption is modulo n exponentiation of the ciphertext c using decryption exponent d.

$$m = c^d \bmod n$$

Alice, who decrypts the ciphertext c, has the values $\{d, n\}$, called the private key. Number n is common part of the public key and the private key. The decryption exponent d is known to Alice only, who is the owner of these public and private keys.

Public key $\{e, n\}$ and private key $\{d, n\}$ are mathematically related to each other, but it is computationally infeasible to derive one from the other. Cryptanalyst or even Bob, who creates the ciphertext c, cannot decrypt c without knowledge of $\{d, n\}$.

9.2.1 RSA Algorithm

Let us now examine the execution of RSA algorithm in steps.

Key Generation

Alice chooses prime numbers p and q. She calculates $n = p \times q$ and totient $\phi(n)$ of n. Since p and q are prime numbers, the totient of n is given by

$$\phi(n) = \phi(p) \times \phi(q) = (p - 1) \times (q - 1)$$

Number n is used as modulus in the modular arithmetic of encryption and decryption. Alice chooses an integer e which is coprime to $\phi(n)$ in $Z_{\phi(n)}$ and determines its multiplicative inverse d in $Z_{\phi(n)}$ such that

$$de = 1 \bmod \phi(n)$$

Since e is coprime to $\phi(n)$, there always exits the multiplicative inverse of e in $Z_{\phi(n)}$. $\{e, n\}$ is the public key for encryption. $\{d, n\}$ is the private key for decryption. Alice sends the public key $\{e, n\}$ to Bob and retains the private key $\{d, n\}$ as a secret.

Encryption

Bob encrypts the message m meant for Alice using her public key $\{e, n\}$ as given below.

$$c = m^e \bmod n$$

Message m is an integer $< n$. Bob sends the encrypted message c to Alice.

Decryption

Alice decrypts the received ciphertext c using her private key $\{d, n\}$ as given below.

$$m = c^d \bmod n$$

The following example illustrates the RSA algorithm.

(a) Let us choose $p = 7$, $q = 11$, thus

$$n = 7 \times 11 = 77, \quad \phi(77) = 6 \times 10 = 60$$

Let us choose $e = 7$ which is coprime of 60 in Z_{60}. Its multiplicative inverse d in Z_{60} is determined such that $ed \bmod 60 = 1$. Extended Euclid's algorithm can be used for this computation. We get $d = 43$. Thus the public key is $\{7, 77\}$ and the private key is $\{43, 77\}$.

(b) The message $m = 9$ is encrypted using the public key $\{7, 77\}$ as given below.

$$c = 9^7 \bmod 77 = 37$$

(c) The encrypted message c is decrypted using the private key $\{43, 77\}$ as given below.

$$m = 37^{43} \bmod 77 = 9$$

9.2.2 Proof of RSA Algorithm

Proof of RSA algorithm is based on the following properties[6] of primes and coprimes.

(a) The following equivalence holds for any two integers x and y, if p and q are prime numbers.

$$\{y \equiv x \ (\bmod \ p), \ y \equiv x \ (\bmod \ q)\} \quad \Leftrightarrow \quad \{y \equiv x \ (\bmod \ pq)\}$$

(b) If $n = p \times q$, p and q being two prime numbers, then totient $\phi(n)$ is given by

$$\phi(n) = \phi(p) \times \phi(q) = (p - 1) \times (q - 1)$$

We proceed with the proof of RSA as follows:
Since $ed = 1 \bmod \phi(n)$, we can say,

$$ed - 1 = k\phi(n) = k(p - 1) \times (q - 1), \text{ where } k \text{ is an integer.}$$

---

6. Refer to Sections 8.2.2 and 8.4 of Chapter 8.

Since p is a prime number, the message m can either be multiple of p or can be coprime to p. If it is coprime to p, then by Fermat's theorem,

$$m^{p-1} \equiv 1 \ (\text{mod } p)$$

Raising both sides of the above congruence by power $k \times (q - 1)$ then multiplying by m, we get

$$m^{1+k(p-1)(q-1)} \equiv m \ (\text{mod } p)$$
$$m^{1+k\phi(n)} \equiv m \ (\text{mod } p)$$
$$m^{ed} \equiv m \ (\text{mod } p)$$

The above congruence is still valid when m is multiple of p because both the sides will be 0 modulo p. Therefore, the above congruence holds for any value of m. Since q is also a prime number, we can say by the same argument

$$m^{ed} \equiv m \ (\text{mod } q)$$

Since p and q are distinct primes, we use the property (a) of the primes given earlier and say

$$m^{ed} \equiv m \ (\text{mod } pq) \equiv m \ (\text{mod } n)$$

In other words,

$$m^{ed} \text{ mod } n = m \text{ mod } n$$

Using the above result, we prove that decryption of ciphertext c using c^d mod n indeed gives the message m as given below:

$$c^d \text{ mod } n = (m^e \text{ mod } n)^d \text{ mod } n = m^{ed} \text{ mod } n = m \text{ mod } n$$

Since $m < n$ always, m mod $n = m$. Therefore,

$$c^d \text{ mod } n = m$$

This completes the proof of RSA scheme. Let us summarize the assumptions we have made.

1. $n = p \times q$, where p and q are prime numbers.
2. $m < n$.
3. $ed = 1$ mod $\phi(n)$, which implies that e has multiplicative inverse d in $Z_{\phi(n)}$. In other words, e is coprime to $\phi(n)$.

9.2.3   Security of RSA Cryptosystem

RSA cryptosystem has been time tested since its introduction. No serious weakness of the cryptosystem has yet been reported. Several potential attacks on inappropriate implementation of RSA and wrong choice of parameters have been suggested. We discuss these in this section.

Brute Force Attack

It involves trying all possible values of decryption key d. The defense against brute force attack is to keep the key space large. This implies larger number of bits for parameters p

and q. But computational complexity of key generation and encryption/decryption slows down algorithm as size of these parameters is increased. Recommended size of parameters p and q is 512 bits. This makes the size of n 1024 bits (309 digits).

Mathematical Attacks

RSA can be attacked mathematically in three ways:

(a) Determine prime factors p and q of modulus n, and then compute totient $\phi(n)$ and decryption key d.

(b) Determine totient $\phi(n)$ directly from knowledge of public key $\{e, n\}$, and then compute $d = e^{-1} \bmod \phi(n)$.

(c) Determine decryption exponent d directly from knowledge of public key $\{e, n\}$.

It can be shown that the complexity of approaches (b) and (c) is equivalent to complexity of factoring n. Therefore, security of RSA against mathematical attacks is determined by the time required for factoring n into p and q. Modulus n greater than 300 digits (or 1024 bits) is considered computationally infeasible to factor presently, but p and q must be chosen carefully. Guidelines for selecting p and q are given below:

- For 1024-bit n, p and q should be of the order of 10^{75} to 10^{100}.
- $p - 1$ and $q - 1$ should have a large prime factor.
- gcd $(p - 1, q - 1)$ should be small.

Chosen-Ciphertext Attack

This attack is based on multiplicative property of RSA algorithm. Let m_1 and m_2 be two messages, and let c_1 and c_2 be their respective RSA encryptions. Now,

$$(m_1 m_2)^e \bmod n = m_1^e m_2^e \bmod n = (m_1^e \bmod n) \times (m_2^e \bmod n) = c_1 c_2$$

In other words, RSA encryption of product of two messages is the product of their respective encryptions. The adversary can use this property to decrypt illegitimately copied ciphertext. Suppose Bob sends to Alice a ciphertext c, which the adversary copies. We assume that Alice will decrypt arbitrary ciphertext from the adversary other than c. The adversary conceals c in c' as $c' = cx^e \bmod n$, where x is a random integer in Z_n^* and has multiplicative inverse in Z_n^*. He sends c' to Alice for decryption. Alice computes m' and returns it to the adversary.

$$m' = (c')^d \bmod n = (cx^e)^d \bmod n = c^d x^{ed} \bmod n = mx \bmod n$$

The adversary computes m by multiplying m' and multiplicative inverse of x.

$$m' x^{-1} \bmod n = m x x^{-1} \bmod n = m$$

This simple attack can be prevented by imposing a structure to the plaintext m, e.g. by appending a pad to m. Alice would notice structural discrepancy of m' when she decrypts c', and she would not return the decrypted message m' to the adversary. The process of appending a pad to plaintext for this purpose is sometimes known as 'salting' the plaintext.

Example 1

Bob sends ciphertext 37 to Alice after encrypting his message $m = 9$ using her RSA public key {7, 77}. The adversary intercepts the ciphertext and launches chosen ciphertext attack based on the multiplicative property of RSA algorithm. He uses a random integer 2 for the attack. Write the steps of chosen-ciphertext attack. Alices private key is {43, 77}.

Solution   (a) The adversary modifies the intercepted message as given below:

$$c' = 37 \times 2^7 \bmod 77 = 39$$

He sends the ciphertext 39 to Alice for decryption.

(b) Alice decrypts 39 using her private key {43, 77} as indicated below.

$$m' = 39^{43} \bmod 77 = 18$$

She returns 18 to the adversary.

(c) The adversary recovers the Bob's original message using multiplicative inverse of 2 in Z_{77}^{*}.

$$m = 18 \times 2^{-1} \bmod 77 = 18 \times 39 \bmod 77 = 9$$

Attacks on Small Encryption Exponent (e)

There may be tendency to keep the encryption exponent (e) as small as possible to improve computational efficiency. The smallest possible value of e is 3. Small value of e can compromise the security of RSA algorithm as described below:

- If the message m is also so small that $m^e < n$, then $c = m^e \bmod n = m^e$. Thus m can be recovered simply by computing $c^{1/e}$.
- If same message m is sent to three entities having public keys {3, n_1}, {3, n_2} and {3, n_3}, the message is encrypted as given below:

$$c_1 = m^3 \bmod n_1$$
$$c_2 = m^3 \bmod n_2$$
$$c_3 = m^3 \bmod n_3$$

Since the moduli n_1, n_2, n_3 are most likely to be pair-wise relatively prime, the adversary observing c_1, c_2, and c_3 can determine $m^3 \bmod n_1 n_2 n_3$ using Chinese remainder theorem. If $m^3 < n_1 n_2 n_3$, which is bound to be true since $m < n_1$, $m < n_2$, and $m < n_3$, $m^3 \bmod n_1 n_2 n_3 = m^3$. Thus the adversary can determine m by computing $m^{1/3}$. Thus a message broadcast is more vulnerable to attack, if exponent e is small.

These attacks can be prevented by 'salting' the plaintext before encryption so that m^e is not less than modulus n or product of moduli $n_1 n_2 n_3$.

Small Message Space

If it is known to the adversary that the message space is small, he can encrypt all the possible messages using the public key. When he intercepts a ciphertext, he can determine the corresponding plaintext simply by matching the intercepted ciphertext with the ones he has. To counter this attack, messages are padded with a random number before encryption.

Small Decryption Exponent (d)

It may seem desirable to select a small decryption exponent d in order to improve the computational efficiency of decryption. However, if $d < 1/3\ n^{1/4}$, Wiener showed that d can be computed from the public key $\{e, n\}$ if $q < p < 2q$. Therefore, to avoid this attack, the exponent e should be carefully chosen to get exponent $d > 1/3\ n^{1/4}$.

Common Modulus Attack

It can be shown that knowledge of public key $\{e, n\}$ and private key $\{d, n\}$ can be used to determine prime factors p and q of n. This poses a threat, if same modulus n is used by a group of entities. An entity of the group having been assigned private key $\{d, n\}$ can determine to the prime factors (p, q) and totient $\phi(n)$ of n. Determining decryption exponents of other members of the group from their public keys is a simple task thereafter since $de = 1$ mod $\phi(n)$. Therefore, it is necessary that the modulus must not be shared.

Cycling Attack

Since $c = m^e$ mod n, encryption maps message m to one of the elements of the message space $Z_n = \{0, 1, \ldots, n - 1\}$. If the encryption is applied repeatedly on c, eventually a stage[7] will arrive when c will get mapped to m. The adversary uses this fact to his advantage. He intercepts a ciphertext c, he carries out repeat encryptions of c till he gets back the intercepted ciphertext c. He goes back by one step because the message encrypted last must be the original plaintext m. It has been shown that computational complexity of this attack is equivalent to the complexity of factoring n.

Example 2   Bob sends ciphertext 37 to Alice after using her RSA public key $\{7, 77\}$. The adversary intercepts the ciphertext and launches cycling attack using the public key of Alice. Write the computation carried out by the adversary to decrypt the ciphertext.

Solution   The adversary encrypts 37 repeatedly as given below:

$c_1 = 37^7$ mod $77 = 16$

$c_2 = 16^7$ mod $77 = 58$

$c_3 = 58^7$ mod $77 = 9$

$c_4 = 9^7$ mod $77 = 37$

In the fourth step he gets $c_4 = 37$. Therefore, he concludes Bob's message is 9.

Unconcealed Messages

An unconcealed message is one that encrypts to itself, i.e., $c = m^e$ mod $n = m$. For example, messages 0, 1, $n-1$ always remain unconcealed. The number of unconcealed messages in Z_n is given by

$$[1 + \gcd(e - 1, p - 1)] \times [1 + \gcd(e - 1, q - 1)]$$

---

7. Order of e in $Z^*_{\phi(n)}$ determines when this stage arrives. In Example 2, order of $e = 7$ in Z^*_{60} is 4. Therefore, m^{e^4} mod $n = m$.

Since $(p - 1)$ and $(q - 1)$ are always even, the number of unconcealed messages is at least 9. By proper choice of e the number of unconcealed messages can be kept small. Unconcealed messages do not pose, in general, a threat to the security.

9.2.4   RSA Implementation

Keeping in view the potential attacks described earlier, the following recommendations on implementation of RSA have been made:

- The modulus n should be at least 1024 bits (309 decimal digits) long to make its factorization an infeasible task.
- The two primes p and q must be at least 512 bits (154 decimal digits) long. Their values should not be close to each other. Both $(p - 1)$ and $(q - 1)$ should have a large prime factor.
- The modulus n should not be shared.
- The value of encryption exponent must be $2^{16} + 1$ or an integer close to this value. This number has only two 1's in its binary representation, and therefore, results in faster encryption.
- If decryption exponent d gets leaked, all the parameters n, e, and d should be changed.
- Short messages should be suitably padded before encryption.

9.2.5   Applications of RSA

RSA algorithm for encryption and decryption is computationally complex and very slow in execution. This makes RSA unsuitable for encryption/decryption of large messages and for messages sent on high data-rate communication links. RSA is suitable for encryption of short messages. Secondly RSA is considered very secure, since no serious threats to it have been encountered so far. These characteristics of RSA make it for the following applications:

- It is used for exchanging secret symmetric keys between two entities before they commence exchange of their messages encrypted using the symmetric key. One such application of RSA is TLS protocol described in Chapter 17.
- As mentioned in the beginning of the chapter, asymmetric-key cryptography can be used for message authentication by reversing the role of private and public keys. Message authentication consists of computing a small image of the message called digest and sending the digest with the message. RSA is used for encrypting the digest using the private key. Encrypted digest constitutes digital signature of the owner of the private key on the message. We discuss message authentication and digital signature in Chapters 11 and 12 respectively.

9.3   RABIN CYPTOSYSTEM

Rabin asymmetric-key cryptosystem uses quadratic congruence as against exponentiation congruence of RSA. It is based on the idea that computing square roots modulo a composite number n is simple when the factors of n are known. But this computation is very complex when the factorization of n is unknown.

The encryption scheme of Rabin cryptosystem involves generating modulo n square of the message m as ciphertext c.

$$c = m^2 \bmod n$$

Modulus integer n is a composite integer consisting of two large prime factors p and q. Decryption involves determination of modulo n square root of the ciphertext c.

$$m = c^{1/2} \bmod n$$

Recall from Chapter 8 that solving a quadratic congruence with composite modulus n is infeasible without knowledge of the prime factors of the modulus n. Therefore, the above equation cannot be solved without knowledge of the prime factors p and q of n. These two prime factors constitute the private key $\{p, q\}$ of Rabin cryptosystem. The private key is known only to its owner. The public key is the modulus n.

9.3.1 Algorithm of Rabin Cryptosystem

Let us now examine the Rabin cryptosystem algorithm in three steps: key generation, encryption and decryption.

Key Generation

Alice chooses two large and distinct prime numbers p and q and calculates $n = pq$. Number n is used as modulus in the modular arithmetic and as the public key for encryption. Alice sends the public key n to Bob and retains the private key $\{p, q\}$ as a secret.

Encryption

Bob encrypts the message m meant for Alice using her public key n as given below.

$$c = m^2 \bmod n$$

Message m is an integer less than n. Bob sends the encrypted message c to Alice.

Decryption

Alice decrypts the received ciphertext c using her private key $\{p, q\}$ as given below.

$$m = c^{1/2} \bmod n$$

Algorithm for computation of square root modulo n involves computation of the square roots modulo p and modulo q and then application of Chinese Remainder Theorem (CRT). There are four square roots of the above equation, and therefore, decryption results in four plaintexts.

The following example illustrates the algorithm.

(a) Alice chooses $p = 7$ and $q = 11$. Thus modulus $n = 7 \times 11 = 77$. Her public key is 77 and private key is $\{7, 11\}$. She sends the public key to Bob.

(b) Bob encrypts the message $m = 5$ using Alice's public key as given below:

$$c = 5^2 \bmod 77 = 25 \bmod 77$$

(c) Alice receives the encrypted message c from Bob. She solves[8] the following quadratic equation using her private key to retrieve the message m.

$$m^2 = 25 \bmod 77$$

She gets the following four values of m:

$$m_1 = 5; \quad m_2 = 16; \quad m_3 = 61; \quad m_4 = 72.$$

Note that Rabin cryptosystem is not deterministic. The receiver who decrypts the ciphertext receiver, is faced with the task of selecting the correct plaintext from among four possibilities. This ambiguity in decryption is easily overcome in practice by padding pre-specified redundancy to the original plaintext prior to encryption. For example, part of the original plaintext can be repeated. The receiver selects one of the four square roots that has this redundancy. The following example illustrates the concept.

Example 3   Alice and Bob use Rabin cryptosystem. They decide that the last two bits of original message will be replicated and appended to the message prior to encryption to resolve decryption ambiguity. The public and private keys of Alice are 77 and {7, 11} respectively. Bob wants to send message 3(0010) to Alice. Write the encryption and decryption steps.

Solution   Bob's original message 3 is 0010 in binary. He pads the message with last two bits to get 001010, which is 10 in decimal notation. Bob encrypts 10 using the public key $n = 77$ as given below:

$$c = M^2 \bmod n = 10^2 \bmod 77 = 23$$

Alice receives ciphertext 23 and decrypts it using private key {11, 7}. She computes the four square roots m_1, m_2, m_3 and m_4 of 23 modulo 77 as follows:

$m_1 = 10 = 001010$ (Binary)
$m_2 = 32 = 100000$ (Binary)
$m_3 = 45 = 101101$ (Binary)
$m_4 = 67 = 100011$ (Binary)

Since $m_1 = 001010$ meets the replication criterion, Alice discards the other three square roots and recovers the original message 0010.

9.3.2   Security of Rabin Cryptosystem

Rabin cryptosystem is secure as long as the private key {p, q} cannot be derived from the public key n. Thus its complexity is at the same level as that of factoring n into its prime factors p and q. From this point of view, Rabin cryptosystem is as secure as RSA.

---

8. Example 8 of Chapter 8 gives the complete solution of this quadratic equation.

Rabin cryptosystem is susceptible to attacks similar to those in RSA. As in RSA, Rabin cryptosystem takes care of these attacks by salting the plaintext before encryption.

9.3.3 Operational Aspects of Rabin Cryptosystem

Rabin encryption is an extremely fast operation as it only involves single modular squaring. RSA encryption, on the other hand, takes minimum one modular multiplication and one modular squaring when encryption exponent $e = 3$. Rabin decryption is slower than encryption, but is comparable in speed to RSA decryption.

The limitation of Rabin cryptosystem is that it necessarily requires building redundancy in the plaintext before its encryption to resolve decryption ambiguity.

9.4 ELGAMAL CRYPTOSYSTEM

The ElGamal cryptosystem is a asymmetric-key encryption scheme, named after its inventor Taher ElGamal. Its security is based on the intractability of the discrete logarithm problem described in Chapter 8. Recall that if p is a large prime and if g a primitive root of the multiplicative group $G = \{Z_p^*, \times\}$, it is easy to compute $g^r \bmod p$ for any integer r. But computing $r = \log_{g,p} g^r$ is infeasible.

ElGamal encryption transforms message m, $0 \leq m \leq (p - 1)$ into ciphertext c as follows:

$$c = mg^r \bmod p$$

The decryption involves modulo p multiplication of c and multiplicative inverse of g^r in Z_p^*.

$$m = cg^{-r} \bmod p = mg^r g^{-r} \bmod p = m$$

9.4.1 Algorithm of ElGamal Cryptosystem

Let us see how the above scheme is implemented as asymmetric-key cipher.

Key Generation

Alice chooses a large random prime p and a generator g of the multiplicative group $G = \{Z_p^*, \times\}$. She selects a random integer d, $1 \leq d \leq (p - 2)$, and computes $g^d \bmod p$. Alice's public key is $\{p, g, g^d\}$ and her private key is d. Alice passes her public key to Bob.

Encryption

Bob represents the message for Alice as an integer m, $0 \leq m \leq (p - 1)$. He selects a secret random number k, $0 \leq k \leq (p - 2)$ and encrypts m using Alice's public key $\{p, g, g^d\}$.

$$c = m (g^d)^k \bmod p = m g^{dk} \bmod p$$

He also computes a hint r.

$$r = g^k \bmod p$$

He sends the hint r and ciphertext c to Alice.

Decryption

Alice decrypts the received ciphertext c using her private key d and the hint r as given below. She computes

$$r^d = (g^k)^d \bmod p = g^{dk} \bmod p$$
$$m = c(r^d)^{-1} \bmod p = mg^{dk} \, g^{-dk} \bmod p = m$$

The following example illustrates the algorithm. Alice chooses $p = 11$, generator $g = 2$, and her private key $d = 3$.

She computes $g^d \bmod p = 2^3 \bmod 11 = 8$. Her public key is $\{p, g, g^d\} = \{11, 2, 8\}$. She sends the public key to Bob.

Bob selects secret random number $k = 4$ and encrypts his plaintext $m = 7$ using k and the public key $\{p, g, g^d\}$ of Alice. He also computes the hint r as given below.

$$c = m \, (g^d)^k \bmod p = 7 \times 8^4 \bmod 11 = 6$$
$$r = g^k \bmod p = 2^4 \bmod 11 = 5$$

Alice decrypts the received ciphertext $c = 6$ using hint $r = 5$ and her private key $d = 3$ as given below:

$$m = c(r^d)^{-1} \bmod p = 6 \times (5^3)^{-1} \bmod 11 = 7$$

9.4.2 Operational Aspects of ElGamal Cryptosystem

Important operational aspects of ElGamal cryptosystem are listed below:

- Note that the plaintext m is masked by a multiplicative factor g^{dk} on encryption. Decryption is carried out by multiplying the ciphertext by the inverse of g^{dk}. In other words, g^{dk} is the key for encryption and decryption. Alice and Bob arrive at this key using their respective secrets d and k. ElGamal cryptosystem is essentially extension of Diffie–Hellman key exchange protocol.
- It is different from its peer asymmetric-key cryptosystems in that its encryption generates two outputs, ciphertext and hint. Therefore, it expands the message size by factor of two.
- If all the communicating entities decide to use same prime p and generator g, these parameters need not be part of the public key. This results in smaller size of the public key.
- We can avoid calculating multiplicative inverse $(r^d)^{-1}$ and carry out decryption in one step. Since p is a prime number and $r = g^k \bmod p$, r is always coprime of p. Therefore, we can say using Fermat's theorem $r^{p-1} \equiv 1 \pmod{p}$. Thus,

$$(r^d)^{-1} \bmod p = r^{p-1}(r^d)^{-1} \bmod p = r^{p-1-d} \bmod p; \text{ and}$$
$$m = c \, (r^d)^{-1} \bmod p = cr^{p-1-d} \bmod p$$

In previous Example, Alice could have decrypted $c = 6$ as given below:

$$m = cr^{p-1-d} \bmod p = 6 \times 5^{(11-1-3)} \bmod 11 = 6 \times 5^7 \bmod 11 = 7$$

9.4.3 Security of ElGamal

ElGamal is susceptible to the following attacks, if it is not implemented properly.

Small Modulus Attack

The adversary knows p, g, g^d, g^k, and the ciphertext $c = mg^{dk} \bmod p$. To recover plaintext m, he needs to know g^{dk} which can be computed as $g^{dk} = (g^d)^k \bmod p = (g^k)^d \bmod p$, if d or k is known. To determine d or k, he needs to solve the following equations:

$$x = \log_{g,p} g^d$$
$$y = \log_{g,p} g^k$$

Thus security of ElGamal cryptosystem depends on infeasibility of solving discrete logarithm in finite field Z_p^* when p is large. The recommended length of the modulus p is 1024 bits.

Known-Plaintext Attack

If the adversary has plaintext–ciphertext pair, $\{m_1, c_1\}$, he can readily calculate $g^{dk} = m_1^{-1} c_1 \bmod p$. Thereafter he can recover plaintext m_2 from subsequent ciphertext $c_2 = m_2 g^{dk} \bmod p$. Therefore, Bob must choose a different random value of k for every message m_i and send the hint h_i with each ciphertext c_i.

By using different random value of k for every message, Bob reduces vulnerability to statistical attack also. Same plaintext is encrypted differently when k is changed in random manner.

Example 4 An adversary intercepts two encrypted messages $c_1 = 19$ and $c_2 = 32$, encrypted using ElGamal public key $\{p, g, g^d\} = \{53, 2, 8\}$. The adversary comes to know that the first message is $m_1 = 17$ and the messages have been encrypted using the same random value. How does he determine the second message m_2?

Solution

$$m_2 = c_2 \times (g^{dk})^{-1} \bmod p = c_2 \times (c_1 \times m_1^{-1})^{-1} \bmod p = c_2 \times (c_1^{-1} \times m_1) \bmod p$$
$$= 32 \times 19^{-1} \times 17 \bmod 53 = 32 \times 14 \times 17 \bmod 53 = 37$$

9.4.4 Generalized ElGamal Cryptosystem

The earlier description of ElGamal cryptosystem is based on multiplicative group $G = \{Z_p^*, \times\}$. ElGamal can be generalized to any finite cyclic group where discrete logarithm problem is infeasible. Some other suitable groups for ElGamal cryptosystem are given below:

- Multiplicative group of finite field $GF(p^n)$
- Multiplicative group of the finite field $GF(2^n)$
- Additive elliptic curve group over a finite field $GF(p^n)$ and $GF(2^n)$

Elliptic curve cryptosystems are taken up in Chapter 10. We illustrate generalized ElGamal cryptosystem over multiplicative group of finite field $GF(2^n)$ with the following example. This example is based on $GF(2^3)$ over irreducible polynomial $x^3 + x + 1$. Table 5.4 of Chapter 5 is used to determine polynomial equivalent for various powers of the generator g. Binary representation of polynomials is shown within brackets.

Key Generation: Alice selects multiplicative group over finite field $GF(2^3)$, whose elements are {000, 001, 010, 011, 100, 110, 111}. The irreducible polynomial for multiplication is $x^3 + x + 1$ (1011). She chooses the generator $g = x$ (010) and the private key $d = 4$. Now,

$$g^d = g^4 = x^2 + x = (110)$$

Therefore, the public key is {1011, 010, 110} which she sends to Bob. Note that instead of prime number p, we specify the irreducible polynomial (1011) in the public key.

Encryption: Bob chooses $k = 5$ to encrypt message $m = (100) = x^2 = g^2$. He computes ciphertext c and hint r as indicated below and sends these to Alice.

$$(g^d)^k = g^{20} = g^6 = x^2 + 1 = (101)$$
$$c = mg^{dk} \bmod (x^3 + x + 1) = g^2 \times g^6 = g = x = (010)$$
$$r = g^k = g^5 = x^2 + x + 1 = (111)$$

Decryption: Alice uses her private key to decrypt c as indicated below.

$$r^d = (g^5)^4 = g^{20} = g^6 = x^2 + 1 = (111)$$
$$m = c\ (r^d)^{-1} \bmod (x^3 + x + 1) = g \times g^{-6} = g^{-5} = g^2 = x^2 = (010)$$

9.4.5 Applications of ElGamal Cryptosystem

ElGamal finds applications where RSA is used.

- It can be used for encrypting small messages. One such typical application, as mentioned in RSA, is exchanging secret symmetric keys between two entities before they commence the exchange of messages encrypted using the symmetric key. ElGamal can be used for encrypting the symmetric key.
- It can be used for generating digital signature which enables authentication of the source. We describe this application in Chapter 12.

9.5 SUMMING UP

We focused on asymmetric-key cryptography and cryptosystems in this chapter.

- Asymmetric-key cryptography uses two different keys, one for encryption and the other for decryption. One of the two keys is made public by its owner and is called public key. The other key is secret key and is retained as private key by him.
- The public key for encrypting the messages meant for the owner of the public key. The private key is used for decryption by its owner.

- Asymmetric-key cryptography can be used for authentication also. The message to be authenticated is encrypted using the private key. The message is verified by decrypting it using the public key.
- RSA is the most common asymmetric-key cryptosystem. RSA encryption function is $c = m^e \bmod n$ and decryption function is $m = c^d \bmod n$, where the modulus n is product of two large prime numbers, the public key is $\{e, n\}$ and the private key is $\{d, n\}$. Security of RSA is based on infeasibility of factorization of a composite of two large prime numbers. No serious weakness of RSA cryptosystem has yet been reported.
- Rabin cryptosystem is based on quadratic congruence. The encryption function $c = m^2 \bmod n$ and decryption function is $m = c^{1/2} \bmod n$ where the modulus n is product of two large prime numbers p and q. The public key is n and the private key is $\{p, q\}$.
- Rabin cryptosystem is not deterministic in the sense that there are four solutions to the quadratic congruence. Therefore, some defined redundancy must be built into plaintext to select the solution that meets the redundancy requirements.
- Security of Rabin cryptosystem is based on the fact that solving a quadratic congruence with composite modulus n is infeasible without knowledge of the prime factors of the modulus n. From this point of view, Rabin cryptosystem is as secure as RSA.
- ElGamal asymmetric-key encryption generates two values, ciphertext $c = mg^{dk} \bmod p$ and hint $r = g^k \bmod p$ where p is a large prime, g is a primitive root of the group $G = \{Z_p^*, \times\}$, d is the private key and k is a random number chosen by the sender. The decryption function is $m = c(\mathrm{H}^d)^{-1} \bmod p$. The public key is $\{p, g, g^d\}$.
- Security of ElGamal cryptosystem is based on the intractability of the discrete logarithm problem. It is susceptible to known-plaintext attack. To defeat the attack, it is necessary that the sender must use a different random number b for each message.
- ElGamal can be generalized to any finite cyclic group.
  - Multiplicative group of finite field $GF(p^n)$
  - Multiplicative group of the finite field $GF(2^n)$
  - Additive elliptic curve group over a finite field $GF(p^n)$ and $GF(2^n)$

In the next chapter, we explore a new exciting field, elliptic curve cryptography which makes asymmetric-key cryptosystems more secure for the same size of the key.

Key Terms		
Digital signature	Private key	RSA cryptosystem
ElGamal cryptosystem	Public key	Rabin cryptosystem
Elliptic curve cryptosystem	Public-key cryptography	

RECOMMENDED READING

ElGamal, T., *A Public-Key Cryptosystem and a Signature Scheme based on Discrete Logarithms*, IEEE Transactions on Information Theory, July 1985.

Forouzan, Behrouz A., *Cryptography and Network Security*, Tata McGraw-Hill, New Delhi, 2007.

Menezes, A., Oorschot, P. and Vanstone, S., *Handbook of Applied Cryptography*, CRC Press, FL, USA, 1997.

Rabin, M., *Digitalized Signatures*. Foundations of Secure Computation, DeMillo, R., et al. (Eds.), Academic Press, NY, USA, 1978.

Rivest, R., Shamir A. and Adleman, L., A Method for Obtaining Digital Signatures and Public Key Cryptosystems, *Communications of the ACM*, February 1978.

Schneier, B., *Applied Cryptography*, John Wiley & Sons, NY, USA, 1996.

Stallings, W., *Cryptography and Network Security*, Prentice-Hall of India, New Delhi, 2008.

Stinson, D., *Cryptography: Theory and Practice*, CRC Press, 2006.

Trappe, W., Washington, L., *Introduction to Cryptography and Coding Theory*, Prentice-Hall, NJ, USA, 2006.

Vaudenay, S., *A Classical Introduction to Cryptography*, Springer, NY, USA, 2006.

Yan, Song Y., *Primality Testing and Integer Factorization in Public-Key Cryptography*, Springer, NY, USA, 2009.

───────────────(**PROBLEMS**)───────────────

1. An RSA cryptosystem has $p = 3$, $q = 11$ and $e = 7$.
   (a) Find decryption key d.
   (b) Encrypt 8.

2. An RSA cryptosystem has $p = 13$, $q = 7$ and $e = 5$.
   (a) Find decryption key d.
   (b) Encrypt 85.
   (c) Decrypt ciphertext 2.

3. Determine private key if the public key $\{e, n\}$ of an RSA cryptosystem is
   (a) $\{5, 35\}$
   (b) $\{17, 3937\}$
   Hint: $3937 = 31 \times 127$.

4. If the order of RSA encryption key e in $Z^*_{\phi(n)}$ is 2, what will be the ciphertext, if the message m is encrypted twice using the same key e?

5. (a) If $n = pq$, where p and q are distinct primes and $s = n + 1 - \phi(n)$, determine roots of $x^2 - sx + n = 0$.
   (b) Find factorization of n using the above equation, if $\{n, \phi(n)\} = \{1457, 1380\}$

6. The adversary intercepts the encrypted message 61 from Bob to Alice whose RSA public key is $\{5, 91\}$. The adversary launches chosen ciphertext attack (Section 9.2.3) using a random integer 2. Write the steps of the chosen ciphertext attack and determine the message. Alice's private key is $\{29, 91\}$.

7. The adversary intercepts the encrypted message 61 from Bob to Alice whose RSA public key is {5, 91}. The adversary launches cycling attack to decrypt the message. Write the steps of the cycling attack and determine the plain text message.

8. Alice and Bob use RSA cryptosystem with common modulus n, but different encryption exponents e_A and e_B respectively. They always begin their exchange with encrypted greeting message m to each other. The adversary notices that e_A and e_B are coprime and modulus n is common. He copies the encrypted opening greeting messages c_A and c_B of Alice and Bob and decrypts the message m using this information. How does he achieve this? (*Hint:* Extended Euclid algorithm.)

9. A community of l users decides to use RSA. For the sake of security of the chosen cryptosystem, the security administrator decides to use different moduli for each user. He makes a pool of prime numbers, and computes the moduli $n_i = p_iq_i$ ($i = 1$ to l) for each user, picking randomly two primes p_i and q_i from the pool. He ensures that the same pair is not picked twice. The prime numbers are returned to the pool after each computation. The adversary comes to know of the approach adopted by the security administrator and attacks their cryptosystem. How does he proceed?

10. Alice and Bob decide to use 56-bit DES for encryption of their messages. They also decide to establish DES session key using RSA algorithm. To achieve high level of security, they use 2048-bit RSA keys.

    (a) Bob publishes his RSA public key {3, n_B}, where n_B is 2048-bit modulus. When Alice wants to send a message to Bob, she uses Bob's RSA public key to encrypt the 56-bit DES session key K. Does this public key provide sufficient security for exchanging the 56-bit DES key? (*Hint:* The adversary attacks the small encryption exponent.)

    (b) Bob realizes his mistake and changes his public key to {e_B, n_B} so that the encryption exponent e_B is sufficiently large. Alice wants to establish DES 56-bit session key K, encrypts it using the new RSA public key of Bob. She did not realize that the session key K selected by her can be written as K = $k_1 \times k_2$, where k_1 and k_2 are 28-bit integers. The adversary learns the encrypted value c of the key K and executes meet-in-the-middle attack to compute K from c. How does he recover K? (*Hint:* Exploit RSA's multiplicative property.)

11. Encrypt $m = 17$ using Rabin public key 77.

12. Alice uses Rabin public and private keys 77 and {7, 11} respectively. She receives encrypted message $c = 58$ from Bob. Determine the four plaintexts she gets on decryption.

13. Alice uses Rabin public and private keys 77 and {7, 11} respectively. She decides with Bob that he will prefix numeral 1 to his messages before encryption. She receives encrypted message $c = 67$ from Bob. Determine the message Bob sent her.

14. Determine the hint and ciphertext when plaintext $m = 5$ is encrypted using ElGamal public key {p, g, g^d} = {11, 7, 2} and random number $k = 4$.

15. Alice receives hint $r = 3$ and ciphertext $c = 3$ from Bob. Her public and private keys are {11, 7, 2} and 3 respectively. Determine the plaintext.

16. An adversary intercepts two encrypted messages $c_1 = 3$ and $c_2 = 10$, encrypted using ElGamal public key $\{p, g, g^d\} = \{11, 2, 8\}$. The adversary comes to know that the first message is $m_1 = 4$ and the messages have been encrypted using the same random value. How does he compute the second message?

17. In Section 9.2.3, we showed that RSA is vulnerable to chosen ciphertext attack. Show that ElGamal cryptosystem too is vulnerable to chosen ciphertext attack. (*Hint:* Choose $c' = xc \bmod p$ for some value x.)

18. RSA decryption is performed using equation $m = c^d \bmod n$, where decryption key d is a large number. Chinese Remainder Theorem (CRT) can be used for fast decryption as given below.

$$c_p \equiv c \bmod p \qquad c_q \equiv c \bmod q$$
$$d_p \equiv d \bmod (p - 1) \qquad d_q \equiv d \bmod (q - 1)$$
$$m_p \equiv c_p^{dp} \bmod p \qquad m_q \equiv c_q^{dq} \bmod q$$
$$m = m_p q (q^{-1} \bmod p) + m_q p (p^{-1} \bmod q) \bmod n$$

Use the above equations to decrypt ciphertext $c = 2$ when $p = 31$, $q = 37$ and $e = 17$. Verify the result by re-encrypting the plaintext so obtained.

19. (a) If the message space is small, the adversary can attack RSA cryptosystem by building a dictionary of encrypted messages since the public key is known to him. Build the dictionary of encrypted English alphabet assuming A is mapped to 65 (ASCII 1000001), B to 66 and so on. The RSA public key $\{e, n\}$ is $\{7, 187\}$.

    (b) Alice sends an encrypted message (113, 91, 86, 86, 50, 61, 56, 113, 8) to Bob. Each letter of the message is encrypted using Bob's RSA public key $\{7, 187\}$. Decrypt the message using the dictionary.

20. The dictionary attack on RSA is on account of the fact that the encryption of a message is always same for a given public key $\{e, n\}$. ElGamal cryptosystem encrypts a message differently using the same public key by introducing a random parameter. In how many ways can a message be encrypted using different values of the random parameter?

10

Elliptic Curve Cryptography

Elliptic curves have been studied for many years, but their application in cryptography has been rather recent. The reason for sudden interest is due to belief that the cryptosystems based on elliptic curve cryptography (ECC) are more efficient for the same level of security as other cryptosystems. We begin this chapter with a brief introduction to elliptic curves. We define the algebraic structures as applicable to the elliptic curves for their use in a cryptosystem. ECC is used for encryption, key exchange and for digital signature. We look at ECC based ElGamal asymmetric-key cryptosystem and Diffie–Hellman symmetric-key exchange. We leave ECC based digital signature for Chapter 12.

10.1 ELLIPTIC CURVE

We are familiar with the simple set of curves, straight line, circle, ellipse, parabola and hyperbola, which can be represented by a general equation $x^2 + axy + by^2 + cx + dy + e = 0$. The next higher set of curves is set of elliptic curves. These are represented by

$$y^2 + axy + by = cx^3 + dx^2 + ex + f$$

We are interested in a simpler form of elliptic curves for cryptography.

$$y^2 = x^3 + ax + b \quad \text{where } 4a^3 + 27b^2 \neq 0$$

Figure 10.1(a) shows plot of the above elliptic curve for some values of the parameters a and b. Note that

– the elliptic curve is symmetric about x-axis because we can write $y = \pm\sqrt{x^3 + ax + b}$
– $x^3 + ax + b$ is a cubic polynomial, and therefore, it has three roots.

We want that all the three roots to be distinct in cryptography. We get three distinct roots when its discriminant $4a^3 + 27b^2$ is not equal to zero. Therefore, parameters a and b are so chosen that discriminant is never zero. An elliptical curve having three distinct roots is referred to as *non-singular*.

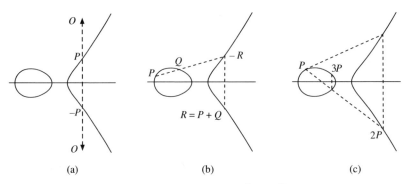

Figure 10.1   Elliptic curve $y^2 = x^3 + ax + b$.

10.1.1   Elliptic Curve as an Abelian Group

Let us construct an abelian (commutative) group E using the points on an elliptic curve as the elements of the set. For example, we say point P at (x_P, y_P) on the curve is an element of set E [Figure 10.1(b)]. The abelian group is constructed as under:

Set E: Set E consists of all the points on the curve and a zero point O, which is at infinity [Figure 10.1(a)].

Identity element: As we shall shortly see, O serves as the identity element.

Additive inverse: Additive inverse of an element P in E is defined as the mirror image of P with respect to x-axis [Figure 10.1(a)]. Since the elliptic curve is symmetric about x-axis, every element of set E has an additive inverse which is also in E.

Group operation: The binary operation for the points on an elliptic curve is, by convention, called addition (+). If P and Q are two points on the elliptic curve, we define the binary operation $P + Q = R$ as shown in Figure 10.1(b).

- Join P to Q with a straight line and extend the straight line to intersect the elliptic curve at a third point $-R$. The mirror image of $-R$ with respect to the x-co-ordinate is the point $R = P + Q$.
- If co-ordinates of P and Q are respectively (x_P, y_P) and (x_Q, y_Q), co-ordinates of R can be determined easily using the following equations. We will not go into their derivation.

$$x_R = \lambda^2 - x_p - x_Q$$

$$y_R = -y_P + \lambda(x_P - x_R)$$

$$\lambda = \frac{y_Q - y_P}{x_Q - x_P}$$

The above definition of binary operation is consistent with definitions of the additive inverse and identity element O. If $Q = -P$, $P + Q = P - P = O$, which is at infinity as shown in Figure 10.1(a).

Now we claim that E with addition operator (+) is an abelian group because it satisfies the rest of the required properties of an abelian group.

Closure   For any P, Q in E, $R = P + Q$ is also in E.
Associative law   We can show that $(P + Q) + R = P + (Q + R)$ for any P, Q, R in E.
Commutative law For any P, Q in E, $P + Q = Q + P$

Closure and commutative laws are obvious from the way we defined the binary operation. Associative law can also be shown mathematically true in this case. Thus {E, +} is an abelian group.

10.1.2   Algebraic Expression for 2P

In elliptic curve cryptography, we add a point P to itself. The addition $P + P$ is denoted by $2P$. To find point $2P$, let us move point Q in Figure 10.1(b) towards P and ultimately coincide it with P. When Q coincides with P, the line joining P and Q becomes tangent at point P and R becomes equal to $P + P = 2P$ [Figure 10.1(c)]. The co-ordinates of point $2P$ are given by the following equations:

$$x_{2P} = \left[\frac{3x_P^2 + a}{2y_P} \right]^2 - 2x_P$$

$$y_{2P} = \left[\frac{3x_P^2 + a}{2y_P} \right] (x_P - x_{2P}) - y_P$$

Having determined $2P$, we can locate $3P$ by adding P to $2P$ [Figure 10.1(c)]. By adding P multiple times, we can locate a point $Q = kP$ where k is a positive integer.

$$Q = kP = \underbrace{P + P + \dots + P}_{k \text{ times}}$$

Given point P and parameter k, we can readily determine Q. But by given points Q and P, it is difficult to compute k. This property of elliptic curves is used in cryptography.

10.2   ELLIPTIC CURVES OVER Z_p

The elliptic curve arithmetic we described earlier is over real numbers. We deal with a finite set of integers only in cryptography. Therefore, we restrict the values of the parameters (a, b) and the variables (x, y) of the elliptic curve to the elements of $Z_p = \{0, 1, 2, \dots, p - 1\}$. Thus the equation of the elliptic curve becomes

$$y^2 \bmod p = (x^3 + ax + b) \bmod p \qquad \text{where } (4a^3 + 27b^2) \bmod p \neq 0 \bmod p$$

Not all the elements of Z_p will satisfy the above equation. We will use the notation $E_p(a, b)$ to represent set of all the points (x, y) that obey the above equation for the given values of a and b. $E_p(a, b)$ also includes the identity element O, the point at infinity.

Although the collection of discrete points in $E_p(a, b)$ satisfies the above equation, these points no longer form a smooth curve on (x, y) plane. Therefore, we cannot use the geometrical construction to illustrate the action of the addition operator. The algebraic expressions for co-ordinates of $2P$ and $R = P + Q$ continue to hold good provided the calculations are carried out modulo p.

Example 1   For the elliptic curve $y^2 \bmod 11 = (x^3 + x + 6) \bmod 11$, determine y when $x = 2$.

Solution $y^2 \bmod 11 = (8 + 2 + 6) \bmod 11 = 5$

$\qquad\qquad y = \pm 4 \bmod 11 = 4$ and 7

Note that for $x = 2$, we get two points $P = (2, 4)$ and $-P = (2, 7)$ on the elliptic curve. These points are inverse of each other. We can determine other points of $E_{11}(1, 6)$ in similar manner. Table 10.1 shows all the points of set $E_{11}(1, 6)$. The values of y^2 for $x = 0, 1, 4, 6$ and 9, do not have a square root modulo 11. We do not have points in $E_{11}(1, 6)$ corresponding these values of x.

TABLE 10.1   Elements of $E_{11}(1, 6)$

x	y^2 (mod 11)	y	P	$-P$
2	5	4, 7	(2, 4)	(2, 7)
3	3	5, 6	(3, 5)	(3, 6)
5	4	2, 9	(5, 2)	(5, 9)
7	4	2, 9	(7, 2)	(7, 9)
8	9	3, 8	(8, 3)	(8, 8)
10	4	2, 9	(10, 2)	(10, 9)
–	–	–	O	O

Example 2   If $P = (3, 5)$ and $Q = (10, 9)$ are two points on $E_{11}(1, 6)$, determine $R = P + Q$.

Solution $\lambda = (9 - 5) \times (10 - 3)^{-1} \bmod 11 = 4 \times 8 \bmod 11 = 10$

$\qquad\qquad x_R = (10^2 - 3 - 10) \bmod 11 = 10$

$\qquad\qquad y_R = [(- 5 + 10 \times (3 - 10)] \bmod 11 = 2$

Thus, $R = (10, 2)$

Example 3   If $G = (2, 7)$ lies on the elliptic curve $y^2 \bmod 11 = (x^3 + x + 6) \bmod 11$, determine $2G$.

Solution

$$x_{2G} = \left[\left[\frac{3 \times 2^2 + 1}{2 \times 7} \right]^2 - 2 \times 2 \right] \bmod 11 = \left[\frac{4}{9} - 4 \right] \bmod 11 = [4 \times 5 - 4] \bmod 11 = 5$$

$$y_{2G} = \left[\left[\frac{3 \times 2^2 + 1}{2 \times 7} \right] \times (2 - 5) - 7 \right] \bmod 11 = \left[\frac{5}{7} - 7 \right] \bmod 11 = [9 - 7] \bmod 11 = 2$$

$$2G = (5, 2)$$

10.2.1 $E_p(a, b)$ as Cyclic Group

If the number of elements in $E_p(a, b)$ is prime, all points on an elliptic curve form a cyclic group with the additive operator defined earlier. Elliptic curve $E_{11}(1, 6)$, for example, is a cyclic group because it has thirteen elements (Table 10.1). If we choose point (2, 7) as the generator G of group $E_{11}(1, 6)$, the other elements can be expressed in terms of G as given in Table 10.2.

TABLE 10.2 Group $E_{11}(1, 6)$ with the Generator G = (2, 7)

G = (2, 7)	$5G$ = (3, 6)	$9G$ = (10, 9)	$13G = O$
$2G$ = (5, 2)	$6G$ = (7, 9)	$10G$ = (8, 8)	
$3G$ = (8, 3)	$7G$ = (7, 2)	$11G$ = (5, 9)	
$4G$ = (10, 2)	$8G$ = (3, 5)	$12G$ = (2, 4)	

Note that we have used notation nG to represent an element of the cyclic group in place of usual g^n because we defined group operation as 'addition'. Since order of the element G is 13, same as the order of $E_{11}(1, 6)$, G = (2, 7) is a primitive element of $E_{11}(1, 6)$.

Example 4 If P = (10, 2), Q = (7, 9) are two points on the elliptic curve $E_{11}(1, 6)$, determine point $R = P + Q$.

Solution P = (10, 2) = $4G$
Q = (7, 9) = $6G$
$R = 4G + 6G = 10G$ = (8, 8)

If we add inverse of a point to it, we get identity element O. Thus, if we add point (3, 5) to its inverse (3, 6), we should get the identity element O.

$$(3, 5) + (3, 6) = 8G + 5G = 13G = O$$

Further, we can compute kG, $k > 13$, as under.

$$15G = 13G + 2G = O + 2G = 2G$$

Example 5 If P = (3, 5) and Q = (10, 9) are two points on $E_{11}(1, 6)$, compute $R = P + Q$.

Solution P = (3, 5) = $8G$,
$Q - (10, 9) - 9G$
$R = 8G + 9G = 17G = 13G + 4G = O + 4G = 4G$ = (10, 2)

$E_{11}(1, 6)$ turned out to be cyclic because its order was prime. But it may not be true in general. Since we are interested in a cyclic group in cryptography, we determine a cyclic subgroup of $E_p(a, b)$ and use this subgroup.

10.3 ELLIPTIC CURVES OVER GALOIS FIELD GF(2^n)

Elements (x, y) of $E_p(a, b)$ and its parameters (a, b) are integers from Z_p. For hardware implementations, it is convenient to use n-bit binary words in place of integers. Therefore, we define elliptic curves over a Galois Field GF(2^n) instead of Z_p. The elements of GF(2^n) are represented by n-bit words. We use the notation $E_2{}^n(a, b)$ to denote set of points (x, y) of the elliptic curve defined over GF(2^n).

It turns out that the following form of elliptic curve needs to be used for cryptography when it is defined over GF(2^n).

$$y^2 + xy = x^3 + ax^2 + b; \quad \text{where b} \neq 0$$

When $b = 0$, we do not get distinct roots. As mentioned before, such curves are not suitable for cryptography. For the elliptic curve given above, we need to redefine the additive group operator as described below.

Inverse: If $P = (x, y)$, then $-P = (x, x + y)$

Addition operation: If $P = (x_P, y_P)$, $Q = (x_Q, y_Q)$ and $P \neq \pm Q$, then point $P + Q$ is determined by

$$x_{P+Q} = \lambda^2 + \lambda + x_P + x_Q + a$$

$$y_{P+Q} = \lambda(x_P + x_{P+Q}) + x_{P+Q} + y_P$$

where $$\lambda = \frac{y_P + y_Q}{x_P + x_Q}$$

If $P = (x_P, y_P)$, then point $2P = (x_{2P}, y_{2P})$ is determined by

$$x_{2P} = \lambda^2 + \lambda + a$$

$$\lambda_{2P} = x_P^2 + (\lambda + 1)x_{2P}$$

where

$$\lambda = x_P + \frac{y_P}{x_P}$$

Element (x, y) and parameters a and b of $E_2n(a, b)$ belong to GF(2^n). Modular polynomial arithmetic using an irreducible polynomial is used for all the above computations. For the purpose of computation, it is convenient to express the elements and parameters of $E_2n(a, b)$ in terms of generator g. Recall[1] that elements of GF(2^n) form a cyclic group under multiplication and can be expressed as powers of the generator element g. For example, Table 10.3 lists the element of GF(2^3) when the irreducible polynomial is $x^3 + x + 1 = 0$ and $g = x = (010)$. Examples below illustrates Table 10.3.

---

1. Refer to Section 5.5.7 of Chapter 5.

TABLE 10.3 Elements of GF(2^3) with the Generator g = (010)

0	000	$g^3 = g + 1$	011
1	001	$g^4 = g^2 + g$	110
g	010	$g^5 = g^2 + g + 1$	111
g^2	100	$g^6 = g^2 + 1$	101

Example 6 If $P = (g^2, 1)$ and $Q = (g^3, g^2)$ are two points on elliptic curve $E_23(g^3, 1)$ defined over GF(2^3) with irreducible polynomial $x^3 + x + 1$, determine

(a) $R = P + Q$
(b) $R = 2P$

Solution

(a) $\lambda = \dfrac{y_P + y_q}{x_P + x_q} = \dfrac{1 + g^2}{g^2 + g^3} + \dfrac{g^6}{g^2 + g + 1} = \dfrac{g^6}{g^5} = g$

$x_{P+Q} = \lambda^2 + \lambda + x_P + x_Q + a = g^2 + g + g^2 + g^3 + g^3 = g$

$y_{P+Q} = \lambda(x_P + x_{P+Q}) + x_{P+Q} + y_P = g^2(g^2 + g) + g + 1 = g^4 + g^3 + g + 1 = g^4$

$R = (g, g^4)$

(b) $\lambda = x_P + \dfrac{y_P}{x_P} = g^2 + \dfrac{1}{g^2} = g^2 + g^5 = g + 1 = g^3$

$x_{2P} = \lambda^2 + \lambda + a = g^6 + g^3 + g^3 = g^6$

$y_{2P} = x_P^2 + (\lambda + 1)x_{2P} = g^{12} + (g^3 + 1) g^6 = g^5 + g^7 = g^2 + g + 1 + 1 = g^4$

$R = 2P = (g^6, g^4)$

10.3.1 E_2n (a, b) as Cyclic Group

As in the case of elliptic curve $E_p(a, b)$, we are interested in the set of only those points on the $E_2n(a, b)$ that form a cyclic group. $E_2n(a, b)$, in general, will not be cyclic. We determine a cyclic subgroup of $E_2n(a, b)$ and use this subgroup. We choose a base point G in $E_2n(a, b)$ as the generator of the subgroup and then determine points $2G$, $3G$ and so on. Table 10.4 lists the elements of such cyclic subgroup of elliptic curve $E_23(g^3, 1)$ with base point $G = (g^2, 1)$ as the generator.

TABLE 10.4 Cyclic Subgroup of $E_23(g^3, 1)$ with $(g^2, 1)$ as the Generator

$G = (g^2, 1)$ = (100, 001)	$6G = (g^5, 1)$ = (111, 001)	$11G = (g^4, g^4)$ = (110, 110)
$2G = (g^6, g^5)$ = (101, 111)	$7G = (0, 1)$ = (000, 001)	$12G = (g^6, g)$ = (101, 010)
$3G = (g^4, 0)$ = (110, 000)	$8G = (g^5, g^4)$ = (111, 110)	$13G = (g^2, g^6)$ = (100, 101)
$4G = (g^3, g^2)$ = (011, 100)	$9G = (g, g^4)$ = (010, 110)	$14G = O$
$5G = (g, g^2)$ = (010, 100)	$10G = (g^3, g^5)$ = (011, 111)	

Example 7   If $P = 3G$, $Q = 8G$ on the elliptic curve $E_23(g^3, 1)$ with base point $G = (g^2, 1)$, $g = (010)$, compute $R = P + Q$.

Solution $R = P + Q = 3G + 8G = 11G = (g^4, g^4) = (110, 110)$

10.4   ELLIPTIC CURVE CRYPTOGRAPHY (ECC)

Elliptic curves over finite fields are used for cryptography. Just as RSA uses 'multiplication' (exponentiation is merely repeated multiplication) as its group operator for encryption, ECC uses the 'addition' (multiplication is merely repeated addition) as group operator for encryption. It is based on the notion that given two points, P and $Q = kP$ on an elliptic curve, it is infeasible to determine integer k. Recovering k from Q is referred to as the discrete logarithm problem of elliptic curves. The fastest known method using discrete logarithm takes 1.6×10^{28} MIPS-years to compute k, if k is 234 bits long. Even the brute force approach of trying all possible values of k is infeasible, if it is kept sufficiently large.

Elliptic curves find several applications in cryptography. We describe two cryptographic applications of elliptic curve for illustrations in this section:

- ElGamal asymmetric key cryptosystem
- Diffie–Hellman key exchange

10.4.1   ElGamal Asymmetric-key Cryptosystem Using ECC

ElGamal algorithm for asymmetric-key encryption is based on multiplicative binary operator. Since elliptic curve cryptography uses additive binary operator, we modify the original scheme, replacing multiplication by addition, and exponentiation by scalar multiplication. We have divided the entire process into three parts: key generation, encryption and decryption. Table 10.2 is referred for computations in the examples used for illustration. We use the notation $E_x(a, b)$ to represent set of points on elliptic curve defined over Z_p or $GF(2^n)$.

Key Generation

Private and public key generation consists of the following steps:

(a) Alice defines an elliptic curve $E_x(a, b)$.
(b) Alice selects
    – a base point G_A on the elliptic curve,
    – an integer d_A as her private key.
(c) Alice computes her public key $P_A = d_A G_A$, where $d_A G_A$ stands for $G_A + G_A + \cdots + G_A$ with G_A making d_A appearances in the expression.
(d) Alice announces $\{E_x(a, b), G_A, P_A\}$ as her public key with other parameters to Bob.

As mentioned above, it is computationally infeasible to determine the private key d_A from G_A and P_A.

Example 8 Alice chooses the base point $G_A = (2, 7)$ in $E_{11}(1, 6)$ and private key $d_A = 5$. Computes her public key.

Solution
$$P_A = d_A G_A = 5G_A = (3, 6)$$

Alice announces $\{E_{11}(1, 6), G_A = (2, 7), P_A = (3, 6)\}$ as her public key with other parameters chosen by her.

Encryption

Encryption using the public key involves the following steps:

(a) Bob selects a point m on the elliptic curve $E_x(a, b)$ announced by Alice. m represents the message that Bob wants to encrypt and send to Alice.
(b) Bob chooses a random number k and encrypts point m by adding kP_A to it.

$$c = m + kP_A.$$

Bob attaches the following hint r to the ciphertext c for Alice.

$$r = kG_A$$

Example 9 Bob receives $\{E_{11}(1, 6), G_A = (2, 7), P_A = (3, 6)\}$ as the public key of Alice. He wants to encrypt his plaintext represented as point $m = (3, 5)$ on the elliptic curve. He chooses a random number $k = 6$. Calculates the hint r and the ciphertext.

Solution
$$r = kG_A = 6G_A = (7, 9)$$

Bob encrypts point m by adding kP_A to it.

$$c = m + kP_A = (3, 5) + 6P_A = 8G + 30G = 12G = (2, 4)$$

Decryption

Alice multiplies the hint r by her private key d_A and subtracts the result from the ciphertext c to get the plaintext m. Subtraction implies adding the inverse.

$$c - d_A\, r = m + kP_A - d_A kG_A = m + k\, d_A G_A - d_A kG_A = m$$

An intruder can retrieve the message m from the ciphertext c, only if he knows the value of k. Computing k from the hint r is difficult.

Example 10 Alice had announced $\{E_{11}(1, 6), G_A = (2, 7), P_A = (3, 6)\}$ as her public key to Bob. She receives hint $r = (7, 9)$ and ciphertext $c = (2, 4)$ from Bob. Decrypt the ciphertext.

Solution Alice decrypts c using her private key d_A as given below.

$$m = c - d_A r = (2, 4) - 5r = (2, 4) - (10, 2) = (2, 4) + (10, 9) = (3, 5)$$

Note that $-(10, 2) \equiv (10, 9)$ since $4G + 9G = O$.

10.4.2 Diffie–Hellman Secret Key Exchange Using ECC

Diffie–Hellman key exchange algorithm described in Chapter 14 can be implemented on elliptic curves. We modify the original scheme here also, replacing multiplication by addition and exponentiation by scalar multiplication.

(a) Alice and Bob choose elliptic curve $E_x(a, b)$, and a base point G on the curve.
(b) Alice selects a secret integer $n_A < n$, n being the order of G. She generates point $P_A = n_A G$ on the elliptic curve. Alice sends P_A and n to Bob.
(c) Bob selects a secret integer $n_B < n$ and generates point $P_B = n_B G$ in similar manner. Bob sends P_B to Alice.
(d) Alice and Bob calculate a shared secret that could subsequently be used as symmetric-key as follows:
  - Alice calculates the shared secret K as
    $$K = n_A P_B$$
  - Bob calculates the shared secret K as
    $$K = n_B P_A$$

The above calculations by Alice and Bob yield the same result K because Alice calculates

$$K = n_A P_B = n_A n_B G = n_B n_A G = n_B P_A = K \text{ as calculated by Bob.}$$

To get the secret K, an attacker would require n_A. Getting n_A from $P_A = n_A G$ involves solving the discrete logarithm problem which, for a properly chosen set of elliptic curve parameters and G, can be extremely hard. To increase the level of difficulty in solving the discrete logarithm problem, we select the base point G having very large order n.

Example 11   Alice and Bob choose base point $G = (2, 7)$ with order $n = 13$ in $E_{11}(1, 6)$ for establishing the secret key using Diffie-Hellman algorithm. Alice selects her secret integer $n_A = 6$ and Bob selects his secret integer $n_B = 8$. What is the shared secret key computed by them?

Solution: Alice computes P_A as given below and conveys it to Bob.

$$P_A = n_A G = 6G = (7, 9)$$

Bob computes P_B as given below and conveys it to Alice.

$$P_B = n_B G = 8G = (3, 5)$$

Alice computes the secret key K using P_B received from Bob.

$$K = n_A P_B = 6P_B = 48G = 13G + 13G + 13G + 9G = 9G = (10, 9)$$

Bob computes the secret key K using P_A received from Alice.

$$K = n_B P_A = 8P_A = 48G = 9G = (10, 9)$$

The following points must be noted in the above example.

- For the sake of illustration, we have equated $6P_B$ and $8P_A$ to $48G$ and determined the key K using Table 10.2. But Alice will have to add P_B six times to get K because she does not know the secret integer selected by Bob. Similarly, Bob will also compute K by adding P_A eight times.

- The secret key K is shown to be a pair of numbers (10, 9). To use this key for conventional encryption, we need to have a single number. We can, for example, use the x co-ordinate (10) or a function of x co-ordinate as the key.
- The order n of the base point G should be large to make discrete logarithm problem infeasible.

10.5 SECURITY AND APPLICATIONS OF ECC

The basis for the security of elliptic curve cryptography is intractability of the following elliptic curve discrete logarithm problem.

"Given an elliptic curve E_x(a, b), point P of order n on the curve, and another point Q such that $Q = kP$, determine the integer k."

This is a discrete logarithm problem, and has received considerable attention during last decade. The best algorithm known to date for the discrete logarithm problem of elliptic curves is the Pollard rho-method which takes about $\sqrt{(\pi n/2)}$ addition steps of elliptic curve E_p(a, b) having order n. Table 10.5 shows the time required for computation of a single discrete logarithm in case of elliptic curves for different values of n. A MIPS year is equivalent to the computational power of a computer that is rated at 1 MIPS and utilized for one year.

TABLE 10.5 Processing Time for Discrete Logarithm Problem of Elliptic Curves

n(bits)	$\sqrt{(\pi n/2)}$	MIPS years
160	2^{80}	9.6×10^{11}
186	2^{93}	7.9×10^{15}
234	2^{117}	1.6×10^{23}
354	2^{177}	1.5×10^{11}
426	2^{213}	1.0×10^{52}

With the algorithms for integer factorization becoming more and more efficient, RSA cryptographic methods require longer keys to foil cryptanalytic attacks. Longer keys increase computational overhead in RSA. Elliptic curve cryptography, on the other hand, provides the same level and type of security as RSA but with much shorter keys. Table 10.6 compares the required key sizes for comparable levels of security against brute force attacks.

TABLE 10.6 Required Key Sizes in Bits for Equivalent Security Level

RSA encryption	Elliptic curve encryption
1024	160
2048	224
3072	256
7680	384
15360	512

Shorter key size gives an edge to ECC over other cryptosystems in the following applications:

- Because of the much smaller key sizes involved, ECC algorithms can be implemented on smart cards without mathematical coprocessors. Contactless smart cards work only with ECC because other systems require too much induction energy.
- Since shorter key lengths translate into faster handshaking protocols, ECC is also becoming increasingly important for wireless communications.
- For the same reasons as listed above, we can also expect ECC to become important for wireless sensor networks.

10.6   SUMMING UP

In this chapter, we introduced elliptic curve cryptography (ECC), which offers signification computational advantage over conventional cryptography based on modular exponentiation. The important learning points of this chapter are listed below:

- The following non-singular elliptic curves with the values of the parameters (a, b) and the variables (x, y) defined over the prime finite field $Z_p = \{0, 1, 2, ..., p - 1\}$ or $GF(2^n)$ are used in ECC.

  1. $y^2 = x^3 + ax + b$ where $4a^3 + 27b^2 \neq 0$
  2. $y^2 + xy = x^3 + ax^2 + b$ where $b \neq 0$

  The elliptic curve (1) is defined over prime finite field $Z_p = \{0, 1, 2, ..., p - 1\}$. $E_p(a, b)$ represents set of points (x, y) of the elliptic curve (1) defined over Z_p. The elliptic curve (2) is defined over $GF(2^n)$. $E_2^n(a, b)$ denotes set of points (x, y) of the elliptic curve (2) defined over $GF(2^n)$.
- Points on an elliptic curve can form an abelian group with addition as the group operation and point at infinity as the identity element. We are interested in cyclic subgroup of the abelian group in ECC.
- ECC can be used for ElGamal asymmetric-key cryptosystem and Diffie–Hellman key exchange. We use additive binary operator of ECC in place of usual multiplicative operator.
- The security of ECC is based on the elliptic curve discrete logarithm problem:

  "Given an elliptic curve $E_x(a, b)$, point P of order n on the curve, and another point Q such that $Q = kP$, determine the integer k."

- ECC provides the same level and type of security as RSA, but with much shorter keys.

We will come across ECC again in Chapter 12 'Digital Signature', where we study use of ECC for signing messages.

Key Terms		
ECC ElGamal cryptosystem	Elliptic curve cyclic group	Non-singular elliptic curve
ECC Diffie–Hellman key exchange	Elliptic curve over $GF(2^n)$	
Elliptic curve abelian group	Elliptic curve over Z_p	

RECOMMENDED READING

Digital Signature Standard (DSS), Federal Information Processing Standards publication #186–4.U.S. Department of Commerce, NIST, Maryland, USA, 2013.

Elliptic Curve Cryptography, Standards for Efficient Cryptography, Certicom Research, Ontario, Canada, 2000.

Forouzan, Behrouz A., *Cryptography and Network Security*, Tata McGraw-Hill, New Delhi, 2007.

Koblitz, N., *Elliptic Curve Cryptosystems*, Mathematics of Computation, 48(177), 203–209, January 1987.

Paar, C. and Pelzl, J., *Understanding Cryptography, A Textbook for Students and Practitioners*, Springer (India), New Delhi, 2009.

RFC 6090, *Fundamental Elliptic Curve Cryptography Algorithms*, IETF.

Stallings, W., *Cryptography and Network Security*, Prentice-Hall of India, New Delhi, 2008.

Vaudenay, S., *A Classical Introduction to Cryptography*, Springer, NY, USA, 2006.

Washington, L., *Elliptic Curves: Number Theory and Cryptography*, Chapman & Hall/CRC, Florida, USA, 2003

----(PROBLEMS)----

1. What are the additive inverses of the following points on the elliptic curve $E_{23}(1, 1)$?
   (a) (7, 12)
   (b) (3, 13)
   (c) (17, 20)

2. If points $P = (4, 2)$ and $Q = (10, 6)$ belong to the curve $E_{13}(1, 1)$, determine $R = P + Q$.

3. If point $P = (5, 2)$ belongs to the curve $E_{11}(1, 6)$, determine $2P$.

4. If point $P = (7, 0)$ belongs to the curve $E_{13}(1, 1)$, determine $2P$.

5. Determine all the points of elliptic curve $E_5(4, 4)$.

6. If the base point G is (2, 7) on the elliptic curve $E_{11}(1, 6)$, determine the point on the curve given by the following expression (*Hint:* Make use of Table 10.2):

    (8, 3) + (7, 9) – 2(2, 4)

7. If $P = (g^3, g^2)$ and $Q = (g^6, g)$ are two points on elliptic curve $E_2^3(g^3, 1)$ defined over $GF(2^3)$ with irreducible polynomial $x^3 + x + 1$ and $g = x$, determine using Table 10.4,
   (a) $R = P + Q$
   (b) $R = 2P$

8. If $P = (g^{12}, g^{12})$ and $Q = (g^6, g^8)$ are two points on elliptic curve $E_2^4(g^4, 1)$ defined over $GF(2^4)$ with irreducible polynomial $x^4 + x + 1$ and $g = x$, determine $R = P + Q$.

9. Alice and Bob negotiate ElGamal encryption based on elliptic curve $E_{11}(1, 6)$. Alice chooses base point $(2, 7)$ and private key $d_A = 3$. Alice conveys her public key and the base point to Bob. Use Table 10.2 for computations.

   (a) Determine Alice's public key.
   (b) Bob encrypts message $(7, 2)$ using Alice's public key and his secret random number $r = 8$. Determine the ciphertext and the hint conveyed by him to Alice.
   (c) Decrypt the ciphertext sent by Bob.

10. Alice and Bob choose base point $G = (2, 7)$ with order $n = 13$ in $E_{11}(1, 6)$ for determination of the symmetric encryption key using Diffie–Hellman algorithm. Alice selects her secret integer $n_A = 5$ and Bob selects his secret integer $n_B = 7$. What is the symmetric encryption key derived by them?

11. (a) Determine all the points of elliptic curve $E_7(3, 2)$. What is the order of the group?
    (b) Given the element $G = (0, 3)$ on the curve, determine the order of G. Is G a primitive element?

11

Message Authentication

We introduce in this chapter the security concerns about message integrity, its origin and disputes between the communicating entities about the transfer of messages. These aspects are addressed by appending an authenticator to the message. We examine two classes of cryptographic functions used for generating the authenticator, customized hash functions designed for specific purpose of authentication and those based on block ciphers. Structural design and security aspects of SHA-512, Whirlpool, HMAC and CMAC are described in brief.

11.1 MESSAGE AUTHENTICATION

Confidentiality of a message is one aspect of message security. The other important aspect of message security is its authenticity. Security concerns about message authenticity are important because an adversary can attack message authenticity in several ways.

(a) The adversary can alter the content of the message, substitute an alternate message or alter the sequence of messages.
(b) He may on send a fraudulent message as having been sent by an authorized source.
(c) He may replay an old valid message.

Encryption does not protect authenticity of a message or provide means to check its authenticity. It merely provides confidentiality, i.e., security against exposure of its information to an adversary.

One may argue that if the adversary cannot decrypt the message, he cannot alter the message. Consider that Alice sends message m encrypted as $c = E(K, m)$ to Bob. The adversary does not have the key K, but he alters c as c' without decrypting c. Bob decrypts c' as m'. It is quite likely that decrypted message m' will be meaningless. But Bob cannot conclude that the message m' is an altered message, since it is possible that Alice had actually sent m'.

Therefore, when Bob receives a message from Alice, he wants to be sure that the message has not been altered or substituted or sent by an imposter. He needs some mechanism to verify message integrity and its origin. The term 'message authentication' refers to both these aspects.

Another important aspect associated with message authentication is non-repudiation. Non-repudiation refers to ensuring that the source cannot deny ownership of its message.

11.1.1 Message Integrity

Integrity of a message refers to its content. Message integrity check enables the receiver to establish genuineness of the content of a message. Figure 11.1 shows the basic scheme for checking message integrity. A cryptographic 'fingerprint' of the message is concatenated to the message by the sender. The 'fingerprint' is computed using an algorithm called cryptographic hash function. The fingerprint is commonly referred to as message digest or hash and is sent along with the message. The receiver verifies the integrity of the received message by re-computing the digest and comparing the received digest with the computed digest. If the received digest is different, it implies that the message has been altered. We assume that the digest attached to the message cannot be altered or substituted by the adversary.

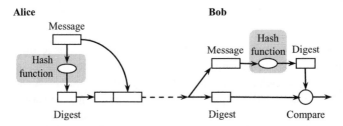

Figure 11.1 Message integrity verification.

The adversary can attack this scheme in number of ways:

- The adversary finds an alternative message that has same digest so that he may substitute the original message. This attempt is countered by designing the hash function so that it is computationally infeasible to find such alternative message.
- The adversary may copy a legitimate message with its digest from Alice to Bob. He may later send this message with its digest to Bob. This is referred to as *replay attack*. To protect against replay attack, Alice appends time, session-id, or sequence number to the message before computing its digest. She sends the message along with these fields and the digest. The receiver accepts the message that
  - is received within a defined time window or sequence number window,
  - bears current session id, and
  - has successful digest verification.
- The hash function used for computing the digest is not a secret. The adversary can create a fraudulent message, compute its digest and substitute both the original message and the digest. This attempt is countered by introducing another security measure, the data-origin authentication, which we discuss next.

11.1.2 Data-origin Authentication

The received message can be a fraudulent message inserted or substituted by the adversary. The receiver, therefore, requires that the sender should 'stamp' the digest with some secret which can be verified by the receiver. For example, the sender may encrypt the digest using the secret symmetric key between him and the receiver (Figure 11.2). The receiver decrypts the digest using the secret key and verifies the message integrity using the digest. If verification is successful, he assumes that the message originated from the authentic source because the adversary cannot generate encrypted digest without knowing the secret key.

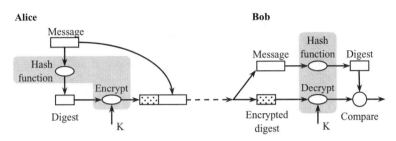

Figure 11.2 Message authentication.

The message authentication scheme, shown in Figure 11.2, requires two cryptographic functions: the hash function and the encryption function. It is possible to have keyed-hash function, which takes the message and the shared secret key as its inputs. The output of keyed hash function is called message authentication code (MAC). We examine keyed hash functions separately, later in this chapter.

11.1.3 Non-repudiation

We tend to assume that security issues arise due to the adversary only. It is possible that the receiver may alter a delivered message to his advantage, or the sender may later deny having sent the message. In other words, there can be dispute between its sender and the receiver.

Consider that Alice sends a message to her bank for transferring from her account certain amount of money to Eve's account. The bank (Bob) carries out the transaction and keeps the message from Alice as record for future reference. Alice later denies having sent the message. The dispute can be about the content (e.g. about the amount of money) or about the origin of the message. The bank produces the recorded message before the arbitrator. It should be possible for the bank to prove to the arbitrator that

- the recorded message is authentic in respect of its origin and its content and
- that it (the bank) could not have altered or fabricated the received message.

Encryption of the digest with the secret symmetric key cannot address the above issues because the symmetric key is a shared secret between the sender and the receiver. The receiver can easily create a fraudulent message and its encrypted digest. Therefore, the sender encrypts the digest with his private key instead (Figure 11.3). The digest so encrypted constitutes 'digital signature' on the message. It is so because

- the private key is known only to its owner, the sender. Therefore, no one else can encrypt the digest and the sender cannot later deny having sent the message.
- integrity of the content can be verified using the decrypted digest. The digest can be decrypted easily using the public key.

– the receiver cannot alter the message, or signed digest without introducing any inconsistency.

The receiver saves the message and signed digest for reference, if there is a dispute. Note that all the three authentication issues message integrity, data-origin and non-repudiation get addressed in this scheme.

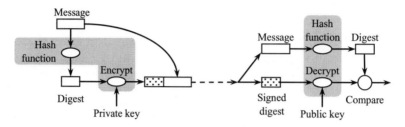

Figure 11.3 Message authentication with non-repudiation.

11.2 CRYPTOGRAPHIC HASH FUNCTION

The cryptographic hash function h maps a variable-size message x to a digest $h(x)$ that has fixed length and is much smaller in size than the size of the message. A trivial example of hash function is given below for illustration:

Alice and Bob use modulo 2 addition of 8-bit words of their messages as the message digest. Alice sends two messages, $m_1 = [00000110, 10011001, 01010011, 10010110]$ and $m_2 = [11100011, 11001100, 11100011, 10010110]$ with their digests as computed below.

$$
\left.\begin{array}{l}
00000110 \\
10011001 \\
01010011 \\
10010110
\end{array}\right\} m_1
\qquad
\left.\begin{array}{l}
11100011 \\
11001100 \\
11100011 \\
10010110
\end{array}\right\} m_2
$$

$$
\underline{01011010} \quad h(m_1) \qquad\qquad \underline{01011010} \quad h(m_2)
$$

Digest is 8-bit word in this example. There are only $2^8 = 256$ possible digests for all the possible messages of various sizes. This is true, in general, because the digest has fixed size, much smaller than the size of message. If the message is n bits long, and the digest is N bit long, $n > N$, we have 2^n possible messages and 2^N possible digests. Therefore, on average there are $2^n/2^N$ messages that generate the same digest. Note that the digests of the two different messages in the given example are same.

Receiving same digest for different messages does not bother Bob, who verifies message integrity using the digest associated with the message. But there is another ramification. It would be possible for one to replace the original message with another message having same digest, and the replacement will go undetected. Alice, Bob or the adversary, any of them, may be interested in replacing the original message.

- Alice can generate two different messages having the same digest. One she sends to Bob and the other she uses before the arbitrator when there is dispute later.
- The adversary intercepts the message and the digest, finds another message having the same digest and replaces the original message with her fraudulent message.
- Bob can also replace the message just like the adversary and claim before the arbitrator that the replaced message is the one Alice sent.

Encryption of digest by Alice using secret key or private key provides no protection, since hash algorithms are public. If the digest is encrypted, the adversary attacks authenticity in the following manner.

- The adversary computes digest of the original message.
- He uses the computed digest to search another message having the same digest.
- Having found an alternative message, the adversary appends the original encrypted digest to the new message.

To thwart the adversarial attack on authenticity, the hash function $h(x)$ is so chosen that it is very difficult to find messages having same digest. The required properties of such a hash function are described next.

Example 1   If hash function is $h(x) = 5x^2 \bmod 9$, compute the digest of $x = 787$.

Solution $h(x) = 5x^2 \bmod 9 = 5 \times 787 \times 787 \bmod 9 = 5 \times 4 \times 4 \bmod 9 = 8$.

11.2.1   Properties of Cryptographic Hash Function $h(x)$

We can define the basic required properties of the hash function $h(x)$ for any message x as follows:

Compression: $h(x)$ can be applied to input x of variable size, but it should produce a fixed-length output for variable length input x.

One way: For any given output y, it is computationally infeasible to find any input x (called pre-image) such that $h(x) = y$. This property is also referred to as *pre-image resistant* property of the hash function.

Weak collision resistant: For a given input x, it is computationally infeasible to find another input x' such that $h(x) = h(x')$. This property is also referred to as *2nd pre-image resistant* property.

Strong collision resistant: It is computationally infeasible to find any two distinct inputs x and x' such that $h(x) = h(x')$. Note that there is free choice of both inputs. This property is referred to as *strong collision resistant*.

Computationally easy implementation: $h(x)$ should be relatively easy to compute for its implementation in software or hardware.

One motivation for each of the three major properties, one-way, weak collision resistant and strong collision resistant, is given below:

- Weak collision resistant property ensures that it is computationally infeasible for the Bob (or the adversary) to find another message having the same digest as that of a message received from Alice.
- Strong collision resistance property makes it computationally infeasible for Alice to generate two different messages having the same hash value. If she is successful in generating two such messages, she can send one message and disown it later before the arbitrator, producing the second message.
- One-way property is the least obvious of the three. Why would one generate a message for a given digest? Consider the situation depicted in Figure 11.3. Adversary wants to generate a message with digital signature of Alice, making use of her RSA public key $\{e, n\}$.

  (a) The adversary picks up a random number r and computes a digest $s = r^e$ mod n.
  (b) He searches for a message m having digest s.
  (c) He sends the message m to Bob with r as digital signature of Alice. r is Alice's digital signature since Alice would have signed s as $r = s^d$ mod n using her private key $\{d, n\}$.
  (d) Bob computes the unsigned digest $s = r^e$ mod n, and verifies integrity of the message.

  One-way property of the hash function renders this scheme infeasible because the adversary cannot execute step (b).

Example 2   Consider hash function $h(x) = x^2$ mod n, where n is a large composite number and x is an integer. Check whether the hash function meets the cryptographic requirements.

Solution
  (a) Size of x can be any length. The digest is always less than n. For example, if $n = 100$, we can always write $h(x)$ as two digit number. Thus the first requirement is met.
  (b) Given digest $h(x)$, we cannot find x because taking square root when modulus is a large composite number is infeasible. Therefore, $h(x)$ is pre-image resistant.
  (c) The hash function is not 2nd pre-image resistant and strong collision resistant because messages x and $-x$ have same of the digest.

11.2.2   Birthday Problems

Since hash function is many-to-one relation, there is always some probability of finding two messages with same digest or finding a message that has a given digest. To determine this probability, we assume that we have

- a message generator that is truly random in its construction of messages, and
- a hash function $h(x)$ that can generate N different digests for various input messages, and each digest is equally probable.

We create a pool of k ($k \le N$) random messages using the message generator. We have imposed the restriction that $k \le N$ because if $k > N$, at least two messages will have same digest. Now, we pose the following questions:

1. What is the 'likelihood' that the pool contains at least one message x for which digest $h(x)$ is equal to a given value H?

2. What is the 'likelihood' that there is at least one pair of messages x and x' in the pool having same digest, i.e. $h(x) = h(x')$?
3. What is the 'likelihood' of having same digest of at least two message x and x' in two different pools?

Before we proceed further, we need define the word 'likelihood' used in the questions above. When probability of an event is greater than 0.5, we say that the event is 'likely' to happen. In other words, we want to determine the size of message pool k, that will make the probability of the event greater than 0.5.

The above questions are collectively addressed as birthday problems as these can be reframed as follows:

1. What is the 'likelihood' of having at least a student in a class having a given birthday?
2. What is the 'likelihood' of having at least two students in a class having the same birthday?
3. What is the 'likelihood' of having at least two students in two different classes having the same birthday?

Solutions to these problems are given in Appendix A2. The results are summarized in Table 11.1. We can now calculate k (number of messages) for a given N (number of possible digests) by setting $P \geq 0.5$. For example, if we assume that $N = 365$, $k = 0.69 \times N = 253$, i.e., there is likelihood of finding a student having a given birthday in a class of 253 students.

TABLE 11.1 Birthday Problems

	Probability (P)	Number of messages (k) for $P = 1/2$
First birthday problem	$P \geq 1 - e^{-k/N}$	$k = 0.69N$
Second birthday problem	$P \geq 1 - e^{-k(k-1)/2N}$	$k = 1.18\sqrt{N}$
Third birthday problem	$P \geq 1 - e^{-k^2/N}$	$k = 0.83\sqrt{N}$

Let us find the answers to the three birthday problems if the size of digest is 64 bits. For the digest size of 64 bits, number of possible digests is $N = 2^{64}$.

(a) To find a message corresponding to given digest, the adversary has to try pool of $k = 0.69 \times 2^{64} = 1.27 \times 10^{19}$ messages. This is very large number. Even if he computes digests of 1 billion messages per second, he will take 500 years to find a matching digest.
(b) If Alice looks for *any two* messages having same digest, she must have a pool of $k = 1.18 \times 2^{64/2} = 1.18 \times 2^{32} = 5.06 \times 10^9$ messages.
(c) Consider that Alice would sign message m, but she would not sign message m'. To take Alice's signature on m', the adversary proceeds as follows:
   • The adversary creates a pool of k variants of message m by adding redundancies (e.g. commas, spaces, etc.) and by using synonyms. He creates another pool of k variants of message m'.

- He selects two variants, one from each pool, that have same digest. He takes signature of Alice on the selected variant of *m*, but attaches the signature to the selected variant of *m'*. He has a valid signed *m'*.

For the probability of success in finding two such variants to be more than 50%, the adversary has to have a pool of $0.83 \times 2^{32} = 3.5 \times 10^9$ messages.

11.2.3   Structure of Cryptographically Secure Iterated Hash Functions

Most cryptographically secure hash functions are iterative processes which can hash inputs of arbitrary length. To compute the digest of a message, it is partitioned into a series of blocks. Then it is hashed block by block using a compression function. Each stage of compression takes one block of the message and the output of previous stage. Figure 11.4 shows the structure of an iterated hash function proposed by Merkle.

- The input message is partitioned into blocks, each of size *b* bits. If necessary, the final block is padded suitably so that it is of the same length as others.
- The final block also includes the total length of the unpadded message. This step enhances the security of the hash function, since it gives some structure to message. The adversary needs to find a fraudulent message which along with the length field hashes to a given value.
- Each stage of processing returns *n*-bit output which is shorter than the block size. There are two inputs, a *b*-bit block of the message and the *n*-bit output of the previous processing stage. The first stage requires a fixed *n*-bit input called the Initialization Vector (IV).
- The compression function *f* itself may involve multiple rounds of processing of the two inputs. The precise nature of *f* depends on the hash algorithm being implemented.

The process can be modelled as below for a message *x* consisting of *N* blocks.

$$z_i = f(x_i, z_{i-1}) \qquad \text{where } z_0 = \text{IV}$$
$$h(x) = z_N$$

It can be easily shown that if the compression function $f(x_i, z_{i-1})$ is collision resistant, the resulting hash function $h(x)$ is also collision resistant for any variable length input *x*.

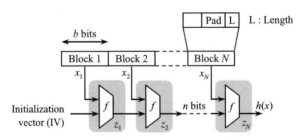

Figure 11.4   Structure of Merkle's hash function.

There are two approaches to design the iterated hash function.

(a) Customized hash functions
(b) Hash functions based on block ciphers

Customized Hash Functions

Customized hash functions are those which are specifically designed 'from scratch' for the explicit purpose of hashing, with optimized performance in mind. MD5 (Message Digest 5) and SHA (Secure Hash Algorithm) are two examples of customized hash functions. SHA being the most current, we describe this function in the next section.

Hash Functions Based on Block Ciphers

The motivation behind using a block cipher for constructing a hash function is that the existing implementation of a block cipher for encryption may be extended for hash function at little additional cost. Though a block cipher E is an invertible function, it can be shown that $f(x) = E(K, x) \oplus x$ is a one-way function for any fixed symmetric key K. Several schemes based on Merkle structure have been proposed. Figure 11.5 shows the structure of Miyaguchi–Preneel scheme.

- The core compression function consists of encryption function E with forward feeds of the key and plaintext. The additional forward feed of the key to ciphertext protects against 'meet-in-the-middle' attack.
- The key and the ciphertext sizes must be same for executing the process in iterative manner.
- Initialization vector acts as key for the first stage. The encryption function parameterized by the key as random input randomizes the input block of the massage.
- The following stage uses the ciphertext output of the previous stage as the key. In effect, the each encryption stage randomizes a message block parameterized by all the previous message blocks. Output of the last stage is the message digest.

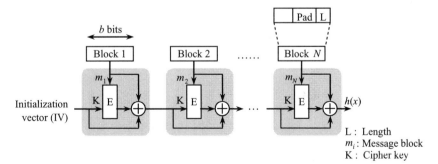

Figure 11.5 Structure of Miyaguchi–Preneel scheme.

We will examine Whirlpool hash function which is based on this scheme later in this section.

11.2.4   Secure Hash Algorithm (SHA)

Secure Hash Algorithm was developed by National Institute of Standards and Technology (NIST) in 1993 and published as a federal information processing standard. There are four versions of the algorithm today: SHA-1, SHA-256, SHA-384 and SHA-512. SHA-256, SHA-384 and SHA-512 are grouped as SHA-2. These versions are similar in structure, modular arithmetic and binary logic operations, except that they produce hash values of lengths 160, 256, 384 and 512 bits respectively (Table 11.2). We describe here SHA-512 in brief. Detailed structural design of SHA-512 can be found in *Secure Hash Standard*, Federal Information Processing Standards Publication#180-4.U.S. Department of Commerce, NIST, 2012.

TABLE 11.2   Versions of SHA

	SHA-1	**SHA-256**	**SHA-384**	**SHA-512**
Hash value length (bits)	160	256	384	512
Maximum message size (bits)	2^{64}	2^{64}	2^{128}	2^{128}
Block size (bits)	512	512	1024	1024
Word size (bits)	32	32	64	64
Number of steps	80	64	80	80

SHA-512 follows Merkle's structure as shown in Figure 11.6. The message is divided into blocks of 1024 bits. The last block is padded and contains 128 bit length field. The padding field consists of 1 followed by 0s to make a full block of 1024 bits. The length field (L) gives the size of the message in bits. Note that if the message is integral multiple of 1024 bits, the last block will consist of padding bits and the length field.

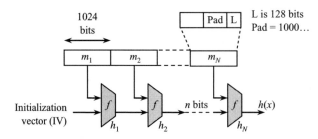

Figure 11.6   Structure of SHA-512.

Structure of SHA-512 is described in terms of words, each word consisting of 64 bits. Thus each block of message consists of 1024/64 = 16 words. SHA-512 produces 512-bit digest. Thus the digest consists of 8 words. The internal structure of ith compression stage is shown in Figure 11.7.

- The inputs to the compression stage are message block m_i and output h_{i-1} of previous compression stage. It generates output h_i.
- The compression function f has a message schedule that expands the length of the message block m_i from 16 words to 80 words (w_0, w_1, ..., w_{79}). Words w_0 to w_{15} consist of the

message block m_i and the rest are generated using an iterative process. The iterative process consists of taking four words at a time, applying rotational transformation followed by their modulo 2 addition to get a new word.
- The compression function has 80 rounds. Each round takes the following three inputs and generates output of eight words:
  - Output of previous round consisting of eight words.
  - One word (w_i) from the message schedule.
  - An additive constant k_i. k_i is a random 64-bit pattern.
- The output of the last round is added to the output of previous stage h_{i-1} to generate the stage output h_i.

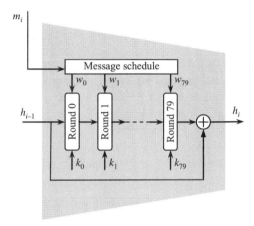

Figure 11.7 A compression stage of SHA-512.

After all the N blocks of the message have been processed, the output of the last stage is the SHA-512 message digest. With message digest of 512 bits, SHA-512 is collision resistant and is reportedly secure against all the attacks.

11.2.5   Whirlpool

Whirlpool is an iterated hash function based on Miyaguchi-Preneel scheme shown in Figure 11.5. The compression function is based on block cipher W which is modified form of AES. Whirlpool has also been adopted by the International Organization for Standardization (ISO) and the International Electrotechnical Commission (IEC) as part of the joint ISO/IEC 10118-3 international standard. Basic features of Whirlpool are listed below.

- Whirlpool takes a message of any length less than 2^{256} bits.
- The block cipher W is modified form of AES to suite the requirements of hash function. It has block size and cipher key size of 512 bits and returns a 512-bit message digest.
- The last block of the message is suffixed with padding bits and 256-bit length field (Figure 11.8). The padding bits are 1 followed by sufficient number of 0s to make block of 512 bits. The length field specifies the message size in number of bits.
- The initialization vector required as the key for first stage is all 0s (Figure 11.8).

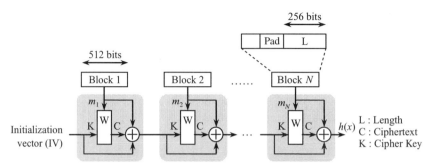

Figure 11.8 Structure of Whirlpool.

11.2.6 Block Cipher W of Whirlpool

As mentioned earlier, the block cipher W of Whirlpool is a modified form of AES. While the operation of the cipher is similar to AES, its major structural differences are given below. It is assumed that the reader is familiar with AES operation.

Number of rounds: W has 10 rounds. The block, the cipher key and the round keys are all 512 bits.

State array: The state array in W is 8×8 bytes matrix. A message block is mapped to the state array row-wise.

Structure of a round: Each round has four stages of transformation—SubBytes, ShiftColumns, MixRows and AddRoundKey [Figure 11.9(a)]. SubBytes is a nonlinear transformation and is carried out using S-box. ShiftColumns transformation is equivalent to ShiftRows of AES, the only difference being columns instead of rows are shifted. MixRows transformation is similar to MixColumns of AES. This transformation involves modulo (0x11D) multiplication of the state array with a constant matrix. AddRoundKey transformation is same as in AES.

The first round is preceded by an additional stage of round key addition as in AES. In all, 11 round keys are required.

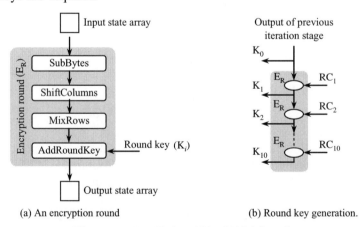

(a) An encryption round   (b) Round key generation.

Figure 11.9 Cipher W of Whirlpool.

Key expansion: Key expansion is entirely different in W. Ten round keys are generated using the output of previous hash iteration stage. The output is transformed by ten stages of 'encryption' using the round function (E_R) and ten round constants RC_i as keys [Figure 11.9(b)]. The round function (E_R) is same as shown in Figure 11.9(a).

Whirlpool is based on robust Miyaguchi–Preneel scheme and block cipher similar to AES which has been proved very resistant to attacks. The length of its message digest is 512 bits which is same as that of SHA-512. It is expected that Whirlpool should be highly collision resistant with its 512-bit digest. Hardware implementation of Whirlpool requires more resources than SHA-512.

11.3   MESSAGE AUTHENTICATION CODE (MAC)

The hash functions described earlier provide message integrity check alone. For data-origin authentication, the digest requires to be further encrypted by the source using the symmetric key or the private key. We describe in this section another class of hash functions which do not require additional encryption stage for source authentication. These hash functions are keyed-hash functions, i.e., the hash algorithm requires a secret key as input. The digest is called Message Authentication Code (MAC) and the keyed-hash function is called MAC algorithm.

Figure 11.10 illustrates the basic scheme. As shown, a secret key (K) is applied as second input to the hash function that generates MAC. MAC is appended to the message. The receiver uses the same key (K) and keyed hash function to generate MAC and compares it with the received MAC. Successful match verifies authenticity of the received message in respect of its origin and integrity. Note the subtle difference in this scheme.

- There is no separate encryption function. The MAC algorithm itself is parameterized by the secret key (K).
- MAC algorithm is symmetric-key function. The receiver uses the same key for re-computing MAC. Therefore, the issue of non-repudiation is not addressed by this scheme. Its use is limited to message integrity and data-origin authentication.

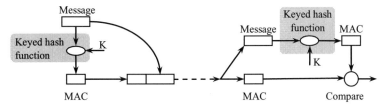

Figure 11.10   Message authentication using keyed hash function.

11.3.1   Properties of MAC Algorithm

We can define the basic required properties of the MAC algorithm $h(K, x)$ for any message x as follows:

Ease of computation: The MAC algorithm $h(K, x)$ given a key K and an input x is easy to compute.

Compression: The MAC algorithm maps an input x of arbitrary finite length to an output $h(K, x)$ of fixed length n.

Computation resistant: Given one or more message-MAC pairs, it is computationally infeasible to find MAC of a new message. This property also implies that the key K used for generating the MAC cannot be recovered from the given one or more message-MAC pairs.

Computation resistant property implies pre-image resistant, 2nd pre-image resistant and strong collision resistant properties when key K is unknown. Recovery of the MAC key by adversary is the most damaging attack, as it allows selective forgery, i.e., the adversary can generate valid MAC for a message of his choice. Key size of MAC is usually large to foil brute force attack on MAC key.

11.4 CONSTRUCTION OF MAC ALGORITHMS

MAC algorithms can be constructed using block ciphers or using iterated hash function. Therefore, we define two classes of MAC algorithms:

- MAC algorithms based on block ciphers.
- MAC algorithms based on iterated hash function.

We describe below these classes of MAC functions with a specific examples of algorithms used in the industry.

11.4.1 MAC Based on Block Ciphers

MAC algorithms based on block ciphers use CBC mode of operation and are referred to as CBC-MAC, in short. Figure 11.11 shows the basic scheme. The underlying block cipher can be DES, triple DES or AES. The message divided into blocks of b bits. The last block is suitably padded to get the required block size b. The block size and key size depend on the block cipher.

The chaining mechanism makes each encrypted output function of previous blocks. The initialization vector (IV) for the first block is all zeros. The last encrypted output constitutes MAC. Instead of limiting to MAC size to the block size of the underlying cipher, the output of last encryption may be truncated to required size of the MAC.

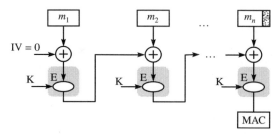

Figure 11.11 CBC mode of block cipher for MAC generation.

Security of CBC-MAC depends on the security of the underlying block cipher. This is true for fixed length messages. It is not secure for variable length messages. Let us see how.

- Suppose the adversary knows two valid message-MAC pairs, (m, h) and (m', h').
- He XORs the MAC h with the first block m'_1 of m' and generates a third message $m'' = m \parallel (h \oplus m'_1) \parallel m'_2 \parallel \ldots m'_N$. Note that the block m'_1 has been replaced with $(h \oplus m'_1)$.
- When CBC-MAC algorithm is used on m'', the last block of prefixed message m generates encryption output h, which is XORed with the next block $(h \oplus m'_1)$ in the following stage. The output of XOR operation is $(h \oplus m'_1) \oplus h = m'_1$, which has no contribution to the MAC from the blocks of the first message m. Hence the resulting MAC value of m'' is also h'.

The adversary is, thus, successful in generating third valid message-MAC pair (m'', h'). This attack is possible only when the message length is variable.

This security weakness can be addressed in two ways:

(a) Prepending the message with a length block.
(b) Encrypting the last block.

The first solution may not be viable, if length of the message is not known in advance. The second solution involves another stage of encryption on the last block of the message using a different key. We will see how this solution is implemented in CMAC algorithm described in Section 11.4.4.

11.4.2 MAC Based on Iterated Hash Function

Motivations for constructing MAC using iterated hash function are twofold. Hash functions such as MD5, SHA-1 and SHA-2 generally execute faster in software than block ciphers, and their library codes for these hash functions are readily available. Since these hash functions are unkeyed functions, the secret key is included as part of input message. The basic scheme shown in Figure 11.12 works as under:

- Alice concatenates a secret key (K) shared with Bob to the message (m) and computes MAC using an iterated hash algorithm. The secret key can be prefixed or suffixed to the message. She sends the message m and the MAC value to Bob. Note that the key is not sent with the message.
- Bob computes MAC value in the same manner and compares the received MAC with the computed MAC. If they are same, the origin and integrity of the message are established.

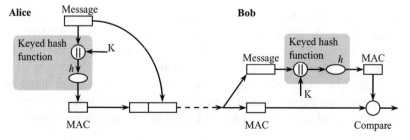

Figure 11.12 MAC using concatenated key.

It is assumed that an adversary cannot manipulate or originate a message without knowledge of the key. One-way property of the hash function precludes the feasibility recovering the key from the message-MAC pair. But there can be alternate ways of attack as described below. We consider the following two ways of constructing MAC algorithm based on iterated hash function.

(a) Prefixed key
(b) Suffixed key

Prefixed Key

Let us assume that key K is prefixed to the message m and MAC of the composite message $H = h(K\|m)$ is computed using an iterated hash function. This construction of message-MAC pair is vulnerable to modification by the adversary. He can append a message m' to the message m and can recompute the MAC as keyed hash $H' = h(K\|m\|m')$ without knowing key K (Figure 11.13). Recall from Figure 11.4 that each stage of compression requires the output of previous stage and the next message block. In this case output of the previous block is H. Thus $H' = h(K\|m\|m')$ is obtained simply by running the hash algorithm for m' with IV = H. The adversary replaces the original message-MAC pair (m, H) with $(m\|m', H')$. The receiver does not detect the modification.

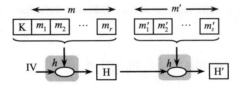

Figure 11.13   Attack on MAC with prefixed key.

Suffixed Key

Let us assume that key K is suffixed to the message m and MAC of the composite message $m\|K$ is computed using an iterated hash function $h(m\|K)$. This construction is vulnerable to the birthday attack. The adversary intercepts a message-MAC pair (m, H), where $H = h(m\|K)$. He finds a message m' such that $h(m) = h(m')$. Since $h(m) = h(m')$, then $h(m\|K) = h(m'\|K)$. This is so because the last hash iteration of the composite message in either case involves compression of the block containing key K using the output of the previous iteration stage, which is $h(m') = h(m)$.

Several variations to above methods have been proposed to avoid their flaws:

- Send only half the bits of the hash $h(K\|m)$ as the MAC with the message. The adversary cannot compute hash of the extended message with the truncated MAC.
- Concatenate the key at both the ends of the message. Prefixed key prevents birthday attack and suffixed key prevents extension of the message.
- Use hash function twice with key prefixed $h[K\|h(K\|m)]$. The prefixed key prevents birthday attack and the outer hash function makes it infeasible to extend the message by adding additional message blocks. HMAC standard, which we discuss next, is based on this scheme.

11.4.3 HMAC

HMAC algorithm is a NIST standard (FIPS 198-1) for generating message authentication code. It has also been issued as RFC 2104. It is used in the IPsec protocol at the Network layer, in SSL/TLS protocol at the Transport layer, and several other applications. HMAC as a hash function can be expressed as:

$$\text{HMAC} = h[k_2 \| h(k_1 \| m)]$$

where

- m is the message consisting of blocks $m_1, m_2, \ldots, m_N$, each having size of b bits. The last block is padded to get the required block size of b bits.
- h is an embedded cryptographic hash function. MD5 or SHA-1, SHA-2 algorithms can be used as the hash function.
- keys k_1 and k_2 are generated from the shared secret key K padded with zeros on the left to the block size b.

k_1 = K $\oplus$ ipad, ipad = 0x363636...36 (Hexadecimal)
k_2 = K $\oplus$ opad, opad = 0x5c5c5c...5c (Hexadecimal)

Size of ipad and opad constants is equal to the block size b. Binary representation of ipad and opad reveals that these constants have one half of the bits as 1. Thus ipad and opad flip one half of the bits of the secret key K.

The structure the HMAC algorithm is shown in Figure 11.14.

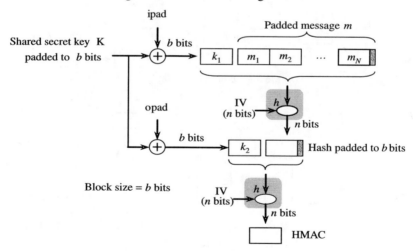

Figure 11.14 Structure of HMAC.

Security of HMAC is to be considered from the following two angles:

- Collision resistance
- Possibility of modifying a message by prefixing or suffixing additional message block

HMAC uses MD5, SHA-1 or SHA-2 as hash function. Therefore, it is as secure as these hash functions from the collision resistance angle. Being a nested function, prefixing or suffixing additional message block is not possible.

11.4.4 CMAC

CMAC is standardized by NIST in its special publication 800-38B. CMAC is abbreviation of cipher-based message authentication code. The underlying cipher can be 3DES or AES. Figure 11.15 depicts the block schematic of the algorithm. It differs from the basic scheme (Figure 11.11) in the following respects:

- The encryption of last block has additional keys, called sub-keys k_1 (or k_2). If the length of the message is multiple of block size, k_1 is used. k_2 is used when the message length is not multiple of block size and the message requires to be padded. Padding bits consist of 1 followed by as many 0s as necessary to make the final block of the required size. The sub-keys k_1 and k_2 are computed as follows:
  - Encrypt a block of 0s using key K and the underlying block cipher.
  - Multiply the encrypted output by polynomial x, if the message does not require padding. The multiplication is carried out in $GF(2^b)$. If the block size is b, irreducible polynomial of degree b is used for multiplication. The result of multiplication is k_1. k_2 is computed in similar manner except that the multiplying polynomial is x^2.
- Leftmost t bits of the encrypted output are used as MAC of size t.

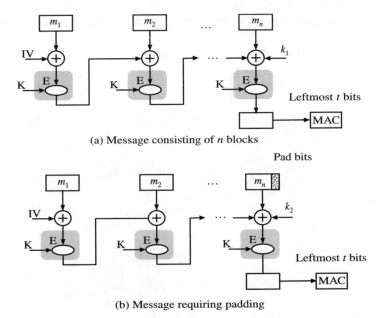

(a) Message consisting of n blocks

(b) Message requiring padding

Figure 11.15 Structure of CMAC.

11.5 SUMMING UP

In this chapter, we covered message authentication aspect of security. We started with the basic schemes for message integrity and data-origin verification using a hash function. After this brief introduction, we examined the cryptographic hash functions used for message integrity verification in detail.

- The desired properties of cryptographic hash functions are one-way, weak collision resistant (2nd pre-image resistant), strong collision resistant and computationally easy implementation.
- Since hash function is many-to-one relation, there is always some probability of finding two messages with same digest or finding a message that has a given digest.
- Cryptographically secure hash functions are iterative processes which can hash series of message blocks into a fixed size digest. Hash functions can be customized functions, or they can be based on block-ciphers.
- MD5 and SHA are examples of customized hash functions. The current version of Secure Hash Algorithm is SHA-512. It produces hash value of 512 bits in 80 iterative steps using block-size of 1024 bits.
- Whirlpool is a block cipher based hash function. Its compression function is based on modified form of AES. It generates 512-bit message digest.
- If data origin verification is also required apart from message integrity, we use keyed hash function. The digest generated using keyed hash function is called MAC (Message Authentication Code). MAC algorithms are based on block ciphers or iterated hash functions.
- CMAC is a standard block cipher based MAC. The underlying cipher can be 3DES or AES. HMAC, another NIST standard, is a based on MD5 or SHA-1, SHA-2 hash algorithms.

We will see many applications of message authentication algorithms in the later chapters of this book.

Key Terms		
Birthday problems	MAC	SHA-1, SHA-2
CBC-MAC	MD5	Strong collision resistant
CMAC	Merkle's structure	Weak collision resistant
Message digest	Miyaguchi–Preneel scheme	Whirlpool
Hash function	One-way hash function	
HMAC	Pre-image	

RECOMMENDED READING

Forouzan, Behrouz A., *Cryptography and Network Security*, Tata McGraw-Hill, New Delhi, 2007.

Hash-functions, Part 3: Dedicated Hash-functions, Information Technology—Security Techniques, International Organization for Standardization, Geneva, 2004.

Kaufman, C., Perlman, R. and Spenciner, M. *Network Security, Private Communication in a Public World*, Prentice-Hall of India, New Delhi, 2007.

Menezes, A., Oorschot, P. and Vanstone, S., *Handbook of Applied Cryptography*, CRC Press, FL, USA, 1997.

Recommendation for Block Cipher Modes of Operation: The CMAC Mode for Authentication, Special Publication 800-38B, NIST, Maryland, USA, 2005.

Schneier, B., *Applied Cryptography*, Wiley India, New Delhi, 2008.

Secure Hash Standard, Federal Information Processing Standards Publication#180-4.U.S. Department of Commerce, NIST, Maryland, USA, 2012.

Stallings, W., *Cryptography and Network Security*, Prentice-Hall of India, New Delhi, 2008.

Stamp, M., *Information Security, Principles and Practice*, John Wiley & Sons, NJ, USA, 2011.

Stinson, D., *Cryptography: Theory and Practice*, CRC Press, FL, USA, 2006.

Trappe, W., Washington, L., *Introduction to Cryptography and Coding Theory*, Prentice Hall, NJ, USA, 2006.

Vaudenay, S., *A Classical Introduction to Cryptography*, Springer, NY, USA, 2006.

(PROBLEMS)

1. If hash function is $h(m) = 5\ m^2 \bmod 9$, compute the digest of the following messages:
   (a) $m = 16$
   (b) $m = 20$
   (c) $m = 786$

2. If a is an integer, p is a prime number that does not divide a, and the hash function $h(x) = a^x \bmod p$, explain why $h(x)$ is not a good cryptographic hash function.

3. If $n = pq$ be the product of two distinct large primes p and a; is the hash function $h(x) = x^2 \bmod n$ collision free?

4. If $h(x) = B_1 \oplus B_2 \ldots \oplus B_n$, where B_i, $1 \le i \le n$ is an 8-bit byte; is $h(x)$
   (a) pre-image resistant?
   (b) 2nd pre-image resistant?
   (c) strong collision resistant?

5. A hash function is defined as $h = (K + \Sigma a_i) \bmod n$ where $a_1, a_2, \ldots, a_N$ are integers constituting a message m, K is a constant, and n is a predefined composite integer.
   (a) Determine h, if $K = 10$, $m = [23, 38, 10, 61, 40]$, $n = 100$.
   (b) Is function $h = (K + \Sigma a_i) \bmod n$ pre-image resistant, 2nd pre-image resistant and strong collision resistant?

6. A hash function is defined as $h = (\Sigma a_i^2) \bmod n$ where $a_1, a_2, \ldots, a_N$ are integers constituting a message m and n is a predefined composite integer with known factors.
   (a) Calculate h, if $m = [3, 8, 0, 6, 20]$, $n = 100$.
   (b) Is function $h = (\Sigma a_i^2) \bmod n$ pre-image resistant, 2nd pre-image resistant and strong collision resistant?

7. Assume that all months have 30 days. Determine the average number of attempts required to find
   (a) a person with the birth date 15th?
   (b) a person born in month of March?
   (c) two persons having same birth date?
   (d) two persons born in the same year after 1950 and before 2001?

8. What is the probability that a family of four persons does not have their birthdays in the same month? Assume all the months are equally probable.

9. How many padding bits are added to a message having 4896 bits, if the hash function is
   (a) SHA-512?
   (b) Whirlpool?

10. Davies and Price suggested the following hash code for a message $m = m_1\|m_2\|....\| m_N$, where m_i is a block of the message.

$$h_i = h_{i-1} \oplus E(h_{i-1}, m_i)$$

$E(m_i, h_{i-1})$ is encryption of h_{i-1} using m_i as the key. The iteration is carried out with initial value h_0 and using all the message blocks to get the message digest $h = h_N$. We assume the DES is used as encryption algorithm. If $h(m, h_0)$ represents hash of m with initial value h_0, show that

$$h(m, h_0) = h(m', \overline{h}_0), \text{ where } m' = \overline{m}_1\|m_2\|...\|m_N$$

(*Hint:* Use complement property of DES, i.e., if $c = E(K, p)$, then $\overline{c} = E(\overline{K}, \overline{p})$.)

11. Meyer and Matyas hash scheme is similar to Davies and Price scheme given in Problem 10. The hash function is defined as given below:

$$h_i = m_i \oplus E(m_i, h_{i-1})$$

Show that $h(m, h_0) = h(m', \overline{h}_0)$, where $m' = \overline{m}_1\|m_2\|...\|m_N$

12. Can we construct a multiple-round block cipher using a one-way keyed hash function? Justify. (*Hint:* Use Feistal structure.)

13. CBC-MAC of a message m having only one block is S. What is the CBC-MAC of two block message $[m, m\oplus S]$?

14. Suppose $h_1(x)$ and $h_2(x)$ are hash functions with the same length output strings. You are told that one of them is strongly collision-free, but you do not know which. Use them to construct a hash function $h(x)$ that is definitely strongly collision-free, and prove that fact. (*Hint:* Let $h(x) = h_1(x)\|h_2(x)$ and prove by contradiction, i.e., assume $h(x)$ is not collision free.)

12

Digital Signature

S ignature on a document establishes the signer's ownership of the contents of the document. Messages exchanged over network also need to be signed by the sender in many applications. Signature on the message establishes its authenticity and ownership. Recall that message authentication using asymmetric-key cryptography covers all the three authentication aspects, message integrity, data-origin authentication, and non-repudiation. A message encrypted with the private key of the sender, in fact, is equivalent to a signed document. We expand this concept to digital signatures in this chapter. We begin this chapter with the required characteristics of digital signatures and differentiate two categories of digital signatures, message transforming and appended signatures. After a brief overview of possible attacks on digital signatures, we study four important digital signature schemes, RSA digital signature, ElGamaal digital signature, Digital Signature Algorithm (DSA), and elliptic curve digital signature. We illustrate the algorithms with examples and analyze their security aspects. Before closing the chapter, we discuss implementation and applications of digital signatures.

12.1 CONCEPT OF SIGNATURE

We are familiar with handwritten signature on a document. A signature is a symbol owned and used exclusively by its owner. When it is put on a document, the document acquires the following characteristics:

- The recipient of the document is convinced that the signer accepts the contents of the document and the signer cannot repudiate its contents later.
- The signer has the confidence that he can readily identify the document he signed. He has the assurance that the document cannot be substituted or altered in any manner.
- The signer also puts the date below his signature as a time stamp so that the document may not misconstrued as having been signed earlier or later.
- The signed document is accepted by third party for adjudication, if there is dispute.

Other less apparent characteristics of the conventional signed document are as follows:

- The paper carrying the written content and the signature is the binding medium between the two. The signature cannot be lifted from one document and put on another document.

- Copy of a signed document can usually be distinguished from the original signed document.

12.1.1 Digital Signature

There is need for the concept of signature in the computing environment also. When Alice sends a message to Bob, disputes can arise between Alice and Bob in several ways.

- Alice can deny having sent the message or she can claim that the contents of the message she sent have been altered.
- Bob can create a fraudulent message in several ways:
  - He can alter a message received from Alice and can claim that the altered message is the one that came from Alice.
  - He can forge a message, and claim that it came from Alice.
  - He can produce an expired or out of context signed message of Alice.

Message authentication code (MAC), we studied in the last chapter, cannot be used as digital signature because it is based on a shared secret between the sender and receiver. It cannot resolve the disputes between them. MAC is suitable only for protection against attacks by the third party. Therefore, we would like to have a scheme for signing the messages that provides all the three following services:

- Message integrity verification
- Data-origin authentication
- Non-repudiation

The digital signature must have the following characteristics to serve its intended purpose:

(a) Digital signature must depend on the content of the message so that the content could be verified using the signature.
(b) Digital signature must bear identity of the signer based on some secret known only to the signer. This requirement ensures that
  - no one else can forge a signature
  - the signer cannot disown his signature later
(c) Digital signature should be verifiable by all without using the signer's secret.
(d) The signature algorithm must somehow 'bind' the signature to the message.
(e) Digital signature should bear the context (e.g. time stamp, session id, etc.) to prevent a signed digital message from being misused.
(f) Digital signature should be easy to compute and verify.

The digital signature schemes are based on use of asymmetric keys. The signing algorithm requires the private key of the signer to produce signed message. Use of private key meets the requirement (b) above. The receiver uses the corresponding public key for signature verification. Use of public key for verification meets requirement (c).

There can be two alternative approaches to generating signed messages.

- The signed message is a transformation of the original message. The verification algorithm recovers the original message. We shall call this approach message transforming digital signature scheme.[1]
- The signed message consists of two parts, the original message and the signature, i.e., the signature is appended to the message. We shall call this approach as appended digital signature scheme.[2]

12.2   MESSAGE TRANSFORMING DIGITAL SIGNATURE SCHEME

Message transforming digital signature approach encrypts the original message using the private key (Figure 12.1). The signature verification algorithm recovers the message using the public key.

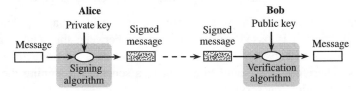

Figure 12.1   Message transforming digital signature.

For example, Alice can use RSA encryption algorithm and her private key to produce signed message. Encryption of the message using the private key does not impart confidentiality to the message. The message can be readily recovered by anyone using Alice's public key. By using her private key, Alice implants her signature on the message. No one other than Alice can generate such signed message. Bob decrypts the signed message using RSA algorithm and Alice's public key to recover the original message. Recovery of the original message using Alice's public key implies successful signature verification.

12.2.1   Redundancy Function

The basic message transforming digital signature scheme has a structural weakness. It is prone to forgery and attack.

- The forger chooses a signed message m', applies verification algorithm to m' using Alice's public key to get m. $\{m, m'\}$ constitutes a valid pair of unsigned message (m) and signed message (m'), though m may not be a meaningful message.
- An adversary alters the signed message from Alice to Bob without decrypting the message. Bob decrypts the altered message. On decryption, the altered message may not be meaningful, but Bob being a software entity cannot decide so.

---

1. Message transforming digital signature scheme is often referred to as 'digital signature scheme with message recovery' scheme.
2. Appended digital signature scheme is often referred to as 'digital signature scheme with appendix'.

These weaknesses can be overcome by applying a predefined redundancy function $R(m)$ to the original message m before signing it. The redundancy function R gives a structure to the message. The signature verification includes verification of the message structure as well. The original message is recovered by applying inverse redundancy function R^{-1} to the output of verification algorithm.

Let us understand this with an example.

- Alice concatenates the message m to itself and signs the concatenated message $m\|m$. She sends the signed concatenated message to Bob.
- Bob uses the verification algorithm with the public key of Alice on the received message. If and only if the output of verification algorithm is in the form $m\|m$, the verification is declared successful.
- Bob recovers the original message m from $m\|m$.

The redundancy function is so designed that the forger cannot find a signed message which on application of verification algorithm generates a message with the required redundancy. The redundancy function R and its inverse R^{-1} are publicly known. There are international standards for the redundancy function.[3]

Two basic limitations of message transforming digital signature are given below:

- The asymmetric key algorithms are slow when used on long messages. The message transforming digital signature scheme is useful for short messages of fixed length.
- The original message is not readily available to the receiver. When required, it is to be recovered from the signed message every time using the verification algorithm and the public key. One alternative is to store the recovered message along with the signed message. But the storage overhead is doubled.

12.3 APPENDED DIGITAL SIGNATURE

In appended digital signature schemes, digest of the message is signed instead of the message (Figure 12.2). The signed digest h' is appended to the message as digital signature. The verification algorithm recovers the original digest from the signed hash h' using the public key and compares the recovered digest with the digest h of the received message. If the two digests are same, the signature verification is declared successful.

Appended digital signature schemes are made resistant to forgery by choosing one-way and collision resistant hash function. An adversary needs to go through the following steps to forge a digital signature:

(a) Choose a signed digest h'.
(b) Apply verification algorithm with the public key on h' to get unsigned digest h.
(c) Find a message m that has digest h.

---

3. ISO/IEC9796, Digital Signature Scheme Giving Message Recovery, Information Technology—Security Techniques, International Organization for Standardization, Geneva, 1991.

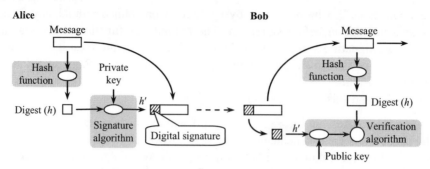

Figure 12.2   Appended digital signature.

The last step (c) is difficult for the forger because the hash function is one way. Also, given a signed message pair {m, h'}, the forger cannot substitute an alternative message in place of m since the hash function is collision resistant.

Other benefits of this approach are as follows:

- Since the digest to be signed has fixed size, computationally efficient and secure signing algorithms can be designed.
- If Bob decides to store the message, he needs to save the message along with its signed digest. Storage overhead of signed digest is a much smaller.
- The original message is always readily available.

12.4   ATTACKS ON DIGITAL SIGNATURE

The goal of an adversary is to forge digital signature which will be accepted as signature of some other entity. He does it without knowledge of the private key of the attacked entity. There are three types of attacks on digital signature:

Key-only attack: The adversary has access to the public key of Alice who generates signed messages.

Known-message attack: The adversary has access to one or more valid message-signature pairs. He wants to forge a valid message-signature pair using this information.

Chosen-message attack: The adversary creates two messages having same digest. He chooses the message that Alice will readily sign and gets signed digest from her. He appends the signed digest to the message he had created.

If the adversary is successful in his attack, he creates forged signed messages. Forgery can be classified into two types: existential forgery and selective forgery.

Selective forgery: An adversary is able to create a valid signature for a particular message chosen by him.

Existential forgery: An adversary is able to forge a signature for a message, but he has little or no control over the message content. It may be meaningless message having no use for the adversary.

Digital signature schemes are designed taking into account the above possible attacks. Each scheme has its own set of vulnerabilities which the adversary tries to take advantage of. We discuss the following digital signature schemes in this chapter. We also examine the possible attacks on each of these schemes.

1. RSA digital signature
2. ELGamal digital signature
3. Elliptic curve digital signature
4. Digital Signature Algorithm (DSA)

12.5   RSA DIGITAL SIGNATURE

RSA algorithm for asymmetric-key encryption can be used both for message transforming digital signature and appended digital signature. We use the notation $\tilde{m}$ as the input to RSA algorithm to represent

- digest h of the message m in case of appended digital signature scheme, i.e., $\tilde{m} = h$.
- message with redundancy function $R(m)$ in case of message transforming digital signature, i.e., $\tilde{m} = R(m)$.

Let us understand the RSA digital signature scheme in its three stages.

Key Generation

The public key $\{e, n\}$ and the private key $\{d, n\}$ are computed as described in Chapter 7. Alice chooses

- two large prime numbers p and q, and computes $n = p \times q$.
- the public key exponent e which is coprime to $\phi(n) = (p - 1) \times (q - 1)$ and computes private key exponent d as multiplicative inverse of e modulo $\phi(n)$.

Her public key is $\{e, n\}$, and her private key is, $\{d, n\}$.

Signing

Alice constructs RSA digital signature s by encrypting $\tilde{m}$ using the private key $\{d, n\}$.

$$s = \tilde{m}^d \bmod n$$

She sends the digital signature s with her public key $\{e, n\}$ to Bob.

Verification

Bob decrypts the digital signature s using Alice's public key $\{e, n\}$ as given below.

$$x = s^e \bmod n$$

If the value (x) so obtained equals $\tilde{m}$, the verification of the signed message is successful.

The following trivial example illustrates the above process.

Example 1   Alice chooses RSA parameters $p = 7$, $q = 11$ and digitally signs the digest h of her message m. She sends her RSA public key, message m and the digital signature s to Bob who verifies the digital signature.

(a) Determine the Alice's public and private keys if the public key exponent $e = 7$.
(b) What is the value of the digital signature s if $h = 9$?
(c) How does Bob verify the signature?

Solution
(a) Alice computes $n = 7 \times 11 = 77$, $\phi(77) = 6 \times 10 = 60$ and determines her private key exponent $d = 7^{-1}$ mod $60 = 43$. Thus her public key is $\{7, 77\}$ and her private key is $\{43, 77\}$.
(b) RSA digital signature $s = 9^{43}$ mod $77 = 58$.
(c) Bob decrypts s using RSA public key of Alice $\{7, 77\}$ as $x = 58^7$ mod $77 = 9$. He computes digest of the message m also, which he gets as 9. Since the received digest and the computed digests are equal, the signature verification is successful.

12.5.1 Security of RSA Digital Signature

No serious attacks have yet been reported on RSA cryptosystem and as such RSA digital signature also considered very secure. Some possible attacks are given below:

Key-only attack: If an adversary is able to factor the modulus n used by Alice as common part of her public and private keys, the adversary can compute totient $\phi(n)$. Once $\phi(n)$ is known, private key d can be readily computed from public exponent e by solving $ed = 1$ mod $\phi(n)$. This constitutes total security breakdown. To guard against this, Alice must select p and q so that factoring n is a computationally infeasible task.

Known-message attack: The RSA algorithm has the following multiplicative property:

If $s_1 = \tilde{m}_1^d$ mod n

$s_2 = \tilde{m}_2^d$ mod n

then $s_1 s_2 = (\tilde{m}_1 \tilde{m}_2)^d$ mod n

In case of message transforming digital signature scheme, $s = s_1 s_2$ will be valid signature for message $\tilde{m} = \tilde{m}_1 \tilde{m}_2$. The adversary can use this property for forging a valid signed message by multiplying two intercepted signed messages. Judicious choice of redundancy function R provides protection against this existential forgery.

In case of appended digital signature, the one way and collision resistant properties of the hash function provide the needed protection against forgery. Even the multiplicative property of RSA is not of much help to adversary.

Chosen-message attack: This attack is also based on the multiplicative property of RSA algorithm. The adversary somehow manages to get Alice's signatures s_1 and s_2 on two chosen messages m_1 and m_2. He computes $s = s_1 s_2 \bmod n$ as the Alice's signature on $m_1 \times m_2$. Judicious choice of the redundancy function R and the hash function can prevent this attack.

12.6 ELGAMAL DIGITAL SIGNATURE

ElGamal digital signature algorithm that we describe in this section is used only as appended digital signature scheme. There are variants of this scheme that can be used as message transforming digital signature scheme[4]. ElGamal asymmetric-key encryption was described in Chapter 7. Recall that ElGamal encryption algorithm generates encrypted message and a hint having size of the message. ElGamal digital signature also consists of two parts: signature s and hint r.

The scheme described below is based on multiplicative group $G = \{Z_p^*, \times\}$. It can be generalized to any finite cyclic group where discrete logarithm problem is infeasible, e.g. $GF(p^n)$, $GF(2^n)$.

Key Generation

Alice chooses a large random prime p and a generator g of the multiplicative group $G = \{Z_p^*, \times\}$. She selects a private key d, $1 \leq d \leq (p - 2)$, and computes $g^d \bmod p$. Alice's public key is $\{p, g, g^d\}$.

Signing

Alice chooses a random number $k < (p - 1)$ and coprime to $(p - 1)$ so that k has its multiplicative inverse in Z_{p-1}^*. She computes the digital signature consisting of two parts, hint r and signature part s.

$$r = g^k \bmod p$$
$$s = (h - dr)\, k^{-1} \bmod (p - 1)$$

where h is the digest of the message to be signed. New value of k is used for each instance of signature generation so that even repetitive message generates a different signature every time.

Alice appends signature $\{r, s\}$ to the message m. She sends the appended message with her public key $\{p, g, g^d\}$ to Bob.

Verification

Verification of the digital signature requires the public key $\{p, g, g^d\}$, digital signature $\{r, s\}$ and hash h of the message m. Verification is a two-step process.

- Bob verifies that $1 \leq r \leq (p - 1)$.

---

4. For example Nyberg–Rueppel digital signature scheme.

- He computes v_1 and v_2 as given below:

$$v_1 = g^h \bmod p$$
$$v_2 = (g^d)^r r^s \bmod p$$

He accepts the signed message if and only if $v_1 = v_2$. This is so because

$$v_2 = (g^d)^r r^s \bmod p = g^{dr}(g^k)^s \bmod p = g^{dr + ks} \bmod p = g^{h \bmod (p-1)} = g^{h+i(p-1)} \bmod p \text{ for}$$
some integer i.

Since $g^{i(p-1)} \bmod p = 1$, we get $v_2 = g^h \bmod p = v_1$.

The following trivial example illustrates the abvoe process.

Example 2   ElGamal digital signature parameters are as follows:

- Public key $\{p, g, g^d\} = \{23, 5, 10\}$,
- Private key $d = 3$,
- Random number $k = 9$

Determine the hint r and the signature s if digest $h = 7$ and verify the digital signature so obtained.

Solution

$$r = g^k \bmod p = 5^9 \bmod 23 = 11$$

$$s = (h - dr)\, k^{-1} \bmod (p - 1) = (7 - 3 \times 11) \times 5 \bmod 22 = 2$$

For verification, we compute v_1 and v_2 as given below:

$$v_1 = g^h \bmod p = 5^7 \bmod 23 = 17$$
$$v_2 = (g^d)^r r^s \bmod p = 10^{11} \times 11^2 \bmod 23 = 17$$

Since $v_1 = v_2$, the verification is successful.

12.6.1   Security of ElGamal Digital Signature

Selective forgery is very difficult to execute in ElGamal digital signature scheme. Private key can be attacked, if Alice repeats the use of same random number k for generating digital signature. Some existential forgery attacks have been reported, but these are inconsequential.

Key-only attack: The goal of an adversary is to find the hint r and signature s for a message m of his choice. He has access to Allice's public key $\{p, g, g^d\}$. He chooses a value for hint r. Then he must find s that meets verification condition $g^h \bmod p = (g^d)^r r^s \bmod p$, where h is digest of the message. s can be calculated from this condition as given below.

$$s = \log_r [g^h (g^d)^{-r}] \bmod p$$

This is a very difficult discrete logarithmic problem. If the adversary chooses s, calculating r that meets the verification condition is even harder. Thus selective forgery is difficult to execute.

Attack on private key: The signer must be careful to choose a different k for each signature and keep k secret. Otherwise, an adversary can deduce the private key d of the signer. Suppose two messages m_1 and m_2, having digests h_1 and h_2 respectively, are sent with signatures $\{r, s_1\}$ and $\{r, s_2\}$ computed using the same value of k. The adversary notices that the value of hint r is same for the two signatures; and concludes that the signatures must be based on the same value of k. He computes k as given below:

$$s_1 = (h_1 - dr) \ k^{-1} \bmod (p - 1)$$
$$s_2 = (h_2 - dr) \ k^{-1} \bmod (p - 1)$$
$$s_1 - s_2 = (h_1 - h_2) \ k^{-1} \bmod (p - 1)$$
$$k = (s_1 - s_2)^{-1} \ (h_1 - h_2) \bmod (p - 1)$$

Knowing k, private key d can be easily computed from the equation of digital signature s.

$$dr = (h - sk) \bmod (p - 1)$$

There can be multiple values of d that satisfy the above equation. To choose the correct value of d, each value of d is verified by computing $g^d \bmod p$ which should match the value given in the public key.

Example 3 Two signed messages having digests $h_1 = 7$ and $h_2 = 4$ have the following ElGamal signature parameters:

ElGamal public key	$\{p, g, g^d\} = \{23, 5, 10\}$
Signatures	$s_1 = 2, s_2 = 9$
Hint	$r = 11$

Determine the private key d of the sender.

Solution

$$k = (s_1 - s_2)^{-1} \times (h_1 - h_2) \bmod (p - 1) = (2 - 9)^{-1} \times (7 - 4) \bmod 22 = 9$$

$$dr = 11a = (h - sk) \bmod (p - 1) = (7 - 2 \times 9) \bmod 22 = 11 \bmod 22.$$

Private key d cannot be 1 since $g^d = 10$. The next value of private key is $d = 3$, which is the right value since $g^d = 5^3 \bmod 23 = 10$.

12.7 DIGITAL SIGNATURE ALGORITHM (DSA)

Digital Signature Algorithm (DSA) was proposed in 1991 and adopted as Digital Signature Standard (DSS) by NIST in 1993 and published as FIPS 186. DSA was the first digital signature scheme accepted as legally binding by a government. It is a variant of ElGamal digital signature scheme. It exploits small subgroups in Z_p^* in order to decrease the size of signatures. It is an appended digital signature scheme.

Key Generation

Alice chooses
- two primes p and q. p has length from 512 to 1024 bits in multiple of 64 bits. q is 160 bits long and divides $p - 1$.
- a generator g ($g > 1$) of multiplicative order q in Z^*_p as $g = a^{(p-1)/q} \bmod p$ where a is any integer, $1 < a < p - 1$. g is generator of the unique cyclic group of order q in Z^*_p. Commonly $a = 2$ is used.
- a private key d, $1 < d < q$.

She computes $g^d \bmod p$. Her public key is $\{p, q, g, g^d\}$.

Signing

To sign the message digest h, Alice chooses a random number k, $0 < k < q$ and computes the digital signature which consists of two parts, hint r and signature part s.

$$r = (g^k \bmod p) \bmod q$$
$$s = (h + dr)\, k^{-1} \bmod q$$

New value of k is used for each instance of signature generation. Since r and s are less than q, DSA signature and hint together are 320 bits in size.

Alice appends the digital signature $\{r, s\}$ to the message m. She sends the appended message with her public key $\{p, q, g, g^d\}$.

Verification

Bob verifies that $1 \leq r, s \leq (q - 1)$ and computes digest h of the message. He proceeds as follows to verify the digital signature. He computes u_1, u_2 and verifier v.

$$u_1 = hs^{-1} \bmod q$$
$$u_2 = rs^{-1} \bmod q$$
$$v = (g^{u_1}(g^d)^{u_2} \bmod p] \bmod q$$

He accepts the signed message if and only if $v = r$. This is so because

$$v = [(g^{hs^{-1} \bmod q}\, (g^d)^{rs^{-1} \bmod q})\, \bmod p] \bmod q = [g^{(h+dr)s^{-1} \bmod q} \bmod p] \bmod q$$
$$= [g^{k \bmod q} \bmod p] \bmod q = [g^k \bmod p] \bmod q = r$$

Let us understand the algorithm with the help of an example.

Key Generation: Alice chooses $p = 23$, $q = 11$, $a = 5$, and computes $g = 2$. Let us verify the value of g.

$$g^q \bmod p = 2^{11} \bmod 23 = 1$$
$$a^{p-1} \bmod p = 5^{22} \bmod 23 = 1$$
$$g^q \bmod p = a^{p-1} \bmod p$$

Alice chooses her private key $d = 8$. Thus

$$g^d \bmod p = 2^8 \bmod 23 = 3$$

Alice's public key is $\{p, q, g, g^d\} = \{23. 11, 2, 3\}$.

Signing: Alice computes digest of the message $h = 12$. She chooses a random number $k = 5$ and computes the hint r and signature s as given below.

$$r = (g^k \bmod p) \bmod q = (2^5 \bmod 23) \bmod 11 = 9$$

$$s = (h + dr)\, k^{-1} \bmod q = (12 + 8 \times 9) \times 5^{-1} \bmod 11 = 8$$

Alice sends the message with hint $r = 9$ and signature $s = 8$ to Bob.

Verification: Bob computes the digest $h = 12$ and verifier v as given below.

$$u_1 = hs^{-1} \bmod q = 12 \times 8^{-1} \bmod 11 = 12 \times 7 \bmod 11 = 7$$

$$u_2 = rs^{-1} \bmod q = 9 \times 8^{-1} \bmod 11 = 9 \times 7 \bmod 11 = 8$$

$$v = [2^7 \times 3^8 \bmod 23] \bmod 11 = 9$$

Bob accepts the signature since $v = r$.

12.7.1 Security of DSA

The security of DSA relies on two distinct, but related discrete logarithm problems. One is the discrete logarithm problem in Z_p^*. If p is a 1024-bit prime, then discrete logarithm problem takes an infeasible amount of computation time. The second discrete logarithm problem is to determine the private key d from given $g^d \bmod p$ where generator g has multiplicative order of q. For large p (e.g., 1024-bits), the best algorithm known for this problem is the Pollard rho method and takes about $\sqrt{(\pi q/2)}$ steps. If $q \approx 2^{160}$, an infeasible amount of computation is required. Thus DSA is not vulnerable to this attack. However, note that there are two primary security parameters for DSA, the size of p and the size of q. Increasing one without a corresponding increase in the other will not result in an effective increase in security. As of now, no serious security weakness of DSA has been found.

12.8 ELLIPTIC CURVE DIGITAL SIGNATURE

Elliptic curve cryptography was described in Chapter 10. Algorithm for elliptic curve digital signature is conceptually similar to ElGamal digital signature algorithm except that it is based on addition operation, while ElGamal digital signature is based on multiplication operation. Elliptic digital signature algorithm is used only as appended digital signature scheme.

Key Generation

Alice chooses

- an elliptic curve $E_p(a, b)$ with p a prime number.
- base point G of prime order q on the curve, the private key d, $1 \le d \le (q - 1)$, and computes point dG.

Her public key is $\{a, b, p, q, G, dG\}$ and the private key is d.

Signing

Alice chooses random $0 < k < q - 1$ and determines point kG having co-ordinates (x_1, y_1) on the elliptic curve. She computes the digital signature consisting of two parts, hint r and signature part s as given below.

$$r = x_1 \bmod q$$

$$s = (h + dr)\, k^{-1} \bmod q$$

where h is digest of the message m. New value of k is used for each instance of signature generation so that even repeated messages generate different signatures.

Alice appends the digital signature $\{r, s\}$ to the message m. She sends appended message and her public key $\{a, b, p, q, G, dG\}$ to Bob.

Verification

Bob verifies that $1 \le r, s \le (q - 1)$ and computes the digest h. He proceeds to compute verifier v as follows:

- Given the points G and dG on the elliptic curve, Bob determines points u_1G and $u_2(dG)$ on the elliptic curve, where $u_1 = hs^{-1} \bmod q$ and $u_2 = rs^{-1} \bmod q$.
- Bob determines point $(x_2, y_2) = u_1G + u_2(dG)$ and computes $v = x_2 \bmod q$

If $v = r$, he accepts signed message. This is so because, if the received signature s is valid,

$$s = (h + dr)\, k^{-1} \bmod q$$

$$k = (hs^{-1} + drs^{-1}) \bmod q = (u_1 + du_2) \bmod q$$

Therefore, point (x_2, y_2) determined by Bob is the point $u_1G + u_2(dG) = (u_1 + u_2d)G = kG$. In other words, point (x_2, y_2) coincides with the point (x_1, y_1), and therefore,

$$x_1 \bmod q = x_2 \bmod q \text{ or } r = v$$

The following example illustrates the above process explicitly. It is based on elliptic curve $E_{11}(1, 6)$ and base point at $G = (2, 7)$ on this curve. Elements of this curve with G as generator that were worked out in Chapter 10, are reproduced in Table 12.1 below for quick reference. Remember that Bob does not know d, the private key. He calculates the co-ordinates of the points using the equations of the elliptic curve.

TABLE 12.1   Group $E_{11}(1, 6)$ with the Generator $G = (2, 7)$

$G = (2, 7)$	$5G = (3, 6)$	$9G = (10, 9)$	$13G = O$
$2G = (5, 2)$	$6G = (7, 9)$	$10G = (8, 8)$	
$3G = (8, 3)$	$7G = (7, 2)$	$11G = (5, 9)$	
$4G = (10, 2)$	$8G = (3, 5)$	$12G = (2, 4)$	

Key Generation: Alice selects elliptic curve $E_{11}(1, 6)$, and base point $G = (2, 7)$ having prime order $q = 13$, and private key $d = 3$. She computes point $3G = (8, 3)$. Her public key of Alice is $\{a, b, p, q, G, dG\} = \{1, 6, 11, 13, (2, 7), (8, 3)\}$.

Signing: Alice has a message m for Bob. She computes digest h of the message as 6. She chooses random number $k = 7$ and determines $7G = (7, 2)$. She computes r and s as given below.

$$r = x_1 \bmod q = 7$$

$$s = (h + dr)\, k^{-1} \bmod q = (6 + 3 \times 7) \times 7^{-1} \bmod 13 = 1 \times 2 \bmod 13 = 2$$

She sends the message m, hint $r = 7$, signature $s = 2$ and her public key to Bob.

Verification: Bob verifies that $1 \leq r, s \leq 12$ and determines the digest h of the message m as 6. He computes u_1 and u_2.

$$u_1 = hs^{-1} \bmod q = 6 \times 7 \bmod 13 = 3$$

$$u_2 = rs^{-1} \bmod q = 7 \times 7 \bmod 13 = 10.$$

Bob determines point $u_1 G = 3G = (8, 3)$ and point $u_2(dG) = 10(dG) = (10, 2)$. He determines point $(x_2, y_2) = u_1 G + u_2(dG)$ as $(7, 2)$ and computes $v = x_2 \bmod q = 7$. Since $v = r$. Bob accepts the signature.

12.8.1   Security of Elliptic Curve Digital Signature

As explained the Chapter 10, the basis for the security of elliptic curve cryptography is intractability of the elliptic curve discrete logarithm problem. On the basis of Table 10.5 (Chapter 10), we can say if 10,000 computers each rated at 1,000 MIPS are available, and $n = 2^{160}$, then a single private key can be recovered from a single public key in 96,000 years. No significant weaknesses have been reported in elliptic curve digital signature till date.

12.9   VARIATIONS AND APPLICATIONS OF DIGITAL SIGNATURES

Digital signatures are used in number of applications some of which we will study in the later chapters of this text. These include TLS (Transport Layer Security) protocol, IPsec protocol and S/MIME protocol for email. Before we close this chapter, let us look at some important implementation related issues and variations of digital signatures.

12.9.1   Public-key Certificates

In our description of digital signature schemes, we have been assuming that Alice passes her public key to Bob for verification of her signature along with the message. The adversary can easily exploit this situation. He can pose as Alice and send a fraudulent message signed using his private key to Bob. He attaches his public key with the signed message. Bob finds the signature in order. To prevent such frauds, it is necessary to establish a trusted statutory certification authority, called CA, who issues public-key certificates to individual users. Every signed message must be accompanied with the sender's public-key certificate issued by the CA. The receiver uses the public-key given in the certificate for sender's signature verification. We will study public-key certificates and CAs in Chapter 15.

12.9.2   Time Stamped Digital Signature

An adversary can intercept signed message from Alice to Bob and he can replay the message later. This replay attack is countered by time stamping each message before generating its signature. Time stamping implies appending a time field to the message. The receiver accepts the messages that carry time stamp within a defined time window. Since there is possibility of the clocks of the sending and receiving systems not in synchronism, an alternative is to attach nonce and session-id to the message. A nonce is a random number used once. When Bob expects a message from Alice, he forwards her a nonce. Alice attaches the nonce to the message while computing the digital signature of her message to Bob. Bob ensures during signature verification that Alice's message is signed using the nonce. This avoids replay attacks of the adversary.

12.9.3   Blind Signature

The concept of blind digital signature was introduced by David Chaum. The signer puts his signature on a disguised message. The resulting blind signature can be verified using public key against the original undisguised message in usual manner. Typical application of blind signature is electronic voting system which requires that each ballot be certified by an election authority before it can be accepted for counting.

To understand this, let us consider a physical ballot system, where the election authority is required to sign blindly each ballot. The voter stamps his choice on the ballot and seals it in a carbon-paper lined envelope. The election authority signs the envelope and its signature gets transferred to the ballot. While counting the votes, each ballot is checked for the signature of the election authority.

In a blind signature scheme, the message is first disguised typically by combining it in some way with a random 'blinding factor'. The disguised message is passed to the signer who signs it using a normal signing algorithm for instance RSA or DSA. The signed message, along with the blinding factor, can be later verified using the signer's public key. In RSA blind signature schemes, it is even possible to remove the blinding factor from the signature before it is verified. Let us see how it is done.

RSA blind signature uses a blinding factor r^e mod n, where r is a random number coprime to n, and $\{e, n\}$ is the public key of the signer (Alice). Bob, who is author of the message m, disguises the message as m'.

$$m' = mr^e \bmod n$$

Bob gives m' to Alice for her signature. m' does not leak any information about m to Alice as r is a random number. Alice calculates the blind signature s' as given below and hands over the signed message to Bob.

$$s' = (m')^d \bmod n$$

Bob can now remove the blinding factor to calculate s, the valid RSA signature of Alice on m.

$$s = s'r^{-1} \bmod n$$

This is so because

$$s'r^{-1} \bmod n = (m')^d \, r^{-1} \bmod n = (mr^e)^d \, r^{-1} \bmod n = m^d \, r^{ed} r^{-1} \bmod n = m^d \, rr^{-1} \bmod n = s$$

There are several potential dangers in blind signatures. Bob could get Alice's signature on a message that may later hurt her.

12.10   SUMMING UP

Digital signature on a message provides message integrity assurance, data-origin authentication and non-repudiation services. In this chapter, we covered various digital signature schemes. There are two broad categories of signature schemes, message transforming digital signature and appended digital signature.

- The message transforming digital signature is formed by applying a redundancy $R(m)$ function to the original message m and then encrypting it using the private key. Redundancy function R foils the adversarial attempts of signature forgery. The message transforming digital signature schemes have limitation of small message size. Secondly, the original message is not readily available.
- In the appended digital signature scheme, digest of the message is signed using the private key. Appended digital signature scheme is made resistant to forgery by choosing one-way and collision resistant hash function. The major benefits of appended digital signature are (a) the secure and computationally efficient signature algorithm can be used on the fixed size digest (b) the appendix has small storage overhead (c) the original message is always readily available.
- The signature forgery is classified as selective forgery and existential forgery. The adversary controls the message content in selective forgery, while there is no such control in existential forgery.
- There are three categories of attacks on digital signature—key-only attack, known-message attack and chosen-message attack.
- Digital signature based on RSA algorithm is considered secure. The possible attacks are based on (a) factorization of RSA modulus n, and (b) multiplicative property of RSA.
- The ElGamal digital signature scheme generates a hint r and signature s. Selective forgery is very difficult in ElGamal digital signature scheme. Private key can be attacked, if the signer repeats the use of same random number for generating digital signature.
- Digital signature algorithm (DSA) is a variant of ElGamal digital signature scheme. Security of DSA relies on discrete logarithm problem in Z_p^*. For 1024-bit p, no serious security weakness of DSA has been found as of now.
- Elliptic curve digital signature is conceptually similar to ElGamal digital signature algorithm except that it is based on addition operation, while ElGamal digital signature is based on multiplication operation. No significant weaknesses have been reported in elliptic curve digital signature till date.

Digital signature algorithms described in this chapter find application in several protocols that we describe in the following chapters.

Key Terms		
Blind signature	ElGamal digital signature	Known-message attack
Certification authority (CA)	Elliptic curve digital signature	Selective forgery
Chosen-message attack	Existential forgery	Redundancy function
Digital signature standard (DSS)	Key-only attack	RSA digital signature

RECOMMENDED READING

ElGamal, T., *A Public-Key Cryptosystem and a Signature Scheme based on Discrete Logarithms*, IEEE Transactions on Information Theory, July 1985.

Elliptic Curve Cryptography, Standards for Efficient Cryptography, Certicom Research, Ontario, Canada, 2000.

FIPS 180–4, *Digital Signature Standard (DSS)*, Federal Information Processing Standards publication #186–2.U.S. Department of Commerce, NIST, Maryland, USA, 2013.

Forouzan, Behrouz A., *Cryptography and Network Security*, Tata McGraw-Hill, New Delhi, 2007.

ISO/IEC 9796, *Digital Signature Scheme Giving Message Recovery*, Information Technology— Security Techniques, International Organization for Standardization, Geneva, 1991.

Kaufman, C., Perlman, R. and Spenciner, M. *Network Security, Private Communication in a Public World*, Prentice-Hall of India, New Delhi, 2007.

Menezes, A., Oorschot, P. and Vanstone, S., *Handbook of Applied Cryptography*, CRC Press, FL, USA, 1997.

Rabin, M., *Digitalized Signatures*, Foundations of Secure Computation, DeMillo, R., et al. (Eds.), Academic Press, NY, USA, 1978.

Rivest, R., Shamir, A. and Adleman, L., A Method for Obtaining Digital Signatures and Public Key Cryptosystems, *Communications of the ACM*, February 1978.

Stallings, W., *Cryptography and Network Security*, Prentice-Hall of India, New Delhi, 2008.

Stamp, M., *Information Security, Principles and Practice*, John Wiley & Sons, NJ, USA, 2011.

Trappe, W., Washington, L., *Introduction to Cryptography and Coding Theory*, Prentice Hall, NJ, USA, 2006.

Vaudenay, S., *A Classical Introduction to Cryptography*, Springer, NJ, USA, 2006.

---(**PROBLEMS**)---

1. In an RSA digital signature scheme $p = 7$, $q = 11$, public key = 13.
   (a) Determine the private key.
   (b) Compute the digital signature on the digest $h = 8$.
   (c) Verify the signature using the public key.

2. Alice and Bob use message transforming digital signature based on RSA algorithm. They decide to concatenate the messages as $m\|m$ to give structure to their messages. Bob receives signed message 110 from Alice whose public key is $\{e, n\} = \{7, 187\}$. Should Bob accept the message? If so, what is the message?

3. Alice agrees to sign prime numbers only when she is approached by a third party. The adversary interested in selective forgery, wants to get Alice signature on $m = 30$. He approaches Alice to sign $m_1 = 2$, $m_2 = 3$, $m_3 = 5$. Alice signs the three messages. What is the value of Alice's valid signature on $m = 30$? Assume Alice uses message transforming RSA digital signature scheme having $p = 7$, $q = 11$, public key $= 13$. Verify the signature on $m = 30$.

4. Alice's public key is $\{7, 77\}$. The adversary notices that RSA encryption of 10 using Alice's public key is 10. He uses multiplicative property of RSA algorithm to forge message transforming Alice's signature as given below:
   - He takes Alice's signature on M = 20. The signed message is $S_{20} = 69$.
   - He splits M = 20 = 2 × 10. Therefore, $S_{20} = S_2 \times S_{10}$, where S_2 and S_{10} are Alice's signed messages on 2 and 10 respectively.
   - He computes S_{10} and determines forged signature S_2.

   Write the computations carried out by the adversary to get S_2. Given that $77 = 7 \times 11$, determine Alice's private key and verify the signature S_2.

5. Alice's RSA public key is $\{13, 77\}$. An adversary wants to exploit existential forgery. He wants the signed message to be 9. What is the unsigned message?

6. Compute the value of ElGamal signature $\{r, s\}$, and public key $\{p, g, g^d\}$ for the following system parameters:

$$p = 23, g = 5, \text{ private key } d = 3, h(m) = 6, k = 9$$

7. Bob receives ElGamal signature $\{r, s\} = \{11, 19\}$ with message having hash value $h = 6$ from Alice. Public key of Alice is $\{p, g, g^d\} = \{23, 5, 10\}$. Verify the signature.

8. An adversary somehow manages to get secret random number $k = 9$, which Alice uses to sign hash value $h = 7$. The ElGamal signature $\{r, s\}$ on the hash value is $\{11, 2\}$. If Alice's public key is $\{p, g, g^d\} = \{23, 5, 10\}$, compute her private key d.

9. Alice's ElGamal digital signature system has public key $\{p, g, g^d\} = \{23, 5, 4\}$. She signs message digests $h_1 = 3$, $h_2 = 6$ as $s_1 = 1$, $s_2 = 10$ respectively. The hint r for both these signatures is 10. She sends the $\{p, g, g^d\}$, h_1, h_2, s_1, s_2 and r to Bob. The adversary notices from the hint r that Alice has used same value of random number k for signing the digests and computes her private key. Show the computation carried out by him.

10. Suppose that the adversary has ElGamal signature $\{r, s\}$ on h. He chooses t coprime to $(p - 1)$ and computes another signature $\{r_1, s_1\}$ as given below.

$$r_1 = r^t \bmod p$$
$$s_1 = s\, r_1 t^{-1} r^{-1} \bmod (p - 1)$$

Show that $\{r_1, s_1\}$ is a valid ElGamal signature on $h_1 = h r_1 r^{-1} \bmod (p - 1)$.

11. The following are several variations of ElGamal signature part s and corresponding signature verification parameters v_1 and v_2. Show that $v_1 = v_2$ in each case.

    (a) $s = (h - kr)\, d^{-1} \bmod (p - 1)$ $v_1 = g^h \bmod p$ $v_2 = (g^d)^s\, r^r \bmod p$

    (b) $s = (dh + kr) \bmod (p - 1)$ $v_1 = g^s \bmod p$ $v_2 = (g^d)^h\, r^r \bmod p$

    (c) $s = (dr + kh) \bmod (p - 1)$ $v_1 = g^s \bmod p$ $v_2 = (g^d)^r\, r^h \bmod p$

12. Random number generator of ElGamal signature scheme gives $k = d$ which is Alice's private key. Alice does not note this and generates signature $\{r, s\}$ on hash h. An eavesdropper observing the message and the signature exploits the weakness of ElGamal to get the private key d. How does

    (a) the eavesdropper detect this incident?

    (b) the eavesdropper calculate d?

13. In a variation of ElGamal signature, Alice refines the signature part s as given below:

$$s = \{h - df(r)\}d^{-1} \bmod (p - 1)$$

where $f(x)$ is any function of x and $f(r) = f(x) \bmod (p - 1)$ for $x = r$. Alice declares her public key $\{p, g, g^d\}$ along with the function $f(x)$. For verification, the following parameters are defined:

$$v_1 = g^h \bmod p$$
$$v_2 = (g^d)^{f(r)}\, r^s \bmod p$$

Show that $v_1 = v_2$ when signature is valid.

14. In a DSA, $p = 23$, $q = 11$, $a = 2$, and $g = 6$.

    (a) Verify that $g = a^{(p - 1)/q}$.

    (b) If private key $d = 6$, compute the public key $\{p, q, g, g^d\}$.

    (c) If digest of the message $h = 9$ and random number $k = 7$, compute the hint r and signature s.

    (d) Verify the signature s using the public key $\{p, q, g, g^d\}$, digest $h = 9$ and hint r.

15. If the DSA algorithm results in value of the signature part $s = 0$, the signature is recomputed using a different value of random number k. How does the value $s = 0$ compromise the security of DSA?

16. An adversary somehow manages to get secret random number $k = 5$, which Alice uses to sign hash value $h = 10$. The DSA signature $\{r, s\}$ on the hash value is $\{2, 7\}$. If Alice's public key is $\{p, q, g, g^d\} = \{23, 11, 3, 2\}$, compute her private key d.

17. A digital signature system is based on elliptic curve $E_{11}(1, 6)$, base point $G = (2, 7)$ having prime order $q = 13$.

    (a) If private key $d = 5$, compute the public key $\{a, b, p, q, G, dG\}$.

    (b) If digest of the message $h = 6$ and random number $k = 7$, compute the hint r and signature s.

    (c) Verify the signature s using the public key, digest $h = 6$ and hint r.

Table 12.1 may be used for computation.

18. A variant of DSA defines the hint r and signature s as given below.

$$r = (g^k \bmod p) \bmod q$$

$$s = hk + dr \bmod q$$

All the parameters h, g, k, p, q and d are the same as defined for DSA in the chapter. The signature is verified by computing u_1, u_2 and verifier v as given below:

$$u_1 = sh^{-1} \bmod q$$

$$u_2 = rh^{-1} \bmod q$$

$$v = (g^{u_1} (g^d)^{-u_2} \bmod p] \bmod q$$

Compute the value of the verifier v for a valid signature.

19. Mr. Lazy Signer uses the same value of k and $r = (g^k \bmod p) \bmod q$ for generating DSA signature. The adversary notices this and recovers his private key using two signed messages from Mr Lazy Signer. Describe the line of attack of the adversary.

20. Alice uses ElGamal signature scheme with the public key $\{p, g, g^d\}$ and her private key d. The adversary somehow manages to bug her random number generator such that it produces numbers that are sequential, i.e., $k_{i+1} = k_i + 1$. Her signature on two consecutive messages m_1 and m_2 are $\{r_1, s_1\}$ and $\{r_2, s_2\}$ respectively. The adversary gets hold of these two signed messages and computes Alice's private key d. Describe the computation carried out by the adversary.

13

Entity Authentication

---

uthentication in cryptography refers to the process of verification of a message or an entity. Message authentication described in Chapter 11 dealt primarily with content integrity and data-origin of a message. In this chapter, our focus is on entity authentication, which refers to establishing identity of the entity that originates the messages. In entity authentication, a claimant entity proves its identity to a verifying entity using a password or through an interactive challenge-response exchange.

We begin this chapter with fixed and one-time password schemes and examine their vulnerability to attacks of an adversary. Then we move on to entity authentication schemes based on challenge-response exchange. We study challenge-response authentication using symmetric-key and public-key. Before we close the chapter, we introduce the concept of zero-knowledge proof and its application in entity authentication using Fiat–Shamir protocol.

The authentication mechanisms we discuss in this chapter are typically used for remote access to private networks through PSTN and/or the public Internet. The networking and authentication protocols, namely PPP, PAP, CHAP and L2TP, required for remote access are given in Appendix A3.

13.1 ENTITY AUTHENTICATION AND MESSAGE AUTHENTICATION

Entity authentication is a process by which the *claimant* entity proves its identity to the *verifier* entity. The claimant entity can be a person, a process, a client or a server. Entity authentication is done just before starting a session of message exchange. The claimant having proven its identity to the verifier is not required to re-authenticate himself for exchange of messages during the course of a session.

Note the subtle difference in entity authentication and message authentication. Message authentication refers to authentication of origin of the messsage and integrity of its content. Each message exchanged during the course of a session between two communicating entities is authenticated. MAC attached to a message assures the receiver of message integrity and its origin. Figure 13.1 shows a typical exchange of messages. The first exchange of messages (User-id, password) and (Accept/Reject) is the entity authentication. The rest of the messages are authenticated for integrity and data origin. We covered message authentication in Chapter 11. We will study methods of entity authentication in this chapter.

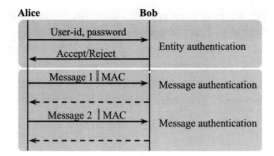

Figure 13.1 Entity authentication and message authentication.

13.1.1 Basis of Identification

Entity authentication techniques are based on broadly three kinds of identification proofs:

Something Known

The claimant produces a proof that he knows some secret. Examples include login passwords, Personal Identification Numbers (PINs) or private keys. In the last case, the claimant demonstrates his knowledge of private key without disclosing it to the verifier.

Something Possessed

This is typically a physical accessory of the claimant, which identifies him. Examples are passport, smart cards, etc.

Something Inherent

This category includes some inherent characteristic or involuntary action of the claimant which can be used for his identification. Examples of inherent physical characteristic for identification are finger prints, retinal pattern and facial features. Typical example of involuntary action is handwritten signature.

Our focus in this chapter is restricted to the first category of entity identification proofs, 'something known'.

13.2 PASSWORDS

The primary purpose of entity authentication is to control access to a resource on a local or remote computer system. The access rights are linked to identity of the user. Typically, Alice sends her user-id and her password to Bob. The password is used as corroborating evidence of the user's identity. Bob checks that it matches Alice's password available in his record and grants access. Password schemes can be broadly categorized as

- Fixed passwords schemes.
- One-time password schemes.

As the name suggests, the password remains same in fixed password schemes, unless it is changed voluntarily by Alice. Eavesdropping and subsequent replay of a password is a major security concern of the fixed-password schemes. One-time password is a password that can be used only once. A new password is dynamically generated, if the application so demands. One-time password schemes are safer from a passive adversary as a password becomes invalid after its use once. The next two sections describe fixed and one-time password schemes.

13.3   FIXED PASSWORDS

A fixed password, associated with a user is typically a string of 6 to 10 or more characters that serves as a shared secret between the user and the system. To gain access to a resource, Alice (claimant) sends her user-id as the claim of his identity and her password as the evidence supporting her claim of identity [Figure 13.2(a)]. The password is sent in clear text. Bob (verifier) verifies that

– the password matches the data it holds against the user-id, and
– the stated user-id is authorized to access the resource.

If verification of password is successful, and if Alice is authorized to access to the resource, the claimed identity is accepted for accessing the resource. There can be several approaches to implementing this basic password scheme for user identification. These approaches differ primarily in the way the password related information is stored by the verifier.

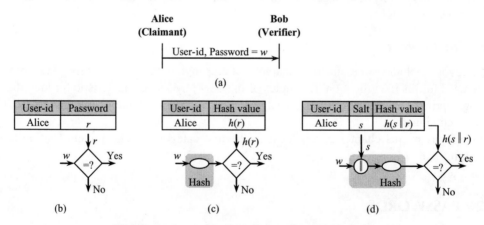

Figure 13.2   Authentication using passward.

13.3.1   Clear-text Password File

The most obvious approach is to store user passwords in clear text in a password file which is both read- and write-protected [Figure 13.2(b)]. Upon receipt of a password, Bob verifies the identity by comparing the received password (w) with the recorded password (r) against the claimed user-id. The drawback of this method is that the passwords are recorded in clear text in the file. If the adversary or any other user gets access to the file, all the passwords get exposed.

13.3.2 Hashed-password File

A more secure approach is to hash of the individual passwords using a one-way hash function. The password file now contains the hash value of the password instead of the password itself [Figure 13.2(c)]. When Alice sends her user-id and password (w), Bob computes the hash value $h(w)$ of the received password and verifies it against the stored hash value $h(r)$. If they match, the password is accepted.

The password file needs only be write-protected, since the hash values of the passwords are no longer secret. The one-way property of the hash function prevents computation of the password from its hash value. However, there is possibility of dictionary attack. The adversary creates a dictionary of all possible values of the passwords and their hash values. If the password is a 6-digit number, he needs to compute 999999 hash values. If he gets hold of the password file, he can determine the password that will work for each user-id.

Example 1 The password file of a system consists of hashed passwords. The passwords are alphanumeric (uppercase and lowercase letters, numerals) and are 9 characters long. The adversary gets hold of the password file. Determine the average number of tries required to decode a password.

Solution The possible number of 9 digits passwords constructed from set of 62 symbols (26 uppercase letters + 26 lowercase letters + 10 digits) is 62^9. Therefore, on average, $62^9/2$ = 6.8×10^{15} hash operations are required to get a matching hash value.

13.3.3 Salted-password File

The dictionary attack can be made less effective by augmenting each password with a t-bit random string (s) before applying the one-way hash function. The random string (s) is called 'salt'. The password file contains salt and hash value against each user-id [Figure 13.2(d)]. When Alice sends her password, the salt is appended to the received password and hash value of augmented string is computed. The result of computation is verified against the stored value. If they match, the password verification is declared successful.

The difficulty of exhaustive search on any particular user's password is unchanged by salting, since the salt is available in clear text in the password file. However, salting increases the complexity of a dictionary attack. Now, the dictionary contains 2^t variations of each trial password, implying thereby the dictionary becomes 2^t times larger. Also note that with salting, two users who choose the same password have different entries in the password file.

13.3.4 Attacks on Fixed Password Schemes

The fixed passwords schemes described above are vulnerable to the following attacks:

Eavesdropping and replay: Since the password is transmitted in cleartext, the adversary can copy it during its transmission from the user to the server. He can later replay the password for gaining access to the resource. In particular, the scheme is not secure when the public network is used for access to the server.

The password file containing password related information (passwords in cleartext, or their hash values) is also a security risk as mentioned earlier.

Exhaustive password search: An adversary can simply try all possible passwords in a systematic manner in hope that the correct password is found. This can be countered by ensuring passwords are chosen from a sufficiently large space and limiting the number of invalid attempts at each instance of access or in a given duration of time.

Password guessing: Most of the users select passwords from a small subset of the full password space. For examples, short passwords, dictionary words, proper names, lowercase strings are common as passwords. An adversary takes advantage of this fact by resorting to systematic password guessing rather than searching through the entire password space. Studies indicate that a large fraction of user-selected passwords are found in dictionaries of only 150000 words. The adversary tries all the words of an online list of words having the given number of characters and finds their hash values. He determines the list of valid passwords by comparing these values with the hash values in the password file. This attack is not generally successful at finding a particular user's password, but it may find many legitimate passwords.

13.4   ONE-TIME PASSWORD

A major security concern of fixed password scheme is eavesdropping and subsequent replay of the password. One-time passwords address this concern to some extent. In this scheme, each password can be used only once and is thus safe from passive adversaries. There are several schemes in this category.

13.4.1   Shared Lists of One-Time Passwords

The user and the system share a sequence of t secret passwords, distributed as a pre-shared list. Each password can be used only once. After its first time use, the password becomes invalid. The replay attack of the adversary is thus thwarted. The drawback of this scheme is maintenance of the shared list of passwords and synchronization of usage of passwords by the user and the system.

A variation of this scheme involves use of a challenge-password table and addresses the synchronization problem mentioned above. The user and the system share a table of challenge-password pairs. Each pair is valid for one-time use. The user sends his user-id, and the system responds with a challenge from a challenge-password table. The user sends the password associated with the challenge. The system verifies the received password against the sent challenge. The challenge-password pair is deleted from the table after single use.

13.4.2 Sequentially Updated One-Time Passwords

In this scheme, only a single secret password is shared initially. During authentication using password w_i, the user creates and transmits to the system a new password w_{i+1}, encrypted under a key derived from the password w_i. w_{i+1} is used as password for the next access. The replay attack of the adversary is thus thwarted. But if he guesses any of the passwords, he can find all the following passwords.

13.4.3 Lamport's One-time Password Scheme

In Lamport's one-time password scheme, a one-way function h is used to define the password sequence: $s, h(s), h(h(s)), \ldots, h^{t-1}(s)$, where

- h^i is the hash function h applied i times,
- s is a secret known to Alice,
- t is a fixed value (e.g., $t = 100$ or 1000) that defines the number of times authentication can be carried out. The password sequence is thereafter restarted with a new value of s.

The password w_i for the ith authentication session is $w_i = h^{t-i}(s)$. These passwords are used in reverse order, i.e., $h^{100}(s)$ is used after $h^{101}(s)$, so that an adversary having copied $h^{101}(s)$, cannot compute the next password $h^{100}(s)$, since the hash function is one way.

To initialize the system, Alice shares with Bob the following values in a secure manner:

- Number of times authentication is carried out, $t = 1000$ (say),
- Hash value $h^{1000}(s)$.

Figure 13.3 shows the basic operation of the scheme. To start with $i = 1$, therefore, Alice sends password $w_1 = h^{999}(s)$. The system verifies the received password after applying the hash function once to the received password, $h(w_1) = h^{1000}(s)$, which should match the available hash value in the Alice's record. If the verification is successful, the system updates the access record of Alice replacing

- the existing hash value with the password received from Alice and
- i by $i + 1$.

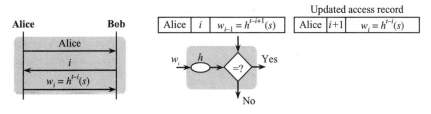

Figure 13.3 Lamport's one-time password scheme.

An enhancement to Lamport's hash is to add salt s' to the secret s. The first hash is now calculated over the concatenation $(s\|s')$. The benefits of adding salt are given below:

- Alice can have different salt values for access to multiple servers. Her secret s remains same.
- When $i = t$, Alice need not change s, she can configure a new value of the salt and convey it to Bob.
- Salt makes the dictionary attack more difficult for Bob.

Lamport's scheme has the following limitations:

- There is no mutual authentication. Alice does not authenticate Bob. Consider the following situation:
  - The adversary diverts the traffic between Alice and Bob to itself. He lets Alice authenticate herself to Bob by relaying their messages.
  - Entity authentication is followed by session key[1] establishment using, for example, Diffie–Hellman exchange. The adversary acts as man-in-the-middle during the session-key establishment.
  - He can, thereafter, monitor/manipulate the exchange of messages between Alice and Bob.
- Lamport's hash is vulnerable to large i attack. Suppose an adversary impersonates Bob and sends a large value of $i = 950$ while he knows that the current value of i is 100 (say) in Bob's database. Alice responds with $h^{50}(s)$ which the adversary intercepts. The adversary can, now, compute all the hash values from $h^{50}(s)$ onwards. He impersonates Alice and responds to Bob with $h^{900}(s)$ when he receives $i = 100$ from Bob. He can impersonate Alice for quite some time. Alice would not detect that someone is impersonating her unless she tracks the values of i she gets from Bob.

13.5   CHALLENGE-RESPONSE AUTHENTICATION

Authentication using password requires the claimant to produce his shared secret password before the verifier. Since the secret is to be revealed, the authentication process becomes susceptible to adversarial interception. The challenge-response approach to entity authentication that we describe in this section, requires the claimant to prove before the verifier that he (the claimant) knows a secret that uniquely belongs to him. The actual secret is not required to be produced. The secret can be the claimant's private key or a shared symmetric key. Figure 13.4 illustrates the basic challenge-response scheme.

  (a) The claimant sends his user-id to the verifier.
  (b) The verifier returns a challenge which consists of a time-variant parameter, e.g. a random number.
  (c) The claimant transforms the received random number into a proof of possessing the secret and returns it to the verifier.
  (d) The verifier checks that the claimant indeed knows the secret by verifying the response.

---

1. Session key is the shared symmetric-key to be used for encryption in the ensuing session.

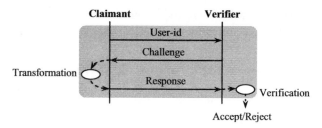

Figure 13.4   Challenge-response authentication.

The challenge is a time variant value, i.e., a different challenge is sent every time the claimant approaches the verifier for authentication. It can be a random number (called nonce[2]), or the time-stamp. Since the challenge is different for every instance of authentication, the replay attack by the adversary is futile.

Challenge-response authentication schemes are based on symmetric-key, public-key, and zero-knowledge identification protocols. We describe these schemes in the following sections.

13.6   SYMMETRIC-KEY CHALLENGE-RESPONSE AUTHENTICATION SCHEMES

Symmetric-key challenge-response authentication requires the claimant and the verifier to share a symmetric key. We assume that the two entities involved in authentication have already established the shared key. The claimant transforms of the challenge into authentication proof either by encrypting the challenge or by computing keyed-hash of the challenge using the symmetric-key. The response from the claimant is verified using the shared symmetric-key.

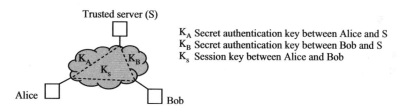

Figure 13.5   Centralized authentication.

Before we proceed further with the symmetric-key challenge-response schemes, it is to be noted that in a small closed system with limited number users, each user-pair can maintain a unique secret key for authentication. In a larger system, the authentication task is made part of centralized key distribution system (Figure 13.5). A trusted server S shares unique secret symmetric-key for authentication with every user. The server carries out two tasks:

(a) *Authentication*   The server authenticates the two users (Alice and Bob) who intend to communicate.

(b) *Key distribution*   The server allots them a temporary session key (K_s). The session key is used by Alice and Bob for exchanging encrypted messages between them.

---

2. Nonce is short form of 'number used once'.

Needham–Schroeder protocol and Kerberos protocol for symmetric key distribution are based on this approach. We describe these protocols in Chapter 14, Symmetric-key Distribution.

13.6.1   Challenge-Response Authentication Using Symmetric-key Encryption

In this case, the claimant proves his identity by encrypting the challenge using the symmetric-key. We consider the following three authentication cases:

(a) Unilateral authentication using a random number
(b) Unilateral authentication using time stamp
(c) Mutual authentication using random numbers

Unilateral Authentication Using a Random Number

As shown in Figure 13.6, Alice, the claimant, sends her user-id to Bob, the verifier. Bob sends a random number R_B as challenge to Alice. Alice responds with $E(K, \{R_B\})$. In this representation of encryption function, the second argument R_B within { } is encrypted using the first argument K, which is the symmetric-key. Bob decrypts the response and checks that his nonce R_B is returned by Alice. If verification is successful, he concludes that sender indeed possesses the symmetric-key K and thus must be Alice.

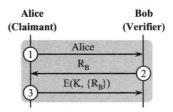

Figure 13.6   Unilateral authentication using random number.

Unilateral Authentication Using Timestamp

Timestamp may be used in place of random number for authentication. Instead of the verifier first sending the challenge, the claimant obtains time-stamp t_A from its host clock and encrypts it using the symmetric key (Figure 13.7).

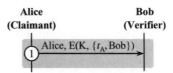

Figure 13.7   Unilateral authentication using timestamp.

Upon reception and decryption, Bob verifies that the timestamp t_A is acceptable. The received time stamp is valid provided the timestamp is within the acceptable time-window. Time-window accounts for the transit and processing time, plus clock skew between the claimant's and verifier's clocks.

The security of timestamp-based verification relies on use of a common time reference. This requires that host clocks of Alice and Bob be 'loosely synchronized' within a defined maximum skew. Time window must be sufficiently small to prevent replay of the claimant's message by the adversary. The identifier 'Bob' in the claimant's message is optional. It helps in two ways:

(a) If Alice shares the same secret key K with several servers, the adversary cannot use Alice's message for Bob for access to another server.

(b) It prevents the adversary from impersonating as Bob and opening a session with Alice. Consider that Alice sends the message to Bob without the identifier 'Bob' in it. The adversary intercepts the Alice's message and sends the message back to her immediately. Alice assumes Bob has initiated a new session and verifies her own message reflected by the adversary. With user-id part of encrypted message, Alice would realize immediately that the message is not meant for her and reject the message reflected by the adversary.

Mutual Authentication Using Random Numbers

To understand the nuances of mutual authentication, let us extend the unilateral authentication scheme shown in Figure 13.6 for mutual authentication as well. We assume that the same secret key is used for authentication in both the directions. For mutual authentication, Alice and Bob both send challenges to each other (Figure 13.8).

1. Alice sends her challenge R_A.
2. Bob sends his challenge R_B as well as his response $E(K, \{R_A\})$.
3. Alice verifies Bob and sends her response $E(K, \{R_B\})$.

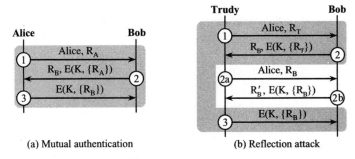

Figure 13.8 Mutual authentication and reflection attack.

This scheme is vulnerable to *reflection attack* of the adversary. Suppose Trudy, the adversary, impersonates Alice and initiates authentication as shown in Figure 13.8(b). Since she does not have the secret key for encrypting the Bob's challenge R_B, she makes Bob to encrypt his own challenge. Trudy proceeds as given below:

1. Trudy starts the authentication protocol with user-id of Alice and a challenge to R_T to Bob.
2. She receives the challenge R_B from Bob, but she cannot proceed further as she cannot encrypt the challenge R_B.
   (a) Trudy opens second session with Bob. This time she uses the challenge R_B received from Bob.
   (b) Bob sends his challenge R'_B and response $E(K, \{R_B\})$ to Trudy's challenge R_B.

3. Trudy completes the first session by sending $E(K, \{R_B\})$ back to Bob. She does not go any further with the second session. Her purpose for opening second session has been served.

There can be several ways of addressing susceptibility of the protocol to the reflection attack.

- Alice and Bob use different encryption keys for responding to the challenge. This will prevent Trudy from using $E(K, \{R_B\})$ of message 2a for her message 3 [Figure 13.8(b)].
- Alice and Bob use different set of numbers as challenges. For example, we may require Alice to use only even numbers and Bob to use odd numbers. Thus Trudy in Figure 13.8(b) cannot reflect the challenge R_B of Bob back to him. Bob would expect an even number from Alice.
- Alice and Bob include user-id in the encrypted response to the challenge. Message 2a in Figure 13.8(b) would become $R'_B, E(K, \{R_B, Alice\})$. Trudy cannot use Bob's response $E(K, \{R_B, Alice\})$ since Bob is expecting message 3 to be $E(K, \{R_B, Bob\})$.

Thus mutual authentication scheme depicted in Figure 13.8(a) is not secure. It is necessary to link the two unilateral authentications of one session to reduce vulnerability to the adversarial attacks. Figure 13.9 depicts such mutual authentication scheme.

1. Alice sends her user-id and challenge R_A to Bob.
2. Bob responds with $E(K, \{R_B, R_A\})$ which includes his challenge R_B. Alice gets Bob's challenge only if she has the secret key K.
3. Alice verifies the Bob's response to authenticate him and sends her response $E(K, \{R_A, R_B\})$ to Bob's challenge. Bob authenticates Alice's response by checking that both the random numbers R_A and R_B match their original values.

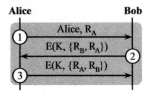

Figure 13.9 Linking of unilateral authentications for mutual authentication.

By incorporating both the challenges R_A and R_B into the encrypted responses, this scheme is protected from several attacks:

- ***Reflection attack***
  Reflection attack is thwarted as the adversary does not get Bob's challenge R_B in message 2. Trudy cannot generate message 1a of Figure 13.8.
- ***Chosen-plaintext attack***
  In chosen-plaintext attack, the adversary chooses plaintext and gets its encrypted with the goal of determining the secret key. In this case, the adversary impersonating as Alice would send chosen-text as R_A to Bob in message 1 to get it encrypted as $E(K, \{R_A\})$ by Bob. But his attempt rendered futile. Bob returns $E(K, \{R_B, R_A\})$ in place of $E(K, \{R_A\})$.

- *Masquerade*

  Note that the order of encryption of R_A and R_B in messages (2) and (3) is reversed. This prevents Trudy from impersonating as Alice. Due to reversed order of encryption, she will not be able to return the message (2) as message (3).

13.6.2 Challenge-Response Authentication Using Keyed Hash Function

Challenge-response mechanisms described in the last section can be implemented using one-way keyed hash function (MAC) in place of encryption algorithm. The verifier independently computes MAC and compares it with the MAC value received from the claimant. If they match, the claimant's authentication is accepted.

Figure 13.10 shows the challenge-response authentication protocols using keyed hash function $h(K, \{x\})$, where the first argument K is the key used in hash computation of the second argument x. In all the three cases shown below, the verifier must have all the fields of which the hash is computed. Therefore, the claimant supplies t_A in message 1 [Figure 13.10(b)] and R_B in message 2 [Figure 13.10(c)]. These fields are sent in clear text.

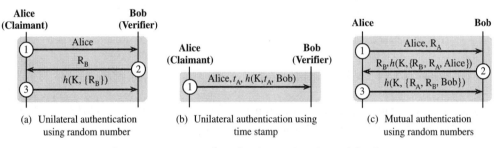

(a) Unilateral authentication using random number

(b) Unilateral authentication using time stamp

(c) Mutual authentication using random numbers

Figure 13.10 Authentication using keyed hash.

13.7 PUBLIC-KEY CHALLENGE-RESPONSE AUTHENTICATION SCHEMES

In the challenge-response authentication based on symmetric-key, the verifier maintains a database of shared secret keys of the users. The adversary can impersonate a legitimate user, if he gets access to the database. This vulnerability is avoided, if the authentication is based on public-key instead of the symmetric-key, since the user database is no longer secret, though it must be protected against unauthorized modification.

The challenge-response authentication using public-key can be done in two ways:

- (a) Authentication based on encrypted challenge
- (b) Authentication based on digital signature

13.7.1 Authentication Based on Encrypted Challenge

Bob (verifier) sends to Alice (claimant) a challenge encrypted using Alice's public key. Alice demonstrates knowledge of her private key by decrypting Bob's encrypted challenge. We consider the following two cases:

(a) Unilateral authentication
(b) Mutual authentication

Unilateral Authentication Based on Encrypted Challenge

Figure 13.11(a) shows the basic authentication scheme. Bob sends the challenge $E(K_{PA}, \{R_B\})$ which is random number R_B encrypted using Alice's public key K_{PA}. Alice decrypts the challenge and returns R_B to Bob, proving to Bob that she possesses the Alice's private key.

This scheme is vulnerable to chosen-ciphertext attack. The adversary could use the scheme to decrypt an encrypted message that was sent by someone to Alice and the adversary copied it. The adversary impersonating as Bob, sends the encrypted message as challenge to Alice, who returns decrypted message to the adversary.

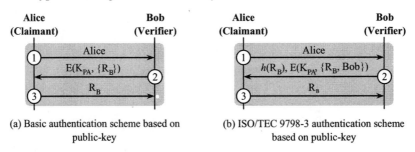

(a) Basic authentication scheme based on public-key

(b) ISO/TEC 9798-3 authentication scheme based on public-key

Figure 13.11 Authentication using public-key (Encrypted challenge).

Figure 13.11(b) shows the authentication scheme as specified in ISO/IEC 9798-3. It is protected against the chosen-ciphertext attack from adversary.

1. Alice sends her user-id.
   Bob chooses a random R_B, computes the evidence $x = h(R_B)$ and constructs the challenge as $E(K_{PA}, \{R_B, Bob\})$. Bob sends the evidence x and the challenge $E(K_{PA}, \{R_B, Bob\})$ to Alice.
   - Here h is one-way hash function. The evidence x tells Alice that Bob indeed knows the value R_B. The adversary trying to get a message decrypted by Alice using authentication protocol cannot produce the evidence x.
   - The challenge is cryptographically linked to Bob by including his user-id in the challenge.
2. Alice decrypts the challenge using her private key to recover R_B. She computes $h(R_B)$ and accepts the challenge only if
   - the received evidence x matches the computed equals $h(R_B)$ and
   - the decrypted challenge contains Bob's user-id.
3. Alice sends R_B as her response to Bob. Bob verifies the response.

Mutual Authentication Based on Encrypted Challenge

Figure 13.12 shows the mutual authentication scheme based on encrypted challenges. Alice sends the challenge $E(K_{PB}, \{R_A\})$ which is random number R_A encrypted using Bob's public key K_{PB}. Bob decrypts the challenge and returns $E(K_{PA}, \{R_A, R_B\})$ to Alice. By returning R_A, Bob proves to Alice that he possesses the Bob's private key. He also sends his challenge R_B to Alice as part of message encrypted using Alice's public key. Alice decrypts the message using her private key and returns R_B to Bob. She, thus, proves to Bob that she possesses Alice's private key.

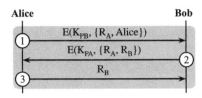

Figure 13.12 Mutual authentication using encrypted challenges.

13.7.2 Authentication Based on Digital Signature

Bob (verifier) sends a challenge to Alice (claimant) who demonstrates knowledge of her private key by digitally signing the challenge. She returns the signed challenge to Bob for verification. We consider the following two cases again:

(a) Unilateral authentication
(b) Mutual authentication

Unilateral Authentication Based on Digital Signature

Figure 13.13(a) shows basic authentication scheme based on digital signature. Here Bob sends a random number R_B as the challenge to Alice. Alice returns the challenge after signing it using her private key K_{RA}. $S(K_{RA}, \{R_B\})$ denotes signature on R_B using the key K_{RA}. Bob verifies the signature using Alice's public key.

This basic scheme can be used by the adversary to trick Alice into signing a chosen text. The adversary impersonating as Bob, sends the chosen text as challenge to Alice, who signs it using her private key.

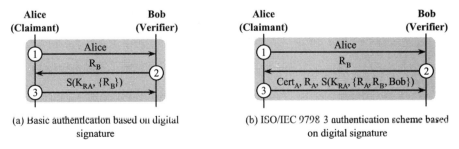

(a) Basic authentication based on digital signature

(b) ISO/IEC 9798 3 authentication scheme based on digital signature

Figure 13.13 Unilateral authentication based on digital signature.

Figure 13.13(b) shows the authentication scheme based on digital signature as specified in ISO/TEC 9798-3.

1. Alice sends her user-id.
2. Bob sends challenge R_B, a random number.
3. Alice chooses a random number R_A and computes her digital signature $S(K_{RA}, \{R_A, R_B, Bob\})$. By adding extra fields R_A and Bob, Alice thwarts any attempt of the adversary to get her signature on chosen-text by him.

   She sends the digital signature along with her public-key certificate[3] $Cert_A$ and R_A to Bob. Bob verifies the digital signature using the Alice's public key given in the certificate to authenticate Alice.

Mutual Authentication Based on Digital Signature

The above scheme for unilateral authentication can be expanded to mutual authentication as shown in Figure 13.14. The first three steps are same as in the case of unilateral authentication. Bob responds to Alice's challenge R_A on the fourth step with his signature $S(K_{RB}, \{R_B, R_A, Alice\})$. He sends his public-key certificate $Cert_B$ as well. Alice verifies Bob's digital signature using his public key given in his public-key certificate.

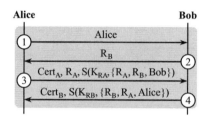

Figure 13.14 Mutual authentication using digital signatures.

13.8 ZERO-KNOWLEDGE INTERACTIVE PROOF

The password and challenge-response authentication mechanisms have one basic drawback. The claimant needs to share with the verifier partial or full information about his secret. Bob can make use of this information to impersonate Alice. Zero-knowledge interactive proofs are designed to address this concern. Here the claimant demonstrates knowledge of a secret while revealing no information that can be reused by the verifier. The only information conveyed is the truth of assertion—the claimant knows the secret. Before we proceed further, let us first understand the concept of zero-knowledge proof.

13.8.1 The Cave Example of Zero-knowledge Interactive Proof

Figure 13.15 shows a cave with a locked door at the far end of the cave. The door can be opened from either side by keying a secret password. Alice claims that she knows the password. To prove to Bob that she knows the password, they agree on the following protocol. To start with, both of them are at the entrance of the cave.

---

3. Public-key certificate contains user-id and the public key of the user certified by a trusted authority. We study public-key certificates in Chapter 15 on Public Key Distribution.

(a) Alice enters the cave and takes left or right arm of the fork to reach the door. Bob does not know which side of the door she is.

(b) Alice calls Bob who comes up to the fork. Bob calls her to come out from left or right arm of the fork. Choice of the selected arm is random and rests with Bob.

(c) Alice comes to the fork on hearing Bob's call. She uses the password of the door, if required.

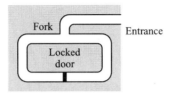

Figure 13.15 The cave example of zero-knowledge proof.

The crux of the protocol is in step (a). In this step, Alice makes a *commitment* by choosing one of the two arms of the fork. The commitment is followed by *challenge* from Bob. Having made the commitment, the Alice can meet the challenge

- always, if she has the secret password,
- sometimes, if she does not have the secret password.

If Alice is successful in the first round, Alice and Bob come out of the cave and repeat the round from step (a). Bob carries out several rounds of this protocol. On the first instance of her failure, he rejects her claim. If Alice has the password of the door, she must be successful in each round. Let us calculate the probability of her success, if she does not know the password.

If Alice does not know the password, she has to make a guess at the time of making commitment, i.e., at the time of choosing left or right arm of the fork. Since it is equally probable that Bob's call may be 'Left' or 'Right', there is 1/2 chance that she would meet Bob's challenge in the round. Thus probability that she is always successful in t rounds is $(1/2)^t$. Bob chooses sufficiently large t to reduce this probability to his comfort level.

Note that Alice does not convey even partial information about the secret password to Bob, yet she proves to Bob that she knows the secret password. This protocol is referred to as zero-knowledge interactive proof.

13.8.2 Fiat–Shamir Protocol

Fiat–Shamir protocol described below illustrates the application of zero-knowledge interactive proof for entity authentication. This version of the protocol is for illustrative purposes. In practice, one would use a more complex variation with multiple 'questions' per iteration rather than one as here.

A trusted third party T selects two large primes p and q and publishes a modulus $n = p \times q$, but keeps p and q secret. Alice, the claimant, selects a secret s, $1 < s < (n - 1)$ and coprime to n. She computes $v = s^2 \bmod n$. She registers v as her public key with T. The security of her secret s relies on the difficulty of computing square root of v modulo large composite integer n of unknown factorization.

Alice proves her knowledge of s to Bob, the verifier, in t rounds, each round consisting of the following steps:

(a) Alice chooses a random number r, between 1 and $(n - 1)$, and sends $x = r^2 \bmod n$ to Bob.
(b) Bob randomly selects a challenge $e = 0$ or 1, and sends e to Alice.
(c) Alice computes $y = rs^e \bmod n$ and sends y as response to Bob. Note that

$$y = r \bmod n \quad \text{if } e = 0$$
$$y = rs \bmod n \quad \text{if } e = 1$$

(d) Bob verifies Alice's response by computing y^2.

$$y^2 = r^2 \bmod n = x \qquad\qquad \text{if } e = 0$$
$$y^2 = (rs)^2 \bmod n = xv \bmod n \qquad \text{if } e = 1$$

Bob can do the above computation because he knows x and Alice's public key v.

Bob rejects Alice's claim, if verification fails. If verification is successful, the next round is initiated with step (a).

Let us examine this protocol in some detail.

Step (a)   Alice makes a *commitment* by choosing a random number r, and sends x as *evidence* of having made commitment. Note that x does not reveal the commitment made by Alice to Bob because it is infeasible for Bob to compute square root of x.

It is necessary that Alice chooses a different random number r in each round. Otherwise an adversary masquerading as Bob (or Bob himself) can extract the secret s from her responses. Example 3 below describes his line of attack.

Steps (b), (c)   Bob throws a random challenge $e = 0$ or 1 to Alice. Alice sends her response to the challenge. The response should be r (if $e = 0$) or $rs \bmod n$ (if $e = 1$).

- When $e = 0$, Bob verifies that Alice knows the commitment r.
- When $e = 1$, Bob verifies that Alice knows the secret s. If she does not know the secret s, she would always fail.

It appears the challenge $e = 1$ really determines whether Alice knows the secret s or not and challenge $e = 0$ is not required. It is not so. An adversary masquerading as Alice can manipulate evidence x in such a manner that would ensure success always when $e = 1$ even though he does not know the secret s. But he would always fail when $e = 0$ in this case. Therefore, Bob's challenge e should be 0 or 1 randomly. Problem 4 at the end of the chapter illustrates this aspect of the protocol.

Step (d)   Bob verifies Alice's response and rejects her claim on the first instance of her failure to respond correctly to the challenge.

Note the following characteristics of zero-knowledge protocol vis-à-vis other entity authentication protocols:

- The secret password of the claimant is not shared with the verifier.
- The random number r used for generating claimant's proof is chosen by the claimant. In the challenge-response authentication schemes described earlier, the random number was chosen by the verifier, which made the schemes vulnerable to chosen-text attack.

Example 2 Let us assume that $n = 35$ in Fiat–Shamir protocol and Alice chooses her secret $s = 16$, which is coprime to n. Her public key $v = (16)^2 \bmod 35 = 11$. Alice chooses $r = 12$ and sends Bob evidence $x = (12)^2 \bmod 35 = 4$.

(a) What is Alice's response if Bob sends $e = 1$? How does Bob verify the response?
(b) What is Alice response if Bob sends $e = 0$? How does Bob verify the response?

Solution

(a) When Bob sends $e = 1$, Alice responds with $y = rs \bmod n = 192 \bmod 35 = 17$. Bob verifies as given below:

$$y^2 \bmod n = 289 \bmod 35 = 9$$
$$xv \bmod n = 4 \times 11 \bmod 35 = 44 \bmod 35 = 9$$

Thus $y^2 \bmod n = xv \bmod n$

(b) When Bob sends $e = 0$, Alice responds with $y = r \bmod n = 12$. Bob verifies as given below:

$$y^2 \bmod n = 144 \bmod 35 = 4 = x$$

Example 3 An adversary masquerading as Bob in Fiat–Shamir protocol sends challenge $e = 1$ in the first round and $e = 0$ in the next round. Alice incidentally commits the same value of r in these two rounds. How does the adversary exploits Alice's choice of r to determine her secret s given the following parameters and Alice's responses:

Modulus $n = 35$
Evidence $x = 4$
Alice's response in the first round $y_1 = 17$
Alice's response in the second round $y_2 = 12$.

Solution

When $e = 1$ $y_1 = rs \bmod n$
When $e = 0$ $y_2 = r \bmod n$

Thus

$$y_1 y_2 = r^2 s \bmod n = xs \bmod n$$
$$s = x^{-1} y_1 y_2 \bmod n$$

The adversary computes the secret s as given below:

$$x^{-1} = (4)^{-1} \bmod 35 = 9, \text{ since } 4 \times 9 \bmod 35 = 1$$
$$s = x^{-1} y_1 y_2 \bmod n = 9 \times 17 \times 12 \bmod 35 = 1836 \bmod 35 = 16.$$

13.8.3 Fiat–Shamir Protocol with Multiple Challenges Per Round

By repeating the Fiat–Shamir protocol t times, we reduce probability of impersonation to $(1/2)^t$. The downside of such serial repetition is that it also requires t round-trip messages between Alice and Bob. This basic version of the protocol can be made more efficient with multiple challenges per round. We illustrate below the principle of multiple challenges in one round with an example of Fiat–Shamir protocol.

The trusted third party T selects two large primes p and q and publishes a modulus $n = p \times q$, but keeps p and q secret. Alice chooses t secrets $(s_1, s_2, ..., s_t)$, all coprime to n. She computes her public key $(v_1, v_2, ..., v_t)$, where $v_i = s_i^2 \bmod n$. She registers her public key with T.

- Alice chooses a random number r, between 1 and $(n - 1)$, and sends $x = r^2 \bmod n$ as evidence of having made a commitment to Bob.
- Bob randomly selects a challenge $e = (e_1, e_2, ..., e_t)$. where $e_i = 0$ or 1 and sends e to Alice.
- Alice computes $y = r \times (s_1^{e_1} s_2^{e_2} ... s_t^{e_t}) \bmod n$ and sends y as response to Bob.
- Bob verifies Alice's response by computing y^2.

$$y^2 = r^2 \times (s_1^{2e_1} s_2^{2e_2} ... s_t^{2e_t}) \bmod n = x \times (v_1^{e_1} v_2^{e_2} ... v_t^{e_t}) \bmod n$$

The probability of impersonation of a verification round is $(1/2)^t$. The following example illustrates this protocol:

Example 4   Assume that $n = 35$ and Alice chooses her secret $s = (9, 12, 17)$.

(a) Determine her public key $v = (v_1, v_2, v_3)$.
(b) Alice chooses $r = 12$. What is the value of her evidence x?
(c) Bob sends challenge $e = (1, 0, 1)$. What is Alice's response y?
(d) Write the computation carried out by Bob to verify Alice's response.

Solution
(a) Alice's public key $v = (9^2, 12^2, 17^2) \bmod 35 = (11, 4, 9)$.
(b) $x = 12^2 \bmod 35 = 4$.
(c) $y = r \times (s_1^{e_1} s_2^{e_2} s_3^{e_3}) \bmod n$
  $= 12 \times 9 \times 1 \times 17 \bmod 35 = 16$.
(d) Bob verifies the response as given below:
  $y^2 \bmod n = 256 \bmod 35 = 11$
  $x \times v_1^{e_1} \times v_2^{e_2} \times v_3^{e_3} \bmod n = 4 \times 11 \times 1 \times 9 \bmod 35 = 11$
  Thus, $y^2 \bmod n = x \times (v_1^{e_1} \times v_2^{e_2} \times v_3^{e_3}) \bmod n$

13.9 SUMMING UP

In this chapter our focus was on entity authentication, which refers to establishing identity of the entity that originates the messages. The claimant entity proves his identity to the verifier entity by producing something known to him or possessed by him or inherent in him. Entity authentication is done just before starting a session of message exchange.

- In the basic form of entity authentication, the claimant produces his password as corroborative evidence of the claimed identity. This basic scheme of entity authentication is vulnerable to eavesdropping and replay, password guessing and exhaustive search attacks from the adversary.

- In one-time password scheme, a password can be used only once and is thus safe from eavesdropping and replay attacks. Shared list of one-time passwords, sequentially updated one-time passwords and Lamport's scheme are typical approaches to implementation of one-time passwords. Lamport's scheme is based on multiple applications of one-way hash function to get new passwords.
- In the challenge-response approach to entity authentication, the verifier sends a challenge to the claimant. The claimant proves his identity to the verifier by transforming the challenge using the secret that uniquely belongs to him. Challenge-response schemes are based on symmetric-key, public-key and zero-knowledge identification protocols.
- Symmetric-key challenge-response scheme uses nonce or timestamp as challenge to be encrypted by the claimant using the secret symmetric-key. This scheme vulnerable to reflection attack from the adversary when the authentication scheme is used for mutual authentication.
- Reflection attack is thwarted by using different encryption keys or different set of nonces in the two directions, or by including user-id in the encrypted response.
- In the challenge-response authentication protocol using public-key, the claimant proves his identity by using his private key to:
  - decrypt the encrypted challenge sent by the verifier.
  - digitally sign the challenge sent by the verifier.
- In the zero-knowledge interactive proof, the claimant demonstrates knowledge of a secret while revealing no information that can be reused by the verifier. This scheme is not deterministic. The verifier identifies the claimant with certain degree of probability. Fiat–Shamir protocol for zero-knowledge challenge-response authentication is based on difficulty of computing square root modulo large composite integer n of unknown factorization.

We had been postponing a very important topic, the key distribution since it requires knowledge of asymmetric-key cryptography, digital signature, hash functions and entity authentication. Having built this background, we can now take up this topic. We study symmetric-key distribution in the next chapter.

Key Terms		
Challenge-response authentication	Lamport's one-time password	Unilateral authentication
Dictionary attack	Mutual authentication	Zero-knowledge interactive proof
Fiat–Shamir protocol	One-time passwords	
Fixed passwords	Reflection attack	

RECOMMENDED READING

Avoine, G., Junod, P. and Oechslin, P., *Computer System Security: Basic Concepts and Solved Exercises*, CRC Press, FL, USA, 2007.

Entity Authentication, Part 3: Mechanisms using Digital Signature Techniques, Information Technology—Security Techniques, International Organization for Standardization, Geneva, 1998.

Feige, U., Fiat, A., and Shamir, A., Zero-Knowledge Proofs of Identity, *Journal of Cryptology*, Vol. 1, pp. 77–94, 1988.

Forouzan, Behrouz A., *Cryptography and Network Security*, Tata McGraw-Hill, New Delhi, 2007.

Kaufman, C., Perlman, R. and Spenciner, M. *Network Security, Private Communication in a Public World*, Prentice-Hall of India, New Delhi, 2007.

Menezes, A., Oorschot, P. and Vanstone, S., *Handbook of Applied Cryptography*, CRC Press, FL, USA, 1997.

Paar, C. and Pelzl, J., *Understanding Cryptography, A Textbook for Students and Practitioners.* Springer, India, New Delhi, 2009.

Vaudenay, S., *A Classical Introduction to Cryptography*, Springer, NY, USA, 2006.

────────────(**PROBLEMS**)────────────

1. Alice and Bob use the following challenge-response authentication scheme based on digital signature. To avoid chosen-text attack (Section 13.7.2), they decide that Alice will sign $R = R_A \oplus R_B$, where R_A is chosen by Alice and R_B is chosen by Bob. They work out the following protocol:

Alice	$\Rightarrow$	Bob	:	Alice, R_A
Bob	$\Rightarrow$	Alice	:	R_B
Alice	$\Rightarrow$	Bob	:	$S(K_{RA}, \{R\})$

   K_{RA} is the private key of Alice. Bob verifies Alice's signature on R to authenticate Alice. An adversary wants Alice to sign on text R_T chosen by him. How does he exploit the protocol for achieving his goal?

2. Alice and Bob realize vulnerability of the protocol of Problem 1 to chosen-text attack. They decide that Alice should have control over $R = R_A \oplus R_B$. They decide that Bob will send R_B and then Alice will select R_A. They work out the following protocol:

Alice	$\Rightarrow$	Bob	:	Alice
Bob	$\Rightarrow$	Alice	:	R_B
Alice	$\Rightarrow$	Bob	:	$R_A, S(K_{RA}, \{R\})$

   (a) Examine this protocol for chosen-text attack by an adversary acting as Bob (verifier).
   (b) Assume that the adversary's goal is to get authenticated to Bob. He copies the above exchange and initiates the dialogue with Bob by sending the identity 'Alice'. He gets random R'_B from Bob. He chooses $R'_A = (R_A \oplus R_B) \oplus R'_B$ and sends

[R'_A, $S(K_{RA}, \{R\})$] to Bob. S is the signature of Alice he had copied earlier. Is he successful in his bid for authentication as Alice?

3. If Alice and Bob had chosen $R = R_A \parallel R_B$ instead of $R = R_A \oplus R_B$ in Problems 1 and 2 above, can the adversary break the protocol impersonating either as Bob or as Alice?

4. In Fiat–Shamir protocol, an adversary impersonating as Alice, the claimant, guesses that the challenge in the next round would be $e = 1$. He plays smart by choosing commitment r, but communicating evidence $x = r^2/v \bmod n$ to Bob. If the challenge $e = 1$, he responds with $y = r$.

   (a) Does his response pass verification test?
   (b) What will happen, if the challenge is $e = 0$?

5. Let us assume that $n = 35$ in Fiat–Shamir protocol and Alice chooses her secret $s = 12$.

   (a) Determine her public key v.
   (b) Alice chooses $r = 8$ and sends evidence $x = r^2 \bmod n$ to Bob. What is the value of her evidence x?
   (c) Bob sends challenge $e = 1$, what is Alice's response? How does Bob verify the response?
   (d) Bob sends challenge $e = 0$, what is Alice's response? How does Bob verify the response?

6. An adversary masquerading as Bob in Fiat–Shamir protocol sends challenge $e = 1$ in the first round and $e = 0$ in the next round. He receives the responses $y_1 = 13$, $y_2 = 9$ respectively for these challenges. Alice incidentally sends the same value of evidence $x = 11$ for these rounds. If $n = 35$, determine Alice's secret s.

7. In Fiat-Shamir protocol, if $n = 35$ and Alice chooses her secret $s = (9, 11, 17)$.

   (a) Determine her public key $v = (v_1, v_2, v_3)$.
   (b) Alice chooses $r = 10$. What is the value of evidence x?
   (c) Bob sends challenge $e = (1, 1, 0)$. What is Alice's response y?
   (d) Write the computation Bob does to verify Alice's response.

8. Here is an application of zero-knowledge proof in RSA encryption. Assume that RSA public key is $\{n, e\}$ and message m is encrypted as ciphertext $c = m^e \bmod n$. The RSA public key and ciphertext c is known to Alice and Bob. But Alice claims that she knows plaintext m also. Alice and Bob decide to use zero-knowledge proof to establish Alice's claim and follow the steps given below:

   1. Alice chooses a random integer r_1 which is coprime to n and computes $r_2 = m \times r_1^{-1} \bmod n$.
   2. Alice computes $x_1 = r_1^e \bmod n$ and $x_2 = r_2^e \bmod n$. She sends x_1 and x_2 to Bob as evidence of having made a commitment.
   3. Bob confirms that $x_1 \times x_2 \bmod n = c$. Bob randomly chooses one of the two parameters r_1 or r_2 as challenge and asks Alice to send the same.

      (a) Describe rest of the verification process carried out by Bob.
      (b) Assume that in the second round, Bob discovers that values of x_1 and x_2 are same as in first round. Bob chooses the challenge of second round such that he manages to get the message m from Alice. How does Bob accomplish this?

14

Symmetric-key Distribution

S ymmetric-key cryptographic algorithms are preferred over asymmetric-key algorithms for the security of bulk data because they are much faster. But establishing shared symmetric-key between communicating entities is a challenging task. In this chapter, we study mechanisms for establishing symmetric keys. We begin the chapter with Diffie–Hellman key exchange between a pair of end entities. Then we examine concept of a centralized system of symmetric key distribution, called Key Distribution Centre (KDC). We study Needham–Schroeder and Otway–Rees protocols for KDC. Finally, Kerberos, a widely implemented KDC and authentication protocol is described in detail.

14.1 SYMMETRIC-KEY DISTRIBUTION

Symmetric key is a shared secret between two entities. It needs to be established securely between the two entities before they commence exchange of messages. Some of the alternatives are given below:

1. Physical delivery of key by an entity to the other entity.
2. Exchanging symmetric key using cryptographic algorithms.
3. Using services of a centralized key distribution centre.

The following factors must also be taken into account to determine suitability of the mode of key exchange:

- If there are n communicating entities, each entity requires $(n - 1)$ keys. Thus n entities will require $n(n - 1)/2$ keys.
- It is possible that an adversary may be successful in determining secret keys after he collects sufficient encrypted data over a time period. Therefore, symmetric keys need to be changed periodically for security.

These considerations rule out the first alternative, the physical delivery of the key because the number of users is very large. The second alternative for exchanging secret keys is used in several protocols. We will examine the following two key exchange methods in this chapter:

(a) Diffie–Hellman key exchange
(b) Symmetric-key exchange using asymmetric-key cryptography

The third alternative involves establishment of a key distribution centre (KDC) which distributes secret session keys to the end entities. KDC maintains n secret *master keys* for communication with n end entities. When the KDC receives request from Alice for a key for a session with Bob, it delivers a session key to Alice and Bob. It encrypts the session key using their master keys for security. The session key has limited life time and can be used for one or more sessions between Alice and Bob. We study the following protocols for symmetric-key distribution using KDC in this chapter:

(a) Needham–Schroeder key distribution protocol
(b) Otway–Rees key distribution protocol
(c) Kerberos

14.2 DIFFIE–HELLMAN KEY EXCHANGE

Diffie–Hellman (DH) key exchange allows two entities to exchange non-secret parameters and calculate a unique shared secret from these parameters. The adversary cannot calculate the shared secret from these parameters. Once established, the shared secret can be used as the symmetric key for encryption or as seed for generating symmetric key.

DH algorithm is based on two parameters p and g. p is a large prime number of the order of 300 decimal digits. g is a generator of the order of $(p - 1)$ of the multiplicative group $\{Z_p^*, \times\}$. p and g are not confidential and can be exchanged in clear text. The steps of DH algorithm are given below:

(a) Alice chooses a large secret random number a, $0 < a < p - 1$. She calculates $K_A = g^a \bmod p$ and sends (p, g, K_A) to Bob. K_A is called DH half key of Alice and is not a secret.
(b) Bob also chooses a large secret number b, $0 < b < p - 1$, and calculates his DH half key $K_B = g^b \bmod p$. He sends K_B to Alice.
(c) Alice and Bob independently calculate the shared secret key K as given below:
Alice calculates $K = (K_B)^a \bmod p = (g^b)^a \bmod p = g^{ab} \bmod p$.
Bob calculates $K = (K_A)^b \bmod p = (g^a)^b \bmod p = g^{ab} \bmod p$.

The following example illustrates the algorithm.

Alice chooses $g = 7$, $p = 23$, and $a = 3$. She computes her half key K_A as given below:

$$K_A = g^a \bmod p = 7^3 \bmod 23 = 21.$$

Alice sends the DH parameters $g = 7$ and $p = 23$, and her half key $K_A = 21$ to Bob. Bob chooses $b = 6$ and computes his half key K_B as given below:

$$K_B = g^b \bmod p = 7^6 \bmod 23 = 4.$$

Bob sends his half key $K_B = 4$ to Alice.

Alice and Bob compute the shared secret key K as given below:

Alice calculates $\quad K = (K_B)^a \bmod p = (4)^3 \bmod 23 = 64 \bmod 23 = 18.$

Bob calculates $\quad K = (K_A)^b \bmod p = (21)^6 \bmod 23 = 18.$

Note that Alice and Bob did not exchange their secret numbers a and b, yet they reached the same value of K. The adversary cannot compute K from the knowledge of p, g, K_A and K_B. He needs one of the two random numbers, a or b. To find a or b, he must calculate one of the following discrete logarithms.

$$\log_{g,\,p} K_A = \log_{g,\,p} g^a = a$$
$$\log_{g,\,p} K_B = \log_{g,\,p} g^b = b$$

where $\log_{g,\,p}$ is the discrete logarithm to base g modulo p. The security of DH key exchange lies in the fact that it is infeasible to calculate discrete logarithms for large prime number p.

14.2.1 Man-in-the-middle Attack

Although it is infeasible for the adversary to calculate the secret key K, he can launch an attack, called man-in-the-middle attack. He fools Alice into believing that he is Bob. Similarly he fools Bob into believing that he is Alice. In simple words, he puts himself in middle of Alice and Bob. The attack proceeds in the following manner:

(a) Alice sends DH parameters g, p and her half key K_A to Bob, which the adversary intercepts.[1]

(b) The adversary chooses a random number x and computes his half key $K_X = g^x \bmod p$. He returns K_X to Alice, posing as Bob. He also sends DH parameters g, p and his half key K_X to Bob, impersonating as Alice.

(c) Bob chooses a random number b and computes his half key $K_B = g^b \bmod p$. He returns K_B to Alice, which the adversary intercepts.

(d) Alice and the adversary calculate the secret $K_{AX} = g^{ax} \bmod p$. Alice does not know that she is sharing this secret with the adversary.

(e) Bob and the adversary calculate the secret $K_{BX} = g^{bx} \bmod p$. Bob does not know that he is sharing this secret with the adversary.

(f) The adversary now acts as an intermediary in the transfer of messages between Alice and Bob. He decrypts the ciphertext from Alice using the key K_{AX}. He re-encrypts the message using the key K_{BX} and forwards the ciphertext to Bob.

(g) Bob assumes that the message has come from Alice. He decrypts the ciphertext using K_{BX}.

(h) Reply from Bob to Alice is intercepted and processed by the adversary in the same way. Alice and Bob exchange messages unaware of the interception that is taking place in the middle.

---

1. Considering that the adversary, Alice and Bob are on a network (or public Internet), it is necessary that the message from Alice to Bob must pass through adversary for the adversary to intercept the message. We examine this aspect in Chapter 21 on Network Vulnerability.

Man-in-the-middle attack was successful because Alice and Bob accepted the adversary's DH half key without verification. They should have verified the origin of DH half key they received from the other end. They can do so, for example, by digitally signing their DH half keys. Alice digitally signs her DH half key and sends it to Bob. Bob verifies Alice's digital signature before accepting the half key. The adversary cannot forge their signatures because he does not have their private keys.

14.3   SYMMETRIC-KEY EXCHANGE USING PUBLIC KEY

Public keys are not secret and can be easily distributed using public-key certificates that we study in the next chapter. But asymmetric-key algorithms are slow for encryption of bulk data. We use these algorithms for exchanging short messages like symmetric key which can be subsequently used for encryption of bulk data. Figure 14.1(a) illustrates the scheme proposed by Merkle.

1. Alice generates a one-time public/private key pair $\{K_{PA}, K_{RA}\}$ and sends her public key K_{PA} with her identifier Id_A to Bob.
2. Bob generates a secret symmetric key K_S and encrypts the key K_S using public key of Alice K_{PA}. He returns the encrypted secret key to Alice. In Figure 14.1(a), the notation $E(K_{PA}, \{K_S\})$ represents encryption of K_S by the public key K_{PA}.

   Alice decrypts the message from Bob using her private key K_{RA} and recovers the secret key K_S.

Alice and Bob now have a shared secret key K_S which they can use for encryption of their bulk data. Though this method is simple, it is vulnerable to man-in-the-middle attack because Alice does not authenticate Bob.

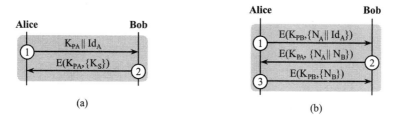

Figure 14.1   Symmetric-key exchange using public key.

Several variations have been proposed that ensure mutual authentication while exchanging the secret symmetric key using public-key encryption. Needham–Schroeder protocol for symmetric key exchange using public key is shown in Figure 14.1(b). As before, the message within curly brackets {...} is encrypted using the key written just ahead of the brackets. We assume that Alice and Bob possess each other's public keys, K_{PA} and K_{PB}. N_A and N_B are random numbers and are used for authentication. These random numbers are called 'nonce' which stands for 'number used once'.

1. Alice sends nonce N_A and her identity Id_A using public key of Bob for encryption.
2. Bob decrypts the message using his private key. He takes note of N_A and Alice's identity. He sends nonces N_A and N_B to Alice, encrypting the message using public key K_{PA} of Alice.
3. Alice decrypts the message using her private key, verifies her nonce N_A. This gives her assurance that the message is from Bob as only Bob could have retrieved N_A from her message (1). Alice takes note of Bob's nonce N_B. She returns N_B to Bob, encrypting it using it Bob's public key K_{PB} to authenticate herself to Bob.
4. Bob decrypts the message (3) from Alice and verifies his nonce N_B. He is assured that Alice is at the other end because only she could retrieve N_B from his message (2).

Having authenticated each other, Alice and Bob compute symmetric key as $K_S = f(N_A, N_B)$, where f is a publically known non-reversible function.

14.4 KEY DISTRIBUTION CENTRE

As mentioned earlier, n communicating entities require $n(n - 1)/2$ secret symmetric-keys to be established. Every instance of entry of new entity entails creating multiple secret keys and distributing these to respective entities. When the number of entities is large, a secure key distribution system is required. The approach adopted for this purpose is to establish a trusted key distribution centre (KDC). Its primary job is to allot symmetric encryption key for each communication session. The KDC shares a master key with each entity. When Alice wants to communicate with Bob, she requests the KDC to allot a secret session key for her communication with Bob (Figure 14.2). The KDC sends the session key K_S to Alice and Bob. Alice and Bob use this session key for communication between them.

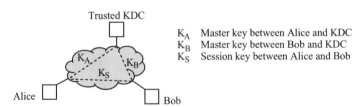

Figure 14.2 Key distribution centre (KDC).

The basic scheme using a trusted KDC needs to be protected from the possible attacks of the adversary who can pose as Alice, Bob or KDC.

- He can pose as Alice and request for a session key from KDC.
- He can pose as KDC and send a session key to Alice and Bob.
- He can intercept the session key sent to Bob and pose as Bob to Alice.

We will address these issues while describing the protocols used for KDC.

14.4.1   Needham–Schroeder Key Distribution Protocol

We assume that Alice wants to establish a secure communication link with Bob. Alice and Bob possess master keys K_A and K_B respectively for communicating securely with a key distribution centre (KDC). The Needham–Schroeder key distribution protocol consists of the following steps (Figure 14.3).

(a) Alice requests KDC for a session key intended specifically for communicating with Bob. She sends the following encrypted message to KDC.

$$E(K_A, \{ID_A \parallel ID_B \parallel N_A\}) \tag{1}$$

where E stands for encryption of the second argument within brackets {...} using the first argument K_A as the key.

    The message (1) sent by Alice to KDC includes Alice's identity ID_A, Bob identity ID_B and a nonce (N_A). Remember that Alice may send several requests for multiple simultaneous sessions with Bob. The nonce is unique to each request sent by Alice to KDC.

(b) When the KDC receives message (1), KDC is assured that this message is from Alice, since the adversary cannot compose this message without knowing K_A. But it can be replay of Alice's old message by the adversary. Therefore, the KDC encrypts its response to ensure that the adversary cannot make use of its response. KDC responds to Alice with the following message encrypted using key K_A:

$$E(K_A, \{K_S \parallel ID_B \parallel N_A \parallel E(K_B, \{K_S \parallel ID_A\})\}) \tag{2}$$

The message consists of the following components:

- The session-key K_S that Alice can use for communicating with Bob.
- The nonce N_A that enables Alice to match the response from KDC to a specific request she sent.
- A 'ticket', $E(K_B, \{K_S \parallel ID_A\})$, for access to Bob. The ticket contains the session key K_S, and Alice's identifier ID_A. It is encrypted using Bob's master key K_B. Note that Alice cannot decrypt this ticket because she does not have Bob's master key K_B.

(c) When Alice receives this message, she is assured that
- it is indeed from KDC. The adversary cannot compose this message as he does not know her master key K_A.
- it also cannot be replay of an old message by the adversary because it contains the current nonce.

Now, Alice has the session key K_S for communication with Bob. Alice forwards the ticket from KDC to Bob so that he also gets the session key K_S.

$$E(K_B, \{K_S \parallel ID_A\}) \tag{3}$$

Note that the ticket is protected from eavesdropping by the adversary, since it is encrypted.

(d) Bob decrypts the ticket received from Alice using the master key K_B. Bob gets
- the session key K_S allotted by KDC and
- identity ID_A of the other communicating entity.

Bob is assured that the message was originated at the KDC because it was encrypted using K_B. But Bob wants to assure that this message was indeed forwarded by Alice. It is quite possible that the adversary may be replaying an old message. Bob sends back the following encrypted message containing his nonce N_B to Alice. The message is encrypted using the session key K_S.

$$E(K_S, \{N_B\}) \tag{4}$$

(e) Alice decrypts the message using the session key K_S and proves to Bob that she possesses the session key K_S allotted to her by the KDC by sending the following message:

$$E(K_S, \{N_B+1\}) \tag{5}$$

When Bob receives this response, and he finds on its decryption that it contains $N_B + 1$, he concludes that
— the sender received his nonce N_B and
— the sender indeed possesses the session key K_S allotted by KDC.

Bob is, thus, assured that the ticket issues by KDC was indeed forwarded by Alice.

Note that Bob authenticated Alice. But Alice did not authenticate Bob. She can authenticate Bob by sending an encrypted nonce $E(K_S,\{N\})$ with message (3). Message (4) from Bob is modified as $E(K_S,\{N_B \| (N+1)\})$. This message assures Alice that Bob possesses K_S, and thus Bob is authenticated.

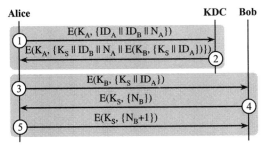

Figure 14.3   Needham–Schroeder key distribution protocol.

If the adversary somehow gets the master key K_A used by Alice with KDC, he can decrypt message (2) and get the session key K_S and the ticket for Bob. Equipped with these, he can establish session with Bob. Even if Alice changes her master key K_A after she comes to know of the key leakage, the adversary can go ahead with his attack because Bob's master key K_B is valid. The Otway–Rees key exchange that we discuss next overcomes this weakness.

14.4.2   Otway–Rees Key Distribution

Figure 14.4 shows one of the several variants of Otway–Rees key distribution protocol.

(a) Alice sends the following message to Bob:

$$ID_A \| ID_B \| N \| E(K_A,\{ID_A \| ID_B \| N \| N_A\}) \tag{1}$$

The message contains identities of Alice and Bob, a common nonce N to be used by the KDC for verification and an encrypted part meant for the KDC. The encrypted part contains identities of the communicating entities, the common nonce N, and Alice's nonce N_A. N_A is used as challenge to KDC to prove its identity. Alice's master key is used for encryption.

(b) Bob sends the following message to KDC:

$$ID_A \parallel ID_B \parallel N \parallel E(K_A,\{ID_A \parallel ID_B \parallel N \parallel N_A\}) \parallel E(K_B,\{ID_A \parallel ID_B \parallel N \parallel N_B\})) \quad (2)$$

The message is basically the message received from Alice with additional encrypted part from Bob to KDC. Bob's part contains identities of Alice and Bob, the common nonce N, and nonce N_B from Bob. N_B is used as challenge to KDC to prove its identity. This part is encrypted using Bob's master key K_B.

(c) The KDC verifies that common nonce is same in both the encrypted messages. The fact that the common nonce is same proves to the KDC that the sender is indeed Bob. The KDC allots a session key K_S and responds to Bob with the following message. It has two parts, one meant for Alice and the other meant for Bob. Each part contains the session key K_S and the nonce send by the respective parties.

$$E(K_A,\{K_S \parallel N_A\}) \parallel E(K_B,\{K_S \parallel N_B\}) \quad (3)$$

(d) Bob decrypts the part meant for him, verifies that it carries the nonce N_B and gets the session key K_S. Bob forwards the other part of the message to Alice.

$$E(K_A,\{K_S \parallel N_A\}) \quad (4)$$

(e) Alice decrypts the message received from Bob, verifies that it carries the nonce N_A and gets the session key K_S. Alice is assured that the sender is Bob because the KDC would not have sent this message to Bob without verification.

Alice sends a recognizable message encrypted with session key K_S to Bob, and establishes her identity to Bob by proving that she could decrypt the message from KDC.

$$E(K_S,\{\text{any recognizable message}\}) \quad (5)$$

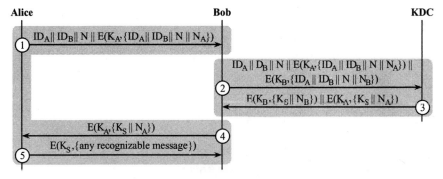

Figure 14.4 Otway–Rees key distribution.

Building a symmetric-key distribution protocol is very tricky job. There are many examples in the security literature of key distribution schemes that have failed because of a clever attack that was found years later. In the rest of this chapter, we shall look a protocol which has withstood careful scrutiny by the experts and has been adopted for use in many applications.

14.5 KERBEROS

When there are number of application servers and user clients on the network, we would like that access to the servers is permitted only to the authorized users. Each server should be able to authenticate every request it receives from the clients for access to it. The simplest way to authenticate the users when they contact a server would be through passwords. Authentication using password in networked environment has its limitations.

- People frequently use passwords that are easy to crack.
- Each application server needs to maintain passwords of all the users.
- Any change in password would require changing the password in each application server.

When the number of users is large, it is likely that the additional task of authentication may place a substantial burden on the application servers. Therefore, we would like to separate the authentication function from the application servers and have a common authentication server [Figure 14.5(a)]. Separation of authentication function results in the following advantages:

- The authentication service is centralized and available to the users for all the application servers.
- Application servers are relieved of authentication function.
- Users update their authentication data (e.g. password) once in the authentication server whenever there is any change. They need not access all the application servers for the update.

The basic authentication server scheme works in the following manner [Figure 14.5(b)]:

- A user client sends request to the authentication server for access to an application server. He produces his authentication data (e.g. a password).
- The authentication server verifies the user password and gives him a secured ticket for the application server.
- The user sends access request to the application server producing the ticket. The application server verifies the ticket and grants access to the user.

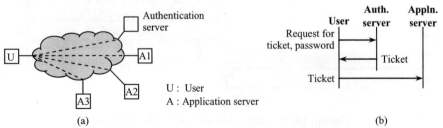

(a)   (b)

Figure 14.5 Authentication server.

Kerberos protocol that we discuss in this section is an authentication and symmetric key distribution protocol for client-server applications. It is based on the work of Needham and Schroeder on key distribution centres and is specified in RFC 4120. Kerberos versions 4 and 5 are in use today. This section is based on Kerberos version 5. Figure 14.5(a) is a typical network environment of Kerberos implementation. The authentication server is part of the key distribution centre (KDC). KDC authenticates the clients, and issues them session key and service tickets for the application servers.

14.5.1 Design Objectives

Kerberos was designed with the following design objectives:

- The user's password must never be stored on the client machine, or stored in an unencrypted form in the KDC, or sent over the network.
- The user is asked to enter his password only once for a session. Thereafter the user is able to transparently access all the services he is authorized to during the session.
- Authentication information is centralized in the KDC so that
  - the administrator can disable the account of any user,
  - when a user changes its password, it is changed for all services at the same time.
- Not only the users are authenticated, the servers must prove their authenticity to the clients to thwart any attempt of the adversary to masquerade as a user or as a server.
- Following the completion of authentication and authorization, the client and server must be able to establish a symmetric encryption key for secure communication.

14.5.2 Key Distribution Centre of Kerberos

KDC resides entirely on a single physical server, but it can be considered having three parts (Figure 14.6):

- Authentication server
- Ticket Granting Server (TGS)
- Database

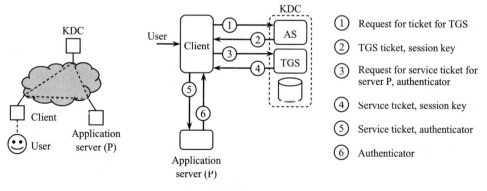

Figure 14.6 Kerberos.

Authentication server (AS):   The authentication server receives the initial request from the user for service and verifies the user from its database. It issues a ticket (called TGT, Ticket Granting Ticket) for access to Ticket Granting Server (TGS).

Ticket granting server (TGS):   The ticket granting server distributes service tickets to the clients for access to the application servers when a client produces TGT.

Database: It contains entries associated users and the services provided by the servers. The entries are indexed by the user name or service name, which is called principal. The database contains the following information:

- The principal
- Encryption key
- Password expiry date
- Maximum validity of the ticket for a service
- Several other parameters

The encryption key for authentication of the users is derived from their passwords using a hash function. There is an encryption key for each application server shared between the TGS and the application server. The service ticket for an application server is encrypted using this key.

14.5.3   Basic Operation of Kerberos

Figure 14.6 depicts the basic operation of Kerberos. It consists of six steps as given below:

1. The user inputs his registered identity when prompted by the client. The client sends its request to the Authentication Server (AS) for access to the Ticket Granting Server (TGS).
2. The AS verifies user's identity from the database and issues an encrypted ticket (TGT) to the client for access to the TGS. The ticket is retrievable only by the client using password of the user. The AS also allots a session key to the client for communicating with the TGS.
3. The client retrieves the ticket using the password of the user and sends its request to the TGS for service from the application server (P). It appends the ticket received from the AS and an authenticator to the request.
4. The TGS verifies user's authorization for access to the application server (P) from the database and issues a service ticket to the client for access to the application server (P) along with a session key for communicating with the application server (P).
5. The client forwards the service ticket to the application server (P) with an authenticator.
6. The application server (P) verifies the authenticator. It responds with another authenticator to prove that it is really the server the client is expecting.

14.5.4   Detailed Scenario

The messages exchanged during the six steps of operation of Kerberos are shown in Figure 14.7. Only the fields essential for explanation have been shown in these messages. It is assumed that the KDC, servers and the clients are part of same administrative domain, called Kerberos realm.

Client

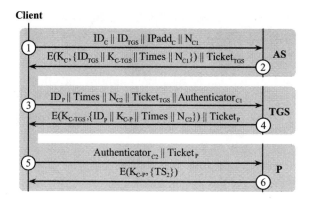

Figure 14.7 Message exchange in Kerberos version 5.

These messages are exchanged over an insecure network. At each step the client and the servers take necessary precautions to defeat the possible attacks from the adversary.

Step 1 When the user inputs his registered user identity, the client sends the following request in clear text to the configured Authentication Server (AS):

$$ID_C \parallel ID_{TGS} \parallel IPadd_C \parallel Times \parallel N_{C1}$$

The request includes

- the registered user identity at the client (ID_C),
- the Ticket Granting Server identity (ID_{TGS}),
- the IP address of the client ($IPadd_C$),
- the start time and till time of requested ticket (Times)
- the nonce of the client N_{C1},
- other options e.g. renewable ticket.

Note that the request does not carry the user password or any useful information for the adversary.

Step 2 The AS checks if the user (ID_C) is registered. If so, it processes the client's request as given below:

- It creates a session key $K_{C\text{-}TGS}$, for the client and the TGS.
- It generates the ticket to TGS ($Ticket_{TGS}$). The ticket contains the three parameters of the client request (ID_C, ID_{TGS}, $IPadd_C$), start-till time parameters and the session key $K_{C\text{-}TGS}$. The contents of the ticket are encrypted using the secret key between AS and TGS, $K_{AS\ TGS}$.

$$Ticket_{TGS} = E(K_{AS-TGS}, \{ID_C \parallel ID_{TGS} \parallel IPadd_C \parallel Times \parallel K_{C\text{-}TGS}\})$$

Note that the contents of ticket cannot be altered by the client or the adversary because they do not know the secret key $K_{AS\text{-}TGS}$.

The AS derives the client key K_C from the password of the user in its database and sends the following encrypted response. $Ticket_{TGS}$ is appended to the response.

$$E(K_C,\{ID_{TGS} \parallel K_{C\text{-}TGS} \parallel Times \parallel N_{C1}\}) \parallel Ticket_{TGS}$$

Note the important features of the message.

- The encryption key K_C is derived from the password of the user available in the database against ID_C. The message can be decrypted only by the client that has the password of the user. In other words, the message is useful only to the authentic user. If the initial request was sent by an adversary, he cannot decrypt this message because he cannot generate K_C without the password.
- The AS returns the nonce N_{C1} so that the AS is authenticated to the client.
- The adversary cannot create this message because he does not have K_C. He cannot replay an old message of the AS due to inclusion of the nonce N_C in the message.

Step 3   On receipt of the message from the AS, the client prompts the user to enter his password. It derives the key K_C using the password, and decrypts the message. It verifies the content (e.g. N_{C1}) to ensure that the message indeed is from the AS in response to its request.

The client creates its credentials in form of an authenticator as given below:

$$Authenticator_{C1} = E(K_{C\text{-}TGS},\{ID_C \parallel IPadd_C \parallel TS_1\})$$

By encrypting its identity ID_C and time stamp TS_1 using the session key $K_{C\text{-}TGS}$, the client proves to the TGS that

(a) the client (ID_C) possesses the session key $K_{C\text{-}TGS}$ allotted by the AS,
(b) the authenticator is not obsolete.

The authenticator is given a short lifetime (2 minutes) after which it becomes obsolete. If the adversary gets hold of the authenticator, he must replay it within two minutes. As a further precaution, the receiver maintains a replay cache containing the received authenticators in last two minutes. A received authenticator is rejected, if it has a replica in the cache. The adversary, therefore, has to be ahead of the client in sending the authenticator to be successful.

The client forwards the following message to the TSG as its service request for access to the application server P.

$$ID_P \parallel Times \parallel N_{C2} \parallel Ticket_{TGS} \parallel Authenticator_{C1}$$

ID_P is the requested service. N_{C2} is the nonce for verification at a later stage.

Step 4   On receipt of the above message, the TGS proceeds as given below:

- The TGS decrypts $Ticket_{TGS}$ and ensures that it is not life expired.
- Using the session key $K_{C\text{-}TGS}$ obtained from the ticket, it decrypts the authenticator and checks it for validity and replay; verifies the user and his authorization from the data base.
- It selects a random session key $K_{C\text{-}P}$ for the client and the application server P, and generates a ticket ($Ticket_P$) to the application server as given below:

$$Ticket_P = E(K_P,\{ID_C \parallel ID_P \parallel IPadd_C \parallel Times \parallel K_{C\text{-}P}\})$$

The ticket contains user id (ID_C), user address ($IPadd_C$), the service id (ID_P), start-till times (Times), the session key $K_{C\text{-}P}$. The contents of the ticket are encrypted using the secret key between TGS and the application server, K_P. The contents of ticket cannot be altered by the client or the adversary because they do not know the secret key K_P.

The TGS sends the following encrypted response to the client. Ticket$_P$ is appended to the response.

$$E(K_{C-TGS}, \{ID_P \parallel K_{C-P} \parallel Times \parallel N_{C2}\}) \parallel Ticket_P$$

Step 5 The client verifies the content (e.g. N_{C2}) to ensure that the message indeed is from the TGS in response to its request. It creates its credentials in form of an authenticator as given below:

$$Authenticator_{C2} = E(K_{C-P}, \{ID_C \parallel IPadd_C \parallel TS_2\})$$

By encrypting its identity ID_C and time stamp TS_2 using the session key K_{C-P}, the client proves its authenticity to the application server P. The client forwards the following request message to the server P:

$$Authenticator_{C2} \parallel Ticket_P$$

Step 6 When the above message arrives, the application server P opens the Ticket$_P$ using its secret key K_P and validates the ticket. It extracts the session key K_{C-P} and uses this key to decrypt the Authenticator$_{C2}$. It verifies that the authenticator is indeed from the user as indicated in the ticket. The timestamp enables him to check the replays.

The application server P responds with the following message to the client:

$$E(K_{C-P}, \{TS_2\})$$

The client decrypts this message using the session key K_{C-P} to verify that the message is indeed from the application server in response to its previous request message.

At the conclusion of these six steps, the client and the application server have established a secret session key that can be used to exchange the future messages between them.

14.5.5 Kerberos Realms

The term realm refers to the administrative domain of a Kerberos implementation. It defines the boundaries within which a KDC has the authority to authenticate a user and issue tickets for services. Each user and service of a realm shares a secret (password/key) with the KDC of that realm.

There can be multiple realms each having its own defined administrative domain. It might be the case that a user of Realm A wants to access resources in Realm B. Kerberos supports inter-realm authentication and service. This is achieved by registering the Kerberos server of Realm B with the Kerberos server of Realm A and vice versa. It is necessary that the participating servers must be willing to trust each other.

Figure 14.8 shows the basic mechanism of inter-realm operation of Kerberos. The client of Realm A follows the usual process to gain access to the local TGS and then requests for a ticket for remote TGS of Realm B. The client then applies to the remote TGS for service ticket to application server P in realm B. The rest of the steps are same as before.

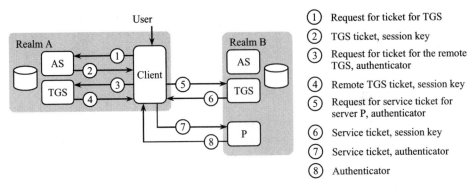

Figure 14.8 Kerberos realms.

14.6 SUMMING UP

Symmetric key, as a shared secret between two entities, needs to be established securely between the two entities before they commence exchange of messages. There are several alternatives available for symmetric-key exchange.

- Diffie–Hellman (DH) key exchange allows two entities to exchange non-secret parameters and calculate a unique shared secret that can be used as seed for generating symmetric key. An adversary can defeat DH key exchange using man-in-the-middle attack.
- When the number of entities is large, a trusted key distribution centre (KDC) is established for symmetric-key distribution. KDC distributes session keys on request. Needham–Schroeder and Otway–Rees are two key distribution protocols for a KDC.
- Kerberos is an authentication and symmetric key distribution protocol for client-server applications. It is based on the work of Needham and Schroeder on key distribution centres.
- The KDC in Kerberos consists of three parts: authentication server (AS), ticket granting server (TGS) and user database. The AS authenticates the users and issues ticket for access to TGS. The TGS in turn issues tickets for access to the requested application service.
- Kerberos implementation can extend to multiple realms so that users of one realm can access services available in another realm.

In the next chapter, we continue with the topic on key distribution. We study public-key distribution using a trusted certification authority.

Key Terms		
Authentication server (AS)	Kerberos realms	Needham–Schroeder key distribution protocol
Diffie–Hellman key exchange	Key distribution centre (KDC)	Otway–Rees key distribution protocol
Kerberos	Man-in-the-middle attack	Ticket granting server (TGS)

RECOMMENDED READING

Avoine, G., Junod, P. and Oechslin, P., *Computer System Security: Basic Concepts and Solved Exercises*, CRC Press, FL, USA, 2004.

Forouzan, Behrouz A., *Cryptography and Network Security*, Tata McGraw-Hill, New Delhi, 2007.

Kaufman, C., Perlman, R. and Spenciner, M., *Network Security, Private Communication in a Public World*, Prentice-Hall of India, New Delhi, 2007.

Menezes, A., Oorschot, P. and Vanstone, S., *Handbook of Applied Cryptography*, CRC Press, FL, USA, 1997.

Needham, R.M. and Schroeder, M.D., Using Encryption for Authentication in Large Networks of Computers, *Communications of the ACM*, Vol. 21, pp. 993–999, 1978.

RFC 4120, The Kerberos Network Authentication Service (V5), IETF, 2005.

Stallings, W., *Cryptography and Network Security*, Prentice-Hall of India, New Delhi, 2008.

Trappe, W., Washington, L., *Introduction to Cryptography and Coding Theory*, Prentice Hall, NJ, USA, 2006.

Vaudenay, S., *A Classical Introduction to Cryptography*, Springer, NY, USA, 2006.

PROBLEMS

1. Describe possible scenario of man-in-the-middle attack in symmetric-key exchange using public key.

2. Compute the half-keys and shared secret for the Diffie–Hellman parameters given below.
   (a) $p = 23$, $g = 5$, $a = 4$, $b = 3$
   (b) $p = 47$, $g = 5$, $a = 3$, $b = 4$
   (c) $p = 23$, $g = 7$, $a = 3$, $b = 5$

3. The adversary notices that Alice and Bob have chosen for their DH exchange prime number $p = 29$ which can be expressed as $29 = 4 \times 7 + 1$. He intercepts their half keys k_A, k_B and modifies them as $(k_A)^7 \bmod 29$ and $(k_B)^7 \bmod 29$. Alice and Bob are unaware of the modification and compute shared secret key using the modified half keys. The adversary readily breaks the key as he has restricted the possible key values to four in number.

   (a) Assume $g = 2$ and compute secret key for the following values of secrets (a, b) chosen by Alice and Bob:

   $$(3, 4), (3, 5), (3, 6), (3, 7), (4, 5), (5, 6), (5, 7)$$

   (b) Explain the reason behind this outcome, i.e., four possible secret keys.

4. In order to prevent man-in-the-middle attack on Diffie–Hellman key exchange, the following modification of Diffie–Hellman key-exchange algorithm is proposed.
   - The public parameters are a large prime p, and generator g of the order of $(p - 1)$ of the multiplicative group $\{Z_p^*, \times\}$.
   - Each user (i) has a secret private key R_i and a public key $P_i = g^{R_i} \bmod p$. The public keys of all the users are available from trusted third party.

   Alice and Bob arrive at a following key agreement:
   - Alice chooses a secret random number a, $0 < a < p - 1$. She calculates $S_A = g^a \bmod p$ and sends S_A to Bob.
   - Bob chooses a secret random number b, $0 < b < p - 1$. He calculates $S_B = g^b \bmod p$ and sends S_B to Alice.
   - Alice computes the secret key K = (Bob's public key)^a × $(S_B)^{\text{Alice's private key}}$ mod p.
   - Bob computes the secret key K = (Alice's public key)^b × $(S_A)^{\text{Bob's private key}}$ mod p.

   What is the common secret key K calculated by Alice and Bob?

5. Assume that the random number b chosen by Bob is a small number in Problem 4. Explain how the adversary can exploit small value of b to impersonate Alice and set up a key with Bob. (*Hint:* Show that K $= (P_B)^a \times (P_A)^b \bmod p$.)

6. Alice, Bob, and Carol want to agree on a common secret key. They publicly choose a large prime p and a generator g. They privately choose random numbers a, b and c respectively. Describe a protocol that allows them to compute a common secret $g^{abc} \bmod p$ securely.

7. A KDC uses the following scheme for symmetric-key distribution:
   - The KDC
     - chooses a large prime number p publically,
     - assigns public keys k_A, k_B, k_C, ... to all the users, $k_i < p$.
     - chooses secret numbers u, v and w, $(u, v, w < p)$.
   - The KDC computes for each user two numbers s and r as given below and sends these numbers confidentially to each user.
     $s = u + v \times k_i \pmod{p}$ $r = v + w \times k_i \pmod{p}$
   - Each user forms a symmetric-key generating polynomial $s + r \times k_i \pmod{p}$.

   When Alice wants to communicate with Bob, she uses this polynomial with Bob's public key k_B to get the symmetric key K_{AB}. Bob also computes the symmetric key K_{BA} using Alice's public key k_A. Show that Alice and Bob arrive at the same value of symmetric key that is $K_{AB} = K_{BA}$.

8. The KDC protocol described in Problem 7 has the following parameters:
   $$p = 31, \ u = 8, \ v = 3, \ w = 1, \ k_A = 11, \ k_B = 3$$
   (a) Show calculations carried out by Alice and Bob to arrive at the symmetric key K_{AB}.
   (b) If Alice and Bob conspire, they can determine the secret numbers u, v and w of the KDC (Problem 7). Show the computation carried out by them.

9. Alice wanting to send secret key K to Bob chooses a nonce n_A and sends message $M_1 = K \oplus n_A$ to Bob. Bob chooses a nonce n_B and returns message $M_2 = M_1 \oplus n_B$ to Alice. Alice computes $M_3 = M_2 \oplus n_A$ and sends it to Bob. Bob computes $K' = M_3 \oplus n_B$ to get the key K.

(a) Show that $K' = K$.

(b) Suppose the adversary copies the messages M_1, M_2 and M_3. How does he compute K?

10. A KDC has master keys with all the end entities for communication with them. The session key distribution scheme is as follows:

(a) Alice chooses a key K_S for a session with Bob and sends the following message to the KDC. The message is a request for issuing encrypted ticket to Bob. The message contains the key K_S encrypted using her master key K_A with KDC.

$$\text{Alice, Bob, } E(K_A, \{K_S\}) \tag{1}$$

(b) KDC sends the following ticket to Alice:

$$E(K_B, \{K_S\}) \tag{2}$$

(c) Alice sends message m encrypted using K_S and ticket received from the KDC to Bob.

$$E(K_S, \{m\}), \ E(K_B, \{K_S\}) \tag{3}$$

(d) Bob retrieves the session key K_S and then the message m.

The mole X in the community of the KDC modifies the message (1) replacing 'Bob' by 'X' in the message. Alice is unaware of these happenings sends message (3) to Bob. X copies (3) and retrieves the message m. Rewrite the exchange of messages and explain how X achieves this fete.

11. As mentioned in the last paragraph of Section 14.4.1, the adversary can launch an attack, if he gets hold of Alice's master key K_A and message (2) from the KDC to Alice, even if the key and the message (2) are obsolete. A proposed solution is to include the following two messages as message (1) and (2). The rest of message sequence remains same.

(a) From Alice to Bob ID_A (1)

(b) Bob to Alice $E(K_B, \{N_B\})$ (2)

N_B is Bob's nonce encrypted using his master key with the KDC. Alice includes this encrypted nonce in her request to the KDC for session key. Complete rest of the message exchange. How do these messages thwart the adversary's potential attack?

12. In message (5) of Needhan–Schroeder protocol, Alice adds one to the nonce N_B received from Bob before returning to him. Why does she do that?

13. Message (5) of Kerberos from the client to application server consists of $\text{Authenticator}_{C2}$ and Ticket_P. What prevents an adversary from copying this message and reusing it?

14. A young cryptographer decides to implement Diffie–Hellman key exchange protocol, using the additive group $\{Z_p, +\}$ instead of the multiplicative group $\{Z_p^*, \times\}$. What is your opinion about his approach?

15. To have secure conference with n participants, a secret conference key is to be established among the participating nodes. Let us consider that there are four nodes A, B, C and D. The conference key is generated in three rounds as given below:

    • The conference coordinator, who is one of the participant, chooses a large prime number p and a generator g of Z_p^* and communicates these parameters to all the other participating nodes.

    • Each node (i) chooses a random number $x_i \in Z_p^*$ and computes $[P_i, Q_i] = [g^{x_i} \bmod p, 1]$ and sends $[P_i, Q_i]$ to the next node ($i + 1$) in the clockwise direction [Figure 14.9(a)].

    • After the first round of sending $[P_i, Q_i]$, each participating node (i) recomputes $[P_i, Q_i]$ as given below.

    $$[P_i, Q_i] = [g^{x_i} P_{i-1}, (P_{i-1})^{x_i} Q_{i-1}]$$

    where $[P_{i-1}, P_{i-1}]$ are the values received by node i from node $i - 1$. In the second round, the recomputed values are sent to the next node. Figure 14.9(b) shows the computation carried out by node A and the values sent out to node B.

    • The previous step is repeated for the third round.

    • Each node computes the conference key K as given below:

    $$K = (P_{i-1})^{x_i} Q_{i-1}$$

    Compute the conference key K.

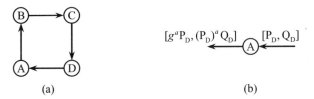

    (a)   (b)

    Figure 14.9   Problem 15.

16. In the DH key exchange, Alice and Bob choose random number a and b from the set $\{2, ..., p - 2\}$. Why are the values 1 and $p - 1$ excluded?

17. Alice and Bob exchange a master key k_0 using DH key exchange and derive the session keys from the master key. They have three alternatives for derivation of the session keys:

    (a) $k_{i+1} = k_i + 1$
    (b) $k_{i+1} = h(k_i)$
    (c) $k_{i+1} = h(k_0 \| i \| k_i)$

    where h is a secure hash function, and k_i is the ith session key. They choose the method of key derivation based on the following criterion.

    "If the adversary manages to get the nth session key, he should not be able to compute other session keys."

    Which is the method chosen by Alice and Bob?

15

Public-key Distribution

In the previous chapter we covered distribution of symmetric keys. Continuing with the same subject of key distribution, we focus on distribution of public-keys in this chapter. We start with conceptual basis of public-key certificate and trusted certification authority. We discuss ITU-T Recommendation X.509 for public-key certificates and the public-key infrastructure required for distribution of the certificates. Before we close the chapter, we introduce hierarchical, cross-certification and hybrid trust models for verification of certificates.

15.1 PUBLIC-KEY DISTRIBUTION

As we saw in the last chapter, the major issue with symmetric-key cryptography is the secret key management and distribution. The asymmetric-key cryptography addresses this issue in a very effective way by declaring one of the encryption keys as public key, which is not a secret key. Its distribution requires authenticity not confidentiality. The other key is secret and is preserved by its owner. It is not to be shared, and therefore, does not require distribution. The following approaches can be adopted for distribution of the public keys.

- Public announcement
- Public-key directory
- Public-key certificates

15.1.1 Public Announcement

There can be several modes of public announcement:

- The public key can be printed like a telephone number on visiting card.
- It can be appended to the messages sent on public forums and emails, or published on the website.
- It can be advertised in newspapers.

Although public announcement is simple and convenient, it is not secure. Anyone can forge such public announcement. The adversary, for example, can advertise his public key as the public key of Alice. When Bob sends his encrypted message to Alice making use of the advertised key, the adversary can read Bob's encrypted messages.

15.1.2 Public-key Directory

An alternative approach for distributing public keys can be similar to telephone directory. A trusted authority can be assigned for maintaining, updating and distributing the public-key directory. The public-key owners register their public keys with the authority. Registration can be done on production of credentials in person or electronically through secure communication. Disbursement of directory information can be formalized and secured as shown in Figure 15.1. It is assumed that the trusted authority's public key is well known.

1. Alice requests the public-key authority for Bob's public key. She appends a nonce N_A that identifies her request.
2. The public-key authority responds with Bob's public key K_B and Alice's nonce N_A. It encrypts the response using its private key K_{AUTH}.
3. Alice decrypts the response using the well-known public key of the authority, identifies her nonce N_A and takes note of Bob's public key K_B. She sends her intent to communicate to Bob by sending her identity, ID_A, and a nonce N_A. She uses Bob's public key K_B to encrypt her message.
4. Bob decrypts the message using his private key and sends request to the public-key authority for Alice's public key. He appends a nonce N_B that identifies his request.
5. The public-key authority responds with Alice's public key K_A and Bob nonce N_B. It encrypts the response using its private key K_{AUTH}.
6. Bob decrypts the response using the well-known public key of the authority, identifies his nonce N_B and takes note of Alice's public key K_A. He responds to Alice with a message consisting of Alice's nonce N_A and his nonce N_B. He uses Alice's public key K_A to encrypt the message.
7. Alice decrypts the Bob's response using her private key and verifies her nonce. She is assured that Bob possesses the private key that corresponds to the public key she obtained from the authority. She returns Bob's nonce encrypted with Bob's public key K_B. On receipt of this message, Bob is assured that Alice possesses the private key that corresponds with the public key he obtained from the authority.

Alice and Bob can now communicate using each other's public keys.

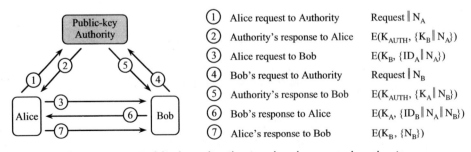

①	Alice request to Authority	Request $\| N_A$
②	Authority's response to Alice	$E(K_{AUTH}, \{K_B \| N_A\})$
③	Alice request to Bob	$E(K_B, \{ID_A \| N_A\})$
④	Bob's request to Authority	Request $\| N_B$
⑤	Authority's response to Bob	$E(K_{AUTH}, \{K_A \| N_B\})$
⑥	Bob's response to Alice	$E(K_A, \{ID_B \| N_A \| N_B\})$
⑦	Alice's response to Bob	$E(K_B, \{N_B\})$

Figure 15.1 Public-key distribution by the trusted authority.

15.1.3   Public-key Certificate

The previous scheme can be further systematized using public-key certificates. The trusted authority is designated as Certification Authority (CA). The CA verifies credentials of the user and issues digitally signed public-key certificate. The certificate binds the public-key of the user to the user's identity (Figure 15.2). The certificate contains the following information:

- User's Id, his public key and applicable public-key algorithm,
- Issuer's Id, his public-key and applicable algorithm for signature verification,
- Validity period of the certificate,
- Digital signature of the issuer on the content of the certificate.

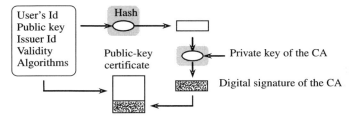

Figure 15.2   Public-key certificate.

When Alice wants to communicate with Bob, she sends her public-key certificate to him. Bob verifies the digital signature of the CA on the certificate. The public key of CA required for signature verification is well known. Similarly, Bob sends his public-key certificate to Alice who verifies Bob's certificate. Now, both Alice and Bob have public keys of each other to have a secure communication session. We will come across use of public-key certificates in IKE, TLS and S/MIME protocols described in the later chapters of the book. For now, we look at the infrastructure required for maintaining and distributing public-key certificates.

15.2   PUBLIC-KEY INFRASTRUCTURE (PKI)

The primary purpose of creating Public-key Infrastructure (PKI), is to provide trusted and efficient management of public-key certificates. As mentioned above there are several security protocols that make use this infrastructure for verifying the public-key certificates. A PKI consists of the following components (Figure 15.3):

- Certification authority (CA)
- Registration authority (RA)
- Certificate and CRL (certificate revocation list) repository
- Certificate user and owner end-entities

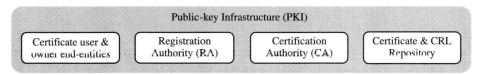

Figure 15.3   Components of PKI.

Certification authority (CA): The CA is responsible for establishing identity and issuing public-key certificate that binds the identity to a public key. It also issues certificate revocation list (CRLs) that contain the certificates revoked before expiration of their validity period.

Registration authority (RA): The RA is responsible for initial registration and authentication of the end-entity. It interfaces with the end-entity for registration, certificate delivery, and certificate life cycle management processes other than issue of certificates and CRLs. It may be a stand-alone component or part of the CA. The following functions are likely to be part of an RA:

- Verification of information submitted by the end-entity for obtaining certificate.
- Validating the entitlement of the end-entity to the requested certificate attributes.
- Generation of public/private key-pairs. If the key pair is generated by the end-entity, RA verifies that the end-entity possesses the private key associated with the public key submitted by it for certification.
- Reporting cases for revocation of certificates to CA.
- Assignment of identities to the end-entities.
- Generation of shared secrets for use during initialization phase.
- Distribution of physical tokens (such as smart cards).
- Other functions as assigned to it by the CA.

Certificate repository: The repository is used for public storage of certificates and CRLs. It has query support for retrieval of the certificates and CRLs.

Certificate user and owner end-entities: An end-entity is the owner of a certificate or a user-client. End-entity can be a person, an organization, a device (e.g. a firewall or a router), or an executable program. As a user-client, an end-entity receives the certificate from its owner and uses it for establishing the identity of the sender. As owner of the certificate, the end-entity produces the certificate for proving its identity.

15.2.1 Functions of PKI

Public-key infrastructure consisting of the above components carries out the following functions:

Registration: Registration is the process whereby an end-entity makes itself known to a CA either directly or through Registration Authority (RA) for obtaining a public-key certificate. Registration involves some online and offline authentication procedure for establishing the end-entity's credentials.

Initialization: Before an end-entity can begin to communicate with PKI, it needs to be initialized for establishing secure communication with the CA or RA and for delivery of public/private key pair.

Certification: This is the process in which the CA issues a public-key certificate for the end-entity. It also posts the certificate in a certificate repository for distribution to the users.

Key generation: Depending on CA's policy, the public/private key pair can either be generated by the owner end-entity, or be generated by the CA. In the latter case, the key material is distributed to the end-entity in an encrypted file or on a physical token such as smart card.

Key-pair recovery: If a CA has generated and issued the public/private key-pair, the end-entity's private key is backed up in CA's key backup system. In the event of the end-entity losing its private key due to forgotten passwords, hard-disc failure, damaged token, or any other reason, PKI provides recovery of the private key from its key backup system.

Key-pair update: A key-pair needs to be replaced with a new key-pair when it expires or it is compromised. In the event of key compromise, the public-key certificate is revoked. A new certificate is issued in either case.

Cross-certification: Cross-certificate is a certificate issued by one CA to another CA to certify the public key of latter CA. Typically cross-certification is required between CA's of two different administrative domains.

Revocation: A certificate may be required to be revoked before expiration of its validity period due to some abnormal circumstances. For example, an employee terminates employment with an organization; the private key is compromised or suspected to have been compromised; or user's identity is changed. The CA revokes the certificate and issues notification in form of Certificate Revocation List (CRL).

15.2.2   X.509 Public-key Certificate

ITU-T Recommendation X.509 is part of X.500 series of recommendations for directory service which provides information (e.g. network address) about the users. X.509 specifically defines a framework for authentication service based on public-key certificates and the IETF adopted this recommendation. Figure 15.4(a) shows general format of the X.509 public-key certificate. Its major fields are described below:

Version: It defines the version of X.509 certificate. The version number started with 0. The value in the field for the current third version is 2.

Serial number: It uniquely identifies this certificate together with the issuer's name.

Signature: This field identifies the signature algorithm used by the CA to sign this certificate. It is followed by the parameters associated with the algorithm.

Issuer name: It is the name of the certification authority that created and signed this certificate.

Validity period: This field defines the earliest time (not before) and the latest time (not after) the certificate is valid.

Subject name: The name of the entity to whom this certificate and therefore the public key given in the certificate belongs.

Subject's public key: This field specifies the public-key algorithm (e.g. RSA), associated algorithm parameters and the public key of the subject.

Issuer's unique identifier: This optional field specifies a unique identifier assigned to the certificate issuer.

Subject's unique identifier: This optional field specifies a unique identifier assigned to the subject.

Extensions: This field consists of a set of optional extensions added to the certificate.

CA's signature: This field specifies the signature algorithm, associated algorithm parameters and CA's digital signature on the certificate. The digital signature is computed over all the other field of the certificate and is put in the sub-field named 'encrypted'. Note that the signature algorithm and the associated parameters specified in the 'signature' field are repeated here.

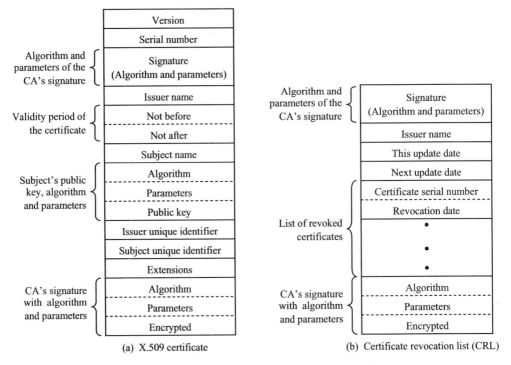

Figure 15.4 Formats of X.509 certificate and CRL.

15.2.3 Extensions Field of X.509 Public-key Certificate

The 'Extensions' field consists of set of extensions. Each extension consists of an extension identifier, criticality indicator and extension value. The extensions fall into three main categories:

- Key and policy information
- Subject's and issuer's attributes
- Certification path constraints

Key and policy information: This extension gives additional information about the subject's public key, issuer's public key and applicable policy framework. The information consists of the following:

- Subject's key identifier, if the subject has multiple public-keys.
- Issuer's key identifier, if the issuer has multiple public-keys.
- Key usage restriction. Public-key types based on permitted usage are described in Section 15.2.5.
- Private key usage period. Usage period of private key associated with the certified public key can be different from the validity period of the public key. For example, private key may have longer usage period than the associated public key used for encryption. This would enable recovery of the stored encrypted data even after expiry of the public key.
- Applicable policies.

Subject's and issuer's attributes: These extensions give additional attributes such as alternative names, picture, email address, etc.

Certification path constrains: This extension is applicable to the certificates issued to the CAs by other CAs. It defines certificate chain length and name space constraints.

15.2.4 Certificate Revocation

The certificate has a validity period. It is renewed by the certificate issuing authority before its expiry. But a certificate may be revoked before its expiry in the following cases:

- If the subject's private key associated with the public key in the certificate is exposed, the certificate needs to be revoked.
- Changed status of the subject may necessitate certificate revocation. For example,
  - The subject no longer works in the organization on whose credentials the certificate was issued.
  - The information (e.g. the subject's name) included in the certificate has changed.
- The issuer's private key that was used to sign the certificate is compromised. In this case, the issuer revokes all the unexpired certificates bearing its signature based on the compromised private key.

When the CA revokes a certificate, it must also advise the users of the revoked status of the certificate. The CA publishes a Certificate Revocation List (CRL) periodically. CRL contains all the revoked certificates that have not expired up to the date of issue of the CRL. Figure 15.4(b) shows the format of the CRL. The list bears digital signature of the issuing CA to ensure that the list cannot be modified by an adversary to his advantage.

15.2.5 Public-key Types

The certified public key of the subject in the certificate has usage restrictions. These restrictions are specified in the extension field of the X.509 certificate. The following key-types based on usage have been defined:

- *Public key for signature verification.* This key (e.g. RSA public key) can be used for signature verification only.
- *Public key for key transport.* This key (e.g. RSA public key) can be used for transporting symmetric session key.
- *Public key for user data transport.* This key (e.g. RSA public key) can be used for transporting user data only.
- *Public key for key agreement.* In this case, the subject's public key field consists of parameters (e.g. Diffie–Hellman key parameters, prime number p, the generator g, and the half key g^x mod p) for generating a shared secret key agreement.
- *Public key for certificate verification.* The use of the public key is limited to verifying the certificate issuer's signature.
- *Public key for CRL verification.* The use of public key is limited to verifying the CRL issuer's signature.

The above key-usage categorization has been made keeping in view the administrative, security and key management policies. There can be statutory restrictions imposed by the government. For example,

- Government security policy may restrict the maximum size of encryption keys. The restriction may not be applicable to signature verification key.
- Signature verification public key, once revoked or expired may not have any further use. On the other hand, the private key associated with the encryption public key may still be required to decrypt the stored encrypted data.

15.3 TRUST MODELS

A public-key certificate binds an identity (e.g. Alice) to an attribute of the identity (e.g. public-key of Alice). It is signed by a certification authority trusted by a community of users. When Alice and Bob belong to the same community, and Alice sends her public-key certificate to Bob, Bob authenticates the certificate by verifying the digital signature of CA on the certificate. He accepts the certificate and its content because he trusts the CA who issued the certificate to Alice. Similarly, when Bob sends his certificate to Alice, Alice authenticates Bob using his certificate. This simple trust model is shown in Figure 15.5(a). An organization can use this model for establishing public-key infrastructure for its own community of users.

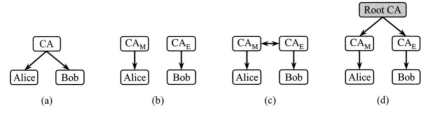

Figure 15.5 Basic trust models.

Assume that Alice and Bob belong to two different arms of an organization, Marketing (M) and Engineering (E) respectively. Each arm has established its own CA [Figure 15.5(b)]. When Alice sends her certificate signed by CA_M to Bob, Bob cannot validate the certificate because he does not trust CA_M. Same situation arises when Bob sends his certificate to Alice.

When there are multiple CAs, there must be trust relationships among the CAs, similar to the trust of Alice and Bob in their respective CAs. This can be achieved through cross certification or having hierarchy of CAs.

15.3.1 Cross Certification

CAs build trust relationships among themselves by cross certifying one another [Figure 15.5(c)]. In the above example, CA_M generates a certificate for CA_E, which binds identity of CA_E and its public key. CA_E also generates certificate for CA_M in the same manner. When Alice sends her certificate to Bob, she also sends CA_M's certificate signed by CA_E. Bob verifies the two certificates sent by Alice. If verification is successful, he accepts the certificates because the chain of certificates ends on CA_E whom he trusts.

If there are n CAs, every CA must obtain certificate from every other CA. In other words, the CA's will have $n(n-1)$ trust relationships [Figure 15.6(a)].

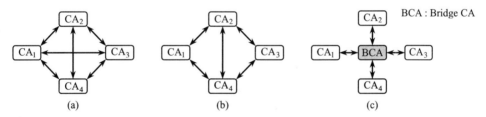

Figure 15.6 Cross certification.

It is not necessary that a trust relationship must be bilateral. For example, in Figure 15.6(a), CA_4 may issue certificate to CA_1, but this relationship may not hold other way round. It is also not necessary to have fully connected mesh of trusts. In Figure 15.6(b), CA_1 and CA_3 do not have any direct trust relationship. In such situation, the trust path needs be built between the two CAs. If Alice has certificate from CA_1 and Bob has certificate from CA_3, there can be several alternate trust paths between them.

$$CA_1 \Leftrightarrow CA_2 \Leftrightarrow CA_3$$
$$CA_1 \Leftrightarrow CA_4 \Leftrightarrow CA_3$$
$$CA_1 \Leftrightarrow CA_2 \Leftrightarrow CA_4 \Leftrightarrow CA_3$$
$$CA_1 \Leftrightarrow CA_4 \Leftrightarrow CA_2 \Leftrightarrow CA_3$$

Trust relationships that extend through minimum number of intermediate CAs are desirable. But it is possible that security policies implemented along a longer path may provide higher level of assurance. This makes certificate distribution and validation more complex and complexity increases exponentially as number n becomes large.

To avoid large number of trust relationships, one alternative is to have a bridge CA [Figure 15.6(c)]. Each CA establishes cross-certification relationship with the bridge CA thus extends the trust relations across the bridge. Note that in this case n CAs will have n trust relationships.

15.3.2 Hierarchical Trust Model

Hierarchical trust model has a hierarchy of CAs with a common root CA_0 [Figure 15.5(d)]. The CA_0 issues certificates to its subordinate CAs, CA_M and CA_E. The CA_0 enjoys the trust of every user and certifies itself. When Alice sends her certificate to Bob, she also sends CA_M's certificate signed by CA_0. Bob verifies the two certificates sent by Alice. If verification is successful, he accepts the certificates because the chain of certificates ends on CA_0 whom he trusts.

The hierarchical model can have multiple levels of hierarchy as shown in Figure 15.7. When E_1 wants to communicate with E_8, he sends chain of certificates up to the root CA_0, i.e., his end-entity certificate and certificates of CA_1, CA_5 and CA_0. E_8 validates each certificate using the respective public key of the issuer.

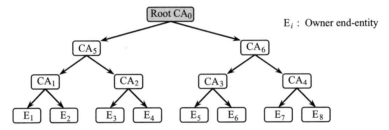

Figure 15.7 Hierarchical trust model.

Hierarchical model is the most widely deployed model today for certification. Its major benefit is certificate distribution. Since root CA enjoys trust of all the users, only the certificate path up to the root CA is required to be validated. Government of India has established Controller of Certification Authorities (CCA) which

- operates the National Root CA,
- maintains the National Certificate Repository,
- issues licenses to organisations for operating as Certifying Authorities (CAs), and
- issues certificates to the licensed CAs.

The licensed CAs issue public-key certificates to the end-entities. The list of authorized CAs in India is given at the website of the CCA.[1]

15.3.3 Hybrid Trust Model

Hierarchical trust model with one root CA may be applicable to an organization, a set of sister organizations, or a country. As can be expected, the public Internet has many root CAs. The

---

1. http://cca.gov.in

root CAs have cross certification so that each hierarchy can reach every other hierarchy via a single cross certificate at the root level (Figure 15.8).

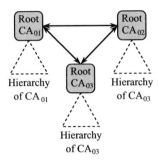

Figure 15.8 Hybrid trust model.

15.4 SUMMING UP

Continuing with the subject of key distribution, we focused on distribution of public keys in this chapter. The key learnings are given below:

- Though public keys are not secret, their authenticity in respect of their owner is the prime security concern. An adversary can easily publish his own key as the key of his victim.
- Public-key distribution is done through a trusted certification authority (CA) who issues public-key certificates that bind identity of an entity to its public key. The entity can be a software entity, a network entity, an organization, or an individual.
- The certificates are digitally signed by the CA and can be readily verified using the well-known public key of the CA.
- ITU-T Recommendation X.509 defines a framework for authentication service based on public-key certificates and format of public-key certificate.
- The public-key certificate specifies the purpose for which the certified public key can be used. A public key certified for encryption cannot be used for signature verification.
- Public-key Infrastructure (PKI) provides trusted and efficient management of public-key certificates. It consists of the following components:
  - Certification authority (CA)
  - Registration authority (RA)
  - Certificate and CRL (certificate revocation list) repository
  - Certificate user and owner end-entities
- The Certification Revocation List (CRL) indicates the certificates revoked before expiry of their validity period. A certificate may be revoked due to changed status of the subject, or due to security reasons, e.g. when the private key of the subject or the certificate issuer is exposed.
- PKI is based on trust models. The users and owners of the public-key certificates lay their trust on the CA of their respective domain. The CAs, in turn, build trust relationships amongst themselves. The trust model can be

– hierarchical in which there is one root CA who is trusted by all the subordinate CAs.
– a mesh or bridged mesh in which the CAs build trust relationships by cross certification.
– hybrid of the above two approaches.

We will come across several protocols which make use of the public-key certificates and public key infrastructure in the following chapters:

Chapter 16   Email Security
Chapter 17   Transport Layer Security (TLS)
Chapter 19   Internet Key Exchange (IKE)

Key Terms		
Bridge CA	Hierarchical trust model	Registration authority (RA)
Certificate revocation list (CRL)	Meshed trust model	Root CA
Certification authority (CA)	Public-key certificate	Trust models
Cross certification	Public-key infrastructure (PKI)	X.509 public-key certificate

RECOMMENDED READING

Avoine, G., Junod, P. and Oechslin, P., *Computer System Security: Basic Concepts and Solved Exercises*, CRC Press, FL, USA, 2004.

Douligeris, C. (Ed), Serpanos, D.N., *Network Security, Current Status and Future Directions*, IEEE Press, John Wiley & Sons, NJ, USA, 2007.

Forouzan, Behrouz A., *Cryptography and Network Security*, Tata McGraw-Hill, New Delhi, 2007.

ITU-T X.509, *The Directory: Public-key and Attribute Certificate Frameworks,* International Telecommunication Union, Geneva, 2012.

Kaufman, C., Perlman, R. and Spenciner, M., *Network Security, Private Communication in a Public World*, Prentice-Hall of India, New Delhi, 2007.

Menezes, A., Oorschot, P. and Vanstone, S., *Handbook of Applied Cryptography*, CRC Press, NJ, USA, 1997.

RFC 4158, *Internet X.509 Public Key Infrastructure: Certification Path Building, IETF.*

RFC 5280, *Internet X.509 Public Key Infrastructure Certificate and Certificate Revocation List (CRL) Profile, IETF.*

Stallings, W., *Cryptography and Network Security*, Prentice-Hall of India, New Delhi, 2008.

Stamp, M., *Information Security, Principles and Practice*, John Wiley & Sons, 2011.

Trappe, W., Washington, L., *Introduction to Cryptography and Coding Theory*, Prentice Hall, NJ, USA, 2006.

Vaudenay, S., *A Classical Introduction to Cryptography*, Springer, NY, USA, 2006.

(PROBLEMS)

1. Assume that CRL is not signed by CA. How can the adversary take advantage of this fact for launching an attack by modifying the CRL?

2. If the public-key certificates had no expiry date, and certificates were revoked when they were no longer required or when they were compromised, apparently it would have simplified management of certificates. The process of their periodic renewal and distribution could be done away with. Give your arguments in favour or against this proposal.

3. Alice owns public-key certificate valid from 1000 hours of 9th November 2013 to 1000 hours of 9th November 2014. The certificate was revoked at 1700 hours on 15 March 2014. The CA publishes the CRL daily at 0000 hours. Determine the dates
   (a) when Alice's certificate appears in the CRL and
   (b) when it disappears from the CRL.

4. Figure 15.9 shows a cross-certification trust model among four CAs. Note that trust relationship is bilateral between CA_2 and CA_4 only. The direction of arrow indicates who issues certificate for whom, e.g. CA_2 certifies CA_1.
   (a) Find all the possible trust paths when the end-entity E_2 authenticates E_1.
   (b) Find all the possible trust paths when the end-entity E_2 authenticates E_3.
   (c) Find all the possible trust paths when the end-entity E_3 authenticates E_1.

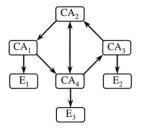

Figure 15.9 Problem 3.

5. Suppose that Bob receives Alice's public-key certificate from a sender. What useful information about the sender does he gain by verifying the signature?

6. What is the security impact when certificates of Alice and Bob as subjects
   (a) certify the same public key?
   (b) have the same signature of the CA?

7. Bob sends his public-key certificate to Alice. The adversary, instead of substituting his own public-key certificate in place of Bob's public-key certificate (which substitution Alice would readily detect), replaces Bob's public key with his own public key in the Bob's public-key certificate. Is he able to fool Alice into accepting his public key as Bob's public key?

16

Email Security

Electronic mail (email) is one of the oldest network applications and has been the most popular Internet service as well. PGP (Pretty Good Privacy) and S/MIME (Secure/Multipurpose Internet Mail Extensions) are examples of two secure email systems deployed widely on various platforms, Windows, UNIX and others. This chapter focuses on the security architecture of these two email systems. We begin the chapter with an introduction of email system based on SMTP and MIME. We look at basic security requirements of an email system and then examine S/MIME and PGP in detail. We also introduce an interesting concept 'web of trust' used in PGP in place of hierarchical trust model that we studied in the last chapter.

16.1 ELECTRONIC MAIL

An email system consists of several components as shown in Figure 16.1.

Message user agent (MUA): MUA process reads and writes email. It fetches mail from the mailbox using protocols POP3 or IMAP4. It appends the outgoing mails to the spool-file.

Spool-file: It contains the mails to be sent. MUA appends the outgoing mails in the spool-file using SMTP protocol. MTA extracts the mails from the spool-file for their delivery.

Message transfer agent (MTA): MTA reads the spool-file and deletes the read mails from the spool-file. It delivers the mails to the mailboxes of the recipients. It forwards the mails to peer MTA using SMTP, if the destination mailbox is in another mail server. There can be intermediate MTAs also that act as transit for transferring mails from one MTA to another.

Mailbox: It is the designated file owned by the receiver. The delivered mails are appended in this file. The user can read and delete the mails from his mailbox file.

Email address: Email address consists of a character string conforming to the format—user@domain. The user part identifies the mailbox of the user in the domain indicated in the domain part of the address. The user part is unique within the domain. Domain part identifies some organization, mail exchange, or a host machine that provides mailbox service, and it is unique globally.

SMTP: SMTP (Simple Mail Transfer Protocol) is based on client-server model. It uses TCP at well-known port TCP port number 25 for the server [Figure 16.1(b)]. All the commands, responses and messages SMTP are in ASCII format (printable characters with binary values from 33 to 126, and control symbols CR, LF).

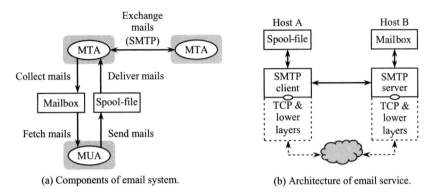

(a) Components of email system.   (b) Architecture of email service.

Figure 16.1 Email service.

16.1.1 Mail Format

Mail format defined in RFC 822 consists of two parts—header and body (Figure 16.2).

Header: The header contains information necessary for transmission and delivery of the mail. It consists of a series of lines each terminated with a pair of ASCII control symbols CR and LF. Each line has a type field followed by colon and the value. The header consists of several fields. It starts with 'Date' field which is followed by 'From' (the sender), 'To' (the recipients), 'Subject', and other fields.

Body: The body of the mail is separated from the header by a blank line. It contains user's message. RFC 822 restricts the maximum size of the body to 1000 characters. The body is followed by optional signature separated from the body by two dashes '--'. It contains personal information of the sender, keys, etc.

```
            ⎧  Date: Wed, 8 Jan 2014
            ⎪  From: Alice <alice@xyz.com>
   Header  ⎨   To: Bob <bob@abc.com>
            ⎩  Subject: Sample message

   Body  ⎧  Hello. This is a sample message.
         ⎩  Alice
```

Figure 16.2 Mail format.

Both the parts of an email, the header and body, are represented in 7-bit ASCII.

16.1.2 Multipurpose Internet Mail Extensions (MIME)

RFC 822 and SMTP together have the following limitations for the email service:

- Executable files, binary objects, text data of other languages (e.g. French, Japanese, Chinese, etc.), non-textual data (pictures, images and video/audio content) cannot be emailed because these are represented in 8-bit codes, while email supports only 7-bit ASCII.
- There is size limitation. SMTP servers may reject mails having size greater than the prescribed size.

Multipurpose Internet Mail Extensions (MIME) is a supplementary protocol that addresses these issues by transforming non-ASCII data into 7-bit ASCII at the sending end. The message is retransformed at the receiving end back to its original data type (Figure 16.3). MIME does so by

- describing the content-type and its format at the sending end. Email content can be text, images, audio/video, HTML pages and application specific data.
- specifying the encoding used to transform the data so that the receiving end may revert the data to its original type.

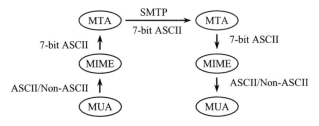

Figure 16.3 MIME.

MIME is realized by adding five additional header fields to the RFC 822 header (Figure 16.4).

RFC 822 header

MIME header
    MIME-Version: 1.1
    Content-Type: type/subtype
    Content-Transfer-Encoding: encoding type
    Content-ID: message ID
    Content-Description: textual explanation of non-textual content

Body

Figure 16.4 MIME header.

Mime version	It indicates the MIME version being used.
Content-type	It describes the type and subtype of data in the body of the message; and how the object in the body is to be interpreted.
Content–Transfer–Encoding	It describes how the object within the body has been encoded to 7-bit ASCII to make it acceptable for mail transport.
Content-ID	It identifies the MIME entities in multiple contexts.
Content-description	It is textual description of the object within the body. This is needed when the object is not displayable (e.g. audio content).

Table 16.1 lists the content-types defined by MIME. There are seven major content-types. The *multipart* type indicates the body consists of multiple parts. The parts are delimited by a boundary parameter defined in the *content-type* header. Each part may have its own *content-type* header as depicted in the following example.

```
From: Alice <alice@xyz.com>
To: Bob <bob@abc.com>
Subject: Sample message

MIME-Version: 1.1
Content-Type: multipart/mixed; boundary=xxx


--xxx
Content-Type: text/plain; charset=us-ascii
This is the first part.
--xxx
Content-Type: text/enriched;
This is the second part.
--xxx--
```

TABLE 16.1 MIME content-types

Type	Subtype	Description
Text	Plain	Unformatted text in ASCII or ISO 8859.
	Enriched	Provides greater format flexibility.
Image	JPEG	JPEG format
	GIF	GIF format
Audio	Basic	Single channel 8-bit μ-law encoding at 8 kbps.
Video	MPEG	MPEG format.
Multipart	Mixed	Mixed parts of various content-types; parts to be presented to receiver sequentially.
	Parallel	Same as mixed, but the order is not defined.
	Alternative	Different parts are alternative versions of same content and are to be used based on capabilities of the receiver.
	Digest	Similar to mixed but default type/subtype of each part is mixed/RFC 822.
Application	Postscript	Abode Postscript.
	Octet-stream	Binary data in 8-bit octets.
Message	RFC822	The body is an encapsulated message that conforms to RFC 822.
	Partial	The body is a fragment of a large mail.
	External-body	Contains pointer to an object that exists elsewhere and is accessible via FTP, TFTP, local file, mail server.

16.1.3   Content–Transfer–Encodings

The content–transfer–encoding field can take six values as listed in Table 16.2.

- The first three values (7-bit, 8-bit and binary) merely specify the representation of content. There is no transfer-encoding. Out of these 7-bit content can be safely sent on SMTP. 8-bit and binary forms may be usable in other email systems.
- x-token is a vendor specific encoding scheme for which a name is to be specified.
- Base64 (also known as Radix-64) encoding maps arbitrary binary input into printable ASCII output. The encoding is carried out as given below:
  - The binary data (stream of 0s and 1s) is divided into 24-bit blocks.
  - Each 24-bit block is further divided into four 6-bit words.
  - Each 6-bit word is mapped to 7-bit ASCII character using Base64 encoding table (Table 16.3).

  For example, three-octet sequence 10110010 01100011 00101001 is expressed as the following four 6-bit words. Decimal equivalent of the word is shown in the brackets.

  101100 (44)   100110 (38)   001100 (12)   101001(41)

  The decimal values of these words are mapped to 7-bit ASCII characters s m M p using Table 16.3. These characters are mail safe when transmitted as ASCII.
- Quoted-printable is useful when the data consist of largely printable characters. ASCII characters outside the range 33 to 61 (decimal equivalent) are represented as two-digit hex representation using an equal sign. For example, ASCII Form Feed (FF) control symbol (0000 1100) is represented as =0C where 0C is its hexadecimal representation of (0000 1100).

Base64 and quoted-printable are the two transfer-encoding schemes of interest for SMTP.

TABLE 16.2   MIME Content–transfer–Encodings

Encoding	Description
7-bit	The body contains 7-bit ASCII characters with maximal length of 1000 characters.
8-bit	The body can contain non-ASCII 8-bit characters with maximal size of 1000 characters.
Binary	Binary 8-bit characters without limitation of 1000 characters in the body.
Quoted-printable	This is useful when the data consist of largely printable ASCII characters. Each non-textual character is replaced with three textual ASCII characters.
Base64	It converts the binary data in a form that is not vulnerable to the mail processing.
x-token	A named non-standard encoding.

TABLE 16.3 Base64 Encoding

6-bit value	ASCII	6-bit value	ASCII	6-bit value	ASCII	6-bit value	ASCII	6-bit value	ASCII	6-bit value	ASCII	6-bit value	ASCII	6-bit value	ASCII
0	A	8	I	16	Q	24	Y	32	g	40	o	48	w	56	4
1	B	9	J	17	R	25	Z	33	h	41	p	49	x	57	5
2	C	10	K	18	S	26	a	34	i	42	q	50	y	58	6
3	D	11	L	19	T	27	b	35	j	43	r	51	z	59	7
4	E	12	M	20	U	28	c	36	k	44	s	52	0	60	8
5	F	13	N	21	V	29	d	37	l	45	t	53	1	61	9
6	G	14	O	22	W	30	e	38	m	46	u	54	2	62	+
7	H	15	P	23	X	31	f	39	n	47	v	55	3	63	/

Consider a MIME message that contains a photograph in GIF representation. The GIF image is converted to 7-bit ASCII using Base64 encoding. The message is formatted as given below:

```
From: Alice <alice@xyz.com>
To: Bob <bob@abc.com>
Subject: Photograph
MIME-Version: 1.1
Content-Type: image/gif
Content-Transfer-Encoding: base64
...base64 encoded data...
```

16.1.4   Security Requirements of Email Service

Email service requires all the aspects of security, namely, confidentiality, message authentication, and non repudiation. The following characteristic features of email service determine the design of its security system.

- Each instance of email is one time, one way activity. There is no session. When Alice sends an email to Bob, reply from Bob is independent and separate activity.
- There can be multiple receivers for the same message. Each receiver should be able to decrypt the message, if it is encrypted, and verify the signature if it is signed.
- Email protocols permits only 7-bit ASCII characters in its body and header. Non-ASCII characters in the body and header must be converted to ASCII characters.

Confidentiality

When Alice wants to send an email to several recipients, she can ensure confidentiality by encrypting the content using

- either public key of each recipient,
- or the symmetric-key she shares with each recipient.

In either case, Alice needs to produce multiple encrypted versions of the same content, one for each recipient. The size of mail gets multiplied by the number of recipients. Having one pre-shared symmetric key for all the recipients does not make sense. Encryption loses its purpose when everyone knows the secret key. Therefore, the way Alice achieves confidentiality is as follows:

1. She chooses a symmetric encryption key K for the email message.
2. She encrypts the message using key K for all the recipients.
3. She encrypts key K for each recipient separately using his public key.
4. She bundles the encrypted message, the multiple versions of encrypted K, encryption algorithm identifiers and sends the entire bundle as one email.

Each recipients gets the secret encryption key K, which he uses it to decrypt the content of the email.

Message Authentication and Non-repudiation

Message authentication implies both message integrity and source authentication. Message authentication can be done using MAC computed using hash function (e.g. HMAC) and the secret key. However, MAC does not address non-repudiation issue. Alternatively, Alice can digitally sign the digest of the message using her private key. Signed digest has several advantages:

- It provides message authentication and non-repudiation.
- The message carries only one signed digest usable by all the recipients for signature verification.

Alice bundles her public-key certificate and signature algorithm identifier in the mail for the recipients. The S/MIME and PGP protocols that we describe later use this approach.

Nested Cryptographic Operations

The cryptographic operations for confidentiality and authentication along with compression can be nested in several ways. For example,

- The content can be encrypted first and the digital signature can be computed for the encrypted content.
- The digital signature can be generated first. The signature and the content can be encrypted thereafter.
- Compression of the content can be done before or after encryption.

We will examine these issues later when we examine specific protocols for email security.

Encoding

Cryptographic transformations (encryption, digest, digital signature) result in output having non-ASCII symbols. Therefore, Base64 encoding is required to convert the binary output into 7-bit ASCII.

S/MIME and PGP are two secure email systems. We examine these email systems in the light of above considerations.

16.2 S/MIME

Secure MIME (S/MIME) as defined in RFC 5751 is the extension of MIME for providing secure email service. S/MIME provides the following security enhancements to the email.

Enveloped data: S/MIME provides confidentiality service by encrypting any type of content in a MIME message. Symmetric-key encryption is used for this purpose. The symmetric-key encrypted using public key of the recipient is sent along with the encrypted content.

Signed data: S/MIME provides authentication service using digital signature. The digest of the selected content of the message is digitally signed using the private key of the sender. The signed content and digital signature are Base64 encoded. A receiver having S/MIME capability only can view the content and verify the signature.

Clear-signed data: This feature of S/MIME is similar to signed data feature except that only the digital signature is Base-64 encoded. A receiver without S/MIME capability can view the content, but he cannot verify the signature.

Compressed data: S/MIME provides for compression of plaintext or encrypted content of a MIME entity.

Multiple operations: Encryption, signing and compression functions can be nested, i.e., a MIME entity can encapsulate another MIME entity. For example, a message can be compressed, signed and then encrypted.

Email is a one-time and one-way activity. It is necessary that the cryptographic algorithm-identifiers, secret keys, public-key certificates and other information required for processing at the receiving end are also communicated with each email. This information along with the encrypted/signed data is sent as one object. PKCS (Public Key Cryptography Standard) defines the syntax of this object.

16.2.1 New MIME Content-types

Security to the Internet email service is provided by way of additional MIME content-types. S/MIME adds the following new content subtypes that describe the content of the MIME entities.

(a) Multipart type has an additional subtype, multipart/signed. This subtype refers to the digital signature part of plaintext content.
(b) Application type has five additional subtypes as shown in Table 16.4. Each subtype is further described by the associated S/MIME parameter.

TABLE 16.4 Additional Application Type MIME Entities for Security

Type	Subtype	S/MIME parameter
	PKCS7-MIME	enveloped-data
	PKCS7-MIME	signed-data
Application	PKCS7-MIME	certs-only
	PKCS7-MIME	compressed-data
	PKCS7-signature	

As mentioned earlier, application-type part of a message requires some processing to retrieve the original content. For example, the part may require decryption, if the content has been encrypted. PKCS-7 defines the standard syntax of the object that carries

– content described by the S/MIME parameter and
– associated information such as encryption key and algorithm identifier, public-key certificate identifier, etc. required for processing the content.

PKCS object is provided with appropriate MIME headers and then sent as the message-body or part of message-body. It is to be noted that application of the security algorithm on the content will result in a binary object in most cases. Therefore, the PKCS object would need Base64 transfer encoding.

We now look at each of these additional subtypes required for S/MIME.

Enveloped Data

The application/PKCS7-MIME subtype with S/MIME parameter 'enveloped-data' is used for the encrypted content data. The steps involved in preparing the enveloped-data MIME are as follows (Figure 16.5):

1. For a chosen encryption algorithm (e.g. tripleDES), a pseudo-random symmetric encryption key (K) is generated.
2. The key (K) is encrypted using the recipient's public key (K_{Pi}) for each recipient.
3. A RecipientInfo block is prepared. It contains recipient's public-key certificate identifier, encryption algorithm identifier for the public key, and the encrypted symmetric key (K).
4. The message content is encrypted using symmetric key (K). The content can be of any type.
5. A ContentInfo block is prepared. It contains content-type, content encryption algorithm and the encrypted content.

The RecipientInfo blocks followed by the ContentInfo block are then Base64 encoded. The encoded entity forms the enveloped-data MIME entity. To recover the message, the recipient removes Base64 encoding, recovers the symmetric encryption key (K) using his private key, and decrypts the received encrypted content.

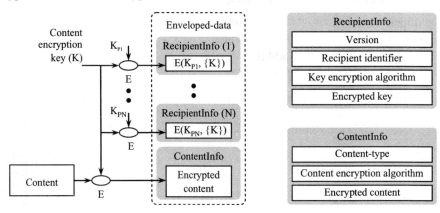

Figure 16.5 Enveloped-data MIME entity.

A simple message (excluding RFC822 header) is given below:

```
Content-Type: application/pkcs7-mime; smime-type=enveloped-data;
Content-Transfer-Encoding: base64

rfvbnj756tbBghyHhHUujhJhjH77n8HHGT9HG4VQpfyF467GhIGfHfYT67n8HHGghyH
hHUujhJh4VQpfyF467GhIGfHfYGTrfvbnjT6jH7756tbB9Hf8HHGTrfvhJhjH776tbB
9HG4VQbnj7567GhIGfHfYT6ghyHhHUujpfyF40GhIGfHfQbnj756YT64Vxxx
```

Signed Data

The application/PKCS7-MIME subtype with S/MIME parameter 'signed-data' is used for authentication based on digital signature. The content can be of any type and there can be multiple signers who sign the digest of the message. The steps involved in preparing the signed-data MIME entity are as follows (Figure 16.6):

1. For each signer, a hashing algorithm (h_i) is selected and the message digest (D_i) is computed.
2. Each message digest (D_i) is digitally signed using signature algorithm (S) and the private key (K_{Ri}) of the signer.
3. A SignerInfo block is prepared for each signer. It contains
   – signer identifier,
   – authenticated attributes,
   – digest encryption algorithm (signature algorithm) identifier,
   – encrypted digest (signature).

Authenticated attributes field is optional and contains attributes like content type, signing time, etc.

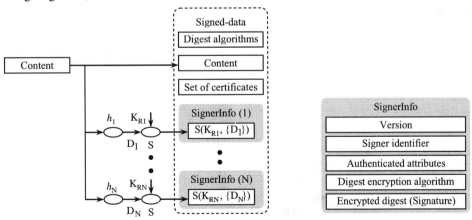

Figure 16.6 Signed-data MIME entity.

SignerInfo blocks together with message content, set of certificates, set of digest algorithms are Base64 encoded. The encoded entity forms the signed-data MIME entity. Inclusion of digest algorithms before the content enables one-pass processing of the content.

To recover the message and verify the digital signature, the recipient removes Base64 encoding. Then he uses the signer's public key to verify the digital signature on the digest of the message.

A simple message (excluding RFC822 header) is given below:

```
Content-Type: application/pkcs7-mime; smime-type=signed-data;
Content-Transfer-Encoding: base64

567GhIGfHfYT6ghyHhHUujpfyF4f8HHGTrfvhJhjH776tbB9HG4VQbnj7
77n8HHGT9HG4VQpfyF467GhIGfHfYT6rfvbnj756tbBghyHhHUujhJhjH
HUujhJh4VQpfyF467GhIGfHfYGTrfvbnjT6jH7756tbB9H7n8HHGghyHh
6YT64V0GhIGfHfQbnj75
```

Clear-signed Data

The signed-data MIME entity described earlier cannot be viewed by the recipients who are not S/MIME compliant. We may want that the recipients, without S/MIME capability but having MIME capability, should be able to read the contents of a message, even though they cannot verify the contents. S/MIME introduces an alternative structure, multipart/signed MIME type that addresses this issue. It allows

– the recipients with S/MIME capability to verify the signature and view the contents,
– the recipients with MIME capability (but without S/MIME capability) to view the message.

The body of the multipart/signed MIME type is made up of two parts.

- The first part, which can be any MIME content type, is left in the 'clear', i.e., it does not undergo any S/MIME transformation. Thus recipients with MIME capability can also view it.
- The second part is S/MIME signed-data object, but without the content field. This object is also referred to as 'detached signature'. It can be processed only by the recipients having S/MIME capability.

A sample message (excluding RFC822 header) is given below. We have left out some optional fields to reduce the clutter. The protocol parameter 'application/PKCS7-signature' indicates that this is a two-part clear-signed entity. The micalg[1] parameter indicates that SHA1 hash algorithm is to be used for digest computation. Since the hash algorithm is specified before the content, computation of digest can be carried out when the first part is being processed.

```
Content-Type: multipart/signed;
        protocol="application/pkcs7-signature";
        micalg=sha1; boundary=boundary42
    --boundary42
    Content-Type: text/plain
    This is a clear-signed message.
    --boundary42
    Content-Type: application/pkcs7-signature;
    Content-Transfer-Encoding: base64
    ghyHhHUujhJhjH77n8HHGTrfvbnj756tbB9HG4VQpfyF467GhIGfHfYT6
    4VQpfyF467GhIGfHfYT6jH77n8HHGghyHhHUujhJh756tbB9HGTrfvbnj
    n8HHGTrfvhJhjH776tbB9HG4VQbnj7567GhIGfHfYT6ghyHhHUujpfyF4
    7GhIGfHfYT64VQbnj756
    --boundary42--
```

---

1. Short for MIC (message integrity code) algorithm.

Compressed Data

The application/PKCS7-MIME subtype with smime-type = compressed-data is used for the compressed content. The compressed-data MIME object consists of version identifier, compression algorithm identifier and EncapContentInfo, which is the compressed message content. The content can be any type of data.

```
Content-Type: application/pkcs7-mime; smime-type=compressed-data;
     name=smime.p7z
  Content-Transfer-Encoding: base64
  Content-Disposition: attachment; filename=smime.p7z

  rfvbnj756tbBghyHhHUujhJhjH77n8HHGT9HG4VQpfyF467GhIGfHfYT6
  7n8HHGghyHhHUujhJh4VQpfyF467GhIGfHfYGTrfvbnjT6jH7756tbB9H
  f8HHGTrfvhJhjH776tbB9HG4VQbnj7567GhIGfHfYT6ghyHhHUujpfyF4
  0GhIGfHfQbnj756YT64V
```

Certificate Only

When a certificate is to be sent, application/PKCS7-MIME subtype with S/MIME parameter 'certs-only' is used. The steps involved are the same as those for creating a signed-data object except that ContentInfo field is absent and other fields are empty.

16.2.2 Multiple Operations

The signed-data, enveloped-data and compressed-data MIME entities subtypes can be nested, i.e., a MIME entity can encapsulate another MIME entity. It is possible to apply the signing, encrypting, and compressing operations in any order. Choice of the order of processing is determined from the following considerations:

- When a message is encrypted first and then signed,
  - the recipient is assured that the encrypted block is unaltered. But he cannot directly correlate the signature and the unencrypted contents of the message.
  - the signatories are exposed,
  - it is possible to verify signatures without decrypting the message content. This feature can be useful in an environment where automatic signature verification is desired.
- When a message is signed first then encrypted,
  - the recipient of a message is assured that the signed message itself has not been altered,
  - authentication can be carried out only after decryption, and
  - the signatories are securely obscured by the subsequent encryption.
- Compression before encryption removes redundancy from the message and thus makes cryptanalysis more difficult.
- Compression of encrypted data does not yield significant compression. However, compression of Base64 encrypted data could be beneficial.

- It is preferable to sign message before compression as one can store uncompressed message together with the signature for verification in future.
- If a lossy compression algorithm is used with signing, compression needs to be carried out first, otherwise the signature will become invalid.

16.2.3 Triple Wrapping

As mentioned earlier, S/MIME specification permits wrapping of a MIME entity into another MIME entity. The S/MIME specification does not limit the number of such wrappings. Triple wrapping, in particular, has been of interest for creating several enhanced security services.

A triple wrapped message is one that has been signed, then encrypted and then signed again. The signers of the inner and outer signatures may be different entities or the same entity.

- The inner signature has an additional purpose apart from message authentication and non repudiation. It binds the authenticated attributes to the original content (Figure 16.6). Authenticated attributes can be used for labelling the message. For example, the attribute field can be used to categorize a message as 'Secret' or 'Restricted'.
- The second wrapping encrypts the body of previous wrapping providing confidentiality that includes confidentiality of the attributes.
- The outer signature is used for
  - hop-by-hop authentication of email message as it transits through intermediate nodes.
  - binding additional attributes that can be used for access control and routing decisions.

16.2.4 Signed Receipt

The sender of a message may require from the recipients of the message a signed acknowledgement of having received the mail. This request is indicated by adding a ReceiptRequest attribute to the authenticated attributes field of the SignerInfo object. The message user agent is configured to create a signed receipt automatically when it receives this attribute. The entire original message is signed and the signature is appended to the original message as returned as receipt.

16.2.5 Cryptographic Algorithms

The cryptographic algorithms for content encryption, key encryption, and signature generation for S/MIME as specified in RFC 5751 are shown in Table 16.5. S/MIME implementations must support AES-128 CBC for content encryption, RSA for symmetric-key encryption, SHA-256 for digest computation and RSA as signature algorithm. The rest are recommended algorithms that can be implemented in addition.

TABLE 16.5 Cryptographic Algorithms for S/MIME

	Must	**Should**
Content encryption	AES-128 CBC	AES-192 CBC
		AES-256 CBC
		3DES CBC
Key encryption	RSA	RSAES-OEAP[2]
		DH-Ephemeral
Signature	RSA/SHA-256	DSA/SHA-256
		RSASSA-PSS[3]/SHA-256
		RSA/SHA-1
		DSA/SHA-1
		RSA/MD5

16.3 PRETTY GOOD PRIVACY (PGP)

Pretty Good Privacy (PGP) was developed by Philip Zimmermann 1991 for securing email messages and storing files securely for future retrieval. There are several versions of PGP that run on variety of platforms, including Windows, UNIX, and others. PGP is now on Internet standards track (RFC 4880) as OpenPGP.

Operation of PGP can be described in the following five steps:

1. Authentication
2. Compression
3. Confidentiality
4. Encoding for compatibility
5. Segmentation

Authentication: Message authentication is carried out using digital signature. Alice as the sender computes digest of the message using SHA-1 and signs the digest using her private key K_{AR} [Figure 16.7(a)]. RSA or DSS is used as the signing algorithm. Bob as the recipient verifies the digital signature using Alice's public key. The signature is usually attached to the message, but PGP supports detached signature also.

Compression: As mentioned before in Section 16.3.2, compression before encryption and after signature is the preferred option [Figure 16.7(b)]. By default, PGP follows this order. PGP uses lossless compression algorithm, ZIP.

Confidentiality: PGP encrypts message using symmetric-key encryption. CAST-128, IDEA or 3DES algorithm in CFB mode. Since email is one-way and one-time operation, a new symmetric key[4] is to be generated for each message and sent with the encrypted message.

---

2. RSAES-OAEP: RSA Encryption Scheme Optimal Asymmetric Encryption Padding
3. RSASSA PSS: RSA Signature Scheme with Appendix—Probabilistic Signature Scheme
4. PGP calls symmetric key as session key, though email application does not have a session.

The symmetric key is protected by encrypting it using the public key of the recipient K_{BP} [Figure 16.7(c)]. RSA or ElGamal algorithm is used for encryption of the symmetric key.

Encoding for compatibility: The message (if encrypted) and its digital signature consist of arbitrary 8-bit octets. As mentioned before, many email systems permit the use of 7-bit ASCII. PGP uses Base64 encoding for converting 8-bit binary stream into 7-bit ASCII.

Segmentation: There is usually limitation of maximum size of a message in email systems. PGP automatically subdivides a message that is too large into smaller segments. Segmentation is done in the last stage of processing, i.e., after Base64 encoding.

At the receiving end, the processing is carried out in reverse order.

1. All the headers of the mail are stripped off and the message segments are reassembled.
2. Base64 encoding is reverted to 8-bit binary.
3. The encrypted symmetric-key K is stripped off and decrypted using recipient's private key.
4. The encrypted block of message and signature is decrypted using key K.
5. The signature block is used to authenticate the message. The public key of the sender is used for verifying the signature.

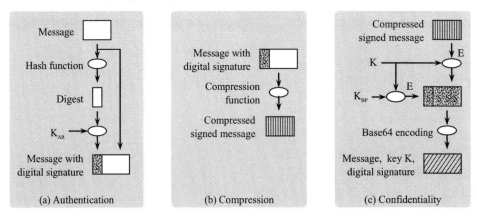

Figure 16.7   PGP cryptographic functions.

16.3.1   General Format of PGP Message

As mentioned before, there are several versions of PGP.[5] We present in this section a general format of a PGP message. It consists of the following three components (Figure 16.8):

(a) Symmetric-key component
(b) Signature component
(c) Message component

---

5. The reader is referred to RFC 4880 on OpenPGP, the IETF version of PGP for detailed description of the PGP message structure.

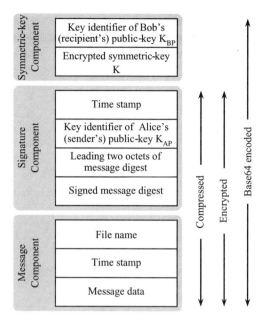

Figure 16.8   General format of PGP message.

Symmetric-key Component

It includes the following parts:

* The encrypted symmetric key that was used for encrypting the message.
* Key identifier of the recipient's public key that was used for encrypting the symmetric key.

The recipient of the mail may have multiple public–private key pairs. The key identifier enables the recipient to select the right private key for decrypting the symmetric key. In PGP, the last 64 bits of the public key are used as the key identifier. Public key is not a secret and it could have been sent in place of its identifier. Identifier is much shorter than the public key which can be a number having hundreds of decimal digits.

Signature Component

The signature component includes the following parts:

* Timestamp, which is the time at which the signature was generated.
* Key identifier of sender's public key, which identifies the public key that is to be used for verifying the signature.
* Leading two octets of the message digest, which provides a quick test to reject some invalid signatures.
* Signed message digest, which is 160-bit SHA-1 digest encrypted with the sender's private key.

The digest is computed over concatenation of the timestamp of signature component and the data part of the message component. Inclusion of timestamp when the message was signed prevents replay attack and supports non repudiation.

Message Component

The message component includes the following parts:

- File-name associated with the message data.
- Timestamp indicating date/time of the file creation.
- Actual data of the message to be transmitted or stored.

The message component and signature component may be compressed using ZIP and then encrypted using the symmetric encryption key.

16.3.2   Key Rings

Alice as sender of PGP email requires the following set of keys:

- Symmetric-key (K) for encryption of the message
  As mentioned before, this is a one-time key associated with a single message. Initialization vector (IV) for CFB mode and the symmetric-key (K) are generated as a pseudorandom numbers.
- Alice's private key (K_{AR}) for signing the digest
  Alice may have multiple public–private key pairs to correspond with different groups of people (e.g. friends, relations, office-colleagues). Thus she has a private-key ring containing her public–private key pairs. Each key pair is identified by the least significant 64 bits of the public key. She sends this key-id with her signature so that the recipient may choose the correct public key for verification of her signature.
- Public keys (K_{BR}) of the recipients for encrypting the symmetric-key K
  Alice needs a key ring carrying public key of all the recipients.

She needs to have an organized data structure that enables maintenance of all the keys with the key-identifiers. Remember that over a period of time, keys get outdated/revoked and new keys are added. PGP provides a pair of data structures at each user node, one for public–private key pairs of the node and the other for public keys of the recipients. These are called private-key ring and public-key ring respectively.

Table 16.6 shows the structure of the private-key ring. Various fields in the private-key ring are given below:

- **Time stamp.**   Date and time when this key pair was created.
- **Key-id.**   The least significant 64 bits of the public key are used as key-id.
- **Public key.**   The public-key part of the key pair.
- **Encrypted private key.**   The private key part of the key pair. Encrypted value[6] of this key is stored for security reasons.

---

6. At the time of creating public–private key pair, the system asks the user for a passphrase. The passphrase is hashed using SHA-1 and 128 bits of the hash code are used as the key for encrypting the private-key using CAST-128.

- **User-id.** Typically user-id is the email address. However, the user may choose to associate a different name with each key pair (e.g. alice.office@abc.com, alice.pals@ xyz.com).

TABLE 16.6   Private-key Ring

Time stamp	Key-id	Public key	Encrypted private key	User-id
---	---	---	---	---
---	---	---	---	---
---	---	---	---	---

Table 16.7 shows the structure of the public-key ring. Various fields in the public-key ring are given below:

- **Time stamp.**   The date and time of creation of this entry.
- **Key-id.**   The least significant 64 bits of the public key are used as key-id.
- **Public key.**   The public key of the owner identified in the user-id field.
- **User-id.**   It identifies the owner of the public key. Typically it is the email address of the owner.
- **Certificate.**   This field contains digital certificate for the public key.
- **Owner trust.**   It indicates the degree to which the owner of public key can be trusted to sign a certificate.
- **Certificate trust.**   The value in this field indicates the degree to which the PGP user trusts the certificate.
- **Key legitimacy.**   This value is calculated by PGP based on the value of certificate trust field.

The last three fields are described in the next section.

TABLE 16.7   Public-key Ring

Time stamp	Key-id	Public key	User-id	Certificate	Owner trust	Certificate trust	Key legitimacy
---	---	---	---	---	---	---	---
---	---	---	---	---	---	---	---
---	---	---	---	---	---	---	---

16.3.3   PGP Trust Model

In the last chapter, we studied a trust model based on a certification authority (CA) who is trusted by a community of users and issues public-key certificates to them. When Alice sends a signed message, she appends her public-key certificate to the message. Bob, the recipient, verifies the certificate issued by the trusted CA and uses the public key given in the certificate to authenticate the message received from Alice. In the extended form of this model, there can be multiple CAs having trust relationships amongst themselves.

PGP provides an alternative trust model, called 'web of trust'. It does not have a central trusted authority who signs certificates of all the users. Instead every user generates and distributes his public-key certificate signed by other users who trust him. For example, Alice gets her public-key certificate signed by Bob, who knows her well. When Alice wants to communicate with Carol, Alice sends Carol a copy of the certificate signed by Bob. Now, if Carol trusts Bob to certify other people's keys, she accepts Alice's certificate. In other words, Bob has introduced Alice to Carol. The users in the community thus create a 'web of trust' and legitimize their public keys. Note that users are free to decide who they trust and who they do not. PGP merely provides mechanisms for associating trust with public keys.

Let us examine this model with an example. PGP defines the following parameters for building trust relationships:

(a) Owner's trust
(b) Certificate trust
(c) Key legitimacy

Owner Trust

Owner trust indicates the degree to which a user trusts the key's owner to sign other public keys. Its value is manually assigned by the user himself. He may assign, for example, the following levels to this parameter:

- Fully trusted (F)
- Partially trusted (P)
- Not trusted (N)

In Figure 16.9, A places full trust in B, but places partial trust in C and D. He does not trust E, F, G, H and I as certificate signers. Note a variation in representation of relation between the certificate signer and the certificate owner. When user X is signed by Y, the direction of arrow head is from X to Y.

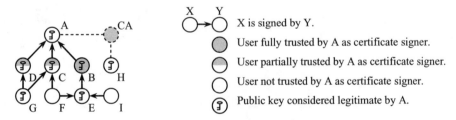

Figure 16.9 Trust model of PGP.

The A's public-key ring has the respective trust levels in the owner trust column as shown in Table 16.8.

TABLE 16.8 A's Public-key Ring

Time stamp	Key-id	Public key	User-id	Owner trust	Certificate signer	Certificate trust	Key legitimacy
- - -	- - -	- - -	A	F			F
- - -	- - -	- - -	B	F	A	F	F
- - -	- - -	- - -	C	P	A	F	F
- - -	- - -	- - -	D	P	A	F	F
- - -	- - -	- - -	E	N	B	F	F
- - -	- - -	- - -	F	N	C, E	P, N	P
- - -	- - -	- - -	G	N	C, D	P, P	F
- - -	- - -	- - -	H	N	CA	F	F
- - -	- - -	- - -	I	N	E	N	N
F : Fully trusted, P : Partially trusted, N : Not trusted								

Certificate Trust

Trust level of a certificate depends on the trust level of its signer. In Figure 16.9, A signs certificates of B, C and D. Since A himself is the signer, the certificates of B, C, D are fully trusted (Table 16.8). Note that A has certified C and D though she does not trust them fully as certificate signers.

A's public-key ring also has certificates of E, F, and G which are signed by B, C and D respectively. The certificate trust levels for E, F and G are the trust levels of the respective signers (Table 16.8). G has another certificate which is signed by C. Its trust level is same as that of C.

There are two more certificates in A's public-key ring. H produces X.509 certificate signed by a certification authority (CA). A decides to accept this certificate after verifying it through root CA. H's certificate is, therefore, fully trusted. I produces its certificate signed by E who is not trusted as certificate signer by A. Therefore, his certificate trust level is N (Not trusted).

Key Legitimacy

Key legitimacy field that indicates the degree to which a user trusts the validity of the public key in its key ring. Its value is determined by sum of the weighted certificate trust levels of a public key. Remember that there may be multiple certificates for a public key, e.g. user G produces two certificates.

Let us assign the following weights to the certificate trust levels:

(a) Fully trusted   1
(b) Partially trusted   0.5
(c) Not trusted   0

Thus to fully trust a public key, A needs one fully trusted certificate or two partially trusted certificates. Thus G's public key is legitimate for A, but F and I fail to meet the legitimacy requirement of A. Of course, nothing prevents A from using the public keys she does not trust. PGP's job is to alert A that the key is not trusted.

16.3.4 Certificate Revocation

It may become necessary for a user to revoke his public-key certificate when the key becomes too old to be safe, or the associated private key is compromised or lost. The user can send a revocation certificate, which should be signed by him using his old private key. The revocation certificate must be sent to all the users.

Certificate revocation is the weakest link of this trust system. It is impossible to guarantee that a revoked public key is removed from all the public-key rings. If the user loses his private key, he cannot generate the revocation certificate which requires his signature.

16.4 SUMMING UP

In this chapter, we studied security implementation at the Application layer for email service. Email is a unique application in the sense that each email is one way and one time communication from a sender to multiple recipients. The sender of email needs to indicate the keys and cryptographic algorithms required for decryption and authentication in his email. We discussed two secure email systems S/MIME and PGP, which provide privacy, integrity and authentication services.

- S/MIME is enhancement of MIME. It defines additional content types for encrypted data, digital signature, public-key certificates and compression. These S/MIME content types can be nested, i.e., data can be compressed, signed and encrypted in any order.
- S/MIME allows triple wrapping in which a message is signed, encrypted and then signed again. The outer signature can be used for hop-by-hop authentication of email message or for binding additional attributes that can be used for access control and routing decisions.
- Pretty Good Privacy (PGP) is another secure email application. A PGM message consists of symmetric-key component, signature component and message component.
- A PGP user needs two key rings, a public-key ring and a private-key ring to prepare a secure email message. The public-key ring contains the public keys of the mail receivers. The private-key ring contains the public-private key pairs of the sender.
- In PGP, public-key certificates can be issued by any user to any other user. The trust model is called 'web of trust'. It is based on the degree of owner's trust on the certificate signer. The degree of trust determines the legitimacy of the key in the public-key ring of the sender.

S/MIME and PGP are examples of application-specific security implementation. Security can be built at a common platform for all applications, e.g. at the Transport layer or at the Network layer. We study Transport Layer Security (TLS) protocol and IPsec protocol in the next two chapters.

Key Terms		
Base64 (Radix-64)	Message transfer agent (MTA)	S/MIME
Certificate trust	Message user agent (MUA)	Signed data
Clear-signed data	Multipurpose Internet Mail Extensions	Signed receipt
Content-transfer-encoding	Owner trust	Triple wrapping
Email address	Pretty Good Privacy (PGP)	Web of trust
Enveloped data	Private-key ring	SMTP
Key legitimacy	Public-key ring	
Mailbox	Quoted-printable transfer encoding	

RECOMMENDED READING

Forouzan, Behrouz A., *Cryptography and Network Security*, Tata McGraw-Hill, New Delhi, 2007.

Garfinkel, S., *PGP—Pretty Good Privacy*, O'Reilly, Cambridge, USA, 1995.

Kaufman, C., Perlman, R. and Spenciner, M., *Network Security, Private Communication in a Public World*, Prentice-Hall of India, New Delhi, 2007.

RFC 822, *Standard for the format of ARPA Internet text messages*, IETF, 1982.

RFC 2045, *Multipurpose Internet Mail Extensions (MIME) Part One: Format of Internet Message Bodies*, IETF, 1996.

RFC 4880, *Open PGP Message Format*, IETF, 2007.

RFC 5321, *Simple Mail Transfer Protocol*, IETF, 2008.

RFC 5751, *Secure/Multipurpose Internet Mail Extensions (S/MIME) Version 3.2, Message Specification*, IETF, 2010.

Stallings, W., *Cryptography and Network Security*, Prentice-Hall of India, New Delhi, 2008.

Trappe, W., Washington, L., *Introduction to Cryptography and Coding Theory*, Prentice Hall, CA, USA, 2006.

Vaudenay, S., *A Classical Introduction to Cryptography*, Springer, CA, USA, 2006.

Zimmermann, P., *PGP Source Code and Internals*, MIT Press, CA, USA, 1995.

(PROBLEMS)

1. Base64 encoding transforms three 8-bit symbols into four 7-bit ASCII characters. If length of the message is not multiple of 3 bytes, formation of 6-bit words may result in the last word having 2 or 4 bits. Therefore, the last incomplete word is padded with 2 or 4 zeros. Padding is indicated to the recipient by appending one '=' symbol, if 2 zeros are padded, or two '=' symbols, if 4 zeros are padded.

Determine the base64 encoding of the following messages:

(a) 11001100   10000001   00111001

(b) 00010101   11010000   00101111   10011110   10110111

(c) 00010101   11010000   00101111   10011110

2. Represent the following non-ASCII symbols as 7-bit quoted-printable encoding.

(a) 10011101

(b) 10001001

(c) 10101100

3. Alice receives a PGP email signed by Tom. Alice had no previous contact with the sender. The email has Tom's public-key certificate signed by Eva and Eva's public-key certificate signed by Bob. Alice does not know Eva, but she has complete trust in Bob as a signer. What is the key legitimacy of Tom's public key?

4. Figure 16.10 shows PGP web of trust where the public keys of B, C and D have been signed by A. P has a certificate from CA. A is in possession of all the certificates issued in this community. Draw the public-key ring of A indicating the following columns:

(a) User-id

(b) Owner trust

(c) Certificate signer

(d) Certificate trust

(e) Key legitimacy

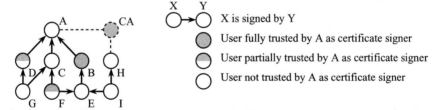

Figure 16.10   Problem 4.

17

Transport Layer Security (TLS)

PGP and S/MIME that we studied in the last chapter are two examples of applications which have inbuilt or embedded security. The advantage of building security into applications is that the security can be tailored to the requirements of the application. On the other hand, there is no leveraging effect. Each application must have its own security. We study in this chapter Transport Layer Security (TLS) protocol which provides a common security platform at the Transport layer for all the applications. TLS consists of four component protocols, namely, Handshake protocol, ChangeCipherSpec protocol, Alert protocol and Record protocol. These protocols are used for negotiating cryptographic algorithms, establishment of shared secret keys and securing the application data. We examine the basic operation of each of these protocols in this chapter.

17.1 SECURITY IMPLEMENTATION AT TRANSPORT LAYER

Considerations for security implementation at the Transport layer (TCP/UDP layer of TCP/IP suite) are several.

(a) The security implementation is transparent to the applications. New applications or new versions of an application run on the common security infrastructure and thus security related incompatibility issues do not arise.
(b) Security implementation is end-to-end and independent of intervening network. Thus secure communication is possible over the public Internet.

Security at the Transport layer is implemented as an additional layer as Transport Layer Security (TLS) sandwiched between the Application layer and TCP layer. Applications that do not need security service of TLS can have direct access to the TCP layer [Figure 17.1(a)]. Applications that make use of TLS service need to have new API[1] for TLS layer [Figure 17.1(b)].

The most common application that uses TLS is the web browser. TLS comes embedded with the web browsers. It was Netscape who developed Secure Socket Layer (SSL) protocol

---

1. API: Application Programming Interface.

for the security of web-based transactions. SSL was later adopted by IETF and released as Transport Layer Security (TLS). Version 3.0 of SSL and version 1.0 of TLS are the most widely deployed versions in the web browsers. We will study the current TLS version 1.2 in this chapter.

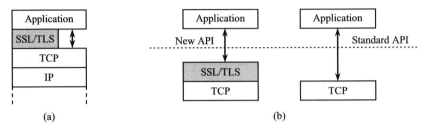

(a)   (b)

Figure 17.1   Transport Layer Security (TLS).

17.2   PURPOSE AND BASIC SERVICES OF TLS LAYER

The basic purpose of TLS protocol is to provide a *secure end-to-end* connection that offers the following services (Figure 17.2):

- Confidentiality of user data by encrypting it.
- Authentication of the source and content using MAC.
- Protection against replay/reordering/deletion of user data using sequence numbers.
- Optional compression of user data.

TLS layer requires the service of TCP layer for reliable end-to-end transport of its data units. TCP layer takes care of errors, sequence-disorder, wrong delivery and loss of TCP segments.

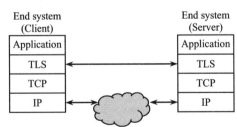

Figure 17.2   End-to-end security.

Figure 17.3 depicts the process of securing application data at the TLS layer[2] after the client and server have negotiated and implemented security algorithms and the secret keys for encryption and authentication.

Fragmentation: The data received from the application layer is fragmented into data units having maximum size of 2^{14} bytes.

---

2. The process of securing data is carried out by TLS Record protocol, one of the component protocol of the TLS layer.

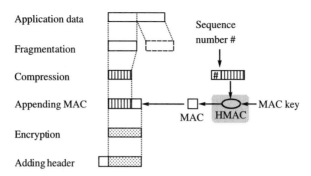

Figure 17.3 Basic operation of TLS layer.

Compression: Fragmented data units are compressed using a compression algorithm, if the client and server agreed to compression. Compression algorithm is lossless so that the receiver at the other end can decompress the data.

Appending MAC: Message authentication code (MAC) computed using a keyed hash function is appended to the compressed fragment. The MAC key is generated from the key material as explained in Section 17.4. A sequence number is appended to the compressed fragment for computing MAC value. The sequence number enables detection of replay and reordering carried out by the adversary. The sequence number is not sent with the message, but is maintained as one of the parameters of the connection state by the server and the client.

Encryption: The compressed fragment along with the MAC is encrypted using one of the following symmetric-key encryption algorithms. Encryption algorithm is negotiated at the time of session establishment.

- Triple DES (EDE) block cipher
- AES (128 or 256 bits key) block cipher
- RC4 (128-bit key) stream cipher

CBC mode is used for block ciphers. The encryption key and the initialization vector (IV) are generated from the key material as explained in Section 17.4.

Adding header: TLS header is attached to the encrypted data unit. The header specifies
- the payload type (e.g. if the payload is application data, the type field is 23),
- TLS version being used, and
- size of the payload in number of octets.

These operations are carried out in reverse order in TLS layer of the receiving end system. It is necessary that the two end systems implement same cryptographic algorithms and keys for encryption and authentication. As we shall shortly see, the TLS layer consists of set protocols to

- establish compression and cryptographic algorithms,
- establish keys for authentication and encryption, and
- perform compression, authentication and encryption as shown in Figure 17.3.

17.3 TLS ARCHITECTURE

To provide the services as mentioned in Section 17.2, the client and server negotiate cryptographic algorithms and establish shared symmetric keys for encryption and authentication. To undertake all these tasks, the TLS layer has set of four component protocols (Figure 17.4):

Handshake Protocol

Handshake protocol is used for negotiating security algorithms for encryption and authentication, and for exchanging secret-key parameters. These key parameters are used for generating symmetric encryption keys, MAC keys and initialization vectors.

ChangeCipherSpec Protocol (CCSP)

ChangeCipherSpec protocol implements the negotiated security algorithms and keys in Record protocol.

Record Protocol

Record protocol carries out required security transformation of the bulk data received from the Application layer. Security transformations include

- symmetric-key encryption for confidentiality and
- appending MAC for data integrity and data origin verification.

Records protocol also carries the messages of Handshake protocol, ChangeCipherSpec protocol and Alert protocol.

Alert Protocol

Alert protocol is used for sending messages whenever any inconsistency of operation or error is noticed.

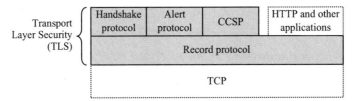

CCSP : ChangeCipherSpec protocol

Figure 17.4 TLS architecture.

TLS operation can be summarized as follows:

- The Handshake protocol *negotiates* the cryptographic algorithms (referred to as cipher suite) and exchanges secret-key parameters.
- ChangeCipherSpec protocol (CCSP) *implements* the cipher suite and the associated encryption/authentication keys in the Record protocol.

- Record protocol *secures* the bulk data received from the application layer by appending MAC and encrypting it. It hands over the secured data to the TCP layer.
- The Alert protocol *reports* errors, operational inconsistencies and notifications by generating alert messages.

17.3.1   Cipher Suite

Secure session establishment between the communicating client and server involves implementation of a cipher suite with secret keys. A cipher suite consists of the following set of cryptographic algorithms:

- Method for establishing a pre-master secret between the client and the server. The premaster secret is used for computing encryption and authentication keys.
- Encryption algorithm for the bulk data, i.e., the data received from the application layer.
- Mode of operation of the symmetric-key encryption algorithm.
- Hash algorithm for generating MAC.

For example, cipher suite TLS_RSA_WITH_AES_128_CBC_SHA256 defines that

- the pre-master secret will be established using RSA method,
- MAC will be generated using SHA256 hash algorithm, and
- bulk data appended with MAC will be encrypted using AES symmetric block cipher in CBC mode of operation. 128-bit symmetric key will be used for encryption.

Once established, the same cipher suite is used for the life of a session.

17.4   PRE-MASTER SECRET AND KEY GENERATION

As mentioned above, the key generation in TLS requires a shared 'pre-master secret' between the client and the server. TLS specifies several alternative methods for establishing the pre-master secret. These are based on RSA and Diffie–Hellman key exchange as described below. The method to be used is agreed as part of the cipher suite.

RSA **[Figure 17.5(a)]:**   The server sends its digital certificate that contains its RSA public key for encryption. The client generates a 48-byte pre-master secret, encrypts it using the server's RSA public key (K_P), and sends the encrypted pre-master secret to the server.

Fixed Diffie–Hellman **[Figure 17.5(b)]:**   The server sends its digital certificate which contains its Diffie–Hellman (DH) key parameters (prime modulus p, generator g, server's half key g^s mod p). The client sends its digital certificate containing Diffie–Hellman key parameters (prime modulus p, generator g, client's half key g^c mod p). The parameters p and g are same in both the digital certificates. The pre-master secret is computed as g^{cs} mod p by the client and the server independently. TLS 1.2 allows use of elliptic-curve-based DH key exchange also.

Ephemeral Diffie–Hellman **[Figure 17.5(c)]:**   Fixed Diffie–Hellman scheme uses the key parameters as indicated in the digital certificate. In ephemeral (one time) Diffie–Hellman scheme, the server generates new set of DH key exchange parameters (prime modulus p, generator g, server's half key $g^s \bmod p$) each time a new session is established. The exchange of messages in this case is as follows:

- The server sends digital certificate containing its public key required for verification of its signature. The digital signature algorithm can be RSA or DSS or elliptic curve DSA.
- The server sends the signed Diffie–Hellman key exchange parameters to the client. TLS 1.2 allows use of elliptic-curve-based ephemeral DH key exchange also.
- The client verifies digital signature using the server's public key given in the digital certificate. The client computes its part of the DH key half key $g^c \bmod p$ and sends it to the server.
- The pre-master secret $g^{cs} \bmod p$ is independently computed by the client and the server.

***Anonymous Diffie–Hellman* [(Figure 17.5(d)]:**   This scheme is similar to ephemeral Diffie–Hellman scheme except that there is no authentication. The server sends Diffie–Hellman key exchange parameters (prime modulus p, generator g, server's half key $g^s \bmod p$) to the client without digital signature. The client computes its DH half key $g^c \bmod p$ and returns it to the server. The pre-master secret is computed as $g^{cs} \bmod p$ by the client and the server independently. This scheme has least verification overhead, but is most vulnerable to attacks.

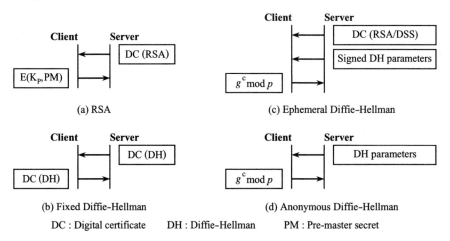

Figure 17.5   Establishment of pre-master secret.

Once the pre-master secret is established, the client and server compute the cryptographic keys independently. We describe the key generation algorithm next.

17.4.1   Key Generation

TLS requires the following three key values for authentication and encryption:

1. MAC secret key for authentication
2. Symmetric key for encryption
3. Initialization vector (IV)

A separate set of the above key values is used for each direction of communication. Thus six key values are required, and these six values must be shared between the server and the client. These key values are generated using a pseudo random function (PRF) and the following parameters.

- Pre-master secret (PM)
- Client random value R_C
- Server random value R_S
- Label

The client and server exchange the random values R_C and R_S during session establishment using the Handshake protocol. The client and the server independently compute the key material from the above parameters. The key material so obtained is divided into MAC keys, encryption keys and initialization vectors (IV) required by the client and server. Figure 17.6 shows the basic scheme.

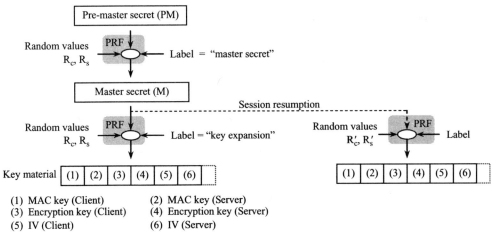

Figure 17.6 Master secret and key material computation.

Note that the computation algorithm for the key material has been divided into two stages. A master secret is computed from the pre-master secret in the first stage. The key material is computed from the master secret in the second stage. Secure exchange of pre-master secret (PM) is expensive in terms of processing time and number of messages exchanged. If a session is to be resumed, instead of re-establishing the pre-master secret, the existing master secret is reused. Only the new values of R'_C, R'_S are exchanged during session resumption, and the key material is recomputed using the existing master secret.

17.4.2　Pseudo Random Function

TLS uses a pseudo random function (PRF) to expand pre-master secret into longer block of data called key material. The key material is divided into six blocks as explained in the last section. The PRF is so designed that the six keys have little correlation amongst themselves.

Figure 17.7 depicts the structure of PRF. It is defined as concatenation of HMAC computations as given below:

PRF = [HMAC (secret, $A_1 \,\|\,$ label $\|$ seed)] $\|$ [HMAC (secret, $A_2 \,\|\,$ label $\|$ seed)] $\|$ [HMAC (secret, $A_3 \,\|\,$ label $\|$ seed)]

where

secret	= Pre-master secret (PM) in computation of master secret
	= Master secret (M) in computation of the key material
A_1	= HMAC(secret, label $\|$ seed)
A_2	= HMAC(secret, A_1)
A_3	= HMAC(secret, A_2)
seed	= $R_C \,\|\, R_S$ for computation of the master secret
	= $R_S \,\|\, R_C$ for computation of the key material
label	= "master secret" for computation of the master secret
	= "key expansion" for computation of the key material
R_C	= Client's random value = Time stamp (4 bytes) $\|$ random number (28 bytes)
R_S	= Server's random value = Time stamp (4 bytes) $\|$ random number (28 bytes)

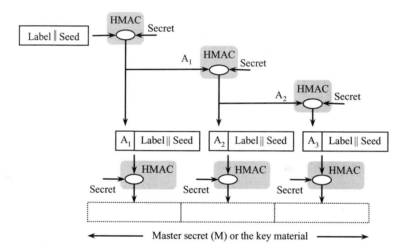

Figure 17.7   PRF.

Note that same PRF is used for computation of master secret and for computation of key material. The inputs to PRF are the seed, the label and the secret. These inputs are different in these two computations. The secret is used as the key in HMAC. HMAC is based on SHA-256 hash algorithm.

17.5   TLS OPERATION

We describe the TLS operation in three parts:

- Secure session establishment

- Secure transfer of application data
- Session closure and resumption

The Handshake protocol and ChangeCipherSpec protocols of TLS are used for establishing a secure session. The Record protocol carries the messages of these protocols. Once the session is established, the Record protocol secures the application data as shown in Figure 17.3 and sends it as its payload to the other end. The Alert protocol is active throughout to report inconsistencies, errors and notifications.

17.5.1   Secure Session Establishment

Establishment of secure session involves several tasks that are carried out in phases primarily by the Handshake protocol and the ChangeCipherSpec protocol (Figure 17.8).

- Phase 1   Cipher suite is negotiated.
- Phase 2   The server sends its part of the parameters required for key generation and authenticates itself.
- Phase 3   The client sends its part of the parameters required for key generation and authenticates itself.
- Phase 4   The cryptographic algorithms and the keys are implemented in the Record protocol.

Phase 1:   *Establishing Security Capability (Handshake Protocol)*

This phase consists of two messages: ClientHello message and ServerHello message. The first message is from the client who initiates the session establishment. The server responds with its message.

ClientHello message: The client sends ClientHello message that contains the following parameters:

- The highest version of TLS it can support.
- Session-id.
  The client leaves this field empty or inserts the previous session-id which it wants to resume.
- 32-byte client's random value R_C.
  R_C consists of 28-byte random number and 4-byte time stamp. It is used in key generation later.
- List of cipher suites that the client can support.
- List of compression methods that the client can support (optional).

ServerHello message: The server responds with ServerHello message that contains the following parameters.

- The selected version of TLS for the session.
- Session-id.
  If the client has specified a session-id in its ClientHello message and the server is willing to resume the session, it responds with the same session-id. If a session is

resumed, it is resumed using the same cipher suite it was originally negotiated with. The server and client proceed directly to the Phase 4.

- 32-byte server's random value R_S.

  R_S consists of 28-byte random number and 4-byte time stamp. R_S is used in key generation later.

- The cipher suite selected from the client's list.

- The compression method selected from the client's list.

Phase 2:   Server Key Exchange and Authentication (Handshake Protocol)

This phase consists of up to four messages from the server.

Certificate message: Server sends digital certificate containing its RSA or DSS public key, or DH public-key parameters. This message is not required, if Anonymous Diffie–Hellman method has been chosen for establishing pre-master secret in Phase 1.

ServerKeyExchange message: In this message the server sends its part of parameters required for computation of pre-master secret. For example, the server sends DH key parameters (prime modulus p, generator g, server's half key g^s mod p) to the client for computation of the pre-master secret.

ServerKeyExchange message is required when the Ephemeral or Anonymous DH methods are used for establishing pre-master secret (Figure 17.5). In the former case, the server sends DH parameters with its digital signature so that the client may use this message for authentication.

CertificateRequest message: A non-anonymous server can optionally request a certificate from the client, if required for the selected cipher suite.

ServerHelloDone message: The last message of Phase 2 is ServerHelloDone message. It is an indication to the client that the server is now waiting for a response from the client.

Phase 3:   Client Key Exchange and Authentication (Handshake Protocol)

This phase consists of up to three messages from the client.

Certificate message: If the server has asked for digital certificate in Phase 2, the client sends this message carrying client's certificate. The public key in the certificate is used for authenticating the client. See Certificate Verify message below.

ClientKeyExchange message: In this message the client sends its part of parameters required for computation of pre-master secret. For example, the client sends DH key parameters (prime modulus p, generator g, client's half key g^c mod p) to the server. If RSA was the chosen method for key exchange, the client sends the pre-master chosen by it to the server using RSA encryption. The server's public key received in ClientHello message is used for encryption.

CertificateVerify message: In this message the client sends signed digest of all the previous messages exchanged so far. The digest is signed using the client's private key so that the server can authenticate the client by verifying the digital signature.

Phase 4: Cipher Suite Implementation (Handshake and ChangeCipherSpec Protocols)

At this stage, both the client and the server can compute the key material and generate the encryption keys, MAC keys and initialization vectors (IV) using the exchanged parameters and PRF as explained in Section 17.4. Implementation security algorithms and security keys is done in this phase which consists of four messages, two from the client and two from the server (Figure 17.8).

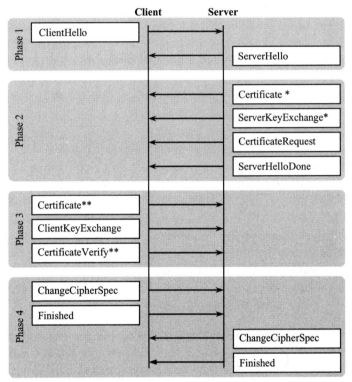

* These messages depend on the key exchange method adopted.
** These messages are applicable in the case of client authentication.

Figure 17.8 Message exchange for session establishment.

ChangeCipherSpec message from the client to the server: This message indicates to the server that the client is changing over to the agreed cipher suite for its *outbound payload* data. After sending the message the client implements the agreed encryption and authentication algorithms with keys in the Record protocol for *outbound payload* data.

The server on receipt of this message gets ready for receiving encrypted payload from the client. It implements the negotiated decryption and authentication algorithms with keys in the Record protocol for *inbound payload* data.

Finished message from the client to the server: A finished message is sent immediately after a ChangeCipherSpec message to verify that the key exchange and authentication processes were successful for the *outbound payload* from the client. This is the first message protected with the just implemented encryption/authentication algorithms and keys in the Record protocol.

The client sends the following payload in its finished message to the server:

PRF(master secret, label "client finished", hash of all the Handshake messages)

On receipt of the finished message, the server verifies successful implementation of the encryption/authentication algorithms and keys by decrypting the payload and verifying the payload as given above.

ChangeCipherSpec message from the server to the client: This message from the server indicates to the client that it (the server) is changing over to the agreed cipher suite for its *outbound payload* data. After sending the message the server implements the agreed encryption and authentication algorithms with keys in its Record protocol for the *outbound payload* data.

The client on receipt of this message gets ready for receiving encrypted payload from the server. It implements the negotiated decryption and authentication algorithms with keys in the Record protocol for *inbound payload* data.

Finished message from the server to the client: This message from the server is used for verification of the encryption/authentication algorithms and keys for the *outbound payload* from the server. The server sends its finished message to the client with the following payload:

PRF(master secret, label "server finished", hash of all the Handshake messages)

This payload is protected by the Record protocol using the just implemented encryption/authentication algorithms and keys for the *outbound payload* data from the server.

On receipt of the finished message, the client verifies successful implementation of the encryption/authentication algorithms and keys by decrypting the payload and authenticating it.

17.5.2   Secure Transfer of Application Data

After the four phases of the session establishment phase, a secure session connection has been established between the client and the server. The client and the server use this connection for transfer of the data received from the Application layer. Application data is fragmented and each fragment is compressed, appended with MAC for authentication, encrypted as explained in Section 17.2. The encrypted fragment is sent as payload of Record protocol. Figure 17.9 shows the process of generating Record protocol message.

- MAC is computed over the data segment consisting of the following fields:
    - 64-bit sequence number,
    - Record type (23 for application data),
    - TLS version,
    - Length of the compressed fragment,
    - Compressed fragment.

    HMAC with one of the following hash algorithms is used for computation of MAC. The hash algorithm is negotiated during the handshake.

    MD5, SHA-1, SHA-256, SHA-384 or SHA-512

    Sequence numbers start with 0 for the first fragment and are incremented for each subsequent fragment.

- After its computation, MAC is appended to the compressed fragment.
- The compressed fragment with the appended MAC is encrypted as shown in the figure.
- The TLS Record header is added to the encrypted block.
- The header consists of three fields, content type (1 byte), TLS version (2 bytes) and length (4 bytes). Note that the sequence number is not part of the TLS record header. It is added only for the computation of MAC. Sequence number addresses security issues relating to replay, deletion and reordering of fragments. The receiver prefixes the same sequence numbers for verification of the MAC.

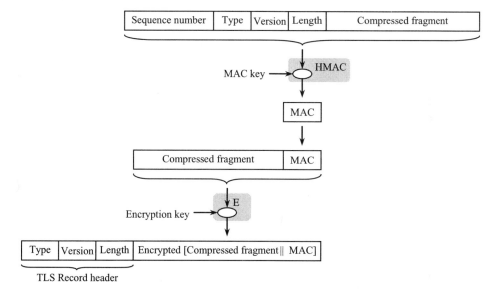

Figure 17.9 Record protocol message.

At the receiving end, the payloads are decrypted, verified for authenticity, decompressed and reassembled before handing over to the Application layer.

The Record protocol uses the TCP protocol for transport of its data units. The TCP protocol provides reliable transport service, i.e., the Record data units are delivered in sequence and acknowledged.

17.5.3   Session Closure and Resumption

Session closure can be initiated either by the client or by the server. A session is closed by sending close_notify message of the Alert protocol. The message is an indication to the receiver that the sender will not send any more messages on this connection. The receiver responds with a close_notify message using the Alert protocol.

Recall that a web browser session may require several connections to be opened. When the HTTP client opens a connection and sends a request, HTTP server responds to the request and simultaneously closes the connection. For the next request, the client opens a new connection to the server. TLS has session resumption feature to handle such situation. The client can resume a closed session, if agreeable to the server. A closed session can be resumed by the client as given below:

- The client sends ClientHello with the Session ID of the session to be resumed and client's new random value R'_C.
- If the server is willing to re-establish the connection, it responds with ServerHello with the same Session ID value and server's new random value R'_S.
- The server and the client compute new key material using the already established master secret and new random values R'_C and R'_S.
- The server sends ChangeCipherSpec message followed by Finished message. The client also responds with these two messages.

Note that Phases 2 and 3 are skipped and thus the overhead of session establishment is reduced substantially.

17.5.4   Alert Protocol

The client and the server use Alert protocol to signal an error condition. Table 17.1 lists some of the important error conditions and their names. There are two severity levels reported by alert messages.

- Severity level 1   warning
- Severity level 2   fatal

TABLE 17.1   Important Alerts Defined in TLS

Error-name (Code)	Description
unexpected_message (10)	An inappropriate message was received. (Fatal)
bad_record_mac (20)	An incorrect MAC was received. (Fatal)
decompression_ failure (30)	Sender was unable to decompress the message. (Fatal)
handshake_failure (40)	Sender was unable to negotiate acceptable set of security parameters. (Fatal)
illegal_parameter (47)	An inconsistent or out of range field was received during handshake. (Fatal)
unknown_CA (48)	CA certificate could not be located or matched with a trusted CA. (Fatal)
decrypt_error (51)	A handshake operation failed due to verification/validation failure. (Fatal)
protocol_version (70)	Protocol version required by the client is not supported by the server. (Fatal)
insufficient_security (71)	Server requires more secure ciphers than what client supports. (Fatal)
close_notify (0)	Sender will not sent any more messages and is ready to close connection.
certificate_revoked (44)	Sender received an expired certificate that was revoked by the CA.
certificate_expired (45)	Sender received an expired certificate.

In case of fatal alert, the client and the server must terminate the connection immediately. Other connections in the session may continue, but no new connection can be established in the session. A session closed with fatal alert cannot be resumed. In case of warning, the system receiving can decide whether to continue the connection.

17.6   TLS MESSAGE FORMATS

TLS uses Record protocol to encapsulate bulk data from the application layer, and messages from Handshake, ChangeCipherSpec and Alert protocols. The Record protocol adds a common header to these payloads. The header consists of the following fields (Figure 17.10):

***Protocol* (8 *bits*):**   It contains identifier of the protocol to which the payload pertains.

ChangeCipherSpec protocol	20
Alert protocol	21
Handshake protocol	22
Bulk data from the application layer	23

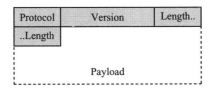

Figure 17.10   Format of TLS Record protocol.

***Version* (16 *bits*):**   First eight bits indicate the major version and the next 8 bits indicate the minor version. Due to historical reasons, TLS version 1.3 is indicated as (3, 3).

***Length* (16 *bits*):**   It indicates size of the payload in number of bytes.

The payload consists of the message of the protocol identified in the protocol field. Figure 17.11 shows format of encapsulated protocols.

- The ChangeCipherSpec protocol consists of only one byte having value 1 to indicate the cipher suite with the keys is being implemented now [Figure 17.11(a)].
- The Alert protocol consists of two bytes which indicate severity level and alert code [Figure 17.11(b)].
- The Handshake protocol has 4-octet header consisting of the following fields [Figure 17.11(c)]:
  - Type field (1 octet):   It carries the message code. Table 17.2 gives the codes of the Handshake messages.
  - Length field (3 octets):   It gives the length of the body of the handshake message.
  The message body itself has a structure depending on the message type. We will not go into structure of each handshake message. There can be multiple messages in one payload. Each message has its own type and length field.
- The Application layer protocol is a compressed fragment appended with its MAC. The compressed fragment and MAC value are encrypted [Figure 17.11(d)].

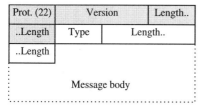

(a) Encapsulated ChangeCipherSpec
protocol.

(c) Encapsulated Handshake protocol.

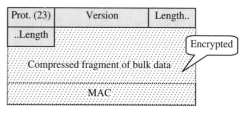

(b) Encapsulated Alert protocol.

(d) Encapsulated Application layer protocol.

Figure 17.11   Encapsulated TLS protocols.

TABLE 17.2   Handshake Messages

Message code	Message
1	ClientHello
2	SeverHello
11	Certificate
12	ServerKeyExchange
13	CertificateRequest
14	ServerHelloDone
15	CertificateVerify
16	ClientKeyExchange
20	Finished

17.7   SUMMING UP

We began this chapter with considerations of implementing security at the Transport layer. We studied Transport Layer Security (TLS) protocol that provides an end-to-end security service platform to the application layer. It uses the reliable transport service of underlying TCP layer.

- TLS provides the following security services:
  Confidentiality, message integrity, data-origin authentication and protection against replay/reordering/deletion of application data
- TLS consists of four component protocols, namely, Handshake protocol, ChangeCipherSpec protocol, Record protocol and Alert protocol.
  1. Handshake protocol is used for negotiating cipher suite, authentication and exchanging secret-key parameters.

2. ChangeCipherSpec is used for signaling implementation of negotiated cipher suite and the encryption/authentication keys in the Record protocol.
3. Record protocol carries out security transformation of the application layer data. It hands over the secured data to the TCP layer.
4. Alert protocol is used for reporting errors and inconsistency of operation.

- The encryption and authentication keys are generated using a pre-master secret. The pre-master secret is established using RSA or Diffie–Hellman algorithms.
- TLS session is established in four phases.
  1. Establishing security capability, i.e., negotiating cipher suite
  2. Server key exchange and authentication
  3. Client key exchange and authentication
  4. Cipher suite implementation
- TLS session is terminated using the Alert protocol. A closed session can be resumed. Session resumption involves phases 1 and 4 of session establishment.

The security implementation at the Application and the Transport layer is end to end. IPsec protocol that we study in the next chapter provides flexibility of implementing security between two routers, between two end systems or between an end system and a router.

Key Terms		
Alert protocol	Finished message	Record protocol
Anonymous Diffie–Hellman	Fixed Diffie–Hellman	Secure Socket Layer (SSL)
ChangeCipherSpec protocol (CCSP)	Handshake protocol	SeverHello
ClientHello	Master secret	ServerHelloDone
ClientKeyExchange	Pre-master secret	ServerKeyExchange
Ephemeral Diffie–Hellman	Pseudo random function (PRF)	

RECOMMENDED READING

Avoine, G., Junod, P. and Oechslin, P., *Computer System Security: Basic Concepts and Solved Exercises*, CRC Press, FL, USA, 2004.

Forouzan, Behrouz A., *Cryptography and Network Security*, Tata McGraw-Hill, New Delhi, 2007.

Kaufman, C., Perlman, R. and Spenciner, M., *Network Security, Private Communication in a Public World*, Prentice-Hall of India, New Delhi, 2007.

Mao, W., *Modern Cryptography*, Pearson Education, New Delhi, 2008.

RFC 5246, *The Transport Layer Security (TLS) Protocol, Version 1.2*, IETF, 2008.

RFC 6101, *The Secure Sockets Layer (SSL) Protocol Version 3.0*, IETF, 2011.

Stallings, W., *Cryptography and Network Security*, Prentice-Hall of India, New Delhi, 2008.

Thomas, S., *SSL and TLS Essentials*, John Wiley & Sons, NY, USA, 2000.

---------------------------------(PROBLEMS)---------------------------------

1. Suppose Alice (Client) sends to Bob (server) a list of cipher suites in her ClientHello message. The adversary removes some of the strong cipher suites from the list with the intent that a weaker cipher suite which he can break would be negotiated. Since the ClientHello message is unprotected, the adversary can make these changes without the server noticing the alteration in the message. What is the protection against this attack in the Handshake protocol and when is the alteration gets detected assuming that the server has not asked for the client's certificate?

2. During the session establishment, several messages authenticate the server. Identify these messages and explain how the authenticity is assured.

3. Except for anonymous DH key exchange method, the server always sends its digital certificate for its authentication in Phase 2 of session establishment. But the similar action for client's authentication is kept optional. Give justification for the same.

4. Table 17.3 shows the state of implementation of cryptographic algorithms (MAC/encryption) and the key material in the Record protocol. The 'Write' state refers to the outbound data and 'Read' state refers to the inbound data. At the commencement of session establishment, no security algorithms/keys are activated, and therefore, we have null state. At the end of the four phases of session establishment, the 'Write' and 'Read' states have the negotiated cryptographic algorithms and the computed key material in the 'Active' column. The 'Pending' column indicates the transition state when the cryptographic algorithms have been negotiated and keys are calculated, but these are yet to be implemented in the Record layer. The client and server negotiate AES (AES_128) for encryption and SHA (SHA256) for MAC computation. The client's key material for outbound data is K_C and server's key material for outbound data is K_S.

Update this state table for the client end immediately after the client

(a) receives ServerHello message from the server.
(b) sends ClientKeyExchange message to the server.
(c) sends ChangeCipherSpec message to the server.
(d) receives ChangeCipherSpec message from the server.

TABLE 17.3   Problems 4 and 5

	Write state		Read state	
	Active	Pending	Active	Pending
MAC	Null		Null	
Encryption	Null		Null	
Key	Null		Null	

5. Update the state table (Table 17.3) for the server end immediately after the server
   (a) sends ServerHello message to the client.
   (b) receives ClientKeyExchange message from the client.
   (c) receives ChangeCipherSpec message from the client.
   (d) sends ChangeCipherSpec message to the client.

6. 'The Finished messages allow both the systems (client and server) to verify that secure session is successfully established and that the security has not been compromised.' Justify this statement.

7. TLS uses reliable services of TCP layer, which ensures that all TCP segments are delivered in sequence. Recall that the header of TCP segment has sequence number field. What is the need to include sequence number in Record protocol as well?

8. Explain how the man-in-the-middle attack is thwarted during TLS session establishment.

9. In Chapter 16, we studied of S/MIME and PGP systems for email security. Emails can be secured using TLS. What would be the difference in the security offered by TLS and that offered by S/MIME or PGP?

10. Let the negotiated TLS cipher suite be TLS_DHE_RSA_WITH_AES_256_CBC_SHA cipher suite. What is the size of key material required for generating MAC keys, encryption keys and initialization vectors?

18

IP Security

Having discussed security implementations at the Application and Transport layers, it is time for examining security provisions at the Network layer. We introduce in this chapter IPsec, a framework for implementing security at the Network layer. IPsec has three component protocols, namely, Authentication Header (AH), Encapsulating Security Payload (ESP), and Internet Key Exchange (IKE). We begin this chapter with the overview of IPsec architecture and then proceed to description of AS and ESP protocols. We illustrate their application in various networking situations using the transport and tunnel modes. We leave IKE, the key exchange protocol for the next chapter.

18.1   SECURITY AT NETWORK LAYER

In a networked environment, communication between users and the applications must be secured for confidentiality, authentication, repudiation and legitimate access. There can be several alternatives for building the required security:

- Building security at the Application layer has the advantage of fine-tuning it to the requirements of the application. But each application needs to have its own inbuilt security. PGP and S/MIME are the examples of applications having inbuilt security.
- Transport Layer Security (TLS) protocol provides a common security infrastructure at the Transport layer for all the applications that need to be secured. The common security infrastructure at the Transport layer overcomes the security related incompatibility issues. But an application must have the API to work with TLS.

Security implementation at the Application and the Transport layer is always end-system to end-system. However, there are situations, where security concerns relate to the network traffic irrespective of the application that generates the traffic. In the next section, we introduce virtual private network (VPN), which is implemented as an overlay network on the public Internet. We would like to provide security at the Network layer so that IP traffic of the VPN is protected from the adversary on the Internet.

18.1.1   Virtual Private Networks

An organization having offices at different locations requires its private network for in-house communications [Figure 18.1(a)]. Private network isolates the traffic from adversarial intrusions, but building and operating a private network is a costly proposition. It may require statutory clearances as well.

An alternative to building private network is to have virtual private network (VPN) build on the public Internet [Figure 18.1(b)]. The private traffic is taken through the public Internet using tunnels that provide virtual isolation between the private and public traffic. There are several technologies for building tunnels:

- GRE (Generic Routing Encapsulation) tunnel
  GRE tunnel is created by encapsulating an IP datagram with private IP addresses in another IP datagram [Figure 18.1(c)].
- MPLS (Multi-Protocol Label Switching) tunnel
  MPLS tunnel is created by applying MPLS label on an IP datagram with private IP addresses [Figure 18.1(c)]. The IP datagram is routed through the Internet using MPLS label attached to it.

GRE and MPLS tunnelling technologies do not address the security threats at the network level. They merely enable routing of private IP addresses through the public Internet. IPsec, as an alternative to GRE and MPLS tunnels, provides secure tunnels for VPNs.

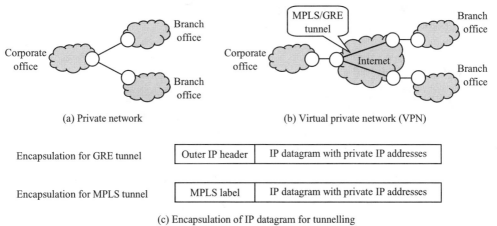

(a) Private network

(b) Virtual private network (VPN)

Encapsulation for GRE tunnel	Outer IP header	IP datagram with private IP addresses

Encapsulation for MPLS tunnel	MPLS label	IP datagram with private IP addresses

(c) Encapsulation of IP datagram for tunnelling

Figure 18.1   Private network and VPN.

18.1.2   Security for IP Datagrams

The public Internet and IP datagrams are inherently insecure.

- An intruder can read contents of an IP datagram and analyze traffic.
- An intruder on the Internet can easily manipulate contents of a datagram including its IP addresses and port numbers. 16-bit checksum in the IP header is of little help because the checksum itself can be readily recomputed and substituted.
- An intruder can copy and replay old IP datagrams.

There is no guarantee that a received datagram originated from the source address in its header, or its content not having been modified or exposed to an adversary. IPsec is designed to provide the following security services for IP datagrams:

- Confidentiality of the payload
- Source and content authentication
- Replay detection and avoidance
- Access control
- Limited traffic flow confidentiality
- Secure tunnels for implementing virtual private networks

Access control refers to discarding the datagrams which are unauthorized. Traffic flow confidentiality refers to hiding

- the source and destination IP addresses,
- TCP/UDP port numbers,
- the payload protocol, and
- the lengths of messages between two nodes.

Note that IPsec does not offer non repudiation. IPsec provides the above services using combination of cryptography algorithms and security protocols. There are two security protocols in IPsec—Authentication Header (AH) and Encapsulating Security Payload (ESP). IPsec enables the IPsec-aware network nodes and end systems to select and implement the required security protocols (AH or ESP), cryptography algorithms for confidentiality and authentication, and the secret keys.

18.1.3 Benefits of IPsec

IPsec with its two protocols AH and ESP provides a very flexible framework for meeting security requirements of various network configurations, network devices and mobile users. Figure 18.2 shows a typical network scenario consisting of a private IP network also called intranet implemented using gateway routers (G) and the public Internet.

- IPsec can be used between gateway routers to protect the intranet traffic as it transits through the public Internet.
- IPsec can be used between the mobile user (C) of the intranet and the gateway router G.
- IPsec can be used between the mobile user (C) of the intranet and the intranet host A.
- IPsec can be used between the intranet hosts A and B.

There can be multiple simultaneous applications of IPsec. For example, IP traffic between hosts A and B is protected using one set of IPsec policies (say authentication). This traffic can be further protected for confidentiality between the two gateway routers, which have their own implementation of IPsec. IPsec, thus, has very flexible framework for its implementation in various networking situations. Its other benefits are highlighted as follows:

- IPsec is application transparent. Therefore, existing applications need not be reconfigured when IPsec is implemented. Applications may not need their own security implementation. If they still do, IPsec places no restrictions.

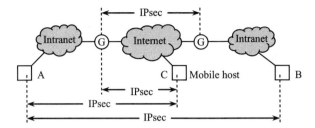

Figure 18.2 Applications of IPsec.

- Consistent security policy independent of various applications can be applied at the Network layer.
- IPsec provides security service to the higher layer which can be TCP or UDP.
- IPsec can provide security service to other protocols carried as payload in IP datagram, e.g. BGP, OSPF, IGMP and ICMP. Security of routing advertisements and updates is vital, since an adversary can divert/disrupt traffic by forged routing advertisements and updates.
- IPsec is implemented at IP layer of end systems, gateway routers, firewalls, mobile hosts, etc. Intermediate routers in the Internet need not be IPsec-aware.
- IPsec can be applied selectively to certain classes of traffic. Other traffic is bypassed from application of security.
- Different security policies can be defined different classes of traffic. Traffic can be classified based on destination address, source address, protocol carried as the payload in IP datagram and combination of these.
- QOS (Quality of Service) can be implemented independent of IPsec.
- IPsec protection can be applied to
  - the payload of IP datagram, or
  - the full IP datagram including the IP header.
- An IP datagram can be provided authentication protection, or privacy protection or both.
- IPsec can provide secure tunnels for creating VPNs on the public Internet.

18.2   IPSEC ARCHITECTURE

IPsec consists of several components as shown in Figure 18.3. These components and their interrelationships comprise the logical architecture of IPsec. RFCs that define the architecture and components of IPsec are listed at the end of this chapter. Before going into the details of each component of this architecture, we look at the overall picture in this section.

18.2.1   Security Policy Database

When an IPsec-aware host or network device (e.g. a router) has an outbound or inbound IP datagram, it needs to know what security processing is to be applied to the datagram. IPsec-aware host/device has a security policy database (SPD). SPD is consulted for each outbound and inbound datagram. A datagram is discarded, allowed to bypass IPsec, or secured according

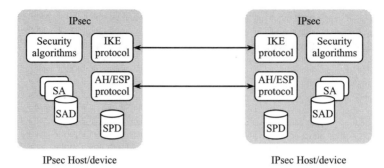

Figure 18.3 Components of IPsec.

to policy specified in SPD. Security policy to be applied to the datagram is determined using subset of various fields in IP datagram.

- Source address, destination address,
- Payload protocol, source port, destination port,
- Flow label (IPv6),
- DSCP, etc.

For example, an outbound IP datagram with the following parameters is secured using ESP protocol in transport mode. The parameters of security policy (e.g. encryption algorithm, key) are specified in security association database, described later.

Source address	Destination address	Source port	Destination port	Policy
192.168.11.11	192.168.22.22	1400	20	Transport ESP

18.2.2 Security Association

Having determined the security policy, the two communicating IPsec-aware peers must agree on the cryptographic key(s) and algorithm(s) to be used. Security association (SA) is set of mutually agreed security algorithms (e.g. HMAC-SHA1 for authentication and 3DES for encryption), associated keys and other parameters (e.g. lifetime of the keys) between the two IPsec peers.

Separate SAs are defined for each direction of communication because security policies can be asymmetric. Therefore, each session requires at least two SAs for both-way communication [Figure 18.4(a)].

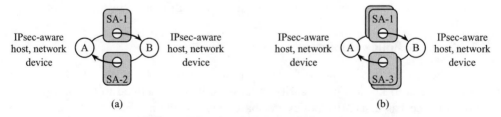

Figure 18.4 Security association (SA).

There are two IPsec protocols, Authentication Header (AH) and Encapsulating Security Payload (ESP). There is separate SA for each IPsec protocol. Therefore, if two IPsec peers decide to use both the protocols, 4 SAs are required for two-way communication between them [Figure 18.4(b)].

Situation depicted in Figure 18.4 holds for an instance of communication between two peers. Figure 18.5 shows an intranet behind two IPsec-aware routers, called gateways. The two gateways will have multiple SAs between them to support several instances of communication among the hosts simultaneously.

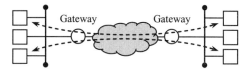

Figure 18.5 Multiple SAs between the gateway routers.

Security associations are negotiated and implemented using Internet Key Exchange (IKE) protocol; and are maintained in the security association database. Each SA is associated with an identifier, security parameter index (SPI). SPI is carried in the IPsec header and is used by the receiving entity for identifying the SA in its security association database.

18.2.3   Security Association Database

Active SAs are held in security association database (SAD). The SAD contains the parameters of each active SA. Some of the SA parameters are listed below.

- IPsec protocol (AH or ESP) and mode of protocol (transport or tunnel)
- Authentication algorithm and its key
- Encryption algorithm, its key and initialization vector
- Sequence number counter
- Anti-replay window
- Life time of SA
- Path MTU (maximum transmission unit)

IKE protocol automatically populates the SAD after an SA is established. Separate SADs are kept for inbound and outbound traffic.

- Outbound traffic SAD is indexed on triplet <SPI, destination address, IPsec protocol>.
- Inbound traffic SAD is indexed on triplet <SPI, source address, IPsec protocol>.

18.2.4   IKE Protocol

IPsec requires support for negotiating and establishing SAs and for key exchange. This support is provided by IKE protocol. When an IPsec node receives an IP datagram, it consults SPD, and if an SA is required to be established, IKE protocol is invoked to establish the SA. We discuss IKE protocol in detail in the next chapter.

18.2.5   AH and ESP Protocols

To provide security at IP layer, IPsec defines two protocols.

Authentication Header (AH):   Authentication header (AH) protocol provides the authentication service, i.e., datagram integrity and source authentication.

Encapsulating Security Payload (ESP):   ESP protocol provides confidentiality service by encrypting the payload of the datagram. Authentication service is optional in ESP.

AH and ESP protocols have two modes of operation:

Transport mode: In transport mode, AH and ESP protocols apply security policy to the payload of an IP datagram[1].

Tunnel mode: In tunnel mode, the security policy is applied to the entire IP datagram and the datagram is encapsulated in an additional IP header.

   The two IPsec protocols (AS and ESP) in two modes (transport and tunnel) modes provide the required flexibility for application of IPsec in various networking situations.

18.2.6   Security Algorithms

As mentioned before, security policy (i.e. AH or ESP in transport or tunnel mode) to be applied to an IP datagram is indicated in SPD. The authentication and encryption algorithms with respective keys are specified in SAD. Authentication service is based on the following MAC algorithms. Recall that authentication based on MAC does not support non-repudiation.

- HMAC-MD5-96
- HMAC-SHA1-96
- AES-XCBC-MAC-96[2]

   The computed value of MAC is truncated to first 96 bits in the above algorithms. Confidentiality service offered by ESP is based on the following symmetric-key algorithms.

- AES-CBC
- Triple DES-CBC
- AES-CTR

   ESP also provides 'NULL' encryption, meaning thereby that the payload is not encrypted, but it is encapsulated in ESP protocol. It may be the case that only authentication option of ESP is used.

18.3   AUTHENTICATION HEADER (AH) PROTOCOL

An unprotected IP datagram can be subjected to manipulation by the adversary in several ways.

---

1. AH protocol, in addition, protects some of the IP header fields as we shall see later.
2. AES-XCBC-MAC-96 is described in RFC 3566, *The AES-XCBC-MAC-96 Algorithm and Its Use With IPsec*.

- The adversary may manipulate fields of the IP header or the payload carrying the higher layer protocol (e.g. TCP or UDP). For example, the adversary may replace the source address of an IP datagram with his own IP address so that the reply comes to him. The checksum field in IPv4 header provides no protection against such attacks because the adversary modifies the checksum as well.
- The adversary can manipulate the payload of an IP datagram. He can modify TCP/ UDP headers or the application data.
- The adversary can insert fraudulent IP datagrams or replay old IP datagrams copied earlier.

AH protocol of IPsec provides protection against any such manipulation by the adversary. AH protocol inserts an additional header just after the IP header[3] of the IP datagram (Figure 18.6). The protocol field in the IP header is changed to 51, which identifies the presence of authentication header following the IP header. Format of authentication header is described as follows:

***Next header* (8 *bits*):** The value in the next header field defines the payload carried by IP datagram. Some of the payloads and the respective next header values are given as:

$$\text{TCP (6)} \qquad \text{UDP (17)} \qquad \text{OSPF (89)} \qquad \text{ICMP (1)} \qquad \text{IGMP (2)}$$

Payload of IP datagram originally defined in the 'Protocol' field of IP header is copied into this field.

***Length* (8 *bits*):** It is the length of the authentication header in 32-bit words minus 2. The 'minus 2' is an artifact of AH protocol being an IPv6 protocol. In IPv6, extension header lengths are always expressed as the total length minus 64 bits. In our case, 64 bits would make two 32-bit words.

***Reserved* (16 *bits*):** These bits are reserved for future use.

***Security parameter index* (32 *bits*):** Security parameter index (SPI) is used for identifying security association (SA) for this datagram. The receiver uses this field to determine the security algorithms and keys to be applied for authentication.

***Sequence number* (32 *bits*):** It is monotonically increasing counter value for protection against replay. It is set to zero when an SA is established. SA is re-established when the sequence number reaches $2^{32}-1$.

Authentication data (variable): It contains the MAC value for integrity and source authentication. The length of this field is integral multiple of 32. The MAC is computed over the following fields:

- IP header with the mutable fields[4] set to zero. The mutable fields are those that change or are likely to change during transit. The following fields of IPv4 are mutable:

---

3. If IP option fields are present, the authentication header is inserted after the option fields.
4. Some of the fields can be mutable but predictable. For example, if source routing is used, the destination address field is mutable, but its ultimate value predictable as specified in the source route. Mutable but predictable fields are included in MAC computation with their predicted value.

- DSCP (Differentiated Service Code point), TOS (Type of service)
- ECN (Explicit congestion notification)
- TTL (Time to live)
- Flags
- Fragment offset
- Header checksum

Some of the option fields are also mutable, e.g. source route, time stamp, record route, etc. If options are present, these mutable fields are also set to zero for computation of MAC.
- The authentication header with authentication data field set to zero.
- Payload.

The secret key and MAC algorithm as specified in SAD are used for MAC computation.

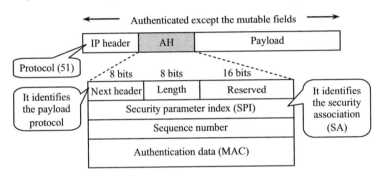

Figure 18.6 AH protocol.

18.3.1 Services of Authentication Header Protocol

The Authentication Header protocol provides the following services:

- IP datagram origin authentication
- IP datagram integrity authentication
- Replay detection and protection

For datagram origin and integrity authentication, AH protocol uses MAC computed using shared secret between the end points. Note that MAC computation covers IP header also.

- Any change in non-mutable fields of the IP header (e.g. source address) renders the MAC invalid. Thus the adversary cannot change the source IP address of an IP datagram to divert the reply to him.
- The adversary cannot insert a fraudulent datagram because he does not know the secret key required for computation of MAC.

The sequence number is used for protection against replay. We discuss replay protection mechanism in Section 18.5.

AH protocol does not provide the following services:

- Non repudiation because it uses symmetric key for data origin authentication.
- Content confidentiality because the content is not encrypted.
- Flow confidentiality because the IP header is not encrypted. The adversary can readily determine the origin and destination of the IP datagram from the IP header.

18.4 ENCAPSULATING SECURITY PAYLOAD (ESP) PROTOCOL

Authentication Header protocol lacks one essential security service when the network is insecure, the confidentiality service. IPSec has ESP protocol for providing confidentiality to the payload of an IP datagram. ESP protocol adds a header and a trailer to an IP datagram as shown in Figure 18.7. The ESP header is inserted just after the IP header[5]. The ESP trailer is added just after the payload. The protocol field in the IP header is changed to 50, which identifies the presence of ESP header following the IP header.

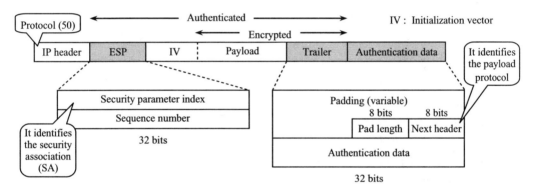

Figure 18.7 ESP protocol.

ESP protocol provides authentication service also as an option. If authentication option is chosen, the MAC field is appended to the ESP trailer. As we shall shortly see, the authentication service of ESP protocol is somewhat different from that provided by AH protocol.

Various fields of the ESP header and trailer are described below.

***Security parameter index* (32 *bits*):** It is used to identify the security association (SA) for this datagram.

***Sequence number* (32 *bits*):** It is monotonically increasing counter value for protection against replay. It is set to zero when an SA is established. SA is re-established when the sequence number reaches $2^{32} - 1$.

***Padding* (*variable*):** Padding octets are all zeros. There can be 0 to 255 octets in this field.

---

5. If the IP option fields are present, the ESP header is inserted after the option fields.

***Pad length* (8 *bits*):**   It is the number of pad octets immediately preceding this field.

***Next header* (8 *bits*):**   The value in the next header field identifies the protocol of encrypted payload carried by IP datagram.

***Authentication data* (*variable, optional*):**   It contains the MAC value for authentication. The length of this field in bits is integral multiple of 32.

The purpose of padding field (0 to 255 octets) requires some elaboration.

- Padding is necessitated during encryption to make the size of plaintext multiple of block size (128 bits for AES and 64 bits for 3DES).
- Padding is required to ensure that the size of payload plus trailer is multiple of 4 octets even if stream cipher or NULL encryption is used.
- The sender may append additional padding octets to the plaintext to hide the length of plaintext message from the adversary.

When the mode of operation (e.g. CBC mode) of the block cipher requires an initialization vector (IV), it is placed just before the payload. IV is kept outside the span of encryption.

18.4.1   Services of Encapsulating Security Payload Protocol

The Encapsulating Security Payload (ESP) protocol provides the following services:

- Payload confidentiality service
- Limited traffic-flow confidentiality service
- Replay detection and protection
- Optional data origin authentication and content integrity service

For the above services, ESP uses symmetric-key encryption algorithm, MAC with shared secret between end points, and sequence numbers. The scope of encryption and authentication services is elaborated as follows:

- Payload field and the trailer are encrypted. It implies that next header field is also encrypted. Thus the payload content and its type (described by the next header field) are not exposed to the adversary.
- MAC is computed over the ESP header, IV, encrypted payload and encrypted ESP trailer. In other words, MAC authenticates SPI, sequence number, IV, payload and the next header fields. Any modification of these fields by the adversary is readily detected.
- Unlike AH, ESP with authentication option does not protect IP header.

There is provision for up to 255 padding octets. If required, the source can use this provision for hiding the size of the payload by appending extra padding octets.

18.5   REPLAY PROTECTION

Internet protocol offers an unreliable connectionless service. IP datagrams may not be delivered in the same order as they were sent or they may not be delivered at all. This situation can be easily exploited by an adversary to launch the replay attack. He obtains copy of an authenticated datagram and later transmits it to the intended destination. The sequence numbering with sliding receiver window in AS and ESP protocols is designed to thwart such attacks.

Sequence Numbering

When a new SA is established, the sequence number counter at the sending end is initialized to zero. The counter is incremented by 1 when a datagram is to be sent. Each datagram carries the current value of the counter. When the counter reaches $2^{32} - 1$, the counter restarts at zero. The sender terminates the current SA and negotiates new SA.

The sequence number scheme with a sliding receiver window is used for preventing replay attacks. The receiver detects replay attack when it finds

- two datagrams with same sequence number in the life time of an SA or
- a datagram with sequence number that is too late.

Sliding Receiver Window Mechanism

The receiver maintains a sliding window for replay detection (Figure 18.8). The window contains sequence numbers of the IPsec datagrams.

- The right edge of the window is at the highest sequence number N of the valid datagram received so far.
- The default window size (W) is 64. Thus the sequence numbers from N – W + 1 to N are within the window.

When an IP datagram is received, the receiver takes the following actions:

- If the datagram fails on authentication validation, it is discarded and the event is logged.
- If the datagram is valid and bears sequence number which is to the left of window, the datagram is discarded and the event is logged.
- If the datagram is valid, and bears sequence number
  - which is to the right of window, it is accepted and the window is advanced so that the sequence number is within the window at its right edge.
  - which is within the window and is uncrossed, the datagram is accepted and the corresponding sequence number is crossed.
  - which is within the window and is already crossed, the datagram is discarded and the event is logged.

It is necessary that the adversary must not be able to manipulate the sequence numbers for the anti-replay window to work effectively. Therefore, authentication option of the ESP protocol must be used to ensure integrity of the IPsec datagram.

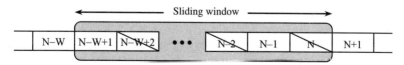

Figure 18.8   Sliding window for replay protection.

18.6 TRANSPORT AND TUNNEL MODES

The IPsec protocols, AS and ESP operate in two modes: transport mode and tunnel mode. In this section, we examine these modes and when we should use one or the other. We examine basic operations of these two modes and some typical networking situations where these modes are used.

18.6.1 Transport Mode

Transport mode is primarily meant for secure transport of the payload of an IP datagram. An IP datagram carries the Transport layer protocols (e.g. TCP) or other protocols (e.g. ICMP, OSPF) as its payload. IPsec provides secure transport of these protocols in terms of confidentiality, content integrity, source authentication and replay protection depending on whether AH or ESP is used.

Typically transport mode is used between two fixed hosts A and B as shown in Figure 18.9(a). The two hosts can be on the same network or part of a VPN across the Internet. In case of VPN, the VPN tunnel carries the IPsec datagram as payload [Figure 18.9(b)].

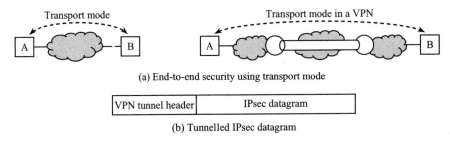

(a) End-to-end security using transport mode

(b) Tunnelled IPsec datagram

Figure 18.9 IPsec in transport mode between two hosts.

IPsec header in transport mode is inserted between the IP header and payload (Figure 18.10).

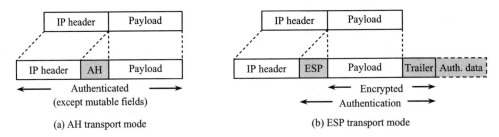

Figure 18.10 IPsec datagram in transport mode.

The following are some specific observations in respect of AH and ESP protocols in transport mode:

AH Transport Mode

- AH transport mode between two hosts is primarily meant for the origin and content authentication.
- There is no content and traffic-flow confidentiality between the two endpoints. This is so even when the IPsec datagram is transported through unsecured VPN tunnel. Traffic flow confidentiality refers to confidentiality of
  - the source and destination IP addresses (IP header),
  - the source and destination port numbers (TCP/UDP header), and
  - the protocol carried by IP datagram (IP header).
- The MAC value authenticates the entire IPsec datagram except the mutable fields in IP header (Section 18.3). The source and destination addresses are protected by authentication. If the adversary manipulates any non-mutable field, including the addresses, the MAC verification will fail.
- If the end-to-end path between the two hosts goes through a NAT[6] device, the MAC verification will fail at the receiving end.

ESP Transport Mode

- ESP transport mode is used to provide confidentiality and authenticity (optional) of the IPsec payload (TCP, UDP, ICMP, other protocols).
- ESP transport mode achieves partial traffic flow confidentiality, since IP addresses cannot be encrypted. Traffic confidentially provided in the following respect:
  - The Next Header field (Figure 18.7) which contains the type of payload protocol is encrypted.
  - The TCP/UDP port numbers which are part of payload are encrypted.
  - The message size is obscured by the padding octets.
- Unlike AH transport mode, ESP transport mode does not protect the source and destination addresses of the endpoint hosts against manipulation by the adversary. For example, if the adversary replaces the source address in a datagram with his IP address, the reply will be routed to him.
- When authentication option is used, ESP header that contains the sequence number is authenticated by the MAC. Thus the adversary cannot manipulate the sequence number to launch replay attack.
- MAC computation in ESP does not include IP header. Thus the adversary can manipulate IP header even if authentication option is used.
- Unlike AH transport mode, ESP transport mode is not restricted in any manner by the NAT device.

---

6. NAT: Network Address Translation. NAT is required for translating private IP addresses (10.0.0.0/8, 172.16.0.0/12, 192.168.0.0/16) into public addresses and vice versa.

18.6.2 Tunnel Mode

Tunnel mode is primarily meant for securing the entire IP datagram including its header. The IPsec datagram is constructed as follows:

- The IP datagram (IP header and the payload) is encapsulated behind IPsec header. The 'Next header' field of IPsec header/trailer is set to 4 indicating that the payload next to IPsec header is IPv4 datagram.
- A new IP header is added in front of IPsec header [Figures 18.11(a), (b)]. The protocol field of the outer IP header indicates the IPsec protocol, AH (51) or ESP (50).

The tunnel mode is so called because the original IP datagram is carried along the route decided by the IP address on the outer IP header.

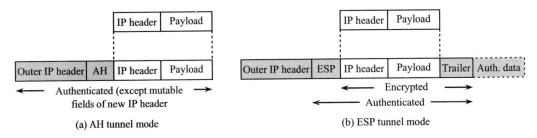

Figure 18.11 IPsec encapsulation in the tunnel mode.

The tunnel mode is typically used between the following endpoints [Figure 18.12(a)]:

(a) Between security gateway routers of the two networks, G_1 and G_2.
(b) Between a remote host (B) and security gateway of a network, G_1.

The addresses on the outer IP header are the IP addresses of tunnel endpoints. The IP addresses of the encapsulated IP header are the ultimate source and destination addresses (A and B). The tunnelling process works in the following manner:

- IP datagram from host A for host B is forwarded to the default gateway G_1.
- Gateway G_1 has security policy database which indicates that the IPsec protocol in tunnel mode is to be used with destination address as G_2. The datagram is encapsulated as shown in Figure 18.12(b).
- The datagram is routed through the internet based on the destination address in the outer IP header.
- The datagram received at the gateway G_2 is processed by the IPsec protocol and the original datagram from host A to B is recovered from the secured payload. The recovered datagram is forwarded to host B.

In the case of the remote host, the gateway function is built into the remote host itself.

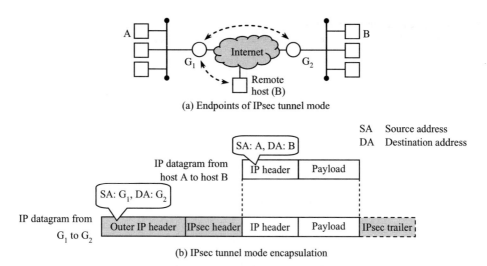

(a) Endpoints of IPsec tunnel mode

(b) IPsec tunnel mode encapsulation

Figure 18.12 IPsec tunnel mode.

The following are some specific observations in respect of AH and ESP protocols in tunnel mode.

AH Tunnel Mode

- AH tunnel mode when used between the gateways G_1 and G_2 provides secure transport of encapsulated IP datagram, but without any content and traffic confidentiality (Figure 18.12).
- The encapsulated datagram with private IP addresses is tunnelled through public Internet without need for address translation.
- Typical application of this mode is seen in the transition phase of IPv4 to IPv6. IPsec allows mixed IP versions of the inner IP header and outer IP header in the tunnel mode. During the transition phase, the Internet will have islands of IPv4 and IPv6. Transporting IPv4 datagrams through IPv6 island and vice versa can be achieved using AH tunnel mode (Figure 18.13).

ESP Tunnel Mode

- ESP tunnel mode when used between the gateways G_1 and G_2 (or between gateway G_1 and remote host) provides full security of the encapsulated IP datagram.
  - Confidentiality of the encapsulated IP datagram.
  - Confidentiality of traffic flow.
  - Source and content authentication of encapsulated IP datagram when authentication option is used.
- The encapsulated datagram with private IP addresses is tunnelled through public Internet without need for address translation.

- In case of a mobile remote host,
    - the IP address of the remote host in the outer IP header is dynamically assigned by the ISP[7].
    - the IP address of the remote host in the inner IP header pertains to the network behind the gateway. It can be fixed address or dynamically assigned by the gateway during SA establishment using IKE protocol.

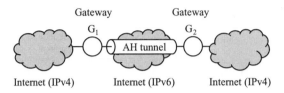

Figure 18.13 AH tunnel for carrying IPv4 datagrams through IPv6 island.

18.6.3 Combining Security Associations

Sometimes it is useful to apply both AH and ESP simultaneously, combining multiple SAs into an SA bundle. There can be several possible combinations tunnel/transport modes and AH/ESP protocols. We present here the following two typical mode combinations for the purpose of illustration:

(a) AH transport—ESP transport
(b) AH transport—ESP tunnel

AH Transport—ESP Transport

This is the simplest situation that combines AH and ESP both in transport mode [Figure 18.14(a)]. AH protocol is used for authentication and ESP is used for confidentiality. Both the protocols are used end-to-end between the two hosts. Note that AH protocol is applied after ESP protocol. This makes sense because we want to authenticate as much of the datagram as possible, including the ESP header.

AH Transport—ESP Tunnel

Figure 18.14(b) shows a VPN consisting of two LANs interconnected through gateways G_1 and G_2 with ESP in tunnel mode between the gateways. The VPN uses private IP addressing scheme. The encrypted IP datagrams with privates IP addresses are transported using ESP protocol in tunnel mode. ESP provides the required confidentiality across the public internet. Within the VPN, the two hosts use AH protocol in transport mode for authentication of IP datagram.

---

7. ISP: Internet service provider.

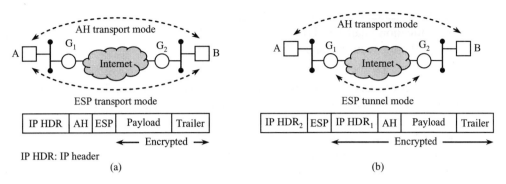

Figure 18.14 Combining security associations.

18.7 IPSEC FOR IPV6

IPsec implementation is optional in IPv4. An ISP may or may not implement IPsec. But IPsec is integral part of the IPv6. It is mandatory to implement IPsec in IPv6 network, though its usage is optional. The basic operation of AH and ESP protocols in IPv6 remains more or less same as in IPv4. There are minor differences due to structural differences of IPv4 and IPv6 datagrams. Figure 18.15 shows basic format of IPv6 datagram. It consists of base header followed by series of extension headers.

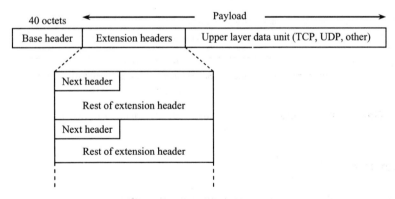

Figure 18.15 IPv6 datagram.

- The base header has fixed length of 40 octets and contains the following fields: Version, traffic class, flow label, payload length, next header, hop limit, source IP address and destination IP address
- Base header is followed by series of extension headers, each of which is optional. There are seven extension headers:

  1. Hop-by-hop options   (0)
  2. Destination options   Header 1   (60)
  3. Routing header   (43)

4. Fragment header   (44)
5. Authentication header (AH)   (51)
6. Encapsulating security payload (ESP)   (50)
7. Destination options—Header 2   (60)

The extension headers are placed in the sequence shown above. The next header field of the base header identifies the first extension header. The next header field of each extension header identifies the following extension header.

We will not go into purpose and other details of these headers. Since destination options—Header 2 follows AH/ESP headers, it needs some explanation. This header notifies the destination host about any special processing needed for this datagram. Having been placed after IPsec header, it is secured by the IPsec protocol.

- The extension headers are followed by the encapsulated data from the upper layer (TCP, UDP, other protocol).

Figure 18.16 shows the AH/ESP encapsulations for the transport and tunnel modes. The encapsulation and span of authentication/encryption are on the same lines as in IPv4.

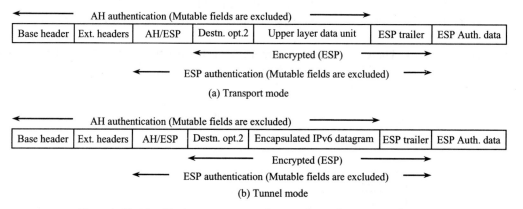

Figure 18.16 IPv6 transport and tunnel mode encapsulations.

18.8 SUMMING UP

This chapter covered implementation of cryptographic mechanisms for privacy and authentication at the Network layer. The main points of learning are summarized as follows:

- IP Security (IPsec) is set of protocols for providing security at the Network layer (IP layer).
- IPsec framework consists of three protocols: Authentication Header (AH), Encapsulating Security Payload (ESP) and Internet Key Exchange (IKE).
- AH protocol provides authentication service for content integrity and data origin authentication. ESP provides confidentiality and authentication (optional) services.
- AH and ESP protocols have two modes of operation, transport mode and tunnel mode. Transport mode is used primarily to provide protection to the IP payload. Tunnel mode provides protection to the entire IP packet by encapsulating it in another IP header.

- AH/ESP in transport/tunnel modes can be applied in a combined mode of operation to meet the security requirements of various networking configurations. IPsec in tunnel mode is typically used for VPN applications.
- IPsec implementation is optional for IPv4 networks, while IPv6 mandates its implementation.

IPsec requires support of IKE (Internet Key Exchange) protocol for negotiating security associations. We study IKE in the next chapter.

Key Terms		
Authentication header (AH)	MPLS tunnel	Sliding receiver window
Encapsulating security payload (ESP)	Security association	Virtual private network (VPN)
GRE tunnel	Security association database (SAD)	Transport mode
IKE protocol	Security parameter index (SPI)	Tunnel mode
Intranet	Security policy database (SPD)	

RECOMMENDED READING

Avoine, G., Junod, P. and Oechslin, P., *Computer System Security: Basic Concepts and Solved Exercises*, CRC Press, FL, USA, 2004.

Doraswamy, H. and Harkins, D., *IPsec*, Prentice-Hall, NJ, USA, 2003.

Douligeris, C. (Ed), Serpanos, D.N., *Network Security, Current Status and Future Directions*, IEEE Press, John Wiley & Sons, NJ, USA, 2007.

Forouzan, Behrouz A., *Cryptography and Network Security*, Tata McGraw-Hill, New Delhi, 2007.

Gupta, Prakash C., *Data Communications and Computer Networks*, PHI Learning, Delhi, 2014.

Kaufman, C., Perlman, R. and Spenciner, M., *Network Security, Private Communication in a Public World*, Prentice-Hall of India, New Delhi, 2007.

Mao, W., *Modern Cryptography*, Pearson Education, New Delhi, 2008.

RFC 4301, *Security Architecture for the Internet Protocol*, IETF, 2005.

RFC 4302, *IP Authentication Header,* IETF, 2005.

RFC 4303, *IP Encapsulating Security Payload (ESP)*, IETF, 2005.

RFC 5996, *Internet Key Exchange (V2)*, IETF, 2010.

Rhee, M., *Internet Security*, John Wiley & Sons, West Sussex, UK, 2003.

Snader, Jon C., *VPNs Illustrated: Tunnels, VPNs, and IPsec*, Pearson Education, New Delhi, 2006.

Stallings, W., *Cryptography and Network Security*, Prentice-Hall of India, New Delhi, 2008.

Stevens, W., *TCP/IP Illustrated, Volume 1: The Protocols*, Pearson Education, New Delhi, 2009.

—————————(**PROBLEMS**)—————————

1. When a valid IPsec datagram is received, the right edge of the replay protection window is advanced so that the sequence number of the received is within the window at its right edge. Window size being fixed, it implies that the left edge of the edge will also be advanced to right by the same amount. If on doing so, some of uncrossed sequence numbers may go out of the window. How does IPsec react when a datagram bearing one of the uncrossed number just pushed out of window is received?

2. IPsec datagrams bearing the following sequence numbers are received when the replay protection window spans from 301 to 332. Indicate if these datagrams will be accepted or discarded. Indicate the position of the right edge of the window after each instance of receiving an IP datagram. Assume that the sequence numbers 310, 315, 320, 325 of the window are already crossed.

   308, 314, 314, 315, 345, 310

3. If a TCP acknowledgement is lost, the TCP segment is retransmitted. Will the IPsec implementation discard the IP datagram carrying retransmitted TCP segment, since it will be carrying a duplicate TCP segment? Explain how the receiving IPsec layer can distinguish between a re-transmitted TCP segment of the legitimate sender and a malicious packet sent by the adversary.

4. Show the span of authentication and encryption in each of the following IPsec configurations:
   (a) AH (Transport mode)
   (b) AH (Tunnel mode)
   (c) ESP (Transport mode with encryption and authentication)
   (d) ESP (Transport mode with encryption and without authentication)
   (e) ESP (Transport mode with null encryption and with authentication)
   (f) ESP (Tunnel mode with encryption and authentication)

5. Among the six IPsec configurations of Problem 4, indicate those which can be used with NAT between the two IPsec endpoints.

6. If one wants to apply ESP and AH to an IP datagram, what should be the order of their application?

7. Some ISPs prohibit IPsec VPNs on home accounts by filtering ESP traffic. Given that the traffic is encrypted, how are the ISPs able to detect the ESP traffic?

8. Suppose the initialization vector (IV) required for CBC mode of operation is not sent with each IPsec datagram. Instead the encrypted payload of previous IPsec datagram is used as IV for decryption. This decision will reduce the size of IPsec datagram significantly.
   (a) How will this decision impact the performance at the receiver?
   (b) IPsec datagrams bearing the following sequence numbers are received in the order as given below. Which of the following IPsec datagrams can be decrypted?

301, 305, 306, 302, 308, 306

Assume that the span of replay protection window is from 300 to 331 when the first datagram is received and all the sequence numbers in the window are uncrossed.

9. Recall that IPsec transport mode is typically used between two hosts, while tunnel mode is used between two gateway routers.

   (a) Why does IESP tunnel mode fail to hide the header information when used from host to host?

   (b) Does IPsec tunnel mode also fail to hide the header information when used between two gateway routers?

19

Internet Key Exchange (IKE)

Security associations of IPsec can be established manually when there is small number of IPsec endpoints and the implementation is restricted to a few sites of an organization. Widespread deployment of IPsec requires automated means of establishing and maintaining SAs. Internet Key Exchange is a supporting protocol to IPsec for this purpose. We begin this chapter with a few enhancements required in Diffie–Hellman key exchange for its use in IKE protocol. We examine the IKE operation, key generation and IKE message formats. It is advised that this chapter be read after thorough study of Chapter 18.

19.1 INTERNET KEY EXCHANGE (IKE)

IP Security (IPsec) provides confidentiality, data integrity, data-origin authentication and access control services for IP datagrams. These services are provided by maintaining a security association (SA) state between the two communicating IPsec endpoints. The SA state comprises

- the cryptographic algorithms to be used for encryption and authentication,
- the secret keys of cryptographic algorithms,
- state of the anti-replay window,
- state of sequence number counter, and
- other parameters, e.g. lifetime of security keys.

The two end-points can be two hosts, two security gateways, or a gateway and a remote host as shown in Figure 19.1.

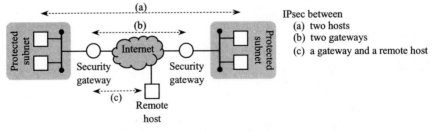

Figure 19.1 IPsec endpoints.

Since establishing SAs manually for each instance of communication does not scale well, a protocol that can establish the SAs dynamically is needed. Internet Key Exchange (IKE) is the automated SA and key management protocol for IPsec.

- IKE establishes IPsec SAs dynamically as they are needed. Establishing SAs implies
  - negotiating cipher suites for authentication and confidentiality, and
  - implementing secret keys for encryption and authentication.
- IKE maintains the IPsec SAs by way of
  - creating new keys and new SAs dynamically as they expire.
  - generating notifications for deleting SAs, rekeying and operational errors.

The IKE messages are sent as UDP payload between two end points. The source and destination UDP ports are 500 (or 4500) for IKE protocol.

19.2   IKE PROTOCOL

IKE is a hybrid protocol that utilizes relevant parts of the following three protocols:

Oakley key creation protocol: It is based on Diffie–Hellman key exchange algorithm with some enhancements.

SKEME key exchange: It is based on public-key authentication during key exchange.

Internet Security Association and Key Management Protocol (ISAKMP):   It defines the framework of

- procedures for exchange of messages
- formats of the messages.

The current version is IKEv2, and it is specified in RFC 5996. Before we go into operation of IKE protocol, let us first understand the enhancements required in Diffie–Hellman key exchange for IKE.

19.2.1   Enhanced Diffie–Hellman Key Exchange

Recall that Diffie–Hellman (DH) key exchange is used for establishing a shared secret (g^{ab} mod p) between Alice and Bob. This secret is established by exchanging the DH half keys, g^a mod p and g^b mod p [Figure 19.2(a)]. DH key exchange is prone to two types of attacks:

- Denial-of-service (DoS) attack
- Man-in-the-middle attack

DoS Attack

DH key exchange algorithm is based on computation-intensive modular exponentiation. An adversary can launch a DoS attack by sending multiple half keys to Bob to exhaust his computing resources. Bob gets so busy with the adversary's half keys that he stops responding to messages from Alice. The adversary launches the DoS attack from forged IP source addresses to avoid detection. DoS attacked can be prevented by introducing a cookie [Figure 19.2(b)].

1. Alice sends request to establish a shared secret.
2. Bob responds with his cookie C_B. The cookie is a secret known only to Bob.
3. Alice returns C_B and her half key g^a mod p.
4. Bob verifies that the received cookie is the one he sent. If it is so, he responds with his half key g^b mod p.

If the adversary uses a forged IP source address in message (1) above, the Bob's response containing the cookie C_B never reaches him. It goes to the forged IP address. The adversary cannot send message (3) which requires cookie C_B to be returned. Bob is, thus, protected from DoS attack.

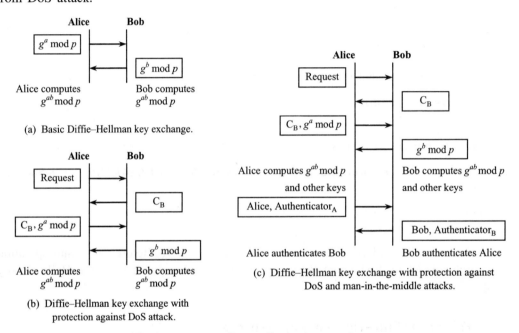

(a) Basic Diffie–Hellman key exchange.

(b) Diffie–Hellman key exchange with protection against DoS attack.

(c) Diffie–Hellman key exchange with protection against DoS and man-in-the-middle attacks.

Figure 19.2 Diffie–Hellman key exchange.

Man-in-the-Middle Attack

Man-in-the-middle attack on DH key exchange was described in Chapter 14. To recall, the adversary places himself between Alice and Bob, impersonating as Bob to Alice and as Alice to Bob. He creates two secret keys using DH key exchange algorithm, one he shares with Alice and the other with Bob. Thereafter he intercepts all the messages exchanged between Alice and Bob.

Man-in-the-middle attack on DH key exchange is thwarted by mutual authentication of communicating entities [Figure 19.2(c)]. Alice and Bob both submit an authenticator as a proof of their identity. The authenticator can be something they individually own or share mutually. For example,

(a) Alice proves that she possesses the private key by sending a signed message along with her digital certificate. Bob verifies the signature using her public key announced in the digital certificate. The adversary cannot forge Alice's signature on the message.

(b) Alice proves that she possesses a pre-shared secret by generating a MAC value using the secret. MAC is computed over concatenation of her identity 'Alice' and her previous message to Bob. Bob verifies the MAC value using the same secret. The adversary cannot forge MAC value as he does not know the secret shared between Alice and Bob.

Bob also authenticates himself to Alice in the same manner. We will look at the structure of authenticator used in IKE later. IKE further improves the DH key exchange by introducing nonces[1], which provide protection against replay-attacks.

19.2.2 IKE Security Association (IKE-SA)

Recall that an IPsec security association is set of mutually agreed security algorithms (e.g. HMAC-SHA1 for authentication and 3DES for encryption), associated keys and other parameters (e.g. lifetime of the keys) between the two IPsec peers. An IP packet is protected between the two IPsec peers using the security algorithms and keys specified in the SA. For example, SA2 is defined for secure transfer of the payload (TCP/UDP segments, tunnelled IP packets) from Alice to Bob (Figure 19.3). Similarly, SA3 is defined for the secure transfer of the payload from Bob to Alice.

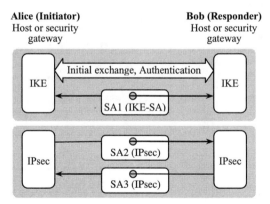

Figure 19.3 IKE-SA and IPsec SA.

To establish these IPsec SAs, the IKE entities at the endpoints have an initial exchange of IKE messages. This exchange of messages negotiates the cipher suites and key parameters of these IPsec SAs. For secure transfer of these IKE messages, a *bidirectional* IKE security association (IKE-SA) is also required (Figure 19.3). IKE-SA specifies the cryptographic algorithms and keys for securing the IKE messages. Secured IKE messages are then encapsulated as UDP payload and sent to the other endpoint.

---

1. Nonce is short for 'number used once'.

Note the subtle differences in IPsec SA and IKE-SA.

- IPsec SA specifies the security algorithms and keys that are used at IP layer. The payload that is protected is user data encapsulated as TCP/UDP segments.
- IKE-SA specifies the security algorithms and keys for securing IKE messages before their UDP encapsulation.

As we shall shortly see, IKE protocol establishes IKE-SA first and then establishes IPsec SAs using the security provided by IKE-SA.

19.2.3 IKE Protocol Operation

IKEv2 protocol consists of the following set of exchanges between an initiator and a responder[2]. Each exchange consists of a pair of messages, a request and a response (Figure 19.4).

(a) IKE_SA_INIT exchange
(b) IKE_AUTH exchange
(c) CREATE_CHILD_SA exchange
(d) INFORMATIONAL exchange

The first two exchanges need to be completed before any other exchange. There can be as many CREATE_CHILD_SA exchanges as required.

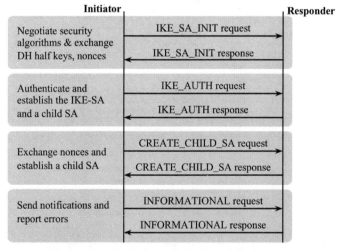

Figure 19.4 IKEv2 protocol operation.

19.2.4 IKE_SA_INIT Exchange

IKE_SA_INIT exchange is the first exchange that establishes the IKE-SA. Its basic purpose is to negotiate the security algorithms and exchange parameters (e.g. DH half keys and nonces) required for setting up the IKE-SA. The exchange consists of the following request and response:

---

2. IKE protocol uses the terms 'initiator' and 'responder' in place of usual Alice and Bob. The entity which sends the request is designated as the initiator. The entity that responds is the responder. During a session, the entities may reverse their roles.

| **Initiator** | IKE_SA_INIT request | $HDR(SPI_I, 0); SA1_I, KE_I, N_I$ | (1) |
| **Responder** | IKE_SA_INIT response | $HDR(SPI_I, SPI_R); SA1_R, KE_R, N_R$ | (2) |

HDR is the common header of all the messages. SPI_I is the initiator's security parameter index which identifies the IKE-SA being set up. It is specified in the header as one of the fields. We describe the header in Section 19.5. The initiator's request contains the following payloads:

- $SA1_I$, the set of cryptographic algorithms proposed by the initiator for the IKE-SA,
- KE_I, the DH half key of the initiator (g^i mod p),
- N_I, the nonce of the initiator to protect against replay.

The responder specifies SPI_R, the security parameter index of the responder for the IKE-SA in the header of his response. The response contains the following payloads:

- $SA1_R$, the set of cryptographic algorithms chosen by the responder,
- KE_R, the DH half key of the responder (g^r mod p),
- N_R, the nonce of the responder to check liveness and to protect against replay.

After this exchange, the initiator and the responder can compute cryptographic keys as explained in Section 19.3. All the IKE exchanges that follow are secured using the negotiated cryptographic algorithms and the IKE-SA keys indicated below:

1. SK_{AI} Authentication key of initiator
2. SK_{AR} Authentication key of responder
3. SK_{EI} Encryption key of initiator
4. SK_{ER} Encryption key of responder

In addition two more keys SK_{PI} and SK_{PR} are generated. These keys are used in IKE_AUTH exchange by the initiator and responder to prove their identities to each other.

DoS Attack

The normal operation of IKEv2 does not include protection against DoS attack. Only when the responder detects several incomplete IKE_SA_INIT exchanges, the responder takes action for detecting DoS attack. In response to the IKE_SA_INIT request from the initiator, it sends a cookie notification, N(Cookie). The initiator resends its IKE_SA_INIT request that includes the cookie notification as the first payload. The responder completes the exchange, if the received cookie is found valid. If there is a DoS attack from a spoofed IP address, the adversary does not get the cookie notification. Therefore, there is no response to the cookie notification.

Initiator	IKE_SA_INIT request	$HDR(SPI_I, 0); SA1_I, KE_I, N_I$	(1)
Responder	Cookie response	$HDR(SPI_I, 0); N (Cookie)$	
Initiator	IKE_SA_INIT request	$HDR(SPI_I, 0); N (Cookie), SA1_I, KE_I, N_I$	(1a)
Responder	IKE_SA_INIT response	$HDR(SPI_I, SPI_R); SA1_R, KE_R, N_R$	(2)

19.2.5 IKE_AUTH Exchange

After the IKE_SA_INIT exchange, the initiator and the responder have set of negotiated security algorithms and associated keys for the IKE-SA. But they are yet to ensure that they are not talking to the adversary. The IKE_AUTH exchange performs this task. The initiator and the responder submit proof of their identity to each other in this exchange. The IKE_AUTH exchange also establishes an IPsec SA from the initiator to the responder. The exchange consists of the following request and response:

Initiator	IKE_AUTH request	HDR; {ID$_I$, [CERT$_I$], [CERT request], AUTH$_I$, SA2$_I$, TS$_I$, TS$_R$}	(3)
Responder	IKE_AUTH response	HDR; {ID$_R$, [CERT$_R$], AUTH$_R$, SA2$_R$, TS$_I$, TS$_R$}	(4)

The payloads within {…} are encrypted and integrity protected using the IKE-SA. The payloads within […] are optional. This exchange contains the following payloads:

- ID$_I$ and ID$_R$, the identity payloads the initiator and the responder.
- [CERT$_I$], and [CERT$_R$], the RSA or DSS public-key certificates of the initiator and the responder. Authentication verification is done using the public key given therein. Certificates are optional.
- AUTH$_I$ and AUTH$_R$, the authentication payloads of the initiator and the sender. The authentication payloads are based on digital signature or MAC. The receiver verifies the authentication payload using sender's public key or the pre-shared secret. The authentication payloads are described later.
- SA2$_I$, the set of proposals from the initiator for the IPsec SA, called the child SA.
- SA2$_R$, the proposal accepted by the responder.
- TS$_I$ and TS$_R$, the traffic selector payloads. TS$_I$ contains the source IP address and port range. TS$_R$ contains the destination IP address and port range. The child SA being created is applicable to TSI and TS$_R$. This information can be used to fill the security policy database (SPD).

At the end of IKE_AUTH exchange, the initiator and responder would have established

1. An IKE-SA
2. A child SA (IPsec) from the initiator to the responder

Additional child SAs can be created now using CREATE_CHILD_SA exchange on the secure IKE-SA channel.

Authentication Payload

IKEv2 supports two options for authentication:

- Signature-based authentication
- Shared secret-based authentication

AUTH payloads for signature-based authentication are as given below:

AUTH$_I$ Signed{IKE_SA_INIT request, N$_R$, HMAC(SK$_{PI}$, ID$_I$)}
AUTH$_R$ Signed{IKE_SA_INIT response, N$_I$, HMAC(SK$_{PR}$, ID$_R$)}

Signature is performed using private keys of the senders. The receiver verifies the signature using the public key given in the received digital certificate. Note that each sender proves his credentials by submitting the following proofs:

- Nonce sent by the other party.
- A message sent by him earlier.
- HMAC of his identity payload. HMAC is computed using the keys SK_{PI}, and SK_{PR} by the initiator and the responder respectively.
- His signature, which can be verified using his public-key certificate.

Authentication using a shared secret (K) is based on HMAC computation as given below:

$AUTH_I$ HMAC{HMAC(K, "Key Pad for IKEv2"), {IKE_SA_INIT request, N_R, HMAC(SK_{PI}, ID_I)}

$AUTH_R$ HMAC{HMAC(K, "Key Pad for IKEv2"), {IKE_SA_INIT response, N_I, HMAC(SK_{PR}, ID_R)}

The shared secret key K between the initiator and responder is established by some other means (e.g. using password).

19.2.6 CREATE_CHILD_SA Exchange

CREATE_ CHILD_SA exchange is used to establish an additional IPsec SA between the two endpoints. There can be multiple CREATE_CHILD_SA exchanges. Either endpoint can be the initiator for creating a child SA.

Initiator   CREATE_CHILD_SA request   HDR; {SA_I, N_I, [KE_I], TS_I, TS_R}
Responder   CREATE_CHILD_SA response   HDR; {SA_R, N_R, [KE_R], TS_I, TS_R}

Here,

- SA_I is the set of proposals of the initiator. SA_R is the accepted proposal from the responder.
- N_I and N_R are nonces of the initiator and the responder respectively.
- KE_I and KE_R are DH half keys of the initiator and the responder respectively.
- TS_I and TS_R are the traffic selectors of the initiator and the responder respectively.

KE payload is optional. It is required, if stronger security is required for the child SA. Otherwise the key SK_D generated after IKE_SA_INIT exchange is used for generating the keys for this SA. Section 19.3 gives the details of key generation.

19.2.7 INFORMATIONAL Exchange

IKE uses INFORMATIONAL exchange for

- Notifications (N).
- Deleting one or more security association (D).
- Configuration information (CP).

Notifications usually carry error and status information. An endpoint may inquire about some configuration information (e.g. IKE software version) using INFORMATIONAL exchange. We will see in the next section how INFORMATIONAL exchange is used for deleting SAs.

As with other exchanges, this exchange also consists of a request and response messages. Each message may contain one or more payloads. INFORMATIONAL exchanges can occur only after the initial exchanges.

Initiator   INFORMATIONAL request   HDR; {[N,...], [D,...], {CP,...]}
Responder   INFORMATIONAL response HDR; {[N,...], [D,...], {CP,...]}

The consolidated payload {...} is cryptographically protected as in CREATE_CHILD_SA exchange. It is possible that for some notification, the responder may not have any payload to send. The protocol requires that response must be sent even if it is empty. An initiator may also send empty INFORMATIONAL request to determine, if the other endpoint is alive.

19.2.8 Deleting SAs Using INFORMATIONAL Exchange

IPsec SAs always exist in pairs, with one SA in each direction. When an IPsec SA is closed, both members of the pair must be closed. Closure is a two-step process (Figure 19.5).

1. The initiator sends INFORMATIONAL request message with Delete payload specifying the SPI of the inbound half (SA3) of the SA pair.
2. On receipt of the request, the responder closes its outbound half (SA3) of the SA pair. The responder sends INFORMATION response messages with Delete payload specifying the SPI of the other half (SA2) of the SA pair.

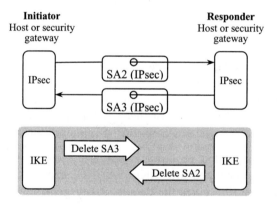

Figure 19.5 Deleting SAs.

The initiator may send multiple Delete payloads in an INFORMATIONAL request message to delete several SAs. The receiver closes the listed SPIs of the SA pairs to be deleted. The response in the INFORMATIONAL exchange will contain Delete payloads for the paired SAs going in the other direction.

For closing an IKE-SA, the initiator sends INFORMATIONAL request message with Delete payload. SPI is not specified in the payload. The main header (HDR) contains the SPI of the IKE-SA. The response to a request that deletes the IKE-SA is an empty INFORMATIONAL response. Deleting an IKE-SA implicitly closes all the child SAs negotiated under it.

19.2.9 Rekeying

IKE and IPsec security associations use the secret keys only for a limited amount of time and to protect a limited amount of data. This limits the lifetime of a security association. When the lifetime of a security association expires as per the lifetime policy[3], and there is requirement to continue the association, a new SA needs to be established. Re-establishment of a security association to replace the one that expires is referred to as 'rekeying'. General principles of rekeying are as follows:

- SAs need to be rekeyed proactively, i.e., the new SA should be established before the old one expires and becomes unusable.
- Rekeying is applicable to the IKE-SA and to child IPsec SAs.
- To rekey a child IPsec SA within existing IKE-SA, a new child IPsec SA is first established and then the old IPsec SA is deleted. The new child IPsec SA inherits the same traffic selectors and algorithms.
- To rekey an IKE-SA, a new IKE-SA is first established and then the old IKE-SA is deleted. The new IKE-SA inherits all the original child IPsec SAs of the old IKE-SA.

Rekeying is carried out using CREATE_CHILD_SA exchange in either case. For rekeying IKE-SA, the following exchange takes place.

| **Initiator** | CREATE_CHILD_SA request | HDR; {SA_I, N_I, KE_I} |
| **Responder** | CREATE_CHILD_SA response | HDR; {SA_R, N_R, KE_R} |

As before,

- SA_I is set of new proposals for the new SA, SA_R is the new accepted proposal.
- N_I and N_R are the new nonces.
- KE_I and KE_R are the DH half keys.

New SPI_I and SPI_R are sent in the SA_I and SA_R payloads.
For rekeying a child IPsec SA, the following exchange takes place:

| **Initiator** | CREATE_CHILD_SA request | HDR; {N (REKEY_SA), SA_I, N_I, [KE_I], TS_I, TS_R} |
| **Responder** | CREATE_CHILD_SA response | HDR;{SA_R, N_R, [KE_R], TS_I, TS_R} |

Notification N (REKEY_SA) is a new payload added in CREATE_CHILD_SA request to indicate that it is rekeying request. This payload contains the SPI of the SA being rekeyed.

19.3 GENERATING KEY MATERIAL

IPsec and IKE protocols require several sets of keys.

- Encryption and authentication keys for each IPsec SA.
- Encryption and authentication keys for IKE-SA.

---

3. The lifetime policy is determined and implemented by the endpoints.

Separate set of keys are required for the initiator and for the responder. These key sets are generated from the common DH secret and nonces (N_I, N_R) using a pseudo random function (PRF). IKEv2 specifies HMAC based on MD5 or SHA1 as the PRF. PRF is negotiated in IKE_SA_INIT exchange.

19.3.1   Keys for IKE-SA

The key material required for IKE-SA is derived from the initial exchange as given below (Figure 19.6).

- The initiator and responder compute common secret g^{ir} mod p from the half keys.

  Initiator computes g^{ir} mod $p = (g^r)^i$ mod p
  Responder computes g^{ir} mod $p = (g^i)^r$ mod p

- The common secret g^{ir} mod p and nonces (N_I, N_R) are used for computing the seed key SKEYSEED.

$$\text{SKEYSEED} = \text{HMAC}(N_I \parallel N_R, g^{ir} \text{ mod } p)$$

  where HMAC is based on MD5 or SHA1.
- SKEYSEED is used for computing the key material required for IKE-SA.

$$\text{Key material} = \text{HMAC}^+(K, S) = T1 \parallel T2 \parallel T3 \parallel \dots$$

where
   K = SKEYSEED,
   S = $N_I \parallel N_R \parallel SPI_I \parallel SPI_R$.

HMAC$^+$ is an iterated HMAC.

   T1 = HMAC(K, S $\parallel$ 0x01)
   T2 = HMAC(K, T1 $\parallel$ S $\parallel$ 0x02)
   T3 = HMAC(K, T2 $\parallel$ S $\parallel$ 0x03)

Iterations are carried out as many times as required to generate the required amount of key material.

- The key material is cut into pieces from left hand side as different keys (Figure 19.6). The following keys are generated from the key material:

  1. SK_D Derived key for key material of child SA.
  2. SK_{AI} Authentication key of initiator.
  3. SK_{AR} Authentication key of responder
  4. SK_{EI} Encryption key of initiator.
  5. SK_{ER} Encryption key of responder.
  6. SK_{PI} Preshared secret key of initiator.
  7. SK_{PR} Preshared secret key of the responder.

SK_D is later used for deriving key material for IPsec child SA. Authentication and encryption keys are used for securing the rest of IKE exchanges that follow IKE_SA_INIT exchange. Preshared secret keys are used for authentication in IKE_AUTH exchange, if this mode of authentication is selected. Note that there are different keys the initiator and for the responder.

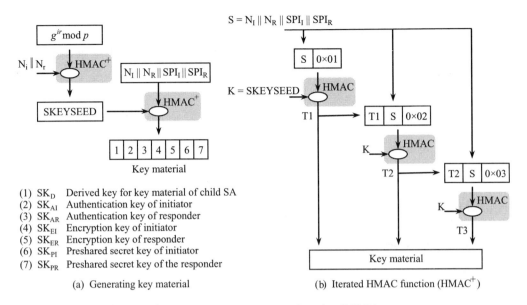

(1) SK_D Derived key for key material of child SA
(2) SK_{AI} Authentication key of initiator
(3) SK_{AR} Authentication key of responder
(4) SK_{EI} Encryption key of initiator
(5) SK_{ER} Encryption key of responder
(6) SK_{PI} Preshared secret key of initiator
(7) SK_{PR} Preshared secret key of the responder

(a) Generating key material

(b) Iterated HMAC function ($HMAC^+$)

Figure 19.6 Key generation for IKE-SA.

19.3.2 Keys for IPsec SA

Keys for IPsec SA are generated in three ways:

(a) IKE_Auth exchange creates one IPsec SA. The key material for this IPsec SA is generated from the derived key SK_D as follows [Figure 19.7(a)]:

$$\text{Key material} = HMAC^+(SK_D, N_I \| N_R)$$

where N_I and N_R are the nonces from the IKE_SA_INIT exchange.

(b) When additional IPsec SAs are created using CREATE_CHILD_SA exchanges, each IPsec SA requires a new set of keys for the initiator and the responder. These keys are generated from the derived key SK_D as above, but new nonces of the CREATE_CHILD_SA exchange replace the earlier nonces.

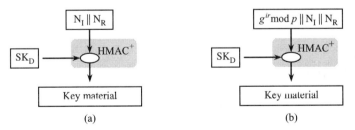

(a)   (b)

Figure 19.7 Key material for IPsec SA.

(c) For stronger security, new KE payload (DH half keys) is also included in CREATE_CHILD_SA exchange. The key material is computed as follows [Figure 19.7(b)].

$$\text{Key material} = \text{HMAC}^{+}(\text{SK}_{\text{D}},\ g^{ir} \bmod p \parallel \text{N}_{\text{I}} \parallel \text{N}_{\text{R}})$$

where $g^{ir} \bmod p$ is computed from the new DH half keys, N_{I} and N_{R} are the new nonces of CREATE_CHILD_SA exchange.

19.4 SECURITY TRANSFORMATIONS

Security transformations refer to various cryptographic algorithms specified in IKEv2 for encryption, authentication and key generation. These transformations are negotiated in the IKE_SA_INIT exchange, IKE_AUTH exchange and CREATE_ CHILD_SA exchange.

Encryption transformation: Encryption transformation is applicable to IKE and ESP protocols. The following encryption algorithms are supported:

    DES, 3DES, RC5, IDEA, CAST, BLOWFISH, 3IDEA, AES-CBC, AES-CTR.

Pseudo random function, PRF: This transformation refers to keyed hash function used for computing key material and for authentication. It is applicable to IKE protocol only. IKEv2 specifies HMAC algorithm with MD5, SHA1 or TIGER[4].

Integrity algorithm: Integrity transformation is applicable to IKE and AH protocols only. It is optional for ESP. IKEv2 specifies the following integrity algorithms.

    HMAC-MD5-96, HMAC-SHA1-96, DES-MAC, KPDK-MD5[4], AES-XCBC-96[4].

Diffie–Hellman group: This transformation defines the Diffie–Hellman group (the prime number and the generator of the group). The DH group is established in the initial exchange. Recall that the derived key SK_{D} computed after initial exchange is used for generating the key material for IPsec SAs. If stronger group is required for an IPsec SA, DH group can be changed in CREATE_CHILD_SA exchange.

    IKEv2 specifies 768, 1024, 1536, 2048, 3072, 4096, 6144, 8192 bits long prime numbers as modulus. The generator is always integer 2. For the specific values of the prime numbers, RFC 5996 may be referred to.

Extended sequence numbers (ESN):   Both AH and ESP protocols use sequence numbers for protection against replay. ESN defines the size of sequence number as 32 bits or 64 bits.

19.5 IKE MESSAGE FORMAT

An IKE message consists of the main IKE header followed by several payloads, each having its own header. The main header of the IKE message consists of the following fields (Figure 19.8).

---

4. TIGER is a hash function having 192-bit hash value.
   KPDK stands for key/pad/data/key. XCBC-96 MAC is a variant of CBC MAC. It is seen for messages of arbitrary length.

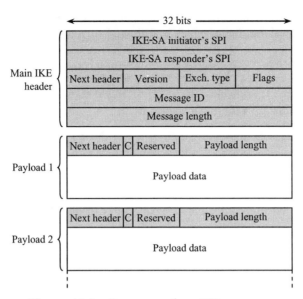

Figure 19.8 Structure of an IKE message.

IKE-SA initiator's SPI **(32 *bits*):** It is the SPI value for the IKE-SA chosen by the IKE-SA initiator.

IKE-SA responder's SPI **(32 *bits*):** It is the SPI value for the IKE-SA chosen by the IKE-SA responder.

Next header **(8 *bits*):** It indicates the type of payload that follows the header.

Version **(4 + 4 *bits*):** It has two parts: major version and minor version. Major version for IKEv2 is 2 and minor version is 0 currently.

Exchange type **(8 *bits*):** It indicates the type of exchange. The following types have been defined currently:

IKE_SA_INIT   34
IKE_AUTH   35
CREATE_CHILD_SA   36
INFORMATIONAL   37

Flags **(8 *bits*):** The flag field xxRVIxxx contains eight flags out of which 3 flags, R V and I, have been defined currently.

    R   It indicates that the message is a response. It is set to 1 in the response.
    V   It indicates that the sender of the message supports higher than the current major version.
    I   'I' flag is set to 1 in the messages sent by the original initiator of IKE-SA.

Message ID **(32 *bits*):** It is used to control retransmission of lost packets and matching of requests and responses. It is essential to the security of the protocol because it is used to prevent message replay attacks.

***Message length* (32 *bits*):** It indicates length of the message (header + payloads) in octets.

As mentioned above, the main header is followed by several payloads of different types depending on type of message. Each payload type has its own header. The first three fields of the payload headers have a generic structure as shown in Figure 19.8.

***Next header* (8 *bits*):** It indicates the type of payload following this payload. The last payload header has value 0 in the next header field.

***C bit* (1 *bit*):** C (critical) bit indicates significance of this payload. If the receiver understands the payload, this bit is ignored. If he does not understand the payload, the value of C bit determines the course of action for him.

- C = 0 implies that the payload is not critical. He is to ignore payload.
- C = 1 implies that the payload is critical. He is to discard the entire message.

***Reserved* (7 *bits*):** These bits are reserved for future use.

***Payload length* (16 *bits*):** It indicates length in octets of the current payload and the header.

The above generic header may have additional fields depending on type of payload. We have described the various payloads in IKE operation. We will not go into structure of individual payloads in this text. RFC 5996 gives the detailed account of all the IKE payloads.

The IKE messages (except the messages of IKE_SA_INIT exchange) consist of the main header followed by a consolidation of several payloads. The encrypted part of an IKE message is always attached as the last payload, if there are other unencrypted payloads. The payload type of encrypted payload is 46, which is indicated in the next-header field of previous header. The structure of encrypted payload is shown in Figure 19.9.

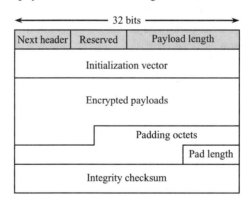

Figure 19.9 Structure of the encrypted payload of an IKE message.

The next header field contains the payload type of the first embedded payload in the encrypted portion. Payload length is the number of octets from header to the last octet of integrity checksum. Initialization vector is the one used in CBC mode for encryption. Integrity checksum is cryptographic checksum computed over the entire message starting from the IKE main header.

19.6   SUMMING UP

We started the subject of IP security in Chapter 18 and covered IPsec protocol. This chapter was a continuation of the same subject and covered the associated protocol IKE used for negotiating cryptographic keys and algorithms for IPsec.

- The Internet Key Exchange (IKE) protocol is used for establishing, maintaining and deleting security associations (SA) for IPsec protocol.
- The security association defines the cryptographic algorithms, secret keys, anti-replay window, lifetime of keys, etc. to be used between two end points.
- IKE creates a secure channel IKE-SA for itself. IKE-SA is bidirectional. IPsec SAs are negotiated on IKE-SA. IPsec SAs are unidirectional.
- IKE protocol consists of the following four types of exchanges, each consisting of a request and a response.
  - IKE_SA_INIT exchange.
  - IKE_AUTH exchange.
  - CREATE_CHILD_SA exchange.
  - INFORMATIONAL exchange.
- IKE_SA_INIT exchange and IKE_AUTH exchange create an IKE-SA and an IPsec SA. An endpoint can create as many SAs as required using CREATE_CHILD_SA exchange. INFORMATIONAL exchange is used for notifications and deleting SAs.
- IKE messages are carried over UDP.

IPsec with IKE provides privacy, authentication, replay protection and access control services for the IP network. Having studied security implementation at the Application, Transport and Network layers, we focus on security implementation at the Data Link layer for wireless local area networks in the next chapter.

Key Terms		
Child SA	IKE-SA	Pseudo random function (PRF)
CREATE_CHILD_SA exchange	IKE_SA_INIT exchange	Rekeying
Diffie–Hellman group	INFORMATIONAL exchange	Security association (SA)
IKE_AUTH exchange	Internet key exchange (IKE)	Traffic selector

RECOMMENDED READING

Doraswamy, H. and Harkins, D., *IPsec*, Prentice Hall, NJ, USA, 2003.

Forouzan, Behrouz A., *Cryptography and Network Security*, Tata McGraw-Hill, New Delhi, 2007.

Kaufman, C., Perlman, R. and Spenciner, M. *Network Security, Private Communication in a Public World*, Prentice-Hall of India, New Delhi, 2007.

Mason Andrew, *IPsec Overview Part Four: Internet Key Exchange (IKE)*, Cisco Press, IN, USA, 2002.

RFC 2408, *Internet Security Association and Key Management Protocol* (*ISAKMP*), IETF, 1998.

RFC 5996, *Internet Key Exchange* (*V2*), IETF, 2010.

Rhee, M., *Internet Security*, John Wiley & Sons, West Sussex, UK, 2003.

Snader, Jon C., *VPNs Illustrated: Tunnels, VPNs, and IPsec*, Pearson Education, New Delhi, 2006.

Stallings, W., *Cryptography and Network Security*, Prentice-Hall of India, New Delhi, 2008.

---(PROBLEMS)---

1. Explain how does the authenticator Signed{IKE_SA_INIT request, N_R, HMAC(SK$_{PI}$, ID$_I$)} proves the identity.

2. To check DoS attack during IKE_SA_INIT phase, the responder sends cookie to the initiator, who resends the IKE_SA_INIT request with the cookie (message 1a, Section 19.2.4). The responder completes the exchange if the received cookie is found valid. Some of the important observations in this context are given below:

    (a) The responder should not be required to remember the cookie it sent for validating the cookie the initiator returns.

    (b) If an adversary sees only the message containing cookie from the responder, he should not be able to construct the message 1a (Section 19.2.4) with his own set of SA$_I$ and send to the responder, thus negotiating a weaker set of algorithms.

    (c) Cookie validation should be dependent on the origin of initiators messages so that the initiators messages could be tied together.

    (d) There can be request for multiple IKE SAs from one initiator. It should be possible to treat these requests separately.

    (e) The adversary, knowing that the responder does not remember the cookie, should not be able to forge a cookie.

    RFC 5996 gives the following example for generating a cookie:

    $$\text{Id of secret} \parallel \text{Hash } [N_I \parallel IP_I \parallel SPI_I \parallel \text{secret}]$$

    Cookie consists of two parts. The first part is the secret identifier. The second part is hash of initiator's nonce (N_I), IP address (IP_I) of the origin of IKE_SA_INIT request, initiator's security parameter index SPI$_I$ and a secret.

    Explain if this construction of the cookie is consistent with the observations made above in the context of DOS attack.

20

Wireless LAN Security

Wireless LAN (WLAN) as the name suggests is a local area network that uses wireless transmission medium. WLAN has flexibility of mobility of the stations and their connectivity to the network. But this flexibility of WLAN comes with added security concerns, since the adversary no longer requires physical connectivity to the LAN cabling. He can easily capture and transmit the wireless signals. He can snoop, masquerade, replay and insert fraudulent messages. Therefore, WLANs need to be secured against the adversarial attacks. We address WLAN security in this chapter.

We begin the chapter with quick review of IEEE 802.11 WLAN configuration, associated terminology, the layered architecture and services. The original IEEE 802.11 specifications provided security called Wired Equivalent Privacy (WEP). WEP was flawed in many ways. We review WEP before proceeding to Robust Security Network (RSN) specified in IEEE 802.11i. We study, RSN security services, operation and key generation. We end the chapter with the two security protocols, TKIP and CCMP specified in IEEE 802.11i.

20.1 WIRELESS LAN CONFIGURATION

Configuration of a WLAN is defined in terms of basic service set, extended service set, access point and distribution system as shown in Figure 20.1.

Basic Service Set: A WLAN consists of wireless stations (STAs) that communicate with one another using wireless transmission medium. A set of such interconnected stations is called basic service set (BSS). A BSS not connected to any other network is called independent BSS (IBSS).

Extended Service Set: Several basic service sets can be interconnected through a distribution system. The extended network so formed is called extended service set (ESS). The ESS appears as a single logical LAN to the LLC sublayer, described in the next section.

Access Point: One of the wireless stations of a BSS has additional functionality and interface built into it for interconnection to the distribution system. This wireless station is called access point (AP). All the STAs in a BSS must 'associate' themselves with the AP to become an active node of the BSS. Association is equivalent to plugging-in a station in a wired network. The AP functions as a relay point between two STAs of the same BSS. If a station wants to communicate with another station in different BSS, then its communication is bridged by the AP over the distribution system towards the destination station.

Distribution System: Distribution system (DS) is a backbone network that interconnects the access points and forwards a received frame towards destination that can be in a BSS or on a network interconnected through a router. The distribution system comprises a bridging engine as part of an AP and a wired or wireless network as backbone network.

In Figure 20.1, the coverage areas of the two BSS are shown overlapping. Overlapping provides uninterrupted service as the mobile STA moves from one BSS to the other. But the STA must 'associate' itself with the new AP when it enters its coverage area.

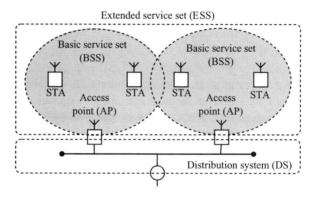

Figure 20.1   Configuration terminology of wireless LAN.

20.1.1   Layered Architecture of WLAN

The layered architecture of a node of WLANs is shown in Figure 20.2. It is similar to the architecture of anode of wired LANs. The data link layer consists of LLC (Logical Link Control) and MAC (Media Access Control) sublayers. The LLC sublayer of WLAN and wired LAN is same and is specified in IEEE 802.2. The MAC sublayer and the physical layer of the WLAN are specified in IEEE 802.11.

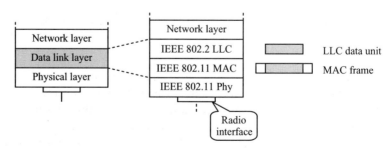

Figure 20.2   Layered architecture of IEEE 802.11 node.

Physical Layer of IEEE 802.11

The basic purpose of the physical layer is to transmit and receive MAC frames[1] over the wireless media. It carries out encoding of bits into wireless signals using digital modulation techniques. The physical layer specifications define the frequency bands, modulation schemes and antenna characteristics for transmission of the MAC frames.

Media Access Control (MAC) Sublayer of IEEE 802.11

All the STAs in a BSS share the capacity of wireless transmission media. The primary purpose of the MAC sublayer is to

- resolve the contention among STAs waiting for transmitting their frames. Contention is resolved by the AP using beacon and poll frames, and an exponential back-off mechanism. Details of this operation are beyond the scope of this text[2].
- encapsulate the data unit received from the LLC sublayer using a header and trailer (Figure 20.2). The MAC frame so formed is reliably[3] delivered to the destination.
- carry out error detection and discard frames received with errors. Recovery from errors is carried out by the LLC sublayer.

In addition to the above primary functions, the MAC sublayer carries out other management and security related functions described in the next section on IEEE 802.11 services.

Logical Link Control (LLC) Sublayer

The LLC protocol is modelled on the HDLC protocol in asynchronous balanced mode (ABM). As mentioned above, LLC protocol carries out the recovery part of error correction. LLC protocol detects the missing frames using sequence numbers and requests their retransmission. In addition, LLC protocol is designed to interface with various next higher layer protocol. The LLC data unit can deliver packets of various protocols[4], e.g. ARP, IP, IPX, etc.

Figure 20.3 shows the architecture of WLAN having an ethernet LAN as the backbone network. The architecture highlights the bridge functionality of the AP at the LLC sublayer. The AP receives IEEE 802.11 MAC frame from the STA, recovers LLC data unit and reconstructs IEEE 802.3 MAC frame for the ethernet.

20.1.2 IEEE 802.11 Services

IEEE 802.11 provides the following nine services. Six of these are used for data delivery and its management, the remaining three are used for WLAN access and security.

---

1. MAC frame is called MPDU—MAC Protocol Data Unit in OSI (Open System Interconnection) terminology.
2. For details refer [Gupta, Prakash C., *Data Communications and Computer Networks*, PHI Learning, Delhi, 2014].
3. An STA sends RTS (Request to send) frame to alert all other STAs that it is going to transmit MAC data frame. The AP responds with CTS (Clear to send) frame. This RTS/CTS exchange allocates the wireless media for a specified duration.
4. *See* Problem 5 at the end of the Chapter.

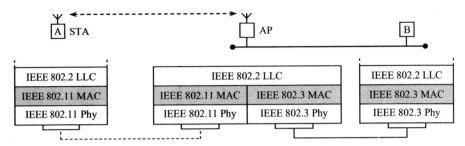

Figure 20.3 Layered architecture of IEEE 802.11 WLAN with ethernet backbone network.

Data delivery and its management
1. Association
2. Disassociation
3. Reassociation
4. Integration
5. Distribution
6. MSDU delivery

LAN access and security
7. Authentication
8. De-authentication
9. Privacy and integrity

Distribution: When a MAC frame is received by an AP, it uses the distribution service to deliver the frame to its destination. The destination may be in the same BSS, different BSS or on the integrated wired LAN.

Integration: Integration service enables transfer of data between an STA on an IEEE 802.11 WLAN and a station on an integrated IEEE 802.x LAN, e.g. between stations A and B in Figure 20.3. The integration service takes care of any address translation and media conversion logic required for the exchange of data.

Association: Before an STA can transmit or receive frames on a WLAN, its identity and address must be known to the distribution system. For this purpose, the STA must establish an association relationship with the AP of the BSS. The AP can then communicate this information to the distribution system. When the distribution system receives a frame for the station, it forwards the frame to the respective AP for delivery to the destination.

Reassociation: When a mobile STA station moves from one BSS to another within the same ESS, reassociation service transfers an established association from the previous AP to the new AP. Reassociation is initiated by the mobile STA. The distribution system updates its records to reflect the accessibility of the mobile station through the new AP.

Disassociation: Disassociation service is used to terminate an existing association. It results in removal of the association data from the distribution system. An STA or the AP can send disassociation notification. The MAC protocol is designed to accommodate stations that leave the network without any notification.

***MSDU delivery*:** MSDU, short for MAC Service Data Unit, is the LLC protocol data unit (LLC PDU) handed over to the MAC sublayer for delivery to the destination. The MAC layer attaches its header and trailer to MSDU to construct MAC frame which is then transmitted to the AP (Figure 20.4). The process is reversed at the destination. MAC header and trailer are stripped and MSDU is delivered to the LLC sublayer. This basic service is referred to as MSDU delivery service.

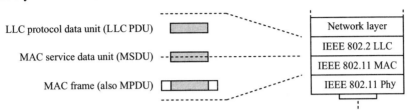

Figure 20.4   LPDU, MSDU and MPDU terminology.

***Authentication*:**   In a wired LAN, a station must be physically connected to the LAN through a data jack (e.g. RJ-45 connector). WLAN does not offer similar level of physical security. Any wireless station within the coverage area of an AP can transmit and receive radio signals. Therefore, additional authentication routines are provided to protect access to the wireless LAN. Authentication is a necessary prerequisite to association, since only the authenticated users are allowed association.

***De-authentication*:**   De-authentication terminates the authenticated relationship. As a side effect, the current association is also terminated. De-authentication notification can be sent by an STA or by the AP.

***Privacy and integrity*:**   Physical security of wired LAN offers some degree of privacy. For example, wiring closets can be locked. WLAN does not offer any physical security. An eavesdropper can catch the radio signals of a WLAN and monitor the messages being exchanged. Privacy and message integrity service of IEEE 802.11 encrypts messages for privacy and generates checksum for integrity verification. This service restricted to the message exchange between an AP and an STA, i.e., to the only wireless segment of the end-to-end link.

20.2   IEEE 802.11 WLAN SECURITY

The original IEEE 802.11b specification defined Wired Equivalent Privacy (WEP) to provide security equivalent to traditional wired networks. WEP had some major security flaws. These flaws were later addressed in IEEE 802.11i. Before going into IEEE 802.11i, we will first examine WEP in brief.

20.2.1   Wired Equivalent Privacy (WEP)

WEP was designed for providing encryption, integrity check and entity authentication services for wireless links of a local area network. These services were provided using a stream cipher for encryption, CRC for integrity check and challenge-response mechanism for authentication.

*Encryption***:** Encryption is based on synchronous stream cipher RC4 [Figure 20.5(a)]. The key stream is generated using concatenation of 40-bit shared secret and 24-bit initialization vector (IV) as the 64-bit seed key.

*Integrity check***:** Integrity check is based on CRC-32[5]. The integrity check value (ICV) is concatenated to the plaintext before encryption [Figure 20.5(a)].

*Authentication***:** Entity authentication is based on challenge-response mechanism. The AP sends a challenge of 128 octets in clear text to the STA. The STA encrypts the challenge using the configured shared secret, which is later used for encryption of data frames as mentioned above.

Figure 20.5(b) shows the structure of the WEP MAC frame. It consists of IEEE802.11 MAC header, followed by a field containing the IV and the shared secret key id. Thereafter we have encrypted LLC PDU and ICV followed by the MAC trailer. Note that IV is sent in clear text as one of the fields of the MAC frame. Different IV is used on each frame.

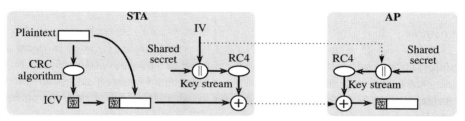

(a) Privacy and integrity check scheme of WEP.

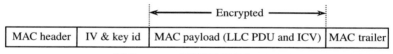

(b) Structure of WEP MAC frame

Figure 20.5 Wired Equivalent Privacy (WEP).

WEP has following major structural weakness:

- WEP is based on symmetric-key stream cipher, but IEEE 802.11 does not specify any mechanism for distribution of shared secret. The shared secret is manually distributed and configured. Administrative burden associated with manual key distribution precludes its frequent revision. Static shared secret makes WEP vulnerable to attacks as explained below:
    - WEP uses RC4 stream cipher for confidentiality. Stream ciphers are vulnerable to cryptanalysis when the key stream is reused[6], which is very likely in WEP.
    - 24-bit IV has 16,777,216 different values, which are soon exhausted when each frame uses a different IV. The reused IV concatenated with the static shared secret

---

5. CRC-32 is 32-bit Cyclic Redundancy Check value computed over the plaintext. CRC is not a one-way or collision free cryptographic hash function. It is used as error detection function in several protocols, e.g. HDLC. But WEP uses it for integrity check.
6. *See* Section 7.2.1 (Chapter 7).

repeats the key stream used earlier. The IV value transmitted in clear text in the frame tips off the adversary when the IV, and therefore, the key stream is reused.

- The encrypted payload of the MAC frame consists of LLC PDU and ICV. Since the first byte of LLC PDU is always 0xAA[7], the adversary can compute the first byte of the key stream by XORing 0xAA with the first byte of encrypted payload. The adversary, thus, knows first 24 bits of IV, and the first byte of key stream. Determining the 40-bit shared secret from this information is easy for the adversary even if he uses brute force.
- The challenge-response authentication mechanism uses the shared secret for encrypting challenge. The adversary can easily capture the challenge and response frames to get plaintext–ciphertext pair. The 40-bit shared secret of WEP can be easily determined from the plaintext–ciphertext pair using brute force attack.
- WEP uses a CRC for integrity check. Although the integrity check value (ICV) is encrypted using RC4, CRC is very weak as a cryptographic hash function. The adversary can make controlled changes in ICV and encrypted data without introducing integrity inconsistency (*see* Section 7.2.1).
- WEP provides unilateral authentication of the STA by the AP. The adversary can use this one-way authentication process to their advantage by masquerading as the AP.

20.2.2   Robust Security Network (RSN) of IEEE 802.11i

IEEE 802.11i task group developed set of capabilities to address the WLAN security issues. The final form of the IEEE 802.11i standard is referred to as Robust Security Network (RSN). In order to accelerate the introduction of strong security into WLANs, Wi-Fi Alliance, a non-profit industry association for inter-operability of WLAN products, has initiated WPA2[8] program for certification of IEEE 802.11i compliant WLAN products.

IEEE 802.11i RSN Security Services

The following security services have been defined in IEEE 802.11i for RSN.

Authentication: Authentication service is used for mutual authentication between an STA and an AP. Extensible Authentication Protocol (EAP) is used for authentication.

Privacy: Privacy service provides encryption of MSDU using the agreed encryption algorithm.

Message integrity: Message integrity service enables verification of integrity and data origin of the MSDU using message integrity code (MIC[9]) and the associated key.

Access control: This service enforces the use of authentication service by keeping the access port closed for the MAC frames containing user data. The port is opened for the user data

---

7. *See* Problem 5 at the end of the Chapter.
8. WPA stands for Wi-Fi Protected Access.
9. While 'MAC' is commonly used in cryptography to refer to a Message Authentication Code, IEEE 802.11i uses MIC instead because MAC has another standard meaning, Media Access Control.

only after successful authentication and implementation of cipher suites and security keys in the STA and the AP.

Negotiable Security Mechanisms

To provide the security services listed above, the STA and the AP negotiate the security mechanisms that will be deployed. IEEE 802.11i offers the following cipher suites for privacy and integrity services. Each cipher suite defines encryption algorithm, integrity verification algorithm and the size of key to be used.

- WEP with 40-bit or 104-bit key.
  Since there can be STAs which continue to use WEP for security in the network, WEP is offered for backward compatibility.
- Temporal Key Integrity Protocol (TKIP).
- CTR with CBC-MAC Protocol (CCMP).
- Vendor-specific cipher suites.

TKIP is a software upgrade for the STAs that were on earlier using WEP. CCMP is a new security cipher suite. There can be cipher suites defined by vendors. We discuss TKIP and CCMP in Section 20.3.4.

Apart from cipher suite, the AP and the STA also agree on Authentication and Key Management (AKM) suite. AKM defines the mechanisms to be used for

- mutual authentication, and
- deriving a root key from which other keys may be generated.

These negotiations are carried out in the first phase of RSN operation described next.

20.3   IEEE 802.11I RSN OPERATION

The operation of an IEEE 802.11i RSN has the following five phases (Figure 20.6):

Phase 1: The first phase is the discovery phase in which, an STA discovers the network, the AP, learns the security capabilities offered by the AP and associates with the AP.

Phase 2: The second phase is authentication phase. The STA and the authentication server (AS) located on the distribution system carry out mutual authentication. The AP does not participate in the authentication process. It merely forwards authentication traffic between the STA and the AS.

Phase 3: The third phase is key generation and confirmation phase. The STA and the AP generate the security keys and implement the keys.

Phase 4: The fourth phase consists of transfer of cryptographically secured MAC data frames. The protection is provided only on the radio segment between the STA and the AP.

Phase 5: The fifth phase is termination phase, in which the STA and the AP terminate the association and teardown the security relationship established in phase 3.

Let us examine each phase in more detail.

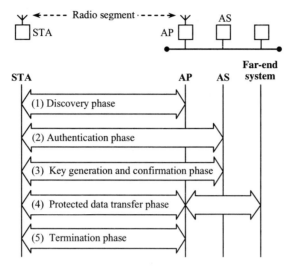

Figure 20.6 Operational phases of IEEE 802.11i.

20.3.1 Discovery Phase

In this phase, an STA and an AP discover each other, agree on a set of security capabilities, and establish an association for communication. It consists of three sets of exchanges (Figure 20.7).

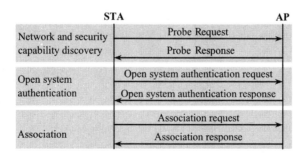

Figure 20.7 Discovery phase.

Network and Security Capability Discovery

During this exchange, the STA discovers the existence of a network and the AP with which to communicate. The AP either periodically broadcasts its security capabilities through the Beacon frame; or it responds to the STA's Probe Request through a Probe Response frame. The STA discovers the AP and its security capabilities by either passively monitoring the Beacon frames or actively probing every channel.

Open System Authentication

The purpose of this exchange is simply to maintain backward compatibility with the old version of IEEE 802.11. The STA and AP simply exchange their identifiers[10].

Association

The purpose of this exchange is to agree on a set of security capabilities to be used. The STA sends an Association Request frame to the AP. In this frame, the STA specifies one set of matching capabilities (one authentication and key management suite, one pairwise key cipher suite, and one group key cipher suite) from among those advertised by the AP. The pairwise key cipher suite is for security of communication between the STA and the AP. The group key cipher suite is for multicast.

20.3.2 Authentication Phase

As mentioned before, the STA and the authentication server (AS) located on the distribution system carry out mutual authentication in this phase. The AP does not participate in the authentication process. It merely forwards authentication traffic between the STA and the AS.

Authentication is based on Extensible Authentication Protocol (EAP). EAP[11] is a general protocol for authentication that supports multiple challenge-response authentication mechanisms. In IEEE 802.11i uses EAP in the following manner:

- Between the STA and the AP, EAP messages are encapsulated as MAC frames. EAP over LAN is referred to as EAPOL protocol.
- The authentication server (AS) and AP use RADIUS (Remote Authentication Dial-In User Service) protocol for carrying authentication information. RADIUS is a client/ server protocol that runs at the Application layer, using UDP as transport. The RADIUS server is implemented in the authentication server and RADIUS client is implemented in the AP.

Thus we have EAPOL between the STA and the AP; and RADIUS between the AP and the authentication server for carrying EAP messages (Figure 20.8). The task of translating the message attributes between EAPOL and RADIUS is carried out by the AP.

Mutual authentication between the AS and the STA proceeds as given below (Figure 20.8).

- The EAP exchange begins with the AP issuing EAP-Request/Identity message to the STA.
- The STA replies with EAP-Response/Identity message, indicating its identity. The AP constructs RADIUS-Access-Request encapsulating the EAP message and sends it to the RADIUS server.
- RADIUS server replies with RADIUS: Access-Challenge message, which is passed on to the STA as EAP-Request/Challenge.

---

10. The identifiers are transmitter address (TA), Receiver address (RA), BSS-Id. See [Gupta, Prakash C., *Data Communications and Computer Networks*, PHI Learning, Delhi, 2014].
11. EAP over PPP (Point-to-point protocol) is described in Appendix A3.

- The STA formulates EAP-Response/f(Challenge) containing the transformation f(Challenge)[12] of the challenge. f(Challenge) corroborates the identity of the STA. The response is translated by the AP into Radius-Access-Request and sent to the RADIUS server. This and the previous steps may repeat several times depending on the EAP method in use.
- The RADIUS server verifies the authentication of the STA and grants access with RADIUS-Access-Accept message. The AP issues an EAP-Success message, which is passed on to the STA by the AP.

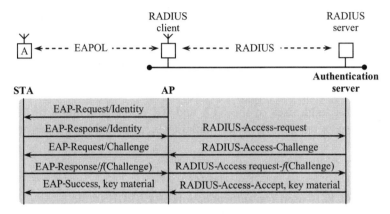

Figure 20.8 EAP operation.

Once authentication is established, the AS generates a master session key (MSK), and sends it to the STA and the AP. 802.11i does not prescribe a method for secure delivery of the MSK but relies on EAP for this. With this exchange, the authentication phase is over, but use of EAP continues to the next phase, the key generation and confirmation phase.

20.3.3 Key Generation and Confirmation Phase

During the key generation phase, several cryptographic keys are generated. These keys are used for protecting the MAC frames containing user data, and for protecting the control frames used setting up the RSN. There are the following two categories of keys:

- Pairwise keys
- Group keys

Pairwise keys are used for communication between an STA and an AP. Group keys are used for multicast communication. We will focus on pairwise keys only in this text.

Key Generation

Figure 20.9 shows the overall structure of the key generation process.

---

12. EAP offers several ways of generating f(Challenge). *See* Appendix A3 for details.

- A pairwise master key (PMK) is established between an STA and the AP. It can be done in two ways:
  - Pre-shared key (PSK)
  - Master session key (MSK)

  Pre-shared key (PSK) is installed in some manner outside the scope of IEEE 802.11i. Alternatively, a master session key (MSK) is generated by the authentication server and passed to the AP and the STA. This is done during authentication phase. By the end of the authentication phase, marked by the EAP-Success message (Figure 20.8), both the AP and the STA have a copy of shared PMK.

- Pairwise master key (PMK) is used by the AP and the STA for generating key material called Pairwise transient key (PTK). A pseudo random function (PRF) based on HMAC-SHA-1 function is applied to the PMK, the MAC addresses of the STA and AP, and the nonces of AP and STA. The nonces are exchanged during key confirmation exchange between the STA and AP, described in the next section.

  Using MAC addresses of the STA and AP in the generation of the PTK provides protection against session hijacking[13] and impersonation; using nonces provides freshness to the keys.

- PTK consists of three keys:
  - EAPOL key-confirmation-key (KCK)

    EAPOL-KCK is used for authentication of EAPOL frame
  - EAPOL key-encryption-key (KEK)

    EAPOL-KEK is used for encryption of the data field of an EAPOL frame.
  - Temporal key (TK)

    The temporal key is used for protecting the MAC data frames that contain user data.

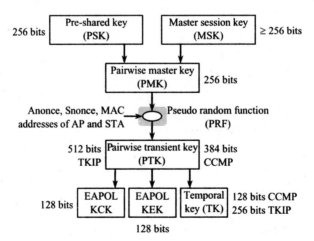

Figure 20.9 Key generation in IEEE 802.11i.

---

13. We study session hijacking attack in Chapter 21.

Key Confirmation Exchange

The STA and the AP use 4-way handshake to confirm the existence of the PMK, and derivation of a fresh PTK for the data session that follows (Figure 20.10). EAP is used for exchanging these messages.

1. The AP sends its nonce (Anonce) to the STA.
2. The STA generates its own nonce (Snonce) and computes a pairwise transient key (PTK) using the PRF on Anonce, Snonce, MAC address of AP, its own MAC address and the PMK.

   It sends a message containing its Snonce, which enables the AP to generate the same PTK. This message is protected using a message integrity code (MIC) generated using HMAC-MD5 or HMAC-SHA-1-128. The key used with the MIC is EAPOL KCK.

   This message demonstrates to the AP that the STA is alive, there is no man-in-the-middle, PTK is fresh. The AP also verifies using the MIC that it has the same EAPOL KCK as the one with the STA.
3. The AP generates the PTK and sends a message to the STA for implementing PTK. The message is protected using the MIC in the same manner before.

   As with message 2, this message demonstrates to the STA that the AP is alive, there is no man-in-the-middle, and PTK is fresh.
4. The STA sends a confirmation message to the AP. This is merely an acknowledgment message, again protected by MIC.

On receipt of message 4, the AP unblocks the controlled port for exchange of user data frames.

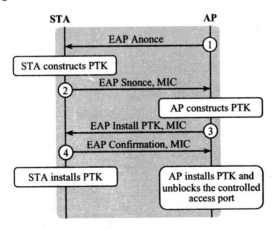

Figure 20.10   Key confirmation exchange.

20.3.4   Protected Data Transfer Phase

As mentioned in Section 20.2.2, IEEE 802.11i defines the following new schemes for protecting integrity, and confidentiality during protected data transfer phase:

- Temporal Key Integrity Protocol
- CTR with CBC-MAC Protocol

Temporal Key Integrity Protocol (TKIP)

TKIP is a software upgrade for WEP implementation. TKIP provides confidentiality, message authentication and replay protection services. The basic scheme of TKIP is shown in Figure 20.11(a). TKIP modifies WEP as follows:

- A transmitter (STA or AP) calculates a keyed cryptographic message integrity code (MIC) over the MAC source and destination addresses, and MSDU. TKIP appends the computed MIC to the MSDU. If required, fragmentation of (MSDU∥MIC) carried out at MAC sublayer.[14]

    TKIP's MIC provides a defense against forgery, redirection, bit flipping, and masquerading attacks because SA and DA cannot be manipulated. The receiver can verify the integrity and data-origin of the defragmented message using MIC.
- TKIP uses a TKIP sequence counter (TSC) to sequence the MAC frames. The TSC is sent in the frame [Figure 20.11(b)]. The receiver accepts the MAC frames received in increasing sequential order. TSC, thus, provides protection against replay.
- TKIP uses a cryptographic mixing function to combine a temporal key (TK), the transmitter address TA, and the TSC into the WEP seed (IV and key). The receiver generates the same WEP seed in the similar manner. TSC is made available to the receiver for this purpose in the MAC frame [Figure 20.11(b)].

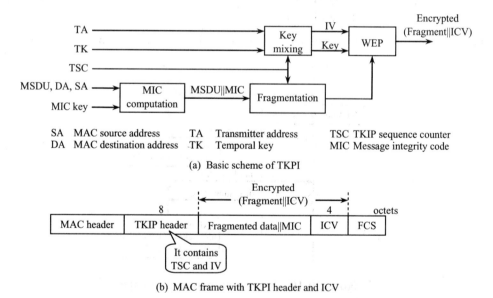

(a) Basic scheme of TKPI

(b) MAC frame with TKPI header and ICV

Figure 20.11 Temporal key integrity protocol (TKIP).

---

14. The MAC header has sequence control field that contains sequence number of the fragment and the sequence number of the unfragmented frame. It also contains flag to indicate if there are more fragments of a frame. *See* [Gupta, Prakash C., Data Communications and Computer Networks, PHI Learning, Delhi, 2014].

The key mixing function is designed to defeat weak-key attacks against the WEP key. Using TSC as one of the inputs to the mixing function makes TKPI secure against sequence number manipulation. Secondly, it produces a dynamic WEP seed that changes with each transmitted frame, thus making cryptanalysis more difficult.

- Each fragment of (MSDU ‖ MIC) is processed using WEP with the seed to generate WEP ICV and to encrypt the fragment and ICV [Figure 20.11(b)]. RC4 is used for encryption.

CTR with CBC-MAC Protocol (CCMP)

While TKIP is used as upgrade for WEP installations, CCMP is intended for new devices having hardware that can support it. CCMP is mandatory for RSN compliance. It is based on RFC 3610 and uses 128-bit AES block cipher for encryption and integrity.

The structure of MAC frame with CCMP is shown in Figure 20.12. CCMP header and the MIC field are the two additions to the MAC frame. CCMP provides the following services:

- Data confidentiality
  Confidentiality service of CCMP is based on 128-bit AES block cipher in counter mode of operation.
- Message authentication
  CCMP provides message integrity and data origin authentication. It uses CBC mode with 128-bit AES for computation of message integrity code (MIC). The same 128-bit AES key is used for both MIC computation and encryption.

  MIC protects integrity of data payload and some of the fields of the MAC header and CCMP header. Note that MIC field is also encrypted along with the data payload.
- Replay protection
  Replay protection is provided by including a nonce in computation of MIC and in encryption using counter mode. Nonce is based on incremental 48-bit packet number and never repeats in a session. The incremental packet number is included in the CCMP header.

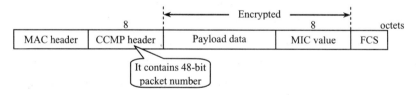

Figure 20.12 MAC frame with CCMP header and MIC.

20.4 SUMMING UP

This chapter covered security of wireless LAN (WLAN). The main points of learning are summarized below:

- IEEE 802.11i is the current version of IEEE 802.11 standard for the architecture and configuration of WLAN. Original IEEE 802.11 specified WEP, Wired Equivalent Privacy, for security. WEP had many flaws and could not provide the required security. IEEE

802.11i specifies Robust Security Network (RSN), which is backward compatible to WEP and is designed to provide the required security on WLAN.

- RSN provides authentication, privacy, message integrity and access control services. It also protects against replay and masquerading attacks.
- RSN specifies two new protocols for security, TKIP and CCMP.
  - TKIP is software upgrade for WEP hardware devices. It provides privacy, authentication, message integrity and replay protection services. It uses RC4 algorithm for encryption.
  - CCMP uses 128-bit AES in counter mode for encryption. 128-bit AES in CBC mode is used for generating MIC for message integrity and data-origin authentication. It uses nonces for protection against replay.

With this chapter, we conclude the discussion on the network security protocols. The next chapter examines the threats to security that emanates from the network. The adversary directs his attacks on availability of the network and the resources available on the network to the legitimate users.

Key Terms		
Access point (AP)	Distribution system (DS)	MAC Sublayer
Association	EAP over LAN (EAPOL)	RADIUS
Basic service set (BSS)	Extended service set (ESS)	Robust security network (RSN)
Beacon frame	Independent BSS (IBSS)	Wired equivalent privacy (WEP)
CCMP	LLC sublayer	TKIP

RECOMMENDED READING

Gupta, Prakash C., *Data Communications and Computer Networks*, PHI Learning, Delhi, 2014.

IEEE 802.11, *Part 11: Wireless LAN Medium Access Control (MAC) and Physical Layer (PHY) Specifications,* IEEE, New York, USA, 2012.

RFC 3610, *Counter with CBC-MAC (CCM)*, IETF, 2003.

RFC 5247, *Extensible Authentication Protocol (EAP) Key Management Framework,* IETF, 2008.

Stallings, W., *Cryptography and Network Security*, Prentice-Hall of India, New Delhi, 2008.

PROBLEMS

1. WEP uses CRC-32 for computation of ICV for message integrity. CRC is computed as the residue of modulo operation using an algebraic polynomial. For the purpose of illustration, compute ICV of (110101010) using (10101) as the modulus.
2. CRC used in WEP for ICV computation is a weak cryptographic hash function. To illustrate the point, recompute ICV by appending four zeros at the end to (110101010) of Problem 1. What do you conclude?

3. A potential weakness of the CRC as an integrity check is that it is a linear function, i.e. CRC(A ⊕ B) = CRC(A) ⊕ CRC(b). Even though WEP encrypts, ICV, an adversary can easily forge an encrypted message with valid ICV as given below. Let c be the encrypted WEP message (m) with encrypted ICV given as follows:

$$c = RC4[m \| CRC(m)]$$

The adversary constructs a WEP message c' as given below.

$$c' = c \oplus [x \| CRC(x)]$$

Show that c' is a valid encrypted WEP message with valid encrypted ICV. What is the modified message?

4. If an attacker captures an encrypted WEP frame, and he later re-transmits this frame, will the frame still be accepted by the AP, assuming the original sending station is still active?

5. The LLC PDU [Figure 20.5(b)] consists of the fields shown in Figure 20.13. DSAP and SSAP are destination and source service access point to the next higher layer, which is SNAP (Subnetwork Access Protocol). The DSAP and SSAP of SNAP are 0xAA. SNAP enables encapsulation of different networking and other protocols, e.g. ARP, IP, IPX, etc. as the payload. The control field is 0x03.

SNAP header consist of two fields. The first field is Organizationally Unique Identifier (OUI) of 3 octets, each being 0x00. It is followed by Type field which 0x0300 for IP payload and 0x0806 for ARP payload.

Considering that WEP encrypts LLC PDU followed by ICV using RC4 stream cipher as shown in Figure 20.5(a), determine the first 8 octets of the stream keys, if the first 8 octets of encrypted LLC PDU are 01 23 45 67 89 AB CD EF (Hexadecimal). The LLC PDU is carrying an IP packet.

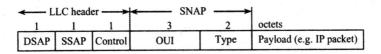

Figure 20.13 Problem 5.

6. The payload of Figure 20.13 consists of IPv4 packet. The adversary knows that the IP header does not contain any option field and QOS (quality of service) is not implemented in the network. List the IP header fields which have fixed values and thus adversary can determine the corresponding stream key octets.

21

Network Vulnerabilities

Today, there is ever growing dependency on the public Internet for business transactions and personal communications. Being a public network, Internet is exposed to many forms of threats which may result in loss of privacy, denial of access to the network services, or unauthorized access to the private resources. We examine various adversarial attacks based on IP/TCP/UDP/ARP/ICMP protocols in this chapter. Before going into details of the attack, we present a brief overview of each protocol.

21.1 THREATS TO A USER NETWORK

Cryptography addresses security issues relating to confidentiality, message integrity, source authentication, user identification and non repudiation. Encryption, message authentication, entity authentication and digital signatures are the basic cryptography mechanisms to deal with these security issues. These mechanisms are required because the adversary is able to access the communication between Alice and Bob. Recall Figure 1.2 of Chapter 1 which depicted the various threats posed by the adversary. The figure is reproduced as Figure 21.1.

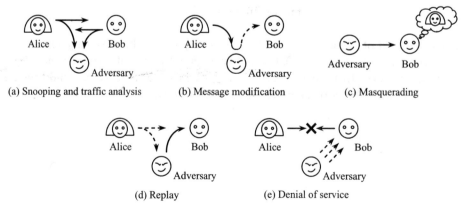

(a) Snooping and traffic analysis   (b) Message modification   (c) Masquerading

(d) Replay   (e) Denial of service

Figure 21.1 Attacks on network security.

- For snooping, traffic analysis, message modification, replay attacks, the adversary should have access to the traffic between Alice and Bob. Remember that Alice, Bob and the adversary may be located on a private network, the public Internet, or both (Figure 21.2). It implies that the adversary must divert the messages between Alice and Bob through him.

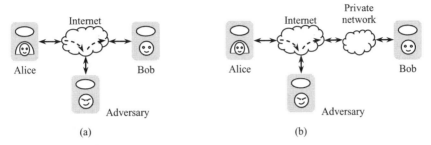

Figure 21.2   Locations of victims and the adversary on the network.

- To gain access to Bob, the adversary impersonating as Alice,
    - logs in through Alice's machine using her password,
    - logs in through his machine using spoofed source IP address of Alice and her password, or
    - hijacks the TCP connection after Alice establishes it.
  In the last case, the adversary needs to divert the traffic between Alice and Bob through him so that he can interject at the right moment. Interjection implies he must synchronize his TCP sequence and acknowledgement numbers with those of Alice. Further he must block the messages from Alice.
- To launch denial of service attacks, the adversary directs his attack on
    - the operating system of the victim, rendering it unworkable or
    - the access network of the victim, blocking it with a flood of traffic.

21.1.1   Network-oriented Reconnaissance

The first stage of the adversarial attacks is reconnaissance stage, when the adversary conducts a survey of the targeted network to gather information about its vulnerabilities, services available, IP addresses, port numbers, version of the operating systems, etc. This reconnaissance operation is carried out in the following sequence:

- First the attacker typically conducts a 'PING Sweep' to determine the active IP addresses of the target network.
- Next he carries out 'Port Scan' on each active IP address to determine which ports or services are active on the active IP addresses. Recall that there are specified server ports for FTP, Email, DNS, Telnet and other services.
- From this information, he carries out 'OS Fingerprinting' to determine the type and version of the application and operating system.

After the reconnaissance stage, the adversary launches his attack. The network attacks are based on networking protocols, typically IP, TCP, UDP, ICMP, and ARP protocols. In the following section we describe these attacks.

Before going into formation of an attack, we will have a quick review of the networking protocol it uses. We will focus only on those aspects of protocol operation that are relevant to the present context, i.e., network security. Secondly, the description of attacks is for purpose of illustration and does not cover the nitty-gritty.

21.2   THREATS AT THE IP LAYER

Internet Protocol (IP) is a connectionless layer-3 protocol based on datagram switching. Each IP packet carries source and destination addresses. The network nodes forward the IP packets towards the destination using a routing table. The routes in the routing table are created and updated manually or dynamically using a routing protocol (e.g. RIP, OSPF).

Connectionless service provided by IP is unreliable in the sense that there is no acknowledgement of delivery of IP packets. IP packets may not be delivered or may be delivered out of sequence to the specified destination.

21.2.1   Format of IP Packet

Format of an IP version 4 packet is shown in Figure 21.3. It consists of the following fields:

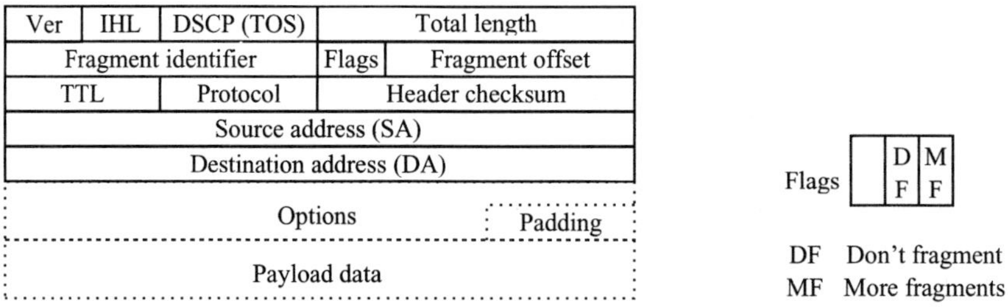

Ver	IHL	DSCP (TOS)	Total length		
Fragment identifier			Flags	Fragment offset	
TTL		Protocol	Header checksum		
Source address (SA)					
Destination address (DA)					
Options			Padding		
Payload data					

(a) Format of IP packet

Flags

	D F	M F

DF   Don't fragment
MF   More fragments

(b) IP flags

Figure 21.3   Format of an IP packet.

Fragment identifier: It identifies fragments of an IP packet.

Flags: There are two fragmentation flags:
    DF   When set, DF flag indicates that the payload cannot be fragmented.
    MF   When set, MF flag indicates that there are more fragments.

Fragment offset: It indicates position of the data fragment relative to the beginning of the unfragmented data. Offset is measured in multiple of 8 octets.

Protocol: It identifies the protocol carried as the payload data, e.g. ICMP (1), TCP (6), UDP (17).

***Source and destination addresses*:** These fields contain the source and destination IP addresses, each of 32 bits.[1]

Other fields:

Version	It indicates version of the Internet Protocol.
IHL	It indicates length of IP header in multiples of 4 octets.
DSCP (TOS)	Differentiated service code point (DSCP) specifies the service quality to be accorded to the IP packet. Old nomenclature of this field is 'Type of Service' (ToS).
Total length	It is the total length of IP packet including the payload in octets.
TTL	Time to live (TTL) is the specified life of an IP packet in seconds.
Header checksum	It is used for detection of transmission errors in the IP header.
Options and padding	It contains various options chosen by the source. Padding bits ensure that the size of the IP header is multiple of 32 bits.

One important option is source route. It enables the source to specify the network nodes of the Internet, through which the IP packet must pass. The IP packet is discarded, if the specified path cannot be followed.

IP fragmentation

An IP packet is fragmented into multiple smaller IP packets, if the network has packet size limitations (Figure 21.4). Fragments of an IP packet are identified by the fragment identifier field, the IP header. Location of the fragment within the original payload is indicated by the fragment offset field.

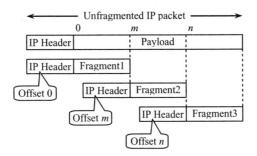

Figure 21.4   IP fragmentation.

Fragmentation of an IP packet is carried out at the source or at any node of the network. But the reassembly of the fragments is carried out at the destination only, since fragments may take different paths and arrive out of sequence. If all the fragments do not reach the destination before expiry of reassembly timer, the received fragments are discarded at the destination.

---

1. 32-bit IP address is usually represented in dotted format a.b.c.d where a, b, c, d are decimal equivalents of 8-bit group, e.g. 192.168.1.0 represents the following 32-bit IP address:
    11000000   10101000   00000001   00000000

21.2.2 IP Fragmentation Attack

An organization protects its private network from attacks by installing a firewall at the point where its network connects to the public Internet (Figure 21.2). Firewall is like a barrier which allows only the authorized traffic in and out of the private network. There can be several types of firewalls. We describe firewalls in detail in the next chapter. For the time being, we assume that a firewall inspects IP/TCP/UDP headers of every IP packet that it receives and then decides whether to block or permit the IP packet. The attacker attempts to cross the firewall barrier by manipulating the fields of IP/TCP/UDP headers. IP fragmentation attack is one such example.

The firewalls usually check only the first fragment of an IP packet and let the other fragments pass. The reason being the first fragment would have all the fields of IP and TCP headers required for the filtering decision. If the first fragment is filtered out by the firewall, the host will discard the rest of fragments after reassembly time out. Only when it is allowed to pass by the firewall, the destination host will be able to reassemble the packet.

In the IP fragmentation attack, the attacker tries to push the first fragment of an IP packet through the firewall that filters IP packets based on port numbers and flags of the TCP/UDP header. He adopts one of the following approaches:

- Tiny fragment
- Overlapping fragments

In the first approach, the attacker keeps a few bytes of the TCP/UDP header in the first fragment. The firewall does not find the required TCP header fields for filtering-decision in the first fragment and lets it pass.

In the second approach, the attacker manipulates the fragment offset numbers. He keeps the offset *m* of second fragment such that the second fragment overwrites some of the bytes of the first fragment at the time of reassembly (Figure 21.5). For example, if the first fragment has 0 to 24 bytes, and he may keep fragment offset $m = 2$ instead of $m = 3$ in the second fragment. In this case, the first eight bytes of second fragment will overwrite the byte numbers 16 to 23 of the first fragment at the time of reassembly[2]. He constructs the first fragment with partly fake TCP/UDP header that will be acceptable to the firewall. He constructs the second fragment with the desired TCP/UDP header.

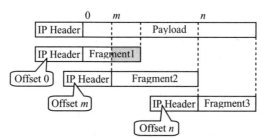

Figure 21.5 Overlapping IP fragments.

---

2. Some operating systems hang or crash when reassembling TCP segments with overlapping fragments. The adversary exploits this weakness of the operating system by sending overlapping TCP segments. This DoS attack is called *teardrop.c* attack.

The tiny fragment attack can be defeated by enforcing the rule that that the first fragment must contain a predefined minimum amount TCP/UDP header. The overlapping fragment can be countered by reassembling the packets in the firewall or by detecting overlapping fragments. But the firewall itself becomes vulnerable to denial of service attack, if it reassembles the IP packet. For example, the attacker can send the IP fragments, withholding the first fragment until the firewall runs out of memory.

21.2.3 IP Spoofing

IP spoofing refers to falsification of IP source address. The goal of an IP spoofing attack is to exploit the trust relationship that exists between two hosts. For example, hosts on a local area network can be so configured that no authentication is required when a host connects to another trusted host. A trusted host is identified by its IP address. For example, in UNIX rhosts file contains the IP addresses of the trusted hosts.

Figure 21.6 depicts the basic scheme of the attack. The attacker sends IP packet with spoofed source address of trusted host B. The victim A sends an IP packet in response. The response is addressed to B. The attacker is able to see the response, since he is on the same local area network[3]. IP spoofing attack is launched with several possible objectives in mind.

- The attacker wants to access the victim, hiding his identity.
- The attacker wants to attack B with unwanted traffic.

In the former case, the attacker must send his next packet before B responds since B having been caught unawares, may respond, for example, with RESET in the case of TCP connection request sent by the attacker.

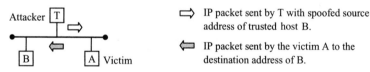

Figure 21.6 IP spoofing attack.

21.2.4 IP Source Routing Attack

IP spoofing attack described in the last section can be useful when the attacker is on the same local area network. If the attacker is on the Internet, he uses IP source routing attack with IP spoofing. IP source routing is an option using which the source can specify the path of the IP packet to the destination. This option is exploited by the attacker by inserting itself in the specified path. Figure 21.7 depicts the basic scheme.

---

3. If the local area network is based on layer 2 switches, the attacker can divert the frames through itself using ARP poisoning described later.

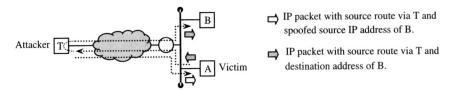

Figure 21.7 IP source routing attack.

The attacker sends IP packet with spoofed source address of B who is trusted by A. The IP packet carries source route option which specifies the route B–T–A. The victim A trusts IP address of B, and therefore, responds with IP datagram with source route A–T–B. The packet reaches the attacker T. The next course of action is decided by the attacker. He may forward the packet to B with or without any modification, or he may simply drop the packet.

21.3 ATTACKS BASED ON ICMP

Internet Control Message Protocol (ICMP) supports IP protocol by way of providing information about the network, e.g. unreachable nodes and destinations, delays in the network, protocol errors, accessibility and other information. ICMP messages are carried as payload of an IP packet with protocol field set to 1 (Figure 21.8). An ICMP message consists of a common header containing type, code and checksum fields.

Type: It identifies type of ICMP message, e.g., Type = 1 is 'Destination unreachable'.

Code: It further qualifies the type, e.g., Code = 3 for Type = 1 indicates that the destination port is unreachable.

Checksum: It is used for detecting errors in ICMP message.

The extension fields are the other fields depending on the type of ICMP message.

IP header with protocol = 1		
Type	Code	Checksum
Extension fields		

Figure 21.8 Format of encapsulated ICMP message.

There are several types of ICMP messages, which can be categorized as follows:

- ICMP error reporting messages
  ICMP error messages are automatically generated whenever an operational error is encountered in delivery of an IP packet. The error message is sent back to the source by the network node or the destination host that encounters delivery problem.
- ICMP query and reply messages
  ICMP query message is sent by a host to determine the network health, e.g. to determine if a network node is up and working.

The following ICMP messages are important in the present context. These ICMP messages are used for several types of attacks.

1. ICMP echo   Query and reply messages
2. Destination unreachable   Error reporting message
3. Redirect   Error reporting message

ICMP Echo (ICMP Type 0 & 8)

When ICMP echo request (Type 8) message is sent to a host, the host returns ICMP echo reply (Type 0) message [Figure 21.9(a)]. The primary purpose of sending an echo request is to ascertain, if the given IP address is reachable. If the ICMP echo reply is not received, we need to look at other responses to determine nature of problem. For example, if the destination IP interface is down, we would receive ICMP 'Destination Unreachable' (ICMP type 3, code 1) message. Ping (Packet Internet Groper) is a utility that sends ICMP echo message. It is used for estimation of round trip delay, packet loss and other parameters.

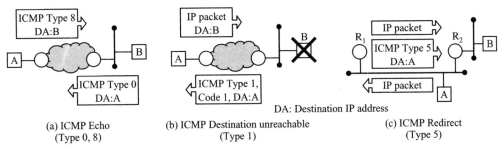

(a) ICMP Echo   (b) ICMP Destination unreachable   (c) ICMP Redirect
(Type 0, 8)   (Type 1)   (Type 5)

Figure 21.9   ICMP messages.

Destination Unreachable (ICMP Type 3)

If an IP packet cannot be delivered to its destination due to any of the reasons given in Table 21.1, ICMP 'Destination Unreachable' message is sent to the source by the router/host that encounters this problem [Figure 21.9(b)].

TABLE 21.1   ICMP Codes for Destination Unreachable Reasons

Code	Description	Sender
0	Network unreachable	Router
1	Destination host unreachable or not responding	Router
2	Protocol given in the IP header is unreachable	Destination host
3	Destination port given in TCP/UDP header is unreachable	Destination host
4	Fragmentation is needed but DF flag in the IP header is set	Router
5	Source route has failed	Router

Redirect (ICMP Type 5)

If the default gateway router configured in a host knows a better path to send an IP packet, it

- sends 'Redirect' ICMP message to the sending host, and
- forwards the IP packet towards the destination.

In Figure 21.9(c), host A sends an IP packet with destination address of host B to its default gateway router R_1. R_1 notices the better path is through R_2. It forwards the IP packet to R_2 and at the same time sends ICMP 'Redirect' message to host A so that the host may send IP packets meant for host B directly to R_2.

21.3.1 ICMP Echo Attacks

The attacker uses ICMP Echo message for two purposes:

- To determine the active IP addresses.
- To launch denial of service (DoS) attacks.

Ping Sweep

During reconnaissance stage, the first mission of the attacker is to determine all the active IP addresses on a subnet. Later he uses these active IP addresses to target specific applications. The ping sweep attack consists of sending ping to all the possible IP addresses of the targeted subnet [Figure 21.10(a)]. He gets all the active IP addresses of the subnet from the replies.

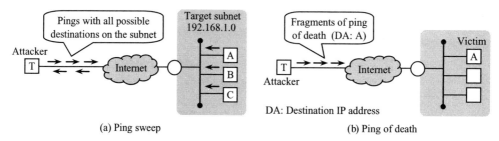

(a) Ping sweep   (b) Ping of death

Figure 21.10   Ping attacks.

Ping of Death

The maximum size of an IP packet is 65535 octets. An IP packet of larger size can cause kernel buffer overflow which may result in collapse of the operating system (OS) of a host. The attacker assembles a ping of size exceeding 65535 octets. He sends the fragments of the ping to the targeted machine [Figure 21.10(b)]. Recall that the reassembly of fragments is done only at the destination. When the fragments are reassembled, the OS of the victim collapses.

Smurf[4] Attack

Smurf attack floods the victim with ICMP echo replies. As shown in Figure 21.11, the attacker (T) sends a, ICMP echo request as directed broadcast[5] to a subnet. The source IP address on this request is spoofed. It is the victim's IP address (X). All the active hosts, which receive this message, respond with ICMP echo reply addressed to the victim.

---

4. The word 'Smurf' comes from comic books. Smurfs are small blue comic creatures that live in mushrooms.
5. Directed broadcast is delivered to all the hosts on a subnet. The host part of the destination address is all1s. For example, in Figure 21.7, the directed broadcast address for subnet 192.168.1. 0/8 is 192.168.1. 255, since 255 in binary is 11111111.

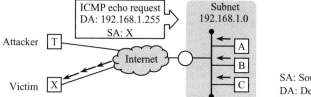

Figure 21.11   Smurf attack.

The victim can be a host on the Internet or on the subnet. In the later case, the ICMP Echo request carries a subnet IP address as the spoofed source address.

To mitigate all such attacks, the firewall between the gateway router and the subnet can be configured to filter

  – unwanted inbound protocols (e.g. ICMP echo requests) from the Internet.
    Echo request is identified by the protocol field in IP header and type field of the ICMP message. The protocol field is 0 for ICMP and ICMP type field for echo request is 8.
  – directed broadcasts from the internet.
    The host part of the destination IP address is all 1s in a directed broadcast.
  – all the IP packets from Internet carrying any subnet IP address as the source address.

21.3.2   ICMP Destination Unreachable Attack

The attacker (T) uses 'Destination Unreachable' ICMP message to cut-off communication between hosts A and B. He sends forged 'Destination Unreachable' ICMP messages (Type 3, code 2 or 3) continuously to host A with spoofed source address B (Figure 21.12). When host A sends an IP packet to host B, he immediately finds a forged ICMP destination unreachable message from B. A is made to believe that the ICMP message is generated as consequence of the IP packet it sent to B. Note that T does not synchronize its ICMP message with the IP packet sent by host A. T sends ICMP 'Destination Unreachable' message continuously. Host A ignores these ICMP messages. It is only when host A sends its IP packet to B, that it takes note of the next forged ICPM message.

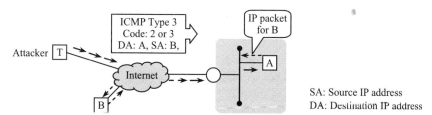

Figure 21.12   Destination unreachable attack.

21.3.3   ICMP Redirect Attack

The attacker uses ICMP redirect to launch the following attacks:

- Man-in-the-middle attack
- Denial of service (DoS) attack

  In the man-in-the-middle attack, the attacker places himself between the two victim hosts so that he can monitor and modify the data exchange between the two hosts. He can even hijack[6] the TCP connection displacing one of the two hosts.

Figure 21.13 shows the man-in-the-middle attack. R is the default gateway router configured in host A. The attacker sends a connection request to the host with a spoofed source IP address (say B). When host A responds, the attacker immediately sends the ICMP redirect message indicating his own IP address as the better route. He uses spoofed source address of the default gateway router R on the ICMP redirect message, giving an impression to host A that the redirect has come from the configured gateway router. Host A updates its routing table. Unlike ARP redirection (Section 21.4.2), this update is not temporary. Thereafter host A sends all its IP packets through attacker T who as man-in-the-middle can monitor/modify the contents of the IP packets [Figure 21.13(b)].

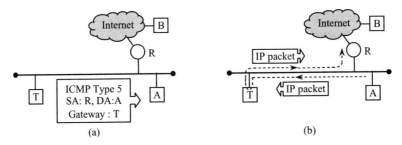

(a)   (b)

Figure 21.13 Man-in-the-middle attack using ICMP redirect message.

In the DoS attack, the attacker (T) corrupts the default geteway router configuration of the victim host. He sends ICMP redirect message to host A indicating a non-existent IP address as the better route. Host A modifies the default gateway router configuration. Since the modified IP address is non-existent, services of host B become unavailable to host A.

21.4 ATTACKS BASED ON ADDRESS RESOLUTION PROTOCOL (ARP)

When a host wants to send an IP packet, it must also know the hardware address (e.g. MAC[7] address) of the destination host, if the host is on the same local area network, or of the default gateway router, if the destination host is on a different network. For example, in Figure 21.14(b), if host A wants to send an IP packet to host B, it must also know the MAC address of B apart from its IP address. Similarly, if host A wants to send IP packet to host C, it must know the MAC address of default gateway router R. For R to deliver the IP packet received from A to host C, it must know the MAC address of host C. MAC address in each of the these cases is determined dynamically using Address Resolution Protocol (ARP).

---

6. See Section 21.5.6 for TCP session hijacking.
7. MAC (Media Access Control) is IEEE 802.3 Ethernet sublayer. MAC address is also commonly referred to as hardware address.

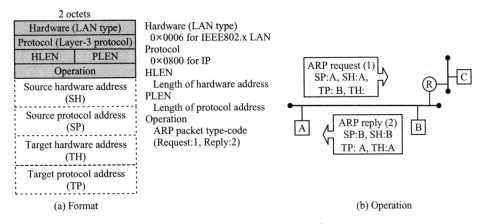

2 octets

| Hardware (LAN type) |
| Protocol (Layer-3 protocol) |
| HLEN | PLEN |
| Operation |
| Source hardware address (SH) |
| Source protocol address (SP) |
| Target hardware address (TH) |
| Target protocol address (TP) |

Hardware (LAN type)
  0×0006 for IEEE802.x LAN
Protocol
  0×0800 for IP
HLEN
  Length of hardware address
PLEN
  Length of protocol address
Operation
  ARP packet type-code
  (Request:1, Reply:2)

(a) Format

(b) Operation

Figure 21.14   ARP packet format and operation.

Format of ARP Packet

ARP is a layer-3 protocol encapsulated by layer-2 frame just like IP packets. The format of ARP packet is shown in Figure 21.14(a). ARP consists of several types of packets. We are interested in ARP request packet (code 1) and ARP reply packet (code 2).

21.4.1   ARP Operation

When host A wants to send IP packet to B, A determines MAC address of host B using ARP request packet as shown in Figure 21.14(b).

- Host A sends ARP request packet indicating
  - A's IP address (source protocol address, SP),
  - A's MAC address (source hardware address, SH) and
  - B's IP address (target protocol address, TP).

  The ARP request packet is encapsulated in a MAC frame with broadcast address so that all devices on the LAN receive it.
- Host B receives the frame and finds that the ARP request packet is meant for it. It updates its ARP cache with A's IP and MAC addresses, and sends ARP reply packet to A. The reply contains B's IP and MAC addresses in the source address fields (SP and SH). The target addresses in the reply are those of A. The reply is encapsulated in a MAC frame with destination address of host A [Figure 21.14(b)].

  Other hosts on the LAN also receive A's ARP request packet. They update their ARP cache with A's IP and MAC addresses.
- Host A receives the ARP reply packet and updates the MAC address of B in its ARP cache. A can now send the IP packet to host B.

When the destination host is on a different network [e.g. C in Figure 21.14(b)], host A determines the MAC address of the default gateway router R using ARP and sends the IP packet for host C encapsulated in a MAC frame. The destination address on the MAC frame is R's MAC address. When router R receives the IP packet from host A for host C, it uses ARP to find the MAC address of host C and forwards the IP packet encapsulated in MAC frame addressed to C.

21.4.2 ARP Poisoning and Redirection Attack

The following attributes of ARP make it vulnerable to attacks:

- ARP request and reply can be forged, since they are not authenticated.
- ARP is stateless, i.e., ARP reply can be sent without a corresponding ARP request.

These vulnerabilities can be exploited in the following manner.

- A forged ARP request or reply can be used to update the ARP cache of the victim host with a forged entry. This attack is called 'ARP Poisoning'.
- The victim's traffic can be redirected to the attacker's host. Thereafter the attacker can copy and modify the data and then forward the frames to their actual destination. He can also block the traffic resulting in denial of service attack.

Figure 21.15 shows a local area network consisting of a layer-2 switch, and three hosts, A, B and T. The attacker owns host T. Let us assume that the attacker knows the IP addresses (IP_A, IP_B) and MAC addresses (MAC_A, MAC_B) of the hosts A and B[8]. At this stage, the status of ARP caches in A and B is as given below:

ARP cache (A)	ARP cache (B)
IP_B MAC_B	IP_A MAC_A

The attacker launches the ARP attack by sending the following two forged ARP replies, one addressed to host A and the other addressed to host B. The source hardware address in these messages is T's address MAC_T (Figure 21.15). Remember that the ARP reply is addressed to specific destination. It is not sent as a broadcast.

	ARP reply to A	ARP reply to B
Source addresses	IP_B, MAC_T	IP_A, MAC_T
Target addresses	IP_A, MAC_A	IP_B, MAC_B

ARP being stateless protocol, A and B accept their respective ARP replies and update their ARP caches as given below:

ARP cache (A)	ARP cache (B)
IP_B ~~MAC_B~~	IP_A ~~MAC_A~~
MAC_T	MAC_T

If there is no traffic between A and B, the ARP cache entries are flushed out after a timeout. Therefore, T continues to poison ARP cache at regular intervals.

---

8. T can send ARP request messages to hosts A and B to determine their MAC addresses.

A and B now send their frames using the MAC address of the attacker T who

- either redirects the frames to their correct destinations. The attacker can monitor/modify the messages as in the typical man-in-the-middle attack.
- or blocks the frames resulting in denial of service attack.

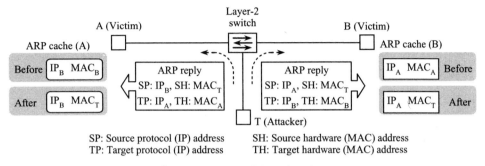

Figure 21.15 ARP poisoning.

ARP poisoning attack is countered by keeping DHCP bindings (IP address↔MAC address) in the switch which filters forged ARP replies using these bindings.

21.5 THREATS AT TCP LAYER

TCP is the most commonly used protocol for Internet services. For example, Telnet, FTP, SMTP and HTTP all are TCP based. TCP is a reliable connection oriented protocol.

- TCP is reliable in the sense that
  - it confirms to the sender that the sent data has been delivered to the destination,
  - it recovers the lost data segments by retransmission, and
  - it delivers data in sequence to the receiver.
- TCP is connection oriented in the sense that the sender and receiver must establish a connection state before transfer of data. The connection state is released when the session of data exchange is over.

TCP uses services of underlying IP at layer-3, which is connectionless and unreliable protocol. Before we look into vulnerability of TCP to various attacks, we will quickly review the TCP protocol. We will restrict this description only to those aspects of TCP operation that are relevant to the context, i.e., network security.

21.5.1 Format of TCP Segment

Format of a TCP segment[9] is shown in Figure 21.16. It consists of the following fields:

---

9. Just like we have frames at layer 2, packets at layer 3, we have segments at the Transport layer.

Source port number			Destination port number	
Sequence number (S)				
Acknowledgement number (A)				
HLEN	Resv	Flags	Window size	
Checksum			Urgent pointer	
Payload data				

U	A	P	R	S	F
R	C	S	S	Y	I
G	K	H	T	N	N

Flags

URG Urgent   ACK Acknowledgement
PSH Push   RST Reset
SYN Synchronize   FIN Final

(a) Format of TCP segment.   (b) TCP flags

Figure 21.16 Format of TCP segment.

Source and destination port numbers: Just like source and destination addresses, these are the service access points to which the user entities (application processes) are attached at the source and at the destination.

- 0 to 1023 port numbers are 'well-known' port numbers reserved for common applications and services. Table 21.2 lists some "well ports". Server applications listen on their well-known ports for incoming service requests.
- The client port numbers are > 1023.

TABLE 21.2 Well-known Ports of TCP and UDP

TCP		UDP	
Applications	**Port number**	**Applications**	**Port number**
FTP	20 (s), 21 (s)	TFTP	69 (s)
Telnet	23 (s)	SNMP	161 (s), 162 (c)
SMTP	25 (s)	DNS	53 (s)
DNS	53 (s)	BOOTP	67 (s), 68 (c)
HTTP	80 (s)	Echo service	7
Name server	42 (s)	Character generator service	19
RPC	111	(s) : server, (c) : client	

Sequence number (S): It is the sequence number of the first user data byte in the payload of this TCP segment.

Acknowledgement number (A): It is the piggy backed acknowledgement of the data bytes received. This number is valid, if the ACK flag is set. If $A = n$, all previous bytes up to $n - 1$ stand acknowledged.

Flags: There are six flag bits. The following four flags are of interest to us.

ACK (Acknowledgement)   If ACK is set, the acknowledgement number (A) is valid.

RST (Reset)   If RST is set, the session is to be cleared immediately.

SYN (Synchronize)   If SYN is set, the sequence number field (S) holds the initial value of the sequence number.

FIN (Final)   If FIN is set, the sender is ready to close the connection.

Checksum: This field is used for detection of content errors in TCP segment and wrong delivery of TCP segment. Checksum is computed over the TCP segment and a pseudo IP header. If destination address of an IP packet is manipulated during its transit, TCP checksum detects wrong delivery.

Other fields:

HLEN   It is the size of TCP header.

Window size   It is the window size prescribed by the sender for the receiver.

21.5.2 TCP Operation

TCP is a connection oriented protocol. Therefore, it has three phases:

1. Connection set-up phase
2. Data transfer phase
3. Disconnection phase

Connection Set-up

TCP connection is established in a three-way handshake between two hosts A and B (Figure 21.17). In this handshake, A and B synchronize their sequence number (SN) and acknowledgement number (AN).

- A sends TCP segment with SYN flag and its initial sequence number SN = 9 to B.
- B responds with SYN and ACK flags and its initial sequence number SN = 29 and acknowledgement number AN = 9 + 1 = 10.
- A sends its TCP segment with ACK flag and acknowledgement number AN = 29 + 1 = 30.

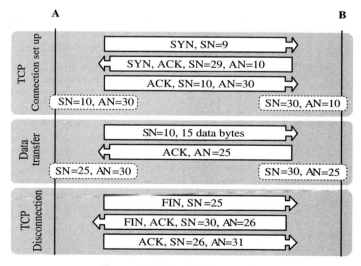

Figure 21.17 TCP operation.

Initial sequence numbers are chosen (or incremented) randomly for each instance of connection establishment. At the end of this exchange, the sequence numbers and the acknowledgement numbers of entities A and B are synchronized as shown below:

	A	B
Sequence number (SN)	10	30
Acknowledgement number (AN)	30	10

Synchronism implies that the sequence number at one end is equal to the acknowledgement number at the other end. In the above example, A is ready to receive data byte number 30 from B and will send byte number 10 to B.

Data Transfer

Data transfer can begin immediately after connection establishment. Figure 21.17 depicts operation of data transfer phase.

- A sends 15 data bytes, the first byte having sequence number 10.
- B is expecting byte number 10 from A. When it receives these 15 bytes of data, it sends acknowledgement number AN = 25. Acknowledgement AN = 25 indicates that B has received byte number 24, and it wants now byte number 25 from A.

Disconnection

Disconnection in TCP can be initiated by either end. Entity initiating disconnection ensures that it has sent all the data bytes in its buffer and received acknowledgement for them. In Figure 21.17, A initiates disconnection and proceeds as given below:

- A sends a TCP segment with FIN flag and SN = 25 to B.
- B acknowledges receipt of FIN and ACK flags with AN = 25 + 1 = 26.
- After A receives the acknowledgement, it closes the outgoing side of the connection. A continues to receive and acknowledge data from B, if B has more data to send.
- When B also sends TCP segment with FIN flag, A responds with ACK flag. B closes its outgoing side of the connection when it receives this acknowledgement.

21.5.3   TCP Port Scanning Attack

Having identified the active IP addresses using ping sweep on a subnet, the attacker's next goal is to determine the open server ports on each active IP address. He carries out port scanning on each IP address by sending TCP connection requests to all the 'well-known' destination ports. If the destination port is open, the server responds with SYN and ACK flags, else it sends RST flag. For example, in Figure 21.18, server A responds with SYN, ACK flags for connection to port number n, and with RST flag for connection to ports l and m.

Having determined the open status of the destination port, the attacker resets the connection request by sending RST flag. Since the connection is not opened, it is likely that the event may not be logged by the operating system of A, and therefore, identity of the attacker may not be revealed. The attacker carries out port scanning on each active IP address of the subnet.

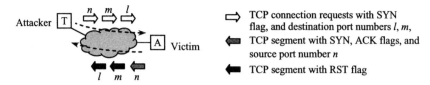

Figure 21.18 TCP port scanning.

Port scanning can be done using other TCP flags as well. For example, the attacker may send FIN flag. Most of the operating systems return RST flag, if the port is closed and ignore FIN flag, if the port is open.

21.5.4 TCP SYN Flooding Attack

When a host (A) receives TCP connection request with SYN flag, it sends back TCP segment with SYN and ACK flags to the connection requesting host (B). To complete the three-way handshake, A must receive TCP segment with ACK flag from B before the connection is established. A needs to keep track of such half open connections where reply from the connection requesting host is awaited.

The attacker T exploits this connection establishment design to incapacitate the victim in the following manner:

- He carries out ping sweep and port scanning to determine the destination IP address and destination port number of the targeted victim.
- He floods the victim with large number of TCP connection requests (Figure 21.19). The attacker (T) uses spoofed source address in its TCP connection requests to hide his identity. The source address is incorrect or nonexistent.
- The victim starts responding to the connection requests by returning SYN, ACK flags while keeping track of all the half open connections.
- The last part of three-way handshake is never completed, since the attacker used nonexistent or incorrect source addresses in its connection requests. Thus number of half open connection quickly builds up. The surge of connection requests exhaust victim's buffer resource allocated for half open connections. The victim is incapacitated to entertain new TCP connection requests from legitimate users. In other words, the victim of the SYN flooding attack becomes inaccessible to the legitimate new users.

Figure 21.19 SYN flooding attack.

RFC 4987 'TCP SYN Flooding Attacks and Common Mitigations' gives several alternatives for minimizing the impact of TCP SYN flooding attack. The impact can be minimized by

- limiting the number of half open connections from a unique source,

- reducing the time for which a connection stays half open, and
- overwriting the oldest half open connection with the new requests.

Other methods suggested in the RFC are based on using proxy to avoid the direct TCP connections to the server and using cookies to avoid tracking of half open connections.

21.5.5 TCP/IP Spoofing Attack

The objective of the TCP/IP Spoofing Attack is to establish TCP connection with the server and give useful commands, e.g. delete a file. To achieve this objective, the attacker impersonates a trusted client of the server and establishes a TCP connection with the server. The attacker proceeds as follows [Figure 21.20(a)]:

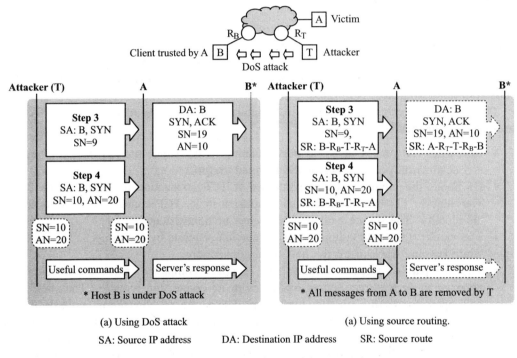

Figure 21.20 TCP/IP spoofing attack.

Step 1: The attacker T figures out the initial sequence numbering pattern of server A by initiating TCP connection with A. A's response reveals its initial sequence numbering pattern.

Step 2: T launches DoS attack on host B (e.g. SYN flooding) so that B is incapacitated to respond.

Step 3: T initiates TCP connection to A using B's IP address as a spoofed source address. Server A responds with SYN, ACK flags and sends response to the destination address of B. Since B is under DoS attack, it cannot reply. If B could process A's SYN, ACK response, B would send a reset to A because it did not initiate the connection request.

Step **4:** Since T does not see the A's response, it does not get the initial sequence number of A. But having already figured out sequence number pattern of A in step 1, T composes the last part of three-way handshake using the guessed initial sequence number[10]. He sends ACK flag to A using B's IP address as the source address.

If T's initial sequence number guess is correct, the server A and the attacker T have synchronized sequence and acknowledgement numbers. A is under the impression that it has set up a TCP connection with B.

Attacker T now has access the application and sends useful commands. He does not get any response from A because A's responses are routed to B. But he does not care so long as his commands get executed by A.

The attack can be further refined using source route [Figure 21.20(b)]. The attacker T specifies source route SR = {B–R_B–T–R_T–A} in its IP packets to the server A. Note that the source route starts from B, passes through T and terminates on A. A sends its response with the source route in reverse order. Thus the attacker gets all the responses. He does not forward the A's responses to B. Thus B is unaware of attack on server A. DoS attack on B is not needed.

21.5.6 TCP Session Hijacking Attack

In the TCP session hijacking, the attacker displaces one of the two communicating hosts of an ongoing session and continues the TCP session with the other host without its knowledge. Usually this attack is used when the server requires client's authentication. For example, the attacker can take over a telnet session after the telnet client establishes the TCP connection and successfully authenticates itself to the server.

The prerequisite for this attack is that the traffic between the two hosts must pass through the attacker's machine. The attacker meets this requirement by launching other attacks (e.g. ARP spoofing, ICMP redirection). The TCP session hijacking attack proceeds as follows (Figure 21.21):

Step **1:** The attacker watches two hosts A (the client) and B (the server) establish TCP connection by exchanging SYN, (SYN, ACK) and ACK flags. When the connection is established, the TCP sequence and acknowledgement numbers are in synchronism at the two ends and the attacker knows these numbers.

	A	**B**
Sequence number (SN)	10	30
Acknowledgement number (AN)	30	10

The attacker initiates step 2 at this stage or after the client (say A) has successfully authenticated itself to server B.

Step **2:** The attacker injects two TCP segments, one towards host A and the other towards host B. The TCP segments contain null data, e.g. IAC NOP in Telnet, and bear the correct

---

10. To improve the chances success, T can send multiple ACKs with different initial sequence numbers. Server A simply rejects the ACKs with wrong sequence numbers.

sequence numbers as synchronized by A and B. The TCP segment for A has B's IP address as spoofed source address. The TCP segment for B has A's IP address as the spoofed source address. The objective of the attacker is to desynchronize the sequence and acknowledgement numbers of A and B.

Hosts A and B accept the TCP segments and respond with acknowledgement to each other. The sequence numbers and acknowledgement numbers at this stage are as given below. The attacker keeps his numbers in synchronism with those of server B.

	A (client)	B (server)	Attacker
Sequence number (SN)	10	30	25
Acknowledgement number (AN)	45	25	30

Hosts A and B realize that their sequence and acknowledgement numbers are desynchronized. They try to resolve this state either by resending acknowledgements or by resetting the connection. The attacker's interests are not served by either of these actions.

Step **4:** The attacker launches DoS attack to silence host A. He continues with the TCP session impersonating as host A to server B. In effect, he takes over the TCP session from host A.

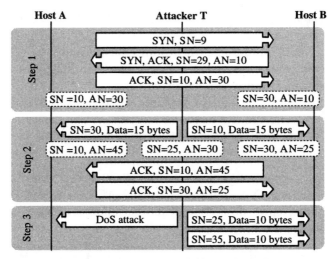

Figure 21.21 TCP session hijacking.

21.6 THREATS AT UDP LAYER

User Datagram Protocol (UDP) is an unreliable connectionless protocol that operates over IP layer. Being a connectionless protocol, it does not ensure sequential delivery of datagrams. It is used for those applications where

- the overhead of connection-oriented service is undesirable, e.g. Domain Name System (DNS) where the data exchange consists of single request datagram followed by a reply datagram,

- the recovery of lost data is not required, e.g. VOIP (voice over IP) where retransmission of a lost voice sample makes no senses.

As a transport layer protocol, UDP adds little but needed capability to IP service:

- While IP addressing delivers a data packet to the logical interface of an end system, UDP port addressing delivers the data bytes to specific application in the end system.
- IP cannot check wrong deliveries of datagrams. UDP ensures that the datagrams delivered rightly are accepted.

21.6.1   Format of UDP Datagram

Figure 21.22 shows format of a UDP datagram. It consists of the following fields:

Source and destination port numbers: Just like source and destination IP addresses, these are the service access points to which the user entities (application processes) are attached at the source and at the destination. Some well-known UDP ports are listed in Table 21.2.

Length: It indicates length of UDP datagram (header plus payload data) in octets.

Checksum: This field is used for detection of content errors in UDP datagram and wrong delivery. Checksum is computed over the UDP datagram and a pseudo IP header. If destination address of an IP packet is manipulated during its transit, the checksum detects wrong delivery.

2 octets	2 octets
Source port number	Destination port number
Length	Checksum
Payload data	

Figure 21.22   Format of UDP datagram.

UDP operation is very simple. The data bytes of application process are encapsulated by the UDP header, and each UDP datagram is sent as independent data unit to the destination.

21.6.2   UDP Storm

This attack is based on UDP echo and character generator (chargen) services.

Echo service: This service is available on UDP port 7. When a UDP datagram with destination port number 7 is received, the echo service returns identical copy of the received data to the sender [Figure 21.23(a)].

Chargen service: This service is available at UDP port 19. When a UDP datagram with destination port number 19 is received, the chargen service returns a random number of characters up to 512 to the sender [Figure 21.23(b)].

The UDP storm is created by crafting a packet with UDP source port 7 (echo) and destination port 19 (chargen) as a trigger. The source and destination IP addresses are addresses of the two victims A and B respectively. This packet creates an endless loop of echo and chargen services. Victim B responds to A's request for chargen service and victim A responds to B's request for echo. This exchange continues until system or network resources are exhausted. The attack proceeds as follows [Figure 21.23(c)]:

- The attacker T sends a UDP datagram to host B with the following IP addresses and UDP port numbers:

Source IP address : Spoofed IP address of A
Destination IP address : IP address of host B
Source UDP port number : 7 (Echo service)
Destination port number : 19 (Chargen service)

This IP packet acts as a trigger for the storm of packets between hosts A and B.
- Host B returns to host A chargen service UDP datagram with the destination port number 7.
- When host A receives the chagen service datagram at its echo port 7, it echoes back the received chargen data. It sends a UDP datagram to host B with the destination port number 19.

Hosts A and B continue responding to each other as fast as their CPUs and the network will allow. The attacker aggravates the situation by releasing multiple triggers. This severely impacts CPU performance and blocks traffic in the network segment between the two hosts.

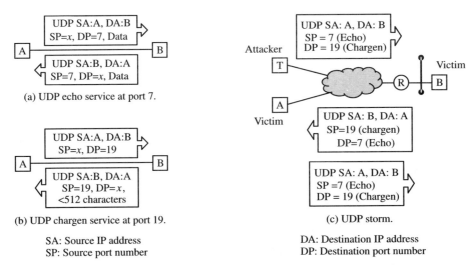

(a) UDP echo service at port 7.

(b) UDP chargen service at port 19.

(c) UDP storm.

SA: Source IP address   DA: Destination IP address
SP: Source port number   DP: Destination port number

Figure 21.23   UDP storm.

If hosts A and B are on the same private network behind a gateway router R, services of the private network can be severely crippled. The attacker can send the trigger packet as directed broadcast towards the gateway router R. The trigger has spoofed source address of host A behind the gateway router R. All the hosts on the subnet respond simultaneously with chargen service datagrams towards host A, flooding host A with multiple echo requests.

UDP storm can be prevented by

- blocking UDP datagrams with port numbers 7 and 19, and directed broadcasts at the gateway router R.
- disabling the ports for chargen and echo services by default in all the hosts.

21.7 DISTRIBUTED DENIAL OF SERVICE ATTACKS

The denial of service (DoS) attack is a malicious attempt by an attacker to cause the victim to deny service to its customers. Distributed denial of service (DDoS) attack amplifies the DoS attack by engaging multiple malicious hosts for launching DoS attack on the victim simultaneously.

To launch a DDoS attack, the attacker first discovers vulnerable hosts on the Internet. Vulnerable hosts are usually those that are either running no antivirus software or that have not been properly configured. Then he installs DDoS client on these hosts. These hosts equipped with the attack tools are known as zombies and can carry out any attack under the control of the attacker.

21.7.1 Direct DDoS

In direct DDoS attack, the army of the attacker consists of master zombies and slave zombies. Zombies are compromised machines that have been infected by malicious code. The attacker coordinates and orders master zombies and they, in turn, coordinate and trigger slave zombies. The slave zombies begin to send a large volume of packets to the victim, flooding its system with useless load and exhausting its resources. The intermediate layer of masters makes tracing the course of the attack more difficult. Figure 21.24(a) shows the direct DDoS attack.

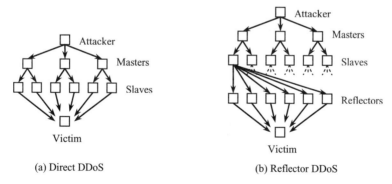

(a) Direct DDoS   (b) Reflector DDoS

Figure 21.24 Distributed denial of service (DDoS) attacks.

21.7.2 Reflector DDoS Attack

Reflector DDoS attack deploys *reflectors* in additions to master zombies and slave zombies. A reflector is any IP host that will return a packet if sent a packet. For example, web servers and DNS servers can be reflectors, since they return SYN ACK or RST in response to SYN or other TCP packets. The attacker locates a very large number of reflectors, say in the order of 1 million. Thus army of the attacker consists of master zombies, slave zombies, and a very large number of reflectors [Figure 21.24(b)].

The attacker launches his attack in the following manner:

- He triggers master zombies to launch the attack. The master zombies, in turn, trigger the slave zombies.
- Each slave zombie sends to all the reflectors or a subset of reflectors a stream of connection requests with the victim's IP address as the source IP address.
- Each reflector responds to the connection request purportedly from the victim. It sends the response (e.g. SYN ACK) to the victim.
- The victim is flooded with large volume of responses from the reflectors.

A few points to note are as follows:

- The reflectors are not compromised hosts. But they mount the attack without being aware of the attack.
- When the victim traces back the source of attack, he finds that the reflectors are legitimate servers.
- The operator of a reflector cannot easily locate the slave that is pumping the reflector, because the connection requests bear the spoofed source IP address of the victim.
- The primary purpose of deploying reflectors is to mask the source of attack. It is not amplification of the attack.

Some well-known tools for DDoS are following:

Trinoo

Trinoo is based on UDP flooding. The attacker-to-master communication is based on TCP, whereas the master to slave communication is based on UDP.

Tribe Flooding Network (TFN)

TFN can cause SYN flooding, UDP flooding and ICMP flooding. Unlike Trinoo which uses UDP to trigger the slaves into launching the attack, TFN uses ICMP. TFN2K is an evolved version of TFN. The major difference is that the slaves do not respond to master, so the latter cannot be traced. But the masters no longer get feedback, if their commands have been received by the slaves. To improve the resilience, the masters can send multiple command packets based on ICMP, TCP and UDP.

Defense approaches to DDoS attacks typically involves the use of a combination of attack detection, traffic classification and response tools, aiming to block traffic that they identify as illegitimate and allow traffic that they identify as legitimate. There is no single point solution.

21.8 SUMMING UP

In this chapter, we examined some adversarial threats at IP, TCP and UDP layers. These threats manipulate use of TCP/UDP/IP/ICMP/ARP protocols to redirect/block the network traffic, block/hijack TCP connections, and incapacitate the servers. The attacks described in this chapter are summarized in Table 21.3.

TABLE 21.3 Attacks on Network Security

Attack	Impact
IP fragmentation attack	The attacker tries to push the first fragment of an IP packet through the firewall that filters IP packets based on port numbers and flags of the TCP/UDP header.
IP spoofing attack	The attacker uses the IP address of a trusted system as the source address on its IP packets to get access to the victim.
IP source routing attack	The attacker exploits the source routing option with IP spoofing to route the victim's IP traffic through his computer. He uses spoofed source address of a trusted system to get the access.
ICMP ping sweep attack	The attacker sends ICMP pings to all the IP addresses to determine active IP addresses on a subnet.
ICMP destination unreachable attack	The adversary sends destination unreachable messages to prevent the victim from establishing a TCP connection.
ICMP redirect attack	The adversary sends redirect message to divert victim's IP traffic via his machine so that he may copy, modify or block the traffic.
ICMP smurf attack	This attack floods the victim with ICMP echo replies.
ICMP ping of death	Ping of death causes kernel buffer overflow when the victim reassembles fragment of an oversized ping.
ARP poisoning attack	The poisoning attack updates victim's ARP cache with a forged entry of the adversary.
TCP port scanning attack	The adversary sends TCP SYN/FIN flags to determine the open TCP ports.
TCP SYN flooding attack	The adversary floods the victim with TCP connection requests to exhaust the victim's resources required for establishing new connections.
TCP/IP spoofing attack	The adversary uses spoofed address for establishing TCP connection with the server and giving useful commands, e.g. delete a file.
TCP hijacking attack	The adversary uses this attack to take over an established TCP connection displacing the legitimate client.
TCP *Land*.c attack	The adversary causes victim's OS to crash by sending TCP connection request with spoofed source address of the victim and same TCP source and destination ports.
UDP storm	The adversary triggers an endless exchange of UDP echo/chargen datagrams between its two victims.
Distributed DoS (DDoS)	The adversary amplifies DoS attack by engaging multiple malicious hosts (zombies) and triggering simultaneous DoS attacks from these hosts. In the reflector DDoS attack, the zombies use DNS servers to reflect the attack towards the victim.

Firewalls and intrusion detection systems are the tools to detect and prevent these attacks. These tools are deployed at the perimeter of a network. We will study these tools in the next chapter.

Key Terms		
ARP poisoning	IP spoofing attack	Smurf attack
Denial of service (DoS) attack	Overlapping fragments attack	SYN flooding attack
Distributed DoS attack	Ping of death	TCP/IP spoofing attack
Fragmentation attack	Ping sweep	Teardrop.c attack
ICMP destination unreachable attack	Port scanning	Tiny fragment attack
ICMP redirect attack	Reflector DDoS attack	UDP storm
IP source routing attack	Session hijacking attack	

RECOMMENDED READING

Avoine, G., Junod, P. and Oechslin, P., *Computer System Security: Basic Concepts and Solved Exercises*, CRC Press, FL, USA, 2004.

Bragg, R., Phodes-Ousley, M., Strassberg, K., *Network Security*, Tata McGraw-Hill, New Delhi, 2004.

Douligeris, C. (Ed), Serpanos, D.N., *Network Security, Current Status and Future Directions*, IEEE Press, John Wiley & Sons, NJ, USA, 2007.

RFC 4987, *TCP SYN Flooding Attacks and Common Mitigations*, IETF, 2007.

Rhee, M., *Internet Security*. John Wiley & Sons, West Sussex, UK, 2003.

Stallings, W., *Cryptography and Network Security*, Prentice-Hall of India, New Delhi, 2008.

──────(**PROBLEMS**)──────

1. A TCP segment is fragmented into two IP packets, each having IHL[11] = 5.

   (a) What are the sizes of two fragments, if the total length field in IP header has values 36 octets in the first IP packet and 44 octets in the second IP packet?
   (b) What is the value in the fragment offset field[12] of the two IP packets?

2. A gateway router filters tiny first fragments of size less than 16 octets. It receives an IP fragment with fragment offset = 1. Should it accept the IP fragment?

---

11. IHL is HP header length in multiple of 4 octets.
12. Fragment offset is defined in multiples of 8 octets.

3. ARP poisoning attack requires the attacker to send forged ARP replies with its MAC address MAC_T (Section 21.4.2). How can the attacker achieve his objective by sending ARP request message in place of ARP reply message?

4. In TCP/IP spoofing and TCP hijacking attacks, the attacker is ultimately able to send TCP segments to the server. What are the basic differences in the two approaches?

5. The adversary monitors the following exchange of TCP segments between Alice and Bob (Figure 21.25) and immediately thereafter inserts a TCP segment addressed to Bob that would be accepted by Bob but would disturb the synchronization of sequence numbers between Alice and Bob. Complete this exchange adding to it the adversary's message carrying 15 bytes of dummy payload and responses of Alice and Bob. How does the attacker's TCP segment affect the communication between Alice and Bob?

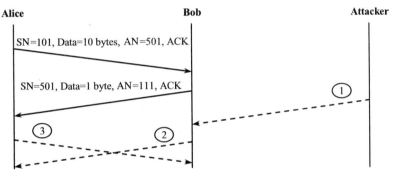

Figure 21.25   Problem 5.

6. Dynamic Host Configuration Protocol (DHCP) is used for dynamically distributing network configuration parameters such as IP address. When a DHCP client sends DHCPDISCOVER request, the DHCP server returns DHCPOFFER containing an IP address along with other configuration information (e.g. validity period, gateway's IP address, DNS server's IP address, etc.).

   (a) An adversary can prevent a DHCP client from obtaining IP addresses. How does the adversary achieve this?
   (b) How can the adversary use the above attack to intercept the outbound traffic from the client?

7. *Land.c* is a DoS attack on TCP implementations. It consists of sending TCP connection request to the victim with
   – source IP address same as the destination IP address of the victim,
   – the same source and destination port numbers, and
   – sequence number, n.

   Describe the sequence of events that can take place when the victim receives this TCP connection request.

22

Firewalls and Intrusion Detection Systems

In the last chapter, we saw variety of attacks an adversary can launch from the public Internet on a private network. Firewall and intrusion detection system are tools to secure the network against these attacks. We begin this chapter with firewalls and describe various types of firewalls, their advantages and limitations. We describe packet filtering, stateful inspection, and proxy firewalls. We also study some typical firewall architectures. Unlike firewall, an intrusion detection system provides protection by monitoring unusual traffic or user behaviour. We study anomaly-based and signature-based intrusion detection systems.

22.1 FIREWALLS

Connectivity to the public Internet is a security risk for the private networks, but at the same time it is indispensable for any organization. The Internet provides

- interconnectivity between geographically separated offices of the organization,
- connectivity to business partners, and
- access to information and services essential for productivity of the organization.

A private network is, therefore, required to be protected against the security threats arising from its connectivity to the Internet. This protection is provided by inserting a firewall at the point where the private network connects to the Internet (Figure 22.1). The firewall provides a single choke point where security policies for protection of the network can be implemented. These policies relate to inbound and outbound traffic. The protection is provided in several ways depending on type of the firewall. For example, a firewall implementation may

- filter the inbound/outbound traffic based on various fields of the IP/TCP/UDP/other protocol headers, or
- provide access to the internal resources through a proxy.

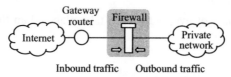

Figure 22.1 Firewall between the Internet and a private network.

But a firewall has its limitations:

- A firewall does not protect against viruses or virus infected email or file transfers.
- A firewall cannot protect against completely new threats. A firewall is configured to protect against known and potential threats.
- A firewall can control the traffic that goes through it. There is nothing a firewall can do about the traffic that does not pass through it. For example, if there is dial-up connectivity through a modem or wireless connectivity, the firewall cannot prevent an intruder from getting in.
- A firewall does not protect against internal threats. Internal threats require host security.
- Firewall can provide little protection against external attacks that are launched with the cooperation of malicious insiders.

22.1.1 Types of Firewalls

Currently there are the following types of firewalls:

- Packet filtering firewall
- Stateful inspection firewall
- Proxy firewalls
  - Application-level
  - Circuit-level

The above categorization has been done based on functionality of each category. The actual firewall implementation may have packet filtering as well as proxy functions, and it may consist of several devices and hosts. We look at firewall architecture later in the chapter.

22.2 PACKET FILTERING FIREWALL

A packet filtering firewall is usually implemented in the gateway router between an untrusted network (e.g. Internet) and an internal network[1] (Figure 22.2). It applies a set of filtering rules to each inbound and outbound packet to determine, if the packet can be permitted to pass through. These rules are typically based on the following fields of IP, TCP/UDP and ICMP headers. There are separate set of rules for inbound and outbound packets.

- Source and destination IP addresses (IP header)
- Protocol field (IP header)
- Total length (IP header)
- Fragmentation offset and fragmentation identifier fields (IP header)
- Source and destination port numbers (TCP/UDP header)
- TCP flags (TCP header)
- ICMP message type (ICMP header)

---

1. The private network is usually called internal network with reference to the firewall.

We studied various attacks types in the last chapter. To fortify against these attacks, typically all the packet filtering firewalls are configured to block

- the directed broadcasts,
- inbound IP packets with internal IP address as source address,
- outbound IP packets with external IP address as source address,
- IP packets with source routing option, and
- tiny IP fragments.

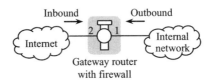

Figure 22.2 Packet filtering firewall.

Table 22.1 is an example of set of rules for a firewall shown in Figure 22.2. This firewall blocks

- all the inbound packets at interface 2 for FTP(21), Telnet(23), TFTP(69) services.
- all the outbound packets for email service (TCP port 25) at interface 1 of the firewall from the subnet 192.168.0.0/16[2].

TABLE 22.1 Rules of Packet Filtering Firewall

Interface of arrival	Source IP address	Destination IP address	Protocol	Source port	Destination port	Action
2	*	*	TCP	*	21 (FTP)	Block
1	192.168.0.0/16	*	TCP	*	25 (Email)	Block
2	*	*	TCP	*	23 (Telnet)	Block
2	*	*	UDP	*	69 (TFTP)	Block

'*' is a wildcard designator that matches every value.

22.2.1 Default Policy and Listing of Filtering Rules

When a packet is received, the firewall goes through the rules in the order they are listed until it finds the matching rule that is applicable to the packet. Then it permits or blocks the packet as specified by that rule. For the packet which is not covered by any of the listed rules, we define default policy. Default policy can be

- 'Permit', i.e., the packet which is not expressly blocked is permitted.
- 'Block', i.e., the packet which is not expressly permitted is blocked.

---

2. /16 specifies the subnet mask, i.e., the first 16 bits of the IP address constitute the subnet address.

In the earlier example (Table 22.1), it is implicit that the packets which are not covered under the above rules are permitted to pass, i.e., the default policy is to 'permit'. The default policy can be explicitly specified as the last rule in the list of filtering rules as shown below.

*	*	*	*	*	*	Permit

The first approach 'Permit' by default is dangerous in a firewall because it is impossible to anticipate all possible attacks in order to prohibit them explicitly. It is much easier to explicitly define the firewall rules that permit the required traffic and filter the rest. Therefore, the second approach 'Block' by default is safer.

The filtering rules are always applied sequentially. Care needs to be taken that the rules are listed correctly. For example, if the above default rule is listed as the first rule, all the traffic in both directions gets permitted.

Consider that we want the firewall to permit access to subnet 192.168.10.0/8 except to destination IP address 192.168.10.5 and configure the following set of rules:

Rule 1	Permit	Destination address	192.168.10.0/8
Rule 2	Block	Destination address	192.168.10.5

In the order listed above, the first rule renders the second rule ineffective, since address range 192.168.10.0/8 covers the address 192.168.10.5 also. For the second rule to be effective, the listing order should be reversed.

22.2.2 Limitations of Packet Filtering Firewalls

Packet filtering firewalls are simple and fast. But they have their limitations:

- Packet filtering firewalls may not prevent application specific attacks, since the filtering decisions do not take into account application layer data. For example, a packet filtering firewall cannot block an IP packet carrying DELETE command for the HTTP server, if the filtering rules permit access to HTTP server port 80. Application-level proxy firewall that we describe later takes into account application level protocol data.
- A packet filtering firewall is blind to application data, which is where viruses and other malware reside.
- Many attacks cannot be prevented merely by packet filtration based on IP/TCP/UDP header fields of individual packets. For example, to detect and block the SYN flooding attack or UDP storm, the firewall needs have state tracking capability as well. Stateful inspection firewall that we describe next addresses this requirement.
- Multitude of services and countermeasures required for various attack types tend to make filtering rules complex and accident prone. Filtering rules need to be thoroughly rechecked whenever a rule is changed.
- Filtering load on the gateway router is significant and impacts its performance.
- Logs of packet filtering firewall provide little additional information other than what the configured filtering rules can generate.
- Packet filtering firewalls are vulnerable to IP address spoofing, source routing, fragmentation and other attacks.

Despite these limitations, packet filtering is invariably used in all the gateway routers as first line of defense. The firewall architecture is, therefore, fortified using additional firewall devices. We study firewall architecture later in the chapter.

22.3 STATEFUL INSPECTION FIREWALL

Simple packet filtering firewall makes filtering decisions without taking into account the 'context' of a communication session. For example, if the firewall gets a TCP connection response with SYN and ACK flags from host B to host A, it does not verify the context, which is 'Had host A sent TCP connection request with SYN flag to host B?' Let us start with some simple example to understand this.

Consider the internal network (subnet 192.168.0.0/16) that allows only the Internet email service to its users [Figure 22.3(a)].

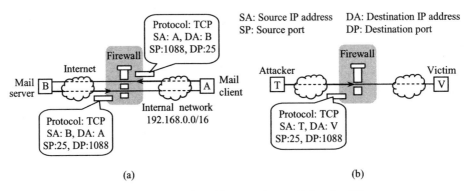

(a)   (b)

Figure 22.3 Packet filtering firewall for SMTP.

The SMTP client of the internal network uses TCP client port number >1023. The mail server on the Internet is available on well-known TCP port number 25. The packet filtering firewall is configured as shown in Table 22.2. It permits only

- the SMTP requests from an internal IP address and source port number > 1023 to the destination TCP port 25 of SMTP server (Rule 1),
- the SMTP replies from TCP port 25 of SMTP server to TCP port > 1023 of an internal IP address (Rule 2).

TABLE 22.2 Packet Filtering Firewall for SMTP

Rule	Interface of arrival	Source IP address	Destination IP address	Protocol	Source port	Destination port	Action
1	Outbound	192.168.0.0/16	*	TCP	>1023	25	Permit
2	Inbound	*	192.168.0.0/16	TCP	25	> 1023	Permit
3	*	*	*	*	*	*	Block

Consider that an attacker on the Internet sends an IP packet with source TCP port 25 (spoofed), destination TCP port > 1023 and destination IP address of an internal host [Figure 22.3(b)]. Rule 2 of the firewall for SMTP replies will permit this IP packet. What is missing in application of Rule 2 is the context. Rule 2 should be applied, if an outbound IP packet carrying SMTP request from an internal user had been permitted a priori by the firewall.

The above example points to the basic limitation of packet filtering firewall that makes filtering decisions on individual packet basis. A stateful inspection firewall tightens up the filtering rules by including the 'state' of each session in its filtering decisions. The following examples illustrate the concept of state.

1. Consider that we want to implement the following filtering rule based on context in a firewall:

   Permit an inbound UDP packet only if it is in response to an outbound UDP packet that was permitted to pass.

   The firewall implements this rule by creating a 'state' record of the outbound UDP packet that was permitted to pass. The state information in this particular case is given as follows:

   <Source IP address, destination IP address, protocol (UDP), source port, destination port, time-out>

   The 'time-out' field gives this record a life-time, on expiry of which it is deleted. When the firewall receives an inbound UDP packet which has IP addresses and port numbers that correspond to this record, the UDP packet is permitted. This is called stateful filtering because the firewall keeps track of state of UDP transactions.

2. The stateful inspection firewall of the private network is to be configured to allow sending and receiving emails only. The internal mail server has IP address 192.168.0.1. Since the stateful inspection firewall keeps track of the state on all TCP connections in progress, firewall rules need to specify the permitted direction of TCP connection. The firewall knows that SYN flag (connection request) in one direction must be followed by {SYN, ACK} flags in response from the opposite direction. The response TCP segments are implicitly permitted. Hence stateful inspection firewall requires only one rule to permit TCP connection in each direction as shown in Table 22.3.

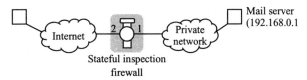

Figure 22.4   Stateful inspection firewall.

Rule 1 permits the internal mail server to connect to port 25 of any mail server on the Internet to deposit emails. Rule 2 permits any machine on the Internet to connect to port 25 of the internal mail server. Once the connection is established, these rules allow the exchange of IP packets that follows over these connections. Rule 3 disallows all the other IP packets.

TABLE 22.3 Filtering Rules of Stateful Inspection Firewall

Rule	Interface of arrival	Source IP address	Source port	Destination IP address	Destination port	Protocol	Action
1	1	192.168.0.1	*	*	25	TCP	Permit
2	2	*	*	192.168.0.1	25	TCP	Permit
3	*	*	*	*	*	*	Block

The characteristic features of stateful inspection firewalls are summarized below:

- A stateful inspection firewall creates a state record for each session and connection request. Its filtering decision is based on the various fields in the IP/TCP/UDP/ICMP headers, and on the state record.
- Apart from IP addresses, port numbers, protocol and time out, the state record may include additional information depending on the protocol. For example,
  - TCP is connection oriented protocol. Therefore, TCP state may include status of SYN, ACK, FIN, RST flags, sequence/acknowledge numbers, number of half open connections, etc.
  - ICMP is a connectionless protocol like UDP. ICMP messages can be error reporting messages or query/responses messages. ICMP state is defined only for query/response messages (e.g. for ICMP echo) and includes ICMP message type as its state parameter.
- The state information is recorded in a state table that tracks the information until a TCP connection is closed, a response is received, or a preconfigured time-out is reached.
- Stateful inspection firewalls are typically configured around the network and transport layer protocols. Some stateful inspection firewalls can create a state taking into account application layer data, but security holes in their implementation render them unsuitable replacement of proxy firewalls.
- Stateful inspection firewall generates more informative logs for analysis than a simple packet filtering firewall.

TCP hijacking and SYN flooding DoS attacks can be defeated using a stateful inspection firewall. Thus stateful firewall is an excellent compromise between a simple packet filtering firewall and proxy firewall from point of view of security and performance.

22.4 PROXY FIREWALLS

A proxy, in general, acts on behalf of its client. Proxy as an application process sits between a client process and a server process. To the client, the proxy appears to be the server, and to the application server, the proxy appears to be a client (Figure 22.5).

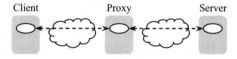

Figure 22.5 Proxy.

Proxy when used as a firewall between a client and an application server protects security interests of each side from risks of direct access. We have two kinds of proxy firewalls from the network security point of view:

- Application-level proxy firewall
- Circuit-level proxy firewall

As the name suggests, the application-level proxy protects security interests by scrutinizing application-layer data that is exchanged between the client and the server. The circuit-level proxy firewall, on the other hand, operates at access level, i.e., it

- authenticates the client,
- checks authorization of the client, and
- relays TCP/UDP segments between the server and the client, hiding the identity of the client from the server.

The circuit-level proxy firewall does not look into the contents of message that it relays.

22.4.1 Application-level Proxy Firewall

Let us start with a simple example to understand the need and operation of the application-level proxy firewall. The web server of a company uses HTTP protocol and is available on well-known TCP port 80. Consider that the company wants to make its selected web pages accessible to its remote users.

The above policy cannot be implemented using packet filtering or stateful inspection firewall, since filtering based on port number 80 will totally block all the requests to the web server. Firewall policy should be based on inspection of the URL contained in each HTTP request. The solution is provided by implementing HTTP proxy in the firewall (Figure 22.6).

- The external client establishes TCP connection to the HTTP proxy in the firewall.
- The proxy in the firewall looks at the URL contained in the HTTP request message.
  - If the requested page is allowed for the source client, the proxy establishes another TCP connection to the web server and forwards the request to the server.
  - If the requested page is not allowed, the proxy returns error message to the source client.
- When the proxy receives response from the web server, it forwards the response to the source client.

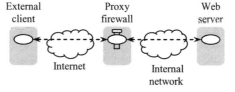

Figure 22.6 Proxy firewall.

In this example, the client was on the external network and the web server was on the internal network. The requests from internal clients for the Internet services are handled in the similar manner. Some of the pertinent observations are given below:

- Application-level proxy firewall operates at the application layer. It understands and interprets the commands of the application protocol. It filters and forwards application-layer data between external client and the application server. Thus it can control both access and scope of services. For example,
  - File Transfer Protocol (FTP) proxy can be configured for RETR (retrieve) command, but block DELE (delete) command.
  - The application-level proxy firewall can filter bad data at the application layer (such as viruses).
- The application-level proxy firewall can consist of several hosts, one for each application, e.g. we have different hosts for FTP and Telnet proxies. We elaborate on architectural aspects of a proxy firewall in the next section.
- The proxy firewall itself requires to be protected from attacks. A host with hardened operating system, called bastion host, is used as proxy. A bastion host has no user accounts, compilers, and has minimal set of programs. Additionally, unused services are disabled.
- The proxy firewall is dual homed, i.e., it has two network interfaces, one for the Internet and the other for the protected internal network. The proxy firewall does not allow direct traffic between the external and the internal networks.
- The host used as proxy also performs logging and auditing functions on the traffic that passes through it. The logs are much more informative than the logs of packet filtering firewall.
- The limitation of application-level proxy firewall is the lack of speed. Since the firewall processes packets to the application layer, it is required to do a great deal more work than packet filtering firewalls.

22.4.2 Circuit-level Proxy Firewall

As mentioned before, the circuit-level proxy firewall authenticates the client, provides access to the server and relays the messages between them. It carries out relaying function by building association between the external and internal connections (Figure 22.7). After having established the association, the circuit-level proxy firewall does not interpret application layer payload of the relayed TCP segments and UDP datagrams. This feature makes the circuit-level proxy firewall a generic proxy server that can be adapted to serve a wide variety of different applications.

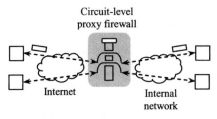

Figure 22.7 Circuit-level proxy firewall.

A common example of circuit-level firewall implementation is using SOCKS (short form of SOCKetS) protocol. The current version of SOCKS is version 5, and it is described in RFC 1928, *SOCKS Protocol Version 5*. From the layered architecture point of view, SOCKS is conceptually a shim layer between the Transport layer (TCP/UDP layer) and the Application layer. As a shim layer protocol between the Application and Transport layers, SOCKS can manage all session requests in an application-independent manner and check the requested sessions for their legitimacy. SOCKS is a client-server protocol. The well-known server ports for SOCKS are TCP 1080 and UDP 1080.

SOCKS for TCP Proxy

Let us start with an example to understand the operation of SOCKS for circuit-level proxy firewall. Consider that a client on the internal network protected by the circuit-level proxy firewall wants to access HTTP service on the Internet.

***Step* 1:** The client starts by opening a TCP connection to the SOCKS proxy available at well-known TCP port 1080.

***Step* 2:** The client sends to the proxy server a 'client negotiation' packet suggesting the authentication methods it supports. The server responds with the 'server negotiation' packet selecting its preferred authentication method from the list.

***Step* 3:** The proxy then proceeds to authenticate the client. The exact procedure at this step depends on the selected authentication method.

***Step* 4:** The client then sends to the SOCKS proxy server 'client request' packet stating
  – the service it wants. For example, the request will be for 'TCP connect' service in this case.
  – the target IP address[3] and target service port of the remote host on the Internet. For HTTP service the target port will be TCP 80.

***Step* 5:** The proxy server evaluates the 'client request' taking into account the client's id, IP address of the client, the target IP address of the remote host on the Internet and the other access control rules as configured in the proxy firewall. If the client is not allowed the type of access it has requested, the proxy server drops the connection with the client. Otherwise, the proxy server establishes TCP connection to the remote server and sends 'server reply' to the socks client. The reply consists of one of the following messages:

Code	Message
00	Successful connection with the remote server.
01	SOCKS proxy error.
02	Connection disallowed by the remote server.
03	Network not accessible.
04	Remote host not accessible.

---

3. The protocol supports IPv4 and IPv6 addresses, along with domain names. Domain name option removes the need for the client to perform a DNS lookup.

05	Connection request with remote host refused.
06	Timeout.
07	SOCKS command not supported.
08	Address type not supported.

The server reply also contains the following IP address and server port, if the connection to the remote server is successful.

- Bound IP address (the Internet-side IP address of the SOCKS proxy server). It is this address that the remote server will communicate with.
- Bound TCP port (the Internet-side port of the proxy server that the remote server sends the TCP segments to).

Step 6: If the connection to the remote host is successful, the proxy server relays the messages received at the 'bound TCP port' from the remote server for the client. Similarly, it relays the messages received from the client to the remote server from the 'bound TCP port'.

Note that SOCKS works independent of the application-level protocols. It can easily accommodate applications that use encryption to protect their traffic. Thus, as far as the SOCKS server is concerned, there is no difference between an HTTP session and an HTTPS session.

SOCKS for UDP Proxy

In the above example, the SOCKS proxy server built association between remote server and the client using two TCP connections. The SOCKS server can build similar association for a service based on UDP datagram service. The process for UDP association is given below:

The client opens TCP connection to the proxy server, negotiates authentication method. The proxy authenticates the client in the same manner as discussed earlier (Steps 1 to 3).

Step 4: The client then sends to the SOCKS proxy server 'client request' packet stating that it wants 'UDP associate' service. It also gives the target IP address and target service port of the remote host on the Internet.

Step 5: The proxy server evaluates the 'client request' taking into account the client's id, IP address of the client, the target IP address of the remote host on the Internet and the other access control rules as configured in the proxy firewall. If the client is not allowed the type of access it has requested, the proxy server drops the connection with the client. Otherwise, the proxy opens an internal UDP relay port sends 'server reply' to the client. The reply contains the UDP port and IP address where the client may send the UDP messages to be relayed.

Step 6: On receipt of the 'server reply', the client wraps its payload in a 'UDP request' datagram with IP address and port number as indicated in step 5 and sends it to the proxy server. The 'UDP request' header consists of the following fields (Figure 22.8):

- Fragment number
- Address type (IPv4, IPv6, or domain name)
- Destination IP address
- Destination port number

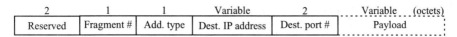

Figure 22.8 UDP request.

The fragment field is optional. Value '0' indicates that this payload is standalone. Values 1 to 127 indicate the fragment position within the sequence of fragments.

The server relays the UDP datagram from the bound IP address and the bound UDP port to the remote server. When the reply from the remote server is received, it adds the above UDP request header to the reply and relays it to the client. The UDP relay port remains open as long as the client keeps the TCP connection to the SOCKS server up.

22.4.3 Benefits and Limitations of Proxy Firewalls

Packet filtering and stateful inspection firewalls provide protection against the vulnerabilities at the network and transport layers. The protection offered by the proxy firewalls, on the other hand, is at application level and has different characteristic features. The benefits and limitations of the proxy firewalls are listed below:

Benefits

- Internal IP addresses and ports are shielded from external attacks because proxy does not allow direct access to internal hosts.
- Proxy firewalls have better event logging facilities than packet filtering routers and provide useful audit information that can be worked upon.
- Proxy firewall is not vulnerable to TCP/IP address spoofing because access is based on service instead of physical connection.
- Filtering rules of proxy firewalls are less complex than packet filtering firewalls.
- Proxy firewalls implement authentication and access control at per user basis.

Limitations

- Proxy firewalls are slower than packet filtering firewalls due to additional processing.
- The proxy server can be a single point of failure for the network or an application.
- Generic proxies may compromise security. Multiple proxy servers are required, if application specific proxies are implemented.
- Each new application protocol requires implementation of a new proxy for it. There is always a lag between introduction of a new service and availability of proxy servers for it.

The basic principle of security is *defense in depth*, which recommends that

- don't depend on one security mechanism, however, strong it may seem to be and
- install multiple mechanisms that back each other up and add to overall security.

Therefore, the packet filtering and proxy firewalls should not be considered in isolation. As we shall see in the next section, a typical firewall implementation may use proxy servers and packet filtering firewalls.

22.5   FIREWALL ARCHITECTURES

Figure 22.1 depicts firewall as a piece of equipment with capabilities of a firewall. It is rather a simplistic view of a firewall. Firewall should be viewed as a capability built into one or more devices which together provide the firewall protection services. Figure 22.9 depicts some simple examples of firewall architectures. Remember that these examples are for illustrative purposes. Firewall architectural design can be much more complex.

(a) **Screening router firewall architecture.**
Firewall using gateway router (G) to do packet filtering.

(b) **Screened host firewall architecture.**
Firewall using a screening router (G) and a bastion host (H) as proxy.

(c) **Screened subnet firewall architecture.**
Firewall using a screening router (G), bastion hosts (H) and interior choke router (I).

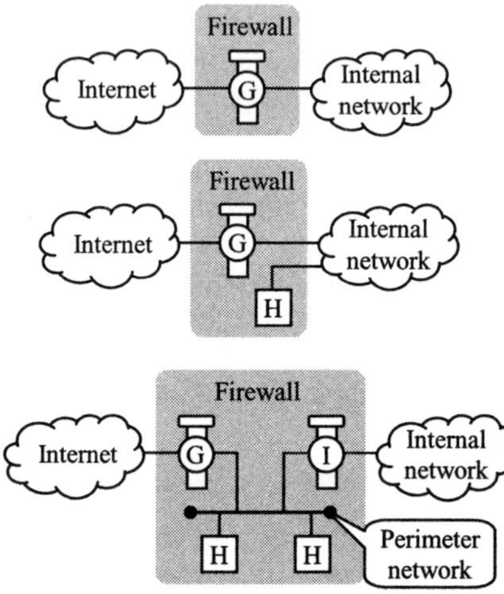

Figure 22.9 Firewall architectures.

22.5.1   Screening Router Firewall Architecture

In Figure 22.9(a), the packet filtering capability of the gateway router is used as the firewall. The gateway router when used as packet filtering firewall is called screening router, since it screens the entire network behind it. Screening router as a firewall offers limited capability from security angle but has high networking performance. It is appropriate for a situation where

– the network being protected has a high level of host security, and
– maximum networking performance at the least cost is the main consideration.

Typically the ISPs (Internet Service Providers) use screening router between their service hosts and the Internet.

22.5.2   Screened Host Firewall Architecture

This firewall architecture includes a bastion[4] host H [Figure 22.9(b)]. Bastion host has a hardened OS platform from security point of view. It resides on the internal network but is a part of firewall function. The bastion host performs authentication and proxy functions. The

---

4. Bastion is highly fortified projection on the outer walls of a castle.

screening router (G) is so configured that the hosts on the Internet can open connections (e.g. to deliver email) only to the bastion host.

As regards the connections initiated by internal hosts to the hosts on the Internet, appropriate security policies can be defined. These policies specify the services that can be accessed only through the bastion host. Certain other services can be accessed directly through the screening router. The packet filtering capability of the gateway router is used as before.

When compared with the previous configuration, this configuration provides additional security by way of

- application level filtering provided by the bastion host as proxy,
- user authentication.

One major point of concern of this configuration is that once an attacker breaks in to the bastion host, the entire internal network is at risk. This is so because the bastion host resides on the internal network and the attacker would be able to snoop the internal traffic. For this reason screened subnet architecture described next is more popular. Screened host firewall architecture is appropriate when

- the inbound connections from the Internet are limited in number.
- the internal network has relatively high level of host security.

22.5.3 Screened Subnet Firewall Architecture

This architecture adds an extra layer of security and configuration flexibility by introducing a perimeter network which further isolates the internal network from the Internet [Figure 22.9(c)]. There are two screening routers, the gateway router (G) and the interior router (I). The bastion host is on the screened subnet (i.e., the perimeter network) between the two routers.

This configuration offers several advantages:

- The configuration provide much needed flexibility:
  - There can be multiple bastion hosts on the perimeter network for different proxy servers.
  - The gateway router can be so configured that all the inbound connections for services can be terminated on the bastion hosts.
  - Packet filtering in the gateway and interior routers can be so configured that internal clients can access the Internet servers directly. For some specific Internet services, the outbound connections can be terminated on the proxy servers.
- To break into the internal network, the attacker would have to get past both the routers.
- Even if bastion host is compromised, the attacker would be able to snoop only the traffic on the perimeter network, i.e., only to and fro Internet traffic. The internal traffic between hosts of the internal network is safe from the prying eyes.
- The gateway router advertises only the existence of screened subnet to the Internet. The internal network is invisible to the Internet.

Screened subnet firewall architecture provides flexibility of tailoring the firewall to the security requirement of an organization.

22.6   INTRUSION DETECTION SYSTEM

Firewalls provide security by forming a barrier that permits only the traffic which is authorized to pass or which meets defined traffic characterization parameters. The security policy implemented by a firewall is based on known threats. A firewall cannot protect against completely new threats. Therefore, we require a second line of defense that

- continuously monitors the network for unusual pattern of activity,
- correlates event logs and
- generates alarms.

Intrusion detection system (IDS) that we discuss in this section provides such services. Typically, the IDS sits within the outer security perimeter of the network (behind the firewall) and monitors all the incoming and outgoing traffic (Figure 22.10).

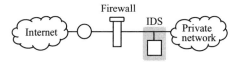

Figure 22.10   Intrusion detection system (IDS).

There are two categories of IDSs:

1. Signature-based intrusion detection system
2. Anomaly-based intrusion detection system

The IDSs are also categorized as host-based IDS and network-based IDS. Host-based IDSs apply their detection methods to activity that occurs on the hosts. These systems have the capability to detect attacks that are visible at the hosts, e.g. buffer overflows. Network-based IDSs apply their detection methods to analyze the network traffic. They detect attacks such as denial of service, port scans, etc.

22.6.1   Signature-based IDS

Signature-based IDS detects attacks that have known 'signature' or pattern. Let us look at some specific examples.

- If the inbound traffic has a packet whose source IP address corresponds to that of an internal host, then we know that we are dealing with IP-spoofing.
- A series of connection attempts on several addresses and ports of protected hosts indicate that the source of these packets is scanning the network.
- Failed login attempts may be indicative of a password cracking attack.

A signature-based IDS has database of 'signatures' of known attack types and an associated security policy to deal with these attacks. For example, the IDS may consider 'n failed login attempts in t seconds' indication or signature of an attack. When the signature is detected, the IDS may log the event or issue an alarm depending on its security policy.

Signature-based IDS is not foolproof. The adversary knowing the signature definitions can avoid detection by the IDS. For example, he will make 'less than n login attempts in t seconds'. It may not be possible for the security administrator to reduce the alarm threshold n to a lower value because it may result in excessive false alarms. Excessive false alarms quickly undermine the confidence level in any security system.

Advantages of signature-based IDS are simplicity, efficiency, and excellent ability to detect known attacks with attack specific warning. The administrator can respond quickly and appropriately.

The limitation of signature detection is that the signature database must be current, since the system can detect only the known attacks. Anomaly-based IDS that we discuss next, attempts to overcome limitations of the signature-based IDS.

22.6.2 Anomaly-based IDS

As the name suggests, anomaly-based IDS looks for unusual or abnormal behaviour. In more objective terms, it looks for statistical deviation of a metric from a trusted baseline value.

The following example illustrates the basic concept of anomaly detection.

The long-term normalized distribution of Alice's number of accesses to servers S_1, S_2, S_3 and S_4 is given at row (1) in Table 22.4.

TABLE 22.4

	a_1	a_2	a_3	a_4
1	0.1	0.4	0.4	0.1
2	0.1	0.4	0.3	0.2
3	0.1	0.4	0.38	0.12

Suppose that recent observations over one week indicate the distribution of server-access as given in row 2 of Table 22.4. Does the recent access pattern represent normal behaviour? To answer this question, we define the following variance $V = \sum (\bar{a}_i - a_i)^2$, where $\bar{a}_i$ is long term average. We define the policy that $V < 0.1$ is to be considered normal. Let us calculate V for the recent observation.

$$V = (0.1 - 0.1)^2 + (0.4 - 0.4)^2 + (0.3 - 0.4)^2 + (0.2 - 0.1)^2 = 0.02$$

We conclude that Allice's server-access is normal. But we must account for this variation in the IDS. We update the long-term distribution of server-access using the following moving average formula:

$$\bar{a}_{i+1} = 0.8\bar{a}_i + 0.2\,a_i$$

where $\bar{a}_{i+1}$ is the new average, $\bar{a}_i$ is the previous average and a_i is the new observation. Row (3) in Table 22.4 contains the updated values.

- A user profile indicates e-mail access and internet access during office hours. Unusual behaviour could be attempts for access other resources (e.g. management system, or accounting system). Maybe an intruder is using his identity.
- There is sudden increase in traffic from a network resource, or the number of sessions in a given time has increased and there is no known reason for the same.

The primary advantage of anomaly detection IDS is that there is chance of detecting previously unknown attacks. But robust anomaly detection IDS is complex to design for several reasons:

- We need to define what constitutes the normal behaviour.
- The definition of normal behaviour must be dynamically adjusted to the changing system usage.
- Mere warning of abnormal behaviour may not provide useful actionable information to the administrator. The signature-based IDS, on the other hand, provides specific information about the suspected attack.
- Statistical thresholding is complex task. We do not want excessive false alarms and at the same time we want IDS to detect every unusual event.

Where anomaly-based IDS fails miserably is in detecting malicious activity that does not violate the accepted behaviour norm. For example, an adversary can port-scan a network with a long enough time interval between each port scanned so that the IDS does not detect the event as statistically significant. Thus, an anomaly-based IDS can be supplement system to signature-based IDS rather than a replacement system.

22.7   SUMMING UP

In this chapter, our focus was on firewalls and intrusion detection systems that are deployed to mitigate the network attacks.

- A firewall provides protection by filtering inbound and outbound traffic, or by providing access to resources through proxies.
- A firewall is configured to protect against known and potential threats. A firewall does not protect against viruses or virus infected email or file transfers.
- A packet filtering firewall applies a set of filtering rules that are based on the fields of IP/TCP/UDP/ICMP headers to the inbound and outbound packets.
- A stateful inspection firewall creates a state record for each session and connection request. Its filtering decision is based on the various fields in the IP/TCP/UDP/ICMP headers, and on the state record.
- Proxy firewall provides protection by acting as a bridge between the client and the server. The application level proxy protects security interests by scrutinizing application layer data.
- The circuit-level proxy firewall authenticates the client, provides access to the server and relays the messages between them. It does not interpret application layer payload of the relayed messages.

- Firewall may be implemented on the gateway router that connects the private network to the Internet. More sophisticated firewall architecture may consist of a screened subnet (perimeter network) with one or more bastion hosts as proxies.
- Intrusion detection system (IDS) supports firewall by generating alarms when it detects abnormal behaviours of users or of traffic, or when it detects symptoms of an attack.
- Anomaly-based IDS looks for deviations in normal behaviour of the users and traffic by profiling their normal behaviour. Signature-based IDS has database of 'signatures' (or symptoms) of known attack types. The primary advantage of anomaly detection IDS is that there is chance of detecting previously unknown attacks.

Key Terms		
Anomaly-based IDS	Host-based IDS	Screened subnet
Application-level proxy firewall	Network-based IDS	Signature-based IDS
Bastion host	Packet filtering firewall	SOCKS proxy server
Circuit-level proxy firewall	Perimeter network	Stateful-inspection firewall

RECOMMENDED READING

Avoine, G., Junod, P. and Oechslin, P., *Computer System Security: Basic Concepts and Solved Exercises*, CRC Press, FL, USA, 2004.

Bragg, R., Phodes-Ousley, M., Strassberg, K., *Network Security*, Tata McGraw-Hill, New Delhi, 2004.

Douligeris, C. (Ed), Serpanos, D.N., *Network Security, Current Status and Future Directions*, IEEE Press, John Wiley & Sons, NJ, USA, 2007.

RFC 1928, *SOCKS Protocol Version 5*, IETF, 1996.

Rhee, M., *Internet Security,* John Wiley & Sons, West Sussex, UK, 2003.

SP800–94, *Guide to Intrusion Detection and Prevention Systems (IDPS)*, NIST, MD, USA, 2007.

Stallings, W., *Cryptography and Network Security*, Prentice-Hall of India, New Delhi, 2008.

Stamp, M., *Information Security, Principles and Practice*, John Wiley & Sons, NJ, USA, 2011.

Zwicky, Elizabeth D., Cooper, S., and Chapman, D.B., *Building Internet Firewalls*, O'Reilly, CA, USA, 2000.

PROBLEMS

1. Suppose it is desired that the packet filtering firewall should block all inbound TCP connections, but should permit all outbound TCP connections. How can this policy be implemented? (*Hint:* Flags field of TCP header.)

2. The scenario implemented in Problem 1, presents a problem for FTP protocol. FTP protocol needs two TCP connections. The PI (Protocol Interpreter) connection is set up by the FTP client. After setting up the PI connection, the client tells server its (client's) port number (say P) for the second connection, the DTP connection. Then the server sets up DTP (Data Transfer Process) connection to this port P. How can the packet filtering policy of Problem 1 be modified to allow outbound TCP connections for FTP? (*Hint:* The port number P can be restricted to a defined range of port numbers not used in the internal network. Alternatively the client can use 'passive' command.)

3. The well-known Telnet server port is TCP 23. In Figure 22.11, we want the firewall to block TCP connection request from the Internet or from subnet 2 to Telnet server H on subnet 1. But we would allow Telnet connections to subnet 2 from the Internet. Explain how to configure the packet filtering policies for the routers G and I.

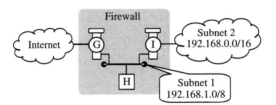

Figure 22.11 Problem 3.

4. Mr. Intern was engaged to configure the packet filtering firewall that allows only inbound and outbound email service to/from network X that has its mail server on IP address 192.168.0.1 (Figure 22.12). The email servers use well-known port number 25 and the client can have any port number > 1023. Mr. Intern comes up with the following filtering rules table (Table 22.5). Rules 1 and 2 permit any external client to access the internal mail server. Rules 3 and 4 permit the internal mail server to access any mail server on the Internet. The other IP packets are blocked.

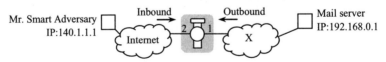

Figure 22.12 Problem 4.

TABLE 22.5 Problem 4

Rule	Interface of arrival	Source IP address	Source port	Destination IP address	Destination port	Protocol	Action
1	2	Any external	> 1023	192.168.0.1	25	TCP	Permit
2	1	192.168.0.1	25	Any external	> 1023	TCP	Permit
3	1	192.168.0.1	> 1023	Any external	25	TCP	Permit
4	2	Any external	25	192.168.0.1	> 1023	TCP	Permit
5	*	*		*	*	*	Block

The smart adversary at source <IP 140.1.1.1, TCP port 25> sends IP packet to destination <IP 192.168.0.1, TCP port 8000> of the internal mail server for connection establishment and succeeds. The adversary can thus attack other ports of the mail server.

(a) Which are the rules of the firewall table that permitted the adversary?

(b) We can prevent the adversarial attack by enforcing that mail server cannot initiate a TCP connection; only a client can. Modify the filtering rules table by adding ACK column to enforce this criterion.

(c) Is there any alternate of implementing the above criterion?

5. Suppose that the server and client exchange encrypted application data. The encryption key is known only to the server and the client. Which type of firewall (packet filtering, stateful inspection, application-level proxy or circuit-level proxy) will work with such packets? Justify your answer.

6. An example given in Section 22.4.1 of this chapter used the 'server access' behaviour as anomaly detection parameter. List any three other possible parameters that could define behavioural pattern.

7. In the example given in Section 22.4.1, the next set of observations reveal access pattern of Alice as <0.2, 0.1, 0.6, 0.1). Is this behaviour normal for Alice?

8. The firewall architecture, shown in Figure 22.13, consists of the following components:

(a) Web server at IP address 10.0.0.2 subnet 10.0.0.0/24.

(b) SMTP proxy at 192.168.10.25 on subnet 192.168.10.0/24.

(c) DNS proxy at 192.168.10.30 on subnet 192.168.10.0/24.

(d) HTTP proxy at 192.168.10.35 on subnet 192.168.10.0/24.

(e) Stateful inspection firewall in the gateway router G and packet filtering firewall in interior router I.

The web server is accessible from the internal network. Write down the filtering table of the outer stateful inspection firewall (G).

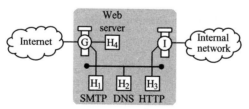

Figure 22.13 Problem 8.

23

Malware

The expression 'malware' is a general term for malicious software, which covers many kinds of undesirable programs that are threat to the security of computer systems. The threat has many forms, e.g. intrusion, data theft, data damage, loss of privacy, performance degradation, etc. We examine in this chapter various kinds of malware. We begin the chapter with broad classification of the malware. Viruses and worms constitute a large section of malware. Therefore, major part of this chapter is devoted to these two classes of malware. We introduce other important classes of malware thereafter. The focus throughout the chapter is on the mode of operation, propagation and the threat posed by malware.

23.1 CLASSIFICATION OF MALWARE

Malware can be subdivided into several different categories, although there is considerable overlap among the various types of malware. We will use the following classification:

Virus A virus is malware that requires another program to propagate from one system to another.

Worm A worm is like a virus except that it propagates by itself without the need of outside assistance.

Trojan horse A Trojan horse is software that has some unexpected and undesirable functionality hidden into it. For example, an innocent-looking game could do something malicious while the victim is playing.

Spyware Spyware is a type of malware that monitors keystrokes, steals data or files.

Rootkit Rootkit malware hides specific running processes or data from the operating system.

Backdoor Backdoor malware allows unauthorized access to a system.

Viruses and worms are the two categories that constitute major section of the malware. We describe these malware in the next two sections. The other categories are covered in the last section.

23.2 COMPUTER VIRUS

Like biological virus, computer virus is a piece of software that 'infects' a computer program by way of injecting a malicious code in that program. The malicious code carries set of instructions for making copies of the virus. Thereafter, the virus spreads to other concurrent programs in the infected computer and to the other computers through swappable media (pen drives, floppy disks) and through the network. For example, an email virus attaches itself to an email and spreads from one user to another.

Apart from replicating itself, a virus can destroy data, degrade system performance, display messages on the infected machine. A virus can even be a harmless virus. Virus is the earliest form of malware, and therefore, many malwares are classified as virus though they are not. *Brain* was the first virus that infected personal computers. It was discovered in 1986. It affects the computer by replacing the boot sector with a copy of the virus. The original boot sector is moved to another sector and is marked as bad sector.

23.2.1 Structure and Activation of a Virus

Structure of computer virus has three parts: infection vector, trigger mechanism and a payload. Infection vector is the mechanism for spreading the virus. Trigger mechanism determines how and when the virus is activated. The payload part of the virus performs the destructive operation, which may include data destruction, file deletion, display of insulting messages.

A virus is always attached or embedded in an executable program. When invoked, the infected program first executes the malicious code of the virus and the then the original code of the program. Thus a virus lies dormant until the infected program is invoked and when certain defined conditions (e.g. particular date and time) prevail.

We can define four phases of virus activation.

Dormant phase   During this stage the virus lies idle attached to an executable file.

Propagation phase   The virus starts propagating, that is, multiplying itself. It copies itself and places the copy into other programs or into certain system areas on the disk. The copy may not be identical; viruses often morph to evade detection. Each infected program will contain a clone of the virus, which multiplies further.

Triggering phase   A virus moves into this phase when it gets activated and the event it was waiting for occurs. The event can be defined in many ways. For example, a virus may be triggered on a particular date, or when the host program has been executed certain number of times. After it is triggered, the virus enters the execution phase.

Execution phase   The virus performs the function for which it was intended. The function may be harmless, such as a message on the screen, or damaging, such as the destruction of data files.

Most viruses are designed to take advantages of architectural weakness and design bugs of specific operating systems and their versions. Thus a virus designed for Windows 98 may not be effective in case of Windows NT.

23.2.2 Classification of Viruses

There can be several ways of virus classification. We present here the following two classifications (Figure 23.1):

Host based classification: This classification is based on the type of host that carries the virus.

- File-infector viruses
- Boot sector and master boot record viruses
- Macro viruses

Concealment strategy based classification: This classification is based on strategy used for concealing the virus.

- Encrypted viruses
- Stealth viruses
- Polymorphic viruses
- Metamorphic viruses

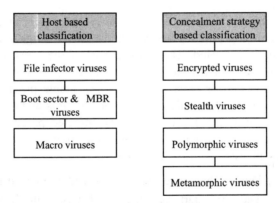

Figure 23.1 Virus classification.

A brief description of each classification-type is given below:

File-infector Virus

File-infector virus infects the executable files, e.g. files with extensions .exe and .com in MS Windows operating system. It is a memory resident virus and once it is loaded into the memory, it remains active until the computer is shut down. It infects other programs that are run when it is active. Win32.Sality.BK was a file-infecting virus that remained among the top ten malware infections in 2011 and 2012.

Boot Sector and Master Boot Record Virus

The boot sector is the first sector of a disk partition. It contains a bootstrapping code to load and launch the operating system installed on the disk. A boot-sector virus overwrites the boot strapping code and becomes memory resident when the user boots the computer from the disk. Every disk including swappable media (e.g. floppy, pen drive), bootable or unbootable, contains the boot-sector and is potential host for the boot sector viruses. If the infected floppy is in the drive while a computer is booting, the virus infects the system.

Master boot record (MBR) is the first sector of the partitioned disk. It points to the boot sector of an active partition. When the system is powered up, MBR points to the boot sector and the booting process starts. Master boot record virus overwrites the master boot record and saves the original record elsewhere. Michelangelo was an MBR and boot sector virus with a March 6th payload. It was discovered in 1991.

Viruses can be multipartite[1] and infect both the master boot record and the program files. Multipartite viruses are nasty because their removal requires cleaning of the master boot sector and the infected program files.

Macro Virus

Applications like MS Word, MS Excel, MS PowerPoint, MS Access have facility of embedding macro commands in the data files. These commands are executed whenever the data file is opened. The macro viruses infect the macros built into these files. Once the macro file is opened, the virus can infect other files opened by the application. A well-known example of a macro virus is the Melissa virus. It is an MS Word 97 macro virus that has a payload to email itself using MS Outlook.

Encrypted Virus

One method of evading signature detection[2] is to use simple encryption to encipher the body of the virus, leaving only the encryption module and a cryptographic key in cleartext. An encrypted virus creates a random encryption key and encrypts the remainder of the virus. The key is stored with the virus. When an infected program is invoked, the virus uses the stored random key to decrypt the virus. Once activated, the virus replicates with a different random key. Because the bulk of the virus is encrypted with a different key for each instance of infection, there is no constant bit pattern to observe. A signature-based virus scanner cannot directly detect the virus.

Stealth Virus

Virus detection software analyzes all the files and the memory of a computer to detect traces of a virus. Stealth virus modifies certain routines of the operating system in such a way that the virus becomes undetectable. Once modified, these routines show uninfected version of a file, even though the file is infected. *Brain* virus mentioned at the beginning of the section used this technique.

Polymorphic Virus

Polymorphic virus is capable of modifying itself after every infection so that its new replication is different from the original. To achieve this, the virus may randomly insert superfluous

---

1. Multipartite virus infects in multiple ways.
2. Signature detection is described in Section 23.2.3.

instructions or interchange the order of independent instructions. The virus code remains same functionally. The objective of the attacker is to evade detection by signature-based virus scanners.

Metamorphic Virus

Metamorphic virus is similar to polymorphic virus in the sense that its replication is different from the original. The difference is that a metamorphic virus rewrites itself completely in each replication, thereby increasing the difficulty of detection. A metamorphic virus may also change its behaviour as well. The longer the virus stays in a computer, the more sophisticated the replications are, making it increasingly hard for antivirus applications to detect, quarantine and disinfect.

23.2.3 Protection against Virus Attacks

Virus in a system can be a mere nuisance or it may be capable of causing massive damage to the system. Protection of a system against virus attack consists of three stages:

Detection stage	This stage determines whether a system is infected with a virus.
Identification stage	This stage identifies the virus.
Removal stage	The stage removes all traces of the virus from the system.

The removal stage may involve

- removal of virus from all the infected files and restoring the files to their original stage.
- quarantining the files that are suspected to be infected so that further spread of the virus is inhibited.
- deletion of the infected files that cannot be cleaned.

There are three general approaches for detecting and identifying viruses in a system.

- Signature detection
- Change detection
- Anomaly detection

We will briefly discuss each of these approaches and consider their relative advantages and limitations.

Signature Detection

Signature detection relies on finding a bit pattern, called signature, associated with a particular virus. The signature is like a fingerprint in that it can be used to detect and identify specific virus. For example, the signature used for the W32/Beast virus is 83EB 0274 EBOE 740A 81EB 0301 0000. To detect presence of this virus, we can search for this signature in all files on a system.

Signature detection is by far the most popular virus detection method. Some of its advantages and limitations are as given below:

- Signature detection is highly effective on virus that is known and for which a common signature can be extracted.

- It places a minimal burden on users and administrators, since all that is required is to keep signature files up to date and periodically scan for viruses.
- A major limitation of signature detection is that signature files keep becoming larger. The number of signatures can be hundreds of thousands of signatures, which can render signature scanning process slow.
- The signature files must be kept up to date, since we can only detect known signatures. Even a slight variant of a known virus might be missed.
- A compressed or encrypted file can make signature detection more complicated.

Change Detection

Since malware must reside somewhere, an unexpected change somewhere in a system, indicates possibility of an infection. That is, if we detect that a file has changed, it may be infected with a virus. One way of detecting changes is to use hash functions. We compute hashes of all files on a system and securely store these hash values. The hash values are recomputed at regular intervals and compared with the stored values. If a file has changed—as it will in the case of a virus infection—we will find that the re-computed hash value does not match the previously stored hash value.

The major advantages and limitations of this approach are given below:

- There are virtually no false negatives in this approach. That is, if a file has been infected, we will detect change in the hash value.
- Another major advantage is that we can detect previously unknown malware.
- Files of a system often change and as a result there will be many false positives, which places a heavy burden on users and administrators.
- If a virus is inserted into a file that changes often, it will be more likely to slip through a change detection regimen.
- If a suspicious change is detected, a careful analysis of log files may be required to decide if the change is unexpected. In the end, it may become necessary to fall back to signature detection.

Anomaly Detection

The third approach is anomaly detection, where the goal is to detect any unusual or virus-like or potentially malicious activity or behaviour. For example, monitored behaviour can include the following parameters:

- Attempts to open, view, delete or modify files.
- Modifications to the logic of executable files and system settings.
- Scripting of emails with executable content.
- Attempts to format disk drives, and other irreversible disk operations.

We discussed similar idea for intrusion detection system in Chapter 22. The fundamental challenge with anomaly detection lies in determining what is normal and what is unusual, and being able to distinguish between the two. Another serious difficulty is that the definition of normal can change, and the system must adapt to such changes, or it will likely overwhelm users with false alarms.

The major advantage of anomaly detection is that there is some hope of detecting previously unknown viruses. Anomaly detection, however, is not robust enough as on date to be used as a stand-alone detection system, so it is usually combined with a signature detection system.

23.3   WORMS

A worm is like a virus except its two distinguishing features. It is autonomous program and does not need a host to replicate itself. Secondly, it has capability to replicate itself in another machine using network. A worm can live independently in a system or inside another file (e.g. an MS Word file), but in that case the whole file is considered as the worm. We drew parallel between biological virus and computer virus in the last section. Worm is like unwanted biological bacterium cell that has its independent existence.

When a system is infected, the worm replicates, propagates and usually performs some unwanted functions depending on its type. It could, for example, implant Trojan horse program which contains hidden malicious functions. Just like its sibling, virus, a worm has dormant phase, propagation phase, triggering phase, and execution phase. To propagate itself a worm makes use of network based applications and services.

- A worm may mail a copy of itself to other systems as an attachment. When the attachment is viewed by the recipient of the mail, its code is executed and replicated in the new system.
- A worm may log onto a remote system as a user and then uses commands to copy itself from one system to the other.
- A worm may carry out port scan[3] to identify the prospective victims.

Some of the worms that appeared during past few years are *LoveLetter* (2000), *CodeRed* (2001), *Nimda* (2001), *BugBear* (2002), *Blaster* (2003), *SQL Slammer (2003)*, *KamaSutra* (2006).

- The *LoveLetter* worm appears as an email with the subject 'I love you' and with attachment in visual basic script. It executes itself when the user opens the email attachment. Then it sends copies of itself to the email addresses it finds in the address book of MS Outlook. Besides replication, it replaces media files on the disk and modifies the opening page of Microsoft Internet Explorer with the intent to capture passwords.
- The *CodeRed* exploits a security hole in the Microsoft Internet Information Server (IIS) to penetrate and spread. It probes random IP addresses to spread to other hosts. It then initiates a DOS attack by flooding the victim with packets from numerous hosts. The worm reactivates periodically. The *CodeRed* worm infected nearly 360,000 servers in 14 hours.

Since worm propagates through network, it can cause large-scale global damage. Therefore, the protection against worms is based on the following approaches:

- Detection of worms resident in a system using signature-based worm scanning.

---

3. See Chapter 21.

- Containment of worm propagation through the network.
- Detection and limiting the impact of a network attack generated by a worm.

Let us briefly examine some of the defense techniques used against worms and worm-attacks.

Signature-based worm scan: This approach is similar to the one used for virus scan. Each worm is identified by its signature which is used to prevent worm from entering/leaving a network/host and for its removal. As in the case of signature-based virus scan, this approach may not be effective against polymorphic worms.

Threshold Random Walk (TRW) scan: To propagate itself, a worm resident in a host machine carries out port scanning picking up different destination addresses. The manner in which the addresses are picked up for port scanning is indicative of the type of the infecting worm.   For example, *Blaster* worm scans port numbers picking up destination addresses sequentially, *CodeRed* worm picks up addresses randomly, and *Nimda* worm is biased towards local addresses. TRW exploits the pattern in picking destinations to detect presence of a worm in host that is generating port scanning traffic.

Worm containment by filtering: In this approach, content of a message is analyzed to determine if it is carrying a worm code or control and data flow structures that suggest presence of a worm in the end systems. If it is so, the message is filtered.

Worm containment by rate limiting and halting: This approach limits the rate of port-scanning traffic from an infected host. Typically port-scanning traffic has high connection failure rate. When such activity is detected on the network, rate-limiting can be invoked to restrict the number of new machines a host can connect to in a given time-window. As an alternative approach, the outgoing connection attempts are blocked when a threshold is exceeded in the outgoing connection rate.

Figure 23.2 shows Proactive Worm Containment (PWC) scheme for containment of worm propagation based on above concepts. Each host has implementation of PWC agent that monitors the worm related activities. The centralized worm management system consists of PWC manager, the security manager and signature extractor.

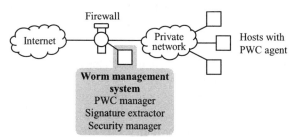

Figure 23.2   Proactive worm containment (PWC).

The PWC agent in each host monitors outgoing traffic for port scan activity, determined by surge in UDP or TCP connection attempts to remote hosts and connection failure rate. If port scan activity is suspected, the PWC agent

- issues an alert to local system,
- blocks all outgoing connection attempts, and
- transmits the alert to the PWC manager.

When the PWC manager receives an alert, it alerts all other PWC agents. When a PWC agent receives the alert from the PWC manager, decides whether to ignore the alert or to proactively initiate action for containment of worm propagation. This decision is based on its own traffic analysis. If it concludes that it might be infected, it also blocks all outgoing connection attempts from the alerted port. All the PWC agents that have blocked the traffic continue monitoring the connection attempts, until the rate of outgoing connection attempts drops below the threshold, at which time the agents remove the block.

Meanwhile, the signature extractor function carries out signature analysis for detecting worms. When a new worm is detected, the security manager sends the signature to the firewall to filter out copies of the worm. The PWC manager sends the signature to PWC agents to identify the infection and disable the worm.

23.4 OTHER MALWARE

In this section we introduce the following classes of malware:

- Trojan horse
- Spyware
- Rootkit
- Backdoor

The objective is to become familiar with their mode of operation and the threat posed by them.

Trojan Horse

A Trojan horse[4] is a stand-alone program that has or appears to have some useful purpose, but it contains hidden malicious code. When the user executes the program, the malicious code performs some unwanted or harmful function. Some typical examples of malicious functions carried out by a Trojan horse are given below:

- A Trojan horse program, when executed, may change the invoking user's file permissions so that the files are readable by any user.
- A Trojan horse may insert additional code into certain programs as they are compiled. For example, it may create a backdoor in the login program that permits the author of the Trojan horse to log on to the system using a special password.
- A Trojan horse may carry other malicious programs (e.g. spyware, rootkit) as its payload and install them when it is executed.

---

4. In Greek mythology, Trojan horse was used by the Greeks during their siege of Troy. A giant hollow wooden horse was constructed and thirty of the most valiant Greek heroes concealed themselves in it. The Trojans dragged the horse into the city. The Greeks emerged from the horse that night and opened the city gates to the Greek army.

The Trojan horse may be well-known software or a useful software tool or game that appears harmless. The author of Trojan horse usually induces users to run the program by placing it in a common directory and naming it such that it appears to be a useful utility program or application. It must be remembered that all Trojan horses require execution by the user, and therefore, they do not spread as fast as worms.

Spyware

A spyware program gathers information on the infected computer and sends it to the attacker. Information can be gathered in several ways, e.g. by logging key strokes, recording the visited websites, scanning the local disks and so on. The spyware may be used to collect confidential data (e.g. passwords, credit card numbers, login ids, etc.) or to collect commercial data (e.g. user's interest areas) in order to send targeted advertisements. As on date spyware is a major threat to user's right to privacy.

Spyware usually infect a machine through the security holes in the web browsers. A malicious website contains a code that attacks the browser of the visiting user and forces download and installation of the spyware. Spyware can also come embedded in a Trojan horse, e.g. a game or bundled with a software which careless user downloads without going through the license conditions. The user installs the legitimate software with the bundled spyware.

Rootkit

A rootkit is a malware designed to hide the specific running processes or programs from the operating system. The term rootkit is a concatenation of 'root', the name of the privileged account on Unix operating system, and the word 'kit', which refers to the software tool. Typical use of the rootkit is to hide a backdoor on the compromised system, but a rootkit with its payload can serve several other malicious objectives.

- Provide an attacker with full access via a backdoor, permitting unauthorized access to, for example, steal or falsify documents.
- Conceal other malware, notably password-stealing key loggers and computer viruses.
- Configure the compromised machine as a zombie[5] computer for attacks on other computers.

Rootkit installation can be automated, or an attacker can install it once he gets root or administrator's access. Once installed, it becomes possible to hide the intrusion, since a rootkit may be able to subvert the software that is intended to find it.

Backdoor

A backdoor is a program that allows remote access to a system bypassing the authentication control and without the knowledge of its administrator. The backdoors open a predefined TCP or UDP port for the remote attacker and wait for his commands. The more sophisticated backdoor sends an email message with IP address and the port number to signal that it is ready to receive the command. In this case, the port number can be arbitrarily selected, which renders the detection of the backdoor even more difficult. Some backdoors use ICMP request

---

5. See *Distributed Denial of Service* (*DDoS*) attacks, Chapter 21.

and reply packets to communicate with the attacker. Examples of backdoors are *Back Orifice 2000* (1999), *Subseven* (1999) and *NetBus* (1998).

23.5 SUMMING UP

In this chapter, our focus was on security of end systems against the threats posed by malicious software, or the malware. We discussed the mode of operation, replication, and propagation besides the security threats of the various types of malware as summarized in Table 23.1.

TABLE 23.1 Characteristic Features of Various Malware Types

Malware category	Description
Virus	Virus is a malicious code that resides in a program and spreads when the host is executed.
Worm	A worm, unlike, virus is autonomous and does not need a host program. It propagates on its own across the network.
Trojan horse	A Trojan horse is apparently a useful program but hides a malicious code, which gets executed when the program is run.
Spyware	Spyware is a type of malware that monitors keystrokes, steals data or files. Usually it comes bundled with free software downloaded from the web.
Rootkit	A rootkit is malware designed to hide the specific running processes or programs from the operating system.
Backdoor	A backdoor is a program that allows remote access to a system bypassing the authentication control and without the knowledge of its administrator.

Key Terms		
Anomaly detection	Malware	Spyware
Backdoor	Master boot record virus	Stealth virus
Boot sector virus	Metamorphic virus	Trojan horse
Change detection	Polymorphic virus	Virus
Encrypted virus	Proactive worm containment	Worm
File infector virus	Rootkit	
Macro virus	Signature detection	

RECOMMENDED READING

Avoine, G., Junod, P. and Oechslin, P., *Computer System Security: Basic Concepts and Solved Exercises*, CRC Press, FL, USA, 2004.

Bishop, D., *Computer Security: Art and Science*, Addison-Wesley, Boston, USA, 2005.

Stallings, W., *Cryptography and Network Security*, Prentice-Hall of India, New Delhi, 2008.

Stamp, M., *Information Security, Principles and Practice*, John Wiley & Sons, NJ, USA, 2011.

PROBLEMS

1. A variant of W32/Beagle worm appears as compressed and encrypted attachment to email. The password is given in the body of the email. If the recipient opens the attached file using the password, the worm infects the computer and then spreads to the next victim chosen from the address book of the current victim. Why is the compressed file encrypted when password is provided in the body of the message?

2. Fred Cohen in 1986 proved that it is impossible to create a program that could decide with absolute certainty, if a file is infected or not. Consider that we have a program $V(x)$ that detects if x is a virus, i.e., it outputs TRUE if x is virus and FALSE if x is not a virus. Suppose one builds the following program P:

```
Program P : =
    { ...
    main-program : =
        {if V(P) then goto next :
            else spread;
        }
next :
    }
```

The module named spread replicates the virus in the executable programs in the memory. Determine if program V can correctly decide whether x is a virus.

3. A mail server has antivirus software installed on it to detect and remove the malware. It also allows blocking/allowing of certain types of files attached to emails from the security point of view. The administrator specifies the list of file extensions (e.g. `.exe`, `.vbs`, `.bat`, etc.) to be blocked. From security point of view what is the flaw in the administrator's approach?

4. CIH virus appeared in 1998. It infects files with extension `.exe` on Windows 95/98 platform. Mr. Smart Administrator manages a network of computers using Windows 95 and Windows NT. AS CIH infects Windows 95/98, should Mr. Smart Administrator run antivirus on all the computers or leave out Windows NT platform?

5. CIH virus of Problem 4 also corrupts the BIOS in certain cases and erases first 2048 sectors of the hard disk. After the suspected attack of CIH, Mr. Smart Administrator notices that the mail server displays message 'Insert a bootable floppy disk' while booting. The web server, on the other hand, does not boot or display any message. Which data is corrupted in these servers?

Appendix A1

Prime Numbers, Primitive Roots, Irreducible Polynomials

- List of prime numbers (P) below than 1000.
- List of the first primitive root (PR) modulo the prime.

P	2	3	5	7	11	13	17	19	23	29	31	37	41	43	47	53	59	61	67	71	73	79	83	89	97
PR	1	2	2	3	2	2	3	2	5	2	3	2	6	3	5	2	2	2	2	2	2	5	3	2	5

P	101	103	107	109	113	127	131	137	139	149	151	157	163	167	173	179	181	191	193	197	199
PR	2	5	2	6	2	3	2	3	2	2	6	5	2	5	2	2	2	19	5	2	3

P	211	223	227	229	233	239	241	251	257	263	269	271	277	281	283	293
PR	2	3	2	6	3	7	7	6	3	5	2	6	5	3	3	2

P	307	311	313	317	331	337	347	349	353	359	367	373	379	383	389	397
PR	5	17	10	2	3	10	2	2	2	7	6	2	2	5	2	5

P	401	409	419	421	431	433	439	443	449	457	461	463	467	479	487	491	499
PR	3	21	2	2	7	5	15	2	3	13	2	3	2	13	3	2	7

P	503	509	521	523	541	547	557	563	569	571	577	587	593	599
PR	5	2	3	2	2	2	2	2	3	3	5	2	3	7

P	601	607	613	617	619	631	641	643	647	653	659	661	673	677	683	691
PR	7	3	2	3	2	3	3	11	5	2	2	2	5	2	5	3

P	701	709	719	727	733	739	743	751	757	761	769	773	787	797
PR	2	2	11	5	6	3	5	3	2	6	11	2	2	2

P	809	811	821	823	827	829	839	853	857	859	863	877	881	883	887
PR	3	3	2	3	2	2	11	2	3	2	5	2	3	2	5

P	907	911	919	929	937	941	947	953	967	971	977	983	991	997
PR	2	17	7	3	5	2	2	3	5	2	3	5	6	7

- List of irreducible polynomials of degree 6 and less.

Degree	x^6	x^5	x^4	x^3	x^2	x^1	x^0	Degree	x^6	x^5	x^4	x^3	x^2	x^1	x^0
1						1	0	5		1	1	0	1	1	1
1						1	1	5		1	1	1	0	1	1
2					1	1	1	5		1	1	1	1	0	1
3				1	0	1	1	6	1	0	0	0	0	1	1
3				1	1	0	1	6	1	0	0	0	1	0	1
4			1	0	0	1	1	6	1	0	0	1	0	0	1
4			1	1	0	0	1	6	1	0	1	0	1	1	1
4			1	1	1	1	1	6	1	0	1	1	0	1	1
5		1	0	0	1	0	1	6	1	1	0	0	0	0	1
5		1	0	1	0	0	1	6	1	1	0	1	1	0	1
5		1	0	1	1	1	1	6	1	1	1	0	0	1	1

Appendix A2

Birthday Problems

A2.1 PROBLEM DEFINITION

Assume that we have

- a message generator that is truly random in its construction of messages, and
- a hash function $h(x)$ that can generate N different digests for various input messages, and each digest is equally probable.

We create a pool of k ($k \leq N$) random messages using the message generator. We impose the restriction that $k \leq N$ because if $k > N$, at least two messages will have same digest. Now, we pose the following questions:

1. What is the 'likelihood' that the pool contains at least one message x for which digest $h(x)$ is equal to a given value H?
2. What is the 'likelihood' that there is at least one pair of messages x and x' in the pool having same digest, i.e., $h(x) = h(x')$?
3. What is the 'likelihood' of having same digest of at least two messages x and x' in two different pools?

When probability of an event is greater than 0.5, we say that the event is 'likely' to happen.

First Birthday Problem

Since all the digests are equally probable, probability that $h(x) = $ H is $1/N$. Therefore,

Probability that $h(x) \neq $ H $= 1 - 1/N$
Probability that all the k messages have $h(x) \neq $ H $= (1 - 1/N)^k$

This can be simplified considering that $(1 - a) \leq e^{-a}$ for all a ≥ 0. Thus

Probability that all the k messages have $h(x) \neq $ H $\leq (e^{-1/N})^k$
Probability p that at least one message has $h(x) = $ H $\geq 1 - e^{-k/N}$
We can now determine k for $p \geq 1/2$.

$$1 - e^{-k/N} = 1/2 \Rightarrow k = N \ln 2 \Rightarrow k = 0.69N$$

Thus, we are likely to find a message with digest $h(x)$ equal to a given value in a pool of $0.69N$ messages, if hash can take N values.

415

Second Birthday Problem

We first determine probability of *not* having any pair of messages with same digest in the pool. If H is the digest of the first message we pick up from the pool, the second message we pick up can have any of the rest $N - 1$ digests. Thus

Probability of 2nd message with any of the rest $N - 1$ digests $= (N - 1)/N$

Probability of 3rd message with any of the rest $N - 2$ digests $= (N - 2)/N$

Probability of k th message with any of the rest $N - (k -1)$ digests $= (N - k + 1)/N$

Probability of all distinct digests $= [1 - 1/N] \times [1 - 2/N] \times [1 - (k - 1)/N]$

This can be simplified considering that $(1 - a) \le e^{-a}$ for all $a \ge 0$. Thus

Probability of having all distinct hash values $\le e^{-1/N}e^{-2/N}...e^{-(k - 1)/N} = e^{-k(k - 1)/2N}$

Probability p of at least a pair messages having the same hash values in the pool of k messages $\ge 1 - e^{-k(k - 1)/2N}$

We can now determine k for $p \ge 1/2$.

$$1 - e^{-k(k - 1)/2N} = 1/2 \Rightarrow k(k - 1) = 2N \ln 2$$

Assuming k is large compared to 1, we get

$$k = 1.18 \sqrt{N}$$

Third Birthday Problem

Let us say that we have two pools A and B, each having k messages. A message in pool A has digest H_1.

Probability that none of k messages of pool B has digest $H_1 = (1 - 1/N)^k$

Probability that none of k messages of pool B has digest equal to that of any message in pool A $= (1 - 1/N)^{k*k}$

Probability p that a message in pool A has the same digest as another message in pool B $= 1 - (1 - 1/N)^{k*k}$

This can be simplified considering $(1 - a) \le e^{-a}$ for all $a \ge 0$. Thus

Probability p that a message in pool A has the same digest as another message in pool B $\ge 1 - e^{-k*k/N}$

We can now determine k for $p \ge 1/2$.

$$1 - e^{-k*k/N} = 1/2 \Rightarrow k^2 \ge N \ln 2 \Rightarrow k \ge 0.83 \sqrt{N}$$

If the digest consists of n-bits, and if all the bit combinations are equally probable, $N = 2^n$. We can summarize the results obtained for the three birthday problems for $N = 2^n$ as below.

Number of messages required to be generated for likelihood of getting

- a message having a given hash value $= 0.69 \times 2^n$
- a pair of messages having same hash value $= 1.18 \times 2^{n/2}$
- a pair of messages having same hash value in two different pools $= 0.83 \times 2^{n/2}$

Note that pre-image and collision resistance of a hash function is determined by the size of digest.

Appendix A3

Networking Protocols for User Authentication

A3.1 POINT-TO-POINT PROTOCOL (PPP)

For dial-in access to the Internet or an intranet[1], authentication service is provided by a network access server (NAS)[2]. NAS has database of users with their authentication data. Figure A3.1(a) shows typical implementation of an intranet with a network access server (NAS). Remote users access the NAS through PSTN connections using Point-to-Point Protocol (PPP). PPP is a data link protocol (layer-2) that can carry authentication data of the user. It is specified in RFC 1661, *The Point-to-Point Protocol (PPP).*

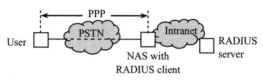

NAS : Network access server
PSTN: Public switched telephone network
RADIUS : Remote authentication dial-in user service

(a) Dial-in remote access   (b) Layered architecture

Figure A3.1 PPP protocol for remote dial-in access.

If the number of users is large, a separate security server, called RADIUS[3] server, is provided. The NAS simply forwards the information from the users to the RADIUS server which completes the authentication process.

Apart from its basic function as data link protocol, PPP performs the following functions required for remote access:

- It configures the layer-3 network protocol, e.g. IP.

---

1. Intranet is a private network based on IP technology.
2. RFC 2881, *Network Access Server Requirements Next Generation (NASREQNG), NAS Model*, IETF, 2000.
3. RADIUS: Remote Authentication Dial-In User Service.

- It carries out endpoint authentication using the following protocols:
  - Password Authentication Protocol (PAP)
  - Challenge-Handshake Authentication Protocol (CHAP)
  - Extensible Authentication Protocol (EAP)

A3.1.1 Layered Architecture of PPP

As shown in Figure A3.1(b), PPP is a layer-2 data link protocol. It can provide service to several network layer protocols, e.g. IP, IPX, NetBios, AppleTalk. The physical layer interface can be a modem interface (EIA 232-D) or high speed data link, e.g. E1 (G.703).

For other access network technologies, Point-to-Point Protocol over Ethernet (PPPoE)[4] and Point-to-Point Protocol over ATM Adaptation Layer 5 (PPPoA)[5] have been defined.

A3.1.2 Component Protocols of PPP

PPP has two component protocols, Link Control Protocol (LCP), and Network Control Protocol (NCP). These protocols perform the following functions:

- LCP manages the establishment, monitoring and termination of the data link. During link establishment, LCP negotiates authentication protocol (PAP, CHAP, EAP) and carries out authentication of the endpoint using the negotiated protocol.
- NCP is used for negotiating the operational parameters of the network layer protocol, e.g. IP address, default gateway, header compression, etc.

A3.1.3 PPP Frame Format

Figure A3.2 shows the format of a PPP frame. It is based on the format of HDLC frame. PPP frame has one additional field, the protocol field.

Flag (**1 octet**):   It identifies start and the end of a PPP frame. Its value is 011111110.

Address (**1 octet**):   Address field is all 1s. This being point-to-point link, the address field is not significant.

Control (**1 octet**):   Control field is 00000011 indicating that the frame is unnumbered information (UI) frame.

Protocol (**2 octets**):   It identifies the protocol encapsulated in the data field. For example, if the information field contains IP datagram, protocol field is 0×0021.

Information (**Variable**):   It contains the protocol as identified by the protocol field.

FCS (**2 Octets**):   Frame check sequence (FCS) contains CRC[6] for error detection.

---

4. RFC 2516, A Method for Transmitting PPP over Ethernet (PPPoE), IETF, 1999.
5. RFC 2364, *PPP Over AAL5,* IETF, 1998.
6. CRC: Cyclic Redundancy Check.

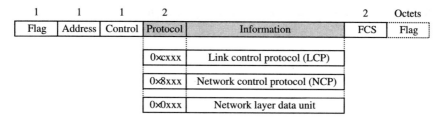

Figure A3.2   Format of PPP frame.

A3.1.4   PPP Operation

PPP operation is spread over five phases, starting from the link establishment and ending at link termination. Each phase may consist of several steps.

***Phase* 1:**   During this phase, LCP negotiates the link parameters (e.g. maximum size of information field) and other options (e.g. authentication protocol—PAP).

***Phase* 2:**   LCP implements the negotiated link parameters and options in this phase. Authentication of user takes place using the authentication protocol negotiated in phase 1. If authentication is successful, PPP continues with phase 3, else the link is terminated by LCP.

***Phase* 3:**   In phase 3, NCP is used for configuring the network layer protocol. For each network layer protocol, there is different NCP, e.g. IPCP (IP control protocol) is used for configuring IP. IPCP configures IP address of the remote device, default gateway address, and several other parameters.

***Phase* 4:**   Exchange of encapsulated data units of the network layer (e.g. IP datagrams) takes place in this phase.

***Phase* 5:**   Termination of the link is carried out using LCP in this phase. It can be initiated by either end of the point-to-point link.

We will not go into description of these phases. In the following sections, we will focus only on user authentication which is carried out in the phase 2 using PAP, CHAP or EAP.

A3.2   PASSWORD AUTHENTICATION PROTOCOL (PAP)[7]

Password Authentication Protocol (PAP) is a simple two-way handshake that establishes identity of an entity. It is carried in the PPP frame. The protocol field of PPP frame is 0xc023 for PAP (Figure A3.2).

A3.2.1   PAP Format

The encapsulated PAP consists of the following fields (Figure A3.3):

---

7.   RFC 1334, PPP Authentication Protocols, IETF, 1992.

***Code* (1 *octet*):** There are three PAP message-types, each identified by the type code.

Authentication-request	Code 1
Authenticate-ack	Code 2
Authenticate-nak	Code 3

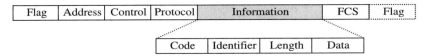

Figure A3.3 PAP/CHAP/EAP message format.

***Identifier* (1 *octet*):** It is used for matching requests and responses.

***Length* (2 *octets*):** It indicates full length of the PAP message from code field to the data field.

***Data* (*Variable*):** It contains data pertaining to the message. For example, this field carries user id and password data in cleartext, if the code is 1.

A3.2.2 PAP Operation

The protocol operation has two messages [Figure A3.4(a)].

- After link establishment the user sends authentication-request (code 1) containing his user id and password in cleartext.
- NAS verifies the password from its database against the user id.
  - If the password is acceptable, NAS responds with authentication-ack (code 2).
  - If the password fails on verification, NAS responds with authentication-nak (code 3) and terminates the data link.

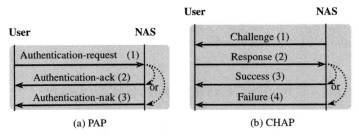

Figure A3.4 PAP and CHAP operation.

A3.3 CHALLENGE-HANDSHAKE AUTHENTICATION PROTOCOL (CHAP)

The Challenge-Handshake Authentication Protocol (CHAP) is used to authenticate the end user in a three-way handshake. CHAP is international standard as specified in RFC 1994.

A3.3.1   CHAP Format

CHAP messages are encapsulated in PPP frame and are identified by the protocol field which has the value $0 \times c223$ (Figure A3.2). The format of CHAP messages is similar to PAP messages (Figure A3.3). The CHAP code field has the following values:

Challenge	Code 1
Response	Code 2
Success	Code 3
Failure	Code 4

A3.3.2   CHAP Operation

The protocol operation has three messages [Figure A3.4(b)].

- After link establishment, NAS sends challenge (code 1) message containing challenge identifier I, a random number R, id of NAS.
- The user computes hash $H = h(I \| S \| R)$, where S is the shared secret between the user and the NAS. The user sends his response (code 2) message consisting of [I, R, H].
- NAS verifies the hash H and responds with either success (code 3) or failure (code 4) message.

A3.4   EXTENSIBLE AUTHENTICATION PROTOCOL (EAP)

The Extensible Authentication Protocol (EAP) is a general protocol for PPP authentication. It supports multiple authentication mechanisms. It also permits the use of a 'back-end' RADIUS server which actually implements the various authentication mechanisms, while the NAS merely acts as 'pass through' for the authentication messages. It is specified in RFC 3748, *PPP Extensible Authentication Protocol (EAP)*.

A3.4.1   EAP Format

EAP messages are encapsulated in PPP frame and are identified by the protocol field which has the value $0 \times c227$ (Figure A3.2). The format of EAP messages is similar PAP/CHAP messages (Figure A3.3). The EAP code field has the following values:

Request	Code 1
Response	Code 2
Success	Code 3
Failure	Code 4

The Request and Response messages are further qualified by a Type field (Figure A3.5). The type field specifies the request and response. Note that EAP supports password (as in PAP) or challenge-response (as in CHAP) or token card[8] for authentication.

---

8. Token card authentication systems require use of a token card which can be a physical card or its software implementation. They are based on challenge-response authentication. When the user receives challenge on his screen, he uses the token card to generate encrypted response which is returned to the NAS.

Identity	Type 1
Notification	Type 2
Nak (Response only)	Type 3
MD5-Challenge	Type 4
One-Time Password	Type 5
Generic Token Card	Type 6

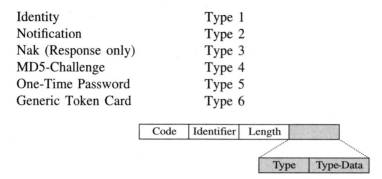

Figure A3.5   Format of EAP Request and Response messages.

***Identity* (1):**   It is used to query the identity of the user.

***Notification* (2):**   It used to send a message from the NAS to the user.

***Nak* (3):**   It is used only for response when the authentication type specified by NAS is unacceptable to the user.

***MD5-challenge* (4):**   It is analogous to CHAP. The request message contains the challenge value for the user. The response message from the user contains MD5 transformation of the challenge.

***One-time password* (5)[9]:**   The request message from NAS contains the one-time password challenge (sequence number and a seed). The user generates one-time password using Lamport's scheme (section 13.3.3) and sends it as response to the NAS.

***Generic token card* (6):**   The request from NAS contains a displayable message (challenge) for the user. The response from the user contains the encrypted message generated by the token card.

A3.4.2   EAP Operation

Typical operation of EAP is as follows (Figure A3.6):

- NAS sends one or more Requests (code 1) to authenticate the user entity. The Request has a type field to indicate what is being requested. Examples of Request types include user identity (Type -1), MD5-challenge, One-time passwords, etc.
- The user entity sends a Response in reply to each Request. As with the Request, the Response contains a type field which corresponds to the type field of the Request.
- NAS ends the authentication phase with a Success or Failure message.

---

9. RFC 2289, A One-Time Password System, IETF, 1998.

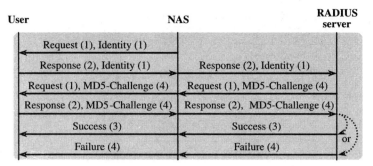

Figure A3.6 EAP operation.

If back-end RADIUS server is provided, authentication is carried out by the RADIUS server. The NAS merely passes through the authentication exchange. RADIUS is a client-server application protocol that runs over UDP. RADIUS client is implemented on the NAS. The RADIUS server provides authorization (user's entitlement) and accounting (usage) services in addition to authentication service.

A3.5 TUNNELLING PROTOCOLS

The dial-in access as shown in Figure A3.1 is a costly proposition, if the remote user is in different city or country. The public Internet can provide a cost-effective alternative to long distance PSTN call. Figure A3.7 shows the basic scheme.

- The remote user connects to the Internet through local PSTN or the access network of the ISP (Internet Service Provider). PPP over Ethernet (PPPoE) or PPP over ATM (PPPoA) is used depending on the type of the access network.
- The ISP implements NAS that provides logical termination point of the PPP link from the user.
- The layer 2 PPP frames are carried in a tunnel across the Internet. Layer 2 Tunnelling Protocol (L2TP) specified in RFC 2661 is used for this purpose.
- The tunnel endpoints are L2TP Access Concentrator (LAC) and L2TP Network Server (LNS). LAC is implemented in the NAS of the ISP and LNS is implanted in the security server of the intranet. The tunnel may be established either by LAC (for incoming calls) or by LNS (for outgoing calls).
- L2TP frames are carried in a UDP datagram. Well-known UDP 1701 port is used for this purpose. Figure A3.7(b) shows the structure of IP packet carrying PPP frame in an L2TP tunnel.
- The authentication process largely remains same as explained earlier. It includes creation of tunnel if it does not already exist.

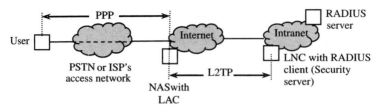

(a) L2TP tunnel over the Internet

IP header	UDP header	L2TP header	PPP frame

(b) Structure of IP packet carrying PPP frame in L2TP tunnel

Figure A3.7   PPP over Internet using L2TP.

RECOMMENDED READING

Kaeo, M., *Designing Network Security*, Pearson Education, New Delhi, 2004.

RFC 1334, PPP *Authentication Protocols*, IETF, 1992.

RFC 1661, *The Point-to-Point Protocol (PPP)*, IETF, 1994.

RFC 1994, *Challenge Handshake Authentication Protocol (CHAP)*, IETF, 1996.

RFC 1998, *A One-Time Password System*, IETF, 1998.

RFC 2364, *PPP Over AAL5*, IETF, 1998.

RFC 2516, *A Method for Transmitting PPP over Ethernet (PPPoE)*, IETF, 1999.

RFC 2661, *Layer Two Tunneling Protocol "L2TP"*, IETF, 1999.

RFC 2881, *Network Access Server Requirements Next Generation (NASREQNG), NAS Model*, IETF, 2000.

RFC, 3748, *PPP Extensible Authentication Protocol (EAP)*, IETF, 2004.

Glossary

Abelian group: A commutative group is also called abelian group.

Access control: A security mechanism that protects against unauthorized or unwanted access to a network or resource.

Access point (AP): In wireless LAN, an entity that contains one station (STA) and provides access to the distribution services, via the wireless medium for associated STAs.

Active attack: An attack that disrupts a service, communication, modifies the data or harms the system.

Additive cipher: An encryption scheme where ciphertext is addition of plaintext and the key.

Additive inverse: Two numbers a and b of $Z_n = \{0, 1, 2, \ldots, n - 1\}$ are additive inverse of one another if $(a + b) \bmod n = 0$.

Affine cipher: A cipher that combines additive and multiplicative encryption components.

Algebraic structure: It has a set of elements and operations that are defined over elements of the set. Group, ring and field are examples of algebraic structures.

Associative law: A binary operation $\bullet$ is said to satisfy associative law if $(a \bullet b) \bullet c = a \bullet (b \bullet c)$.

Asymmetric-key encryption: A cryptosystem in which the encryption and decryption keys are different.

Authentication: A security service that verifies the integrity of message content and the source of a message.

Authentication header (AH): It is one of the two protocols of IPsec that provides verification of integrity of an IP packet.

Authentication server: One of the two components of KDC (key distribution centre), which authenticates the users.

Authenticator: Authenticator is appended to message to enable the receiver to verify that the message is authentic.

Base64: See *Radix64*.

Binary operation: Mathematical operation involving two inputs and one output.

Birthday problems: Classical probabilistic problems of having a given birthday in a set of people.

Blind signature: A digital signature scheme wherein a message is signed without revealing the contents of the message to the signer. The scheme can be used, for example, for notarizing a message.

Block: A group of bits treated as a unit.

Block chaining: A procedure used in block encryption that makes the encrypted output function of current plaintext block and of previous encrypted block.

Block cipher: A cipher that encrypts a block of bits as one unit.

Broadcast: A method of delivering a packet to every host on a particular network.

Brute force attack: Attack that involves trying all possible key values to find the cipher key.

CA (Certification authority): An entity that signs security certificates, thereby promising that the public key contained in the certificate belongs to the entity named in the certificate.

Certificate: A digitally signed document that certifies the name and public key of an entity. It is used for distributing public keys.

Challenge-response authentication: An authentication method in which the claimant proves his identity by transforming the challenge using the secret he knows.

Chinese remainder theorem (CRT): A method of solving a set of congruent equations with one variable and relatively prime moduli.

Chosen-ciphertext attack: The adversary somehow gets Alice to decrypt ciphertext of his choice. Later he analyses ciphertext–plaintext pairs to derive the key.

Chosen-plaintext attack: The adversary makes somehow gets Alice to encrypt plaintext of his choice. Later he analyses ciphertext–plaintext pairs to derive the key.

Cipher: An encryption–decryption algorithm.

Cipher block chaining (CBC): A cryptographic mode of operation in which each plaintext block is XORed with the previous block of ciphertext before encryption.

Cipher suite: Set of key exchange, authentication and encryption algorithms.

Ciphertext: An encrypted message.

Ciphertext-only attack: An attack on encryption scheme using encrypted messages only.

Client: The requester of a service in a distributed system.

CMAC: A standard algorithm based on symmetric block cipher for keyed message authentication code.

Collision resistant: The property of a cryptographic hash function that ensures that two messages having the same value of digest cannot be found.

Commutative group: A group in which the binary operation satisfies commutative law.

Commutative law: A binary operation • is said to satisfy commutative law, if $a \bullet b = b \bullet a$.

Composite number: A positive integer with more than two divisors.

Congruence: Two numbers a and b are said to be congruent modulo n, if a mod $n = b$ mod n. Congruence is expressed as $a \equiv b$ (mod n).

Connectionless protocol: A protocol in which data may be sent without any advance connection-setup. IP is an example of such a protocol.

Coprime: See *relatively prime.*

Cryptanalysis: The science and art of breaking cryptographic codes.

Cryptography: The science and art of transforming messages to make them secure.

Cyclic subgroup: A subgroup that can be generated by repeated application of the binary operation of the group.

Datagram: The basic transmission unit in the Internet architecture. A datagram contains all of the information needed to deliver it to its destination.

DDoS (Distributed denial of service): A denial of service attack in which the attack originates simultaneously at a set of nodes. Each attacking node may put only a marginal load on the target machine, but the aggregate load from all the attacking nodes swamps the target machine.

Deauthentication: The service in WLAN that voids an existing authentication relationship.

Deciphering: See *decryption.*

Decryption: The act of reversing an encryption process to recover the data from an encrypted message.

Diagram: A string of two letters.

Dictionary attack: An attack in which the adversary tries all the possible passwords regardless of the user-id to get one valid user-id and password pair.

Diffusion: A desired property of a block cipher that hides the relationship between the plaintext and ciphertext.

Digest: A much shorter output obtained by applying a hash function to a message. To be useful, the hash function must be preimage and collision resistant.

Digital signature: A security mechanism in which the signing entity encrypts the message or its hash using its private key, certifying thus, the ownership of the contents of the message.

Discrete logarithm: An integer d is discrete logarithm modulo n of a to base r if $r^d = a$ mod n, where r is primitive root of n and a and n are coprime.

Distributive property: An algebraic structure with binary operations • and ∇ has distributive property of • over ∇ for all a, b, c elements of the underlying set, if $a \bullet (b \nabla c) = (a \bullet b) \nabla (a \bullet c)$.

DNS (Domain name system): The distributed naming system of the Internet, used to resolve host names into IP addresses.

DoS (Denial of service): A situation in which an attacking node floods a target node with so much work that it effectively keeps legitimate users from accessing the node, hence, they are denied service.

ElGamal cryptosystem: An asymmetric-key cryptosystem devised by ElGamal based on complexity of discrete logarithm problem.

Elliptic curves: Cubic equations of the type $y^2 + axy + by = cx^3 + dx^2 + ex + f$.

Encapsulation: The operation, performed by a lower-level protocol, of attaching a protocol-specific header to a message passed down by a higher-level protocol.

Encryption: The act of applying a transforming function to data, with the intention that only the receiver of the data will be able to read it (after applying the inverse function *decryption*). Encryption generally depends on either a secret shared by the sender and receiver or on a public/private key pair.

Entity authentication: A mechanism for proving identity of a claimant entity to a verifier entity.

ESP (Encapsulating security payload): One of the two IPsec protocols, that provides authentication and confidentiality services.

Euler's theorem: It states that for every positive integer n and every a that is coprime to n, $a^{\phi(n)} \equiv 1 \pmod{n}$ where $\phi(n)$ is totient of n.

Euler's totient (ϕ) function: For a given positive integer n, ϕ is the number of positive integers less than n that are coprime to n.

Feistal cipher structure: A block cipher structure devised by Feistal. It is based on non-invertible scrambling function.

Fermat's little theorem: Fermat's little theorem states that if p is a prime number and a is any positive integer, then $a^p = a \bmod p$.

Fiat-Shamir protocol: A zero-knowledge challenge-response authentication protocol.

Field: An algebraic structure with two operations, under both of which, the elements of the set satisfy properties relating to closure, associative law, commutative law, existence of identity element and existence of inverse. The additive identity element does not have multiplicative inverse.

Finite field: Field with finite number of elements.

Firewall: An implementation of routers, and proxy servers configured to filter inbound and outbound IP packets to/from a network secured by the firewall.

Fragmentation/reassembly: A method for transmission of messages larger than the network's MTU. Messages are fragmented into small pieces by the sender and reassembled by the receiver.

Galois field: Field having finite number of elements.

GCD (Greatest common divisor): The largest integer that can divide two integers.

Group: An algebraic structure with one operation that satisfies properties of closure, associative law, existence of identity element and inverse.

Hardware address: The data link level address used to identify the host adaptor on the local network.

Hash function: A function that creates a much shorter output from an input. See also *digest*.

HMAC: A standard algorithm for keyed message authentication code.

Host: A computer attached to one or more networks that supports users and runs application programs.

Identity element: An element e in group $\{G, \bullet\}$ such that $a \bullet e = e \bullet a = a$ for every a in G.

IETF (Internet engineering task force): The body responsible for the specification of standards and protocols related to the Internet.

IKE (Internet key exchange): A protocol for creating security associations in IPsec.

Integrity: In the context of network security, a service that protects data from modification.

Invertible function: A function that assigns each element in the range with exactly one element in the domain.

IPsec (IP security): An architecture for authentication, privacy, and integrity of IP packets.

Irreducible polynomial: A polynomial which cannot be factored.

ISKMP (Internet security association and key management protocol): A framework that defines the exchanges and the formats of IKE messages.

IV (Initialization vector): A block used in the first iteration of block cipher in some modes of operation.

JPEG (Joint photographic experts group): Typically used to refer to a widely used algorithm for compressing still images.

KDC (Key distribution centre): A trusted third party that establishes a shared secret key between two entities.

Kerberos: A authentication and symmetric-key distribution protocol developed at MIT, for client-server applications.

Key expansion: Process of generating round keys from the cipher key for multi-round encryption algorithm.

Key material: It consists of encryption and authentication keys, and initialization vectors required for a secure session. It is generated from a secret seed value.

Key-only attack: An attack on digital signature when only the public key is known.

Key ring: A set of public keys and private keys used in PGP.

Key space: Set of all possible keys.

MAC (Message authentication code): A cryptographic hash used for verification of message integrity and source authentication.

Man-in-the-middle attack: Typically used in context of Diffie–Hellman key exchange algorithm. The attacker impersonates as Bob to Alice and as Alice to Bob, and establishes secret keys with them to read their messages.

Masquerading: A type of attack on security, in which the adversary impersonates one of the two communicating entities.

MD5: A cryptographic checksum algorithm commonly used to verify that the contents of a message are unaltered.

Media access control (MAC) protocol data unit (MPDU): The unit of data exchanged between two peer MAC entities using the services of the Physical layer.

Media access control (MAC) service data unit (MSDU): Information that is delivered as a unit between MAC service access points.

Meet-in-the-middle attack: Used to attack double DES encryption when a plaintext–ciphertext pair is available to the adversary.

Message integrity code (MIC): An equivalent term in WLANs for message authentication code. It authenticates the message for its content and its origin.

Message transfer agent (MTA): A client server program for transfer of emails to mail server.

MIME (Multipurpose Internet Mail Extensions): Specifications for converting binary data (such as image files) to ASCII text, which allows it to be sent via email.

Modes of operation: A set of schemes of deploying symmetric-key block ciphers for encryption of message of arbitrary length.

Monoalphabetic cipher: A substitution cipher where ciphertext characters are defined as a random mapping of plaintext alphabet.

MPEG (Moving Picture Experts Group): Typically used to refer to an algorithm for compressing video streams.

MTU (Maximum transmission unit): The size of the largest packet that can be sent over a physical network.

Multiplicative inverse: Two numbers a and b of $Z_n = \{0, 1, 2, \ldots, n - 1\}$ are multiplicative inverse of one another, if $(a \times b) \bmod n = 1$.

Name resolution: The action of resolving host names into their corresponding IP addresses.

Needham–Schroeder protocol: A secure protocol used by KDC for distributing a session key to Alice and Bob for communication between them.

NIST (National Institute for Standards and Technology): The official U.S. standardization body.

Node: A generic term used for individual computers that make up a network. Nodes include general-purpose computers, switches, and routers.

Non repudiation: One of the security services that protects against denial by the sender of a message of having sent the message or its content.

Nonce: It is random number used for establishing a secure session between two communicating entities. It is used only once, i.e., each new session has a new number.

One-way function: It is characteristic of a hash function used for to generating message digest. One way characteristic makes it impossible to get the pre-image given a message digest.

Order of a group: The number of elements in a group.

OTP (One time pad):   A polyalphabetic cipher which uses a key pad to encrypt a message. Each character on the key pad is used once as substitution key to encrypt one character of plaintext message.

Packet: A data unit of layer 3 typically.

Passive attack: A passive attack involves monitoring, copying, analyzing the communication between two entities without disrupting or modifying the communication. A passive attacker uses the captured data later, e.g., for extracting information or replying the data.

PGP (Pretty good privacy):   An email security protocol that provides privacy, integrity and authentication.

Ping: A utility used to test the round trip time and accessibility to nodes/hosts of the Internet.

Plaintext: The unencrypted message input to an encryption algorithm.

PPP (Point-to-point protocol):   Data link protocol typically used to connect computers over a dial-up line.

Pre-image resistant: A desired property of cryptographic hash function h, which ensures that given the hash value x, it is infeasible to find any m such that $x = h(m)$.

Pre-master secret: It is a secret established between the client and server and used in computation of the key material for TLS.

PRF (Pseudo random function):   A function used by the client and server for generating key material for TLS protocol. It takes as inputs the premaster secret, the master secret, the random numbers of the client and server, other inputs.

Primitive root: If the order of an element in the group $G = \{Z_n^*, \times\}$ is same as $\phi(n)$, the element is called primitive root of the group.

Private key: One of the two keys of asymmetric-key cryptosystem, that is not shared by its owner is called private key. He uses it sign messages and for decrypting the messages encrypted with his public key.

Proxy: An agent sitting between a client and server that acts 'stand in' for the server by responding to client requests. It intercepts client's messages and forwards them to the server. Similarly, it forwards the server's response to the client.

Public key: One of the two keys of asymmetric-key cryptosystem, which is made public for encrypting messages to the owner of the key. It is also used for verification of digital signature of the owner.

Public key cryptosystem: Any of several encryption algorithms (e.g., RSA) in which each user has a private key (shared with no one else) and a public key (available to everyone).

Public key infrastructure: A framework of creating and distributing public-key certificates based on X.509.

Radlx64:   A scheme for converting 8-bit symbols into printable ASCII characters. It is used in email systems that permit transmission of printable characters only. It is also called Base64 encoding.

RC4: A byte oriented stream cipher devised by Ronald Rivest.

Record protocol: The protocol of TLS that carries the secured data from the upper layer.

Relatively prime: Two integers are relatively prime, if their GCD is 1.

Replay attack: A type of attack in which the adversary resends an intercepted message.

RFC (Request for comments): Internet reports that contain, among other things, specifications for protocols like TCP and IP.

Ring: An algebraic structure with two binary operations. The first operation must satisfy the five properties of abelian group, and the second operation satisfies closure, associative and distributive properties.

RSA cryptosystem: A public-key encryption algorithm named after its inventors: Rivest, Shamir and Adleman.

SA (Security association): Security Association is set of mutually agreed security algorithms for authentication and encryption, associated keys and other parameters (e.g. lifetime of the keys) between the two IPsec peers.

SAD (Security association database): Active SAs are held in security association database. It contains the parameters of each active SA, e.g. IPsec protocol (AH or ESP), mode (transport or tunnel), authentication/encryption algorithms with keys, life time of SA, etc.

Salting: Adding a string called salt to the password to counter the dictionary attack.

Second pre-image resistant: A desired property of cryptographic hash function, which makes it difficult to find second pre-image m' such that $h(m') = h(m)$, given m and $h(m)$.

Self-synchronizing stream cipher: A stream cipher in which each key of the key stream is generated from the previous the ciphertext so that the sending and the receiving ends have synchronized stream of keys.

Server: The provider of a service in a client/server distributed system.

Session key: A secret symmetric-key used during a session between two communicating entities for confidentiality.

Set of residues (Z_n): Set of positive integers modulo n.

SHA (Secure hash algorithm): A family of cryptographic hash algorithms, standardized by NIST.

Shift cipher: A cipher in which each character of the alphabet is shifted by the amount equal to the key. For example, if key = 2, A is encrypted as C.

S/MIME: An enhancement to MIME designed to provide security to email.

Source routing: Routing decisions performed at the source before the packet is sent. The route consists of the list of nodes that the packet should traverse on the way to the destination.

SPD (Security policy database): It contains the security policy to be applied to the datagram. A datagram is discarded, allowed to bypass IPsec, or secured according to policy specified in SPD.

SSL (Secure socket layer):   A protocol layer that runs over TCP to provide authentication and encryption of TCP segments. See also *TLS*.

Statistical attack: Attack on encrypted symbols or blocks based on the statistical frequency of occurrence of plaintext symbols or blocks.

Stream cipher: A category of ciphers in which encryption/decryption is carried out on one symbol or bit at a time.

Subgroup: A subset of a group G is a subgroup H if it is group in itself with the same binary operation of G.

Substitution cipher: A cipher that replaces one symbol with another.

Symmetric-key encryption: A cryptosystem that uses the same key for encryption and decryption.

Synchronous stream cipher: A stream cipher in which the key stream is independent of the plaintext and ciphertext, and it is generated in synchronism at the sending and receiving ends.

TGS (Ticket granting server):   A component of Kerberos, which grants ticket for access to the application server.

Ticket: An encrypted message handed over to the requestor for access to the application server, who verifies the ticket. See also *TGS*.

TLS (Transport layer security):   Security services build at the transport layer. It is often used by HTTP to perform secure transactions on the web. It is the IETF version of SSL. See also *SSL*.

Transport mode: One of the two modes of IPsec, in which the IPsec protection is provided to the IP payload data.

Transposition cipher: A cipher that permutates the symbols (or bits) of plaintext to encrypt.

Trigram: A three letter string.

Triple DES: In triple DES, DES algorithm is applied three times for encryption using either three different keys or two keys, the first and third stage sharing the same key. It is also written as 3DES.

Trojan horse: A computer program that appears to have a useful function, but also has a hidden and potentially malicious function that evades security mechanisms, sometimes by exploiting legitimate authorizations of a system entity that invokes the program.

Tunnel mode: A mode in IPsec that protects entire IP packet by encapsulating it in IPsec header/trailer and adding a new IP header.

UDP (User datagram protocol):   Transport protocol of the Internet architecture that provides a connectionless datagram service to application-level processes.

URL (Uniform resource locator):   A text string used to identify the location of Internet resources. A typical URL looks like http://www.cisco.com. In this URL, http is the protocol to use to access the resource located on host www.cisco.com.

User agent: The entity that prepares an email message.

Virus: Code embedded within a program that causes a copy of itself to be inserted in one or more other programs. In addition to propagation, the virus usually performs some unwanted function.

VPN (Virtual private network): A logical network overlaid on an existing network. For example, a company with sites around the world may build a virtual network on top of the Internet.

Web of trust: The trust model that determines public key legitimacy in PGP. The trust model is not hierarchical or centralized, but it is based on cumulative degree of trust one places on certificate issuers.

Well-known port: A port number that is, by convention, dedicated for use by a particular server. For instance, the Domain Name Server receives messages at well-known UDP and TCP port number 53 on every host.

Worm: A malware that can replicate itself and send copies from computer to computer across network connections. In addition to propagation, the worm usually performs some unwanted function.

X.500: ITU directory services standard, which defines an attribute-based naming service.

X.509: ITU standard for digital certificates.

Zero-knowledge authentication: An entity authentication method in which the claimant demonstrates knowledge of a secret while revealing no information that can be reused by the verifier.

Answers to Selected Problems

Chapter 2

1. (a) 4   (b) 9   (c) 2   (d) 0
2. 17 and −4, 13 and 27
3. 2
4. (a) 4   (b) 1
5. (0, 0), (1, 16), (2, 15), (3, 14), (4, 13), (5, 12), (6, 11), (7, 10), (8, 9)
6. HZCV
7. INDIA
8. (5, 5), (7, 7), (11, 11)
9. B
10. K
11. $\begin{bmatrix} 6 & 7 & 8 \\ 0 & 4 & 6 \\ 8 & 5 & 0 \end{bmatrix}$
12. B is multiplicative inverse.
13. (a) 3   (b) 6   (c) 12
14. (a) 6   (b) 37
15. 9, 5, 8

Chapter 3

1. (a) WTZYJ   (b) ARMY
2. K = 3
3. (a) FEPZ   (b) CODE   (c) 1, 3, 5, 7, 9, 11, 15, 17, 19, 21, 23, 25   (d) (5, 15)
4. O

5. CSYBHNJVML

6. IYYSIYGSYDBCS

7. $a = 3$, K $= 4$

8. The Government has hiked duty on import of all types of automobile parts. This amendment will have impact on our margins. We need to revise the expansion planned this year. Chief has agreed to revise the targets.

9. (a) AHMFOHARKENV   (b) CRYPTOGRAPHIC

10. ASUNEF. Cyclic rotation of rows and columns leads to equivalent substitutions.

11. RPGK

12. M $= \begin{bmatrix} 7 & 13 \\ 2 & 5 \end{bmatrix}$

13. $K^{-1} = \begin{bmatrix} 1 & 11 \\ 22 & 23 \end{bmatrix}$, ARMY

14. LDC

15. $c = 11p + 14 \bmod 26$

16. ESKY ERSC TAEM TRSE

17. LMNAAASMI

18. MLIT

19. (a) Encrypted message of Alice $c_2 = \{R\ H\ T\ M\ H\ G\ R\ T\ K\ M\ W\ W\ W\ H\ T\ M\}$.

    (b) $K_3 = \{F\ D\ P\ S\ H\ M\ C\ T\ S\ C\ E\ D\ F\ D\ P\ S\}$.

      $K_3 \equiv K_1 + K_2 \pmod{26}$.

      Size of the key word K_3 is 12.

    (c) Not really. The adversary cracking the code will directly hit the key K_3.

20. 7 or 14.

21. Shift key K $= 5$.

    The increased use of computer and communication systems by industry has increased the risk of theft of proprietary information.

22. $a = (m_1 - m_2)^{-1}(c_1 - c_2) \bmod n$, $b = c_1 - am_1 \bmod n$. The attacker chooses m_1 and m_2 such that $(m_1 - m_2)^{-1} \bmod n$ exists.

Chapter 4

1. (a) 1001

   (b)

	00	01	10	11
00	0011	1001	1100	0001
01	1110	0100	0110	1010
10	1000	1011	1101	0101
11	0111	0000	0010	1111

2. (a) 1000 1010 1100 1111   (b) 1100 1000 0100 1110
3. 1000 0110 0100 0000
4. NETWORKS
5. (a) Output of two rounds = $M_0 \oplus K \oplus M_1$, M_0. Thus M_0 is known and $K \oplus M_1$ can be calculated using M_0, but K cannot be obtained.
   (b) Output of three rounds = M_0, M_1, which is plaintext block.
7. (b) K = 000...000
11.

Round key	(a) $g(x, K_i) = 0$		(b) $g(x, K_i) = x$		(c) $g(x, K_i) = K_i$	
	L_0	R_0	L_0	R_0	L_0	R_0
K_1	L_0	R_0	$L_0 \oplus R_0$	R_0	$L_0 \oplus K_1$	R_0
K_2	L_0	R_0	$L_0 \oplus R_0$	L_0	$L_0 \oplus K_1$	$R_0 \oplus K_2$
K_3	L_0	R_0	R_0	L_0	$L_0 \oplus K_1 \oplus K_3$	$R_0 \oplus K_2$
K_4	L_0	R_0	R_0	$L_0 \oplus R_0$	$L_0 \oplus K_1 \oplus K_3$	$R_0 \oplus K_2 \oplus K_4$

13. $S_1(x_1) \oplus S_1(x_2) = 1010$, $S_1(x_1 \oplus x_2) = 1101$

Chapter 5

1. No. 0, 2, 3, 4 do not have multiplicative inverses in Z_6.
2. G is cyclic since its every element can be expressed as 3^k.
3. (a) $x^3 + x^2$ (b) $x^5 + x^4 + 1$ (c) x (d) $x^2 + 1$
4. (a) $x^3 + 4x^2 + 5x + 1$ (b) $x + 6$ (c) $6x^2 + 2x + 5$
5. (a) $(x + 1)(x + 1)$ (b) $(x + 1)(x^2 + x + 1)$
6. (a) $x + 1$ (b) $x^2 + x + 1$
7. (a) (010) (b) (111)
8. $x^2 + 1$
9. (100)
10. (110)
11. (a) $g^1 = x + 1 = (011)$, $g^2 = x^2 + 1 = (101)$, $g^3 = x^2 = (100)$, $g^4 = x^2 + x + 1 = (111)$, $g^5 = x = (010)$, $g^6 = x^2 + x = (110)$, $g^7 = 1 = (001)$
    (b) $g^2 = (101)$

Chapter 6

2. {7c}

3.

(a)			
00	04	08	0C
01	05	09	0D
02	06	0A	0E
03	07	0B	0F

(b)			
01	05	09	0D
00	04	08	0C
03	07	0B	0F
02	06	0A	0E

4. (a) W(4) = W(5) = W(6) = W(7) = {62 63 63 63}

5. (a) W(4) = W(6) = {E8 E9 E9 E9}, W(5) = W(7) = {17 16 16 16}

6. {1F}

8. {AC 77 66 F3}

9. $\begin{bmatrix} E9 & E9 & E9 & E9 \\ E9 & E9 & E9 & E9 \\ E9 & E9 & E9 & E9 \\ E9 & E9 & E9 & E9 \end{bmatrix}$

Chapter 7

1. 1 0 0 0 1 0 0 1 1 0 1 0 1 1 1 0 0 0 1

2. S = [0, 1, 2, ..., 255]

3. (a) S = [1 3 2 0],   (b) k = 0, 2, 1, 3

4. (a) B_1 to B_8 will be in error. B_9 to B_{32} will be decrypted correctly.

   (b) Bytes B_1 to B_8 are lost. Rest of the bytes will be decrypted correctly.

   (c) Received sequence will be B_{16}, B_1 to B_8, B_{17} to B_{32}.

5. (a) B_1 to B_{16} will be in error. B_{17} to B_{32} will be decrypted correctly.

   (b) Bytes B_1 to B_8 will be lost. B_9 to B_{16} will be in error. Rest of the bytes will be decrypted correctly.

   (c) B_1 to B_{24} will be in error. B_{25} to B_{32} will be decrypted correctly.

6. (a) B_1 to B_9 bytes will be in error. The rest B_{10} to B_{32} will be decrypted correctly.

   (b) Bytes B_1 is lost. Bytes B_2 to B_9 will be in error. The rest B_{10} to B_{32} will be decrypted correctly.

   (c) B_1 to B_{10} bytes will be in error. The rest B_{11} to B_{32} will be decrypted correctly.

7. (a) B_1 will be decrypted with error. B_2 to B_{32} will be decrypted correctly.

   (b) All the bytes will be decrypted with error.

   (c) B_1 and B_2 will be decrypted with error. B_3 to B_{32} will be decrypted correctly.

8. (a) B_1 to B_8 will be in error. B_9 to B_{32} will be decrypted correctly.

   (b) Bytes B_1 to B_8 are lost. Rest of the bytes will not be decrypted correctly.

   (c) B_1 to B_{16} will be in error. B_{17} to B_{32} will be decrypted correctly.

9. (a) 9 11 6 13 3

   (b) Yes. Each byte of the pad will have value equal to the size of the block in bytes.

10. $m_i \oplus m_j$. From XOR of previous encrypted blocks, XOR of plaintext blocks can be computed.

11. (a) The OFB mode is basically one-time pad with the random sequence which is generated using the IV and the secret key. If they remain fixed, the sequence generated is always the same for different messages because it is independent of plaintext or ciphertext. The adversary recovers the random sequence by XORing the known plaintext and ciphertext pair. Once the sequence is known, any ciphertext of same or shorter length can be decrypted.

    (b) The CFB mode is better than OFB mode but it is still vulnerable to known plaintext attack to some extent. The first encrypted block is XOR of the first plaintext block and the encrypted IV. This encrypted IV remains same for all the messages if IV is not changed. Thus XOR of the first blocks of the known plaintext–ciphertext pair, gives the encrypted IV, which can be used for decrypting the first block of all the other encrypted messages.

    CBC mode is not vulnerable to this kind of attack.

12. (a) $m_i = D(K, c_i \oplus c_{i-1})$.

13. (c) Compared to CBC mode, the counter mode is very insecure if constant IV is used.

14. (a) Second option is better because bit flipping is not possible and brute force effort to determine IV is tripled.

    (b) Second option is better since parallel execution of DES algorithm is possible for multiple blocks.

15. (a) The last block c_N is decrypted first. Since the size of c_{N-1} block is r bits, the first r bits of decrypted output are the last segment m_N of the message. The rest $n - r$ are the stolen bits of the previous encrypted block. These are attached to c_{N-1} and the n-bit block so obtained is decrypted to get m_{N-1}.

Chapter 8

2. (a) 16   (b) 60   (c) 8

4. (a) 54   (b) 64

5. (a) 10   (b) 14

6. 6

10. 276

11. (a) 54   (b) 30

12. (a) 5, 6   (b) (11, 8)   (c) No solution exists

13. (a) 71, 27, 50, 6   (b) 67, 32, 45, 10
14. (a) 12
    (b) 1(1), 2(12), 3(3), 4(6), 5(4), 6(12), 7(12), 8(4), 9(3), 10(6), 11(12), 12(2). Order is indicated within bracket.
    (c) 2, 6, 7, 11
    (d)

x	$\log_{2,13} x$	$\log_{6,13} x$	$\log_{7,13} x$	$\text{Log}_{11,13} x$
1	12	12	12	12
2	1	5	11	7
3	4	8	8	4
4	2	10	10	2
5	9	9	3	3
6	5	1	7	11
7	11	7	1	5
8	3	3	9	9
9	8	4	4	8
10	10	2	2	10
11	7	11	5	1
12	6	6	6	6

15. (a) 4   (b) 1(1), 5(2), 7(2), 11(2). Order is indicated within brackets.
    (c) There is no primitive root.
17. 17
18. (a) 4   (b) 7

Chapter 9

1. (a) 3   (b) 2
2. (a) 29   (b) 50   (c) 32
3. (a) {5, 35}   (b) {3113, 3937}
4. m
5. (a) p, q (b) 31, 47
6. 3
7. 3
8. The adversary computes $(c_A)^x \times (c_B)^y \equiv (m^eA)^x \times (m^eB)^y \equiv m^{xe_A + ye_B} \equiv m(\text{mod } n)$.
10. (a) No. The adversary can easily determine K.
11. 58
12. 60, 38, 39, 17

13. 2
14. $r = 3, c = 3$
15. 5
16. 6
18. $m = 721$
19. (a) $142 \rightarrow$ A, $110 \rightarrow$ B, $67 \rightarrow$ C, $51 \rightarrow$ D, $86 \rightarrow$ E, $60 \rightarrow$ F, $113 \rightarrow$ G, $30 \rightarrow$ H, $61 \rightarrow$ I, $167 \rightarrow$ J, $114 \rightarrow$ K, $32 \rightarrow$ L, $121 \rightarrow$ M, $56 \rightarrow$ N, $139 \rightarrow$ O, $75 \rightarrow$ P, $38 \rightarrow$ Q, $91 \rightarrow$ R, $8 \rightarrow$ S, $50 \rightarrow$ T, $68 \rightarrow$ U, $103 \rightarrow$ V, $43 \rightarrow$ W, $11 \rightarrow$ X, $166 \rightarrow$ Y, $95 \rightarrow$ Z.
    (b) GREETINGS
20. $p - 3$

Chapter 10

1. (a) (7, 11) (b) (3, 10) (c) (17, 3)
2. (11, 2)
3. (10, 2)
4. O
5. (0, 2), (0, 3), (1, 2), (1, 3), (2, 0), (4, 2), (4, 3), O.
6. (5, 9)
7. (a) (101, 111) (b) (111, 110)
8. $(1, g^6)$
9. (a) Public key $\{E_{11}(1, 6), G_A = (2, 7), P_A = (8, 3)\}$ (8, 3)
    (b) $c = (3, 6)$, $r = (3, 5)$
10. K = (10, 9)
11. (a) $\{(0, 3), (0, 4), (2, 3), (2, 4), (4, 1), (4, 6), (5, 3), (5, 4)\}$. Group order is 9.
    (b) $G = (0, 3)$, $2G = (2, 3)$, $3G = (5, 4)$, $4G = (4, 6)$, $5G = (4, 1)$, $6G = (5, 3)$, $7G = (2, 4)$, $8G = (0, 4)$, $9G = O$. Order of G is 9. G is primitive element.

Chapter 11

1. (a) 2 (b) 2 (c) 0
2. $h(x) = h(x + p - 1)$ since $a^{p-1} \bmod p = 1$. Thus it is easy to construct collisions.
3. No, since $h(n - x) \bmod n = (n^2 + 2nx + x^2) \bmod n = x^2 \bmod n$.
4. (a) No, since $h(B1) = B1$
    (b) No, since $h(B1) = h(B1 \oplus 0)$
    (c) No, since messages B1, B1 $\oplus$ 0, B1 $\oplus$ 0 $\oplus$ 0, ... have same value of the digest.
5. (a) 82
    (b) Pre-image resistant – No, since if $h(x) = y$, $x = (y - K) \bmod n$.
    2nd pre-image resistant and strong collision resistant – No, since it is easy to find messages having same hash value, e.g. by adding zero or n.

6. (a) 9
   (b) If n is predefined composite with known factors, $h = a^2$ mod n can be solved for message a. Therefore the function is not pre-image resistant. Since hash of messages $[a]$ and $[a, 0]$ is same, it is not 2nd pre-image resistant or strong collision resistant.
7. (a) 21   (b) 8   (c) 22   (d) 8
8. 0.573
9. (a) 96 bits   (b) 480
13. S

Chapter 12

1. (a) {37, 77}   (b) 57   (c) 8
2. yes, 6
3. 2
4. Alice's signature on 2 = 30
5. 58
6. $\{p, g, g^a\} = \{23, 5, 10\}$, $r = 11$, $s = 19$
7. $v_1 = v_2 = 8$
8. 3
9. 4
12. (a) The adversary notices $r = g^a$, and concludes $k = a$.
    (b) He computes a using $s = (h - ar)\, a^{-1}$ mod $(p - 1)$.
14. (b) $\{p, q, g, g^x\} = \{23, 11, 6, 12\}$
    (c) $\{r, s\} = \{3, 7\}$
    (d) $v = r = 3$
15. Private key x can be readily calculated since $s = 0 = k^{-1}(h + xr)$ mod q.
16. 7
17. (a) Public key $\{a, b, p, q, G, xG\} = \{1, 6, 11, 13, (2, 7), (3, 6)\}$
    (b) $\{r, s\} = \{7, 4\}$
18. rAS
19. $x = (s_1 k - h_1)\, r^{-1}$ mod q, where $k = (h_1 - h_2) \times (s_1 - s_2)^{-1}$ mod q.

Chapter 13

1. The adversary chooses $R_B = R_A \oplus R_T$.
2. (a) Secure   (b) Yes
3. No.
4. (a) Yes.
   (b) The adversary fails to give the acceptable response $y = r/v^{1/2}$.

5. (a) Her public key $v = 4$ (b) $x = 29$ (c) $y = 26$ (d) $y = 8$

6. $s = 17$

7. (a) $v = (11, 16, 9)$ (b) 30   (c) 10   (d) $y^2 \bmod 35 = 30$

8. (a) The rest of the protocol proceeds as given below:

     (4) Alice sends r_1 or r_2 as per Bob's request. Bob verifies that $x_i = r_i^e$. If it is so, Bob asks Alice for the second round.

     (5) Alice chooses a different random integer as r_1 and repeats the steps starting from (a). If the verification fails Bob rejects Alice's claim. Else Bob asks Alice for another round if he is still unconvinced.

    (b) Bob uses the other challenge in second round so that he has r_1 and r_2. He computes $r_1 \times r_2 \bmod n = r_1 \times m \times r_1^{-1} \bmod n = m$.

Chapter 14

2. (a) 4, 10, 18   (b) 31, 14, 18   (c) 21, 17, 14

3. (a) 1, 17, 28, 12, 1, 28, 17

   (b) Effectively the adversary has changed the generator from $g = 2$ to $g = 2^7 = 128$. 128 as generator has order of 4. Thus $g^x \bmod 29$ for any x can have one of the only four possible values.

4. $K = g^{aR_B + bR_A}$

6. They calculate part key values $g^a \bmod p$, $g^b \bmod p$, $g^c \bmod p$ respectively. They circularly rotate the part values amongst them and recomputed $(g^c)^a \bmod p$, $(g^a)^b \bmod p$, $(g^b)^c \bmod p$ respectively. These part keys are again rotated and each of them computes $g^{abc} \bmod p$.

7. $K_{AB} = K_{BA} = u + v \times (k_A + k_B) + w \times k_A \times k_B$

8. (a) 21

9. (b) $M_1 \oplus M_2 \oplus M_3 = K$

10. Alice, X, $E(K_A, \{K_S\})$ ...(1)

    $E(K_X, \{K_S\})$ ...(2)

    $E(K_S, \{m\})$, $E(K_X, \{K_S\})$ ...(3)

    X copies the last message (3), decrypts the session key K_S and recovers the message m from Alice.

11. Alice to Bob ID_A ...(1)

    Bob to Alice $E(K_B, \{N_B\})$ ...(2)

    Alice to KDC $E(K_A, \{ID_A \| ID_B \| N_A\}) \| E(K_B, \{N_B\})$ ...(3)

    KDC to Alice $E(K_A, \{K_S \| ID_B \| N_A \| E(K_B, \{K_S \| ID_A \| N_B\})\})$ ...(4)

    Alice to Bob $E(K_B, \{K_S \| ID_A \| N_B\})$ ...(5)

    Bob to Alice $E(K_S, \{N_B\})$ ...(6)

    Alice to Bob $E(K_S, \{N_B + 1\})$ ...(7)

    When the adversary sends (5) to Bob, Bob notices the obsolete nonce N_B.

12. Alice proves to Bob that she actually decrypted the nonce received from him. The adversary would fail in this test.

13. The application server will not accept the adversary's message because the authenticator has time stamp which would have expired. The adversary cannot modify the authenticator as he does not know the session key.

15. $K = g^{ab+ac+ad+bc+bd+cd} \bmod p$

Chapter 15

1. The adversary can add a certificate serial number in the CRL for launching DOS attack. The validation of the certificate will fail and thus the owner will be denied the services. He can also delete a serial number from the list for circumventing the revocation process so that may use the spoofed identity and the compromised private key of its original owner.

2. It will not be ever possible to purge CRL. It will always be getting longer. By keeping an expiration date, the expired certificates can be removed from the CRL.

3. (a) 16th March 2014   (b) 10th November 2014

4. (a) $CA_1 \Leftarrow CA_2 \Leftarrow CA_3$ (b) $CA_4 \Leftarrow CA_1 \Leftarrow CA_2 \Leftarrow CA_3$, $CA_4 \Leftarrow CA_2 \Leftarrow CA_3$
   (c) $CA_1 \Leftarrow CA_2 \Leftarrow CA_4$, $CA_1 \Leftarrow CA_2 \Leftarrow CA_3 \Leftarrow CA_4$

5. Bob does not gain any information about the sender. The certificate merely tells him the public key of Alice.

6. (a) Same public key means that each can read encrypted messages meant for the other. It will be impossible to distinguish between their digital signatures.

   (b) It implies that the hash values of the two certificates are same. It is not impossible though this situation is unlikely. It is possible that one of the certificates is fake.

Chapter 16

1. (a) IE5   (b) F d A v n r c =   (c) F d A v n g = =

2. (a) =9D   (b) =89   (c) =AC

3. Not trusted.

4.

User Id	Owner trust	Certificate signer	Certificate trust	Key legitimacy
A	F			F
B	F	A	F	F
C	N	A	F	F
D	P	A	F	F
E	N	B	F	F
F	P	C, E	N, N	N
G	N	C, D	N, P	P
H	N	CA	F	F
I	N	P, E	N, N	N

Chapter 17

1. The Finished message from the client will reveal the inconsistency to the server.

4.

	(a)				(b)				(c)				(d)			
	Write state		Read state		Write state		Read state		Write state		Read state		Write state		Read state	
	Act.	Pend.	Act.	Pend.	Act.	Pend.	Act.	Pend.	Act.	Pend.	Act.	Pend.	Act.	Pend.	Act.	Pend.
MAC	Null	SHA	Null	SHA	Null	SHA	Null	SHA	SHA		Null	SHA	SHA		SHA	
Encrypt	Null	AES	Null	AES	Null	AES	Null	AES	AES		Null	AES	AES		AES	
Key	Null		Null		Null	K_C	Null	K_S	K_C		Null	K_S	K_C		K_S	

5.

	(a)				(b)				(c)				(d)			
	Write state		Read state		Write state		Read state		Write state		Read state		Write state		Read state	
	Act.	Pend.	Act.	Pend.	Act.	Pend.	Act.	Pend.	Act.	Pend.	Act.	Pend.	Act.	Pend.	Act.	Pend.
MAC	Null	SHA	Null	SHA	Null	SHA	Null	SHA	Null	SHA	Null	SHA	SHA		SHA	
Encrypt	Null	AES	Null	AES	Null	AES	Null	AES	Null	AES	Null	AES	AES		AES	
Key	Null		Null		Null	K_S	Null	K_C	Null	K_S	Null	K_C	K_S		K_C	

7. The two sequence numbers have different purposes. TCP sequence number ensures reliable transfer of user data (TLS Record protocol data unit).

   Sequence number used during computation of MAC in the Record Protocol protects against replay and reordering of application data. The adversary can manipulate (reorder or replay) the encrypted blocks of [compressed application data ‖ MAC] if the sequence number is not used during computation of MAC.

8. Public key certificates used for authentication prevent man-in-the-middle attack.

Chapter 18

1. Rejected.

2. 308: Accepted, Window [301,332]; 314: Accepted, Window [301,332]; 314: Rejected, Window [301,332]; 315: Rejected, Window [301,332]; 345: Accepted, Window [314, 345]; 310: Rejected, Window [314, 345].

3. No.

5. ESP in tunnel mode.

6. ESP and then AH. Order of processing is reversed is reversed at the receiving end. Thus only the authenticated packet is decrypted. Authentication filters replays, and packets with mutilated/manipulated fields. This order also facilitates parallel processing at receiver. Decryption can be carried out in parallel with authentication verification.

7. The protocol field is 50 for ESP. ISP applies filter based on the protocol field.

8. (a) IP is unreliable service. If an IP packet is lost, the following IP datagram cannot be decrypted.

   (b) 302, first 306.

Chapter 19

2. N_I addresses observation (b), IP_I addresses observation (c), SPI_I addresses observation (d), Secret addresses observation (e). As regards observation (a), since N_I and SPI_I are available in message 1a, IP_I available in the IP header of the message, the secret whose Id is part of the cookie is already available with the responder, the original cookie can be regenerated.

Chapter 20

1. 1011
2. 1011
3. $m \oplus x$
4. Yes.
5. $k_1 = 0xAB$, $k_2 = 0x89$, $k_3 = 0x46$, $k_4 = 67$, $k_5 = 0x89$, $k_6 = 0xAB$, $k_7 = 0xCE$, $k_8 = 0xEF$

Chapter 21

1. (a) 16, 24 octets   (b) 0, 2
2. No. The first fragment would have only 8 octets.
3. The attacker sends the following ARP request messages to A and B in non-broadcast mode.

	ARP request to A	**ARP reply to B**
Source addresses	IP_B, MAC_T	IP_A, MAC_T
Target addresses	IP_A, ? ·	IP_B, ?

5. Adversary sends to Bob   (1) S = 111, Data = 15 bytes, A = 502, ACK.
   Bob responds to Alice   (2) S = 502, A = 126, ACK.
   Bob receives from Alice   (3) S = 111, A = 502, ACK.

   The sequence number S = 111 of Alice and acknowledgement number A=126 of Bob get desynchronized by the adversary's message. Alice may reset the TCP connection.

6. (a) The adversary sends DHCPDISCOVER messages (indicating different fake MAC addresses required in DHCPDISCOVER message) until the IP addresses available in the DHCP server are exhausted. Other DHCP clients do not get IP address during the validity period of the IP addresses allotted to the adversary.

   (b) The adversary activates its fake DHCP server that sends DHCPOFFER message in response to DHCPDISCOVER message from a client. It

   – allocates one of the stolen IP addresses from the original DHCP server and
   – provides its own IP address as the gateway/DNS server's IP address.

   The adversary can thereafter intercept the outgoing communication of the victim.

7. The TCP of the victim host replies to itself. The operating system becomes trapped in this endless loop and either crashes, slows down badly.

Chapter 22

1. Block inbound TCP packets with SYN flag set and ACK flag not set.

3. Router G blocks inbound traffic to the Telnet server port, unless the destination is subnet 2. Router I blocks all Telnet traffic from subnet 2 to subnet 1.

4. (a) Rules (3) and (4).

(b)

Rule	Interface of arrival	Source IP address	Source port	Destination IP address	Destination port	Protocol	ACK flag	Action
1	2	Any external	> 1023	192.168.0.1	25	TCP	*	Permit
2	1	192.168.0.1	25	Any external	> 1023	TCP	Set	Permit
3	1	192.168.0.1	> 1023	Any external	25	TCP	*	Permit
4	2	Any external	25	192.168.0.1	> 1023	TCP	Set	Permit
5	*	*	*	*	*	*	*	Block

(c) IP packets from server with SYN = 1 and ACK = 0 are blocked.

5. The application data is not examined by the packet filtering firewall, stateful inspection firewall, and circuit-level proxy firewall. Only these firewalls can work when the application data is encrypted.

7. V = 0.1486. Not the normal behaviour as V should be less than 0.1 per the specified policy.

8.

	Source IP address	Source port	Destination IP address	Destination port	Protocol	Action
For subnet 192.168.10.0/24	*	*	192.168.10.25	25	TCP	Permit
	*	*	192.168.10.30	53	UDP	Permit
	*	*	192.168.10.35	80	TCP	Permit
	*	*	192.168.10/24	*	*	Block
	192.168.10.25	*	*	25	TCP	Permit
	192.168.10.30	*	*	53	UDP	Permit
	192.168.10.35	*	*	80	TCP	Permit
	192.168.10/24	*	*	6	*	Block
For subnet 10.0.0.0/24	*	*	10.0.0.2	80	TCP	Permit
	*	*	10.0.0.0/24	12	*	Block
	10.0.0.0/24	*	*	*	*	Block
	*	*	*	*	*	Block

Chapter 23

1. The attachment is encrypted to evade detection by the antivirus software in the mail server and the recipient's computer.
2. V always returns the wrong answer.
3. The administrator's approach is not based on *default deny* principle.
4. All the computers.
5. BIOS of the web server is corrupted. BIOS of the mail server is not corrupted but the data on its hard disk is damaged.

Index